Index to the 1800 Massachusetts Federal Census
for the County of
Middlesex

Rebecca M. Sullivan
Deborah Lee Larsson

Index to the 1800 Massachusetts Federal Census
for the County of
Middlesex

November 2014

ISBN: 978-1503255869

Manufactured in the United States

FOREWARD:

This is the ninth volume of several containing the heads of household that were enumerated in the 1800 United States Federal Census in Massachusetts. Our ninth volume is comprised of those towns in Middlesex County. In order to make it easy for the researcher, towns are alphabetized, followed by an alphabetical index of Middlesex county.

We have made every attempt at correctly transcribing each town. However, many of these documents are torn, covered with ink, tape marks, rips and poor handwriting. Spelling errors have been left as they were originally written. Any names & enumerations illegible are denoted with an asterisk.

This book should be used as a guide and research aid. When possible the actual image should be obtained for proper verification and citation. Visit the National Archives website to find out more on how to obtain census images. www.archives.gov/research/census.

In order to get all of the information on one page to make for easy reading we had to reduce the size of the font.

Drop us a line, we'd love to hear what you're researching: rsulli1219@aol.com

Becky & Deb
November 2014

Check out our other books:

INDEX

Middlesex County

INDEX

Middlesex County

Middlesex County Stats

Microfilm Reel Number: M32-17

Town:	Page Numbers:	Enumerated By:
Acton	16-20	Unknown
Ashby	34-37	Unknown
Bedford	161-163	Unknown
Billerica	173-178	Unknown
Boxborough	199-201	Unknown
Burlington	154-156	Unknown
Cambridge	220-230	Caleb Brooks
Carlisle	20-23	James Barrett
Charlestown	79-92	Unknown
Chelmsford	155-173	Unknown
Concord	2-11	James Barrett
Dracut	44-49	Unknown
Dunstable	215-217	Unknown
East Sudbury	65-69	Unknown
Framingham	70-78	Unknown
Groton	206-213	Unknown
Hollistown	236-239	Unknown
Hopkinton	240-245	Unknown
Lexington	156-160	Unknown
Lincoln	12-15	Unknown
Littleton	201-205	Unknown
Malden	93-98	Unknown
Marlborough	187-195	Unknown
Medford	99-103	Unknown
Natick	245-248	Unknown
Newton	117-125	Unknown
Pepperell	30-34	Unknown
Reading	127-138	James Bancroft
Sherburn	248-251	Unknown

Middlesex County Stats

Microfilm Reel Number: M32-17

Town:	Page Numbers:	Enumerated By:
Shirley	213-215	Unknown
Stoneham	138-140	Unknown
Stow	195-199	Unknown
Sudbury	57-65	William Rice
Tewksbury	49-53	Unknown
Townsend	25-29	Joseph Heald
Tyngsborough	40-43	Parker Varnum
Waltham	112-116	Unknown
Watertown	231-235	Unknown
Westford	179-184	Unknown
Weston	105-111	Ebenezer Hobbs
Wilmington	140-144	James Bancroft
Woburn	148-153	Unknown

TOWN	PG#	LN#	LAST NAME	FIRST NAME	M under 10	M 10 to 16	M 16 to 26	M 26 to 45	M 45 and over	F under 10	F 10 to 16	F 16 to 26	F 26 to 45	F 45 and over	TOTAL ALL OTHER	TOTAL SLAVES	TOTALS	DISTRICT/ TOWNSHIP	NOTES
Acton	16	1	Wright	Samuel	1	1		1	2		1		1				7		
Acton	16	2	Prescott	Benjamin			1	2				1		2			6		
Acton	16	3	Law	Stephen			2	1	1		1	3		1			9		
Acton	16	4	Law	Stephen Jr	2		1		1	1	1		1				7		
Acton	16	5	Shirland	James	3				1					1			5		
Acton	16	6	Cole	John	2	1	1		1					1			6		
Acton	16	7	Cole	Joseph	2			1					1				4		
Acton	16	8	Barker	Joseph Jr		1	2		1	2				1			7		
Acton	16	9	Barber	Robert				1			1		1	1			4		
Acton	16	10	Adams	John Jr		1		2	1	1		1		1			7		
Acton	16	11	Barker	Ebenezer			1			2			1	1			5		
Acton	16	12	Thomas	Sarah	1							1		1			3		
Acton	16	13	Wheeler	Timothy B.	3			1						1			5		
Acton	16	14	Hayward	John			2	1				1		1			5		
Acton	16	15	Chaffin	Stephen	1			1			1		1				4		
Acton	16	16	Linfield	Nathaniel				1			1		1				3		
Acton	16	17	Robbins	Phillip			1		1			1	1	1			5		
Acton	16	18	Dudley	Joseph	1			1		1			1				4		
Acton	16	19	Hayward	Simeon			1		1	2	1		1				6		
Acton	16	20	Hayward	John Jr	2		1	1		1	2		1				8		
Acton	16	21	Adams	John				1					1	1			3		
Acton	16	22	Adams	Ammi F			1			3		1	1				6		
Acton	16	23	Linfield	Nathaniel Jr			2							1			3		
Acton	16	24	Brooks	Jonas		1		1	1	1	1		2				7		
Acton	16	25	Brooks	Daniel		1		1			1		1				4		
Acton	16	26	Law	Thomas				1	4				1				6		
Acton	16	27	Wheeler	Rebekah										3			3		
Acton	16	28	Tuttle	Thaddeus	1			1		1			1				4		
Acton	16	29	Piper	Silas	1		1	1	1	5		1	1	1			12		
Acton	16	30	Brown	Daniel				1					1				2		
Acton	16	31	Reed	William			1		1			1		1			4		
Acton	16	32	Tinney	Peter	1	1		1		1		1					5		
Acton	16	33	Faulkner	Francis		1	2	1	1				1	1	1		8		
Acton	16	34	Faulkner	Obedience										1			1		
Acton	16	35	Hapgood	Abraham	2	1	1		1	2		2		1			10		
Acton	17	1	Hapgood	Ephraim		2	1		1	4	1	1	1	1			12		
Acton	17	2	Smith	Eben		1		1					1				3		
Acton	17	3	Brooks	Joseph			1	1	1			1	1	1			6		
Acton	17	4	Fitch	Noah	2			1					1				4		
Acton	17	5	Smith	Thomas	2			1		2			1				6		
Acton	17	6	Furbush	Ephraim	2		1	1	1	2	2		1				10		
Acton	17	7	Fletcher	Peter		1		1					1				3		
Acton	17	8	Hunt	Simon	1			1				1	1	1			5		
Acton	17	9	Durant	Henry		1		1		1		1					4		
Acton	17	10	Robbins	George		1	1		1	1	1	1	4				10		
Acton	17	11	Robbins	Tilg			1			1			1				3		
Acton	17	12	Furbush	David				1			2		1				4		
Acton	17	13	Furbush	Simeon	1		1					1					3		
Acton	17	14	Jones	Samuel				1					2				3		
Acton	17	15	Jones	Aaron	2	2	1		1	3	1	1	1				12		
Acton	17	16	Jones	Oliver			1	1	1			3		1			7		
Acton	17	17	Hunt	John		1	2	1	1			1	1				7		
Acton	17	18	Faulkner	Aaron			1					2	1	1			5		
Acton	17	19	Faulkner	Nathaniel			1		1		1	1	1				5		
Acton	17	20	Houghton	Oliver	1			1		1			1				4		
Acton	17	21	Houghton	Joseph				1					1				2		
Acton	17	22	Hayward	Benjamin		2	1		1	3	1	1	1				10		
Acton	17	23	Hayward	Stephen		1	1	1		1		1	1				6		
Acton	17	24	Davis	Sarah	1			1				1					3		
Acton	17	25	Dole	Joseph Jr	1			1		2		1					5		
Acton	17	26	Ramsdell	Abigail				1			1	1	1				4		
Acton	17	27	Wheeler	Kiah	2			1		1	1	1	1				7		
Acton	17	28	Eule	Asahel	2		1	1				1					5		
Acton	17	29	Wheeler	Samuel				1					2				3		
Acton	17	30	Wheeler	Nathan		1	1	1				1					4		
Acton	17	31	Wheeler	Roger				1			1	1	1				4		
Acton	17	32	Hayward	samuel	3	1		1		1		1	1				8		
Acton	17	33	Wheeler	John		2		1		1		1					5		
Acton	17	34	Hosmer	Jonathan	1		3	1	1	1		2		1	1		11		
Acton	17	35	Hosmer	Stephen		1		1	1			3		1			7		
Acton	17	36	Hosmer	Nathan			1			1		1					3		
Acton	17	37	Hosmer	Ephraim	2		1	1					1	1			7		
Acton	17	38	Hosmer	Samuel	2			1		3	1		1				8		
Acton	17	39	Cutting	William			2		1			2		2			7		
Acton	17	40	Dole	Joseph				1					1				2		
Acton	18	1	Barker	Joseph				1			1		1				3		
Acton	18	2	Marsh	James	2	1		1		1	1		1				7		
Acton	18	3	Brown	Joseph	4	1	1		1	1		1	1				10		
Acton	18	4	Richardson	Moses	2	2	1		2		1		1				9		

TOWN	PG#	LN#	LAST NAME	FIRST NAME	FREE WHITE MALES					FREE WHITE FEMALES					TOTAL ALL OTHER	TOTAL SLAVES	TOTALS	DISTRICT/ TOWNSHIP	NOTES
					under 10	10 to 16	16 to 26	26 to 45	45 and over	under 10	10 to 16	16 to 26	26 to 45	45 and over					
Acton	18	5	Noyes	Josiah	1		1	1		2	1		1				7		
Acton	18	6	Robbins	John Jr			1						3				4		
Acton	18	7	Dudley	Ephraim				1					1	1			3		
Acton	18	8	Harras	John			1			1		1					3		
Acton	18	9	Noyes	Thomas		1	1	1	1	1		1		1			7		
Acton	18	10	Chaffin	David				1					1				2		
Acton	18	11	Chaffin	Sarah		1					1		1				3		
Acton	18	12	Gilbert	Jude		2		1	1				1				5		
Acton	18	13	Conant	Samuel P	2	1		1		2			1				7		
Acton	18	14	Parlin	Samuel	1		2	1		2	1		1				8		
Acton	18	15	Jones	Hannah			1			1			1				3		
Acton	18	16	Law	Danforth		1		1				1					3		
Acton	18	17	Tuttle	Simon	1			1		1				2			5		
Acton	18	18	Tuttle	Simon Jr	4		2	3		1			1	1			12		
Acton	18	19	Sergeant	Solomon	1			1		1	1		1				5		
Acton	18	20	Handley	Charles	2	1		1		3	2	1	1				11		
Acton	18	21	Skinner	Abraham	3			1		1	1		1				7		
Acton	18	22	Dexter	John		1	1		1			2	1				6		
Acton	18	23	Handley	Amos	3			1		1		1					6		
Acton	18	24	Barnard	David	1			2		3	1		1				8		
Acton	18	25	Barker	Francis				1		1			1				3		
Acton	18	26	Chaffin	Simon	1			1		3	1		1				7		
Acton	18	27	Adams	Moses	1		2		1	1	2	2	1	1			11		
Acton	18	28	Brooks	Paul			2	1					1	1			5		
Acton	18	29	Fletcher	James	1	1		1			1		1				5		
Acton	18	30	Billings	James		1	1		1	1			1	1			6		
Acton	18	31	Billings	Ephraim	1	1				2		1	1				6		
Acton	18	32	Dudley	Paul	2			1	1		1		1				6		
Acton	18	33	Davis	Stephen	2			1		2			1	1			7		
Acton	18	34	Lock	Joseph	1	1			1	1	1		1				6		
Acton	18	35	Brabook	Benjamin		1		1				1		1			4		
Acton	18	36	Woodson	Ebenezer			1			1		1					3		
Acton	18	37	Barker	Samuel				1						1			2		
Acton	18	38	Robbins	John	1	1		1		3		1	1				8		
Acton	18	39	Harras	Joseph	1			1		1		1	1	1			6		
Acton	19	1	Robbins	Ruth			2				1		1				4		
Acton	19	2	Wetherbee	Edward	1	1	2		1	2	1	1		1			10		
Acton	19	3	Edward	John		1	2	2		3		1	2	2			13		
Acton	19	4	Brooks	Seth			2	1		1	1		1				6		
Acton	19	5	Brooks	Nathan	2			1					1				4		
Acton	19	6	White	Samuel	1	1		2				1	1	1			7		
Acton	19	7	Brabook	Joseph		1				1	1			1			4		
Acton	19	8	Chamberlain	Joseph	1	1		1		2	1		1				7		
Acton	19	9	Thorpe	Thomas	2	1		1		2			1				7		
Acton	19	10	Wood	Moses	2		1		1	3		2	1				10		
Acton	19	11	Davis	James			1		1	6	2	1	1				12		
Acton	19	12	Lovejoy	Samuel			1			2			1				4		
Acton	19	13	Wheeler	Phinehas			1						1				2		
Acton	19	14	Davis	Elijah	2	1			2	2			1	1			9		
Acton	19	15	Temple	Samuel	3			1		1	2		1				8		
Acton	19	16	Davis	David	3			1		1			1				6		
Acton	19	17	Davis	Jonathan	1		1		1	2	4	3	1	1			14		
Acton	19	18	Brown	Timothy	1	1		1		1	1	1					6		
Acton	19	19	Heald	John	1			1						1			3		
Acton	19	20	White	Daniel	2	1	1	1			1		1				7		
Acton	19	21	Davis	Daniel			3		1	2		2		1			9		
Acton	19	22	Lamson	John				1				2		1			4		
Acton	19	23	Lamson	Nathan			1			3		1					5		
Acton	19	24	Morse	Abel		1		2					1				4		
Acton	19	25	Robbins	Rebekah	1						1		1				3		
Acton	19	26	Handley	John	1	1		1		1			1				5		
Acton	19	27	Procter	Abel	2			1		2	1		1				7		
Acton	19	28	Hager	Joseph				1						1			2		
Acton	19	29	Gold	Benjamin				3						2			5		
Acton	19	30	Smith	Solomon	2			1		2	1	1					7		
Acton	19	31	Noyes	Amos	1			2					1				4		
Acton	19	32	Chaffin	Joseph	1	1		1		1			1	1			6		
Acton	19	33	Reed	John	2	1		1		2			1				7		
Acton	19	34	Davis	Ephraim	2		1	1		2		1		1			8		
Acton	19	35	Heywood	Calven	2			1		2			1	1			7		
Acton	19	36	Emerson	Augustus			1	1					1				3		
Acton	19	37	Tuttle	Samuel			2	1			1		1				5		
Acton	19	38	Melven	Eathon	2			1		2			1				6		
Acton	19	39	Burges	Solomon	2	1		1			1	1	1				7		
Acton	19	40	Robert	Chaffin	2		1		1	1	2	1	1				9		
Acton	20	1	Oliver	John											5		5		

TOWN	PG#	LN#	HEADS OF HOUSEHOLD		FREE WHITE MALES					FREE WHITE FEMALES					TOTAL ALL OTHER	TOTAL SLAVES	TOTALS	DISTRICT/ TOWNSHIP	NOTES
			LAST NAME	FIRST NAME	under 10	10 to 16	16 to 26	26 to 45	45 and over	under 10	10 to 16	16 to 26	26 to 45	45 and over					
Ashby	34	1	Abbott	John	2	1		1		3	1	1	1				10		
Ashby	34	2	Abbott	Jonh	3			1		2	1		1				8		
Ashby	34	3	Brown	Zach		1	1		1		2	1	1	1			8		
Ashby	34	4	Badlam	Stephen	1				1	2	1	1	1	1			8		
Ashby	34	5	Bennet	Phinehas					1					1			2		
Ashby	34	6	Brown	Daniel	1	2		1		2			1	1			8		
Ashby	34	7	Bain	*	3		3	2		1			2				11		
Ashby	34	8	Barr	Robt. W.	1		1	1		2		1					6		
Ashby	34	9	Barrett	Jona		2	1		1			1		1			6		
Ashby	34	10	Barrett	Zebn	1	1		1		1	1	1					6		
Ashby	34	11	Barrett	Benja				1				1					2		
Ashby	34	12	Barrett	Benja Jr	1	1	1	1		2		1	1				8		
Ashby	34	13	Barrett	Jonas	1	2	1	1	1	2	1	1	1				11		
Ashby	34	14	Patche	Abrm	2	1	1		1	1	1	3		1			11		
Ashby	34	15	Carver	Thos	1			1				1					3		
Ashby	34	16	Colman	Benja	1	2	3		1		1	1		1			10		
Ashby	34	17	Carver	Thos Jr			1		1		1			2			5		
Ashby	35	1	Damon	Jacob								1	1				2		
Ashby	35	2	Damon	Jacob Jr			1			2		1					4		
Ashby	35	3	Damon	David				1						1			2		
Ashby	35	4	Ditson	Thos				1		1				1			3		
Ashby	35	5	Damon	Jacob			2					1		1			5		
Ashby	35	6	Damon	Benja	1	2	1	1		3	1		1				10		
Ashby	35	7	Damon	Joseph Jr	2			1		3			1				7		
Ashby	35	8	Chamberlin	Thos	3	1		1		2		1	1				9		
Ashby	35	9	Davis	Joseph			2	3	1	1		1		1			9		
Ashby	35	10	Eaton	Benja	3	1		1		1		1	1				8		
Ashby	35	11	Eaton	Joseph	2			1		1	1		1				6		
Ashby	35	12	Edwards	Abram	1	2	2	1		2	1		2	1			12		
Ashby	35	13	Chamberlin	Ephm				1						1			2		
Ashby	35	14	Flant	Edmund	1	1		1		2	1		1				7		
Ashby	35	15	Flagg	Wm		1		1						1			3		
Ashby	35	16	Fletcher	James				1		1	2	2		1			7		
Ashby	35	17	Fletcher	Jonas			1			1			1				3		
Ashby	35	18	Foster	David	1			1		2			1				5		
Ashby	35	19	Foster	Abram	2			1		1	2	1	1				8		
Ashby	35	20	Foster	John	3	1		1		1	2	1		1			10		
Ashby	35	21	Foster	Jona			1			1			1				3		
Ashby	35	22	Flagge	Allen	1			1			1	1					4		
Ashby	35	23	Farr	Wm	1	1		1		1	1	1	1				7		
Ashby	35	24	Damon	Joseph				1			1	1		1			4		
Ashby	35	25	Hodgmon	Willard	1		1					1					3		
Ashby	35	26	Page	Jona	1		1					1					3		
Ashby	35	27	Wellington	Roger				1						1			2		
Ashby	35	28	Gregory	Isaac				1			1			1			3		
Ashby	35	29	Gregory	Josiah			1			2			1				4		
Ashby	35	30	Greene	Isaac	1		1				2		1				5		
Ashby	35	31	Greene	Wm	2	1		1		3		1	1				9		
Ashby	35	32	Gates	Abrm		2		1		2	1			1			7		
Ashby	35	33	Gibson	Abrm	1	1		1		2	1	1	1				8		
Ashby	35	34	Gibson	Stephen	1	1		1						1			4		
Ashby	35	35	Gibson	Ephrm		1								1			2		
Ashby	35	36	Gibson	Israel	1		1					1					3		
Ashby	35	37	Hodgmon	Benja Jr		1		1		1		1					4		
Ashby	35	38	Hill	Betty							2		1				3		
Ashby	35	39	Hill	Ralph		2	1		1	4		1	1				10		
Ashby	35	40	Houghton	Elijah				1						1			2		
Ashby	35	41	Houghton	Elijah Jr	1			1		1	1	1	1				6		
Ashby	35	42	Hodgmon	Jonas			1			4			1				6		
Ashby	35	43	Howard	Daniel	2		1		1	2	2	1	1	2			12		
Ashby	35	44	Hodgmon	Benja		1		1		1	2	1		1			7		
Ashby	35	45	Hall	John	4			1		2		1					8		
Ashby	35	46	Jones	John				1						1			2		
Ashby	35	47	Jones	Daniel		1	1					1					3		
Ashby	35	48	Jaquith	John		1	1		1		1	1		1			6		
Ashby	36	1	Jaquith	Alford		1			1		1	1		1			5		
Ashby	36	2	Johnson	Wm	1		1	1		3			1				7		
Ashby	36	3	Gibson	Silas		1	1	1		2	1		1				7		
Ashby	36	4	Lymond	James	2	1	1		1	1		1		1			8		
Ashby	36	5	Shid	Betty		1		1		2				1			5		
Ashby	36	6	Spaulding	Eleazer	3			1			1	1					6		
Ashby	36	7	Wood	David	1	1	1					1					4		
Ashby	36	8	Whitney	Josiah Jr	2	1		1		2		1	1				8		
Ashby	36	9	Taylor	Abel		1		1		2			1				5		
Ashby	36	10	Wright	Henry Jr				1		1				1			3		
Ashby	36	11	Wright	Abel	2			1		1		1	1				6		
Ashby	36	12	Wright	Elijah			1			3			1				5		
Ashby	36	13	Wright	Abram B.	2								1				4		
Ashby	36	14	Wright	Stephen	1	1		1		3			1				7		

11

TOWN	PG#	LN#	HEADS OF HOUSEHOLD LAST NAME	FIRST NAME	FWM under 10	FWM 10 to 16	FWM 16 to 26	FWM 26 to 45	FWM 45 and over	FWF under 10	FWF 10 to 16	FWF 16 to 26	FWF 26 to 45	FWF 45 and over	TOTAL ALL OTHER	TOTAL SLAVES	TOTALS	DISTRICT/ TOWNSHIP	NOTES
Ashby	36	15	Wyman	Abijah	2		2	1	1		1	2	1	2			12		
Ashby	36	16	Worth	Levi	3	1		1		1	1		1				8		
Ashby	36	17	Wellington	Benja		1	1		1			3		1			7		
Ashby	36	18	Wellington	Amos					1			3		1			5		
Ashby	36	19	Wellington	Elias Jr			1	1				1					3		
Ashby	36	20	Wilden	Rufus	1		1		1	2	1			1			7		
Ashby	36	21	Whitney	Josiah	1	2		1				1		1			7		
Ashby	36	22	Whitney	Selas		1	2	1		3	1		1				9		
Ashby	36	23	Whitney	Isaac		2		1		4			1				8		
Ashby	36	24	Weatherbee	Israel	2	1	1		1		1	1		1			8		
Ashby	36	25	Waller	Benja	2			1		3	1		1				8		
Ashby	36	26	Walker	Zach	1	2			2		1	2		1			9		
Ashby	36	27	Walker	Isaac	1			1		1	1		1				5		
Ashby	36	28	Walker	Asa		1	1		1					1			4		
Ashby	36	29	Whitney	Judah	1			1		2			1				5		
Ashby	36	30	Warner	Wm					1					2			3		
Ashby	36	31	Wellington	Oliver	4	1		1		1	1		1				9		
Ashby	36	32	Wyman	Stephen				1			1		1				3		
Ashby	36	33	Waters	*	2	1		1	1	2	2	2	1				12		
Ashby	36	34	Woster	Joseph Jr	1			1			1		1				4		
Ashby	36	35	Winship	Abel	1	2		1			1	1	1				7		
Ashby	36	36	Walker	Asa Jr	1			1		1			1				4		
Ashby	36	37	Wellington	Elias Jr			1	1		1	2	2	1				8		
Ashby	36	38	King	James				1		1				1			3		
Ashby	36	39	Hartwell	Timo	3			1		1			1				6		
Ashby	36	40	Kendall	Oliver			2	1		2			1				6		
Ashby	36	41	Kendall	Asa					1					2			3		
Ashby	36	42	Kendall	Asa Jr	4	1		1		2	1		1				10		
Ashby	36	43	Kendall	Pierpoint	1		2	1		1			1	1			7		
Ashby	36	44	Kendall	Benja	1	2	1			1		1					6		
Ashby	36	45	Kendall	Joseph	1		2					1					4		
Ashby	36	46	Locke	David		1	1	1		1			1				5		
Ashby	36	47	Laurence	Josh	1			1		2			1				5		
Ashby	37	1	Laurence	Isaac		1		1		1		1					4		
Ashby	37	2	Laurence	Charles		2		1			1	1	1				6		
Ashby	37	3	Laurence	Reuben	1			1		2			1				5		
Ashby	37	4	Laurence	El*			1			1		1		1			4		
Ashby	37	5	Laurence	John		1	1		1	1		4		1			9		
Ashby	37	6	Laurence	Jona Jr	1			1		2	2	1	1				8		
Ashby	37	7	Laurence	Benja	2			1					1	1			5		
Ashby	37	8	Laurence	Oliver				1		1			1				3		
Ashby	37	9	Locke	John	1			1		1		1					4		
Ashby	37	10	Laurence	Jacob	2			1		1	1		1				6		
Ashby	37	11	Laurence	Thos	2		1	1		1			1				6		
Ashby	37	12	Laurence	Jonas		1	1		1		1			1			5		
Ashby	37	13	Lees	Jonas	1	3		1				1	1				7		
Ashby	37	14	Locke	Jonas		1	1		1	1	1	3	1				9		
Ashby	37	15	Manning	John		2			1	2		1	1				7		
Ashby	37	16	March	Saml				1						1			2		
Ashby	37	17	March	Josh W.	3		1			1		1					6		
Ashby	37	18	Patch	Stephen	1	2	1		1	1	1		1				9		
Ashby	37	19	Prescott	Elijah			1			1		2					4		
Ashby	37	20	Piper	Jona	1	1		1		1		2					6		
Ashby	37	21	P*	Jacob			2			3		1	1				7		
Ashby	37	22	Gates	Paul		1		1					1				3		
Ashby	37	23	Rice	Saml	2	2		1				1	1				7		
Ashby	37	24	Rice	John		1		1		2		1					5		
Ashby	37	25	Rice	Saml Jr				1		2	1		1				5		
Ashby	37	26	Ross	Jona	2			1		1		1					5		
Ashby	37	27	Raymond	Daniel	2	1		1		1	2		1				8		
Ashby	37	28	Richardson	Abel	2	1		1		2		1	1	1			9		
Ashby	37	29	Stone	John L.	1		1					1					3		
Ashby	37	30	Stearns	Thos				1						1			2		
Ashby	37	31	Sta*	Abel	1	2		1		1			1				6		
Ashby	37	32	Stone	John E.	3	1		1					1				6		
Ashby	37	33	Stone	Josh	2			1		2			1				6		
Ashby	37	34	Stone	Saml				1						1			2		
Ashby	37	35	Shattuck	Elias Jr	1	1	2		1	1	2	1		1			10		
Ashby	37	36	Cutler	Thos	1	1		1		2		1					6		
Ashby	37	37	Whitson	Jonah	1			1		2		1					5		
Ashby	37	38	Worth	Joseph				1				1					2		
Ashby	37	39	Willard	Tarbill			1					1					2		
Ashby	37	40	Whiting	Saml				1				1					2		
Ashby	37	41	Rice	Asa		1						1					2		
Ashby	37	42	Mosman	Mathias	1	1		1	1	2	1	2		1			10		
Ashby	37	43	Allen	Benja	1		3					1					5		
Ashby	37	44	Wright	Henry Jr		1		1		1			1				4		
Ashby	37	45	Pa*	Elian	3		1		1	2			1				8		
Ashby	37	46	Taylor	Abram				1			1	1	2				5		

TOWN	PG#	LN#	HEADS OF HOUSEHOLD		FREE WHITE MALES					FREE WHITE FEMALES					TOTAL ALL OTHER	TOTAL SLAVES	TOTALS	DISTRICT/ TOWNSHIP	NOTES
			LAST NAME	FIRST NAME	under 10	10 to 16	16 to 26	26 to 45	45 and over	under 10	10 to 16	16 to 26	26 to 45	45 and over					
Ashby	37	47	Wheeler	John	2			1		2	1		1				7		
Ashby	37	48	*	John		1											1		

TOWN	PG#	LN#	HEADS OF HOUSEHOLD		FREE WHITE MALES					FREE WHITE FEMALES					TOTAL ALL OTHER	TOTAL SLAVES	TOTALS	DISTRICT/ TOWNSHIP	NOTES
			LAST NAME	FIRST NAME	under 10	10 to 16	16 to 26	26 to 45	45 and over	under 10	10 to 16	16 to 26	26 to 45	45 and over					
Bedford	161	1	Abbott	Moses	2				1					1			4		
Bedford	161	2	Abbott	Henry			1										1		
Bedford	161	3	Abbott	Moses Jr	2	1		1		1	1	1	1				8		
Bedford	161	4	Bacon	Thompson	3	3		1		2			1				10		
Bedford	161	5	Bacon	Benjamin				1					1				2		
Bedford	161	6	Bacon	Benjamin Jr	1	1		1		2		1	1				7		
Bedford	161	7	Bacon	Jonah & Joseph Frank	3			1					1	1			6		
Bedford	161	8	Bacon	Solomon		1		1					1				3		
Bedford	161	9	Bacon	Flagg	1		3	1		3		1					9		
Bedford	161	10	Brown	Edward		1				1		1					3		
Bedford	161	11	Brown	Nathaniel		1	1			1			1				4		
Bedford	161	12	Blodgett	Aaron	1			1		1		1					4		
Bedford	161	13	Brown	Nathan				1				1		1			3		
Bedford	161	14	Convers	Joseph		1	1	1	1			2		1			7		
Bedford	161	15	Chamberlain	Phincas			2	1		2		1	1				7		
Bedford	161	16	Catowell	John	3			1		1			1				6		
Bedford	161	17	Dean	Thaddeus	2				1	3	1			1			8		
Bedford	161	18	Davis	Thaddeus	1	1	1		1	2	1	2	1				10		
Bedford	161	19	Davis	Eleazer Jr				1		1	1	1					4		
Bedford	161	20	Davis	Eleazer					1		1	1	1				4		
Bedford	161	21	Dix	Jonathan	2		1							1			4		
Bedford	162	1	Fitch	Matthew		1		2					3	1	1		8		
Bedford	162	2	Fitch	Moses	1		1		1	1	1		1				6		
Bedford	162	3	Fitch	David				1				1	1				3		
Bedford	162	4	Fitch	Jeremiah		1	1		1			1		1			5		
Bedford	162	5	Fitch	Thaddeus	2				1			2	1	1			7		
Bedford	162	6	Fitch	David Jr			1					1					2		
Bedford	162	7	Gleason	Jonas		2	1		1			2	1	1			8		
Bedford	162	8	Goodridge	William	1			1		2			1	1			6		
Bedford	162	9	Goodwin	Uriah	3			1		3			1				8		
Bedford	162	10	Hutchinson	Benjamin		1		1						2			4		
Bedford	162	11	Hill	Josiah	3	1	1			2	1		1				9		
Bedford	162	12	Hartwell	Samuel		1	1			1	1	1					5		
Bedford	162	13	Hartwell	Joseph		1		1					2				4		
Bedford	162	14	Hartwell	William	3		1	1				1	1				7		
Bedford	162	15	Hadley	Simon	4			1		2			1	1			9		
Bedford	162	16	Hosmer	John	3	1	1		1	2	2		1				11		
Bedford	162	17	Hutchinson	James			1			1			1				3		
Bedford	162	18	Haywood	Mather			2					3					5		
Bedford	162	19	Jones	Timothy	1	1	1		1	1	2	2		2			11		
Bedford	162	20	Jones	James C	2	1		1	1		1		1	1			8		
Bedford	162	21	Lane	Stephen		1		1		1			1				4		
Bedford	162	22	Lane	Samuel	1		1		1			2		1			6		
Bedford	162	23	Lane	Samuel Jr	1			1		1	1	1		1			6		
Bedford	162	24	Lane	Jonathan	1	1	1	1		2	1	1	1				9		
Bedford	162	25	Lane	James				1									1		
Bedford	162	26	Lane	David	2	1		1		1		1		1			7		
Bedford	162	27	Lane	Solomon	1	1		1			1	1		1			6		
Bedford	162	28	Lane	Luke	3			1		1			1				6		
Bedford	162	29	Lane	Elizabeth								1		1			2		
Bedford	162	30	Meriam	William		1			1	2	1		1				6		
Bedford	162	31	Meriam	John		1	2					1	1	1	1		6		
Bedford	162	32	Meed	Stephen			1	1			1	2					5		
Bedford	162	33	Maxwell	William		1			2	2	1	1	1	1			9		
Bedford	162	34	Meriam	Samuel	1	1			1	3			1				7		
Bedford	162	35	Moar	John & Bradley Bowans	1	1		1	2				1	1	1		8		
Bedford	162	36	Meriam	Nathaniel				1		1			1				3		
Bedford	162	37	Pike	John	2			1			1		1				5		
Bedford	162	38	Penniman	Mesheck				1				1		1			3		
Bedford	162	39	Porter	William		2		1		3	1	1	1				9		
Bedford	162	40	Page	Nathaniel		1	1				1	1		1			6		
Bedford	163	1	Pollard	Matthew		1		1						2			4		
Bedford	163	2	Page	Christopher		1		1		1	1	1	1	1			7		
Bedford	163	3	Page	William				1						1			2		
Bedford	163	4	Pollard	Oliver			2	1			1	1	1				6		
Bedford	163	5	Page	David		1	1	1		1	1			3			8		
Bedford	163	6	Page	Thomas		1		1				1		1			4		
Bedford	163	7	Page	John			2	1		3			1				7		
Bedford	163	8	Preston	Amaraiah	2			1		1	1	1	1				7		
Bedford	163	9	Reed	David	1	1			1	1		1	1	1			7		
Bedford	163	10	Reed	Oliver				1						1			2		
Bedford	163	11	Reed	Oliver Jr			1	1				1	1				4		
Bedford	163	12	Reed	Reuben	3		1	1		2			1				8		
Bedford	163	13	Robbinson	Jesse	1			1		1		1					4		
Bedford	163	14	Ross	John				1		1				1			3		
Bedford	163	15	Reed	John			1	1		1		1	1				5		
Bedford	163	16	Reed	John Jr	2			1		1		1	1				6		
Bedford	163	17	Stearns	Samuel			1		1				4	1	1		8		
Bedford	163	18	Simonds	Aaron			2			1		1					4		
Bedford	163	19	Stearns	Elijah		1			2			1		1			5		

TOWN	PG#	LN#	LAST NAME	FIRST NAME	FREE WHITE MALES					FREE WHITE FEMALES					TOTAL ALL OTHER	TOTAL SLAVES	TOTALS	DISTRICT/ TOWNSHIP	NOTES
					under 10	10 to 16	16 to 26	26 to 45	45 and over	under 10	10 to 16	16 to 26	26 to 45	45 and over					
Bedford	163	20	Skilton	Dryz	4		1	1						1			7		
Bedford	163	21	Sprague	John	1	1	1	1	1	3	2	1	1	1			13		
Bedford	163	22	Simonds	Lemuel		1		1					1				3		
Bedford	163	23	Smith	Isaac			1	1		1		2					5		
Bedford	163	24	Tidd	Samuel				1					1	1			3		
Bedford	163	25	Wright	James			2	1		1	1		1				6		
Bedford	163	26	Wright	James Jr	1		2			1	1						5		
Bedford	163	27	Webber	John			2		1				1				4		
Bedford	163	28	Webber	John Jr		1		1		2			1				5		
Bedford	163	29	Wyman	Nathaniel		1			1	2	1		1				6		
Bedford	163	30	Webber	William	2		1	1		1			1				6		
Bedford	163	31	Wilson	James		1	2	1					1	1			6		
Bedford	163	32	Webber	Joseph	1			1		1			1				4		
Bedford	163	33	Woodward	David				1					2		2		5		
Bedford	163	34	Wheeer	Abner	1			1		1	1		1				5		

TOWN	PG#	LN#	LAST NAME	FIRST NAME	FWM under 10	FWM 10 to 16	FWM 16 to 26	FWM 26 to 45	FWM 45 and over	FWF under 10	FWF 10 to 16	FWF 16 to 26	FWF 26 to 45	FWF 45 and over	TOTAL ALL OTHER	TOTAL SLAVES	TOTALS	DISTRICT/ TOWNSHIP	NOTES
Billerica	173	1	Abbot	Nathan		1		1		1	2		1				6		
Billerica	173	2	Abbot	David				2	1				1				4		
Billerica	173	3	Abbot	James	3	1	3	2		2		1	1	1			14		
Billerica	173	4	Abbot	Joshua			1		1			1		1			4		
Billerica	173	5	Allen	Mala'		2			1	2				1			6		
Billerica	173	6	Allen	Jerem'	3	1	1		1			1	1	1			9		
Billerica	173	7	Amory	Nath'															
Billerica	173	8	Banres	Isaac	1	2			1	1		1		2			8		
Billerica	173	9	Batchelor	Jos'			1					1					2		
Billerica	173	10	Brown	Nath'					1			1	2				4		
Billerica	173	11	Brown	John		3	1		1		1		1	1			8		
Billerica	173	12	Brown	Saml'	1	1		1		3							6		
Billerica	173	13	Brown	Mary									1	1			2		
Billerica	173	14	Brown	Nath' Jr			1					3					4		
Billerica	173	15	Brown	Tho'	2	2			1			1		1			7		
Billerica	173	16	Brown	Tho' Jr	3	1	1		1	1	1		1				8		
Billerica	173	17	Bowars	Wm		1			1					1			3		
Billerica	173	18	Bowars	Jon'		1	1		1			1		1			5		
Billerica	173	19	Bowars	Benja'	3	2	1		1		1	1		1			10		
Billerica	173	20	Bowars	Saml	1	3	2		1	2	2	1		1			13		
Billerica	173	21	Bowars	Jona' Jr			1	1			1	1	1	1			6		
Billerica	173	22	Beard	Isaac					1				1	1			3		
Billerica	173	23	Beard	Isaac Jr	1		1			3			1				6		
Billerica	174	1	Beard	Mary	1								1	1			3		
Billerica	174	2	Beard	Benja'					1		1			2			4		
Billerica	174	3	Beard	Benja' Jr		1		1					1				3		
Billerica	174	4	Bond	Jona'	1	1	1	1				1	1				6		
Billerica	174	5	Blanchard	Saml'				1		1			1	1			4		
Billerica	174	6	Blanchard	Saml' Jr	2	2		1			1	4		1			11		
Billerica	174	7	Blanchard	Jerem'	2	1		1					1				5		
Billerica	174	8	Blanchard	Isaac	2	1		1		1	2		1				8		
Billerica	174	9	Blanchard	Joseph		1			1	3				1			6		
Billerica	174	10	Blanchard	Fra'			1					1					2		
Billerica	174	11	Bratten	Mary									1	1			2		
Billerica	174	12	Bowman	Abel		2	1	1		1	1	2	1				9		
Billerica	174	13	Bacon	John	1	1		1			1	1	1				6		
Billerica	174	14	Bromfield	John					1		1	2	1	1			6		
Billerica	174	15	Balch	Tho'					1					1			2		
Billerica	174	16	Bacon	Jonas	3	1		1		2	1		1				9		
Billerica	174	17	Baldwin	Nahum	1			1		1	2		1				6		
Billerica	174	18	Baldwin	Benja'					1	2	2			1			6		
Billerica	174	19	Baldwin	John					1					1			2		
Billerica	174	20	Baldwin	Joel		1	1	1					1				4		
Billerica	174	21	Baldwin	Reuben	2	1		1		3			1				8		
Billerica	174	22	Bradstreet	Elijah	2			1		4		1	1				9		
Billerica	174	23	Barrett	Steph'			2	1		3		1	1				8		
Billerica	174	24	Batchelor	Jos' Jr	2	2	1	1			1	1					8		
Billerica	174	25	Baldwin	Wm	2	1	1	1	1	1	1			1			9		
Billerica	174	26	Bridge	Saml	2	1	1	1		1	1	1					8		
Billerica	174	27	Barron	Isaac		1	1			2	1	1					6		
Billerica	174	28	Bridge for Leland	Saml			46	40	3								89		
Billerica	174	29	Brown	Nathl Jr			1							2			3		
Billerica	174	30	Carlton	Amos		1		1		2			1				5		
Billerica	174	31	Carlton	John		1			1	1				1			4		
Billerica	174	32	Carlton	John Jr	1			1		1			1				4		
Billerica	174	33	Cook	Sears	1	1	1		1			3		1			8		
Billerica	174	34	Carr	Walter	3			1						1			5		
Billerica	174	35	Cummings	Henry					1		1		1	1			4		
Billerica	174	36	Colburn	Phins	1		1			1		1					4		
Billerica	174	37	Crosby	Josiah			1		1			1		1			4		
Billerica	174	38	Crosby	Oliver	1				1		1	1					6		
Billerica	174	39	Crosby	Timo'	1				1		2			1			5		
Billerica	174	40	Crosby	Josiah		3	1		1					2			7		
Billerica	174	41	Crosby	Eph'					1					1			2		
Billerica	174	42	Crosby	Eph' Jr	3			1	1	2			1				8		
Billerica	174	43	Crosby	John		1		1									1		
Billerica	174	44	Crosby	Hez'			1		1		1		1	1			5		
Billerica	174	45	Crosby	Jerem'			1	1		1	1		1				5		
Billerica	175	1	Crosby	Seth					1			1		1			3		
Billerica	175	2	Crosby	Seth Jr				1		2			1				4		
Billerica	175	3	Cragg	Tho'		1	1	1		2	2	1	1				9		
Billerica	175	4	Cragin	Aaron	1		1	1		1	1		1				6		
Billerica	175	5	Cragin	Silas	1	1	2				1	2					7		
Billerica	175	6	Durel	Ann			1			1			1				3		
Billerica	175	7	Dike	John		2		1		1			1				5		
Billerica	175	8	Duren	Reuben		1	1		1	1				1			5		
Billerica	175	9	Duren	Reuben Jr	1		2	1					1				5		
Billerica	175	10	Danforth	Jan*	1	1							1	1			4		
Billerica	175	11	Danforth	Jos'	1			1		3		1	1	1			8		

16

TOWN	PG#	LN#	HEADS OF HOUSEHOLD LAST NAME	FIRST NAME	FREE WHITE MALES under 10	10 to 16	16 to 26	26 to 45	45 and over	FREE WHITE FEMALES under 10	10 to 16	16 to 26	26 to 45	45 and over	TOTAL ALL OTHER	TOTAL SLAVES	TOTALS	DISTRICT/ TOWNSHIP	NOTES
Billerica	175	12	Danforth	John	2	1		1		1	1						6		
Billerica	175	13	Danforth	Benja'			1		1					1			3		
Billerica	175	14	Danforth	Eliz'	1	1							1	2			5		
Billerica	175	15	Davis	Benja'	1	2			1	3	1	2		1			11		
Billerica	175	16	Davis	Timo'	1	1		1		2		2	2				9		
Billerica	175	17	Dale	Jos'		2	1		1	1	1						6		
Billerica	175	18	Dexter	John			2										2		
Billerica	175	19	Dowse	Jos'		1		1		3		2	1		1		9		
Billerica	175	20	Dowse	Benja'	1		1		1	2	2		1				8		
Billerica	175	21	Duren	John	4			1					1				6		
Billerica	175	22	Easty	Ebenz'				1					1	1			3		
Billerica	175	23	Farmer	Edw'		1		1		1				1			4		
Billerica	175	24	Farmer	Edw' Jr	1		1		1					1			4		
Billerica	175	25	Farmer	Edw' 3rd	1	1	1	1		2			1				7		
Billerica	175	26	Farmer	John	1		1		1	1		1		1			6		
Billerica	175	27	Farmer	Mary									1	1			2		
Billerica	175	28	Farmer	Oliver		1		1	1					1			4		
Billerica	175	29	Farmer	Oliver Jr	2	1		1		2			2				8		
Billerica	175	30	Foster	Timo'				1		1	2	2	1				4		
Billerica	175	31	Frost	Wm	2	1			1	2				1			7		
Billerica	175	32	French	Isaac	1	1	1		1	1			1	1			7		
Billerica	175	33	French	Isaac Jr	1	3			1	1	1	1		1			9		
Billerica	175	34	French	Isaac 3rd	1	1	1			1		1					5		
Billerica	175	35	French	Jesse				1					1				2		
Billerica	175	36	French	Seth	1			1		1			1				4		
Billerica	175	37	French	Jonas				1					1				2		
Billerica	175	38	Friend	Reuben	4	1		1		2			1				9		
Billerica	175	39	Fuller	Silas				1				1	1				3		
Billerica	175	40	Farmer	Jotham	2		1			1			1				5		
Billerica	175	41	Gleason	Jos'	2			1					1				4		
Billerica	175	42	Gleason	Wm				1				1	1				3		
Billerica	175	43	Gleason	Wm Jr		1		1		1			1				4		
Billerica	176	1	Goodwin	Tho'	2			1		2	1		1				7		
Billerica	176	2	Heardman	Tho'	1			1		1				1			4		
Billerica	176	3	Hickle	Wm	1			1		1			1				4		
Billerica	176	4	Hill	Lot				1		2			1				4		
Billerica	176	5	Hill	Peter		1	1	1	1	1		1		1			7		
Billerica	176	6	Hill	Wm	1	2			1	2	1		1				8		
Billerica	176	7	Hill	John				1									1		
Billerica	176	8	Hill	John Jr			1						1				2		
Billerica	176	9	Hill	Mary				1						1			2		
Billerica	176	10	Hill	Jona'		1	1						1	2			6		
Billerica	176	11	Hill	Job	4		1		1	1	1	1	1				10		
Billerica	176	12	Hill	Thad'	1			1		1			1				4		
Billerica	176	13	Hill	Noah				1					1				2		
Billerica	176	14	Hill	Alph'	1	1		1		1	1		1				6		
Billerica	176	15	Jeffs	Henry				1				1		1			3		
Billerica	176	16	Jeffs	Mary									2	1			3		
Billerica	176	17	Jaques	Jos'		1			1	1	1			1			5		
Billerica	176	18	Jaques	Jos' Jr	1			1		1			1	1			5		
Billerica	176	19	Jaques	Timo'				1						1			2		
Billerica	176	20	Johnson	James				1		4			1	1			7		
Billerica	176	21	Kidder	John	2	2	1	1					1				8		
Billerica	176	22	Kidder	Ephrm			1	1						1			3		
Billerica	176	23	Kidder	Eph' Jr			1	1		1	1	1					5		
Billerica	176	24	Kitteridge	Nehem'		1	3		1	1	2		1				9		
Billerica	176	25	Kendal	Reuben				1									1		
Billerica	176	26	Kendal	Jos'	1	1	1	1		3		1	1				9		
Billerica	176	27	Lewis	John				1					1				2		
Billerica	176	28	Love	Wm				1					1				2		
Billerica	176	29	Lewiston	Wm	2		1	1		2			1				7		
Billerica	176	30	Lewiston	Tho'				1					1				2		
Billerica	176	31	Lewiston	John			1						1				2		
Billerica	176	32	Manning	Isaac				1				1		1			3		
Billerica	176	33	Manning	Jacob		1		1						1			3		
Billerica	176	34	Manning	Jesse	1			1				1	1				4		
Billerica	176	35	Manning	Wm		1	2		1	2	1	3		1			11		
Billerica	176	36	Marshall	Isaac				1					1				2		
Billerica	176	37	Marshall	Isaac Jr	1		1	1		2			1				6		
Billerica	176	38	Marshall	Saml			1	1					1				3		
Billerica	176	39	Mears	Tho'	1			1	1	1	1		1				6		
Billerica	176	40	Miller	John				1					1				2		
Billerica	176	41	Miller	John Jr			1						1				2		
Billerica	176	42	Manning	Jesse Jr			1			1			1				3		
Billerica	177	1	Needham	Asa	2		1			1			1				5		
Billerica	177	2	Osgood	Phins	1		1			2			1				5		
Billerica	177	3	Orne	Hannah								3	1	1			5		
Billerica	177	4	Pollard	Jona' P.	3	2		1				1	1				9		
Billerica	177	5	Pollard	Sols'			1	1	1					2			5		

TOWN	PG#	LN#	LAST NAME	FIRST NAME	FREE WHITE MALES under 10	10 to 16	16 to 26	26 to 45	45 and over	FREE WHITE FEMALES under 10	10 to 16	16 to 26	26 to 45	45 and over	TOTAL ALL OTHER	TOTAL SLAVES	TOTALS	DISTRICT/ TOWNSHIP	NOTES
Billerica	177	6	Pollard	Wm			1						1				2		
Billerica	177	7	Pollard	Edw'		1		1						1			3		
Billerica	177	8	Pollard	Jona'				1				1	1	1			4		
Billerica	177	9	Pritchard	Burly			1										1		
Billerica	177	10	Parker	John	2	2	1	1	1	2			2	1			12		
Billerica	177	11	Parker	John Jr		3	2		1		1	1	1				9		
Billerica	177	12	Parker	Steph'		1		1		3			1				6		
Billerica	177	13	Patten	John			2		1			2		1			6		
Billerica	177	14	Patten	John Jr	2	1		1		1	1		1				7		
Billerica	177	15	Patten	Asa		2			1				2	1			6		
Billerica	177	16	Patten	Wm		1	1		1				1	1			5		
Billerica	177	17	Pemberton	Ebenz'	1	2			1	1			1	1			7		
Billerica	177	18	Rupell	Benja		1	1			1			1				4		
Billerica	177	19	Ruggles	Joseph				1					1				2		
Billerica	177	20	Richardson	Oliver		1	1		1		1	2		5			11		
Billerica	177	21	Richardson	Tho'	1	1	1		1	2	1	4		1			12		
Billerica	177	22	Richardson	Saml				1						1			2		
Billerica	177	23	Richardson	Saml Jr		1	1	1		1	1		1				6		
Billerica	177	24	Richardson	John	2	1		1		1	1		1				7		
Billerica	177	25	Richardson	Eben'				1						1			2		
Billerica	177	26	Richardson	Eben' Jr	1	2	1		1	3	2	1	1				12		
Billerica	177	27	Richardson	Asa	2			1		1	1	1	1	2			9		
Billerica	177	28	Richardson	Josiah			1	1		1	1			1			5		
Billerica	177	29	Richardson	Silas	1	1		1					1				4		
Billerica	177	30	Richardson	Steph'				1				2		2			5		
Billerica	177	31	Richardson	Jacob		1	3		1		2	1	1	1			10		
Billerica	177	32	Richardson	Josiah		1							1				2		
Billerica	177	33	Rogers	Zeb				1						1			2		
Billerica	177	34	Rogers	Zeb Jr	3	1			1	1			1				7		
Billerica	177	35	Rogers	Micaijah	1	1	1	1			1	1					6		
Billerica	177	36	Rogers	Tho'	2		1	1		1			1	1	1		8		
Billerica	177	37	Rogers	Josiah	3	3	1	1		2	1		1				12		
Billerica	177	38	Rogers	John	3			1					1				5		
Billerica	177	39	Rogers	Wm	3		4	1	1	2		1	1				13		
Billerica	177	40	Russell	John	1			1		1			1	1			5		
Billerica	177	41	Simonds	John	2			1	1	1			1				6		
Billerica	177	42	Stickney	Jona'				1	1			1		2			5		
Billerica	177	43	Skilton	John		1	1			2			1				6		
Billerica	178	1	Stearns	Elijah			1			1			1				3		
Billerica	178	2	Stearns	Saml				1					1	2			4		
Billerica	178	3	Stearns	Isachar	2		1	1		2			1				7		
Billerica	178	4	Stearns	Isaac				1				1		1			3		
Billerica	178	5	Stearns	Timo'	2	1		1					1				5		
Billerica	178	6	Stearns	John				1									1		
Billerica	178	7	Stearns	Joseph	2	1		1		2			1				7		
Billerica	178	8	Stearns	Jona	3			1		1			1				6		
Billerica	178	9	Soley	John					1				1		1		3		
Billerica	178	10	Snow	John	2			1					1	1			5		
Billerica	178	11	Saunders	John	1				1			1		1			4		
Billerica	178	12	Saunders	Hannah							1			2			3		
Billerica	178	13	Shed	Zach	3		1	1		3			1				9		
Billerica	178	14	Shed	Jos'	1					2	1	1					6		
Billerica	178	15	Shed	Tho'				1						1			2		
Billerica	178	16	Symmes	Steph'		1		1						1			3		
Billerica	178	17	Sprague	Levi		1		1		3	1		1				7		
Billerica	178	18	Sprague	Mary	1					1	1		1				4		
Billerica	178	19	Spaulding	Benoni	1	1		1		5			1				9		
Billerica	178	20	Spaulding	Asa			2	1	2				2	1			8		
Billerica	178	21	Spaulding	Tho'	1		1		1	2			1				6		
Billerica	178	22	Thompson	Wm			2		1		1		1				5		
Billerica	178	23	Tarble	Wm	1		1		1	1		1	1				6		
Billerica	178	24	Tarble	Wm Jr			1										1		
Billerica	178	25	Tufts	Geo	1	1		1		3			1				7		
Billerica	178	26	Trull	Saml				1					1				2		
Billerica	178	27	Trull	Elijah	1		1	1		1		1	1				6		
Billerica	178	28	Trull	David	1			1	1	1	1		1	1			7		
Billerica	178	29	Taylor	Richd				1						1			2		
Billerica	178	30	White	Mary										1	1		2		
Billerica	178	31	Wilson	Seth	3	1		1		1			1	1			8		
Billerica	178	32	Wilson	John				1				1		1			3		
Billerica	178	33	Wilson	Jos'	2			1		2			1				6		
Billerica	178	34	Walker	Dudly	1	1	1	1		3		1	1				9		
Billerica	178	35	White	John				1				1		2			4		
Billerica	178	36	Weatherly	John	1			1		1			1				4		
Billerica	178	37	Whiting	Saml	1	4	1	1		2	1	1		1			12		
Billerica	178	38	Webber	Leonard			1										1		
Billerica	178	39	Wilkins	Wm	2		4	1		2	1	1	1				12		
Billerica	178	40	Wright	John	1	1		1		1	1	1	1				8		
Billerica	178	41	Wright	Danl		1	1		1		1		1	1			6		

18

TOWN	PG#	LN#	HEADS OF HOUSEHOLD		FREE WHITE MALES					FREE WHITE FEMALES					TOTAL ALL OTHER	TOTAL SLAVES	TOTALS	DISTRICT/ TOWNSHIP	NOTES
			LAST NAME	FIRST NAME	under 10	10 to 16	16 to 26	26 to 45	45 and over	under 10	10 to 16	16 to 26	26 to 45	45 and over					
Billerica	178	42	Weston	Saml				1					1				2		
Billerica	178	43	Wyer	Martha		3	2			1				2			8		

TOWN	PG#	LN#	LAST NAME	FIRST NAME	FREE WHITE MALES					FREE WHITE FEMALES					TOTAL ALL OTHER	TOTAL SLAVES	TOTALS	DISTRICT/ TOWNSHIP	NOTES
					under 10	10 to 16	16 to 26	26 to 45	45 and over	under 10	10 to 16	16 to 26	26 to 45	45 and over					
Boxborough	199	1	Taylor	Silas	1	1	1		1		1	2		1			8		
Boxborough	199	2	Taylor	Israel	1	1		1		1	1	1	1	1			8		
Boxborough	199	3	Cameron	Hugh					1					1			2		
Boxborough	199	4	Hayward	Paul		1	2		1		1	1	1	1			8		
Boxborough	199	5	Bachelor	Nehemiah	1	1			1	1		1		1			6		
Boxborough	199	6	Wood	Oliver	1	1	2		1	2	2		2	1			12		
Boxborough	199	7	Raymond	Molly	1					1		1					3		
Boxborough	199	8	Searjants	Samuel	2			1			1	1	1				6		
Boxborough	199	9	Wyman	Oliver					1			1		1			3		
Boxborough	199	10	Whitney	Joshua	3	1		1					1				6		
Boxborough	199	11	Warren	Joseph		1			1	1		1		1			5		
Boxborough	199	12	Raymond	Joseph	1				1	1	1		1	1			7		
Boxborough	199	13	Whitcomb	Samuel	2	1	1					1	1	1			7		
Boxborough	199	14	Lawrence	Thomas			2		1		2			1			6		
Boxborough	199	15	Fletcher	Eleazer			1		1					1			3		
Boxborough	199	16	Fletcher	Eleazer Jr	2	1		1		1			1				6		
Boxborough	199	17	Phillips	Ebenezer					1					1			2		
Boxborough	199	18	Foster	John		2		1		1			1				5		
Boxborough	199	19	Walker	Augustus	2			1		1			1				5		
Boxborough	199	20	Fox	Peter				1					1				2		
Boxborough	199	21	Kidder	John	1			1		2		1		1			6		
Boxborough	199	22	Davis	Oliver T.	1	1		1		3	1		1				8		
Boxborough	199	23	Fletcher	Abel	1	1	1		1		1	1		1			7		
Boxborough	199	24	Whitcomb	Ephraim		1	1		1		1	1		2			7		
Boxborough	199	25	Draper	Triphena	1		1						2	1			5		
Boxborough	199	26	Brown	Edward				1						1			2		
Boxborough	199	27	Whitcomb	Ephraim Jr	1			1		1	1						4		
Boxborough	200	1	Nourp	John	1			1		1		1					4		
Boxborough	200	2	Robbins	Daniel		1		1		2	1		1				6		
Boxborough	200	3	Witherbee	Silas				1					1				2		
Boxborough	200	4	Burges	Levi	1		1			1			1				4		
Boxborough	200	5	Willard	Joseph		1			1		2	5		1			10		
Boxborough	200	6	Brooks	Calvin	1			1		1		2					5		
Boxborough	200	7	Witherbee	Levi		1			1	1	1		1				5		
Boxborough	200	8	Holt	Thomas		1		1		1			1				4		
Boxborough	200	9	Witherbee	Phinehas				1					1				2		
Boxborough	200	10	Witherbee	Phinehas Jr		1		2	1				2	1			7		
Boxborough	200	11	Hastings	John	1		1						1				3		
Boxborough	200	12	Moore	Jonathan	1	1		1		2			1				6		
Boxborough	200	13	Whitcomb	Moses	2			1		3			1				7		
Boxborough	200	14	Robbins	Elisha	2			1		1	1	2	1				8		
Boxborough	200	15	Witherbee	Reuben	1			1		1		1					4		
Boxborough	200	16	Taylor	Ephraim		1	1	1				1		1			5		
Boxborough	200	17	Cooledg	Henry				1									1		
Boxborough	200	18	Cooledg	James D.	3	2		1		1	1		1				9		
Boxborough	200	19	Graham	Reuben		1		1				1					3		
Boxborough	200	20	Stevens	Benjamin	2	1	1	1		1		1	1				8		
Boxborough	200	21	Stone	Silas		1	2	1			1	2	2	1			10		
Boxborough	200	22	Taylor	Oliver	1		2	1		1			1				6		
Boxborough	200	23	Taylor	Mary									1				1		
Boxborough	200	24	Taylor	Hezekiah		1						1					2		
Boxborough	200	25	Whitcomb	Abel	1	1		1		1	2	1	2				9		
Boxborough	200	26	Mead	Oliver	2	2		1		2	1	2	1			2	13		
Boxborough	200	27	Witherbee	Samuel				1					1				2		
Boxborough	200	28	Witherbee	Simeon	1		1	1		3			1				7		
Boxborough	200	29	Witherbee	Samuel Jr		1		1		2			1				5		
Boxborough	200	30	Sawyer	Lemuel	1			1					1				3		
Boxborough	200	31	Whitcomb	William				1				1		1			3		
Boxborough	200	32	Whitcomb	Jotham				1		1		1	1	1			5		
Boxborough	200	33	Crouch	John				1					1				2		
Boxborough	200	34	Crouch	John Jr	2		1			1			1				5		
Boxborough	200	35	Morse	Benjamin	1		1			1	1		1				5		
Boxborough	200	36	Crouch	Amos	2		1			1			1				5		
Boxborough	200	37	Stearns	Miriam				1					1				2		
Boxborough	200	38	Hayward	Paul Jr	3			1		1			1				6		
Boxborough	200	39	Sawyer	Nathaniel		2		1			1	1	1				6		
Boxborough	200	40	Crouch	Timothy	3		1	1		2			1				8		
Boxborough	200	41	Crouch	Jonathan	2	1	1	1		1	1		1				8		
Boxborough	200	42	Chester	Prince											5		5		
Boxborough	200	43	Holten	Phinehas	3			1		1	1		1				7		
Boxborough	200	44	Wheeler	Peter	4	1		1		1	1		1				9		
Boxborough	201	1	Coy	John W.				1						1			2		
Boxborough	201	2	Canada	John				2						2			2		

TOWN	PG#	LN#	LAST NAME	FIRST NAME	under 10	10 to 16	16 to 26	26 to 45	45 and over	under 10	10 to 16	16 to 26	26 to 45	45 and over	TOTAL ALL OTHER	TOTAL SLAVES	TOTALS	DISTRICT/ TOWNSHIP	NOTES
			HEADS OF HOUSEHOLD		FREE WHITE MALES					FREE WHITE FEMALES									
Burlington	154	1	Abbott	William		1			1					2			4		
Burlington	154	2	Abbott	William Jr			1				1		1				3		
Burlington	154	3	Alexander	Giles			2		1			1	1	1			6		
Burlington	154	4	Blanchard	Benjamin	2		1	1		1	1	1	1				8		
Burlington	154	5	Blanchard	Josiah	1			1		2			1				5		
Burlington	154	6	Blanchard	David	2				1	1	1	1	1				7		
Burlington	154	7	Berry	James		1	1		1		1	1		1			6		
Burlington	154	8	Burton	Rebekah		1							1	1			3		
Burlington	154	9	Baldwin	Isaac	3	2		1					1	1			8		
Burlington	154	10	Center	Bill				1						1			2		
Burlington	154	11	Caldwell	Sarah	1								1	1			3		
Burlington	154	12	Caldwell	Joseph	2	1		2					1				6		
Burlington	154	13	Cutler	Samuel	2		1	1		1	1		1				7		
Burlington	154	14	Cutler	Nathaniel				1					1				2		
Burlington	154	15	Cutler	Nathaniel Jr		1	3	1					1				6		
Burlington	154	16	Carter	James	1	2	1	1		2	1	1	1				10		
Burlington	154	17	Carter	William	1		3	1				1	1				7		
Burlington	154	18	Carter	Joshua		2		1	1	1		1					6		
Burlington	154	19	Carter	Jonas	1		1	1		1	2	1	1				8		
Burlington	154	20	Dean	Jesse		1	2		1		1	1	1				7		
Burlington	154	21	Dean	Thomas		1		2		1		2	1				7		
Burlington	154	22	Flagg	Goliah		1		1		2			1				5		
Burlington	154	23	Farrington	Mathw				1	1	1			1				3		
Burlington	154	24	Fowle	Samuel	1	2			1	1	1	1		1			8		
Burlington	154	25	Goodwin	Thomas	1				1					1			3		
Burlington	154	26	Goodwin	Reuel		1	1	1		1			1				5		
Burlington	154	27	Gleason	Thomas				1		1			1				3		
Burlington	154	28	Homer	Robert		1		1				1		1			4		
Burlington	154	29	Hopkins	Jesse				1		1			1				3		
Burlington	154	30	Howard	Ebenez			1						1				2		
Burlington	154	31	Heath	James	2		1					1					4		
Burlington	154	32	Johnson	Rebekah		1	1						1				3		
Burlington	154	33	Johnson	William				1				1	1				3		
Burlington	154	34	Johnson	Jotham	2		1		1	1	2		2				9		
Burlington	154	35	Jones	Abigail									1		1		2		
Burlington	154	36	Jaquith	Andrew			1			1			1				3		
Burlington	154	37	Johnson	Abijah			1			2		1	1				5		
Burlington	154	38	Johnson	Abiathar				1					1				2		
Burlington	154	39	Kendall	John	1	1		1		3	1	1	1				9		
Burlington	154	40	Kimbal	Reuben		1			2			1		1			5		
Burlington	154	41	Kendall	Joshua				1					1				2		
Burlington	154	42	Kendall	William		1						1					2		
Burlington	154	43	Kendall	Daniel			1						1				2		
Burlington	155	1	Lawrence	Jonathn	2		1			1	1		1				6		
Burlington	155	2	Lovering	John	1		1			1			1				4		
Burlington	155	3	Munro	Ishmael	1		1	1	1	1			2				7		
Burlington	155	4	Marion	Isaac			1		1	1	1			3			7		
Burlington	155	5	McIntier	Joseph	5		1						1				7		
Burlington	155	6	Marrett	John				1				1	2				4		
Burlington	155	7	Mullet	Robert	1		1			1			1				4		
Burlington	155	8	Nevers	Samuel	2	2			1	3	1		1	1			11		
Burlington	155	9	Parker	Simeon			1				2		1				4		
Burlington	155	10	Procter	Ruth			1				2		1	3			7		
Burlington	155	11	Peters	Phillip			1				2	3		1			7		
Burlington	155	12	Pasho	John A	2	1		1		2	1		1	1			9		
Burlington	155	13	Reed	Prudence									1				1		
Burlington	155	14	Reed	Jonathn	3			1		2			1				7		
Burlington	155	15	Reed	George		1			1				1				3		
Burlington	155	16	Reed	Jonas		2		1		3			1				7		
Burlington	155	17	Reed	James	1	2	1		1	1	1		2		1		10		
Burlington	155	18	Reed	James Jr	2	1		1		3		3	1				11		
Burlington	155	19	Reed	Samuel				1					1				2		
Burlington	155	20	Russell	Amos		1		1		3		1					6		
Burlington	155	21	Russell	Molly						1			1				2		
Burlington	155	22	Stevens	Jedidiah			3			1		1					5		
Burlington	155	23	Smith	Jonathan	1			1		1		1	1				5		
Burlington	155	24	Simonds	Gideon	2			1		2	1	1					7		
Burlington	155	25	Skilton	Matthew	2	1			1		1		1				6		
Burlington	155	26	Skilton	Thomas			2		1			1		1			5		
Burlington	155	27	Skilton	Dayz	2		2		1	1	1			1			8		
Burlington	155	28	Simonds	Caleb	3	2	1	1		2	1		1				11		
Burlington	155	29	Simonds	Jonathan			1		1	3	2		1				8		
Burlington	155	30	Simonds	Calvin	2	2	2		1		1		2	1			11		
Burlington	155	31	Shed	Samuel	1	1		1		2			1				6		
Burlington	155	32	Skilton	Matthw Jr			1						1				2		
Burlington	155	33	Taylor	John	1			1					1				3		
Burlington	155	34	Trull	Soloman			1			3			1				5		
Burlington	155	35	Tay	Isaiah	1			1				1					3		
Burlington	155	36	Tu*	Timothy				1					1				2		

TOWN	PG#	LN#	LAST NAME	FIRST NAME	FREE WHITE MALES					FREE WHITE FEMALES					TOTAL ALL OTHER	TOTAL SLAVES	TOTALS	DISTRICT/ TOWNSHIP	NOTES
					under 10	10 to 16	16 to 26	26 to 45	45 and over	under 10	10 to 16	16 to 26	26 to 45	45 and over					
Burlington	155	37	Tu*	Edward		1	1		1	3		1					7		
Burlington	156	1	Wood	John		1			1	1				1			4		
Burlington	156	2	Wood	John Jr	1	1	1	1		2	1	1	1				9		
Burlington	156	3	Wyman	Abel		2	3		1	1		2		1			10		
Burlington	156	4	Wyman	Ezra					1		1	1	2	1			6		
Burlington	156	5	Walker	Josiah					1				1	2			4		
Burlington	156	6	Walker	Josiah Jr			1	1		1			1				4		
Burlington	156	7	Winn	Joseph					1		1	2		1			5		
Burlington	156	8	Walker	James				1			1		1				3		
Burlington	156	9	Walker	Samuel	2	1		1		2	2		1				9		
Burlington	156	10	Walker	Edward	1	1	2	1		4	1	1	1				12		
Burlington	156	11	Wilson	Rebekah									1	1			2		
Burlington	156	12	Winn	David	1	1			2		1	2		1			8		
Burlington	156	13	Winn	Timothy			3	1	1	1		1	1	3			11		
Burlington	156	14	Wyman	Ahira					1					1			2		
Burlington	156	15	Winn	Jeremiah					1	1	1						2		
Burlington	156	16	Walker	John	1	2		1		1			1				6		
Burlington	156	17	Wood	Edward	2			1			1		1	1			6		
Burlington	156	18	Wilson	James			1			1		1					3		
Burlington	156	19	Winn	Abel				1		2			1				4		

TOWN	PG#	LN#	LAST NAME	FIRST NAME	FREE WHITE MALES					FREE WHITE FEMALES					TOTAL ALL OTHER	TOTAL SLAVES	TOTALS	DISTRICT/ TOWNSHIP	NOTES
					under 10	10 to 16	16 to 26	26 to 45	45 and over	under 10	10 to 16	16 to 26	26 to 45	45 and over					
Cambridge	220	1	A*	James	2		2	2		2		3					11		
Cambridge	220	2	Allen	Abijah				1	3	1	1						6		
Cambridge	220	3	Adams	John	2		1		1	2	1	1	2	1			11		
Cambridge	220	4	Aspenwall	Saml				1		3	1	1	1				7		
Cambridge	220	5	Adams	Daniel	1		1	1		2	1		1				7		
Cambridge	220	6	Adams	Hanah									1	1			2		
Cambridge	220	7	Beals	Thon			1		2	1	1	1					6		
Cambridge	220	8	Belnap	Jason	1			1						1			3		
Cambridge	220	9	Belnap	Joseph		1			1			2					4		
Cambridge	220	10	Butterfield	Deborah	1			2				1		1			5		
Cambridge	220	11	Butterfield	Saml	2	1	1		1	2	1		1				9		
Cambridge	220	12	Butterfield	John		1			1	3			1				6		
Cambridge	220	13	Boardman	William	1			1		1			1				4		
Cambridge	220	14	Boardman	Aaron				1		1	2	1	1				6		
Cambridge	220	15	Blake	Oliver				1					1				2		
Cambridge	220	16	Bettleship	Levis			2	2						1	1		6		
Cambridge	220	17	Buckman	Jacob	2			1					1				4		
Cambridge	220	18	Blackington	Wm	1			1		2			1				5		
Cambridge	220	19	Blackington	Israel			1					2					3		
Cambridge	220	20	Blackington	Edward		1						1					2		
Cambridge	220	21	Bell	Daniel		1	1			1		1		1			5		
Cambridge	220	22	Bates	Joseph		2			1			2		1			6		
Cambridge	220	23	Bartlett	Eben	1				1					1			3		
Cambridge	220	24	Bartlett	Joseph		1	3	1				1	1				7		
Cambridge	220	25	Bradish	William	1				1	1		4		1			8		
Cambridge	220	26	Bigelow	Abel	1	1		1		3		2					8		
Cambridge	220	27	Bonner	George	1			1		2		1					5		
Cambridge	220	28	Brown	John			1		1	2			1				5		
Cambridge	220	29	Boardman	Richard			1			1	1	1					4		
Cambridge	220	30	Bartlett	Saml		3			1	2	2	3		1			12		
Cambridge	220	31	Brattle	Thos	1	2			1			2					6		
Cambridge	220	32	Bliss	Theordore				1					1				2		
Cambridge	220	33	Brown	Daniel			1	1				1	3				6		
Cambridge	220	34	Bacon	Norman			1			2			1	1			5		
Cambridge	220	35	Backer	Benjn		1	1	1		1				1			5		
Cambridge	220	36	Brown	Ebenr		1	1	1		2	1	1	1				8		
Cambridge	220	37	Bliss	Eli	3		1		2	1							9		
Cambridge	220	38	Bush	Levi	4		7	1			3	2	1				18		
Cambridge	220	39	Cook	Mary	3	1				4		1	3	1			13		
Cambridge	220	40	Cutter	Washington		1	1			1							3		
Cambridge	220	41	Cutter	James	3	1		1		2		1	1				9		
Cambridge	220	42	Clark	Ballard	1	1				1		1					4		
Cambridge	220	43	Cook	Betsy			1	1						2			4		
Cambridge	221	1	Childs	Phinias			1			2				1			4		
Cambridge	221	2	Crafts	Saml	1			1		1			1				4		
Cambridge	221	3	Cutter	Nehemiah	3	2			1	2	2		1				11		
Cambridge	221	4	Cutter	Charles	1	1		1					1				4		
Cambridge	221	5	Cook	Ephm		1	4	1		1	3						10		
Cambridge	221	6	Cutter	Gersham					1					1			2		
Cambridge	221	7	Cutter	Aaron	1			1		3	1		1				7		
Cambridge	221	8	Cutter	Ephraim	3			1		2			1				7		
Cambridge	221	9	Cutter	Frances		2	1	5	1	2	1	1	1				14		
Cambridge	221	10	Cole	Caleb	2			2		1			1				6		
Cambridge	221	11	Cutter	Jona	2			1		1			1	1			6		
Cambridge	221	12	Cutter	William Jr	2	2	1	1			2		1				9		
Cambridge	221	13	Cutter	Amos				2						1			3		
Cambridge	221	14	Cutter	Stephen		1			1	1	1			1			5		
Cambridge	221	15	Cutter	Lucy										1			1		
Cambridge	221	16	Cutter	Hannah	2	1					1	1	1	1			7		
Cambridge	221	17	Cutter	John		1	1			1			1				4		
Cambridge	221	18	Cutter	William		1		1	1	1		1		1			5		
Cambridge	221	19	Crosby	Simeon	4			1					1				6		
Cambridge	222	1	Cox	Saml	2		3	4				1					11		
Cambridge	222	2	Chandler	Lois			1					1		1			3		
Cambridge	222	3	Chatburn	Sarah	1			1				1		1			4		
Cambridge	222	4	Cox	Walter		1	2	1		2		1					7		
Cambridge	222	5	Cutter	Mary						2	1		1	1			5		
Cambridge	222	6	Colstone	John			1		1				1	1			4		
Cambridge	222	7	Clark	Charles	2		3	1	1	1			1	1			10		
Cambridge	222	8	Chickering	Joseph			1										1		
Cambridge	222	9	Childs	Saml	1	1	1		1	1			1				6		
Cambridge	222	10	Cunningham	Wm	1			1		2		1					5		
Cambridge	222	11	Craige	Andrew			1		1	1		1	1	1			6		
Cambridge	222	12	Cook	Thos				1					1				2		
Cambridge	222	13	Champney	Nathl	2	1		1		1			1	1			7		
Cambridge	222	14	Crafts	Joseph	1		2			1		1					5		
Cambridge	222	15	Coolidge	Caleb	2				1	1				1			5		
Cambridge	222	16	Capen	Benjn	2	2			1				2				8		
Cambridge	222	17	Cook	William		1	1	1		1			1				5		

TOWN	PG#	LN#	LAST NAME	FIRST NAME	FWM under 10	FWM 10 to 16	FWM 16 to 26	FWM 26 to 45	FWM 45 and over	FWF under 10	FWF 10 to 16	FWF 16 to 26	FWF 26 to 45	FWF 45 and over	TOTAL ALL OTHER	TOTAL SLAVES	TOTALS	DISTRICT/ TOWNSHIP	NOTES
Cambridge	222	18	Capen	Jona	1			1		1			1				4		
Cambridge	222	19	Coolidge	Caleb Jr	1			1					1				3		
Cambridge	222	20	Champaney	Isaac				1		2	1		1				5		
Cambridge	222	21	Dickinson	Edward				1						2			3		
Cambridge	222	22	Dickinson	Isiah	1				1	2			1				5		
Cambridge	222	23	Danforth	Elizabeth										4			4		
Cambridge	222	24	Deforis	Stephen	1	1		1				2		1			6		
Cambridge	222	25	Dana	Francis			3	1	2	1	3	1	1	1	2		15		
Cambridge	222	26	Dana	Joseph	1			1		3			1	1			7		
Cambridge	222	27	Davis	John		1	1			2		1	1	1			7		
Cambridge	222	28	Davis	John Jr	1		3						1				5		
Cambridge	222	29	Dickenson	Henry				1			1				1		3		
Cambridge	222	30	Dickenson	Gilbert				1		1	1	1					4		
Cambridge	222	31	Dewing	Jabez	1	1	1	1	1	1	1	1					8		
Cambridge	222	32	Dana	Stephen	1			2	1	2		1		1			8		
Cambridge	222	33	Dana	Henry	2			1		2	1	1					7		
Cambridge	222	34	Dana	James	1			1						1			3		
Cambridge	222	35	Dana	Caleb	3			1		3			1				9		
Cambridge	222	36	Emerson	Elias	3	1	1	1		1		1	1				9		
Cambridge	222	37	Easterbrooks	Nehemiah				1		1							2		
Cambridge	222	38	Easterbrooks	Eliakim	3			1		1		1					6		
Cambridge	223	1	Easterbrooks	John			3										3		
Cambridge	223	2	Emerson	Joseph			1										1		
Cambridge	223	3	Ellis	Andrew			1	1				1					3		
Cambridge	223	4	English	Thos	1	1	1	2	1	1		1	2				10		
Cambridge	223	5	English	John		1	2					1					4		
Cambridge	223	6	Fisk	Thaddeus		1		1		3	1	1					8		
Cambridge	223	7	Frost	Sarah		2						2	1	2			7		
Cambridge	223	8	Frost	Sarah	1									3			4		
Cambridge	223	9	Frost	Ephhm	2		2	1	1	2		1	2				11		
Cambridge	223	10	Frost	John	3		1	1		2	1	1	1				10		
Cambridge	223	11	Frost	Seth	1	2		1		2	1	1	1				9		
Cambridge	223	12	Frost	Amos	3	2		1	1	2		1	1	1			12		
Cambridge	223	13	Frost	Stephen	1		1		1	1	3	2		1			10		
Cambridge	223	14	Foster	Noah	1			1					1				3		
Cambridge	223	15	Frost	James		1		1			1	2	1				6		
Cambridge	223	16	Foxcraft	John				2		2	1						5		
Cambridge	223	17	Fowl	Martha										1			1		
Cambridge	223	18	Fessenden	Icabud	3	1		1					1	1			7		
Cambridge	223	19	Frost	John	2			1		2	1	2		1			9		
Cambridge	223	20	Frost	Cooper	2			1		2				1			6		
Cambridge	223	21	Farthingham	Willm			3	1		1				1			6		
Cambridge	223	22	Farthingham	Charles	1		1		4	1		1					8		
Cambridge	223	23	Frost	Walter	2	2	2	1		1	2		1				11		
Cambridge	223	24	Frost	Gideon				1					1	2			4		
Cambridge	223	25	Frost	Willm			1					1					2		
Cambridge	223	26	Frost	David		1	1						1				3		
Cambridge	223	27	Frost	James				2		1							3		
Cambridge	223	28	Fluker	Mima							1	1	1	1			4		
Cambridge	223	29	Fillebrown	James	1	1		3					1	1			7		
Cambridge	223	30	Flagsawyer	Samll			2	2					1				5		
Cambridge	223	31	Fillebrown	James Jr	1		1			2			1				5		
Cambridge	223	32	Farrer	Samll			1										1		
Cambridge	223	33	Foster	Bassender	1	2	2	2	1	1		1	1	1			12		
Cambridge	223	34	Fairweather	Thos			1		1			1	1	1			5		
Cambridge	223	35	Fortner	Nathl				1		1			1				3		
Cambridge	223	36	Foster	John	2	2		1		3			1	1			10		
Cambridge	223	37	Fuller	Ebenz	1			1		2			1				5		
Cambridge	223	38	Frost	Nepton											3		3		
Cambridge	223	39	Fillebrown	Edward				1		1	1	1		1			5		
Cambridge	223	40	Freeman	Ruth									1	1			2		
Cambridge	224	1	Gould	Elizabeth	1	1	1			1	2	1					8		
Cambridge	224	2	Gervis	Leonard	2	1	5		2		1	4	2	1			18		
Cambridge	224	3	Godard	Thos		1	1		1	1				1			5		
Cambridge	224	4	Gervis	Nathl			3	1	1	2			2	1			10		
Cambridge	224	5	Gannett	Caleb		1	2		1	1		1	1	1			8		
Cambridge	224	6	Gammage	Wm	1	3	1		1	2		2	1	1			12		
Cambridge	224	7	Gerry	Elbridge	3		2	1		4		1	2	3			16		
Cambridge	224	8	Godden	Jona	1	2	1	1		3		2		1			11		
Cambridge	224	9	Greenwood	Nevin			1										1		
Cambridge	224	10	Gookin	Esquise	2		1	1		2			1				7		
Cambridge	224	11	Gookin	Edmund	1	1	1	1		2			1				7		
Cambridge	224	12	Griggs	Nathl			1	1				1					3		
Cambridge	224	13	Griggs	Moses	1	2	3		1		1	2		1			11		
Cambridge	224	14	Gardner	Thos		1	3	1	1	2			2	1			11		
Cambridge	224	15	Gardner	Richd	1		3	1				2	3				10		
Cambridge	224	16	Gardner	Jethro											3		3		
Cambridge	224	17	Hill	David	1		1					1	1				4		
Cambridge	224	18	Hill	Dorcas			1						1	1			3		

24

TOWN	PG#	LN#	HEADS OF HOUSEHOLD LAST NAME	HEADS OF HOUSEHOLD FIRST NAME	M under 10	M 10 to 16	M 16 to 26	M 26 to 45	M 45 and over	F under 10	F 10 to 16	F 16 to 26	F 26 to 45	F 45 and over	TOTAL ALL OTHER	TOTAL SLAVES	TOTALS	DISTRICT/ TOWNSHIP	NOTES
Cambridge	224	19	Hill	Wm		1	2		1		1	3	1	1			10		
Cambridge	224	20	Hill	Wm Jr	2			1		1	1		1				6		
Cambridge	224	21	Hill	Abrm					1				1				2		
Cambridge	224	22	Hill	James		1		1		1	1	1					5		
Cambridge	224	23	Hall	Thos	1	1	1	1		2	3	1	1				11		
Cambridge	224	24	Hill	Mathew	1		1						1				3		
Cambridge	224	25	Hunt	Saml	2		1			1		1					5		
Cambridge	224	26	Hill	Zachr	3	1		1		1		1	1				8		
Cambridge	224	27	Haynes	Joseph			1						1				2		
Cambridge	224	28	Hastings	Lydia					1				4	1			6		
Cambridge	224	29	Hill	Joseph	1			1		3			1				6		
Cambridge	224	30	Hastings	Saml				3			1	1					5		
Cambridge	224	31	Hovey	Josiah				2		1			1				4		
Cambridge	224	32	Hovey	Phineas		1				3		1	1				6		
Cambridge	224	33	Hayden	John	1	4	2			1	1	1					10		
Cambridge	224	34	Harlow	Asaph		1		1		3			1	1			7		
Cambridge	224	35	Harrington	Benjn	1		1			2	1		1				6		
Cambridge	224	36	Hill	Lydia	1						1		1	1			4		
Cambridge	224	37	Hill	Sarah										1			1		
Cambridge	224	38	Hall	Ebenz	3	1		1		1	2		1				9		
Cambridge	224	39	Hovey	Moses	1			1		2			1				5		
Cambridge	224	40	Howard	Charles	1			1		2	1						5		
Cambridge	225	1	Hancock	Mary			1			1			2				4		
Cambridge	225	2	Hunnawell	Eunos			2	1				2	1	1			7		
Cambridge	225	3	Hayles	Tabor	2			1		2		1					6		
Cambridge	225	4	How	Nancy								3					3		
Cambridge	225	5	Henry	Jona	3		1	1		2		2					9		
Cambridge	225	6	Hunnawell	Elizath	2					2			1	1			5		
Cambridge	225	7	Hedge	Levi			1										1		
Cambridge	225	8	Hill	Aaron	1	2	1	1		3	2	1	2				13		
Cambridge	225	9	How	Hannah				1		2			2				5		
Cambridge	225	10	Hubard	Wm	1			1		3	1		1				7		
Cambridge	225	11	Hill	Benjn Jr	1	1		1					1				4		
Cambridge	225	12	Hill	Benjn		1	1		1	1			1				5		
Cambridge	225	13	Hill	Edward			1			2			1				4		
Cambridge	225	14	Hastings	Reuben	1	1		2	1		1	1	1				8		
Cambridge	225	15	Hovey	Thos	2	1	1	1		1	1						8		
Cambridge	225	16	Haryd	Dudly	1		1				1	1	1				5		
Cambridge	225	17	Holten	Benjn	1		1					1					3		
Cambridge	225	18	Holbrook	John	2	2		1		1	1		1				8		
Cambridge	225	19	Hastings	Edward		1	1		1	2			1	1			7		
Cambridge	225	20	Hovey	James	1	1		1		1			1				5		
Cambridge	225	21	Hovey	Ebenz		1	1	1		1		1					5		
Cambridge	225	22	Jenks	Samll		1	2		1				1				5		
Cambridge	225	23	Jones	Samll	1			1		1			1				4		
Cambridge	225	24	Jenks	Wm	1	1	1				1	1					5		
Cambridge	225	25	Jonneson	Timothy L.	2	1		1		2			2				8		
Cambridge	225	26	King	Lemuel	2		1			1			1				5		
Cambridge	225	27	Kendall	Joshua	2	1	1	1	1		2	1		1			10		
Cambridge	225	28	Kidder	Samll	2	1			1	3		2	3	2			14		
Cambridge	225	29	Kendall	Jabez		1			1	1	1	1		1			6		
Cambridge	225	30	Kidder	Mary						1		1		1			3		
Cambridge	225	31	Kneeland	Elizath					1	1	3		1				6		
Cambridge	225	32	Kerr	Wm	1		1			1		1					4		
Cambridge	225	33	Lock	Saml	1	3	2	1	1	1		1		1			11		
Cambridge	225	34	Lane	Ebenz	1			1		1	1						4		
Cambridge	225	35	Loseing	David	2			1		1			1	1			6		
Cambridge	225	36	Lopas	Kathm									2				2		
Cambridge	225	37	Lock	Joseph	2		2	1				1		1			7		
Cambridge	225	38	Lock	Wm		1		1			1		1				4		
Cambridge	225	39	Lock	Benjm	3			1		1	1		1	1			8		
Cambridge	225	40	Lock	Nathn				1		2		1					4		
Cambridge	226	1	Lock	Francis	2	1	2		1			1		2			9		
Cambridge	226	2	Lock	Joseph			2	1									3		
Cambridge	226	3	Lane	John	1	4	2		1	1				1			10		
Cambridge	226	4	Learned	Thos		1			1			1		1			4		
Cambridge	226	5	Learned	Aaron					1	2		1					4		
Cambridge	226	6	Lock	Saml Jr	1		1			1		1					4		
Cambridge	226	7	Lee	Jane				1	1	1	1	1	1	1			7		
Cambridge	226	8	Lee	Joseph		1		2		2			1				6		
Cambridge	226	9	Learned	Josiah	1	1	1	1			1		1				6		
Cambridge	226	10	Linch	John	1			1		2			1				5		
Cambridge	226	11	Learned	Saml					1				1				2		
Cambridge	226	12	Livanos	Jona	1	2		1		3	1		1				9		
Cambridge	226	13	Lee	Mark											3		3		
Cambridge	226	14	Mason	Josiah Jr		1	1			2			1				5		
Cambridge	226	15	Mackey	James	2		1					1					4		
Cambridge	226	16	Mannen	Wm		1			1				1				3		
Cambridge	226	17	Manson	Frederick			1			1		1					3		

TOWN	PG#	LN#	LAST NAME	FIRST NAME	FREE WHITE MALES under 10	10 to 16	16 to 26	26 to 45	45 and over	FREE WHITE FEMALES under 10	10 to 16	16 to 26	26 to 45	45 and over	TOTAL ALL OTHER	TOTAL SLAVES	TOTALS	DISTRICT/ TOWNSHIP	NOTES
Cambridge	226	18	Moredoc	Jacob W	1		1						1				3		
Cambridge	226	19	Mason	Thadd					1	4	1		3	1			10		
Cambridge	226	20	Mason	Daniel		2		1		1			1				5		
Cambridge	226	21	Moore	Francis			1		1	1	1			1			5		
Cambridge	226	22	Morse	William				1									1		
Cambridge	226	23	Moore	Josiah		2	3	1			2		1	2			11		
Cambridge	226	24	Mason	Thos		1		1			1		1				4		
Cambridge	226	25	Mullen	John	1	1		1		2		1	1				7		
Cambridge	226	26	Morse	Susanna	1		1		2	2	1	2	1	1			11		
Cambridge	226	27	Morse	Arnold		1				2		1					4		
Cambridge	226	28	Mills	Samll	1	1		1		1	1		2				7		
Cambridge	226	29	Mannen	Samll		1		1						1			3		
Cambridge	226	30	Mason	Jacob	1			1		1	1		1				5		
Cambridge	226	31	Nutting	Elizabeth					5	1		2		7			15		
Cambridge	226	32	Norton	Elizth						1			1				2		
Cambridge	226	33	Noreross	John			1	1		1			1				4		
Cambridge	226	34	Perry	James	1	1		1				1		1			5		
Cambridge	226	35	Patterson	Joseph				1					1				2		
Cambridge	226	36	Parks	Leonard	2			1		4	1		1				9		
Cambridge	226	37	Pierce	Solomon		1	3		1	1		2		1			9		
Cambridge	227	1	Pierce	Jonas	2		1	1		4			1				9		
Cambridge	227	2	Parker	David	1			1		2			1				5		
Cambridge	227	3	Prentice	John	2			1		2		1					6		
Cambridge	227	4	Prentice	Henry		3		1					1				5		
Cambridge	227	5	Prentice	Wm		1		1		2				1			5		
Cambridge	227	6	Prentice	Henry			1	1		2	2						6		
Cambridge	227	7	Prentice	George	1	1	1	1	1			2	1				9		
Cambridge	227	8	Prentice	Soloman				1					1				2		
Cambridge	227	9	Prentice	Ebenz	1	1		1		1			1				5		
Cambridge	227	10	Page	Jacob	2	1		1		1			1				6		
Cambridge	227	11	Porter	Israel	1	2	1		1	1		2		1			9		
Cambridge	227	12	Palmer	John	1	3		1	1	2			1				9		
Cambridge	227	13	Pearsons	Eliphalet	1	1	1		1			2	2	1			9		
Cambridge	227	14	Porter	Joseph			1			1			1				3		
Cambridge	227	15	Palmer	Stephen				1					1				2		
Cambridge	227	16	Pearsons	Gorom		1	1	1		1			4	1			9		
Cambridge	227	17	Pearsons	Thos	2			1		3	1	1					8		
Cambridge	227	18	Pomson	Samll	1	3		5	1	1	2	3	2				18		
Cambridge	227	19	Phillips	Nathan	3			1		1			1				6		
Cambridge	227	20	Robbins	Nathan	1	1	1						1				4		
Cambridge	227	21	Russell	Edward	1	1		1		3			1	1			8		
Cambridge	227	22	Russell	Josiah	1			1		2			1				5		
Cambridge	227	23	Russell	Elizth			1							1			2		
Cambridge	227	24	Russell	Daniel				1					1				2		
Cambridge	227	25	Russell	Patten					1					1			2		
Cambridge	227	26	Russell	Nathan	2	1		1				2	1				7		
Cambridge	227	27	Russell	Ichabod			1	2					2				5		
Cambridge	227	28	Russell	Samll				1					2				3		
Cambridge	227	29	Rust	Wallis		1	1	1		2		1					6		
Cambridge	227	30	Russell	Thos			2	1				2		1			6		
Cambridge	227	31	Russell	Noah	1	1		1		2	1	1	1				8		
Cambridge	227	32	Richardson	Raham	2			1					1				4		
Cambridge	227	33	Reed	Joseph					1	1	2			1			5		
Cambridge	227	34	Richardson	Giles	3			1	1	1	1		2				9		
Cambridge	227	35	Richardson	Elias	1	1		1		4		1	2	1			11		
Cambridge	227	36	Richardson	Richd	3	1	5		1	1	1	1	1				14		
Cambridge	227	37	Reed	Josiah				1					2				3		
Cambridge	227	38	Russell	David	2			1		1			1				5		
Cambridge	227	39	Robbins	Philemon	1	1		1		2		1	1				7		
Cambridge	227	40	Robbins	Elisha	1			1		3			1				6		
Cambridge	228	1	Row	Isaac	4	2		1		1	1		1				10		
Cambridge	228	2	Row	James	2		2		1		3		2	1			11		
Cambridge	228	3	Robbins	Anna									1				1		
Cambridge	228	4	Reed	James				1					1				2		
Cambridge	228	5	Russell	Mongo											3		3		
Cambridge	228	6	Swan	George	1	1	1		1	1	1	2		1			9		
Cambridge	228	7	Swan	Sarah	1							1	1				3		
Cambridge	228	8	Straton	Nathan			1						1				2		
Cambridge	228	9	Swaney	Willm			1	1			2	1		1			6		
Cambridge	228	10	Stone	Mary	1					3	3	1		3	1		12		
Cambridge	228	11	Swan	Timf	4			2		1			1				8		
Cambridge	228	12	Swan	Ebenz	1			1					1	1			4		
Cambridge	228	13	Swan	Gershom	2		3	1		2			2	1			11		
Cambridge	228	14	Shed	John	3	1		1		1			1				7		
Cambridge	228	15	Sterley	Saml M.				1					1				2		
Cambridge	228	16	Sawing	Joseph				1		1			1				3		
Cambridge	228	17	Shed	Frances			2						1				3		
Cambridge	228	18	Spooner	Andrew		1		1	1	1	3	1					8		
Cambridge	228	19	Smith	Cathn							3		1				4		
Cambridge	228	20	Stedman	Ebenz	1	1	1	1	1	1	3		1				10		

TOWN	PG#	LN#	LAST NAME	FIRST NAME	FREE WHITE MALES					FREE WHITE FEMALES					TOTAL ALL OTHER	TOTAL SLAVES	TOTALS	DISTRICT/ TOWNSHIP	NOTES
					under 10	10 to 16	16 to 26	26 to 45	45 and over	under 10	10 to 16	16 to 26	26 to 45	45 and over					
Cambridge	228	21	Shed	Nathan		1	4	2	1			2					10		
Cambridge	228	22	Sparrowhawk	Mary										2	1		3		
Cambridge	228	23	Sparrowhawk	David			1	1			1		1	1	1		6		
Cambridge	228	24	Slever	John				2						1			3		
Cambridge	228	25	Seaver	Ebenz		2		1				1		1			5		
Cambridge	228	26	Sparrowhawk	Hannah	2	2	2	1				1	2	1			11		
Cambridge	228	27	Sparrowhawk	Saml				1					2				3		
Cambridge	228	28	Stearns	Stephen	1	1			1					1			4		
Cambridge	228	29	Storier	Charles	1	1		1		1	1		1				6		
Cambridge	228	30	Thompson	Ebenz	1		1	1		1	1	1	1				7		
Cambridge	228	31	Thayer	Richard	1		1	1		1			1				5		
Cambridge	228	32	Tufts	Stephen	1		1					1					3		
Cambridge	228	33	Tufts	John		1	1			1		1		1			5		
Cambridge	228	34	Tapley	Isaac	2			1				1					4		
Cambridge	228	35	Thatcher	Mary			1			1		3		1			6		
Cambridge	228	36	Tappan	David	1	2	1		1	2			1	1			9		
Cambridge	228	37	Twing	Amos	1			1		2		1					5		
Cambridge	228	38	Twing	Thos		1		1					1	1			4		
Cambridge	229	1	Tiliston	Josiah		2						1					3		
Cambridge	229	2	Twing	Nathl	3				1	1	1		1				7		
Cambridge	229	3	Taylor	Mical	1		1	1					1				4		
Cambridge	229	4	Townsend	Saml		1		1		1			1				4		
Cambridge	229	5	Vose	Robert	1		3	2		2	1	1	1	1	1		13		
Cambridge	229	6	Vaughan	Charles	2		1			2							5		
Cambridge	229	7	Willington	Jedun		1	1		3	2	1		2				10		
Cambridge	229	8	Wilson	Josiah	1	2		1	1				1				6		
Cambridge	229	9	William	Gershom		1	2		1	1		2	1				8		
Cambridge	229	10	Whittemore	Saml		1		4		2		2					9		
Cambridge	229	11	Wyman	Saml		1		1		1		1					4		
Cambridge	229	12	Whittemore	Wm	1				1			1	1	1			5		
Cambridge	229	13	Whittemore	Saml	3		1					1	1				6		
Cambridge	229	14	Whittemore	Thos	1	2		1	1	2	1		1				9		
Cambridge	229	15	Whittemore	Jona		1	3	2		3			1				10		
Cambridge	229	16	Wyeth	Noah	2	1	1		1				1	1			7		
Cambridge	229	17	Watson	Wm	2	1				1	1	3	1				10		
Cambridge	229	18	Winthrop	James									1				1		
Cambridge	229	19	Winship	John	1	1			1					1			4		
Cambridge	229	20	Winthrop	Wm		1		1			1			1			4		
Cambridge	229	21	Winship	Wm			3	1				1		1			6		
Cambridge	229	22	Winship	Wm Jr			1			1	1		1				4		
Cambridge	229	23	Williams	Thos			1	1									2		
Cambridge	229	24	Whittemore	Wm	3			2		2	2	1	2				12		
Cambridge	229	25	Whittemore	Amos	2		1	1		3	2	1	1				11		
Cambridge	229	26	Watson	Nathan	1		1	1				2	1	1			7		
Cambridge	229	27	Watson	Jacob	1					1	1			1			4		
Cambridge	229	28	Watson	Daniel				1						1			2		
Cambridge	229	29	Watson	Saml		1		2		1							4		
Cambridge	229	30	Watson	Nathl P.	2			1						1			4		
Cambridge	229	31	Worth	Saml	1		1			1		1					4		
Cambridge	229	32	Williams	Amasa	2			1		1		1					5		
Cambridge	229	33	Wyeth	Jonas		1	1	1	1				1	1			6		
Cambridge	229	34	Waterhouse	Benjn	3	2			1	2	2	2		1			13		
Cambridge	229	35	Nelsen	Priscilla										1			1		
Cambridge	229	36	Webber	Saml	3			1		3	1	2	2	1			13		
Cambridge	229	37	Warland	Thos		1	1	1		1	2	3	1				10		
Cambridge	229	38	Watson	Jacob Jr	1			1	2	2		1	1	1			9		
Cambridge	230	1	Wright	Hannah									2	2			4		
Cambridge	230	2	Wells	Ebenz	4	2	1		1	3	1		1				13		
Cambridge	230	3	Wendall	Cathn					1					1			3		
Cambridge	230	4	Watson	John	1		3		1			1		1			7		
Cambridge	230	5	Willard	Mary	1			1				1	1	1			5		
Cambridge	230	6	Willard	Joseph	1	1	2		1	2	2	4	1	1			15		
Cambridge	230	7	Warland	John		2	2		1				1	1			7		
Cambridge	230	8	Wyeth	Jacob	1	2		2			1	2					8		
Cambridge	230	9	Wyeth	Ebenz	1	4			1		1			1			8		
Cambridge	230	10	Winship	Saml	2			1		2			1				6		
Cambridge	230	11	Warren	Wm	1	2							1				4		
Cambridge	230	12	Winship	Edmund	2			1		1	1		1	1			7		
Cambridge	230	13	Warren	Josiah	2			1					1				5		
Cambridge	230	14	Woods	Coolidge	2		1	1	1	2		1		1			9		
Cambridge	230	15	Walker	Saml	1	1		1		1	1	1					6		
Cambridge	230	16	Warren	Joseph	2	1	3	2		2		1		1			12		
Cambridge	230	17	White	Elijah	1		2			1	1	1					6		
Cambridge	230	18	Winship	Jona		3	5		1		1	3		1	1		15		
Cambridge	230	19	Whipple	Joseph	1				2			2	1				6		
Cambridge	230	20	White	Charles		1	1		1			2		2			7		
Cambridge	230	21	White	Easter										2			2		
Cambridge	230	22	White	Joseph			3						1				4		
Cambridge	230	23	White	Daniel A			1										1		
Cambridge	230	24	Whittemore	Josiah	2	1		3		3	2	1	1	1			14		
Cambridge	230	25	Waters	Bettern	2	2	5	3	1	3	2	4	1	5	4		32		

TOWN	PG#	LN#	LAST NAME	FIRST NAME	FREE WHITE MALES					FREE WHITE FEMALES					TOTAL ALL OTHER	TOTAL SLAVES	TOTALS	DISTRICT/ TOWNSHIP	NOTES
					under 10	10 to 16	16 to 26	26 to 45	45 and over	under 10	10 to 16	16 to 26	26 to 45	45 and over					
Carlisle	20	1	Heald	Israel					1			1	1	1			4		
Carlisle	20	2	Heald	Timothy	2	1		1		1	1		1				7		
Carlisle	20	3	Parkins	Nathan	1	1		1				1	1	1			6		
Carlisle	20	4	Raimond	Daniel	2			1		1	1		1				6		
Carlisle	20	5	Wheeler	Sampson				1						1			2		
Carlisle	20	6	Wheeler	Simon	1			1		1		1					4		
Carlisle	20	7	Wheeler	Oliver				1						1			2		
Carlisle	20	8	Wheeler	Reuben	4			1		2			1				8		
Carlisle	20	9	Wheeler	Joseph P	1			1		1	1	1		1			6		
Carlisle	20	10	Heald	John	1	1	1	1	1	1		3		1			10		
Carlisle	20	11	Russell	Amos						1				1			2		
Carlisle	20	12	Hutchinson	Nathaniel Jr	1	1		1		2	1		1				7		
Carlisle	20	13	Hutchinson	Nathaniel		1	2	1		1			1	1			7		
Carlisle	20	14	Parkin	Asa		1		1						1			3		
Carlisle	20	15	Robbins	John Jr			2	1			1			1			5		
Carlisle	20	16	Waters	John		1		1				1	1	1			6		
Carlisle	20	17	Durant	Jonas			1	1		3			1				6		
Carlisle	20	18	Hutchinson	Thomas	4			1	1				2	1			9		
Carlisle	20	19	Barnes	Elias	3		1	1		3			1				9		
Carlisle	20	20	Robbins	John		1	1	1		1		3		1			8		
Carlisle	21	1	Flint	Henry	2	1		1		2		1	1				8		
Carlisle	21	2	Robbins	John 4th			1					1					2		
Carlisle	21	3	Tower	Sarah	2					2			1	1			6		
Carlisle	21	4	Blasdel	William	2	1		1		2	1		1	1			9		
Carlisle	21	5	Crosby	Benjamin		1	1	1				1	1	1			6		
Carlisle	21	6	Parker	William	2	1	1	1		2	1	1	1				10		
Carlisle	21	7	Robbins	Ephraim	1			1		2		1	1				6		
Carlisle	21	8	Robbins	Benjamin				1				2	1	1			5		
Carlisle	21	9	Foster	John	2			1		2			1				6		
Carlisle	21	10	Kemp	James	1			1		2	1		1				6		
Carlisle	21	11	Litchfield	Paul	1	1	3	1						2			8		
Carlisle	21	12	Spauldin	Jonas	1			1		2	1		1	1			7		
Carlisle	21	13	Barrett	Benjamin	1	1	1	1		2	2		1				9		
Carlisle	21	14	Hunt	Joshua	2			1		1		1	1				6		
Carlisle	21	15	Parker	Sarah										1			1		
Carlisle	21	16	Barrett	Joseph				1						1			2		
Carlisle	21	17	Spauldin	Zebulon		1	2	1		1		2	3	1			11		
Carlisle	21	18	Wilson	Samuel	2			1	1					1			5		
Carlisle	21	19	Stearns	Nathaniel	2			1		2			1				6		
Carlisle	21	20	Parker	David				1			1		1	1			4		
Carlisle	21	21	Kidder	Amos				1				2		2			5		
Carlisle	21	22	Ingals	James	2			1		1			1				5		
Carlisle	21	23	Jamison	Matthew				1						1			2		
Carlisle	21	24	Foster	Jane									1				1		
Carlisle	21	25	Adams	Timothy	2	2	1	1		2			1				9		
Carlisle	21	26	Webber	Thomas				1	1		2			1			5		
Carlisle	21	27	Dutten	Nathaniel	4			1					1				6		
Carlisle	21	28	Brown	John	3			1		3			1				8		
Carlisle	21	29	Nicklas	John Jr		1	1	1	1	1	1	1		1			8		
Carlisle	21	30	Durant	Willard	1			1		2			1				5		
Carlisle	21	31	Nicklas	James		1		1			1	1		1			5		
Carlisle	21	32	Nicklas	John				1		1				2			4		
Carlisle	21	33	Nicklas	Job	2			1		1			1				5		
Carlisle	21	34	Green	Samuel		1	1	1				2		1			6		
Carlisle	21	35	Heald	Samuel			1	1				3		1			6		
Carlisle	21	36	Nutting	Amos	2			1					1				4		
Carlisle	21	37	Wheeler	Nathan	1			1		3	1		1				7		
Carlisle	21	38	Russell	James	1		1	1		1				1			8		
Carlisle	22	1	Russell	James Jr	1		1	1					1				4		
Carlisle	22	2	Blood	Jonas				1						1			2		
Carlisle	22	3	Heald	Silas	1	1		1				1	1	1			6		
Carlisle	22	4	Green	Leonard	2			1		1		1	1	1			8		
Carlisle	22	5	Heald	Jonathan		1	1	1				2		1			6		
Carlisle	22	6	Hartwell	David	1	1		1	1				2				6		
Carlisle	22	7	Hartwell	Asa	1			1					1	1			4		
Carlisle	22	8	Munroe	Jonas	1	1	2	1	4	2	1		1	1			14		
Carlisle	22	9	Heald	Thomas	4			1		2	1		1				9		
Carlisle	22	10	Partin	David				1						1			2		
Carlisle	22	11	Partin	David Jr	1			1		1			1				4		
Carlisle	22	12	Heald	Gershum				1						1			2		
Carlisle	22	13	Heald	Eleazer	3			1		1		1	1				7		
Carlisle	22	14	Partin	Josiah	3			1	1			1		1			8		
Carlisle	22	15	Foster	Smith	2			1				1	1	1			6		
Carlisle	22	16	Foster	Benjamin	1	1		1		4	1		1				9		
Carlisle	22	17	Dutton	Hannah									2	1			3		
Carlisle	22	18	Taylor	Abraham	1	1		1		1			2				6		
Carlisle	22	19	Taylor	Abel				1				1		1			3		
Carlisle	22	20	Brown	Samuel			1	1				1					3		
Carlisle	22	21	Wilkin	Timothy Jr	1	1		2		2			1				7		

TOWN	PG#	LN#	LAST NAME	FIRST NAME	FREE WHITE MALES					FREE WHITE FEMALES					TOTAL ALL OTHER	TOTAL SLAVES	TOTALS	DISTRICT/ TOWNSHIP	NOTES
					under 10	10 to 16	16 to 26	26 to 45	45 and over	under 10	10 to 16	16 to 26	26 to 45	45 and over					
Carlisle	22	22	Wheat	Daniel	1			1		3			1				6		
Carlisle	22	23	Green	John			1						1				2		
Carlisle	22	24	Flint	Amos	3	1	1		1	1	1	2	1				11		
Carlisle	22	25	Jacobs	John	2			1		2	2		1				8		
Carlisle	22	26	Wilkins	James	1			1		3	1		1				7		
Carlisle	22	27	Wilkins	Isaac					1				1	1			3		
Carlisle	22	28	Durant	Reuben	1	1	2	1					1				6		
Carlisle	22	29	Wheeler	Judah				1									1		
Carlisle	22	30	Spauldin	William			1	1		1		1	1				5		
Carlisle	22	31	Wilkins	Timothy	3		2		1	1		1	1	1			10		
Carlisle	22	32	Green	Amos			1						1				2		
Carlisle	22	33	Blood	David		1	1		1				1	1			5		
Carlisle	22	34	Green	Zacheus		1	2	2	1		1	2					9		
Carlisle	22	35	Green	Asa			1						1				2		
Carlisle	22	36	Green	Nathan		1		1				1	1	1			5		
Carlisle	22	37	Green	Jesse	2		1						1				4		
Carlisle	23	1	Procter	Ezekiel	1		1			2			1				5		
Carlisle	23	2	Nicklas	Joseph	2			1				1		1			5		
Carlisle	23	3	Hodgman	John	4	1	1		1	1			1				9		
Carlisle	23	4	Perry	Jonathan	2			1		2			1				6		
Carlisle	23	5	Parker	Nathaniel		1	1		1		1	2		1			7		
Carlisle	23	6	Anderson	Nehemiah			2				1	1					5		
Carlisle	23	7	Andrews	Edmund					1		1	1		1			4		
Carlisle	23	8	Andrews	Solomon				1					1				2		
Carlisle	23	9	Blood	Stephen				1		1		1	1				4		
Carlisle	23	10	Kimbell	William	1		1			1			1				4		
Carlisle	23	11	Winn	Peter			1			1			1				3		
Carlisle	23	12	Blood	Frederick				1		2		1	1				5		
Carlisle	23	13	Blood	Jonathan			3	2	1			2		1			9		
Carlisle	23	14	Blood	Zebulon			1	1					1				3		
Carlisle	23	15	Blood	Phinehas	2		1		1					2			6		
Carlisle	23	16	Blood	Sarah										1			1		
Carlisle	23	17	Hodgman	Abijah		1	2		1	2	1	1	1				9		
Carlisle	23	18	Hodgman	John		1		1		3		1					6		
Carlisle	23	19	Hodgman	Thomas	1			1		2	1		1				6		
Carlisle	23	20	Nicklas	Isaac											4		4		

TOWN	PG#	LN#	LAST NAME	FIRST NAME	FREE WHITE MALES under 10	10 to 16	16 to 26	26 to 45	45 and over	FREE WHITE FEMALES under 10	10 to 16	16 to 26	26 to 45	45 and over	TOTAL ALL OTHER	TOTAL SLAVES	TOTALS	DISTRICT/ TOWNSHIP	NOTES
Charlestown	79	1	Adams	Wm			1	1		1	1		1				5		
Charlestown	79	2	Adams	Jos'			3	1				1	1				6		
Charlestown	79	3	Adams	Nathn	3	1		1				2	1				8		
Charlestown	79	4	Adams	Nathn Jr			2	1					1				4		
Charlestown	79	5	Abraham	Eliza'									2				2		
Charlestown	79	6	Abraham	Jos'				1					1				2		
Charlestown	79	7	Armstead	James	1		1			1		1					4		
Charlestown	79	8	Austin	John		1		1				1	1				4		
Charlestown	79	9	Austin	Ebenz			1	1				1					3		
Charlestown	79	10	Austin	Nath			2	1	1		1			3			8		
Charlestown	79	11	Allen	Saml				1				1	1				3		
Charlestown	79	12	Ames	Robt			1										1		
Charlestown	79	13	Ango	John	3			1		2			1				7		
Charlestown	79	14	Ando	Tho'	1			1			1		1				4		
Charlestown	79	15	Bodge	Nath		1	1					1					3		
Charlestown	79	16	Bridge	Mary									1				1		
Charlestown	79	17	Brigden	Micah			1				1	1	1				4		
Charlestown	79	18	Breed	Ebenz		2		2		1	1	1		1			8		
Charlestown	79	19	Bancroft	James		3		1		1	1						6		
Charlestown	79	20	Bootman	Jno'				1									1		
Charlestown	79	21	Brazier	Tho'	2			1					1				4		
Charlestown	79	22	Bradstreet	Saml			1		1	1			2	1	2		8		
Charlestown	79	23	Blanchard	Simon	1		2	2		3			1	1			10		
Charlestown	81	1	Blanchard	Joshua	4		1						1				6		
Charlestown	81	2	Blanchard	Hezk	3	2		1		3			1				10		
Charlestown	81	3	Bradshaw	Lois								1		1			2		
Charlestown	81	4	Boston	Peter	1			1					1				3		
Charlestown	81	5	Brown	Jos'			2	1					1				4		
Charlestown	81	6	Brown	Nich'	1			1		2		1					5		
Charlestown	81	7	Brown	Farwel			1			1							2		
Charlestown	81	8	Brown	Tho'				1				1					2		
Charlestown	81	9	Barker	David	1	1	1		1			1		1	2		8		
Charlestown	81	10	Barker	Josi'	2	1		1		1	1	1	1				8		
Charlestown	81	11	Burket	Wm	2		1			2			1				6		
Charlestown	81	12	Breelat	Jno'	1		1					1					3		
Charlestown	81	13	Blair	Jno'				1					1				2		
Charlestown	81	14	Burdit	Jno	1			1				1					3		
Charlestown	81	15	Burdit	Saml			1					1					2		
Charlestown	81	16	Bradish	Catha'									2				2		
Charlestown	81	17	Brinkley	Jno'	1			1		2			1				5		
Charlestown	81	18	Bartlett	Josiah	5	1		2			2	1	2				13		
Charlestown	81	19	Bailey	Kendal			2	1									3		
Charlestown	81	20	Briant	Timo'	1			1		1			1				4		
Charlestown	81	21	Bartlett	Geo'	2		2	2		3	1		2				12		
Charlestown	81	22	Barker	Eliza	1					3	1	3	1				9		
Charlestown	81	23	Brooks	Tho'	1	3	1	1	1	2	2	1	1				13		
Charlestown	81	24	Brooks	Pomp											5		5		
Charlestown	81	25	Barrell	Jos'	1		2	4	2	1		2	2	1			15		
Charlestown	81	26	Bassett	Mary	2					1			1	1			5		
Charlestown	81	27	Brazier	Abigl									1	1			2		
Charlestown	81	28	Bridge	Mathew	1		3		1		1	2	1				9		
Charlestown	81	29	Bradshaw	Tho'	1	1		1		2			1				6		
Charlestown	81	30	Bell	Wm	1			1		1			1				4		
Charlestown	81	31	Bucknam	Saml		1		1		3			1				6		
Charlestown	81	32	Bond	Wm		2			1		1	1		1			6		
Charlestown	81	33	Bodge	Henry	1		1			1		1					4		
Charlestown	81	34	Bispham	Wm	1			1		3			1				6		
Charlestown	81	35	Bird	Comfort									1				1		
Charlestown	81	36	Bird	Jos'	3			1			1	1					6		
Charlestown	81	37	Bennett	Fra'			1										1		
Charlestown	81	38	Babb	Jos'				1		3			1				5		
Charlestown	81	39	Bailey	Danl	2	1		1					1				5		
Charlestown	81	40	Boylston	Richd				1	2			1	1	1			6		
Charlestown	81	41	Burbank	Elisha				1		2			1				4		
Charlestown	81	42	Conant	Saml				1					1	1			3		
Charlestown	81	43	Center	Saml	1		1	1		1			1	1			6		
Charlestown	81	44	Cary	Saml	1			1					1				3		
Charlestown	81	45	Carter	John		1	1		1					2			6		
Charlestown	82	1	Carter	Danl	2			1		1			1				5		
Charlestown	82	2	Carter	Saml	1					1		1	1	1			5		
Charlestown	82	3	Carter	John Jr				1		1			1				3		
Charlestown	82	4	Calder	Eliz'						1				1			2		
Charlestown	82	5	Calder	Geo'				1			1	1		2			5		
Charlestown	82	6	Calder	Robt	3		1	1		2	1		2				10		
Charlestown	82	7	Cole	Cha'		1		1		1		2					5		
Charlestown	82	8	Coster	John D.		1		1	3					1			6		
Charlestown	82	9	Cutter	Gershom	1	1	1	1					1				5		
Charlestown	82	10	Cutter	Jos'	1			1	1	1		2	1				7		
Charlestown	82	11	Cox	Saml		1		1				1		1			4		

30

TOWN	PG#	LN#	LAST NAME	FIRST NAME	under 10	10 to 16	16 to 26	26 to 45	45 and over	under 10	10 to 16	16 to 26	26 to 45	45 and over	TOTAL ALL OTHER	TOTAL SLAVES	TOTALS	DISTRICT/ TOWNSHIP	NOTES
					FREE WHITE MALES					FREE WHITE FEMALES									
Charlestown	82	12	Clapp	Gates			1	1				1					3		
Charlestown	82	13	Caldwell	Saml	2			1		1	1	1					6		
Charlestown	82	14	Carver	Reuben	1			1		1	1		1				5		
Charlestown	82	15	Choat	John		2		1		2		1	1				7		
Charlestown	82	16	McCluer	Peter											4		4		
Charlestown	82	17	Calder	Wm			1		1			2		1			5		
Charlestown	82	18	Child	Saml	4			1		2		1	1				9		
Charlestown	82	19	Call	Jona'			2	2					1				5		
Charlestown	82	20	Cutter	Ammi	1		1		1	2	2	1					8		
Charlestown	82	21	Cook	Wm			1			1		1					3		
Charlestown	82	22	Carterett	Saml		1						1					2		
Charlestown	82	23	Christy	Tho'			1			2		1					4		
Charlestown	82	24	Cox	Tho'			1			2		1	1				5		
Charlestown	82	25	Curtis	Steph	2		1			1		1					5		
Charlestown	82	26	Center	Cotton	1		1	1		4		2					9		
Charlestown	82	27	Center	Roland	1		1					1					3		
Charlestown	82	28	Carlton	Jno'		1	1				1						3		
Charlestown	82	29	Chubb	Tho'	2			1					1				4		
Charlestown	82	30	Clement	Elijah			1					1					2		
Charlestown	82	31	Chadwick	Benja'	2	1	3					1					7		
Charlestown	82	32	Carter	Richd	1	1	2	1				1					6		
Charlestown	82	33	Cross	Danl	1			1				1					3		
Charlestown	82	34	Call	James					1					2			3		
Charlestown	82	35	Cockran	Mary		1	1	1				1	1				5		
Charlestown	82	36	Cutter	Ebenz	2			1		1			1				5		
Charlestown	82	37	Cutter	Isaac	1	2		1		1	1		1				7		
Charlestown	82	38	Cutter	Saml	2	1		1		3	1		1				9		
Charlestown	82	39	Cutter	Benja'		1		1				1	1		1		5		
Charlestown	82	40	Cook	Isaac	2			1		1		1	1				6		
Charlestown	82	41	Choate	Saml	3			1		1		1	1				7		
Charlestown	82	42	Cary	Han'					1				1				2		
Charlestown	82	43	Cary	Saml															Enumeration blank
Charlestown	82	44	Carrel	Peggy	1							1					2		
Charlestown	82	45	Chadwick	John	2			1		1			1	1			6		
Charlestown	82	46	Carlton	Isaac	2		9	2				2					15		
Charlestown	82	47	Carterett	Richd	1			1					1				3		
Charlestown	83	1	Carrol	Tho'			1					1					2		
Charlestown	83	2	Dammon	Wm			1										1		
Charlestown	83	3	Davidson	Geo'	1			1		1	1	1					5		
Charlestown	83	4	Dowse	Ann								1	2				3		
Charlestown	83	5	Devens	Richd	1				2			1	1	1			6		
Charlestown	83	6	Dolliver	Peter			2	1			1	4	1				9		
Charlestown	83	7	Dickson	John	1	1		1				1	1				5		
Charlestown	83	8	Daniels	John			1	1		1		1					4		
Charlestown	83	9	McDonnaugh	Tho'	2	1	1		1	3	1	2	3		2		16		
Charlestown	83	10	Dexter	Nathan	1		1		1	2	3		1				9		
Charlestown	83	11	Dexter	Geo' B.			1										1		
Charlestown	83	12	Dean	Mary								1					1		
Charlestown	83	13	Dunkley	John	1			1		2			1				5		
Charlestown	83	14	Dunkley	Isaac	1			1					1				3		
Charlestown	83	15	Direr	Ann		1		1					1	1			4		
Charlestown	83	16	Dupee	Ellias			1			1			1				4		
Charlestown	83	17	Dunbar	John				1				2					3		
Charlestown	83	18	Dexter	Saml	1		1			1	1	2					6		
Charlestown	83	19	Dickson	Wm				1					1				2		
Charlestown	83	20	Dickson	Wm Jr	1			1		2			1				5		
Charlestown	83	21	Dickson	Aaron	1		1	1				1					4		
Charlestown	83	22	Dickson	Jona'	1			1					1				3		
Charlestown	83	23	Dunham	Sarah									1				1		
Charlestown	83	24	Dodge	Tho'		2		1		1		1					5		
Charlestown	83	25	English	Wm			1										1		
Charlestown	83	26	Edes	Peter	1	1		1		1	3		1				8		
Charlestown	83	27	Edes	Saml				1						1			2		
Charlestown	83	28	Edes	Tho'	3	1		1		2			1				8		
Charlestown	83	29	Edmands	John		1		1				1	1				4		
Charlestown	83	30	Edmands	John Jr	2	1	2					1					6		
Charlestown	83	31	Edmands	David	1			1			2	1	1				7		
Charlestown	83	32	Edmands	David Jr	1		1			1		1					4		
Charlestown	83	33	Edmands	James		1	1	1					1	1			5		
Charlestown	83	34	Edmands	Tho'		1		1				1					3		
Charlestown	83	35	Eaton	Edm'	1			1		2			1				5		
Charlestown	83	36	Eaton	Benja'	1	1		1		1	1						5		
Charlestown	83	37	Elliot	Tho'			1		1	2	2		1	1			8		
Charlestown	83	38	Ethridge	Saml		2	2	2		2	2		1				11		
Charlestown	83	39	Fox	John	2	1		1					1				5		
Charlestown	83	40	Fox	Ann									1				1		
Charlestown	83	41	Foster	Tho'	2			3		2			1				8		
Charlestown	83	42	Fesendon	Eliza'								1		1			2		
Charlestown	83	43	Fosdick	David	1	2		1		2	1	3	1				11		
Charlestown	83	44	Fillebrown	John			1			1	1						3		

TOWN	PG#	LN#	LAST NAME	FIRST NAME	FREE WHITE MALES under 10	10 to 16	16 to 26	26 to 45	45 and over	FREE WHITE FEMALES under 10	10 to 16	16 to 26	26 to 45	45 and over	TOTAL ALL OTHER	TOTAL SLAVES	TOTALS	DISTRICT/ TOWNSHIP	NOTES
Charlestown	84	1	Frothingham	Richd		3	3		1	2	1			2			12		
Charlestown	84	2	Frothingham	Jabez				1				2	1				4		
Charlestown	84	3	Frothingham	Benja'		1	3		1		1		1	1			8		
Charlestown	84	4	Frothingham	Benja' Jr			1										1		
Charlestown	84	5	Frothingham	Tho'		2			1								3		
Charlestown	84	6	Frothingham	James					1				1				2		
Charlestown	84	7	Frothingham	James Jr		1	1		1	3	1		1				8		
Charlestown	84	8	Frothingham	Debor'									1				1		
Charlestown	84	9	Fayerweather	David				1					1		2		4		
Charlestown	84	10	Fillebrown	Tho'				1					1				2		
Charlestown	84	11	Fezendon	John			1										1		
Charlestown	84	12	Farnsworth	Marcy	2	1							1				4		
Charlestown	84	13	Ferguson	Wm			1					1					2		
Charlestown	84	14	Farwell	James			1					1					2		
Charlestown	84	15	Farley	John			1				1	1					3		
Charlestown	84	16	Foster	Jacob	1	3	5	2		3	1	1	1				17		
Charlestown	84	17	Frost	Mary									1				1		
Charlestown	84	18	Frost	Marg'	1							1					2		
Charlestown	84	19	Farnsworth	Elias	2			1					1				4		
Charlestown	84	20	Goodwin	Edw'		1		1					1				3		
Charlestown	84	21	Goodwin	Benja				1		1			1				3		
Charlestown	84	22	Goodwin	Wm		1		1			1		1				4		
Charlestown	84	23	Goodwin	Saml				1				1					2		
Charlestown	84	24	Goodwin	David		2		1					1				4		
Charlestown	84	25	Goodwin	David Jr	3	1	1	1		1			1	1			9		
Charlestown	84	26	Goodwin	John	2	1	2	1		1			1				8		
Charlestown	84	27	Goodwin	Edw' Jr		1	2					2					5		
Charlestown	84	28	Gibson	Asa	2		1						1				4		
Charlestown	84	29	Griffith	James	1			2		2			2		1		8		
Charlestown	84	30	Green	John				1					1				2		
Charlestown	84	31	Green	Fra'		1			1	3	2	1		1			9		
Charlestown	84	32	Green	Charlotte								1					1		
Charlestown	84	33	Getty	James	1	1		1		1			1				5		
Charlestown	84	34	George	Wm			1										1		
Charlestown	84	35	Gibbs	James		1	1		1	2	1		1				7		
Charlestown	84	36	Gilman	Jona'		1	1						1				3		
Charlestown	84	37	Gould	Joanna								1					1		
Charlestown	84	38	Gage	Ebenz	2	1	1	1				1	1				7		
Charlestown	84	39	Grover	Simon			2				1		1				4		
Charlestown	84	40	Grover	Ebenz			1						1				2		
Charlestown	84	41	Gray	Benja'	4			1		1	1		1				8		
Charlestown	84	42	Green	Benja'	3			1		1			1				6		
Charlestown	84	43	Green	James	1	1		1			1	1	1				6		
Charlestown	84	44	Green	Wm	1	1		1				1					4		
Charlestown	84	45	McGoon	That'		1											1		
Charlestown	84	46	Gardner	Martha								1		1			2		
Charlestown	85	1	Gardner	*	1			1		1		1					4		
Charlestown	85	2	Gardner	John Jr	2			1					1	1			5		
Charlestown	85	3	Gardner	John			1		1		4	1	1				8		
Charlestown	85	4	Gardner	Edw'	1		1		1		2		2				7		
Charlestown	85	5	Gardner	Saml			1	1		1	1		1				5		
Charlestown	85	6	Gorham	Nath	2			1		1		1	1				6		
Charlestown	85	7	Gorham	Rebecca								1		1			2		
Charlestown	85	8	Goddard	Step'			1		1		1	2					5		
Charlestown	85	9	Goddard	Benja'				1					1				2		
Charlestown	85	10	Goddard	Nath'				1					1				2		
Charlestown	85	11	Gould	John				1		1			1				3		
Charlestown	85	12	Harris	John		1	1		1				1				4		
Charlestown	85	13	Harris	Sarah									1				1		
Charlestown	85	14	Harris	Josiah		1	1					1					3		
Charlestown	85	15	Hooper	Joshua	1			1		2			1	1			6		
Charlestown	85	16	Hooper	Tho'				1		2			1				4		
Charlestown	85	17	Holden	Oliver	4	1	3	1		2			2	1			14		
Charlestown	85	18	Holden	John	2			1		1	1		1				6		
Charlestown	85	19	Hadley	Moses	2		1		1	1	1			1			7		
Charlestown	85	20	Harley	Solomon	3			1					1				5		
Charlestown	85	21	Henly	Cath'	1		1					2	1	1			6		
Charlestown	85	22	Hailey	Danl				1					1				2		
Charlestown	85	23	Hailey	Charles	1		1					1					3		
Charlestown	85	24	Hersy	Wm				1		1	1		1				4		
Charlestown	85	25	Haskel	Jerem		1		2		1			1				5		
Charlestown	85	26	Hoppen	Nich'				1					1				2		
Charlestown	85	27	Hawkins	Nath'		2	2	1		1			1				8		
Charlestown	85	28	Harrison	Wm	1	1		1		2		2	1				8		
Charlestown	85	29	Hazwell	Robert	1		1	1				3			1		7		
Charlestown	85	30	Harden	Wm				1		1			1				3		
Charlestown	85	31	Hagar	Joel	2		1	1		1			1				6		
Charlestown	85	32	Howard	Tho' C.			2										2		
Charlestown	85	33	Hill	James				1									1		

TOWN	PG#	LN#	LAST NAME	FIRST NAME	M under 10	M 10 to 16	M 16 to 26	M 26 to 45	M 45 and over	F under 10	F 10 to 16	F 16 to 26	F 26 to 45	F 45 and over	TOTAL ALL OTHER	TOTAL SLAVES	TOTALS	DISTRICT/ TOWNSHIP	NOTES
Charlestown	85	34	Hall	Ebenz			1										1		
Charlestown	85	35	Hay	John				1									1		
Charlestown	85	36	Hay	Wm	2		1				1	1					5		
Charlestown	85	37	Hay	Ann		1					1		1				3		
Charlestown	85	38	Hurd	Benja'				1					1	1			3		
Charlestown	85	39	Hurd	Benja' Jr	1	3	2		1	2		4		1			14		
Charlestown	85	40	Hurd	Jos'		1	1	1		1		2		1			7		
Charlestown	85	41	Hunt	Simon			1										1		
Charlestown	85	42	Hayden	John				1				1		2			4		
Charlestown	85	43	Holden	Nehm				1				1		1			3		
Charlestown	85	44	Holden	Nehm Jr	2		1			2		1					6		
Charlestown	85	45	Hunt	Jona'	2			1		1				1			5		
Charlestown	85	46	Hill	Tho'			1										1		
Charlestown	86	1	Hall	Jona'	4		1			2			2				9		
Charlestown	86	2	Holden	Richd															Enumeration blank
Charlestown	86	3	Henderson	Mary										1			1		
Charlestown	86	4	Hildrith	Tho'			1			1			1				3		
Charlestown	86	5	Hoppen	Hannah										1			1		
Charlestown	86	6	Hunniwell	Wm	2		1	1		1			1				6		
Charlestown	86	7	Harris	Tho'	1		2		1	1	2	2		1			10		
Charlestown	86	8	Harris	John Jr	3	1		1		1			1				7		
Charlestown	86	9	Hyde	Fredr'		2	1			1		1					5		
Charlestown	86	10	Hancock	John	1		1			1		1					4		
Charlestown	86	11	Houghton	Oliver	1		1			1		1					4		
Charlestown	86	12	Hooker	James		1	1	1		2			1				6		
Charlestown	86	13	Heyden	Danl			1										1		
Charlestown	86	14	Holden	Richd	1			1		2			1				5		
Charlestown	86	15	Hutchinson	John	1	1	2		1		1	1		1			8		
Charlestown	86	16	Ireland	Tho'				1		1			1	1			4		
Charlestown	86	17	Ireland	Saml		1		1			1			1			4		
Charlestown	86	18	Ireland	Jona'	2	1		1		2	1	1	1				9		
Charlestown	86	19	McIntire	John		1				1		1					3		
Charlestown	86	20	Johnson	Jos'				1						1			2		
Charlestown	86	21	Jaques	Saml		1											1		
Charlestown	86	22	Jack	David	1	2	1		1	1		1		1			8		
Charlestown	86	23	Jones	Ebenz	1			1			1	2					5		
Charlestown	86	24	Jones	Peter		4	1			3		1					10		
Charlestown	86	25	Joy	Benja			1			1		1					3		
Charlestown	86	26	Jepson	John				1				1		1			3		
Charlestown	86	27	Johnson	Tho'			1					1		1			3		
Charlestown	86	28	Johnson	Saml			1			1		1					3		
Charlestown	86	29	Johnson	Edmd	2			1		2		1					6		
Charlestown	86	30	Jackson	Saml	1		1	1		1		1					5		
Charlestown	86	31	Jenkins	Israel		1	1	1				2					5		
Charlestown	86	32	Jarvis	James			1			2				1			4		
Charlestown	86	33	Johnson	John				1						1			2		
Charlestown	86	34	Jones	Ruth								1					1		
Charlestown	86	35	Knight	Mary									1				1		
Charlestown	86	36	Keith	Timo'		3				1		2					6		
Charlestown	86	37	Kidder	Isaac				1					2				3		
Charlestown	86	38	Kidder	John	1	2		1		1	1		1				7		
Charlestown	86	39	Kettell	John				1				2					3		
Charlestown	86	40	Kettell	Andr'				1			1	2	1				5		
Charlestown	86	41	Kettell	Jona'		1		1		2	1	1					6		
Charlestown	86	42	Kendal	Isaac		1						1	1				3		
Charlestown	86	43	Kinsman	Wm			1					1					2		
Charlestown	86	44	Kent	Mary									1				1		
Charlestown	86	45	Kent	Saml	4	2	1			1			1				9		
Charlestown	86	46	Keys	John				1									1		
Charlestown	86	47	Larkin	Saml		2		1				1	1				5		
Charlestown	87	1	Lock	Jona'	2	1	1		1	1		2	1				9		
Charlestown	87	2	Long	Benja'	3	1						1					5		
Charlestown	87	3	Lane	Geo'			4	2		2	1	2	4		1		16		
Charlestown	87	4	Larrabee	Jona'	2	1			1	2			1				7		
Charlestown	87	5	Lawrence	Isaac	1		1	1		1		1					5		
Charlestown	87	6	Leathers	Benja	1			1					1				3		
Charlestown	87	7	Lewis	Debo'								1					1		
Charlestown	87	8	Lewis	James	2			1			2	1					6		
Charlestown	87	9	Lincoln	Hezl		1											1		
Charlestown	87	10	Lewiston	James		1				2	1						4		
Charlestown	87	11	Larkin	John				1			1		2	1	1		6		
Charlestown	87	12	Larkin	Mary	1						2			1			5		
Charlestown	87	13	Larkin	Eben	2			1		2		1	2				8		
Charlestown	87	14	Larkin	Isaac	1			1		1		2					5		
Charlestown	87	15	Leman	Danl		1						1					2		
Charlestown	87	16	Leman	Eliz'								1	1	1			3		
Charlestown	87	17	Lamson	Caleb			1			2			1				4		
Charlestown	87	18	Lamson	Iza'			1							1			2		
Charlestown	87	19	Lanson	Jos'	3			1		1			1				6		
Charlestown	87	20	Merick	Esther						4			1	1			6		

TOWN	PG#	LN#	LAST NAME	FIRST NAME	FREE WHITE MALES					FREE WHITE FEMALES					TOTAL ALL OTHER	TOTAL SLAVES	TOTALS	DISTRICT/ TOWNSHIP	NOTES
					under 10	10 to 16	16 to 26	26 to 45	45 and over	under 10	10 to 16	16 to 26	26 to 45	45 and over					
Charlestown	87	21	Miller	Tho'		2	2		1		1	2		1			9		
Charlestown	87	22	Mercy	Sophia									1				1		
Charlestown	87	23	Manning	Wm H.	1			1		1			1	1			5		
Charlestown	87	24	Manning	Pheebe			2						1	1			4		
Charlestown	87	25	Mirick	Benja'	2			1		1	2		1				7		
Charlestown	87	26	Mallet	Isaac	2		1		1	4	1	1					10		
Charlestown	87	27	Merriam	Lott		1	2	1		3		1	1				9		
Charlestown	87	28	Mincher	Edw'				1		3		1					5		
Charlestown	87	29	Mallet	Ann									1	1			2		
Charlestown	87	30	Mitchel	Ann	1								1				3		
Charlestown	87	31	Munroe	Sal	3			1					1				5		
Charlestown	87	32	Maxwell	Wm			2			1		1					4		
Charlestown	87	33	Makepeace	Geo'					1			1		1			3		
Charlestown	87	34	Murray	Mary		1				1			1				3		
Charlestown	87	35	Mullet	Eprm	4	2	2	1		1	1		1				12		
Charlestown	87	36	Miller	Jos'	1		2	1		2	2		1	1			10		
Charlestown	87	37	Miller	Sarah									1				1		
Charlestown	87	38	Mansir	Saml	1		1	1		1		1					5		
Charlestown	87	39	Mansir	Eben	2	1	2		1	2	1		1	1			11		
Charlestown	87	40	Manning	Rachl		1				1		1		1			4		
Charlestown	87	41	Manning	Wm			1			2		1					4		
Charlestown	87	42	Moore	Wm			1	1		1			1				4		
Charlestown	87	43	Moore		1			2		4		1	1	1			10		
Charlestown	87	44	Moore	John					1	2		1					4		
Charlestown	87	45	Morse	Jedh	2			1				1	2				6		
Charlestown	87	46	Manning	John	2			1					1				4		
Charlestown	88	1	Mansfield	Arnold			1			1		1					3		
Charlestown	88	2	Newhall	Wm		1		1		1		1					4		
Charlestown	88	3	Newhall	NapR	1			1		1		1					4		
Charlestown	88	4	Newell	Eliz'							1		1				2		
Charlestown	88	5	Newell	Susan	1					2			1				4		
Charlestown	88	6	Newell	Hannah								1	1				2		
Charlestown	88	7	Newell	Eliphl	1			1		1			1				4		
Charlestown	88	8	Newell	Andr'				1					1				2		
Charlestown	88	9	Nutting	Jona'				1					1				2		
Charlestown	88	10	Nutting	John				1		1		1					3		
Charlestown	88	11	Nickols	Jona'											3		3		
Charlestown	88	12	Nickolson	Saml	1	3		1		2	1	3	1		2		14		
Charlestown	88	13	Niles	Silas	2			1				1		1			5		
Charlestown	88	14	Niles	Silas Jr		1	4	1		1			1				8		
Charlestown	88	15	Nason	Micah			1			1		1					3		
Charlestown	88	16	Norton	Solo'		1		1		3		1	1				7		
Charlestown	88	17	McNeal	Archb		2	2		2			5		1			12		
Charlestown	88	18	Oakes	Edw'			1			1		1					3		
Charlestown	88	19	Oakes	Rebecca						1		1					2		
Charlestown	88	20	Oliver	John		1		1					1				3		
Charlestown	88	21	Odin	Saml				1									1		
Charlestown	88	22	Oates	James	2		1			1		1					5		
Charlestown	88	23	Payson	Saml	3		1			2	1		2				9		
Charlestown	88	24	Payson	Phillips	2		1			1		1	1				6		
Charlestown	88	25	Payson	Tho'	1		1			2	1	2	1				8		
Charlestown	88	26	Page	Jona'	2	2	5	8	2	1	1	2	2				25		
Charlestown	88	27	Page	John			1			2		1					4		
Charlestown	88	28	Phipps	Jos'		2	2		1	1	2		1				9		
Charlestown	88	29	Phipps	Saml	2		1			1		1					5		
Charlestown	88	30	Phipps	Solo'		2		1		3		1	1				8		
Charlestown	88	31	Parker	Jos'	1		1	1					1				4		
Charlestown	88	32	Parker	Danl	1		1	1				1	1				5		
Charlestown	88	33	Pratt	Tho' W.	1	1		1					1				4		
Charlestown	88	34	Pratt	Isaac		1	1						1				3		
Charlestown	88	35	Putnam	Susan								1		1			2		
Charlestown	88	36	Putnam	Aaron	1	1	2	1		1	1		2				9		
Charlestown	88	37	Polly	Geo'											3		3		
Charlestown	88	38	Polly	Robt				1						1			2		
Charlestown	88	39	Pratt	Wm	2		1			2		2	1				8		
Charlestown	88	40	Perry	Cushman	2		1					1					4		
Charlestown	88	41	Perry	Jos'	2	1		1		2	2	1					9		
Charlestown	88	42	Peirce	Saml		1											1		
Charlestown	88	43	Peirce	James				1									1		
Charlestown	88	44	Peirce	Mary								1					1		
Charlestown	88	45	Prentice	Nath'		1	1		1	1	1	1	1				7		
Charlestown	89	1	Prentice	Geo'				1				1	1				3		
Charlestown	89	2	Prentice	Mary									1	1			2		
Charlestown	89	3	Parsons	Ruth									1				1		
Charlestown	89	4	Pollard		5		1	1		1		1					9		
Charlestown	89	5	Paul	Clerk		1						1					2		
Charlestown	89	6	Palmer	Joshua			1			3		1					5		
Charlestown	89	7	Pilsbury	Saml	2		1	1		1	1						5		
Charlestown	89	8	Powars	Batting	2		1	1	8	6		2	5	6	1		32		
Charlestown	89	9	Robbins	Tho'			1	1	1	1		3	1	1			9		
Charlestown	89	10	Russell	Mary						1		2					3		
Charlestown	89	11	Rayner	Ann								1		1			2		
Charlestown	89	12	Rand	Tho'		1	1						1	1			4		
Charlestown	89	13	Runey	John	2	1	1	2		1		3	1				11		
Charlestown	89	14	Runey	Hannah							1		1	1			3		
Charlestown	89	15	Romny	James				1					1				2		
Charlestown	89	16	Rand	Nath'	1			1		1			1				4		
Charlestown	89	17	Rand	Richd		1						1	1				3		
Charlestown	89	18	Rand	Mary									1				1		

TOWN	PG#	LN#	HEADS OF HOUSEHOLD		FREE WHITE MALES					FREE WHITE FEMALES					TOTAL ALL OTHER	TOTAL SLAVES	TOTALS	DISTRICT/ TOWNSHIP	NOTES
			LAST NAME	FIRST NAME	under 10	10 to 16	16 to 26	26 to 45	45 and over	under 10	10 to 16	16 to 26	26 to 45	45 and over					
Charlestown	89	19	Rand	Caleb		1			1					1			3		
Charlestown	89	20	Rand	Tho'		1		1					1				3		
Charlestown	89	21	Rand	Abra'	1			1				1		1			4		
Charlestown	89	22	Rand	Anna	1									1			2		
Charlestown	89	23	Rand	Hepz'										1			1		
Charlestown	89	24	Rand	Esther								2	2				4		
Charlestown	89	25	Rand	Tho'	3	2		1		2			1	1			10		
Charlestown	89	26	Rand	Tho' Jr			1				1						2		
Charlestown	89	27	Robbins	Eben			1	1		1			1				4		
Charlestown	89	28	Robbins	John		2						2					4		
Charlestown	89	29	Robbins	Aaron	1	1						1					3		
Charlestown	89	30	Robbins	Jos'	2			1					1				4		
Charlestown	89	31	Robbins	Jona'		1											1		
Charlestown	89	32	Raymond	Danl	1		1	1		2	1		1				7		
Charlestown	89	33	Raymond	Bartho'		1		1					1				3		
Charlestown	89	34	Raymond	Bartho' Jr	1		1				1						3		
Charlestown	89	35	Reed	Jos'		1	3				1	2					7		
Charlestown	89	36	Reed	Danl Jr	1		1			2	1	1					6		
Charlestown	89	37	Reed	Danl				1				1		1			3		
Charlestown	89	38	Rayner	Ann										1			1		
Charlestown	89	39	Richards	Peaton		1											1		
Charlestown	89	40	Richardson	Jona'	2	1		1		2			1				7		
Charlestown	89	41	Richardson	Asa				1			1	2	1				5		
Charlestown	89	42	Richardson	Asa Jr			1					1					2		
Charlestown	89	43	Richardson	Tho'			1			2			1				4		
Charlestown	89	44	Reynolds	Jona'				1									1		
Charlestown	89	45	Roulston	Andr'	3	1		1				2					7		
Charlestown	89	46	Roulston	James	2		1	1		1		1					6		
Charlestown	89	47	Reynolds	Hannah								1					1		
Charlestown	90	1	Rogers	Wm			1	1		1			1	1	1		6		
Charlestown	90	2	Rogers	Israel				1		1	2		1				5		
Charlestown	90	3	Ryan	Rehica									1	1			2		
Charlestown	90	4	Russell	Philm	3		2	1				1	1				8		
Charlestown	90	5	Russell	James		2	3	2				1	2	1			11		
Charlestown	90	6	Russell	Walter	2	1	3	1		2	1		1				11		
Charlestown	90	7	Rand	Prince											5		5		
Charlestown	90	8	Rand	Eunice	1					1			1				3		
Charlestown	90	9	Rice	Tho'	2	1		1		1			1	1			7		
Charlestown	90	10	Richards	Saml			1						1				2		
Charlestown	90	11	Stimpson	Andri'	2		1		1	2	1	1					8		
Charlestown	90	12	Stimpson	Wm	1	1			1	2			1				6		
Charlestown	90	13	Sprague	Saml	2			1		1			1	1			6		
Charlestown	90	14	Sprague	Jos'				1		1			1	2			5		
Charlestown	90	15	Smith	Isaac	1			1		1		2					5		
Charlestown	90	16	Smith	Ann											1		1		
Charlestown	90	17	Smith	Eben				1					1				2		
Charlestown	90	18	Smith	Eliza'									1				1		
Charlestown	90	19	Stevens	John	4	2	1	1			1		1				10		
Charlestown	90	20	Stevens	Eliza'						2			1	1			4		
Charlestown	90	21	Stevens	Pelet'	2		1			2		1					6		
Charlestown	90	22	Sargeant	Saml L.	1			1		2			1				5		
Charlestown	90	23	Sargeant	Saml G.			1			2		1	1				5		
Charlestown	90	24	Swan	Saml		1	1						1				3		
Charlestown	90	25	Swan	Benja B.	1	1					1						3		
Charlestown	90	26	Swan	Saml Jr			1						1				2		
Charlestown	90	27	Swan	Tho'	1		1			1		1					4		
Charlestown	90	28	Swan	John		1	3		1	1	1		1				8		
Charlestown	90	29	Symonds	Wm	1	2	1						1				5		
Charlestown	90	30	Symonds	Silas	1			1					1				3		
Charlestown	90	31	Scott	John			1			1	1						3		
Charlestown	90	32	Scott	Robt				1				1					2		
Charlestown	90	33	Sweetsin	Caleb		2				1	1		1				5		
Charlestown	90	34	Sweetsin	Jos'	1	1		1		3	1		1				8		
Charlestown	90	35	Sweetsin	Richd	2		1						1	1			5		
Charlestown	90	36	Sweetsin	Benja				1				1		1			3		
Charlestown	90	37	Sweetsin	Pheebe							1	1					2		
Charlestown	90	38	Stanton	John				1					1	1			3		
Charlestown	90	39	Shattuck			1											1		
Charlestown	90	40	Soley	Saml	1			1		1	1	1					5		
Charlestown	90	41	Snow	Mary										1			1		
Charlestown	90	42	Sampson	Amos	2	1			1	3	2		1				10		
Charlestown	90	43	Stetson	David	1	1	9	2		1		1	2				17		
Charlestown	90	44	Stetson	Jos'	2		1	2				1	1				7		
Charlestown	90	45	Stone	John	1	2		1		2		2	2				10		
Charlestown	90	46	Shed	Eben				1				1	1	1			4		
Charlestown	90	47	Shed	Saml				1				1		1			3		
Charlestown	91	1	Sheppard	Saml	2			1		1	1						5		
Charlestown	91	2	Shed	Saml		2		1					1				4		
Charlestown	91	3	Smith	Sarah									1				1		
Charlestown	91	4	Sargeant	Jesse			1			3			1				5		
Charlestown	91	5	Saunders	John		1											1		
Charlestown	91	6	Symonds	Jos'	2			1				1					4		
Charlestown	91	7	Skinner	John	2			1		2			1				6		
Charlestown	91	8	Skinner	Richd	1		1			2							4		
Charlestown	91	9	Skilton	Saml			1					1	1				3		
Charlestown	91	10	Smith	Ebz' Jr						1		1					2		
Charlestown	91	11	Sheppard	Leml															
Charlestown	91	12	Townsend	Saml			1	1		1			2				5		
Charlestown	91	13	Trumbal	Richd		1	1	2					1		1		6		
Charlestown	91	14	Turner	John					1			2		1			4		

TOWN	PG#	LN#	LAST NAME	FIRST NAME	FREE WHITE MALES under 10	10 to 16	16 to 26	26 to 45	45 and over	FREE WHITE FEMALES under 10	10 to 16	16 to 26	26 to 45	45 and over	TOTAL ALL OTHER	TOTAL SLAVES	TOTALS	DISTRICT/ TOWNSHIP	NOTES
Charlestown	91	15	Turner	John Jr	2	1		2		1	1		1				8		
Charlestown	91	16	Turner	Barnab		1	1	2			1		1				6		
Charlestown	91	17	Turner	Benja'				1				1					2		
Charlestown	91	18	Turner	Nath'			1	1		1		1					4		
Charlestown	91	19	Tufts	Ammi	1			1			2		1				5		
Charlestown	91	20	Tufts	Jos'	1	2	1	1		4	2		1				12		
Charlestown	91	21	Tufts	Ann									1	1			2		
Charlestown	91	22	Tufts	John	2	1	3		1	1	2		2	1			13		
Charlestown	91	23	Tufts	Timo' Jr	2	2		1		1	1	1					8		
Charlestown	91	24	Tufts	Simon	1			1		3			1				6		
Charlestown	91	25	Tufts	Danl		1	3	1				1	1				7		
Charlestown	91	26	Tufts	Nath'		2	1	1				1	1				6		
Charlestown	91	27	Tufts	Amos	2		2	1		2	1		1				9		
Charlestown	91	28	Tufts	Jos' Jr				1		1			1				3		
Charlestown	91	29	Tufts	Peter Jr	1	1	1			1		1					5		
Charlestown	91	30	Teal	Blany	3				1			1	1				6		
Charlestown	91	31	Teal	Jona'	3	1	1		1	1	1	2	1				11		
Charlestown	91	32	Townsend	Ezra			1			2		1					4		
Charlestown	91	33	Taply	John	1		1					1					3		
Charlestown	91	34	Tyng	Danl	1			1				1					3		
Charlestown	91	35	Trask	Nath'	2	1	2	1		1		1	1				9		
Charlestown	91	36	Trask	Isaac					1		1			1			3		
Charlestown	91	37	Thayer	Zenas				1									1		
Charlestown	91	38	Trull	Joel		1											1		
Charlestown	91	39	Thompson	Timo'	3		4		1	2	2			1			13		
Charlestown	91	40	Thompson	Timo' Jr	2		2					2					6		
Charlestown	91	41	Taylor	Wm	2			1				1	1				5		
Charlestown	91	42	Thompson	Hugh	2		1	1					1				5		
Charlestown	91	43	Trumbal	Fra'								1	1				2		
Charlestown	91	44	Tufts	Timo' Esq				1						1			2		
Charlestown	91	45	Tufts	Isaac		1	1			2		1					5		
Charlestown	91	46	Tufts	Jos'			1			1		1					3		
Charlestown	91	47	Tufts	Saml		1			1		1	2		1			6		
Charlestown	91	48	Tufts	Saml' Jr			3			1	1	1					6		
Charlestown	92	1	Turner	James	3			1				2	1				7		
Charlestown	92	2	Vose	Danl			1			1		1					3		
Charlestown	92	3	Veron	Stephn	2	1		1	1	2	1		1				9		
Charlestown	92	4	Underwood	Jos'	1			1				1	1				4		
Charlestown	92	5	Watson	Moses	2	1	2	1				1	1				8		
Charlestown	92	6	Wallace	Susan								2	1				3		
Charlestown	92	7	Wood	Jona'			1					1					2		
Charlestown	92	8	Wood	John			1										1		
Charlestown	92	9	Wealer	Simon			1					1					2		
Charlestown	92	10	Winship	Henry	1	2		1			1		1				6		
Charlestown	92	11	Wellington	Josiah		1	1		1			1		1			5		
Charlestown	92	12	Wright	Jos'			1										1		
Charlestown	92	13	Warren	Amos		1	1		1	1		2		1			7		
Charlestown	92	14	Wyman	Seth	1		1	1	1	2		2	1	1			10		
Charlestown	92	15	Whittemore	Wm			1			1		1					3		
Charlestown	92	16	Welsh	Ezra	3			1		1	1		1				7		
Charlestown	92	17	Welsh	Eunice									1				1		
Charlestown	92	18	Winship	Jona'		1											1		
Charlestown	92	19	Wait	Benja'		1											1		
Charlestown	92	20	Wade	Eben		1				2							3		
Charlestown	92	21	Waters	Abra'	1			1		1		1					4		
Charlestown	92	22	Wiley	Wm	1	1	1	1		3	1		1				9		
Charlestown	92	23	Wood	David					1		1	1	1				4		
Charlestown	92	24	Wyer	David		1	1		1	1		3		1			8		
Charlestown	92	25	Whittemore	Nathan		1	1	1		2	2		1				8		
Charlestown	92	26	Wyer	Lydia							1	2		1			4		
Charlestown	92	27	Wright	Benja'			1					1	1				3		
Charlestown	92	28	Welman	John				1				1					2		
Charlestown	92	29	West	Saml			1										1		
Charlestown	92	30	Wyman	Nehm		3	1	1		4			1				10		
Charlestown	92	31	Walker	Timo'	1	2	2	2		2		1	1				11		
Charlestown	92	32	Whitney	Amazh	2			1		2		1	1				7		
Charlestown	92	33	Wood	Wm			1			1		1	1				4		
Charlestown	92	34	Whittemore	Phillip	2	1		1		3	1		1				9		

TOWN	PG#	LN#	LAST NAME	FIRST NAME	FREE WHITE MALES					FREE WHITE FEMALES					TOTAL ALL OTHER	TOTAL SLAVES	TOTALS	DISTRICT/ TOWNSHIP	NOTES
					under 10	10 to 16	16 to 26	26 to 45	45 and over	under 10	10 to 16	16 to 26	26 to 45	45 and over					
Chelmsford	166	1	Abbott	Joseph				1		2		1					4		
Chelmsford	166	2	Ames	Nathan		1	2	1		2			2				8		
Chelmsford	166	3	Adams	Wm	3			1		2	1		2				9		
Chelmsford	166	4	Adams	Saml Jr		1	1		1	2		1		1			7		
Chelmsford	166	5	Adams	Joseph	2	1		1				1	1				6		
Chelmsford	166	6	Adams	Benja		1	1		1			1		1			5		
Chelmsford	166	7	Adams	Abel		1	2			1		1					5		
Chelmsford	166	8	Adams	Olive			1					1		1			3		
Chelmsford	166	9	Adams	Sarah										1			1		
Chelmsford	166	10	Adams	John					1	1				1			3		
Chelmsford	166	11	Adams	Isaac	1	1		1		1		1					5		
Chelmsford	166	12	Adams	Saml					1	1	2			1			5		
Chelmsford	167	1	Butterfield	Benja Jr	2	2	1		1	1		2	1				10		
Chelmsford	167	2	Blanchard	Joshua	1	1			1	2		1	1				7		
Chelmsford	167	3	Bowars	Luke	2	1			1	2			1				7		
Chelmsford	167	4	Bateman	Jno'		1		2		4	2	2	1				12		
Chelmsford	167	5	Butterick	Charles				1				1					2		
Chelmsford	167	6	Brown	Saml		1		1		1			1				4		
Chelmsford	167	7	Bridge	Ebenz			1	1				3	1				6		
Chelmsford	167	8	Butterfield	John		1		1	1	2		1	1	1			8		
Chelmsford	168	1	Blodget	Simeon				1					1				2		
Chelmsford	168	2	Blodget	Simeon Jr		1	1					1					3		
Chelmsford	168	3	Bowars	Wm			2	1		1			1				5		
Chelmsford	168	4	Baldwin	Cyrus		1	1			1		1					4		
Chelmsford	168	5	Bowars	Phillip	1			1				1					3		
Chelmsford	168	6	Barret	Joel				1		1			1				3		
Chelmsford	168	7	Barron	Oliver				1					1				2		
Chelmsford	168	8	Barron	Jona'	1	1		3		2		2			1		10		
Chelmsford	168	9	Byan	Benja'				1				1					2		
Chelmsford	168	10	Byan	Wm	1			1				1					3		
Chelmsford	168	11	Byan	John			1	1				1		1			4		
Chelmsford	168	12	Byan	Solo'	1			1		3		1					6		
Chelmsford	168	13	Byan	Sarah								1					1		
Chelmsford	168	14	Byan	Lucy	1	2					1	2		1			7		
Chelmsford	168	15	Bridge	Wm	1		3		1			1		1			7		
Chelmsford	168	16	Baldwin	David	1			1		3			1				6		
Chelmsford	168	17	Blaizdel	Henry	2			1		2	1		1				7		
Chelmsford	168	18	Betty	John		1	1	1				1		1			5		
Chelmsford	168	19	Blaizdel	Aaron	3	1		1		2			1				8		
Chelmsford	168	20	Bridge	Joanna									2		1		3		
Chelmsford	168	21	Barker	Mary								1		1			2		
Chelmsford	168	22	Barker	Asa	3		1	1					1				6		
Chelmsford	168	23	Butterfield	John Jr		1		1		2			1				5		
Chelmsford	168	24	Butterfield	Benja'					1			1		1			3		
Chelmsford	168	25	Chandler	Roger	2			1					1				4		
Chelmsford	168	26	Crosby	Nathan					1					1			2		
Chelmsford	168	27	Coburn	Henry		1	1			1		1		2			7		
Chelmsford	168	28	Cory	Ezra			1			?		1					4		
Chelmsford	168	29	Crosby	John			1			1	3	1	1				7		
Chelmsford	168	30	Cornwell	Foster											6		6		
Chelmsford	168	31	Chambers	Jos'	1			1		2			1				5		
Chelmsford	168	32	Chamberlin	Roger	2			1					1				4		
Chelmsford	168	33	Chamberlin	Phins			2		1		1			1			5		
Chelmsford	168	34	Chamberlin	Jos'	1	1		1					1				4		
Chelmsford	168	35	Chamberlin	Jacob	1		2	1		3	1		1				9		
Chelmsford	168	36	Chamberlin	Benja'				1				1		1			3		
Chelmsford	168	37	Chamberlin	Aaron		1		1		1		1	1	1			5		
Chelmsford	168	38	Chamberlin	Aaron	2	1	1		1	2	2			1			10		
Chelmsford	168	39	Chamberlin	Saml				1					1				2		
Chelmsford	168	40	Chamberlin	Issac	1	1	1	1		1			1	2			8		
Chelmsford	168	41	Davis	Moses					1			2		1			4		
Chelmsford	168	42	Davis	Joshua	1			1		1			1				4		
Chelmsford	169	1	Davis	Abijah	1		5	1		4			1				12		
Chelmsford	169	2	Davis	Johnson	1			1		1			1				4		
Chelmsford	169	3	Dutton	John				1					2	2			5		
Chelmsford	169	4	Dane	Wm	3	1			1	2			1				8		
Chelmsford	169	5	Dunn	John			1	1	1			1		2			6		
Chelmsford	169	6	Dunn	John Jr	2			1				1					4		
Chelmsford	169	7	Dunn	James	1	2		1		2	1	2	1				10		
Chelmsford	169	8	Dunn	Mary	1					1			1	1			4		
Chelmsford	169	9	Estabrook	Moses			2	1		1			1				5		
Chelmsford	169	10	Emerson	Saml	2			1					1				4		
Chelmsford	169	11	Emerson	Asa					1			1		1			3		
Chelmsford	169	12	Emerson	Owen	2	1		1		1		1		2			8		
Chelmsford	169	13	Foster	Isaiah				1									1		
Chelmsford	169	14	Foster	Jacob			1	1		1	1		1				5		
Chelmsford	169	15	Furbush	Silas	1			1		1		1					4		
Chelmsford	169	16	Farmer	Simeon			1		1								2		
Chelmsford	169	17	Farmer	John	1	2		1		2			1				7		

TOWN	PG#	LN#	LAST NAME	FIRST NAME	FREE WHITE MALES					FREE WHITE FEMALES					TOTAL ALL OTHER	TOTAL SLAVES	TOTALS	DISTRICT/ TOWNSHIP	NOTES
					under 10	10 to 16	16 to 26	26 to 45	45 and over	under 10	10 to 16	16 to 26	26 to 45	45 and over					
Chelmsford	169	18	Farmer	Jonas					1					1			2		
Chelmsford	169	19	Farrar	Jonas		1		1						1			3		
Chelmsford	169	20	Frost	Ebenz				1						1			2		
Chelmsford	169	21	Frost	Asa	2		3	1		2			1				9		
Chelmsford	169	22	Foster	Mary	1		1						1	1			4		
Chelmsford	169	23	Freeland	John			1	1						1			3		
Chelmsford	169	24	Farrar	Nath'			2					1					3		
Chelmsford	169	25	Ford	John			3	1	1	1		1	1	1			8		
Chelmsford	169	26	Fletcher	Andr'			1										1		
Chelmsford	169	27	Fletcher	Levi'	2			1		2			1	1			7		
Chelmsford	169	28	Fletcher	Susan									1	1			2		
Chelmsford	169	29	Fletcher	Joseph	3			1		1			1				6		
Chelmsford	169	30	Fletcher	Josiah				1									1		
Chelmsford	169	31	Fletcher	Josiah Jr	2		1	1					1	2			7		
Chelmsford	169	32	Fletcher	Nehson'	1			1		2			1				5		
Chelmsford	169	33	Fletcher	Wm		1	1		1	1			1				5		
Chelmsford	169	34	Fletcher	Benja			1		1	1	1		1				5		
Chelmsford	169	35	Fletcher	Benja' Jr			1	1				1	1	1			5		
Chelmsford	169	36	Fletcher	Saml				1						1			2		
Chelmsford	169	37	Fletcher	Solomon			1						1				2		
Chelmsford	169	38	Gload	John			1					2	1	1			5		
Chelmsford	169	39	Gload	Wm			1			2			1				4		
Chelmsford	170	1	Glinn	John	3		1			1			1				6		
Chelmsford	170	2	Gilson	Ichab'			1			1		1					3		
Chelmsford	170	3	Gould	Ebenz	1			1						1			3		
Chelmsford	170	4	Gould	Benja'	1			1		3	2		1				8		
Chelmsford	170	5	Harrington	Wm	1			1		1			1				4		
Chelmsford	170	6	Hale	Moses			2	1		3	1		1				8		
Chelmsford	170	7	Hoar	Silas	1			1		2			1				5		
Chelmsford	170	8	Hunt	Saml			1					1					2		
Chelmsford	170	9	Hunting	Nathan	1		2	1		4			1				9		
Chelmsford	170	10	Howard	Saml		1		1				1	1				4		
Chelmsford	170	11	Howard	Nath'			1			1		1					3		
Chelmsford	170	12	Howard	Jacob	1		1	1					1				4		
Chelmsford	170	13	Howard	Willard			1	1						2			4		
Chelmsford	170	14	Hodgman	Asa	1			1		3	3		1				9		
Chelmsford	170	15	Hodgman	Josiah				1					1	1			3		
Chelmsford	170	16	Heywood	Jos'	1	1	1	1		3	2	1	1				11		
Chelmsford	170	17	Heywood	Sarah									1				1		
Chelmsford	170	18	Harwood	John	1	1	2		1	1	1	2		1			10		
Chelmsford	170	19	Johnson	Ezra			1										1		
Chelmsford	170	20	Johnson	David			1										1		
Chelmsford	170	21	Keyes	David	1			1		2			1				5		
Chelmsford	170	22	Kimbal	Dema*	2			1		2	1		1				7		
Chelmsford	170	23	Kidder	Jacob	1			1		1			1				4		
Chelmsford	170	24	Lewiston	Seth	1	2	1		1	1				1			7		
Chelmsford	170	25	Lewiston	Seth Jr			1										1		
Chelmsford	170	26	Lewis	Wm	1	1		1				1		1			5		
Chelmsford	170	27	Mears	Robert			1			2			1				4		
Chelmsford	170	28	Marshal	James	2	1		1		2	2		1				9		
Chelmsford	170	29	Marshal	Peter			2					2		1			5		
Chelmsford	170	30	Marshal	Saml				1						1			2		
Chelmsford	170	31	Marshal	Saml Jr	3		2		1	3	1	1					11		
Chelmsford	170	32	Marshal	Abel	2	1		1		3	1		1				9		
Chelmsford	170	33	Manning	Jona'	1		2		1	1	2	3		1			11		
Chelmsford	170	34	Manning	Timo'			3		1		2			1			7		
Chelmsford	170	35	Manning	Jacob	2		2	1					1				6		
Chelmsford	170	36	Moore	Jos'				1					1	1			3		
Chelmsford	170	37	Moore	Mial	3			1		1			1				6		
Chelmsford	170	38	Melvin	Benja'	2		1		1	3				1			8		
Chelmsford	170	39	Minot	John				1						1			2		
Chelmsford	170	40	Mansfield	John		1	2							1			5		
Chelmsford	171	1	Osgood	Eph'			1	1									2		
Chelmsford	171	2	Parker	Ebenz		1	1	1		2			1				6		
Chelmsford	171	3	Parker	Jos'	2	1		1	1	1	1		1	1			9		
Chelmsford	171	4	Parker	Moses	2			1		1			1				5		
Chelmsford	171	5	Parker	Wm				1						1			2		
Chelmsford	171	6	Parker	Henry L			1					1					2		
Chelmsford	171	7	Parker	Simon	1	1		1		2			2	1			8		
Chelmsford	171	8	Parker	Benja'			1	1				1		1			4		
Chelmsford	171	9	Parker	Jeduth	1			1		2	1		1				6		
Chelmsford	171	10	Parker	Zebul'	4			1					1				6		
Chelmsford	171	11	Parker	Jona'	1		1		1				1	1			5		
Chelmsford	171	12	Parker	Willard	1	1	2		1			1	1	1			8		
Chelmsford	171	13	Parker	David			2	1	1				1	1			6		
Chelmsford	171	14	Peirce	Oliver			1		1			1	2	1			6		
Chelmsford	171	15	Peirce	Steph'	3	2	1		1	1	1			1			10		
Chelmsford	171	16	Peirce	Hannah									1	1			2		
Chelmsford	171	17	Peirce	Silas			1		1			2	1	2			7		

TOWN	PG#	LN#	LAST NAME	FIRST NAME	FREE WHITE MALES under 10	10 to 16	16 to 26	26 to 45	45 and over	FREE WHITE FEMALES under 10	10 to 16	16 to 26	26 to 45	45 and over	TOTAL ALL OTHER	TOTAL SLAVES	TOTALS	DISTRICT/ TOWNSHIP	NOTES
Chelmsford	171	18	Peirce	Robert	2	1	1		1	1				1			7		
Chelmsford	171	19	Peirce	James		1	1		1		2	1		1			7		
Chelmsford	171	20	Peirce	Rebecca									1	1			2		
Chelmsford	171	21	Pitts	Saml	1	1	3	1	1	1	1	1					10		
Chelmsford	171	22	Pettengail	Nathl	1			1	2	2			1				7		
Chelmsford	171	23	Procter	Amos	1			1					1				3		
Chelmsford	171	24	Procter	Levi				1				1	1				3		
Chelmsford	171	25	Procter	Danl'			1		1					1			3		
Chelmsford	171	26	Procter	Eldad	2	1		1		1			1				6		
Chelmsford	171	27	Procter	Elijah			1		1			3		1			6		
Chelmsford	171	28	Packard	H*z'	2	1	3	1				2					9		
Chelmsford	171	29	Parkis	Danl'		1	1	1	1	1		1		1			7		
Chelmsford	171	30	Parkhurst	Epm'		1	1			1				2			6		
Chelmsford	171	31	Parkhurst	Phillip			4	1	1					2			8		
Chelmsford	171	32	Parkhurst	Josiah	3	1		1		1			1				7		
Chelmsford	171	33	Parkhurst	Saml	2	1		1		1			1				6		
Chelmsford	171	34	Perham	Jona'		2							1	1			5		
Chelmsford	171	35	Putnam	Danl'	1	1		1		2	1		1	1			8		
Chelmsford	171	36	Picking	John		2	1		1			2	1				7		
Chelmsford	171	37	Pelsuc	Benja'	1	1	2		1	1	1	1		1			9		
Chelmsford	171	38	Richardson	Jona'				1						1			2		
Chelmsford	171	39	Richardson	Elijah			1	1				1	1				4		
Chelmsford	171	40	Richardson	Oliver	3	1	1	1		1	1		1				9		
Chelmsford	171	41	Richardson	Eleazer															Enumeration blank
Chelmsford	171	42	Richardson	Josiah			1	1						1			3		
Chelmsford	171	43	Richardson	Josiah Jr		1		1		3			1				6		
Chelmsford	172	1	Spaulding	Az'	1	1	1			1			1				6		
Chelmsford	172	2	Spaulding	Simeon	1	1		1		3	1		1				8		
Chelmsford	172	3	Spaulding	Micah	4	1	1		1	1	1		1	1			11		
Chelmsford	172	4	Spaulding	Joel			2		1		1	1		1			6		
Chelmsford	172	5	Spaulding	Noah			1	1			1	1	1	1			6		
Chelmsford	172	6	Spaulding	Ephm		1		1					1				3		
Chelmsford	172	7	Spaulding	Jona'			2	1				1	1	1			6		
Chelmsford	172	8	Spaulding	Abijah			1							1			2		
Chelmsford	172	9	Spaulding	Job		1	1	1						1			4		
Chelmsford	172	10	Spaulding	Job Jr	1	1		1		1	1		1				6		
Chelmsford	172	11	Spaulding	Jesse	2			1		3		1	1				8		
Chelmsford	172	12	Spaulding	Steph'				1									1		
Chelmsford	172	13	Spaulding	Peter Jr					1								1		
Chelmsford	172	14	Spaulding	Zebul'		1			1			1	2	1			6		
Chelmsford	172	15	Spaulding	Zebul' Jr	2			1		1			1				5		
Chelmsford	172	16	Spaulding	John					1					1			2		
Chelmsford	172	17	Spaulding	John Jr	3	1		1		1	1	1	1				9		
Chelmsford	172	18	Spaulding	Henry Jr				1					1				2		
Chelmsford	172	19	Spaulding	Saml	2				1				1				4		
Chelmsford	172	20	Spaulding	Joseph	2		2		1	1				1			7		
Chelmsford	172	21	Spaulding	Hevz'			1					1		1			3		
Chelmsford	172	22	Spaulding	Robert	4	1		1		1	2		1				10		
Chelmsford	172	23	Spaulding	Henry	2	1			1	1	1	2		2			10		
Chelmsford	172	24	Spaulding	Andrew			1	1		4	2	1					9		
Chelmsford	172	25	Spaulding	Benja'		1			1	1	3		1				7		
Chelmsford	172	26	Spaulding	Ira	1			1		2			2				6		
Chelmsford	172	27	Spaulding	Eli			1										1		
Chelmsford	172	28	Spaulding	Peter				1		1				1			3		
Chelmsford	172	29	Spaulding	Esther								1		2			3		
Chelmsford	172	30	Sherburn	Saml			1						1				2		
Chelmsford	172	31	Simonds	Josiah			1						1				2		
Chelmsford	172	32	Stevens	Abel			1										1		
Chelmsford	172	33	Stevens	Simeon		1		1				3		1			6		
Chelmsford	172	34	Stevens	Lampron	1			1		3			1				6		
Chelmsford	172	35	Stevens	Saml		1	1	1		1			1				5		
Chelmsford	172	36	Stevens	Jona'	1				1		1	1		1			5		
Chelmsford	172	37	Stearns	John	2			1		1			1				5		
Chelmsford	172	38	Snow	Jona'		1		1		3			1				6		
Chelmsford	172	39	Shed	Ebenz	2	1	1		1					1			6		
Chelmsford	172	40	Shed	Eliza'										1			1		
Chelmsford	172	41	Tyler	Mary									1	1			2		
Chelmsford	172	42	Tyler	Nathan	5	1	1	1		1	1	1	1				12		
Chelmsford	172	43	Tyler	Jos'	4	2	1	1		1			1				10		
Chelmsford	172	44	Tuttle	Sarah			1					1	1	1			4		
Chelmsford	173	1	Varnum	Lucy						1			1				2		
Chelmsford	173	2	Walker	Ezek'		1		1		1			1				4		
Chelmsford	173	3	Walker	David		1		1			1						4		
Chelmsford	173	4	Wilson	Simeon	1			1		2			1				5		
Chelmsford	173	5	Worcester	Osgood	1			1			1	1					4		
Chelmsford	173	6	Willey	Andr		1		1		1			1				4		
Chelmsford	173	7	Whiting	Phin'			1	1				2	1		3		8		
Chelmsford	173	8	Williams	Benja'	2			1					1				4		
Chelmsford	173	9	Williams	Jona'	1	1	3	1			1	2		1			10		
Chelmsford	173	10	Williams	Seth			1				1		1				3		

TOWN	PG#	LN#	LAST NAME	FIRST NAME	FREE WHITE MALES under 10	10 to 16	16 to 26	26 to 45	45 and over	FREE WHITE FEMALES under 10	10 to 16	16 to 26	26 to 45	45 and over	TOTAL ALL OTHER	TOTAL SLAVES	TOTALS	DISTRICT/ TOWNSHIP	NOTES
Chelmsford	173	11	Williams	Isaac	2				1	1	1						5		
Chelmsford	173	12	Whitney	Amos	1			1					1				3		
Chelmsford	173	13	Wilson	Saml					1								1		
Chelmsford	173	14	Warren	Isaac			1		2			2	1	1			7		
Chelmsford	173	15	Warren	Issac Jr			1			1		1					3		
Chelmsford	173	16	Warren	Jos'			1		1	2	1	1	1				7		
Chelmsford	173	17	Warren	Jerem'	1			1		2	1	1					6		
Chelmsford	173	18	Warren	Jos' Jr	1	1		1		4		1		1			9		
Chelmsford	173	19	Wright	Zach'	1	1		1				1	1				5		

TOWN	PG#	LN#	HEADS OF HOUSEHOLD LAST NAME	FIRST NAME	FREE WHITE MALES under 10	10 to 16	16 to 26	26 to 45	45 and over	FREE WHITE FEMALES under 10	10 to 16	16 to 26	26 to 45	45 and over	TOTAL ALL OTHER	TOTAL SLAVES	TOTALS	DISTRICT/ TOWNSHIP	NOTES
Concord	2	1	White	John		1			1	1	1	1	1				6		
Concord	2	2	Noreau	John	1	1			1	2	3	1	1				10		
Concord	2	3	Clark	Benjamin		1			1					1			3		
Concord	2	4	Minott	Timothy		1			1		1	1	1				5		
Concord	2	5	Wyman	Oliver		1	1	1		1		5					9		
Concord	3	1	Hosner	Nathan			1	1				1					3		
Concord	3	2	Jarvis	Francis	1		1	1		2		1	1				7		
Concord	3	3	Wood	Stephen	1		1	1		2		1	1				7		
Concord	3	4	Loring	Henry	1			3				1	1				6		
Concord	3	5	Breed	John C	1			1					1				3		
Concord	3	6	Brown	Abel Jr	2			1		3	1		1				8		
Concord	3	7	Bryant	Reuben	1			1				1	1				5		
Concord	3	8	Barrett	James	2	1	2	1	1	1		2	2	2			14		
Concord	3	9	Hadley	Joseph		1			1	1	1						4		
Concord	3	10	Ross	James	1			1		2			1				5		
Concord	3	11	Barrett	Peter	2	2	3		1		1	2	1	1			13		
Concord	3	12	Barrett	Mary									2				2		
Concord	3	13	Barrett	Samuel			2	1			1		1				5		
Concord	3	14	Cutter	Thomas	1			1		1			1				4		
Concord	3	15	Stone	Martha		1		1				4		2	1		9		
Concord	3	16	Handley	John	1			1				1	1				4		
Concord	3	17	Brown	James		1	3	2				1	1				8		
Concord	3	18	Hibrett	Jonathan	3	1	3	3	1	2	1	1	1	2			18		
Concord	4	1	Jones	Mary		1	1				1	1		2			6		
Concord	4	2	Heywood	William	1		3	1		2	1	1	1				10		
Concord	4	3	Prescott	Willoughby		1			1	2	2	1	1				8		
Concord	4	4	Heywood	Jonas				1		1	1		2				5		
Concord	4	5	Heywood	Jonas Jr	1		1	1		2		1					6		
Concord	4	6	Brown	Abel	1	1		1		3			1				7		
Concord	4	7	Baker	Daniel	1		1					1					3		
Concord	4	8	Hunt	Reuben		4		1	1	1	2	3	1				13		
Concord	4	9	Brown	David		1	1	1	1		2	2	2				10		
Concord	4	10	Prescott	Abel		1		1		1	1		1				5		
Concord	4	11	Curtis	John	2			1		1	1		1				6		
Concord	4	12	Stow	Joseph				1					1				2		
Concord	4	13	Richard	Louis				1		5			1				7		
Concord	4	14	Brown	Zachariah	2		1					1					4		
Concord	4	15	Kettell	John			1	1					1				3		
Concord	4	16	Meriam	Sarah		1						1					2		
Concord	4	17	Piper	Joshua	1			1					1				3		
Concord	4	18	Phillips	Lemuel				1		1		1		1			4		
Concord	4	19	Hutton	Nathaniel				1					1	2			4		
Concord	4	20	Prescott	Benjamin			1	1						1			3		
Concord	4	21	Prescott	Benajmin Jr	2			1		2			1				6		
Concord	4	22	Brooks	Susanna		1				3	1		1				6		
Concord	4	23	Hoar	Daniel	4			1		1	1	1					8		
Concord	4	24	Bateman	Jonas		1			1				1				4		
Concord	4	25	Hardy	Ebenzer	1	1	1	2		2	2		1	1			12		
Concord	4	26	Hosmer	Elijah		1	1		1			1	1	2			7		
Concord	4	27	Brooks	Ebenezer		1						1					2		
Concord	4	28	Rogers	Abigail						1			1				2		
Concord	4	29	Hunt	Jeremiah				1				2	1				4		
Concord	4	30	Durant	Keturah										1			1		
Concord	4	31	Jones	Asa		1						1					2		
Concord	4	32	Allen	George				1				2		1			4		
Concord	4	33	Stow	Nathan		1			1			2		2			6		
Concord	5	1	Shaw	Joseph Jr		1							1				2		
Concord	5	2	Stratton	Elizabeth									1	1			2		
Concord	5	3	Stearns	Peter	1			1		3			1				6		
Concord	5	4	Curtis	Jonathan	3			1		1			1				6		
Concord	5	5	Gregory	Marshall				1		1		1					3		
Concord	5	6	Wheeler	Peter	1	2	1		1	1	1	1	1				9		
Concord	5	7	Hubard	Ebenezer			1	1					1				3		
Concord	5	8	Davis	Nathaniel	2		1	1		2	1	1	1				9		
Concord	5	9	Vose	John	1	1	1	1					2				6		
Concord	5	10	Condy	Mary						1	1	2		1			5		
Concord	5	11	Stone	Joshua	2			1		1			1				5		
Concord	5	12	Jones	Joshua			4	1		1			1	1			8		
Concord	5	13	Minott	Stephen			2	1					1				4		
Concord	5	14	Potter	Ephraim		1			1				1				3		
Concord	5	15	Richardson	John		1		2		2		3					8		
Concord	5	16	Prison				2	6	8						1		17		
Concord	5	17	Hunt	Thadeus			2	1					1	2			6		
Concord	5	18	Hoar	Jonathan	1		1	1			1		1	1			6		
Concord	5	19	Wood	Nathan	2		1	1			1		1				6		
Concord	5	20	Potter	Samuel	4			1		1			1				7		
Concord	5	21	Potter	Jonas	2	1			1		1	1		1	1		8		
Concord	5	22	Potter	Ephraim Jr	2			1		1			1	1			6		
Concord	5	23	Clapp	Salma		1							1				2		

TOWN	PG#	LN#	LAST NAME	FIRST NAME	FWM under 10	FWM 10 to 16	FWM 16 to 26	FWM 26 to 45	FWM 45 and over	FWF under 10	FWF 10 to 16	FWF 16 to 26	FWF 26 to 45	FWF 45 and over	TOTAL ALL OTHER	TOTAL SLAVES	TOTALS	DISTRICT/ TOWNSHIP	NOTES
Concord	5	24	Underwood	Joseph	1			1		2			1				5		
Concord	5	25	Hurd	Isaac		1	1	1			1	2	2		1		9		
Concord	5	26	Crosby	Elizabeth										1			1		
Concord	5	27	Merrick	Tilly	1	2			1			1	1				6		
Concord	5	28	Pain	Phenihas	2		1		1		1	4		1	2		12		
Concord	5	29	Wheelock	Jonathan			1	1		2			1				5		
Concord	5	30	Bond	Martha									1				1		
Concord	5	31	Jones	Ephraim		1			1	2		1	2				7		
Concord	5	32	Turner	Thomas	2				1		1	1	2				7		
Concord	5	33	Parkman	William	1				1		1		1				4		
Concord	6	1	Flint	Abishai	1	1		2		2		1	1				8		
Concord	6	2	Brown	Ephraim	1			1		4	1		1				8		
Concord	6	3	Ripley	Ezra	1	1	1		1	1		2		1			8		
Concord	6	4	Jones	Elisha		1	2		1			2		2			8		
Concord	6	5	Knight	Jonathan	1	2		1		2			3				9		
Concord	6	6	Jones	Samuel Jr		1		1				1	2				5		
Concord	6	7	Barrett	Humphrey		1	1	1	1		1	1	1				7		
Concord	6	8	Whiting	Thomas	1	1			1	2		1	1				7		
Concord	6	9	Gill	Silas				1		3	1		1				6		
Concord	6	10	Mulliken	Joseph			1	1		3			1				6		
Concord	6	11	Harley	John				2				1					3		
Concord	6	12	Jones	Stephen		1			1	2	2		1				7		
Concord	6	13	Spauldin	Ithamar				1		1	1	1					3		
Concord	6	14	Lee	Jonas		1	1		1	2	1	1					7		
Concord	6	15	Barrett	Stephen		1				1		2					4		
Concord	6	16	Jones	William	1	1	1	1				2					6		
Concord	6	17	Coggswell	Emerson	1				1	2	2	1	1	1			9		
Concord	6	18	Bailey	David				1		2			1				4		
Concord	6	19	Coggswell	James				1		2		1					4		
Concord	6	20	Brown	Jesse				1			2		1				4		
Concord	6	21	Robinson	Jeremiah	1		1	1	1		1		1				6		
Concord	6	22	Bowen	William	1	1	1	1				1					5		
Concord	6	23	Hartshorn	Martha									1				1		
Concord	6	24	Hunt	Joseph		1			1			1	1				4		
Concord	6	25	Hoar	Mary						1		1	1				3		
Concord	6	26	William	Oliver			1					1					2		
Concord	6	27	Prescott	Rebecka		1				4			1				6		
Concord	6	28	Page	David	1			1		4	2		2				10		
Concord	6	29	Brown	Reuben	1	2	2	1	1			1		2			10		
Concord	6	30	Fay	Jonathan		1		1		1	1	3		1	1		9		
Concord	6	31	Heywood	Abiel		1						1	1				3		
Concord	6	32	Heywood	Asa		1	1				2	1					5		
Concord	6	33	Turner	Joseph		2	1					1					4		
Concord	6	34	Stebins	John			1			1		1					3		
Concord	6	35	Heywood	Jonathan		2						1	1				4		
Concord	6	36	Maynard	Aaron	1			1				1					3		
Concord	6	37	Shaw	Joseph		1		1		1			1				4		
Concord	7	1	*	Joseph				1			2						3		
Concord	7	2	Hadley	Samuel				1			2	1	1	1			6		
Concord	7	3	French	Nathaniel	2		2	1		3	2		1				11		
Concord	7	4	Derby	Eunice									2				2		
Concord	7	5	Cargill	Reuben		1	1				1		1	1			5		
Concord	7	6	Brown	Jacob		1		1	1				1				4		
Concord	7	7	Wood	Thadeus		1			1	1	1	2		1			7		
Concord	7	8	Procter	John				1					1	1			3		
Concord	7	9	Davis	Abel		2		1	1	3	1	1	1				10		
Concord	7	10	Melven	Samuel	1	1		1		3	2		1				9		
Concord	7	11	Melvin	Isaac			1			2			1				4		
Concord	7	12	Estabrook	Robert		1		2				1	1				7		
Concord	7	13	Davis	Dorothy				1					1	1			3		
Concord	7	14	Melvin	Jacob	1			1		1	1	1	2		1		8		
Concord	7	15	Wood	Daniel	4	1		1		1			1				8		
Concord	7	16	Brown	Samuel	2	3		1	1			1	2	3			13		
Concord	7	17	Chandler	Joseph			1		1		1	1		1	1		6		
Concord	7	18	Ha*well	David		1		1		1			1				4		
Concord	7	19	Barrett	Stephen	1	1	1		2			3	1	1			10		
Concord	7	20	*	Stephen									1	1			2		
Concord	7	21	Jones	Peter		1		1		1	2	1			1		7		
Concord	7	22	Melven	Amos	2	1	1		1	1	1		1				8		
Concord	7	23	Farrar	Reuben	1			1		3			1				6		
Concord	7	24	Farrar	Timothy			1	1					1				3		
Concord	7	25	Farrar	Ephraim	4	2		1		1		1					9		
Concord	7	26	Farrar	Jacob	3	1				1		1					8		
Concord	7	27	Dakin	Samuel			1	2	1			1		1			6		
Concord	7	28	Barrett	Thomas				1			1	2		1			5		
Concord	7	29	Conantt	Abel		1		1		1			1				4		
Concord	7	30	Law	David	1			2					1				4		
Concord	7	31	Temple	Peter	2	1	2		1	1	1		1				9		
Concord	7	32	Temple	Benjamin				1			1		1				3		

TOWN	PG#	LN#	LAST NAME	FIRST NAME	FREE WHITE MALES					FREE WHITE FEMALES					TOTAL ALL OTHER	TOTAL SLAVES	TOTALS	DISTRICT/ TOWNSHIP	NOTES
					under 10	10 to 16	16 to 26	26 to 45	45 and over	under 10	10 to 16	16 to 26	26 to 45	45 and over					
Concord	7	33	Barnes	Josiah	3	2			1		2			1			9		
Concord	7	34	Dakin	Samuel Jr	1		2	1		1	1		1				7		
Concord	7	35	Buttrick	Nathan			1	1					1				3		
Concord	7	36	Buttrick	Eli	3			1	1	2			1				8		
Concord	7	37	Buttrick	John	1	1		1		1		1	2				7		
Concord	7	38	Buttrick	Jonas	2		2	2		1	1	2	2				12		
Concord	7	39	Hosmer	Abigail						1			1				2		
Concord	8	1	Minott	Jonas Jr			1	1		2		1	1				6		
Concord	8	2	Mercer	William		2		1				1		1			5		
Concord	8	3	Jones	Abigail										3			3		
Concord	8	4	Meriam	Ephraim	2		1	1		1		1	1				7		
Concord	8	5	Meriam	John Jr			2						1				3		
Concord	8	6	Prescott	John				1				1	1				3		
Concord	8	7	Prescott	Samuel	1			1				1					3		
Concord	8	8	Prescott	Abel Jr	1			1		2			1				5		
Concord	8	9	Bowman	Edmond				1					1				2		
Concord	8	10	Meriam	John	3	1	1		1			2	1				9		
Concord	8	11	Minott	Jonas	1		1		1	2		1	1				7		
Concord	8	12	Minott	George	1	1			1		1	1		2	1		8		
Concord	8	13	Flint	Edward	1	1	2		1	1	2	2		2			12		
Concord	8	14	Hubbard	Thomas			1		1			1		1			4		
Concord	8	15	Hubbard	Thomas Jr	3			1		1	1		1				7		
Concord	8	16	Jones	Farwell			1	2		2	1	1	1	1			9		
Concord	8	17	William	John	1			1		2			1				5		
Concord	8	18	Wheler	Ephraim				1				1	1				3		
Concord	8	19	Wheeler	Ephraim Jr		1		1		1		2					5		
Concord	8	20	Colburn	James		1		1				1	1				4		
Concord	8	21	Hannon	Henry				1	2				1				4		
Concord	8	22	Conant	Eli				1	1	1	1		1				4		
Concord	8	23	Hunt	Hannah								1					1		
Concord	8	24	Jones	Samuel		1	3		1		2			1			8		
Concord	8	25	Simmon	Micah	1	3	2	1	1		1		1				10		
Concord	8	26	Harrington	Edward	2			1				2		1			6		
Concord	8	27	Brown	Paul				1									1		
Concord	8	28	Wood	Ephraim		1			1		1		1	1			5		
Concord	8	29	Lee	Lucy		2	1			1	1		1		1		7		
Concord	8	30	Hosmer	Joseph		2		1				1	1				5		
Concord	8	31	Hosmer	Cyrus	2	1	1	1		2	1		1				9		
Concord	8	32	Wheeler	Thomas		1		1				1		2			5		
Concord	8	33	Marhsal	Robert	1			1			1		1				4		
Concord	8	34	Hosmer	Benjamin				1					1				2		
Concord	8	35	Wood	Amos				2					1				3		
Concord	8	36	Wood	Amos Jr	2	1		1			1	1					6		
Concord	8	37	Shaw	William				1					1				2		
Concord	9	1	Wheeler	Abel	2				1	2	2	2	1				10		
Concord	9	2	Hosmer	Bethiah									2				2		
Concord	9	3	Hosmer	John	3	1	?		1	2	1	1	1	1			13		
Concord	9	4	Holden	Hannah									1				1		
Concord	9	5	Baker	James		1			1		1	1		1			5		
Concord	9	6	Willington	Lucy	1					1	2		1				5		
Concord	9	7	Hosmer	David			1					1					2		
Concord	9	8	Derby	Joseph		1			1			2		2			6		
Concord	9	9	Derby	Robert				1					1				2		
Concord	9	10	Heywood	Edward	1				1				1				3		
Concord	9	11	Hosmer	Daniel				1		2	1	1		1			6		
Concord	9	12	Piper	Lucy										1			1		
Concord	9	13	Brown	Roger		1	3		2		1	2		1			10		
Concord	9	14	Conant	Ezra				1					3	1			5		
Concord	9	15	Conant	Lot	2			1			1		1				5		
Concord	9	16	Heywood	Josiah				1					1				2		
Concord	9	17	Heywood	Reuben	3		1	1					1				6		
Concord	9	18	Heywood	Cyrus				1				1					2		
Concord	9	19	Noyes	Adam	1	1						1					4		
Concord	9	20	Conant	Andrew		1	1	2	1			1		1			7		
Concord	9	21	Heywood	Ephraim				1				1					2		
Concord	9	22	Wright	Joseph				1					1				2		
Concord	9	23	Wright	Jonas	3		1	1				1	1				7		
Concord	9	24	Price	James	1	1	1	1	1	1	1		1		2		10		
Concord	9	25	Wheeler	Mary									1				1		
Concord	9	26	Hosmer	Jesse	2	1			1	2	3			1			10		
Concord	9	27	Minot	John	1		1		1		1			1			5		
Concord	9	28	Miles	James	1			1		1		1					4		
Concord	9	29	Prescott	Charles				1									1		
Concord	9	30	Miles	Ezekiel			2	1					1				4		
Concord	9	31	Miles	Charles	1		1	1					2	1			6		
Concord	9	32	Hosmer	Stephen		1			1				1				3		
Concord	9	33	Benney	Elizabeth							2	1					3		
Concord	9	34	Hosmer	Silas	3	1		1					1				6		
Concord	10	1	Wood	Abigail									1				1		

TOWN	PG#	LN#	HEADS OF HOUSEHOLD LAST NAME	FIRST NAME	FREE WHITE MALES under 10	10 to 16	16 to 26	26 to 45	45 and over	FREE WHITE FEMALES under 10	10 to 16	16 to 26	26 to 45	45 and over	TOTAL ALL OTHER	TOTAL SLAVES	TOTALS	DISTRICT/ TOWNSHIP	NOTES
Concord	10	2	Holden	Daniel		1	1	1	1	1	1			1			7		
Concord	10	3	Jones	Redit	2		1	1	1	1	1		1				8		
Concord	10	4	Conant	Abel			1		1				1	1			4		
Concord	10	5	Melven	Sarah										1			1		
Concord	10	6	Lee	Isaac	2	1		1		2		1	1	1			9		
Concord	10	7	Wheeler	Noah		1	3		1	2	1	1		1			10		
Concord	10	8	Wheeler	Samuel	2	1	2		1				1	1			8		
Concord	10	9	Hayward	Joseph			1	1						1			3		
Concord	10	10	Hayward	John	3			1		2	2		1				9		
Concord	10	11	Parker	Phinehas				1		1		2		1			5		
Concord	10	12	Wheeler	Mary		1		1					1	1			4		
Concord	10	13	Hosmer	Amos		2	1		1	1		1	2	1			9		
Concord	10	14	Lee	Betty										1			1		
Concord	10	15	Miles	Oliver		1			1			1		1			4		
Concord	10	16	Miles	Joseph	2			1					1	1			5		
Concord	10	17	Wheeler	Phinehas		1	2		1	2	1			1			8		
Concord	10	18	Hosmer	Israel		1	1					1	1	1			5		
Concord	10	19	Price	Joel		1		1				1	1	1			5		
Concord	10	20	Ball	Lydia									1	1			2		
Concord	10	21	Ball	Reuben	2	1			1	1			1				6		
Concord	10	22	Smith	Elisha			1										1		
Concord	10	23	Robbinson	Keen	2		1		1	2			1				7		
Concord	10	24	Brooks	Abel		1		1		1			1				4		
Concord	10	25	Brook	Samuel		1		1	1		1		1	1			6		
Concord	10	26	Brook	Asa	2		2		1	1	1	1	1				9		
Concord	10	27	Ball	Benjamin	1				1					1			3		
Concord	10	28	Ball	Abner			2						2				4		
Concord	10	29	Green	Reuben	3			1					1				5		
Concord	10	30	Wood	Moses			1										1		
Concord	10	31	Barron	Oliver				1						1			2		
Concord	10	32	Barns	Benjamin	2			1		2	1		1				7		
Concord	10	33	Blood	Willard				1				1					2		
Concord	10	34	Blood	Timothy				1				1					2		
Concord	10	35	Blood	James	2			1		1			1	1			6		
Concord	11	1	Blood	Jotham				1		2		1					4		
Concord	11	2	Brown	Charles		1		1	1	1	1		1				6		
Concord	11	3	Lawrence	John				1		2	1		2	1			7		
Concord	11	4	Barrett	John		3	2		1	3	1		1	1			12		
Concord	11	5	Buttrick	David	1	1		1		2	1		2				8		
Concord	11	6	Flint	Mary	1					2			1				4		
Concord	11	7	Buttrick	Joseph			1	1		1				1			4		
Concord	11	8	Buttrick	Samuel	2			1	2	2		1	2	1			11		
Concord	11	9	Buttrick	Samuel Jr	3		1	2		2			1	1			10		
Concord	11	10	Hunt	Nehemiah	2			1		2	1	1	1	1			9		
Concord	11	11	Barrett	Nathan	2	1		2			1	1	1	1			9		
Concord	11	12	Clark	Benjamin Jr		2			1	1	1	2		1			8		
Concord	11	13	Wayman	John	3		1	1	1	2	1		1				10		
Concord	11	14	Merriam	Josiah Jr	2	1		1		2		2	1				9		
Concord	11	15	Meriam	Josiah		1		1				1		1			4		
Concord	11	16	Meriam	Joseph			1						1				2		
Concord	11	17	Kibby	Elizabeth										1			1		
Concord	11	18	Estabrook	John		1		1		2			1				5		
Concord	11	19	Harris	Jonathan				1	1	1	1		1	1			4		
Concord	11	20	Wheeler	David			1	2	1			2		1			7		
Concord	11	21	Wheeler	David Jr	3		1	1		2			1				8		
Concord	11	22	Wheeler	Jotham		2			1	1				2			6		
Concord	11	23	Case	Huldy									1				1		
Concord	11	24	Tower	Elizabeth										2			2		
Concord	11	25	Case												1		1		
Concord	11	26	Robbinson	Cesar											3		3		
Concord	11	27	Freeman	Brister											4		4		
Concord	11	28	Ingraham	Cato											4		4		
Concord	11	29		Zilpah											1		1		
Concord	11	30	Dugan	Thomas											4		4		

TOWN	PG#	LN#	LAST NAME	FIRST NAME	FREE WHITE MALES					FREE WHITE FEMALES					TOTAL ALL OTHER	TOTAL SLAVES	TOTALS	DISTRICT/ TOWNSHIP	NOTES
					under 10	10 to 16	16 to 26	26 to 45	45 and over	under 10	10 to 16	16 to 26	26 to 45	45 and over					
Dracut	44	1	Varnum	Parker	1	2		2	1	2	2	3			1		14		
Dracut	44	2	Bradley	Amos Jr	5	1	1	1		1	2		1				12		
Dracut	44	3	Bradley	Amos			1		2			1	1	1			6		
Dracut	44	4	Bradley	Joshua	3		1	1		2		1	1				9		
Dracut	44	5	Bradley	Joseph	1			1		2		1	1				6		
Dracut	44	6	Bradley	Isaac		1		1	1	2	1		1				7		
Dracut	44	7	Bradley	Isaac Jr	1	1	1	1		1		2					7		
Dracut	44	8	Hovey	Saml			2	1					1				4		
Dracut	44	9	Hovey	Henry A		1		1		4	1		1				8		
Dracut	44	10	Hovey	Thom			4	2	1			1		1			9		
Dracut	44	11	Hildreth	William	1	1		1		1	1	1	2				8		
Dracut	44	12	Hildren	Micah			2			1			1				4		
Dracut	44	13	Sherborn	James	2		1					1					4		
Dracut	44	14	Durant	Nathan			1	1				1					3		
Dracut	44	15	Abbott	Daniel	1		1	2		1			1	1			7		
Dracut	44	16	Durant	Saml		1			1	1			1				4		
Dracut	44	17	Hamblet	Jona	2	1			1	1			1				6		
Dracut	44	18	Coburn	Ezra					1				1				2		
Dracut	44	19	Cohen	J* W	1		1	1		1		1	1				6		
Dracut	44	20	Littlehale	James		1	2		1			1		1			6		
Dracut	44	21	Coburn	Ephm		1	1		1			2					5		
Dracut	44	22	Marble	David		1	1			1		1		1			5		
Dracut	44	23	Osgood	Solomon			1	1		1	2						5		
Dracut	44	24	Osgood	Henry C	1		1			1		1	1				5		
Dracut	44	25	Abbott	Solomon	1	1		1		4	1		1				9		
Dracut	44	26	Varnum	Jona		2		1				1		1			5		
Dracut	44	27	Varnum	Jona Jr			1					1					2		
Dracut	44	28	Varnum	Thomas	3	1	1		1	2	2		1	1			12		
Dracut	44	29	Coburn	Elijah		2	1		1					1			5		
Dracut	44	30	Hildreth	John					1					1			2		
Dracut	44	31	Putnam	John			5	1		1			1				8		
Dracut	44	32	Varnum	Joseph M	2	3	1		1	1		2		1	1		12		
Dracut	44	33	Dane	Joseph	1	1			1	1	1	1					6		
Dracut	44	34	Barron	Saml				1		2	1	1	1				6		
Dracut	44	35	Varnum	Daniel	2		1	1		3		1					8		
Dracut	44	36	Coburn	Simon	1	1		1		1		1					5		
Dracut	44	37	Coburn	Simeon				1		1	1		1				4		
Dracut	44	38	Hunt	Israel	4			1			1		1				7		
Dracut	44	39	Coburn	Kezia		1								1			2		
Dracut	45	1	Richardson	Saml	1			1		1			1				4		
Dracut	45	2	Coburn	Thomas			2		1			2	1	1			7		
Dracut	45	3	Blood	Abraham	1	1	1	1	1			1	4	1			11		
Dracut	45	4	Wilson	David	1	1	1	1		1	1	1					7		
Dracut	45	5	Marble	Jonath				1		1			1				3		
Dracut	45	6	Coburn	Willard		1		1				2		1			5		
Dracut	45	7	Coburn	Willard Jr	2			1		3			1				7		
Dracut	45	8	Barker	Andrew			1			3		1					5		
Dracut	45	9	Didson	Seth	1			2		1			1	1			6		
Dracut	45	10	Brown	Osgood	2			1		1			1				5		
Dracut	45	11	Coburn	Timo		1		1		1		1		1			5		
Dracut	45	12	Brown	Timothy	1				1			1		1			4		
Dracut	45	13	Coburn	Mary Jr						1	1		1				3		
Dracut	45	14	Coburn	Moses B.	1	2		1		1	1		1				7		
Dracut	45	15	Coburn	Mary		1	1			1	1		1				5		
Dracut	45	16	Austin	Lewis	3	1	1		1	1	4		1				12		
Dracut	45	17	Varnum	James		1	2		1	1	1	2	1				9		
Dracut	45	18	Thompson	Leonard		1		1		1			1				4		
Dracut	45	19	Varnum	Joseph			2			1			1				4		
Dracut	45	20	Coburn	Micah	1								1				2		
Dracut	45	21	Varnum	Joseph Brett	1		1				1	1		1			5		
Dracut	45	22	Buttrick	Willard			1		1	1	1						4		
Dracut	45	23	Goodhue	Zach	1				1	1		2	2	1			8		
Dracut	45	24	Doak	William			1		1		1	1		1			5		
Dracut	45	25	Hasseltine	James			1		1					1			3		
Dracut	45	26	Frye	Timothy			2		1	1		2		1			7		
Dracut	45	27	Coburn	Jeptha	1	1		1			1	2	1				7		
Dracut	45	28	Goodhue	Moses		1	1	1				2	1				6		
Dracut	45	29	Flint	Nehemiah			1		1		1	3					6		
Dracut	45	30	Jones	Hugh					1					1			2		
Dracut	45	31	Jones	Oliver	2	1			1	2	1		1				8		
Dracut	45	32	Jones	Zebediah	1		1		1	2	1		1				7		
Dracut	45	33	Jones	Nathl	1	1	1		1	1	1	1	1				8		
Dracut	45	34	Hasseltine	Peter	1	2			1	2		2		1			9		
Dracut	45	35	Hildreth	Josiah	1		1		1			1		4			8		
Dracut	45	36	Hildreth	James	1		1					1					3		
Dracut	45	37	Aiken	Solomon	3			1		1	1		1				7		
Dracut	45	38	Hildreth	Josiah Jr	2			1		2		1					6		
Dracut	45	39	Morgan	Jona	3	1		1			1		1				7		
Dracut	46	1	Thayer	Elizabeth	2			1		1			1				5		

TOWN	PG#	LN#	HEADS OF HOUSEHOLD — LAST NAME	FIRST NAME	FREE WHITE MALES — under 10	10 to 16	16 to 26	26 to 45	45 and over	FREE WHITE FEMALES — under 10	10 to 16	16 to 26	26 to 45	45 and over	TOTAL ALL OTHER	TOTAL SLAVES	TOTALS	DISTRICT/ TOWNSHIP	NOTES
Dracut	46	2	Richardson	Obadiah	1				1	3	3		1				9		
Dracut	46	3	Richardson	Moses				1					1				2		
Dracut	46	4	Richardson	Jonathan	3	2		1		2	1	1	1				11		
Dracut	46	5	Richardson	Reuben	3		1			2			1	1			8		
Dracut	46	6	Wood	Abijah		1		1					1				3		
Dracut	46	7	Wood	Hiram	1		1					1					3		
Dracut	46	8	Friend	Isaac	1			1		2			1				5		
Dracut	46	9	Cheever	Moses	4			1			1	1	1				8		
Dracut	46	10	Coburn	Job		1		1		1			1				4		
Dracut	46	11	Coburn	Uriah			1		1	1	1		1				5		
Dracut	46	12	Parker	Daniel	1		1			1	1	1	1				6		
Dracut	46	13	Parker	Peter	4	1		1		1	1		1				9		
Dracut	46	14	Parker	John Jr		1	1					1					3		
Dracut	46	15	Parker	Jona	2			1		2		1					6		
Dracut	46	16	Barker	Isaac	3			1		1			1				6		
Dracut	46	17	Sawyer	Henry	1			1		3		1					6		
Dracut	46	18	Richardson	Robert	2			1		1			1				5		
Dracut	46	19	Norwell	Moses	1			1		1	1	1					5		
Dracut	46	20	Sawyer	Nathan		1	1			1		1					4		
Dracut	46	21	Sayer	Reuben	1				1				1	1			4		
Dracut	46	22	Sawyer	Eben	2			1		3	2		1				9		
Dracut	46	23	Harris	Peter	1	1		1		2		1					6		
Dracut	46	24	Harris	Simon	2			1		2	1		1				7		
Dracut	46	25	Harvey	James				1		1	2	2	1	1			8		
Dracut	46	26	Mears	Samll	1		1	1		2	2	1	1				9		
Dracut	46	27	Davies	Moses	2	2		1		2			1				8		
Dracut	46	28	Richardson	William	2	2		1		3			1				9		
Dracut	46	29	Snell	David	3		1		1		1	1	1				8		
Dracut	46	30	Austin	Solomon	1	1		1		2	1	1	1				8		
Dracut	46	31	Austin	David		1	1		2	1	1	1		1			8		
Dracut	46	32	Austin	David Jr		1						1					2		
Dracut	46	33	Jones	David				1					1				2		
Dracut	46	34	Jones	David Jr		1						1					2		
Dracut	46	35	Clark	Timothy	2		1					1					4		
Dracut	46	36	Fox	Abijah	1		1		1	2	1	1		1			8		
Dracut	46	37	Fox	Joel	1	3		1		2			1				8		
Dracut	46	38	Varnum	Prescot	2		1	1	2	4	1		1				12		
Dracut	46	39	Bailey	Moses	1	1		1		3	1		1				8		
Dracut	46	40	Manfure	Samll		1	1	1				2	1	1			7		
Dracut	47	1	Manfure	J* W	2		1		1	1	3	2		1			11		
Dracut	47	2	Richardson	Stephen Jr	2	2		1		3	1		1				10		
Dracut	47	3	Holl	Ephraim		1			1	1			1				4		
Dracut	47	4	Holl	Phinehas			1					1					2		
Dracut	47	5	Davis	Timo		1	1		1	1	1	3		1			9		
Dracut	47	6	Davis	Eben			1						1	1			3		
Dracut	47	7	Clough	William		1		1				1		1			4		
Dracut	47	8	Gardner	Samll		1		1		2			2				7		
Dracut	47	9	Banon	Samll				1		2	1	1					6		
Dracut	47	10	Ellingswood	Robert		1		1		3		1		1			7		
Dracut	47	11	Hanich	Israel			1						1				2		
Dracut	47	12	Hall	Timothy	1			1		2	1		1				6		
Dracut	47	13	Coburn	Hezeh		2		1					1		4		7		
Dracut	47	14	Marshall	Joshua	2	2	1		1	2	1		2				11		
Dracut	47	15	Webster	William	2	1		1		3			1				8		
Dracut	47	16	Varnum	Jonas	1	2			1	1	1	1	1				8		
Dracut	47	17	Coburn	Jabeth	1	1	1		1	1	2	3	1				11		
Dracut	47	18	Ham*	John	1			1				1		1			5		
Dracut	47	19	Coburn	Peter				1					1				2		
Dracut	47	20	Coburn	Peter Jr	2	2		1		1	1	1	1				9		
Dracut	47	21	Cummings	Samll		1		1					1				3		
Dracut	47	22	Williams	Simeon	1		1	1					2				5		
Dracut	47	23	Clements	Moses	3	1	1			2	2		1				10		
Dracut	47	24	Wilson	Joseph		1	2	1				1	1				6		
Dracut	47	25	Coburn	Jacob		2		1			1		1	1			6		
Dracut	47	26	Coburn	Jonas				1					1				2		
Dracut	47	27	Coburn	Saul	3	1		1		1			1				7		
Dracut	47	28	Coburn	Thaddeus		2		1		1			2				6		
Dracut	47	29	Coburn	Jonas Jr	1	1		1		3	2		1				9		
Dracut	47	30	Crosby	Jona				1					1				2		
Dracut	47	31	Crosby	Jona Jr		1	2	1			1			1			6		
Dracut	47	32	Bowen	John	2		1	1		2	1	1	1				9		
Dracut	47	33	Piper	Samll	2		1		1	2	3	1	1				11		
Dracut	47	34	Fox	Josiah		2		1		2	2	1					8		
Dracut	47	35	Fox	Peter			1			1		1					3		
Dracut	47	36	Fox	Eliphalet	1	3		1		2	2			2			11		
Dracut	47	37	Parker	Kindal Jr	2			1		1		1					5		
Dracut	47	38	Jones	Solomon		1		1		1		1					4		
Dracut	48	1	Peabody	*	1			1		1			1	1			5		
Dracut	48	2	Peabody	*	3	1		1		1	1		1				8		

TOWN	PG#	LN#	LAST NAME	FIRST NAME	FREE WHITE MALES					FREE WHITE FEMALES					TOTAL ALL OTHER	TOTAL SLAVES	TOTALS	DISTRICT/ TOWNSHIP	NOTES
					under 10	10 to 16	16 to 26	26 to 45	45 and over	under 10	10 to 16	16 to 26	26 to 45	45 and over					
Dracut	48	3	Fox	David		2	3		1	1	2		1				10		
Dracut	48	4	Fox	Daniel			1			2		1					4		
Dracut	48	5	Barnes	Benejah	3	2	1	1		1			1	1			10		
Dracut	48	6	Frye	Jedidiah	1			1				1					3		
Dracut	48	7	Gilcrest	John	3			1			2	1	1				8		
Dracut	48	8	Stevens	Benja	1	2			1	3	1		1				9		
Dracut	48	9	Harvey	Joseph	1			1		2			1				5		
Dracut	48	10	Reed	James	2		1	1						1			5		
Dracut	48	11	Hildreth	Israel	2		1	1	1	1	1	1	2	1			11		
Dracut	48	12	Harvey	Benja		1				1			1				3		
Dracut	48	13	Taylor	Isaac	5		1			1		1					8		
Dracut	48	14	Taylor	John	1			1		1		1	1	1			6		
Dracut	48	15	Barker	Timothy				1						2			3		
Dracut	48	16	Barker	Timothy Jr			1	1					1	1			4		
Dracut	48	17	Harvey	John D	2	1		1		3	1		1				9		
Dracut	48	18	Hall	Richard		3				1	1	1					6		
Dracut	48	19	Sawyer	Caleb	4		1			1			1				7		
Dracut	48	20	Austin	William	1	1	1	1		2	1		1				8		
Dracut	48	21	Smith	Dudley		1		1		1	1	1		1			6		
Dracut	48	22	Clough	Abigal		1	1							1			3		
Dracut	48	23	Richardson	Acquilla	1		1			1			1				4		
Dracut	48	24	Richardson	Stephen		1		1		1			1				4		
Dracut	48	25	Kelly	George Jr	3		1					1					5		
Dracut	48	26	Richardson	Ephm		1		1		1			3				6		
Dracut	48	27	Mallone	William				1				1		1			3		
Dracut	48	28	Cheever	John	1		1			3	1						6		
Dracut	48	29	Wood	Solomon	2		1			3	2		1				9		
Dracut	48	30	Wood	Daniel	3		1			1			1	1			7		
Dracut	48	31	Wood	Amos	1	1		1		2			1				6		
Dracut	48	32	Parker	John	3		1			2			1				7		
Dracut	48	33	Parker	Ephraim				1					1	1			3		
Dracut	48	34	Parker	Warren		1							1		1		3		
Dracut	48	35	Thissell	Joshua	3		1						2	1			7		
Dracut	48	36	Coburn	Isaac		2				1		1					4		
Dracut	49	1	Richardson	Obadiah Jr	1	1							1				3		
Dracut	49	2	Abbott	David		1	1			1			1	1			5		
Dracut	49	3	Kimbal	Samll	1	1			1	3			1				7		
Dracut	49	4	Cheever	Ezehl			1	1			1	1		1			5		
Dracut	49	5	Blanchard	Caleb	2	2		1		2			1	1			9		
Dracut	49	6	Blanchard	Samll				1						1			2		
Dracut	49	7	Wood	William			1						1				2		
Dracut	49	8	Cheever	Solomon		1				1	1			1			4		
Dracut	49	9	Kelly	George				1						1			2		
Dracut	49	10	Kelly	John	1			1		2		1					5		
Dracut	49	11	Wood	Joseph	2			1		2				2			7		
Dracut	49	12	Barker	Richard				1						1			2		
Dracut	49	13	Hall	Asa	4	1		1		1	1		1	1			10		

TOWN	PG#	LN#	LAST NAME	FIRST NAME	FREE WHITE MALES					FREE WHITE FEMALES					TOTAL ALL OTHER	TOTAL SLAVES	TOTALS	DISTRICT/ TOWNSHIP	NOTES
					under 10	10 to 16	16 to 26	26 to 45	45 and over	under 10	10 to 16	16 to 26	26 to 45	45 and over					
Dunstable	216	1	Blodgett	Josiah			2		1	1				1			5		
Dunstable	216	2	Blodgett	Zebulon	1	1			1	1		1	1	1			7		
Dunstable	216	3	Butterfield	Leonard Capt.	1		1	1	1	1		2	1	1			9		
Dunstable	216	4	Butterfield	Phillip Capt.	2	2	1	2		2		2	1				12		
Dunstable	216	5	Blood	Silas	3	1			1	1			1	1			8		
Dunstable	216	6	Blood	Peter	3		1		1		1	1	1	1			9		
Dunstable	216	7	Blood	Caleb					1	1	2	2		1			7		
Dunstable	216	8	Blood	Caleb Jr			2			1			1				4		
Dunstable	216	9	Blood	Henry	1	1	1	1		1		1	1				7		
Dunstable	216	10	Cummings	Oliver Capt.				1		1			1				3		
Dunstable	216	11	Cummings	Simeon		1		1	1	2	2		1				8		
Dunstable	216	12	Cummings	James	1			1		3	1	1	1				8		
Dunstable	216	13	Cummings	Nathl			3	1					1		1		6		
Dunstable	216	14	Cummings	Joshiah Capt.				1		1	1		1				4		
Dunstable	216	15	Cummings	Jeremiah	2	1		1		2			1	1			8		
Dunstable	216	16	Cummings	Nathl Jr				1					1				2		
Dunstable	216	17	Chancy	John	1	1	1		1	1		1					6		
Dunstable	216	18	Carter	Michal	1			1		3			1				6		
Dunstable	216	19	Emerson	Mary Wid		2					1	2	1				6		
Dunstable	216	20	Eldridge	Micah Doct.	1		1			1		1					4		
Dunstable	216	21	Fletcher	Thomas		1		1				2		1			5		
Dunstable	216	22	Fletcher	Jona Capt.		1	1		1		1	1		1			6		
Dunstable	216	23	Fletcher	Joseph	1		1		1	1	1	1	1				7		
Dunstable	217	1	Fletcher	Phinehas		1	1	1		3	1	2	1	1			11		
Dunstable	217	2	Fletcher	Nathl Capt.			1	1				2					4		
Dunstable	217	3	Fletcher	Saml	1			1		1	1	1					5		
Dunstable	217	4	French	Ebenz		1	1	1				1		1			5		
Dunstable	217	5	French	Jonas	1	1	1	1				2					6		
Dunstable	217	6	Farwell	Ebenz				1						2			3		
Dunstable	217	7	Hardy	Moses		1		1			2		1				5		
Dunstable	217	8	Ingoll	John	1		1		1	1		1	1	1			7		
Dunstable	217	9	Johnson	Silas	2	1		1		1		1	1				7		
Dunstable	217	10	Jewett	Joseph				1		1	1		1				4		
Dunstable	217	11	Kendall	John				1				1	1				3		
Dunstable	217	12	Kendall	Jacob				1					1				2		
Dunstable	217	13	Kendall	Temple			1	1				1	1				4		
Dunstable	217	14	Kendall	Edward				1					1				2		
Dunstable	217	15	Kendall	Zebed* Dea.	2	2	2	1			1		1				9		
Dunstable	217	16	Kendall	Josiah			1			1			1				3		
Dunstable	217	17	Kendall	Temple Jr	2	1		1		2			1	1			8		
Dunstable	217	18	Kendall	Jonas	1	1		1		1			2	1			7		
Dunstable	217	19	Lawrence	Isaac				1					1				2		
Dunstable	217	20	Parkhurst	Joel Equ				1		1		1	1				4		
Dunstable	217	21	Parkhurst	Joseph				1					1				2		
Dunstable	217	22	Parkhurst	Joseph Jr		1		1		1	1	2	1				7		
Dunstable	217	23	Parkhurst	Ebenz	3	1	1	1			1		1				8		
Dunstable	217	24	Parkhurst	Leonard	3		1	1		3			1				9		
Dunstable	217	25	Parker	Levi		1		1		1	2	1		1			7		
Dunstable	217	26	Proctor	Jonas	1	1	1		1	1			1				6		
Dunstable	217	27	Proctor	Gershom	2	2		1				1	1	1			8		
Dunstable	217	28	Proctor	Nathan	1			1			2		1				5		
Dunstable	217	29	Proctor	Peter	1		2	1				1	1				6		
Dunstable	217	30	Pratt	Jerathmul C.				1		1			1				3		
Dunstable	217	31	Reed	Eleazr				1		1		2		1			5		
Dunstable	217	32	Reed	Caleb	2			1		1			1				5		
Dunstable	217	33	Roby	Joseph W		1		1					1	1			4		
Dunstable	217	34	Robbins	Elijah	4			1					1				6		
Dunstable	217	35	Richardson	Zachariah			1						1				2		
Dunstable	217	36	Swallow	Amiziah		1		1		1				1			4		
Dunstable	217	37	Swallow	Benjm			1	1				1	1	1			5		
Dunstable	217	38	Swallow	Peter	1		1		1	1	1			1			6		
Dunstable	217	39	Swallow	Jonas	1			1		3	1		1				7		
Dunstable	217	40	Swallow	Asa	2		1	1		2			2				8		
Dunstable	217	41	Swallow	Abraham	2	1		1		2			1				7		
Dunstable	217	42	Spaulding	Abel		1		1				2		1			5		
Dunstable	217	43	Spaulding	Joseph	1	2		1		1		1					6		
Dunstable	217	44	Stevens	Saml Capt.			2		1			1		1			5		
Dunstable	217	45	Stevens	Jesse	2		1	1		1			1				6		
Dunstable	217	46	Stevens	Parker		1		1				1	1				4		
Dunstable	217	47	Stevens	Josiah			3	1		3		1		1			9		
Dunstable	217	48	Taylor	David			1	1					1	1			4		
Dunstable	217	49	Taylor	Jonas		1						1	1				4		

TOWN	PG#	LN#	LAST NAME	FIRST NAME	M <10	M 10-16	M 16-26	M 26-45	M 45+	F <10	F 10-16	F 16-26	F 26-45	F 45+	TOTAL ALL OTHER	TOTAL SLAVES	TOTALS	DISTRICT/TOWNSHIP	NOTES
East Sudbury	65	1	Adams	Benjamin			2		1	3	2	2	1				11		
East Sudbury	65	2	Adams	Seth	2			1	1				1	1			6		
East Sudbury	65	3	Abbott	Ephraim		1		1	1	1			3	1			8		
East Sudbury	65	4	Allen	John			1	1					1				3		
East Sudbury	65	5	Rice	Nathaniel	3				1	1			1				6		
East Sudbury	65	6	Baldwin	David	2	2		2		1	1	2	1				11		
East Sudbury	65	7	Bryant	Joel	1		1	1		1			1	2			7		
East Sudbury	65	8	Bracket	William	2	2		1		2		1	1				9		
East Sudbury	65	9	Bent	William	3	2	1		1			1		2			10		
East Sudbury	65	10	Bond	Phinehas				1	1				1				3		
East Sudbury	65	11	Bond	Nathan	1			1		4			1				7		
East Sudbury	65	12	Berry	John					2					1			3		
East Sudbury	65	13	Curtis	William		1	1				1			1			4		
East Sudbury	65	14	Cutting	Elisha	2	1			1	2		2	1	2			11		
East Sudbury	65	15	Cutting	John		3	1	1		2			1				8		
East Sudbury	65	16	Cutting	Robert	1				1			1	1				4		
East Sudbury	65	17	Clark	William				1		1				1			3		
East Sudbury	66	1	Thompson	Abel	2				1	2	2		1				8		
East Sudbury	66	2	Cory	Isaac	2		2		1	1	1	1		1			9		
East Sudbury	66	3	Damon	Thomas	2	1		2	1	2			2	3			13		
East Sudbury	66	4	Damon	William	1			1	1				1	1			5		
East Sudbury	66	5	Damon	Isaac	1		1		1	2			1	1			8		
East Sudbury	66	6	Dudley	Joseph	3		1	1	1	1			1	1			9		
East Sudbury	66	7	Dudley	William				1				1					2		
East Sudbury	66	8	Dudley	Benjm	2		1		1	1			1	1			7		
East Sudbury	66	9	Dudley	William Jr	1			1		1			1				4		
East Sudbury	66	10	Dudley	Daniel	3	2		1		1			1				8		
East Sudbury	66	11	Flagg	John	2	1		2		3	1	1	1				11		
East Sudbury	66	12	Morse	Asarelah		1		1		1		1		1			5		
East Sudbury	66	13	Griffin	Samuel		1	1		1	1		1	1	1			7		
East Sudbury	66	14	Gleason	Isaac			1						1				2		
East Sudbury	66	15	Gleason	Nathan	1			1		3			1				6		
East Sudbury	66	16	Gleason	Luther	1			1		1			1				4		
East Sudbury	66	17	Gleason	Reuben		2				2		1		1			6		
East Sudbury	66	18	Gould	James		1				1		1		2			5		
East Sudbury	66	19	Goodnow	Micah	1			1	1		1	1		1			6		
East Sudbury	66	20	Goodnow	Asahel	3			1	1	2	1		1				8		
East Sudbury	66	21	Grout	Silas		1	1		1	3			1				7		
East Sudbury	66	22	Heard	Thomas	1	1			1	1	1	2		1			8		
East Sudbury	66	23	Heard	Zeuheriah	2	2			1			1		1			7		
East Sudbury	66	24	Heard	David	2	1		1		1	1	1	1				8		
East Sudbury	66	25	Heard	Richard	2	1			1	1	1	1	1				8		
East Sudbury	66	26	Haynes	Samiel			1	1		2		1	1	1			7		
East Sudbury	66	27	Jenkison	Abraham		1		1		1	1	1		1			6		
East Sudbury	66	28	Bevis	William				1						1			2		
East Sudbury	66	29	Johnson	William			2			1	1	1					5		
East Sudbury	66	30	Johnson	Peter	1		2		1	1	1	2		1			9		
East Sudbury	66	31	Johnson	Ebenezer	1	1	2		1	1				1			7		
East Sudbury	66	32	Loker	Bulah			1						1	1			3		
East Sudbury	66	33	Loker	John			1						1				2		
East Sudbury	66	34	Loker	Ebenezer	2		1					1		1			5		
East Sudbury	66	35	Loker	Isaac	2		1			1		1					5		
East Sudbury	66	36	Loker	Alpheus			1	1		1		1	1				5		
East Sudbury	67	1	Loker	Paul			1			1		1					3		
East Sudbury	67	2	Moore	Israel	3			1		2	1		1				8		
East Sudbury	67	3	Maynard	Daniel		1		1				1	1				4		
East Sudbury	67	4	Maynard	Deborah			1	2		2			1				6		
East Sudbury	67	5	Maynard	Micah	2		1	1				1		1			6		
East Sudbury	67	6	Meriam	Elisha	1		1	1		3			1	1			8		
East Sudbury	67	7	Bridge	Josiah		1	1	2	1				2	1			8		
East Sudbury	67	8	Brown	William			1			1		2					4		
East Sudbury	67	9	Moore	Caleb	1			1		1		1	1				5		
East Sudbury	67	10	Moulton	Caleb			1		1		1	1		1			5		
East Sudbury	67	11	Moulton	William				1						1			2		
East Sudbury	67	12	Moulton	Windsor	2		1	1					1				5		
East Sudbury	67	13	Moulton	Aaron	1				2					1			4		
East Sudbury	67	14	Noyes	John		1	1	1	1			2	2	1	1		10		
East Sudbury	67	15	Noyes	Tabitha			1							1			2		
East Sudbury	67	16	Abbott	Amos	1			1		1			1				4		
East Sudbury	67	17	Gleason	Edward			1		1		1	3		1	1		8		
East Sudbury	67	18	Noyes	Anna									2	1			3		
East Sudbury	67	19	Parmenter	Jona	3		1		1				1	1			7		
East Sudbury	67	20	Pratt	Simeon	2	1		1		1	1	1	1				8		
East Sudbury	67	21	Pool	Hannah			1	1						1			3		
East Sudbury	67	22	Herington	Elisha			1				1		1				3		
East Sudbury	67	23	Drummond	Rebecka	1									1			2		
East Sudbury	67	24	Bent	Rufus		1			1				1				3		
East Sudbury	67	25	Carter	Jonathan				1			2	1		1			5		
East Sudbury	67	26	Tyler	Othneil	2			1			1		1				5		

49

TOWN	PG#	LN#	LAST NAME	FIRST NAME	FREE WHITE MALES					FREE WHITE FEMALES					TOTAL ALL OTHER	TOTAL SLAVES	TOTALS	DISTRICT/ TOWNSHIP	NOTES
					under 10	10 to 16	16 to 26	26 to 45	45 and over	under 10	10 to 16	16 to 26	26 to 45	45 and over					
East Sudbury	67	27	Roby	William	2			1		1		1	1	2			8		
East Sudbury	67	28	Butter	Thomas	1		2		1	1		1	1				7		
East Sudbury	67	29	Rice	Isaac		1	1		1		1			1			5		
East Sudbury	67	30	Butter	Joseph			1		1	1	2	1	1				7		
East Sudbury	67	31	Reeves	Nathaniel		1			1		1			1			4		
East Sudbury	67	32	Rice	Edmund	2	1			1	2	2		1				9		
East Sudbury	67	33	Rice	Elisha	2			1		2	2		1				8		
East Sudbury	68	1	Rice	Ezekiel		1	1		1			1	1	1			6		
East Sudbury	68	2	Rice	Elisabeth						1				1			2		
East Sudbury	68	3	Russell	Thadeus		1			1		1			1			4		
East Sudbury	68	4	Rivers	Jacob	3	2	1	1		1	1		2	1			12		
East Sudbury	68	5	Sherman	Timothy	1		1	1	1		1	1		1	1		8		
East Sudbury	68	6	Sherman	Reuben	2			1		2			2				7		
East Sudbury	68	7	Sherman	Jona		1		1		1	1		1	1			6		
East Sudbury	68	8	Sherman	Edward				1					1				2		
East Sudbury	68	9	Sherman	Ephraim	2	2		1			1		1				7		
East Sudbury	68	10	Payson	Joseph					1		1	2		1			5		
East Sudbury	68	11	Maples	Ebenezer			1		1	1		1		1			5		
East Sudbury	68	12	Sanderson	James	1	1	1		1			2		1			7		
East Sudbury	68	13	Smith	Joseph					1				1	1			3		
East Sudbury	68	14	Smith	David	1			1		2		1	1				6		
East Sudbury	68	15	Hawes	Jeremiah		1		1				1	1				4		
East Sudbury	68	16	Smith	Ephraim		2	2		1	1	1		1				8		
East Sudbury	68	17	Stone	John					2			2		1			5		
East Sudbury	68	18	Stone	Aaron	1		1				1						3		
East Sudbury	68	19	Stone	Isabel	2	1	1	1		1			1	2			9		
East Sudbury	68	20	Stone	Purchas	1	1		1		2			1				6		
East Sudbury	68	21	Tilton	John			2		1	1	1	1		2			8		
East Sudbury	68	22	Tilton	Samuel	1		1		1					1			4		
East Sudbury	68	23	Thomas	Josiah	1	1	1	1	2		1		1	2			10		
East Sudbury	68	24	Wyman	William	2	1	1		1	1		2	1				9		
East Sudbury	68	25	Smith	Simeon				1		1				2			4		
East Sudbury	68	26	Stone	John Jr	3	1	2	1		1	1	2	3				14		
East Sudbury	68	27	Peirce	Thomas		1		1					1				3		
East Sudbury	68	28	Whitney	Elisabeth								1		1			2		
East Sudbury	68	29	Underwood	Jona	1		1		1		1	1	1				6		
East Sudbury	68	30	Underwood	Jona Jr	1	1			1	1	1		1				6		
East Sudbury	68	31	Burbanks	Thos						1	2	1	1				5		
East Sudbury	68	32	Smith	Alexander	1			1		4	1		1				8		
East Sudbury	68	33	Sawin	Benjm	1		1	1					1				4		
East Sudbury	69	1	Tilton	John Jr		1	3					1	1				6		
East Sudbury	69	2	Griffin	Daniel		1		1		2		1	1				6		
East Sudbury	69	3	Brackett	John	2	1		1		2			1				7		
East Sudbury	69	4	Loker	Stephen	3				1	2	2		1				9		
East Sudbury	69	5	Loker	Ephraim		1				3		1					5		
East Sudbury	69	6	How	Willard			1					1					2		
East Sudbury	69	7	Brown	Rebeckah						1		1					2		
East Sudbury	69	8	Cutlar	Abel	1	2	3	1		3		1	3				14		
East Sudbury	69	9	Oliver	John	3			1		2		1					7		
East Sudbury	69	10	Parmenter	Jason					1			1	1				3		
East Sudbury	69	11	Rice	Daniel	1			1	1	1		1					5		
East Sudbury	69	12	Thorning	John	2			1		1			1				5		
East Sudbury	69	13	Underwood	Benjm	2			1		2		1					6		
East Sudbury	69	14	Dane	Susannah									1	1			2		
East Sudbury	69	15	Allen	Deborah								1		1			2		
East Sudbury	69	16	Livermore	Joseph					1			1		1			3		
East Sudbury	69	17	Butter	Micah M		1	1						1				3		
East Sudbury	69	18	Moulton	Daniel	2			1		2			1				6		
East Sudbury	69	19	Harris	Amos	1		1					1		1			4		
East Sudbury	69	20	Joy	Reuben			1			2		1					4		
East Sudbury	69	21	Travis	Joel			1			3		1	1				6		
East Sudbury	69	22	Murdock	Aaron			1						1				2		
East Sudbury	69	23	Parmenter	Susannah								1	1	2			4		
East Sudbury	69	24	Parris	Abigail									1				1		

TOWN	PG#	LN#	LAST NAME	FIRST NAME	FWM under 10	FWM 10–16	FWM 16–26	FWM 26–45	FWM 45 & over	FWF under 10	FWF 10–16	FWF 16–26	FWF 26–45	FWF 45 & over	TOTAL ALL OTHER	TOTAL SLAVES	TOTALS	DISTRICT/TOWNSHIP	NOTES
Framingham	70	1	Ainger	Joseph	2	1		1		2			1	1			8		
Framingham	70	2	Abbott	Josiah			1				2			1			4		
Framingham	70	3	Arnold	William		1			1		2			1			5		
Framingham	70	4	Belknap	Jeremiah					1		2			1			4		
Framingham	70	5	Belknap	Jesse	1	1		1		4			1				8		
Framingham	70	6	Belknap	Abraham		1		1		1			1	1			5		
Framingham	70	7	Belknap	Luther			1						1				2		
Framingham	70	8	Belknap	Daniel		1						1					2		
Framingham	70	9	Banister	Berzellia		1		1		1	1	1					5		
Framingham	70	10	Belcher	Jacob	1			1			1	1	1				5		
Framingham	70	11	Belcher	Ezra	2			1		2			1				6		
Framingham	70	12	Belcher	Joseph	2	1		1		1	1		1				7		
Framingham	70	13	Belknap	Enoch			1			1			1				3		
Framingham	70	14	Bent	John				1					1				2		
Framingham	70	15	Bent	John Jr		1		1			2	1		1	1		6		
Framingham	70	16	Bent	Matthias				1		1	1		1	1			5		
Framingham	70	17	Bennet	Joseph	1	1	2		1	1		2	2				11		
Framingham	71	1	Buckminster	Dawson		2	2	1	1	3	2	3	1	1			16		
Framingham	71	2	Cutting	Samuel				1		1	2	2	1				7		
Framingham	71	3	Clayes	James		1	1		1				1				4		
Framingham	71	4	Childs	Josiah				1		1			1				3		
Framingham	71	5	Childs	Abel	2	2	1	1		3	1		1				11		
Framingham	71	6	Dedman	Jonathan		1	1					1	2				6		
Framingham	71	7	Dedman	Timothy	2		1	1				1		1			6		
Framingham	71	8	Edmunds	Jonathan		1		2						2			5		
Framingham	71	9	Dedman	Joseph	3			1		2		1					7		
Framingham	71	10	Edgel	Simon				1					1				2		
Framingham	71	11	Edgel	Aaron	1			1		2			1				5		
Framingham	71	12	Eaton	Noah				1					1				2		
Framingham	71	13	Eaton	Nathan	1	1	1	1		1			2				7		
Framingham	71	14	Eames	Timothy	1		1	1					1				4		
Framingham	71	15	Eaton	John	2	1	3	1	1	1	1	1	1	1			13		
Framingham	71	16	Eaton	Ebenezer		1	1		1	1	2	2		1			9		
Framingham	71	17	Eaton	Luther	2	1		1		1			1				6		
Framingham	74	1	Fay	Ruben	2			1		1	1	1					6		Stamped pg# was x'd out
Framingham	74	2	Frost	Samuel		1			1	1	2	2	1				8		Stamped pg# was x'd out
Framingham	74	3	Frost	Elisha	3	1		1		2	1	1	1				10		Stamped pg# was x'd out
Framingham	74	4	Fairbanks	Joshua	3		1	2	1	1	1	2	1	1			13		Stamped pg# was x'd out
Framingham	74	5	Fish	Micah	1	1	1	1				1	1				6		Stamped pg# was x'd out
Framingham	74	6	Clayes	Elijah	2			1		3			1				7		Stamped pg# was x'd out
Framingham	74	7	Gibbs	Phinehas	2	1	1	1	1	3	2	1	1	1			14		Stamped pg# was x'd out
Framingham	74	8	Goddard	Ruth		1						1		3			5		Stamped pg# was x'd out
Framingham	74	9	Gibbs	Jonathan				1		1	1						3		Stamped pg# was x'd out
Framingham	74	10	Nichols	Alpheus				1			2	2	1	1			7		Stamped pg# was x'd out
Framingham	74	11	Hervey	John	2			2		2	1	1	1				9		Stamped pg# was x'd out
Framingham	74	12	Hemenway	Danl		1	1		1					1			4		Stamped pg# was x'd out
Framingham	74	13	Hemenway	John	1		1		1			1	1	2			7		Stamped pg# was x'd out
Framingham	74	14	Haven	Moses	1	1		1		4			1				8		Stamped pg# was x'd out
Framingham	74	15	Haven	Jesse			1					2					3		Stamped pg# was x'd out
Framingham	74	16	Hemenway	Rebecka	1	1				1		1		1			5		Stamped pg# was x'd out
Framingham	72	1	Hemenway	Abijah	1	2		1				2	1				7		
Framingham	72	2	Hemenway	Jacob	1		2		1	3		2	1	1			11		
Framingham	72	3	Hemenway	Saml		1		1						1			3		
Framingham	72	4	Hoton	John			2	1		4			1				8		
Framingham	72	5	Hager	Ephraim	3			1		2			1				7		
Framingham	72	6	How	Ezekiel		2	1	1		1	1	3	1				10		
Framingham	72	7	Hemenway	Benjm S	2	1		1				2		1	1		8		
Framingham	72	8	Hemenway	Ebenezer		1	4		1			1	1	2			10		
Framingham	72	9	Hemenway	Josiah	3			1					1				5		
Framingham	72	10	Hill	Jonathan			2		1			2	1	1			7		
Framingham	72	11	Hill	Aaron				1		1	1		1				4		
Framingham	72	12	How	Isaac	1	2		1		1	1		1				7		
Framingham	72	13	Hastings	William	1			1		1			1				4		
Framingham	72	14	Jones	John	2	2				3			1				6		
Framingham	72	15	Jones	Daniel	2	1		1		3			1				8		
Framingham	72	16	Kendall	John	1		2		1	2	2		1	1			10		Stamped pg# was x'd out
Framingham	72	17	Kendall	Nathan		2		1		2	1		1				7		Stamped pg# was x'd out
Framingham	72	18	Mixer	John		2	1		1			1	1	2			8		Stamped pg# was x'd out
Framingham	72	19	Manson	Frederick	1			1		1	1	1		1			7		Stamped pg# was x'd out
Framingham	72	20	Morse	Asa	1	1	1		1	1		1		1			7		Stamped pg# was x'd out
Framingham	72	21	Morse	James				2		1	1	2		1			7		Stamped pg# was x'd out
Framingham	72	22	Moulton	Caleb	1			1		2			1	1			6		Stamped pg# was x'd out
Framingham	72	23	Maynard	Jonathan	1	1		1	1			1	1	1			7		Stamped pg# was x'd out
Framingham	72	24	Nixon	Thomas	2			1		2			1	1			7		Stamped pg# was x'd out
Framingham	72	25	Parmenter	Amos				1						1			2		Stamped pg# was x'd out
Framingham	72	26	Pratt	Benoni	1	1		2	2	2	1	1	1	1			12		Stamped pg# was x'd out
Framingham	72	27	Parmenter	Joshua	1		2		1	1		1		1			7		Stamped pg# was x'd out
Framingham	72	28	Parhust	Josiah		1	1	1						1			4		Stamped pg# was x'd out
Framingham	72	29	Patterson	David	1		1	1	1			1	1	2			8		Stamped pg# was x'd out
Framingham	72	30	Winch	Reuben	1			1		2		1					5		Stamped pg# was x'd out
Framingham	72	31	Stearns	Timothy Jr				1		1			1				3		Stamped pg# was x'd out
Framingham	72	32	Stearns	Timothy				2					1				3		Stamped pg# was x'd out
Framingham	73	1	Stearns	Timothy 3	2			1		2			1				6		

TOWN	PG#	LN#	LAST NAME	FIRST NAME	FWM under 10	FWM 10 to 16	FWM 16 to 26	FWM 26 to 45	FWM 45 and over	FWF under 10	FWF 10 to 16	FWF 16 to 26	FWF 26 to 45	FWF 45 and over	TOTAL ALL OTHER	TOTAL SLAVES	TOTALS	DISTRICT/TOWNSHIP	NOTES
Framingham	73	2	Haven	Timothy		2		1		3	2		1				9		
Framingham	73	3	Stones	Thomas					1					2			3		
Framingham	73	4	Stone	Peggy								1		1			2		
Framingham	73	5	Stone	Abner	1		2		1	1			1	1			7		
Framingham	73	6	Stone	Micah		1			1	1				1			4		
Framingham	73	7	Stone	Benjamin				1					1				2		
Framingham	73	8	Stone	Josiah	1	2	1	1		2	1		1	1			10		
Framingham	73	9	Stone	Daniel					1			1		1			3		
Framingham	73	10	Stone	Daniel Jr	1			1		2	1		1	2			8		
Framingham	73	11	Trowbridge	John		1		1		1				1			4		
Framingham	73	12	Trowbridge	John Jr	1		1	1					1				4		
Framingham	73	13	Trowbridge	Joshua			1	1		1				1			4		
Framingham	73	14	Underwood	Jonas			1	1					1	1			4		
Framingham	73	15	Underwood	Nathan	2			1		2			1	1			7		
Framingham	73	16	Walker	Samuel	2			1		1	3		1				8		
Framingham	73	17	Stone	Thomas Jr	3			1	1	1			1				7		
Framingham	70	1	Warren	Josiah	3		1	1					1	1			7		
Framingham	70	2	Winch	Silas				1			3		1				5		Stamped pg# was x'd out
Framingham	70	3	Winch	Joseph	3			1	1	2	1		1	1			10		Stamped pg# was x'd out
Framingham	70	4	Winch	Nathan		1		1					1	1			4		Stamped pg# was x'd out
Framingham	70	5	Kellogg	David	2	1		1				2	2	2	1		11		Stamped pg# was x'd out
Framingham	70	6	Walkup	William		1	2		1	1		1	2	1			9		Stamped pg# was x'd out
Framingham	70	7	Winch	Jesse		1		1		2			1				5		Stamped pg# was x'd out
Framingham	70	8	Walker	Matthias	2			1		2	1		1	2			9		Stamped pg# was x'd out
Framingham	70	9	Gleason	Jonathan			1	1					2				4		Stamped pg# was x'd out
Framingham	70	10	Wilson	James				1		1	1	1	1				5		Stamped pg# was x'd out
Framingham	70	11	Winch	Josiah	3			1				1	1				6		Stamped pg# was x'd out
Framingham	70	12	Winzell	John	1	1		1	2	2			1	5			13		Stamped pg# was x'd out
Framingham	70	13	Wheeler	Abner	1			1				2					4		Stamped pg# was x'd out
Framingham	70	14	Parmenter	Ezra				1		5			1				7		Stamped pg# was x'd out
Framingham	70	15	Eames	Phinehas	2		1	1		2			1				7		Stamped pg# was x'd out
Framingham	70	16	Belcher	John	2	1		1					1				5		Stamped pg# was x'd out
Framingham	70	17	Greenwood	William				1					1	1			3		Stamped pg# was x'd out
Framingham	74	1	Winch	Rebeckah										1			1		
Framingham	74	2	Dorothy	Martha										1			1		
Framingham	74	3	Brackett	Solomon	2			1		2		1					6		
Framingham	74	4	Parmenter	Peter	2			1			2		1				6		
Framingham	74	5	Parmenter	Phinehas					1					1			2		
Framingham	74	6	Brewer	Jason				1		2	2			1			6		
Framingham	74	7	Clark	Jonas				1		1				1	1		4		
Framingham	74	8	Churchill	Mary										1			1		
Framingham	74	9	Maynard	William	1	1		1					1				4		
Framingham	74	10	Stearns	John				1									1		
Framingham	74	11	Woolson	Pervis						1			1				2		
Framingham	74	12	Hemenway	Susannah		1							1				2		
Framingham	74	13	Adams	Stephen			2						1				3		
Framingham	74	14	Evens	Sherebiah	1			1					1				3		
Framingham	74	15	Fish	John	2	1	1		1			1	2	1			9		
Framingham	74	16	Flagg	Jonathan	1		1			1		1		1			5		
Framingham	74	17	Haven	Luther			1						1				2		
Framingham	68	1	Buckminster	Tho	1	2	1		1	2	2	1	1		1		12		Stamped pg# was x'd out
Framingham	68	2	Brewer	David	3	2	3		1	1			1	1			12		Stamped pg# was x'd out
Framingham	68	3	Brown	Andrew			2	1				1		1			5		Stamped pg# was x'd out
Framingham	68	4	Brown	Ebenezer	3			1		2	1		1				8		Stamped pg# was x'd out
Framingham	68	5	Eaton	Silas		1	1		1	3	1		1				8		Stamped pg# was x'd out
Framingham	68	6	Biglow	Asaph					1		1	2		1			5		Stamped pg# was x'd out
Framingham	68	7	Bullard	Eli	1			1		2		2					6		Stamped pg# was x'd out
Framingham	68	8	Warren	Isaac			2						1				3		Stamped pg# was x'd out
Framingham	68	9	Baley	Joseph	3	1		1		2			1	1			9		Stamped pg# was x'd out
Framingham	68	10	Burnam	Job		1		1				1	1				4		Stamped pg# was x'd out
Framingham	68	11	Bixby	Sarah	1		1				1	2		1			6		Stamped pg# was x'd out
Framingham	68	12	Ballard	William		5		2		1	2			1			11		Stamped pg# was x'd out
Framingham	68	13	Ballard	Samuel	1			1		3	1		1	1			8		Stamped pg# was x'd out
Framingham	68	14	Bullard	Aaron	2	1		1					1				4		Stamped pg# was x'd out
Framingham	68	15	Burnam	Joshua		1		1		1			1	1			5		Stamped pg# was x'd out
Framingham	68	16	Biglow	Daniel	1	2		1		1			1				7		Stamped pg# was x'd out
Framingham	68	17	Benson	Abel												8	8		Stamped pg# was x'd out
Framingham	68	18	Gallett	Peter				1				2					3		Stamped pg# was x'd out
Framingham	75	1	Gallett	John	1			1		1			1				4		
Framingham	75	2	Clayes	Josiah	2			1		2	1		1				7		
Framingham	75	3	Cutting	Daniel				1	1	1	3			1			6		
Framingham	75	4	Claflin	Cornelius		1	1	1		3	1						7		
Framingham	75	5	Claflin	Daniel				1						2			3		
Framingham	75	6	Claflin	Asa	3			1					1	1			6		
Framingham	75	7	Coolidge	Joel	3		1	1		1	2	1	1				10		
Framingham	75	8	Cole	Anesimus	1		1	1		4			1	1			9		
Framingham	75	9	Clayes	Peter	3	1		1		1	4	2	1				13		
Framingham	75	10	Drewry	Caleb		2	3	1					1	1			8		
Framingham	75	11	Drewing	Thomas	3			1					2	1			7		
Framingham	75	12	Dudley	John	3			1	1	1			1	1			8		
Framingham	75	13	Darling	Job				1	1					1			3		
Framingham	75	14	Dedman	Nathan		1	1					1	3	1			8		
Framingham	75	15	Dedman	Martha		1						2	1	1			5		

TOWN	PG#	LN#	LAST NAME	FIRST NAME	\<FWM under 10\>	10 to 16	16 to 26	26 to 45	45 and over	\<FWF under 10\>	10 to 16	16 to 26	26 to 45	45 and over	TOTAL ALL OTHER	TOTAL SLAVES	TOTALS	DISTRICT/ TOWNSHIP	NOTES
Framingham	75	16	Dunn	John	1			1		1		1		1			5		
Framingham	75	17	Dalrymple	James	1	2	1	1		2	1		1				9		
Framingham	66	1	Edwards	Benj		1			1			1		1			4		Stamped pg# was x'd out
Framingham	66	2	Newton	Ephraim		1		1		3		1	1				7		Stamped pg# was x'd out
Framingham	66	3	Eaton	Jonas	1	1	1	1	1				1				6		Stamped pg# was x'd out
Framingham	66	4	Eames	Henry	1	1		1			2	1	1				7		Stamped pg# was x'd out
Framingham	66	5	Eames	John			1	1				1	1	1			5		Stamped pg# was x'd out
Framingham	66	6	Eames	Nathaniel	1	2		1		1	1	1		1			8		Stamped pg# was x'd out
Framingham	66	7	Eames	Moses	3			1		3	2		1				10		Stamped pg# was x'd out
Framingham	66	8	Everett	Jesse			1	2	1			1	1	1			7		Stamped pg# was x'd out
Framingham	66	9	Greenwood	Abel	1	1	3		2	3	1	2	1	1			15		Stamped pg# was x'd out
Framingham	66	10	Bullard	Henry	1			1					1				3		Stamped pg# was x'd out
Framingham	66	11	Greenwood	James	1	1			1	2				3			8		Stamped pg# was x'd out
Framingham	66	12	Gregory	Daniel		1		1		1		1					4		Stamped pg# was x'd out
Framingham	66	13	Gleason	John	1		1	1			1	1		1			6		Stamped pg# was x'd out
Framingham	66	14	Goodnow	Jonathan	3		1				2		1				7		Stamped pg# was x'd out
Framingham	66	15	Haven	David				1		1			1				3		Stamped pg# was x'd out
Framingham	66	16	Haven	Abner	4		3	2		1	2		1				13		Stamped pg# was x'd out
Framingham	66	17	Hunt	John	3			1		1	2		1				8		Stamped pg# was x'd out
Framingham	66	18	How	Pearly		4	1	1		1	1	1			1		10		Stamped pg# was x'd out
Framingham	76	1	How	Francis	3	2	1	1					1				8		
Framingham	76	2	Hanker	Cato									1		2		3		
Framingham	76	3	Hancock	Nathan	1	1	1		1		1		2				7		
Framingham	76	4	Daniels	Israel	1			1		1	1	1					5		
Framingham	76	5	Haven	Benj	1	1	1		1		1	2	2	2			11		
Framingham	76	6	Haven	Jesse	1	1	1		1	3	1		2				10		
Framingham	76	7	Johnson	Amos	2			1		3	2		1				9		
Framingham	76	8	Kendal	Jemima			2								1		3		
Framingham	76	9	Kitteridge	John B.			1								1		2		
Framingham	76	10	Littlefield	Asa			1	1		2		1		1			6		
Framingham	76	11	Lamle	David	2	1		1				1	1	1			7		
Framingham	76	12	Learnard	Sarah				1					1				2		
Framingham	76	13	Lovering	Amos	1		1			1		1					4		
Framingham	76	14	Metcalf	Levi			1		1			1		1			4		
Framingham	76	15	Mellen	Abner	1	2		1		2	1		1				8		
Framingham	76	16	Mayhew	John	1		2	1		1	1			1			7		
Framingham	76	17	Marshall	Gilbert	1		1	1		5	1		1				10		
Framingham	64	1	Meriam	Timothy	3		1	1		1	2	1	1				10		Stamped pg# was x'd out
Framingham	64	2	Nurse	John		2		1		2	1	2	1	1			10		Stamped pg# was x'd out
Framingham	64	3	Nurse	Asa	1				1	3	3						8		Stamped pg# was x'd out
Framingham	64	4	Nurse	Lawson		1		1		1	1	1	1				6		Stamped pg# was x'd out
Framingham	64	5	Newton	Jonas	1	1		1		1	1		1				6		Stamped pg# was x'd out
Framingham	64	6	Parker	Peter	2		1	1	1	2	1		2				10		Stamped pg# was x'd out
Framingham	64	7	Parker	John	2			1		3	1	1		1			9		Stamped pg# was x'd out
Framingham	64	8	Pratt	Aaron	2			1		3			1				7		Stamped pg# was x'd out
Framingham	64	9	Park	John	3		2	1		2		2	1	1			12		Stamped pg# was x'd out
Framingham	64	10	Parkhurst	Ephraim	2	1		1		3		1	1				9		Stamped pg# was x'd out
Framingham	64	11	Sanger	Daniel Jr	1			1		2		1					5		Stamped pg# was x'd out
Framingham	64	12	Pratt	John	3	1		1			2	1		1			9		Stamped pg# was x'd out
Framingham	64	13	Rice	Ezekiel					2	1				1			4		Stamped pg# was x'd out
Framingham	64	14	Richards	Thomas	4		1	1		2			1				9		Stamped pg# was x'd out
Framingham	64	15	Rugg	Jonathan		1	2		1	1	1			1			7		Stamped pg# was x'd out
Framingham	64	16	Knowlton	Isaiah	1			1					2				4		Stamped pg# was x'd out
Framingham	64	17	Rice	Samuel	3			1	1	2	1		1				9		Stamped pg# was x'd out
Framingham	77	1	Rice	David	2			1				1	1	1			6		
Framingham	77	2	Rice	Thomas	4			1		2	1	1					9		
Framingham	77	3	Rice	Peter	1			1	1	1	2	1	1	1			9		
Framingham	77	4	Rice	Josiah				1									1		
Framingham	77	5	Rider	Jonas		1			1			1		2			5		
Framingham	77	6	Eames	Alexander				1				1					2		
Framingham	77	7	Rice	Phinehas		2	2		1	4			1	1	1		12		
Framingham	77	8	Rice	Ezra	3			1		1			1				6		
Framingham	77	9	Stone	Elijah			1	2	1		1	2	1	1			9		
Framingham	77	10	Sanger	Joseph		2			1	1	1			1	1		7		
Framingham	77	11	Stone	Isaac		1	2		1	1	2			1			8		
Framingham	77	12	Sanger	Daniel					1		1	1	1	1	1		5		
Framingham	77	13	Tucker	Abel				1		1			1				3		
Framingham	77	14	Temple	Josiah		2	1	1	1		1	1		1			8		
Framingham	77	15	Tombs	Nathan	1			1		2			1				5		
Framingham	77	16	Tower	Joseph					1		1		2				4		
Framingham	77	17	Torry	Reuben					1		1		1				3		
Framingham	78	1	Fish	Richard	1	1	1		1		2		1				7		
Framingham	78	2	Fish	Moses	1		2	1		1	3		1	1			10		
Framingham	78	3	Campbell	Daniel	2	1				3	1		1				9		
Framingham	78	4	Buckminster	Joseph			1					1					2		
Framingham	78	5	Stone	Rebeckah		1	1					1	1				4		
Framingham	78	6	Drewry	Lydia	1					1	2	1					5		
Framingham	78	7	Goodnow	Ephraim	1	1		1		2			1				6		
Framingham	78	8	Pratt	Ephraim	2			1		4			1				8		
Framingham	78	9	Davis	Amos	2				1	1	1	1	1				7		
Framingham	78	10	Pratt	Jonathan	1			1		2	1	1					6		
Framingham	78	11	Knowlton	Nathan				1		3	2			1			7		
Framingham	78	12	Amsdel	Joseph	1			1				1					4		

TOWN	PG#	LN#	LAST NAME	FIRST NAME	FREE WHITE MALES under 10	10 to 16	16 to 26	26 to 45	45 and over	FREE WHITE FEMALES under 10	10 to 16	16 to 26	26 to 45	45 and over	TOTAL ALL OTHER	TOTAL SLAVES	TOTALS	DISTRICT/ TOWNSHIP	NOTES
Framingham	78	13	Benj	Holdin	1				1	1				1			4		
Framingham	78	14	Morse	Daniel	2			1		2			1				6		
Framingham	78	15	Pratt	John Jr	3			1		3			1				8		
Framingham	78	16	Pratt	Nathl	1	1		1		2	1		1				7		
Framingham	78	17	Jones	Nathl A.					1	1		2		1			5		
Framingham	78	18	Marshall	Eben					1					1			2		

TOWN	PG#	LN#	LAST NAME	FIRST NAME	FREE WHITE MALES under 10	10 to 16	16 to 26	26 to 45	45 and over	FREE WHITE FEMALES under 10	10 to 16	16 to 26	26 to 45	45 and over	TOTAL ALL OTHER	TOTAL SLAVES	TOTALS	DISTRICT/ TOWNSHIP	NOTES
Groton	206	1	Ames	Amos					1	1	1			1			4		
Groton	206	2	Adams	Natha		1			1								2		
Groton	206	3	Bennett	Wm				1		2			1				4		
Groton	206	4	Bigelow	Aaron			1	1			1			1			4		
Groton	206	5	Blood	Oliver Jr			1		1		2			1			5		
Groton	206	6	Blood	Caleb		1	1		1	1	1	2		1			8		
Groton	206	7	Bancroft	Wm	1	2	1	1	1	4		1	1	1			13		
Groton	206	8	Blood	Jonas		1		1				1		1			4		
Groton	206	9	Buttrick	Benjm			1			1				1			3		
Groton	206	10	Blood	Oliver 3rd		2						1					4		
Groton	206	11	Blood	Thomas		1						1					2		
Groton	206	12	Buttrick	Tilly		1		1		2	2						6		
Groton	206	13	Burgess	John	1			1	1	4		1	1				9		
Groton	206	14	Bancroft	Sarah Wid.		1											1		
Groton	206	15	Bigelow	Timothy Esq	3		1	2		1		3	1				11		
Groton	207	1	Allin	Joseph		1	2	1	1			2		2			9		
Groton	207	2	Adams	John		1			1				1				3		
Groton	207	3	Adams	John Jr			1					1					2		
Groton	207	4	Ames	Peter	1			1				1					3		
Groton	207	5	Ames	Berkley	1		2	1				1					5		
Groton	208	1	Br*er	James Esq	1	1	2	1			1		1	1			8		
Groton	208	2	Blood	James		1		1				1		2			5		
Groton	208	3	Blood	Levi			1	1	1	1		1		1			5		
Groton	208	4	Blood	Oliver				1						1			2		
Groton	208	5	Blood	Henry	2			1		3			1				7		
Groton	208	6	Blood	Shattuck				1						1			2		
Groton	208	7	Blood	Shattuck Jr		1		1					1				3		
Groton	208	8	Bowern	Isaac			1	1	1	1		1		1			5		
Groton	208	9	Bennett	James				1						1			2		
Groton	208	10	Bennett	Thomas	2	1	1		1		1	1	1				8		
Groton	208	11	Blood	Jona	3	1		1		1			1				7		
Groton	208	12	Blanchard	Nathl	2			1			1		1	1			6		
Groton	208	13	Blood	Royal	3	1		1			1		1				7		
Groton	208	14	Bancroft	Saml	3	1		1		1			1				7		
Groton	208	15	Blood	Eben	1			1		2			1				5		
Groton	208	16	Boynton	Calvin	2		1	1		1		1					6		
Groton	208	17	Bennett	Jona		1	1			1							3		
Groton	208	18	Bennett	Ebenzr	2	1		1		1			1				6		
Groton	208	19	Blood	Wm	1			1	1	1			1				5		
Groton	208	20	Bailey	John	1			1					1				3		
Groton	208	21	Bruce	Jonas			1			1		1					3		
Groton	208	22	Benteroth	Wm				1			1			1			3		
Groton	208	23	Cooper	Simon			1		1					1			3		
Groton	208	24	Cook	Samuel	2			1				1	1				5		
Groton	208	25	Carlton	Solomon	1		1	1				1					4		
Groton	208	26	Carlisle	Levi		1	1			1		1					4		
Groton	208	27	Chase	Moses	2			1			1		1				5		
Groton	208	28	Capel	John	1	1	1		1	4	2			1			11		
Groton	208	29	Chaplin	Jeremiah				1		4	1		1		1		8		
Groton	208	30	Champney	Francis	3			1		2	1		1				8		
Groton	208	31	Cory	Elisha	2	1	1		1		1			1			7		
Groton	208	32	Culter	Jemima Wid										1			1		
Groton	208	33	Cory	Nathan	1			1		1	3	1		1			9		
Groton	208	34	Cook	Peter				1		1		1					3		
Groton	208	35	Childs	Abraham Capt.	1			1		2	1		1				6		
Groton	208	36	Cory	Saml	2			1				1	1				5		
Groton	208	37	Chaplin	Daniel Revd	1	1	2		1	1	3	1	1				11		
Groton	208	38	Dickson	Walter	1		2	1		3	1	2	1				11		
Groton	208	39	Davis	Joshua	1			1		2	2	1					7		
Groton	208	40	Dodge	Saml	5	1	1	1	1	1		1	1	1			13		
Groton	208	41	Dolbt	Frederick				1						1			2		
Groton	208	42	Davis	David		1		1	1		1		1				5		
Groton	208	43	Day	Moses		1						1					2		
Groton	208	44	Dana	Saml Esq	1		1	1		1	1		1		1		7		
Groton	209	1	Davis	Abel	2		1	1				1					5		
Groton	209	2	Eaton	Calvin			1			3		1					5		
Groton	209	3	Edes	Isaiah	1	1		1		2		2					7		
Groton	209	4	Eaton	Jonas				1					1				2		
Groton	209	5	Eaton	Jonas Jr	2			1		2		1					6		
Groton	209	6	Fish	Jonathan				3			1		1				5		
Groton	209	7	Farwell	Henry Jr		2		1					1				4		
Groton	209	8	Farrar	Stephen		1	1	1	1	2		2					8		
Groton	209	9	Flint	Elisha	2					1		1	1				5		
Groton	209	10	Farnsworth	Betty Wid.		2	3				1	2		1			9		
Groton	209	11	Farnsworth	Isaac Dea.				1									1		
Groton	209	12	Farnsworth	Oliver				1				1		1			3		
Groton	209	13	Farwell	Henry Capt.	1			1	1				2				5		
Groton	209	14	Fitch	Zacht Capt.		1	2					1	1	2			8		
Groton	209	15	Farnsworth	John	4		1	1	1	2		1					11		

TOWN	PG#	LN#	HEADS OF HOUSEHOLD		FREE WHITE MALES					FREE WHITE FEMALES					TOTAL ALL OTHER	TOTAL SLAVES	TOTALS	DISTRICT/ TOWNSHIP	NOTES
			LAST NAME	FIRST NAME	under 10	10 to 16	16 to 26	26 to 45	45 and over	under 10	10 to 16	16 to 26	26 to 45	45 and over					
Groton	209	16	Frost	Solomon	2	1		1			1		1				6		
Groton	209	17	Farnsworth	Samson Capt.	2			1					1				4		
Groton	209	18	Farnsworth	Aaron	2			1		1	1		1				6		
Groton	209	19	Faran	Ebenzr				1									1		
Groton	209	20	Farnsworth	Lydia Wid.									1				1		
Groton	209	21	Fletcher	David	1		2	1		1			1	1			7		
Groton	209	22	Farnsworth	Jonas	1	1	1		1	2		2		1			9		
Groton	209	23	Farnsworth	Amos Dea.	2	2			1		1	1	1				8		
Groton	209	24	Fish	John	2	1	1		1	2	3			1			11		
Groton	209	25	Farnsworth	Saml	1	1		1		2							5		
Groton	209	26	Fletcher	Peletiah	4	1		1		1	2	1	1				11		
Groton	209	27	Farwell	Wm				1				1	1				3		
Groton	209	28	Fletcher	Oliver				1		1			1				3		
Groton	209	29	Fletcher	Sador	1			1		2			1				5		
Groton	209	30	Fletcher	Ezekiel		1		1				3					5		
Groton	209	31	Fletcher	Ezekiel Jr	3			1		1	1		1				7		
Groton	209	32	Fletcher	Zryling	1			1		1							3		
Groton	209	33	Fletcher	Lyman			1					1					2		
Groton	209	34	Farmer	Jessa			1			1		1					3		
Groton	209	35	Graves	Peter		2		1		1		1		1			6		
Groton	209	36	Gap	Thomas	2			1					1				4		
Groton	209	37	Gillson	Nehemiah		2		2		1		1		2			8		
Groton	209	38	Gillson	Asa	2		1			1			1				5		
Groton	209	39	Gillson	Nathl	1			1		2			1	1			6		
Groton	209	40	Gillson	Amasa				1					1				2		
Groton	209	41	Gillson	Simon	2			1		3			1				7		
Groton	209	42	Gillson	Simeon	1	2		1		3	1		1				9		
Groton	209	43	Gillson	Jonas	3			1		1			1	1			7		
Groton	209	44	Gillson	Nehh Jr	3	1		1		1			1	1			8		
Groton	210	1	Gragg	Thomas		1			1			1		2			5		
Groton	210	2	Gragg	Joseph	2	1		1		2			1				7		
Groton	210	3	Green	Eleazr	2	1			1	1			1				6		
Groton	210	4	Green	David				1									1		
Groton	210	5	Gardner	Thomas Maj.	4		2	1		2		1	1		1		12		
Groton	210	6	Green	Jonas	1	1	1		1	1	2			1			8		
Groton	210	7	Gillson	Peter	2	1		1		1	1		1				7		
Groton	210	8	Gardner	Mary Ann Wid.	1		2			2	1	3	1				10		
Groton	210	9	Graves	John			1										1		
Groton	210	10	Graves	Hannah Wid.									1	1			2		
Groton	210	11	Green	Joshua		1											1		
Groton	210	12	Hemenway	Saml	2	2	1		1		1	1		1			9		
Groton	210	13	Hubbard	Nathan				1					1				2		
Groton	210	14	Hubbard	Thomas		1	1	1		1	1			1			6		
Groton	210	15	Hubbard	Thos Jr	1		1	1		1			1				5		
Groton	210	16	Hopkins	Ebenzr	3		1	1		1		1	1				8		
Groton	210	17	Hall	Isaiah		2	1			2		1					6		
Groton	210	18	Hobart	Jeremiah				1					1				2		
Groton	210	19	Hobart	Nathl	3			1		2	2		1				9		
Groton	210	20	Hobart	Josiah	1			1	1	2		1					6		
Groton	210	21	Huzen	Benjm		1	1	1						1			4		
Groton	210	22	Huzen	David		2	1	1			1		1				6		
Groton	210	23	Hartwell	Saml			1			1		1					3		
Groton	210	24	Holden	Mabel Wid.				1		1	1		1				3		
Groton	210	25	Jaquith	Benjm				1				1	1				3		
Groton	210	26	Johnson	John	2	1		1				1	1				6		
Groton	210	27	Jewett	Joshua A.		1		1					1				3		
Groton	210	28	Johnson	George		1											1		
Groton	210	29	Kemp	Saml				1					1				2		
Groton	210	30	Kemp	Saml Jr		2	1		1	1		2		1			8		
Groton	210	31	Kemp	Capt. Levi		1	2		1	2	1	2		1			10		
Groton	210	32	Kemp	Ephraim	1	1	1		1	1	1						6		
Groton	210	33	Kemp	John	1			1		1			1				4		
Groton	210	34	Keyzer	Jona	1	1			1	1	1		1				7		
Groton	210	35	Lawrance	Jona				1						2			3		
Groton	210	36	Lawrance	Saml Esq	1	1	2	1	1	2	1		2	1			12		
Groton	210	37	Loreing	John	1		1	1		1		1	1				6		
Groton	210	38	Lawrance	Joel	2			1		2			1				6		
Groton	210	39	Lewis	Reuben	1	1			1			1		1			5		
Groton	210	40	Lewis	Eunice Wid.								1		1			2		
Groton	210	41	Lawrance	Isaac	1	2			1	1		2		1			8		
Groton	210	42	Lampson	Amos				1					1				2		
Groton	210	43	Lawrance	Asa Jr	2		1	1		1			1				6		
Groton	210	44	Lewis	James Capt.				1						2			3		
Groton	210	45	Lewis	James Jr Capt.	3	3	1	1					1	1			10		
Groton	211	1	Lewis	Ebenzr	5	2			1	1	1			1			11		
Groton	211	2	Lawrance	Roland	2			1		3	1		1				8		
Groton	211	3	Lawrance	Benjm				1						1			2		
Groton	211	4	Lawrance	Salmon	2	1		1		2			1				7		
Groton	211	5	Lawrance	John		1	1			2	2	1		1			8		

56

TOWN	PG#	LN#	HEADS OF HOUSEHOLD		FREE WHITE MALES					FREE WHITE FEMALES					TOTAL ALL OTHER	TOTAL SLAVES	TOTALS	DISTRICT/ TOWNSHIP	NOTES
			LAST NAME	FIRST NAME	under 10	10 to 16	16 to 26	26 to 45	45 and over	under 10	10 to 16	16 to 26	26 to 45	45 and over					
Groton	211	6	Lakin	Lemuel		1											1		
Groton	211	7	Lakin	Levi	1		1		1	1	2		1				7		
Groton	211	8	Lawrance	Ephraim	3	1		1		2			1				8		
Groton	211	9	Lawrance	John Jr	3			1					1				5		
Groton	211	10	Lakin	David	1	2	1		1	1		1	1				9		
Groton	211	11	Lepcar	Wm		2			1					1			4		
Groton	211	12	Lawrance	Abel	1		1			1		1		1			5		
Groton	211	13	Lawrance	Wm		1	1			1		1	1				5		
Groton	211	14	Lawrance	Asa Capt.				1					1				2		
Groton	211	15	Lawrance	John 3rd	1		1						1				3		
Groton	211	16	Moore	Joseph Esq		2	3	1	3	1		1	2		1		14		
Groton	211	17	Morse	Benjm Doct.		1		1					1				3		
Groton	211	18	Morse	Abel		1		1					1				3		
Groton	211	19	Morse	Saml	3	1		1		1			1				7		
Groton	211	20	Munroe	Stephen	3	1	2		1	1		1	2				11		
Groton	211	21	Moore	Lydia Wid.									1				1		
Groton	211	22	McLorn	Edward	1			1		2	2		1				7		
Groton	211	23	Nutting	Abijah	1	1		1		1			1				5		
Groton	211	24	Nutting	Phinehas	2		1			2			1				6		
Groton	211	25	Nutting	Wm	1	1	1		1	1	1	2		1			9		
Groton	211	26	Nutting	Jona		1		1		3	1	1	1				8		
Groton	211	27	Nutting	Ephm	1	1	1	1		4			1	1			10		
Groton	211	28	Nash	Ephm		1	1						1	1	1		5		
Groton	211	29	Nutting	Ezekiel	1	1		1		2			1				6		
Groton	211	30	Nutting	Daniel				1					2				3		
Groton	211	31	Nutting	Isaac				1		1			1				3		
Groton	211	32	Prescott	Oliver Jr Esq	2	1	3	1		3		2	1				13		
Groton	211	33	Parker	Nathan		1			1	1		1					3		
Groton	211	34	Pierce	Elijah	2		1						1				4		
Groton	211	35	Pierce	Saml	1	1		1		1			1				5		
Groton	211	36	Park	John	2	1	1	1		1			1	1			8		
Groton	211	37	Page	Simon		1	1		1			1		1			5		
Groton	211	38	Prentice	Daniel				1									1		
Groton	211	39	Page	Benjm		2	1		1	1	1		1	1			8		
Groton	211	40	Pushey	Jonas	1		1			1		1					4		
Groton	211	41	Pierce	Abner			1			3			1				5		
Groton	211	42	Pushey	John Jr	3		1					1					5		
Groton	211	43	Parker	Ezekiel	1			1		1			1				4		
Groton	211	44	Parker	Eleazr	1		1	1				1	1	1			6		
Groton	211	45	Priest	Timothy		1	1		1				1	1			5		
Groton	211	46	Parker	Jacob L.		1		1	1	2		2	1				8		
Groton	212	1	Prescott	Susanna Wid.			2						2	1			5		
Groton	212	2	Parker	Imla		1	1	1		1			1	1			6		
Groton	212	3	Prescott	Oliver Esq			2		1		1	2		3			9		
Groton	212	4	Parker	Phinehas	1		1							1			4		
Groton	212	5	Proctor	James Jr		1	1	1	1	2			1				7		
Groton	212	6	Parker	Winslow	2	2	2		1	3	1			1			12		
Groton	212	7	Prescott	Jonas				1			3			1			5		
Groton	212	8	Prescott	Abel	2		1	1		1			1	1			7		
Groton	212	9	Prescott	David	1			1		1	1	1		1			6		
Groton	212	10	Prescott	Samson	2	1		1		3			1				8		
Groton	212	11	Parker	Joshua	2			1		2	1		1				7		
Groton	212	12	Parker	Wm	3	3		1		3	1		1				12		
Groton	212	13	Parker	Oliver	2		1			1			1				5		
Groton	212	14	Pushey	John				1		1				1			3		
Groton	212	15	Parker	Benjm	2	3		1		2			1				9		
Groton	212	16	Protor	Ebenzr	1			1		1			1				4		
Groton	212	17	Parker	Abigail Wid.									1				1		
Groton	212	18	Prescott	Isaac	1		1			2			1				5		
Groton	212	19	Patch	Jacob L.		1	1		1		2			1			6		
Groton	212	20	Parker	Ebenzr	2	2	1		1	2	1	1		1			11		
Groton	212	21	Phillips	Jonas	1		1			1		1		1			5		
Groton	212	22	Pratt	Jona				1						1			2		
Groton	212	23	Parker	Betty										2			2		
Groton	212	24	Parker	Silas		1	1	1		1			1	1			6		
Groton	212	25	Quailes	Charles		1		1		1			1	1			5		
Groton	212	26	Rockwood	Saml Dea.	3	1	2		1	1			2				10		
Groton	212	27	Rockwood	Joseph		1	1	1			2			1			6		
Groton	212	28	Rockwood	Joseph Jr	3		1	1		1	1		1				8		
Groton	212	29	Richardson	Jephh Capt.	1		4	1			1	1	1				9		
Groton	212	30	Russell	Peteliah	1		1	1	1	1	1	1					7		
Groton	212	31	Robbins	John				1			1		1				3		
Groton	212	32	Ramsdel	Rebekah Wid.							1		1				2		
Groton	212	33	Reed	Saml			1						1				2		
Groton	212	34	Richardson	Alpheus	2	1	1						1				5		
Groton	212	35	Richardson	Wm M.		3	1		1	1		1	1				7		
Groton	212	36	Robbins	Willard	2		1		1	1		1	1	1			7		
Groton	212	37	Reed	John	1			1		2			1				5		
Groton	212	38	Robbins	John Jr	1			2		1			1				5		

TOWN	PG#	LN#	HEADS OF HOUSEHOLD		FREE WHITE MALES					FREE WHITE FEMALES					TOTAL ALL OTHER	TOTAL SLAVES	TOTALS	DISTRICT/ TOWNSHIP	NOTES
			LAST NAME	FIRST NAME	under 10	10 to 16	16 to 26	26 to 45	45 and over	under 10	10 to 16	16 to 26	26 to 45	45 and over					
Groton	212	39	Seever	Herman	1		2	1				2	1				7		
Groton	212	40	Symms	Caleb	2	1		1		2	1		1	1			9		
Groton	212	41	Sawtell	Richard			1		1		1	1	1	1			6		
Groton	212	42	Sawtell	Richard Jr		1		1		2			1				5		
Groton	212	43	Simonds	John			1	1	1			1		1			5		
Groton	212	44	Stone	Levi	2	2			1	1	1	3	1	1			12		
Groton	212	45	Stone	Jona	1				1			1		1			4		
Groton	212	46	Stone	Jonas		1			1			2		2			6		
Groton	212	47	Stone	Amos	1	2	1		1	2	1	2		1			11		
Groton	212	48	Sawtell	Joseph Jr	3	1	1	1	1			1	1	1			10		
Groton	212	49	Shed	Oliver				1	1					1			3		
Groton	212	50	Sheple	Wilder	1	2		1					1	1			6		
Groton	212	51	Stone	Joseph	1		2					1					4		
Groton	212	52	Swallow	Rachel Wid.						3			1				4		
Groton	212	53	Stone	Natha Wid.							1			1			2		
Groton	212	54	Sheple	Jona	1			1		1	2		1				6		
Groton	212	55	Sheple	Wm				1						1			2		
Groton	212	56	Sheple	Wm Jr	1	1		1		1			1				5		
Groton	212	57	Shattuck	Job Capt.			1		1			1		2			5		
Groton	212	58	Shattuck	Noah	1		1	1		1		1		2			7		
Groton	212	59	Shattuck	Job Jr	1	2	1	1		1	1	1	1				9		
Groton	212	60	Sheple	James	2	2	1		1				1				8		
Groton	212	61	Sawtell	Joseph				1				1					3		
Groton	212	62	Sawtell	Joseph 3rd	1		2	2		3			1	1			10		
Groton	212	63	Shattuck	Ezekiel	2	1		1		2	1	1	1				9		
Groton	212	64	Shed	Joseph		1		1						1			3		
Groton	212	65	Sheple	John	1	2		1						1			5		
Groton	212	66	Simson	Benjm	1					3			1				5		
Groton	212	67	Sawtell	Nathl				1						1			2		
Groton	212	68	Stevens	Jona	1			1		3	1		1				7		
Groton	212	69	Sawtell	Elnathan	4			1		1	1	2	1				10		
Groton	212	70	Shattuck	Nathl	1			1		1	2			1			6		
Groton	212	71	Spaulding	Timothy		1		1				1	2				5		
Groton	212	72	Shattuck	Daniel		1	1	1		1	1	1					6		
Groton	212	73	Shattuck	John			1			1		1					3		
Groton	212	74	Sawtell	Abel	1			1		4			1				7		
Groton	212	75	Simmons	Moses	1			1		3	2		1				8		
Groton	212	76	Shattuck	Jeremiah	3		1			1			1				6		
Groton	212	77	Tufts	Asa	2			1		2	1		1				7		
Groton	212	78	Tarbell	Solomon	1			1		1			2				5		
Groton	212	79	Tarbell	Thomas		1		1	1	2	1		1				7		
Groton	212	80	Tarbell	Eben			1			2	1		1				5		
Groton	212	81	Tarbell	Benjm			1		1			1		1			4		
Groton	212	82	Tarbell	John		1	1	2	1			1	1	1			8		
Groton	212	83	Tarbell	Wm	1	1	1	1		3			1				8		
Groton	212	84	Tarbell	Mary Wid.		1				2			1				4		
Groton	212	85	Tarbell	Nehh				1				1		1			3		
Groton	212	86	Tufts	Ebrakim	1			1		3	1		1				7		
Groton	212	87	Trowbridge	Abigail Wid.	1	2	1	1				1		1			7		
Groton	212	88	Trowbridge	Thomas				1			1			1			3		
Groton	212	89	Woods	Samson Maj.	1		2	1		2	1	1	1				9		
Groton	212	90	Wait	Phinehas			1		1	1			1	1			5		
Groton	212	91	Williams	Aaron				1				1					2		
Groton	212	92	Wood	Mary Wid.	1	1						1		1			5		
Groton	212	93	Wheeler	Asa			1			1	1	1		1			5		
Groton	212	94	Wythe	Joseph				1				1		1			3		
Groton	212	95	Williams	Jason			1		1			1	1	1			5		
Groton	212	96	Williams	Daniel	3	2		1		1		1	1				9		
Groton	212	97	Williams	Jacob L.	2	2	1			1		1	1				8		
Groton	212	98	Williams	Simeon Capt.	1			1		2		1	1	1			7		
Groton	212	99	Williams	John Capt.	1			1		1	2	1	1	1			8		
Groton	212	100	Woods	Timothy				1		1	2		1	1			6		
Groton	212	101	Woods	Abel				1						1			2		
Groton	212	102	Woods	Nahum	1	1	1	1		3	2		1				11		
Groton	212	103	Woods	Eber	1			1		2			1				5		
Groton	212	104	Woods	John			1	1				2		1			5		
Groton	212	105	Whitman	Nehh	1			1			1	3		1			7		
Groton	212	106	Wood	John A.				1									1		
Groton	212	107	Wood	Daniel				1						1			2		
Groton	213	1	Wright	Oliver	1			1		1	1	1	1				6		
Groton	213	2	Woods	Caleb	2			1		4			1				8		
Groton	213	3	Woods	Jotham	1	1		1		3			1				7		
Groton	213	4	Wood	John	1			1		3			1				6		
Groton	213	5	Woods	Oliver				1			2			1			4		
Groton	213	6	Wythe	Jonathan	1		1					1					3		
Groton	213	7	Woods	Jona	1	1		1			1		1				5		
Groton	213	8	Wright	John C.	1	1		1		1			2				6		
Groton	213	9	Wetherbee	Parker				1		1		1					3		
Groton	213	10	Young	Elisha	1			1		3	1	1	1				8		

TOWN	PG#	LN#	HEADS OF HOUSEHOLD LAST NAME	FIRST NAME	FREE WHITE MALES under 10	10 to 16	16 to 26	26 to 45	45 and over	FREE WHITE FEMALES under 10	10 to 16	16 to 26	26 to 45	45 and over	TOTAL ALL OTHER	TOTAL SLAVES	TOTALS	DISTRICT/ TOWNSHIP	NOTES
Hollistown	236	1	Adams	Timothy	2	1		1		1	1		1				7		
Hollistown	236	2	Adams	Jona	1		1		1	1	1		1				6		
Hollistown	236	3	Adams	Levi				1					1				2		
Hollistown	236	4	Adams	Ezekiel				1					1				2		
Hollistown	236	5	Bullard	Henry		1		1		1			1				4		
Hollistown	236	6	Bullard	Nathan		1	1	1					2	1			6		
Hollistown	236	7	Bond	Aaron				1				1		1			3		
Hollistown	236	8	Bond	Aaron Jr	2		1	1		1			1				8		
Hollistown	236	9	Bullard	Walter	3	1		1		2			1				8		
Hollistown	236	10	Bullard	Asa		1	1	1				1		1			5		
Hollistown	236	11	Bullard	Benjm		1		1				1					3		
Hollistown	236	12	Briant	Jona	1		1					1					3		
Hollistown	236	13	Bridge	Benjm		1	1						1				3		
Hollistown	236	14	Brown	Ezra	2		1	1		1	1		1				7		
Hollistown	236	15	Brick	Jona			1			1			1				3		
Hollistown	236	16	Bigelow	Ephm	1	1	1	1		1			1				6		
Hollistown	236	17	Bullard	Isaac Jr		1	1				1		1				4		
Hollistown	236	18	Beals	Elizth										3			3		
Hollistown	236	19	Bullard	Hezekh		1	2	1					1				5		
Hollistown	236	20	Bullard	Ebenz	1	1		1		1			1				5		
Hollistown	236	21	Bridge	Nathan	1		1				1						3		
Hollistown	236	22	Bullard	Samll			2	1				1		2			6		
Hollistown	236	23	Bullard	Isaac				1				1	1				3		
Hollistown	236	24	Bullard	Joel	1		2			1		2					6		
Hollistown	236	25	Cutter	Elizth		1					1		1				3		
Hollistown	236	26	Clarck	Nathan				1					1				2		
Hollistown	236	27	Carroll	Elijah	2		1			2		1					6		
Hollistown	236	28	Clafton	John	1	1	1	1		1		1	1				7		
Hollistown	236	29	Clark	Naham	1	2		1		1	1	1	1				8		
Hollistown	236	30	Clafland	Wm	1			1		2			1				5		
Hollistown	236	31	Chamberlain	Enoch		1	1	1		3	1		1				8		
Hollistown	236	32	Clark	Abijah	2		1						1				4		
Hollistown	236	33	Cobbett	Nathan	2			1		2	2		1				8		
Hollistown	236	34	Chamberlain	Jason	2	1	1	1		2			2	2			11		
Hollistown	236	35	Cutter	Ebenz		1		1				1	1				4		
Hollistown	236	36	Cozens	Isaac	2			1		2	2		1	1	1		10		
Hollistown	236	37	Cutter	Elihu	1	1		1				1					4		
Hollistown	236	38	Daniels	Japhet				1				1	1				3		
Hollistown	236	39	Daniels	Amonasa	1			1					1				3		
Hollistown	236	40	Daniels	Daniel				1				1	1				3		
Hollistown	236	41	Daniels	Elisha	1	1		1					1				4		
Hollistown	236	42	Daniels	Saml				1					1				2		
Hollistown	237	1	Daniels	Jesse	1	1		1					2				6		
Hollistown	237	2	Daniels	John		1	1						1				3		
Hollistown	237	3	Daniels	Perry	1		1					1					3		
Hollistown	237	4	Death	John	2		1			1		1					5		
Hollistown	237	5	Death	Rachel									1				1		
Hollistown	237	6	Dixon	Timothy	3		1	1		2			3	2			12		
Hollistown	237	7	Eames	Daniel		1	1	1				2		2			7		
Hollistown	237	8	Eames	Wm		1	1						1				3		
Hollistown	237	9	Eames	Hopsil	1		1	1			1	1		1			6		
Hollistown	237	10	Eames	Reuben		1	1	1		1		2	1				7		
Hollistown	237	11	Eames	Aaron		1		1		1	1	1					5		
Hollistown	237	12	Eames	Ezra		1		1	1		2	3	1				10		
Hollistown	237	13	Fisk	David		2	1	1		1			1	1			7		
Hollistown	237	14	Fisk	John	1		1						1				3		
Hollistown	237	15	Fisk	Nathan	2		1						1				4		
Hollistown	237	16	Fisher	Lewis		1		1		1		1					4		
Hollistown	237	17	Fairbanks	Adams	3		1					2	1				7		
Hollistown	237	18	Fisk	Levi	2		1			2			1				6		
Hollistown	237	19	Fairbanks	Reuben				1		1			1				3		
Hollistown	237	20	Frail	Sarah									2				2		
Hollistown	237	21	Fairbanks	John	3	2	1	1			1	1	1				10		
Hollistown	237	22	Fisk	Asa	1		3	1		1			1				7		
Hollistown	237	23	Foster	Isaac	1	1		1		2		2					7		
Hollistown	237	24	Giles	Paul	1	1	2	1		2	1	1	1				10		
Hollistown	237	25	Green	Close	1			1		1	1	2	1				7		
Hollistown	237	26	Hescock	Moses	1			1		4			1				7		
Hollistown	237	27	Hemenway	Daniel	2		1	1		1	1	1					7		
Hollistown	237	28	Haven	Jessa		1		1				2	1				5		
Hollistown	237	29	Haven	Luther			1			2		1					4		
Hollistown	237	30	Hardy	Fairbush	3			1							1		5		
Hollistown	237	31	Harrod	John	1	1		1		1	1		1				6		
Hollistown	237	32	Hill	Ebenz				1							1		2		
Hollistown	237	33	Hill	Rachel	1						1		1				3		
Hollistown	237	34	Hill	Moses	1			1					1				3		
Hollistown	237	35	Johnson	Nathl	3	1	1	1		1	1		1				9		
Hollistown	237	36	Johnson	Levi		1						1					2		
Hollistown	237	37	Jones	David				1					1				2		

TOWN	PG#	LN#	LAST NAME	FIRST NAME	FWM under 10	10 to 16	16 to 26	26 to 45	45 and over	FWF under 10	10 to 16	16 to 26	26 to 45	45 and over	TOTAL ALL OTHER	TOTAL SLAVES	TOTALS	DISTRICT/ TOWNSHIP	NOTES
Hollistown	237	38	Jennens	Isaac	1			1			3		1	1			7		
Hollistown	237	39	Jennens	Daniel				1		1		1	1				4		
Hollistown	237	40	Knolton	Elias	2	1		1		1			1				6		
Hollistown	237	41	Kilburn	Josiah				1		2			1				4		
Hollistown	237	42	Kilburn	John	1			1		1		2	1				6		
Hollistown	237	43	Laland	Oliver	4			1		1			1				7		
Hollistown	237	44	Littlefield	John				1				1		1			3		
Hollistown	237	45	Littlefield	John Jr	2			1		2			1				6		
Hollistown	238	1	Lovering	Eli*		1	1						1	1			4		
Hollistown	238	2	Leland	Asa		1	1		1			1		1			5		
Hollistown	238	3	Lovering	Craft				1						1			2		
Hollistown	238	4	Lovering	Wm			1			1			1				3		
Hollistown	238	5	Leland	Abner	2		2		1			1		1			7		
Hollistown	238	6	Littlefield	Simeon				1				1		1			3		
Hollistown	238	7	Lovering	Elias			1					1					2		
Hollistown	238	8	Lincoln	Asa	2		1	1			1		1				6		
Hollistown	238	9	Lewis	Samll				1						1			2		
Hollistown	238	10	Leland	Daniel	1	1	2		1	1		3		1			10		
Hollistown	238	11	Leland	Asapher Jr	2		1	1		1	2		1				8		
Hollistown	238	12	Leland	Timothy			1		1	1			1				4		
Hollistown	238	13	Leland	Henry		1			1				1				3		
Hollistown	238	14	Leland	Parley			1			1			1				3		
Hollistown	238	15	Leland	Asapher				1						1			2		
Hollistown	238	16	Littlefield	Jotham	1			1				1	1				4		
Hollistown	238	17	Littlefield	Ephm		2		1		1	1		1				6		
Hollistown	238	18	Leland	Jeremh	1		1	1		1	1	1	1				7		
Hollistown	238	19	Leland	Daniel	1		2		1	2	1		1				8		
Hollistown	238	20	Mellen	John			2					1					3		
Hollistown	238	21	Mellen	Jacob				1						1			2		
Hollistown	238	22	Mellen	Obediah	1		1					1					3		
Hollistown	238	23	Messenger	Cathn		1	1	2			1	1	1				7		
Hollistown	238	24	Messenger	Joseph	2		1					1					4		
Hollistown	238	25	Morse	Isaac	1	1	1		1	2	1		1				8		
Hollistown	238	26	Mellens	Wm	1			1		1			1	1			5		
Hollistown	238	27	Mellens	James	1	1	1		1	1	2	1	1				9		
Hollistown	238	28	Mellens	Robert		1		1						1			3		
Hollistown	238	29	Mellens	John	1		1	1		3		1	1				8		
Hollistown	238	30	Marsh	Ezekl	1	3			1	2	1	1		1			10		
Hollistown	238	31	Norcross	Asa	1			1						1			3		
Hollistown	238	32	Nichols	Samll	1		1					1					3		
Hollistown	238	33	Newton	Simeon				1						1			2		
Hollistown	238	34	Newhall	Theodore	2			1		1			1				5		
Hollistown	238	35	Phipps	Aaron	1	2		1		1			1				6		
Hollistown	238	36	Perry	Abner		1		1				1					4		
Hollistown	238	37	Perry	Abner Jr	3	1		1			1		1				7		
Hollistown	238	38	Perry	James				1		1	1		1				4		
Hollistown	238	39	Pond	Jona			1			2		1	1				5		
Hollistown	238	40	Parks	Solomon	2			1		3	1		1				8		
Hollistown	238	41	Parks	Samll				1						1			2		
Hollistown	238	42	Parks	Samll Jr		1	1			2		1					5		
Hollistown	238	43	Rider	Joseph				1						1			2		
Hollistown	239	1	Rider	Asa			1	1		1	1	1					5		
Hollistown	239	2	Rockwood	Asa				1		1			1	1			4		
Hollistown	239	3	Rockwood	Naham				1				1					2		
Hollistown	239	4	Rockwood	Timothy			2		1			1		1			5		
Hollistown	239	5	Rockwood	Timothy Jr	1	2	1		1	1	1			1			8		
Hollistown	239	6	Richardson	Joshua Jr		1	1			1	2	1	1				7		
Hollistown	239	7	Stone	James	1	1		1		1		2	1				7		
Hollistown	239	8	Snell	John				1						1			2		
Hollistown	239	9	Smith	Richard				1				2		1			4		
Hollistown	239	10	Stone	John		1		1				1	1				4		
Hollistown	239	11	Smith	Israel	1		1					1	1				5		
Hollistown	239	12	Stone	John Jr			1						1				2		
Hollistown	239	13	Smith	Isaa	1		1		1	1	2	1					7		
Hollistown	239	14	Stedman	John		2		1		2			1				6		
Hollistown	239	15	Thair	Elim		2		1		1	3		1				8		
Hollistown	239	16	Underwood	Joshua Jr		1		2		2			1				6		
Hollistown	239	17	Wiswell	Jona				1				1		1			4		
Hollistown	239	18	Walkens	Elijah	1			1					1				3		
Hollistown	239	19	Whitney	Samll			1	1				1		1			4		
Hollistown	239	20	Winship	Jacob	1			1		1			1				4		
Hollistown	239	21	White	James	1		1	1				2					5		
Hollistown	239	22	Whitney	David	2	2		1		1	1		2	1			11		
Hollistown	239	23	Wier	George	2		1		1				1				5		
Hollistown	239	24	Watkins	Andrew		1		1				1		1			4		
Hollistown	239	25	Walker	Solomon		1			1		1	1	1				5		

TOWN	PG#	LN#	LAST NAME	FIRST NAME	M <10	M 10-16	M 16-26	M 26-45	M 45+	F <10	F 10-16	F 16-26	F 26-45	F 45+	TOTAL ALL OTHER	TOTAL SLAVES	TOTALS	DISTRICT/ TOWNSHIP	NOTES
Hopkinton	240	1	Adams	Moses				1	1	2		2	1	2	1		10		
Hopkinton	240	2	Adams	Elisha		1	2		1	2		1	1				8		
Hopkinton	240	3	Adams	Benjm	1		1			2	3		1				9		
Hopkinton	240	4	Andrews	Joshua					1					1			2		
Hopkinton	240	5	Andrews	Wm	1				1			1		1			4		
Hopkinton	240	6	Adams	Asa Jr		1		1		3			1				6		
Hopkinton	240	7	Bullard	Daniel	1			1		1			1				4		
Hopkinton	240	8	Bowker	Uriah	1	1	1			1			3				8		
Hopkinton	240	9	Bowker	John	2	2		1		1		1	1				8		
Hopkinton	240	10	Bowker	Abiether	1		1	1		1	1		1	1			7		
Hopkinton	240	11	Bowker	Asa	1		2	1		2			1	5			12		
Hopkinton	240	12	Bachelder	Thos		1						1					2		
Hopkinton	240	13	Bruce	Elisha	1			1						1			3		
Hopkinton	240	14	Brigsby	Joel	3			1				2					6		
Hopkinton	240	15	Barns	Joseph	1	1			1	1	1	1					6		
Hopkinton	240	16	Ball	Abram				2		1			2				5		
Hopkinton	240	17	Burlingham	Benjm				1					1				2		
Hopkinton	240	18	Bachelder	Benjm				1		3		2	1				7		
Hopkinton	240	19	Burnup	Isaac	1	1	1	1	1	1	2		2				10		
Hopkinton	240	20	Burnam	Zadock	2	2		1		1	1	1					8		
Hopkinton	240	21	Briggs	Philip	1	1	1	1					1				5		
Hopkinton	240	22	Buckler	Thos		1	1			1	1						4		
Hopkinton	240	23	Barret	Ames		1		1		2			1				5		
Hopkinton	240	24	Butlar	Aaron	2		1			1	1		1	1			7		
Hopkinton	240	25	Bigsby	Peletiah	1		1	1				1	1				6		
Hopkinton	240	26	Bullard	Benjm				1		1	1		1				4		
Hopkinton	240	27	Burnam	Josiah	2	1	1	1					2	2			9		
Hopkinton	240	28	Bigsby	Abijah			1			1			1				3		
Hopkinton	240	29	Clark	Peter	1	1	1	1		1			1				6		
Hopkinton	240	30	Clapton	Caleb			1			1		1					3		
Hopkinton	240	31	Clapton	Elisha	1			1		1		1					4		
Hopkinton	240	32	Chamberland	Ebenz			1			2		1					4		
Hopkinton	240	33	Chamberlain	John						1			1				2		
Hopkinton	240	34	Chamberlain	Moses	1			1		2		1					5		
Hopkinton	240	35	Cheany	Wm		1		1					1				3		
Hopkinton	240	36	Clafton	Amaziah			2				1		1				4		
Hopkinton	240	37	Chamberlain	Nathl			1			2		1					4		
Hopkinton	240	38	Carter	Daniel		1	1	1		1	1	1					6		
Hopkinton	240	39	Crook	Eleazer				1					1				2		
Hopkinton	240	40	Cory	Jona			1	1				1	1				4		
Hopkinton	240	41	Comey	John	1		1	1				1	1				5		
Hopkinton	240	42	Cunningham	Joseph	2	2		1		1		1					7		
Hopkinton	240	43	Clemons	John Jr	1			1		1		1					4		
Hopkinton	240	44	Cutter	David	1			1	1	1	1	1	1				7		
Hopkinton	240	45	Claflan	Aaron	1		1		1	1	1						5		
Hopkinton	241	1	Claflan	Isaac		1	1	1		1		1		1			6		
Hopkinton	241	2	Clark	Isaac	2	2		2		1	1		2	1			11		
Hopkinton	241	3	Crooks	Abrm	1				1			4	2	2	2		12		
Hopkinton	241	4	Clark	Sarah			1					1	1				4		
Hopkinton	241	5	Clemmons	John					1			1		1			3		
Hopkinton	241	6	Daniels	Obediah		1		1					1				3		
Hopkinton	241	7	Day	Uriah	2			1		1		1					5		
Hopkinton	241	8	Dewing	John	1				1	2	1		1				6		
Hopkinton	241	9	Dickman	John	2	2	2		1	2	2		1	1			13		
Hopkinton	241	10	Dench	Gilbert		2	1		1		1	2		1			8		
Hopkinton	241	11	Daniels	Simeon		1		1		3			1				6		
Hopkinton	241	12	Eames	Asa	1	1		1		1	1		1				6		
Hopkinton	241	13	Eames	David	1	1		1		1	1		1				6		
Hopkinton	241	14	Eames	Jessa	1	1		1		2			1				6		
Hopkinton	241	15	Fisk	Abial			1	1		1		1		1			5		
Hopkinton	241	16	Fitch	Hannah		1	1					1	2	1			6		
Hopkinton	241	17	Foster	James	2	1			1	3			1				8		
Hopkinton	241	18	Fairbanks	Adam	3			1		2	1		1				8		
Hopkinton	241	19	Frail	Saml	1	1	1			1	1	1					6		
Hopkinton	241	20	Frail	Joseph		1			1	2	2			1			7		
Hopkinton	241	21	Flagg	Wm		1	1		1			1		1			5		
Hopkinton	241	22	Farland	Joseph				1		2	1		1				5		
Hopkinton	241	23	Fay	Nathan	3		3	1		2		1					8		
Hopkinton	241	24	Freeland	Wm	1	2	1		1	1	1		1				8		
Hopkinton	241	25	Freeland	Abrm		1		1		1			1				4		
Hopkinton	241	26	Freeland	Thos	1	1	1		1			2	1	1			8		
Hopkinton	241	27	Gibbs	Jacob				1						1			2		
Hopkinton	241	28	Gibbs	Wm	3		2	1	1	2		1	2	1			13		
Hopkinton	241	29	Guild	Wm			1			2			1				4		
Hopkinton	241	30	Gody	John	1		1	2	1	2	3		1				11		
Hopkinton	241	31	Gody	Joseph				1					1				2		
Hopkinton	241	32	Greenwood	Moses	3	2		1					2				8		
Hopkinton	241	33	Golden	John	2	1	1	1		1	1	1	1				10		
Hopkinton	241	34	Gilson	John			2		2			2	2	1			9		

61

TOWN	PG#	LN#	LAST NAME	FIRST NAME	FREE WHITE MALES					FREE WHITE FEMALES					TOTAL ALL OTHER	TOTAL SLAVES	TOTALS	DISTRICT/TOWNSHIP	NOTES
					under 10	10 to 16	16 to 26	26 to 45	45 and over	under 10	10 to 16	16 to 26	26 to 45	45 and over					
Hopkinton	241	35	Gibson	James			1		1	2		1	1				6		
Hopkinton	241	36	Graves	Nathan	2			1					1	1			5		
Hopkinton	241	37	Godard	Saml	2		1	1				2	1	1			8		
Hopkinton	241	38	Godfry	Saml	1			1		2			1				5		
Hopkinton	241	39	Gossett	Seth			3		1			1					5		
Hopkinton	241	40	Godard	Edward		1		1		1	2		1				6		
Hopkinton	241	41	Gibbs	Saml			1	1		1			1				4		
Hopkinton	241	42	Hall	Saml				1				1		1			3		
Hopkinton	241	43	Haven	Moses				1						1			2		
Hopkinton	241	44	Haven	Isaac	1	1	1		1					1			5		
Hopkinton	241	45	Hardy	Seth				1						1			2		
Hopkinton	242	1	Haven	Sedde		1			1	1				1			4		
Hopkinton	242	2	Homer	John			1	1		4	2	2	1				11		
Hopkinton	242	3	Homes	Francis			1	1		1		1	1				5		
Hopkinton	242	4	Hayden	Elisha				1				1	1				3		
Hopkinton	242	5	Hayden	Wm	1		1					1	1				4		
Hopkinton	242	6	Hayden	John	1			1		4			1				7		
Hopkinton	242	7	Hayden	John Jr			1			3			1				5		
Hopkinton	242	8	Howard	Jason	2		1						1				4		
Hopkinton	242	9	How	Nathan	1		1		2		1	1					6		
Hopkinton	242	10	Howard	Alexr			1			1		1					3		
Hopkinton	242	11	Haven	Jotham	3		1	1		2			1				8		
Hopkinton	242	12	Howard	Joshua	1			1		3	2			2			9		
Hopkinton	242	13	Hitchcock	Thos		1		1		2							4		
Hopkinton	242	14	Homes	John Jr	2	1	2		1	1	1	2		1			11		
Hopkinton	242	15	Haven	John		2		1	1	1							5		
Hopkinton	242	16	Homer	Mitchel		1	1	2						1			5		
Hopkinton	242	17	How	Phineas		2	1	1		1	1			1			7		
Hopkinton	242	18	How	Nehemiah	1			1				2	2				6		
Hopkinton	242	19	Jones	Isaac		1		1		2	1		1				6		
Hopkinton	242	20	Ingram	Nathan				1		1				1			3		
Hopkinton	242	21	Jennings	Noses	1			1		1		1	1	1			6		
Hopkinton	242	22	Jones	Mary			1					1	1	1			4		
Hopkinton	242	23	Johnson	Reuben			2	1	1	1		1					6		
Hopkinton	242	24	Jones	John	1	1	1	1		3	2	1	1				11		
Hopkinton	242	25	Jones	Elisha	2			1		2			1				6		
Hopkinton	242	26	Johnson	Syvannus	1			1		4			1				7		
Hopkinton	242	27	Kinsman	Aaron	1			1		1			1				4		
Hopkinton	242	28	Kenny	Wm				1		1		1		2			5		
Hopkinton	242	29	Kenny	Asa				1		1				1			3		
Hopkinton	242	30	Loring	Nathan	1		1	1					1				4		
Hopkinton	242	31	Leaky	Simeon		1	1			1			1				4		
Hopkinton	242	32	Lyon	Orpheus		1		1					1	1			4		
Hopkinton	242	33	Littlefield	Pelletiah			1				1		1				3		
Hopkinton	242	34	Littlefield	Jeremh		1		1			1	1		1			5		
Hopkinton	242	35	Mellens	Henry				1						1			2		
Hopkinton	242	36	Millenge	Thos			2				1	1					4		
Hopkinton	242	37	Mellens	Thos				1				1		1			3		
Hopkinton	242	38	Mellens	Henry			1				1						2		
Hopkinton	242	39	Marsh	Lydia			3			1		1		1			6		
Hopkinton	242	40	Morse	Joel	1			1		1			1				4		
Hopkinton	242	41	Mifflin	Walter	1	1	2		2	1	1	2		1			11		
Hopkinton	242	42	Motten	John	1			1		2	1			1			6		
Hopkinton	242	43	Morse	Parrias		2	2	1					1				6		
Hopkinton	243	1	Morse	Joseph	1	1		1		3	1		1				8		
Hopkinton	243	2	Morse	Elisha	3		1	1		1			1				7		
Hopkinton	243	3	Morting	Nathan		1		1				1	1				4		
Hopkinton	243	4	Morting	Jame			1						1				2		
Hopkinton	243	5	Mayhew	John		1							1				2		
Hopkinton	243	6	Medeay	Mathew		2	1	1		1		2		1			8		
Hopkinton	243	7	Norcross	Daniel		1		1		1				1			4		
Hopkinton	243	8	North	Daniel	1			1				1	1				4		
Hopkinton	243	9	Norcross	Benjm				1						1			2		
Hopkinton	243	10	Norcross	Joel	2	1		1		1			1				6		
Hopkinton	243	11	Perry	Nathan	1			1		1				1			4		
Hopkinton	243	12	Pike	Aaron	4			1		4		1					10		
Hopkinton	243	13	Pratt	Moses				1		2		1					4		
Hopkinton	243	14	Phipps	Saml	1	1		1				1	1	1			6		
Hopkinton	243	15	Pierce	Jonas				1						1			2		
Hopkinton	243	16	Piercing	Jonas	3			1		2			1				7		
Hopkinton	243	17	Phipps	David		1						1					2		
Hopkinton	243	18	Parks	Joseph				1						1			2		
Hopkinton	243	19	Pettis	James	2			1	1			1	1	2			8		
Hopkinton	243	20	Perry	Moses			1	1		4	1		1				8		
Hopkinton	243	21	Prentice	Saml	1		1	1					1	1			5		
Hopkinton	243	22	Pierce	Ebenz	1			1		1			1				4		
Hopkinton	243	23	Pierce	Aaron	2			1		1			1				5		
Hopkinton	243	24	Pierce	Aaron Jr	2			1		1			1				5		
Hopkinton	243	25	Pierce	Francis				1						1			2		

TOWN	PG#	LN#	LAST NAME	FIRST NAME	under 10	10 to 16	16 to 26	26 to 45	45 and over	under 10	10 to 16	16 to 26	26 to 45	45 and over	TOTAL ALL OTHER	TOTAL SLAVES	TOTALS	DISTRICT/ TOWNSHIP	NOTES
Hopkinton	243	26	Pierce	Saml	1				1	3	2		1				8		
Hopkinton	243	27	Pond	Zadoc				1		2			1				4		
Hopkinton	243	28	Pierce	Wm		1			1		1	1		2			6		
Hopkinton	243	29	Perkins	Reubin	2			1					1				4		
Hopkinton	243	30	Pierce	Nathan	3			1		2	1		1				8		
Hopkinton	243	31	Pike	Jona Jr			1					1					2		
Hopkinton	243	32	Pike	Nathan			1		1			2	1	2			7		
Hopkinton	243	33	Pike	Jona			2			1	2	2	1	2			10		
Hopkinton	243	34	Pike	Timothy				1					1				2		
Hopkinton	243	35	Pierce	Icabud	1			1		1			1				4		
Hopkinton	243	36	Pond	Painjm	1	1	1	1		2	1		1				8		
Hopkinton	243	37	Rice	Jason				1					1				2		
Hopkinton	243	38	Rice	Moses	2	1		1		4		1	1				10		
Hopkinton	243	39	Rocket	Nathan	1			1		2			1				5		
Hopkinton	243	40	Rocket	Josiah			1	1		1		1	1	1			6		
Hopkinton	243	41	Rice	Hezekiah			1		1	1	1		1				5		
Hopkinton	243	42	Reed	Ephm	1	1		1		2	1		1	1			8		
Hopkinton	243	43	Rand	Jona	2			1		2			1				6		
Hopkinton	243	44	Richards	Joseph	1	1	1	1		3	2		1				10		
Hopkinton	244	1	Snell	Saml	2			1		4			1				8		
Hopkinton	244	2	Snell	John				1					1				2		
Hopkinton	244	3	Smith	Richard			3		1		1	2		1			8		
Hopkinton	244	4	Stimpson	Jeremh	1	1		1		3	1		1		1		10		
Hopkinton	244	5	Stone	John	1	2	1	1		1	3		1				10		
Hopkinton	244	6	Stearns	Jona	2	3		1		2	2		1				11		
Hopkinton	244	7	Sheffield	Daniel	2			2		1		1					6		
Hopkinton	244	8	Spring	Thadeus	2			1				2					5		
Hopkinton	244	9	Stimpson	Saml Jr	3		1			2			1				7		
Hopkinton	244	10	Stimpson	Saml		1			1	2	2		2				8		
Hopkinton	244	11	Stimpson	Ebenz	1		4					1	1				8		
Hopkinton	244	12	Smith	Joseph	1			1		1		1	1	1			6		
Hopkinton	244	13	Smith	Benjm		1		1	1	1		1		1			5		
Hopkinton	244	14	Smith	Aaron	2			1			1		1				5		
Hopkinton	244	15	Smith	Moses				1		1			1				3		
Hopkinton	244	16	Smith	Abiel		1		2		1		1	1				6		
Hopkinton	244	17	Serridge	Isaac	2			1	1	1		1	1	1			8		
Hopkinton	244	18	Singletery	Ebenz		1	1		1	1			1				5		
Hopkinton	244	19	Stepherd	Timothy		1		1	1	3	2		2				10		
Hopkinton	244	20	Show	Saml	1				1			1	1	1			5		
Hopkinton	244	21	Thayer	Araba		1		1		1	1						4		
Hopkinton	244	22	Tumbs	Joseph	2	1			1	2	2		1				9		
Hopkinton	244	23	Tilton	Abrm	1		1	1	1	2	1	1	1	1			10		
Hopkinton	244	24	Tidd	Daniel	1	1	1	1		2		1					7		
Hopkinton	244	25	Tidd	John	2	2			1	1		2	1	1			10		
Hopkinton	244	26	Temple	Abner	1	3			1	2	1		1				9		
Hopkinton	244	27	Twitchel	Jonas	1	1			1				1				4		
Hopkinton	244	28	Townsend	Timothy	1	1		1	1	2	1	2	1				10		
Hopkinton	244	29	Titus	Primas											3		3		
Hopkinton	244	30	Underwood	Daniel	1			1		1			1				4		
Hopkinton	244	31	Vollentine	Wm Jr	3	1	1					1					6		
Hopkinton	244	32	Vollentine	Wm	3	3	1		2		1	3		1			14		
Hopkinton	244	33	Vollentine	Joseph			1	1		1		1					4		
Hopkinton	244	34	Vollentine	Saml	2	1	1		1	3			1				9		
Hopkinton	244	35	Watkins	Moses	1	1			1	1	1	3		1			9		
Hopkinton	244	36	Walken	Henry	3			1			1		1	1			7		
Hopkinton	244	37	Weatin	Levi	1			1		2	1		1				6		
Hopkinton	244	38	Walker	Joseph		1		1			1		1				4		
Hopkinton	244	39	Warren	Naham		1		1		1			1				4		
Hopkinton	244	40	Walker	Sarah							1		1				2		
Hopkinton	244	41	Ward	Joseph			1	1		1		1	1				5		
Hopkinton	244	42	Warren	Daniel		1				1	1						3		
Hopkinton	244	43	Walkins	Jona			1			1		1					3		
Hopkinton	244	44	Ware	James				1					1	1			3		
Hopkinton	245	1	Ware	James Jr			1			2	1		1				5		
Hopkinton	245	2	Walker	Israel		1	2		1			1		1			6		
Hopkinton	245	3	Walker	Timothy	3	1			1	5	1	1	1				13		
Hopkinton	245	4	Ward	Peter	1			1					1				3		
Hopkinton	245	5	Wesson	Aaron			2					2					4		
Hopkinton	245	6	Wesson	Abiel	3			1		1		1					6		
Hopkinton	245	7	Wood	Wm	3			1		2	2	1					9		
Hopkinton	245	8	Walker	Joseph	2	2		1		2			1				8		
Hopkinton	245	9	Wesson	John		1		1					1				3		
Hopkinton	245	10	Whuler	Saml	1			1		2			1				5		
Hopkinton	245	11	Works	Jane			3		1		1	1		2			8		
Hopkinton	245	12	Works	James	1			1					1				3		
Hopkinton	245	13	Wilson	John O.	2	1	1	1	1	2		1	1	1			11		
Hopkinton	245	14	Young	John	3					2	2		1	1			9		

TOWN	PG#	LN#	HEADS OF HOUSEHOLD		FREE WHITE MALES					FREE WHITE FEMALES					TOTAL ALL OTHER	TOTAL SLAVES	TOTALS	DISTRICT/ TOWNSHIP	NOTES
			LAST NAME	FIRST NAME	under 10	10 to 16	16 to 26	26 to 45	45 and over	under 10	10 to 16	16 to 26	26 to 45	45 and over					
Lexington	156	1	Ainger	John	2	1		1		1		1					6		
Lexington	156	2	Adams	Katharine								1	1				2		
Lexington	156	3	Adams	George				1					1				2		
Lexington	156	4	Blodgett	Isaac			1		1	1	1		1	1			6		
Lexington	156	5	Blodgett	Isaac Jr	1		1					1					3		
Lexington	156	6	Bridge	John				1			1						2		
Lexington	156	7	Bridge	Jonas	3		1	1		2	2		1	1	1		12		
Lexington	156	8	Brown	Benjamin				1			1		1	1			4		
Lexington	156	9	Blodgett	Nathan	4		1		1	1			1	1			9		
Lexington	156	10	Bridge	Jonathan	1	1		1		1	2		1	1			8		
Lexington	156	11	Bowman	Francis	1	1		1			1		1				5		
Lexington	156	12	Brown	James	1	1	2	1		1	1		1				8		
Lexington	156	13	Brown	James Jr			1	1		1			1	1			5		
Lexington	156	14	Benjamin	William	3			1		2			1				7		
Lexington	156	15	Blodgett	James	2	1		1		3	1		1				9		
Lexington	156	16	Childs	Abijah			1	1						1			3		
Lexington	156	17	Chandler	John				1						1			2		
Lexington	156	18	Chandler	John Jr	3	3		1		3			1				11		
Lexington	156	19	Chandler	Nathan	1	1		1		1			1				5		
Lexington	156	20	Chandler	Joseph			1	1		2			1	1			6		
Lexington	156	21	Cutler	Thomas	1	1	2		1	1	1			1			8		
Lexington	156	22	Cutler	Nathaniel	1	1		1		1	1						5		
Lexington	156	23	Clark	Jonas					2		2	1	1				6		
Lexington	157	1	Caldwell	Thomas I			1	1		2			1				5		
Lexington	157	2	Caldwell	John		1		1					1				3		
Lexington	157	3	Dudley	Nathan	1		1	1		2	1		2				8		
Lexington	157	4	Downing	Susanna	2						1		1				4		
Lexington	157	5	Davis	Peter	2	1	3	1		1				1			9		
Lexington	157	6	Eaton	Rebekah						1	1			2			4		
Lexington	157	7	Estabrook	Benjamin		1	2	1		1		1		1	1		8		
Lexington	157	8	Estabrook	Benjamin Jr	1	1		1		1			1				5		
Lexington	157	9	Estabrook	Nehemiah	1			1				2	1				5		
Lexington	157	10	Fessendon	Thomas	1		2	1		1	2		1				8		
Lexington	157	11	Fessendon	Nathan	1			1		1			1				4		
Lexington	157	12	Fisk	David				1					1				2		
Lexington	157	13	Fisk	David Jr		1	1	1				1	1				5		
Lexington	157	14	Fisk	David 3rd	3	1		1		2	2		1	1			11		
Lexington	157	15	Fisk	Joseph			1	1		1			1	1			5		
Lexington	157	16	Fisk	Joseph Jr	2	1		1		1			1	1			7		
Lexington	157	17	Fassett	Abiel	1	1	1	1					1				5		
Lexington	157	18	Harrington	Jonathan				1									1		
Lexington	157	19	Harrington	Jonathan Jr	3		1	1		2			1				8		
Lexington	157	20	Harrington	Abijah				1					1				2		
Lexington	157	21	Harrington	Isaac	1			1	1	1			1	2			7		
Lexington	157	22	Hartwell	Stephen		1			1			1	1				4		
Lexington	157	23	Harrington	Daniel				1				2		1			4		
Lexington	157	24	Harrington	Jeremiah				1						1			2		
Lexington	157	25	Harrington	Moses	2	2		1					1	1			7		
Lexington	157	26	Harrington	Levi	2	1		1		2	1		1				8		
Lexington	157	27	Hastings	Isaac	2	2	1	1			1	2	1				10		
Lexington	157	28	Hastings	Samuel				1			1	1		1			4		
Lexington	157	29	Harrington	Samuel	2			1		4	1		1				9		
Lexington	157	30	Harrington	Joseph	3		2			1			1				7		
Lexington	157	31	Harrington	Peter	1			1		1		1					4		
Lexington	157	32	Harrington	Solomon	3	1		1					1				6		
Lexington	157	33	Hunt	Jonathan		1	2	1		1		1					6		
Lexington	157	34	Harrington	Charles	1			1		2	1		1				6		
Lexington	157	35	Hadley	Benjamin	2			1		3			1				7		
Lexington	157	36	Harrington	Ebenezer	1	2		1		2	1		1	1			9		
Lexington	157	37	Johnson	Ab*son			4	1		2			1				8		
Lexington	157	38	Kendall	Oliver				1					1				2		
Lexington	158	1	Lock	Thomas		2		1		3		2	1				9		
Lexington	158	2	Lawrence	Phinehas	1		1			2	1	1					6		
Lexington	158	3	Lawrence	Jonathan			1			1	1	1					4		
Lexington	158	4	Lawrence	Sarah									2	1			3		
Lexington	158	5	Lock	Amos	2	1		1						1			5		
Lexington	158	6	Lock	Jonas		1	2	1		1	1			1			7		
Lexington	158	7	Lock	Samuel				1									1		
Lexington	158	8	Lock	Asa B	3		1	1				2					7		
Lexington	158	9	Lock	Benjamin	2			1		2			1				6		
Lexington	158	10	Lock	Reuben	1	1		1					1	1			5		
Lexington	158	11	Lock	Mehitabel								1	1	1			3		
Lexington	158	12	Loring	Joseph	1		1			1			1	1			5		
Lexington	158	13	Loring	Jonathan	2			1		1	2		1				7		
Lexington	158	14	Munro	Thaddeus	2		1	1						1			5		
Lexington	158	15	Marrett	Amos				1		1				1			3		
Lexington	158	16	Marrett	Amos Jr		1		1		3	2		1				8		
Lexington	158	17	Meriam	Rufus	1	1	1	1		3	1	1	1				10		
Lexington	158	18	Muzzy	Amos Jr	1			1		2		1	1				6		

TOWN	PG#	LN#	LAST NAME	FIRST NAME	FREE WHITE MALES under 10	10 to 16	16 to 26	26 to 45	45 and over	FREE WHITE FEMALES under 10	10 to 16	16 to 26	26 to 45	45 and over	TOTAL ALL OTHER	TOTAL SLAVES	TOTALS	DISTRICT/ TOWNSHIP	NOTES
Lexington	158	19	Muzzy	Amos					1				1	2			4		
Lexington	158	20	Meed	Josiah				1		3			1	1			6		
Lexington	158	21	Mullikin	John	1	1	2	1		1		2	1	1			10		
Lexington	158	22	Moor	Robert		1		1						2			4		
Lexington	158	23	Munro	Nathan	2		1	1				2	1	1			8		
Lexington	158	24	Munro	John				1				2	1				4		
Lexington	158	25	Munro	Joseph	2		1			1	1		1				6		
Lexington	158	26	Munro	William Jr		2	1			3	1		1				8		
Lexington	158	27	Munro	Phil*n	2	3		2		3			1				11		
Lexington	158	28	Meed	Levi	1	2	1	1					1	2			8		
Lexington	158	29	Muzzy	John		2		1					1	1			5		
Lexington	158	30	Munro	Ebenezer		1		1				2		1			5		
Lexington	158	31	Munro	Abigail	3								1	2			6		
Lexington	158	32	Mason	Joseph				1						2			3		
Lexington	158	33	Mason	Daniel				1					1				2		
Lexington	158	34	Munro	William		1	2	1				3	1				8		
Lexington	158	35	Meriam	Benjamin				1				2		1			4		
Lexington	158	36	Muzzy	Ebenezer	1	1		1		1	1	1	1	2			8		
Lexington	158	37	Nichols	Adna	2			1		2	1	1	1				8		
Lexington	159	1	Peak	John	1	1	1		1	1	1	1		1			8		
Lexington	159	2	Phinney	Benjamin	1		1		1	1		1		1			6		
Lexington	159	3	Parker	John	1	1			1	2	2		1	1			9		
Lexington	159	4	Parker	Robert	1			1		1			1				4		
Lexington	159	5	Parker	Mary										1			1		
Lexington	159	6	Parkhurst	John		1	1		1				1	1			5		
Lexington	159	7	Perry	Widow										1			1		
Lexington	159	8	Parker	Obediah		4	3	1					1				9		
Lexington	159	9	Penney	David	1	2			1	1	1	1	1				8		
Lexington	159	10	Porter	William		1		1		1	1	2		1			7		
Lexington	159	11	Pierce	Abijah		1	2					2					5		
Lexington	159	12	Pierce	Reuben	1			1				1	1	1			5		
Lexington	159	13	Pierce	Isaac		1		1		2	1		1				6		
Lexington	159	14	Robbins	Thomas		1		1	1			1	1	1			6		
Lexington	159	15	Russell	Nathan	3	1		2	1				1	1			9		
Lexington	159	16	Robbinson	Jacob	4		1	1		1			1				8		
Lexington	159	17	Reed	Nathan	1		2	1	1		2	2		1			10		
Lexington	159	18	Russell	Joshua		1	6	3					1		1		12		
Lexington	159	19	Reed	Hammond			1	1					1	1			4		
Lexington	159	20	Reed	Hammond Jr		1		1		2			1				5		
Lexington	159	21	Robbinson	Joseph		1		1			1	2		1			6		
Lexington	159	22	Reed	Joshua		1	1	1		2			1	1			7		
Lexington	159	23	Russell	Joseph				1					1	1			3		
Lexington	159	24	Reed	William				1		2			1	1			5		
Lexington	159	25	Reed	Thaddeus	3	1	1		1	2			1				9		
Lexington	159	26	Robbins	Stephen		2	1	2		1		2	1				9		
Lexington	159	27	Reed	Elizabeth		1	1					1		2			5		
Lexington	159	28	Reed	Sweethen				1		2	1			2			6		
Lexington	159	29	Robbinson	Jonathan			1						1				2		
Lexington	159	30	Stearns	Asahel	4	3	1		1	1	1	1	1				13		Joel Smith included on line
Lexington	159	31	Stone	Samuel	3	1		1					1				6		
Lexington	159	32	Stone	Jonas		1			1	1				2			5		
Lexington	159	33	Simonds	David	1			1	1	2			1	1			7		
Lexington	159	34	Simonds	John			1	1		1	1		1				5		
Lexington	159	35	Simonds	Joshua			1	1		1	1	1	1				6		
Lexington	159	36	Simonds	Joshua Jr	2			1		1	1		1				6		
Lexington	159	37	Simonds	Joseph		1	1	1	1	1				1			6		
Lexington	159	38	Simonds	William			1				1	1					3		
Lexington	159	39	Smith	Jonathan Jr	2		1		1	2			1	1			8		
Lexington	160	1	Swan	Joshua						1	2	1					4		
Lexington	160	2	Stearns	Benjamin			2	1		2				1			6		
Lexington	160	3	Stearns	Isaac	3			1	1	1			1	1			8		
Lexington	160	4	Smith	William				1						1			2		
Lexington	160	5	Smith	Nathan	2		1	2					1	1			8		
Lexington	160	6	Smith	William Jr		1		1		1	1		1				5		
Lexington	160	7	Smith	Josiah	1	1	1		1	1	1			1			7		
Lexington	160	8	Smith	Jonas		1		1		1			1				4		
Lexington	160	9	Smith	Joseph	2	2	2	1	2	1			1				13		
Lexington	160	10	Smith	Abraham	1	1		1					2				5		
Lexington	160	11	Smith	Abel	2			2					1				5		
Lexington	160	12	Smith	James	1	2		2		1	1	1	1		1		10		
Lexington	160	13	Tufts	Thomas	1	1	1	1		1			1				6		
Lexington	160	14	Tidd	John		1	1	1		1		2					6		
Lexington	160	15	Tidd	William				1						1			2		
Lexington	160	16	Thorning	William	3	2		1		2	1		1				10		
Lexington	160	17	Viles	Joel	1	1	1		1	1		1	2		1		9		
Lexington	160	18	Underwood	Joseph			3		1		2	2		1			9		
Lexington	160	19	Wyeth	John				1						1			2		
Lexington	160	20	Wyman	James Jr	1			1					1	1			4		
Lexington	160	21	Winship	Simon	2		1		1	1			1	1			7		
Lexington	160	22	Winship	Isaac	1		1		1	1		1	1				6		

TOWN	PG#	LN#	LAST NAME	FIRST NAME	FREE WHITE MALES					FREE WHITE FEMALES					TOTAL ALL OTHER	TOTAL SLAVES	TOTALS	DISTRICT/ TOWNSHIP	NOTES
					under 10	10 to 16	16 to 26	26 to 45	45 and over	under 10	10 to 16	16 to 26	26 to 45	45 and over					
Lexington	160	23	Winship	Jonathan	1			1	1	1	1	1	1	2			9		
Lexington	160	24	Wyman	James	2	1			1			3		1			8		
Lexington	160	25	Willington	Benjamin		2	2		1		1		1	2			9		
Lexington	160	26	Walker	Abiel				1				1					2		
Lexington	160	27	Winship	Stephen	1		1	1		5			2				10		
Lexington	160	28	Williams	Elizabeth			1			1				2			4		

TOWN	PG#	LN#	LAST NAME	FIRST NAME	under 10	10 to 16	16 to 26	26 to 45	45 and over	under 10	10 to 16	16 to 26	26 to 45	45 and over	TOTAL ALL OTHER	TOTAL SLAVES	TOTALS	DISTRICT/ TOWNSHIP	NOTES
					FREE WHITE MALES					FREE WHITE FEMALES									
Lincoln	12	1	Garfield	Thadeus	3	1			1	1			1				7		
Lincoln	12	2	Farrar	Nehemiah	1			1		4	1		2				9		
Lincoln	12	3	Farrar	Zebediah		1		1					1				3		
Lincoln	12	4	Minot	Abel	3			1					1				5		
Lincoln	12	5	Adams	Joseph		2	1		1			2	1	1			8		
Lincoln	12	6	Toleman	Elisha	1		3	1		1		1	1				8		
Lincoln	12	7	Adams	James			1		1			2		1			5		
Lincoln	12	8	Adams	Andrew			1						1				2		
Lincoln	12	9	Jones	Eli		1		1		3	3	2	1		1		12		
Lincoln	12	10	Brown	Abjah				1					1				2		
Lincoln	12	11	Hunt	Samuel		1		1					2				4		
Lincoln	12	12	Warren	Daniel	1		2	1		2			1				7		
Lincoln	12	13	Easty	Ebenezer		2						1					3		
Lincoln	12	14	Parks	Charles	1		1	1		2		1					6		
Lincoln	12	15	Cornwall	Thomas		1				1		1	1				4		
Lincoln	12	16	Parks	Willard				1		1	2		1				5		
Lincoln	12	17	Farrar	Samuel		1	2	1	1	1	1		2				9		
Lincoln	12	18	Sherman	Jonas	1			1		1	1			1			6		
Lincoln	12	19	Babcock	Seth	4			1		3	1		1				10		
Lincoln	13	1	Underwood	Peter	1			1		2			2				6		
Lincoln	13	2	Parks	Daniel	2			2		3		1	1				9		
Lincoln	13	3	Whiting	Hosea	1		1				1	1	1				5		
Lincoln	13	4	Woods	Nehemiah	1			1		2		1	1				7		
Lincoln	13	5	Underwood	Peter				1				1		1			3		
Lincoln	13	6	Parks	Isaac		1	1	1		1			1				5		
Lincoln	13	7	Parks	Samuel		2	2	1		1	2		1				9		
Lincoln	13	8	Fisk	Phinehas		1		1		2		1					5		
Lincoln	13	9	Garfield	Enock			1			1		1					3		
Lincoln	13	10	Parks	Josiah	2	1	1	1		2			1				8		
Lincoln	13	11	Derby	Samuel	2			1		4	1		1				9		
Lincoln	13	12	Codman	John	3			1		2	1	2	3		1		13		
Lincoln	13	13	Goodenough	Isaac			5	1				1	1				8		
Lincoln	13	14	Bapson	Theodore	1		3	1		1	1	1					8		
Lincoln	13	15	Billings	Jonathan B	1		1	1				1		1			5		
Lincoln	13	16	Billings	Timothy	1	1			1				1				4		
Lincoln	13	17	Baker	Nathaniel		1			1	1	1		2				6		
Lincoln	13	18	Baker	Amos	3	1		1			2		1	1			9		
Lincoln	13	19	Jones	Silas	2			1		1			1				5		
Lincoln	13	20	Billings	Joseph			1		1	1			1				4		
Lincoln	13	21	Billings	Nathan	1			2	1			1	1	1			7		
Lincoln	13	22	Brooks	John				1					1	1			3		
Lincoln	13	23	Brook	Daniel	2	1	1	1		2	1	1	1				10		
Lincoln	13	24	Brooks	Noah	1	1	1	1				1	1				6		
Lincoln	13	25	Brooks	Joshua	1	2	2		1	3	1	1	1				12		
Lincoln	13	26	Brooks	Hannah									1	1			2		
Lincoln	13	27	Mason	Jonas				1		1	2	1	2				7		
Lincoln	13	28	Hartwell	John	1	1		1	1	1	2	2		2	1		12		
Lincoln	13	29	Brooks	Levi	3		1	1		1	1		2				10		
Lincoln	13	30	Hartwell	Samuel		2	2		1			2	1	1			9		
Lincoln	13	31	Collwell	William	1	2			1	2	1		1				8		
Lincoln	13	32	Brooks	Aaron			1	1	1		1						4		
Lincoln	13	33	Winship	Benjamin		2			1				1				4		
Lincoln	13	34	Nelson	Josiah		2	2		1	1		2					8		
Lincoln	13	35	Nelson	Thomas						1					1		2		
Lincoln	13	36	Hastings	Samuel	3	1	1	1		2	2	2	2				14		
Lincoln	13	37	Abbot	Nehemiah	1	1			1		1			1			5		
Lincoln	13	38	Brown	Daniel		1		1	1			1		1			5		
Lincoln	13	39	Abbot	Joseph	2	1	1		1	2		1		1			9		
Lincoln	14	1	Abbot	Abiel	1			1		1			1				4		
Lincoln	14	2	Hoar	Leonard	3	1		2		3			1	3			13		
Lincoln	14	3	Stone	Gregory	1			1		4	1		1				8		
Lincoln	14	4	Adams	Buckley		1		1				2	1				5		
Lincoln	14	5	Harington	Daniel	2			1				1		1			5		
Lincoln	14	6	Weston	Nathan	4	1			2		1		1	1			10		
Lincoln	14	7	Peirce	Abijah		1		1				1	1	1			5		
Lincoln	14	8	Colowin	Joseph	1	1	1	1		1	1	1	1	1			9		
Lincoln	14	9	Gove	Nathaniel	1	1	1		1	1	2	1		1			9		
Lincoln	14	10	Gove	Nathaniel Jr	1		1			1		1					4		
Lincoln	14	11	Bernis	Phinehas	2			1		2			1				6		
Lincoln	14	12	Parkhurst	Nathaniel				1					1				2		
Lincoln	14	13	Flag	Silas	2	1		1					1				5		
Lincoln	14	14	Willington	Elijah	2	1			1	2	2		1				9		
Lincoln	14	15	Brown	Sarah									1	2			3		
Lincoln	14	16	Brown	Ephraim	1	2	1	1		2		1	1				9		
Lincoln	14	17	Brown	Hannah		1	3				1			2			7		
Lincoln	14	18	Bemis	Jonas	3			1		2			1				7		
Lincoln	14	19	Munroe	Benjamin	1	1		1	1	1			1				6		
Lincoln	14	20	Colburn	Joseph	2			1		1			2				6		
Lincoln	14	21	Foster	Solomon		1	1					1		1			4		

TOWN	PG#	LN#	LAST NAME	FIRST NAME	FREE WHITE MALES under 10	10 to 16	16 to 26	26 to 45	45 and over	FREE WHITE FEMALES under 10	10 to 16	16 to 26	26 to 45	45 and over	TOTAL ALL OTHER	TOTAL SLAVES	TOTALS	DISTRICT/ TOWNSHIP	NOTES
Lincoln	14	22	Peirce	Jonas	1	1		1	1	1	1		1	1			8		
Lincoln	14	23	Flint	Ephraim			2		1		1	2	2				8		
Lincoln	14	24	Dudley	Benjamin	1				1				1	1			4		
Lincoln	14	25	Garfield	Elisha				1	1					1			3		
Lincoln	14	26	Fisk	Elijah			1	1				2	1				5		
Lincoln	14	27	Colburn	Joseph	4	1		1		2	2		1				11		
Lincoln	14	28	Smith	Jonathan			1		1		2			1			5		
Lincoln	14	29	Hoar	Samuel		3	1	1	1	2		1		1			10		
Lincoln	14	30	Underwood	Moses					1	1		1		1			4		
Lincoln	14	31	Carter	Benjamin	1		1	1		3			1				7		
Lincoln	14	32	Tower	Daniel			1						1				2		
Lincoln	14	33	Laurence	William	2	2			1	2	2		1				10		
Lincoln	14	34	Turner	Henry	2			1	1	1				1			5		
Lincoln	14	35	Billings	Joseph Jr	1	1		1		2	2		1				8		
Lincoln	14	36	Tower	Jonathan	3			1			1		1				6		
Lincoln	14	37	Hollowell	Benjamin	1			1		3			1				6		
Lincoln	14	38	Baker	Jacob		2			1	2	1		1				7		
Lincoln	14	39	Bemis	Amos	1			1		3			1				6		
Lincoln	15	1	Smith	*amiah	2	2	1		1			2	1				9		
Lincoln	15	2	Stearns	Charles	2	2			2	2	2	1	1	1			13		
Lincoln	15	3	Weston	Daniel	2			1		1			1				5		
Lincoln	15	4	Weston	Zacariah			2	1					2	1			6		
Lincoln	15	5	Cole	Abraham	1	1		1		2			1	1			7		
Lincoln	15	6	Adams	John					1					1	1		3		
Lincoln	15	7	Adams	Jonas		1		1		2	2						6		
Lincoln	15	8	Emes	Ephraim	1	1		1					1				4		
Lincoln	15	9	Gage	Lydia	1								1	1			3		
Lincoln	15	10	Estey	John	1	1		1		2			1				6		
Lincoln	15	11	Lawrence	Love		1						2	1	1			5		
Lincoln	15	12	Jones	Jacob				1					1				2		
Lincoln	15	13	Matthews	Abner	1			1			1		1				4		
Lincoln	15	14	Child	Elijah				1					1	1			3		
Lincoln	15	15	Child	Joshua		1	1		1		1	1	1				6		
Lincoln	15	16	Wheeler	Edmund			1	2	1				1				5		
Lincoln	15	17	Wheeler	Thomas	1	1		1		1			1				5		
Lincoln	15	18	Meriam	James				1					1				2		
Lincoln	15	19	Child	Elisha	2			1	1	1			1				5		
Lincoln	15	20	Child	Anna									1	1			2		
Lincoln	15	21	Bemis	Joel	2			1		2	1		1				7		
Lincoln	15	22	Brook	Timothy		1			2			1		1			5		
Lincoln	15	23	Baker	Amos Jr	1		1						1				3		
Lincoln	15	24	Brook	Timothy Jr			1	1					1				3		
Lincoln	15	25	Brooks	Eleazer		1	1		1			2		2			7		
Lincoln	15	26	Wheeler	Abner	1	1	3		1		2	1		1			10		

TOWN	PG#	LN#	LAST NAME	FIRST NAME	FREE WHITE MALES under 10	10 to 16	16 to 26	26 to 45	45 and over	FREE WHITE FEMALES under 10	10 to 16	16 to 26	26 to 45	45 and over	TOTAL ALL OTHER	TOTAL SLAVES	TOTALS	DISTRICT/ TOWNSHIP	NOTES
Littleton	201	1	Hunt	Peter			1	1						1			3		
Littleton	201	2	Bulkely	Joseph	2		1			1			1				5		
Littleton	201	3	Bulkely	Charles				1						1			2		
Littleton	201	4	Tuttle	John			1		1	2	2	2	1	1			10		
Littleton	201	5	Grimes	William		1	1	1				1		1			5		
Littleton	201	6	Hartwell	Simon	2		1			2			2				7		
Littleton	201	7	Powers	Robert				1				1		1			3		
Littleton	201	8	Wood	Martin			1										1		
Littleton	201	9	Priest	Jacob	3	2	1	1			1		2				10		
Littleton	201	10	Longley	Anna										1			1		
Littleton	201	11	Hartwell	Daniel	1		1	1			2		1				6		
Littleton	201	12	Farmer	Nathaniel		1		1					1	1			4		
Littleton	201	13	Hunt	Jane										1			1		
Littleton	201	14	Harwood	Joseph	1	2			1	2		1		1			8		
Littleton	201	15	Reed	Potter		1		1		3			1	1			7		
Littleton	201	16	Hoar	Oliver	4		1	1		1		1	1				9		
Littleton	201	17	Hoar	Heber	2		2			2			1				7		
Littleton	201	18	Baker	Edward	1		1			2		1	1				7		
Littleton	201	19	Hoar	Abel			1			3			1				5		
Littleton	201	20	Chase	Francis										1			1		
Littleton	201	21	Foster	Edmond	3	2		1		2	2		2				12		
Littleton	201	22	Whitcomb	Oliver				1		1			2	1			5		
Littleton	201	23	Whitcomb	John	3	2		1			1	1	1				9		
Littleton	201	24	Kelley	Nathan	2		1			1			1				5		
Littleton	201	25	Dix	John	1		1		2	1			1	1			7		
Littleton	201	26	Hoping	Thomas	2	1		1		3			1				8		
Littleton	201	27	Rogers	Daniel		1			1	2	1						5		
Littleton	202	1	Reed	Daniel		1		1	1	1			1				5		
Littleton	202	2	Reed	Thomas Jr	2			2		2			1				7		
Littleton	202	3	Warren	James	1			1		2			1				5		
Littleton	202	4	Dutton	James	1			1			1			1			4		
Littleton	202	5	Hartwell	Thomas	3		1		1	2	1	1	1				10		
Littleton	202	6	Hoar	Peter		1		1		2			1				5		
Littleton	202	7	Rice	Daniel	2	1			2	3	1		1	1			11		
Littleton	202	8	Williams	Miriam											1		1		
Littleton	202	9	Newell	Jonathan A.	1	1		1			1	1					5		
Littleton	202	10	Tuttle	William	3	1	2		1	1		3	1				12		
Littleton	202	11	Fagon	Mentus											1		1		
Littleton	202	12	Tuttle	Samuel	1	1		1		3	2		1	1			10		
Littleton	202	13	Herwood	Vilet											4		4		
Littleton	202	14	Wilson	Henry	1			1		2			1				5		
Littleton	202	15	Howell	Jesse	1		1	1		1		1					5		
Littleton	202	16	Holden	Phinehas	1		2	1		1		1			1		7		
Littleton	202	17	Proctor	Nathaniel				1					1				2		
Littleton	202	18	Proctor	Nathaniel Jr.	2	1		1		1	1	1	1				8		
Littleton	202	19	Fletcher	Joseph		1	3	1		2	1		1				9		
Littleton	202	20	Warren	Elizabeth									1	1			2		
Littleton	202	21	Cogswell	Jeremiah		2		1		2	2		1				9		
Littleton	202	22	Lawrence	David	1		1	1		1			2		1		7		
Littleton	202	23	Bracket	Samuel	2	1	1		1	2			1				8		
Littleton	202	24	Baley	Joseph	3			1		1		1					6		
Littleton	202	25	Bowers	Lucy	2					1	1		1				5		
Littleton	202	26	Wright	Ezekiel	3			1		3			2	1			10		
Littleton	202	27	Sawtell	Mercy	1								1	1			3		
Littleton	202	28	Woods	Phillips				1		1	1						3		
Littleton	202	29	Flagg	Daniel		1	1			2		1					5		
Littleton	202	30	Sanger	David	2		1							1			4		
Littleton	202	31	Spalding	Isaac				1						1			2		
Littleton	202	32	Spalding	David			1						1				2		
Littleton	202	33	Lindley	James											2		2		
Littleton	202	34	Young	William		1		1		2	1	1					6		
Littleton	202	35	Raymond	Joseph	3		1						1				5		
Littleton	202	36	Jacobs	Braddock	1		1			3			1				6		
Littleton	202	37	Russell	John			1	1		1			3				6		
Littleton	202	38	Wilson	Charles	1			1		3			1				6		
Littleton	202	39	Russell	Thomas				1			1		1	1			4		
Littleton	202	40	Dix	Benjamin	2	3	1					1	1				8		
Littleton	202	41	Hartwell	John	3			1		1	2	2	1	1			11		
Littleton	202	42	Haskell	Solomon		1		1		1	1			1			5		
Littleton	202	43	Davis	Jonathan				1						1			2		
Littleton	202	44	Warren	Samson		2	1		2	1	1	2	1	1			11		
Littleton	202	45	Durant	Henry	1	1			1					1			4		
Littleton	202	46	Ingols	Daniel	1	1			1	2			2	1			8		
Littleton	202	47	Adams	Joseph	1		1	1		4			1				8		
Littleton	202	48	Treadwell	Tane			1						2	1			4		
Littleton	202	49	Wright	Peter	3			1		2	1		1				8		
Littleton	202	50	Elsworth	Edward			1	1						1			3		
Littleton	203	1	Jewett	Aquilla		1		1				1		1			4		
Littleton	203	2	Jewett	Israel H.			1			1		1					3		

69

TOWN	PG#	LN#	LAST NAME	FIRST NAME	FREE WHITE MALES under 10	10 to 16	16 to 26	26 to 45	45 and over	FREE WHITE FEMALES under 10	10 to 16	16 to 26	26 to 45	45 and over	TOTAL ALL OTHER	TOTAL SLAVES	TOTALS	DISTRICT/ TOWNSHIP	NOTES
Littleton	203	3	Sanderson	Samuel	1			1		1	1		1				5		
Littleton	203	4	Pingery	Stephen	3	1		1	1	2		1	1	1			11		
Littleton	203	5	Porter	John	1	1			1			1		1			5		
Littleton	203	6	Wright	Ephraim	3			1		1	2		1				8		
Littleton	203	7	Shierer	William				1						1			2		
Littleton	203	8	Whitcomb	Jonathan		2	2	1	1		1	4	1	1			13		
Littleton	203	9	Humfries	John		1		1			2	2		1			7		
Littleton	203	10	Baker	Ezra	2			1		2	2		1				8		
Littleton	203	11	Sprague	Hezekiah	1			1					1				3		
Littleton	203	12	Wood	Jane		1				1			1				3		
Littleton	203	13	Lawrence	Abijah	1		1		1	1		1					5		
Littleton	203	14	White	John	1			1		2		1					5		
Littleton	203	15	White	Samuel	1	1		1		5		1					9		
Littleton	203	16	White	Elenor								1	1	1			3		
Littleton	203	17	Farnsworth	Edmond	1	1		1		1				2			6		
Littleton	203	18	Brooks	Matthew	1	1	1		2			3		2			10		
Littleton	203	19	Humfries	Richard				1				1	1				3		
Littleton	203	20	Gardner	Bela			1						1				2		
Littleton	203	21	Proctor	John	2			1		2			1				6		
Littleton	203	22	Wood	Samuel		1	1	1		1			1				5		
Littleton	203	23	Wood	Josiah	1			1					1				3		
Littleton	203	24	Tulle	Samson				1		2	1	1					5		
Littleton	203	25	Brown	Abel			1				1		1				3		
Littleton	203	26	Kidder	Francis	3	1	2	2	1		2	1	1		1		14		
Littleton	203	27	White	Joseph	2			1		3			1				7		
Littleton	203	28	Wright	Jotham			1				1						2		
Littleton	203	29	Webber	Job	2			1		2			1		1		7		
Littleton	203	30	Vinal	Christian		1							1				2		
Littleton	203	31	Reed	Peter	2			1		4	1		1				9		
Littleton	203	32	Kimball	Daniel	1	1	3		1	3	1			1			11		
Littleton	203	33	Reed	Thomas		1		1		1	2		1				6		
Littleton	203	34	Tenney	John	1		1	1		3			1				7		
Littleton	203	35	Reed	Samuel		1	2	1					1				5		
Littleton	203	36	Vinal	Melzer	2			1	1	3			1	1			9		
Littleton	203	37	Cowing	Anna	1					1	1	1					4		
Littleton	203	38	Litchfield	Andrew	1			1		1							3		
Littleton	203	39	Litchfield	Penelope							1	1		1			3		
Littleton	203	40	Vinal	Luftanus	1			1				1					3		
Littleton	203	41	Proctor	Simeon Jr	1			1		3	1		1				7		
Littleton	203	42	Proctor	Simeon				1						1			2		
Littleton	203	43	Proctor	William		1		1					1				3		
Littleton	204	1	Freeman	Jacob											3		3		
Littleton	204	2	Harris	Noah			1	1					1	1			4		
Littleton	204	3	Johnson	William	4	2		1	1	2		1	1	1			13		
Littleton	204	4	Tenney	Stephen	2			2		1			2				7		
Littleton	204	5	Tenney	William				1						1			2		
Littleton	204	6	Merriam	Willard		1		1						1			3		
Littleton	204	7	Flint	Josiah			1					1					2		
Littleton	204	8	Dole	Lemuel	1			1		3	1		1				7		
Littleton	204	9	Flint	Willard	1	1		1				1					4		
Littleton	204	10	Jewett	Lucy									1	1			2		
Littleton	204	11	Robbins	Joseph				1					1		1		3		
Littleton	204	12	Robbins	Peter				1									1		
Littleton	204	13	Fletcher	Samuel	2			1				1					4		
Littleton	204	14	Allen	Zadock		1		1		1			1				4		
Littleton	204	15	Robbins	Benjamin				1					1	1			3		
Littleton	204	16	Harding	Jesse		1		1						1			3		
Littleton	204	17	Crosby	Michael	2			1		3			1				7		
Littleton	204	18	Beard	Ithamer	1	1	2	1		1			1				7		
Littleton	204	19	Wheeler	Thomas	2			1		2		1	1				7		
Littleton	204	20	Worster	Benjamin		1	1	1				1	1	2			7		
Littleton	204	21	Worster	Bridges	1			1				1					3		
Littleton	204	22	Tuttle	Daniel	2	1	1	1		1	1		1				8		
Littleton	204	23	Tuttle	Jeremiah	2		1	1				1					5		
Littleton	204	24	Patch	John		1	1		1		1	1		1			6		
Littleton	204	25	Patch	Abraham				1					1				2		
Littleton	204	26	Patch	Moses		1		1		2	1		1				6		
Littleton	204	27	Jewett	Joseph	2			1		1			1				5		
Littleton	204	28	Hoar	Paul	1	2		1				2		1			7		
Littleton	204	29	Hoar	Samuel Jr	2		2		2	1	1		1				9		
Littleton	204	30	Keyes	Solomon		1	1			2			1				5		
Littleton	204	31	Wheeler	Peter				2						1			3		
Littleton	204	32	Fuller	Ebenezer W.	2			1					1				4		
Littleton	204	33	Tenney	Cheney				1					1	1			3		
Littleton	205	1	Jennings	Stephen		1		1			1	1	1	1			6		
Littleton	205	2	Blanchard	Abigail	1	1	3				2		1	1			9		
Littleton	205	3	Brown	Stephen	3		1	1					1				6		
Littleton	205	4	Patch	Isaac	1	1		1						1			4		
Littleton	205	5	Patch	Hannah									1	1			2		

TOWN	PG#	LN#	LAST NAME	FIRST NAME	FREE WHITE MALES					FREE WHITE FEMALES					TOTAL ALL OTHER	TOTAL SLAVES	TOTALS	DISTRICT/ TOWNSHIP	NOTES
					under 10	10 to 16	16 to 26	26 to 45	45 and over	under 10	10 to 16	16 to 26	26 to 45	45 and over					
Littleton	205	6	Cobleigh	Nathaniel	1			1		2			1				5		
Littleton	205	7	Cobleigh	Rachel	2			1					1	1			5		
Littleton	205	8	Cobleigh	John	2			1				1					4		
Littleton	205	9	Cobleigh	Mary									1				1		
Littleton	205	10	Whitcomb	Daniel		1			1				1				3		
Littleton	205	11	Hartwell	John Jr	2	1	1		1	2			1	1			9		
Littleton	205	12	Taylor	Elizabeth										1			1		
Littleton	205	13	Wood	John	1			2		1		1	2				8		

TOWN	PG#	LN#	HEADS OF HOUSEHOLD		FREE WHITE MALES					FREE WHITE FEMALES					TOTAL ALL OTHER	TOTAL SLAVES	TOTALS	DISTRICT/ TOWNSHIP	NOTES
			LAST NAME	FIRST NAME	under 10	10 to 16	16 to 26	26 to 45	45 and over	under 10	10 to 16	16 to 26	26 to 45	45 and over					
Malden	93	1	Ally	John			1										1		
Malden	93	2	Allen	John			1						1				2		
Malden	93	3	Bradbury	Wymond			2	1					2	1			6		
Malden	93	4	Bradbury	Cha'	1		1			1			1				4		
Malden	93	5	Breed	Nathan	1			1		2			1				5		
Malden	93	6	Briant	John			1				1		1				3		
Malden	93	7	Breeden	John			1			2			1				4		
Malden	93	8	Bell	Eliza'									1				1		
Malden	93	9	Buckman	Benja'		1	1	1			1		2				6		
Malden	93	10	Buckman	Aaron	1	2	1		1	1	1	1		1			9		
Malden	93	11	Baldwin	John	1		1						1				3		
Malden	93	12	Burdit	Nathan					1	1	1			1			4		
Malden	93	13	Banks	Wm				1					1				2		
Malden	93	14	Blodget	Phins	1			1		2			1				5		
Malden	93	15	Barrett	Jos'	1		1		1	3	1		1				8		
Malden	93	16	Bulfinch	Jno'				1									1		
Malden	93	17	Bacon	Wm	1			1					1				3		
Malden	93	18	Blanchard	Sylvanus		2		1					1	1			5		
Malden	93	19	Burdit	Saml	2	1	2	1		1	1		1				9		
Malden	93	20	Burdit	Hannah										1			1		
Malden	93	21	Barrett	Jona'			1			1			1				3		
Malden	93	22	Brintnal	Rebecca										1			1		
Malden	93	23	Burdit	Tho' Jr			1										1		
Malden	93	24	Barret	Mary		1	1				1	1		1		2	7		
Malden	93	25	Burdit	Tho'	1			1					1	1			4		
Malden	93	26	Buckman	Elisha			1			1			1				3		
Malden	93	27	Becham	John				1					1	2			4		
Malden	93	28	Barnes	Robt				1					3	1			5		
Malden	93	29	Blany	Andros	1		1						1				3		
Malden	93	30	Blany	Benja'			1	1						1			3		
Malden	93	31	Blany	Benja' Jr			1			1			1				3		
Malden	93	32	Cheever	Jos'	2				1	1		1	3	1			9		
Malden	93	33	Connery	Jno'		1		1		2			1				5		
Malden	93	34	Clarenbone	Tho'				1									1		
Malden	93	35	Chittendon	Clavin		1		1		1				1			4		
Malden	93	36	Chittendon	Isaac	1			1						1			3		
Malden	93	37	Crane	John	3	1	1		1	1		1		2			10		
Malden	93	38	Coleman	Dorothy										1			1		
Malden	93	39	Call	John		1		1		1	1		1				5		
Malden	93	40	Cox	Unite	2	3			1	2		1		1			10		
Malden	93	41	Dexter	Wm		1			1	1		2		1			6		
Malden	93	42	Dexter	Rich'	2		1	1		2		1	1	1			9		
Malden	93	43	Dager	Jos'			1			2			1				4		
Malden	93	44	Dager	Jno'				1						1			2		
Malden	93	45	Dyer	Jno'	1			1		1	1		1				5		
Malden	93	46	Dyer	James	1		1			1	1	1					5		
Malden	94	1	Dyer	Jos'	3		1			1			1	1			7		
Malden	94	2	Dyer	Naomi										1			1		
Malden	94	3	Dimond	Hall				1					1			3	5		
Malden	94	4	Edmands	John	2		1	1		2	1		1				8		
Malden	94	5	Everet	Epm	1								1		1		4		
Malden	94	6	Eaton	Sarah									1	1			2		
Malden	94	7	Emerson	Wm	2	2			1	1	1	1		1			9		
Malden	94	8	Faulkner	David	1			1		2			1				5		
Malden	94	9	Faulkner	Benja'	1		1	2		3		1					8		
Malden	94	10	Forbes	Cha'				1									1		
Malden	94	11	Floyd	Jos'	1	2			1	2		1	1	1			9		
Malden	94	12	Green	John				1		1				1			3		
Malden	94	13	Grover	Hanh										1			1		
Malden	94	14	Green	Lois								1		1			2		
Malden	94	15	Grover	Peter			1	1									2		
Malden	94	16	Green	Barnard	2				1			1	1				6		
Malden	94	17	Green	Aaron	1	1		1					2				5		
Malden	94	18	Green	Ezra	1			1		1			1				4		
Malden	94	19	Green	James				1					1	1			3		
Malden	94	20	Green	Wm	1			1		1	1		1				5		
Malden	94	21	Green	Eliza'									1	1			2		
Malden	94	22	Green	Jonas		1		1			1		1				4		
Malden	94	23	Green	Phins		1		1				1		1			4		
Malden	94	24	Green	Phins Jr		1	1	1		2	1	1					6		
Malden	94	25	Green	Saml		1	2		1				1	1	1		7		
Malden	94	26	Gill	Joshua				1					1	1			3		
Malden	94	27	Grover	Martha										1			1		
Malden	94	28	Hersey	John	1			1					1	1			4		
Malden	94	29	Hemenway	Israel	1			1		1			1				4		
Malden	94	30	Howard	John	1	1		1		1	1		1				6		
Malden	94	31	Howard	Jabez	1			1		2			1				5		
Malden	94	32	Howard	Wm				1					1	1			3		
Malden	94	33	Howard	Eunice								1					1		

TOWN	PG#	LN#	LAST NAME	FIRST NAME	FREE WHITE MALES under 10	10 to 16	16 to 26	26 to 45	45 and over	FREE WHITE FEMALES under 10	10 to 16	16 to 26	26 to 45	45 and over	TOTAL ALL OTHER	TOTAL SLAVES	TOTALS	DISTRICT/ TOWNSHIP	NOTES
Malden	94	34	Howard	Jos'	1	1		1		1			2				6		
Malden	94	35	Howard	Ezra					1		1	2		1			5		
Malden	94	36	Howard	Amos					1			2		1			4		
Malden	94	37	Howard	Amos Jr	2	1		1		2	2	1					9		
Malden	94	38	Hill	Tho'	1			1		1		1	1				5		
Malden	94	39	Hill	Benja'				1									1		
Malden	94	40	Hill	Cha'	1		1	1		2	3	1					9		
Malden	94	41	Hill	Cha' Jr			1			1		1			1		4		
Malden	94	42	Hunt	Tho'		1		1		1			1				4		
Malden	94	43	Hart	Asa	3		1						1				5		
Malden	94	44	Hovy	Nathan		1											1		
Malden	94	45	Hall	Chri		1											1		
Malden	94	46	Hatch	Lou'									1				1		
Malden	94	47	Hitchens	James	1		1			2		1					5		
Malden	95	1	Haskins	Wm	1		1			2		1					5		
Malden	95	2	Hatch	Nalar		1	1	1				1	2				6		
Malden	95	3	Harnden	Jno'				1					1				2		
Malden	95	4	Harnden	Eben	1	1		1		1	1	1	2				8		
Malden	95	5	Hay	John	2		1						1				4		
Malden	95	6	Holden	Tho'	3	1							1				5		
Malden	95	7	Haskins	Robt		1				1	1	1					4		
Malden	95	8	Jenkins	Jno'				1				1	1				3		
Malden	95	9	Jenkins	Abigl									1				1		
Malden	95	10	Johnson	Tho'			1	1									2		
Malden	95	11	Jackson	Isaac		1											1		
Malden	95	12	Knowah	Jona'				1					1				2		
Malden	95	13	Knowah	Ann	2					1		1					4		
Malden	95	14	Knight	Mary									1				1		
Malden	95	15	Lear	Peter	1		1			3		1					6		
Malden	95	16	Lear	John	1		1			1	1	1					5		
Malden	95	17	Ladd	Wm	2		1			1	1		4		2		11		
Malden	95	18	Learned	Tho		1											1		
Malden	95	19	Leatherly	Saml		2		1			1	1	1				6		
Malden	95	20	Lynde	Rachl								1	1				2		
Malden	95	21	Lynde	Mary									1				1		
Malden	95	22	Lynde	Jabez	1			1					1				3		
Malden	95	23	Lynde	Benja'	1	1		1		2	2	1					8		
Malden	95	24	Lynde	Jos'				1			1	1	1				4		
Malden	95	25	Lynde	Jso'	1		1			1		1					4		
Malden	95	26	Lynde	Nathn		1		1					1		2		5		
Malden	95	27	Lynde	Nathn Jr	3		1	1		1	1	1	1				9		
Malden	95	28	Lynde	Jos' Jr			1										1		
Malden	95	29	Merrill	Moses			1										1		
Malden	95	30	Merchant	Mary									1				1		
Malden	95	31	Martin	Mary				1				1	4				6		
Malden	95	32	Nickols	Eben	2		1			3		1					7		
Malden	95	33	Nickols	David			1			1		1					3		
Malden	95	34	Nickols	Jno'	3			1		2		1	1				8		
Malden	95	35	Nickols	Nathn			1			3		1	2		1		8		
Malden	95	36	Nickols	Wm	3		1	1				1	1				7		
Malden	95	37	Neagles	Ann									1				1		
Malden	95	38	Neagles	Micah	3	1		1		1	1		1	1			9		
Malden	95	39	Newell	Mary									1				1		
Malden	95	40	Newell	Eliz'	1	1	1			1			1				5		
Malden	95	41	Newell	Edw'				1									1		
Malden	95	42	Oakes	Edw'				1					1				2		
Malden	95	43	Oakes	Nehem			1										1		
Malden	95	44	Oakes	Jona'		1	2	1		2	2	1					9		
Malden	95	45	Oakes	Esther						1	1		1				3		
Malden	95	46	Oliver	Robt	3	2		1		1	2	1					10		
Malden	96	1	Oliver	Edw'			1	1									2		
Malden	96	2	Polly	Saml	1		1	1		2	1	1					7		
Malden	96	3	Paul	John					1			1	1				3		
Malden	96	4	Phillips	Fra'	1	1		1					2				5		
Malden	96	5	Perkins	Jacob	4	1	2	1		2	2		1	1			14		
Malden	96	6	Popkins	Jno'	1	1		1		2	2	2	1				10		
Malden	96	7	Pain	Jno'				1		1			1				3		
Malden	96	8	Pain	Step'				1					1				2		
Malden	96	9	Pain	Step' Jr	1		2	1		1		2	1				8		
Malden	96	10	Paine	Eben	1			1		1		1	1				5		
Malden	96	11	Parker	Abigl									1				1		
Malden	96	12	Parker	Amos		1											1		
Malden	96	13	Parker	Jno'		1											1		
Malden	96	14	Parker	Wm		1	1										2		
Malden	96	15	Peirce	Jos'		1											1		
Malden	96	16	Parker	Jacob	1		2	1				1	1				6		
Malden	96	17	Parker	May									1	2			3		
Malden	96	18	Pratt	John	1	1		1		1		1	2				7		
Malden	96	19	Pratt	John	1	2	1	1		3	1		1				10		

73

TOWN	PG#	LN#	LAST NAME	FIRST NAME	FREE WHITE MALES					FREE WHITE FEMALES					TOTAL ALL OTHER	TOTAL SLAVES	TOTALS	DISTRICT/ TOWNSHIP	NOTES
					under 10	10 to 16	16 to 26	26 to 45	45 and over	under 10	10 to 16	16 to 26	26 to 45	45 and over					
Malden	96	20	Pratt	Nath'	3		1	1		1			1				7		
Malden	96	21	Pratt	Jacob	1	2	3	1		2		1	1				11		
Malden	96	22	Pratt	Tho'					1					1			2		
Malden	96	23	Pratt	Tho' Jr			1										1		
Malden	96	24	Pratt	Jacob Jr			1										1		
Malden	96	25	Reed	James				1		1	1	1					4		
Malden	96	26	Richardson	Wm			1										1		
Malden	96	27	Rand	Edmd Jr			1										1		
Malden	96	28	Rand	Edmd					1					1			2		
Malden	96	29	Ramsdal	John					1					1			2		
Malden	96	30	Ramsdal	John Jr	2			1					1				4		
Malden	96	31	Rantam	Mary										1			1		
Malden	96	32	Reynolds	Jno'				1									1		
Malden	96	33	Richardson	Bradbury			1										1		
Malden	96	34	Sargeant	Ezra	1		1	1				1		2			6		
Malden	96	35	Sargeant	Debor'										3			3		
Malden	96	36	Sargeant	David				1					2	1			4		
Malden	96	37	Sargeant	David Jr				1		2	2		1				7		
Malden	96	38	Sargeant	David 3rd			1			1		1					3		
Malden	96	39	Sargeant	Amos	3	1	1	1		1	1		1	1			10		
Malden	96	40	Sargeant	Mary										1			1		
Malden	96	41	Sargeant	Winslow		1	1	1	1		1	2		1			8		
Malden	96	42	Sargeant	Ruth										1			1		
Malden	96	43	Sargeant	Jos'				1									1		
Malden	96	44	Sargeant	Nath'			1										1		
Malden	96	45	Sprague	John	2	1	1		1	1	1		1				8		
Malden	96	46	Sprague	Phins				1						1			2		
Malden	96	47	Sargeant	Benja'			1			1							2		
Malden	97	1	Sprague	Phins Jr	1		1		1	2	1	1		2			9		
Malden	97	2	Sprague	Cotton		1		1		3		1					6		
Malden	97	3	Sprague	Jona	1	2		1		3	1		1				9		
Malden	97	4	Sprague	Step'	4			1		1	1		1				8		
Malden	97	5	Sprague	John Jr			1										1		
Malden	97	6	Smith	Lydia									1				1		
Malden	97	7	Shute	Pheebe										1			1		
Malden	97	8	Shute	Saml				1		1			1				3		
Malden	97	9	Shute	Han'									4				4		
Malden	97	10	Shute	Geo'	1			1		1			1				4		
Malden	97	11	Shute	Solo'				1		1			1				3		
Malden	97	12	Shute	Wm			1										1		
Malden	97	13	Shute	Tho'			1										1		
Malden	97	14	Shute	Jacob		1	1							1			3		
Malden	97	15	Shute	Richd		1	1	1				1	1	1			6		
Malden	97	16	Shute	Eben				1									1		
Malden	97	17	Shute	Isaac		1											1		
Malden	97	18	Sweetsir	James	1			1		1	1		1				5		
Malden	97	19	Tufts	Mary				2						1			3		
Malden	97	20	Tufts	David	4	2		1		2		1					10		
Malden	97	21	Tufts	Step'	1	1		1		1	1	1	1				7		
Malden	97	22	Tufts	Josiah	1	1		1	2			1					6		
Malden	97	23	Tufts	Saml	1	1	1	1		1	2		1				8		
Malden	97	24	Townsend	Eben		1											1		
Malden	97	25	Townsend	John	1			1		3	1	1					7		
Malden	97	26	Townsend	Esther								1		1			2		
Malden	97	27	Todd	Joshua		1											1		
Malden	97	28	Trevalley	John	3			1					1				5		
Malden	97	29	Upham	Wm		1		1		1	1			1			5		
Malden	97	30	Upham	Lois										1			1		
Malden	97	31	Upham	Sarah	1					2			1				4		
Malden	97	32	Upham	Lydia										1			1		
Malden	97	33	Upham	Amos		1	1	1			1			1			5		
Malden	97	34	Upham	Amos Jr	2		1				1						4		
Malden	97	35	Upham	Saml L.	1		1			1	1						4		
Malden	97	36	Upham	Jesse			1	1						1			3		
Malden	97	37	Vinton	Mary									1	1			2		
Malden	97	38	Wait	John				1									1		
Malden	97	39	Wait	Jno' Jr				1						1			2		
Malden	97	40	Wait	Jno' 3rd	1			1		2			1				5		
Malden	97	41	Wait	Saml				1				1	1				3		
Malden	97	42	Wait	Saml' Jr			1			1	1	1					4		
Malden	97	43	Wait	Andr'		1						1					2		
Malden	97	44	Wait	Aaron	1	1						1					3		
Malden	97	45	Wait	Wm				1						1			2		
Malden	97	46	Wait	Wm Jr	1			1		1	2	1					6		
Malden	97	47	Wait	David				1									1		
Malden	98	1	Wait	Isaac			1										1		
Malden	98	2	Wait	Micah	1		3	1		1	1		1				8		
Malden	98	3	Wait	James	2	1					1						4		
Malden	98	4	Wait	Eben			1		1			1	1	1			5		

TOWN	PG#	LN#	LAST NAME	FIRST NAME	under 10	10 to 16	16 to 26	26 to 45	45 and over	under 10	10 to 16	16 to 26	26 to 45	45 and over	TOTAL ALL OTHER	TOTAL SLAVES	TOTALS	DISTRICT/ TOWNSHIP	NOTES
					FREE WHITE MALES					FREE WHITE FEMALES									
Malden	98	5	Wait	Tho'		1			1			1		1			4		
Malden	98	6	Wait	Ezra			2		1	1				1			5		
Malden	98	7	Wait	Pheebe						2	1						3		
Malden	98	8	Wait	Mary										1			1		
Malden	98	9	Wait	Ruth										1			1		
Malden	98	10	Wait	Sarah										1			1		
Malden	98	11	Wait	Step'			1		1					1			3		
Malden	98	12	Wait	Step' Jr				1					1				2		
Malden	98	13	Wait	Nathn	1		1		1				2	1			6		
Malden	98	14	Wait	Danl	1		2	1		1		1					6		
Malden	98	15	Wait	Ezra Jr	1	1	1	1		1	1	1					7		
Malden	98	16	Wait	Benja'	1				1		1			2			5		
Malden	98	17	Wilson	Saml	1	1	1	1		1		1					6		
Malden	98	18	Wealer	Ann										1			1		
Malden	98	19	Wade	Edw	1		1		1	1		1		1			6		
Malden	98	20	Willis	Eliakm				1						1			2		
Malden	98	21	Waters	Danl		1	2		1			1		1	1		7		
Malden	98	22	Whittemore	Jos'			1		1					1			3		
Malden	98	23	Williams	Jane						2		1					3		
Malden	98	24	Wealer	Saml	1	1		1			1	1					5		
Malden	98	25	Wealer	Isaac	2			1				1					4		
Malden	98	26	Wade	Fitch			1										1		
Malden	98	27	Watts	Isaac	1			1				1	1				3		
Malden	98	28	Young	Tho'				1									1		

TOWN	PG#	LN#	HEADS OF HOUSEHOLD LAST NAME	FIRST NAME	FREE WHITE MALES under 10	10 to 16	16 to 26	26 to 45	45 and over	FREE WHITE FEMALES under 10	10 to 16	16 to 26	26 to 45	45 and over	TOTAL ALL OTHER	TOTAL SLAVES	TOTALS	DISTRICT/ TOWNSHIP	NOTES
Marlborough	187	1	Barns	Edward	1		1		1	2	1	1		1			8		
Marlborough	187	2	Wood	Peter					1	1				1			3		
Marlborough	187	3	How	Thomas					1					1			2		
Marlborough	187	4	How	Francis	1		2		1	2	2		1				9		
Marlborough	187	5	How	Francis Jr			1				1						2		
Marlborough	187	6	Stevens	Francis			2		2	1	1			1			7		
Marlborough	187	7	Woods	Sarah		1								1			2		
Marlborough	187	8	Guliker	Jane							1	1		1			3		
Marlborough	187	9	Williams	Thomas	2			1					1				4		
Marlborough	187	10	Rice	William		1		1			1		1				4		
Marlborough	187	11	Sawin	Mannings					1					1			2		
Marlborough	187	12	Sawin	John	1		1		1		1			1			5		
Marlborough	187	13	Sherman	Isaac	1				1	2	1			1			6		
Marlborough	187	14	Cory	Enoch			1			1			1				3		
Marlborough	187	15	Brigham	Joseph Jr	1		2	1		3		2					9		
Marlborough	187	16	Prentiss	Nathaniel S.	3			1		1	1		1				7		
Marlborough	187	17	Cotting	Amos	5			1	1				1	2			11		
Marlborough	187	18	Bender	Peter		1	1	1			1	1		1			7		
Marlborough	187	19	Temple	David		1		2	1			1		1			6		
Marlborough	187	20	Maynard	Hezekiah	1	2	4	1	1			2		1			12		
Marlborough	187	21	Woods	Moses	1		1	1	1			2		1			7		
Marlborough	187	22	Barns	Stephen	2			1		1	1		1				6		
Marlborough	188	1	Caldwell	John	1	1		1					1				4		
Marlborough	188	2	Woodward	Moses				1				1					2		
Marlborough	188	3	Dexter	Mary			1			1			1	1			4		
Marlborough	188	4	Munroe	David Jr	1		3			1	1	1					7		
Marlborough	188	5	Cogswell	William	2	1	1		1	3	1	4		1			14		
Marlborough	188	6	Newton	Joseph				1				1					2		
Marlborough	188	7	Souther	Lucy		1	1				1		1				4		
Marlborough	188	8	Brigham	Jotham	2	1		1		1	1		1				7		
Marlborough	188	9	Rice	Noah	1	2	2		1	2	2	1		3			14		
Marlborough	188	10	How	Lovewell	1	2			1				1				5		
Marlborough	188	11	How	Simon		1		1	1	2			2	1			8		
Marlborough	188	12	How	Aaron	2			1		1			1				5		
Marlborough	188	13	Phillips	Nathaniel				1					1				2		
Marlborough	188	14	Rice	Benjamin		1	1	1	1	1			1	1			7		
Marlborough	188	15	Cook	Ananias		2		1		2	3		1				9		
Marlborough	188	16	Phelps	Roger	3		1	1		1	1		1				8		
Marlborough	188	17	Loring	William	1		1		1	1	4			1			9		
Marlborough	188	18	Packard	Asa	2	1		1		3		1	1	1			10		
Marlborough	188	19	Arnold	William	3		1	1		1			1	1			8		
Marlborough	188	20	Gibbon	Samuel	3		1	1		2			2				9		
Marlborough	188	21	Morse	Windsor	3			2		1			1	1			8		
Marlborough	188	22	Moore	Carley	2			1			1		1				5		
Marlborough	188	23	Rice	Ephraim B.	1			1		2	1	1					6		
Marlborough	188	24	How	Joseph Jr	1			1				1					3		
Marlborough	188	25	Smith	Zeduthun	1			1		1		1					4		
Marlborough	188	26	Bruce	James				1		1				1			3		
Marlborough	188	27	Bent	Peter		1		1			1						3		
Marlborough	188	28	Bent	Jabez		1		1			1		2				5		
Marlborough	188	29	Maynard	Elihu	1	1		1		3		1	1				8		
Marlborough	188	30	Maynard	Mary									2				2		
Marlborough	188	31	Brigham	Paul	3	2		1			1		1				8		
Marlborough	188	32	Brigham	Abner	2			1		1		1	1				6		
Marlborough	188	33	Brigham	Mary				1						1			2		
Marlborough	188	34	How	Luther				1									1		
Marlborough	188	35	Rice	Jabez	1	1		2			1		1				6		
Marlborough	188	36	Holyoke	Sarah	1						2		1				4		
Marlborough	188	37	Hall	Paul	1	1		1	1		1	1	1				7		
Marlborough	188	38	Bond	John	1	1		1		2			1				6		
Marlborough	188	39	Brigham	Warren		1		1		1		1	1	1			6		
Marlborough	188	40	Brigham	Joseph				1				1	1				3		
Marlborough	188	41	Ames	Moses		1		1		1	1		1				5		
Marlborough	189	1	Gassett	John		1		1					1				3		
Marlborough	189	2	Brown	Samuel	2			1		1	1		1				6		
Marlborough	189	3	How	Samuel	1		1		1			2		1			6		
Marlborough	189	4	Rice	Gershom	1		2		1	1	1		1				7		
Marlborough	189	5	Webster	James				1		3		1					5		
Marlborough	189	6	Hudson	Elijah				1						1			2		
Marlborough	189	7	Hudson	Francis			1				1						2		
Marlborough	189	8	Pease	Levi		1		1		4	1		1	1			9		
Marlborough	189	9	Russell	Oliver	2	1	1			2		1	1				9		
Marlborough	189	10	Bartley	Jonas		1	2		1	1		2		1			8		
Marlborough	189	11	Brigham	Mattathias R.			1	1					1				3		
Marlborough	189	12	Brigham	Noah				1		1			1				3		
Marlborough	189	13	Rice	Seth	1			1		2		1					5		
Marlborough	189	14	Cunningham	Simeon	2			1		2			1				6		
Marlborough	189	15	Baley	Samuel		1			1	1				1			4		
Marlborough	189	16	Felton	Joel	3	1	1	1	1		1		2				10		

TOWN	PG#	LN#	LAST NAME	FIRST NAME	FREE WHITE MALES					FREE WHITE FEMALES					TOTAL ALL OTHER	TOTAL SLAVES	TOTALS	DISTRICT/ TOWNSHIP	NOTES
					under 10	10 to 16	16 to 26	26 to 45	45 and over	under 10	10 to 16	16 to 26	26 to 45	45 and over					
Marlborough	189	17	Rice	Thomas	2	2	1		1			3	1	1			11		
Marlborough	189	18	Rice	Peter		1	1		1			1		1			5		
Marlborough	189	19	Rice	Eli			1					1					2		
Marlborough	189	20	Rice	Joel					1					1			2		
Marlborough	189	21	Weeks	William	2	1		1		2	1		1				8		
Marlborough	189	22	Wheeler	Asa	3			1	1	1			1				7		
Marlborough	189	23	Felton	Stephen	2	1	1		1			2	2				9		
Marlborough	189	24	Rice	Jonah	2		1		1	2	1		1				8		
Marlborough	189	25	How	Benjamin	3	1			1	1		1	1				8		
Marlborough	189	26	How	Abraham	2	1		1		1		1		1			7		
Marlborough	189	27	Rice	Nathan	1		1					1					3		
Marlborough	189	28	Biglow	William	3	2		1					1				8		
Marlborough	189	29	How	Eleazer	2			1				1	1	1			6		
Marlborough	189	30	Gates	William	1		2	1		1	2		1				8		
Marlborough	189	31	Gleason	James	1	1		1		3			1				7		
Marlborough	189	32	Gleason	Joseph				1			1		1				3		
Marlborough	189	33	Goodell	Abner	1	1	2	1		3	1	1	1	1			12		
Marlborough	189	34	Priest	Shadrick	2		1						1				4		
Marlborough	189	35	Moore	Edmond	1			1		2	1	1		1			7		
Marlborough	189	36	Brigham	Ashbel S.	1			1					1				3		
Marlborough	189	37	Boyd	William		1	2	1				2	2				8		
Marlborough	189	38	Stevens	Daniel Jr	1		1	1		1		1	1				6		
Marlborough	189	39	Benson	Lydia									1				1		
Marlborough	189	40	Loring	John	2	1			1	2	2		1				9		
Marlborough	190	1	Williams	George		1	1	1	3	1			1	1			9		
Marlborough	190	2	Williams	Betty						1			1	1			3		
Marlborough	190	3	Fay	Josiah	2	1		1		3			1				8		
Marlborough	190	4	Mack	John P.	1			1		1		1					4		
Marlborough	190	5	Gates	Elizabeth							1		1	1			3		
Marlborough	190	6	Brigham	Aaron	1			1		1	2		1				6		
Marlborough	190	7	Morse	Francis		1			1		1	1	1				5		
Marlborough	190	8	Barber	Ephraim			1		2		1		1				5		
Marlborough	190	9	How	Ephraim	2		2	1		1	1		1				8		
Marlborough	190	10	How	Elizabeth										1			1		
Marlborough	190	11	How	Mary										3			3		
Marlborough	190	12	Brigham	Asa				1	1					2			4		
Marlborough	190	13	Brigham	Lewis		1			1	2			1				5		
Marlborough	190	14	Brigham	Ithamer	3	2	1	1		1			1				9		
Marlborough	190	15	Brigham	Fortunalus	2	1		1		1	1	1	2	2			11		
Marlborough	190	16	How	Phinehas		1			1	1	1			1			5		
Marlborough	190	17	How	Sylvanus	2			1		1			1				5		
Marlborough	190	18	Taylor	John	2			1					2				5		
Marlborough	190	19	Carley	Silas				1		2	1	1		1			6		
Marlborough	190	20	Brown	Delivarance	1		1	1				1	1				5		
Marlborough	190	21	How	John Jr	2	2		1		2	1		1				9		
Marlborough	190	22	How	Archelas	3			1		1	1		1				7		
Marlborough	190	23	How	Gilbert				1				1					2		
Marlborough	190	24	Biglow	Gershom Jr	2			1		2	1		1				8		
Marlborough	190	25	Carley	Joseph	1			1						1			3		
Marlborough	190	26	Carley	Sarah										1			1		
Marlborough	190	27	Park	Thomas	1				1	2			1				5		
Marlborough	190	28	Carley	Job				1						2			3		
Marlborough	190	29	How	Noah					1		1			1			3		
Marlborough	190	30	How	Winslow	1			1		2			1				5		
Marlborough	190	31	How	Levi	1		1	1						1			4		
Marlborough	190	32	How	Aaron				1						1			2		
Marlborough	190	33	How	Fortunalus	3	2		1		2			1				9		
Marlborough	190	34	Biglow	Ivory	1	2			1	1		3		1			9		
Marlborough	190	35	Brigham	Caleb			2	1						1			4		
Marlborough	190	36	Stevens	Daniel		1		1		2	3		1				8		
Marlborough	191	1	Barns	Lovewell	4	1		1		1	1		1				9		
Marlborough	191	2	Barns	Sarah							1		1				2		
Marlborough	191	3	Phelps	Stephen	1			1				1					5		
Marlborough	191	4	Wilder	Eunice								1	1				2		
Marlborough	191	5	Bruce	Daniel	2	1		1		3	1		1				9		
Marlborough	191	6	Hudson	Stephen	1			1		3			1				6		
Marlborough	191	7	Gleason	Zacheus		1		1					1				3		
Marlborough	191	8	Whitney	Thomas	1	1	1			1		1					5		
Marlborough	191	9	Moore	Phinehas				1					1				2		
Marlborough	191	10	Fay	Micijah					1								1		
Marlborough	191	11	Newton	Jerusha					1					3			4		
Marlborough	191	12	Brigham	Solomon	1			1	2	5			2				11		
Marlborough	191	13	Brigham	Ivory				1				1					2		
Marlborough	191	14	Sawyer	Phinehas	1			1		4			1				7		
Marlborough	191	15	Cranston	Joel			2	2		1			1	1			7		
Marlborough	191	16	Bruce	Zeduthun			1			1		1					3		
Marlborough	191	17	Bruce	William				1		1		1		1			4		
Marlborough	191	18	Bruce	Nathaniel		1	1			1			1				4		
Marlborough	191	19	Felton	Silas			1					1					2		

TOWN	PG#	LN#	LAST NAME	FIRST NAME	M under 10	M 10 to 16	M 16 to 26	M 26 to 45	M 45 and over	F under 10	F 10 to 16	F 16 to 26	F 26 to 45	F 45 and over	TOTAL ALL OTHER	TOTAL SLAVES	TOTALS	DISTRICT/ TOWNSHIP	NOTES
Marlborough	191	20	Nurse	Francis	1			1		1		1					4		
Marlborough	191	21	Barnard	William	2	1		1		2	1		3	1			11		
Marlborough	191	22	Will	Ebenezer	1			1		2	1		1				6		
Marlborough	191	23	Barnard	Stephen	1			1						1			3		
Marlborough	191	24	Bruce	Moses	1		1					1					3		
Marlborough	191	25	Carr	Ephraim	1		1			1		1		1			5		
Marlborough	191	26	Goodenow	Jonathan					2					2			4		
Marlborough	191	27	Cox	Elisha	4			1					1				6		
Marlborough	191	28	Tayntor	John	3			1				2	1				7		
Marlborough	191	29	Smith	John			1	1	1					1			4		
Marlborough	191	30	Smith	William	2			1	1	2	3		1	1			11		
Marlborough	191	31	Smith	Jonas	1		1		1	1	1		1				6		
Marlborough	191	32	Priest	Benjamin	3	1		1			1		1				7		
Marlborough	191	33	Walnutt	Ephraim	3			1		1			1				6		
Marlborough	191	34	Priest	Abraham			1	1		1				1			4		
Marlborough	191	35	Brown	Isaac	2			1		1	1		1				6		
Marlborough	191	36	Hapgood	John		1	2		1	3	2						10		
Marlborough	191	37	Hardy	Rachel							1			1			2		
Marlborough	191	38	Hapgood	Jonathan	1	1	1	1		2	2		1	1			10		
Marlborough	191	39	How	Azlemas	2	2	2		1	1		2	1	1			12		
Marlborough	191	40	Stow	Joab		1	2	2		1	1	1					8		
Marlborough	191	41	Bruce	Jonathan	4	1		1		2			1				9		
Marlborough	192	1	Brigham	Ephraim	3	1		2		1		2					9		
Marlborough	192	2	Barns	Mary									1	1			2		
Marlborough	192	3	Rice	Elisha	2			1		2	1		1				7		
Marlborough	192	4	How	Joseph		1			1					1	1		4		
Marlborough	192	5	How	Joseph 3rd		1							1				2		
Marlborough	192	6	Tayntor	Jonathan				1					1	1			3		
Marlborough	192	7	Tayntor	Joseph			1						1				2		
Marlborough	192	8	Gleason	John				1					1	1			3		
Marlborough	192	9	Gleason	John Jr		1	1	1				2	1				6		
Marlborough	192	10	Barns	Solomon					1					1			2		
Marlborough	192	11	Barns	William	4		1	1		2	1	1	1				11		
Marlborough	192	12	How	William	1	1		1					1	1			5		
Marlborough	192	13	Manson	Loring	1		1	1		2			1				6		
Marlborough	192	14	Parker	John				1			1		1	1			4		
Marlborough	192	15	Winchester	Caleb			2	1					1				4		
Marlborough	192	16	How	Jonah	1			1		4			1				7		
Marlborough	192	17	Dexter	Charles	2			1				1					4		
Marlborough	192	18	Trobridge	Joseph	1	1		1		2			1				6		
Marlborough	192	19	Stow	Hannah		1						1	1				3		
Marlborough	192	20	Maynard	Simon	1		1	1					1	1			5		
Marlborough	192	21	Maynard	Benjamin		1		1		1		1	1	1			6		
Marlborough	192	22	Wesson	James			1	1	1				1	1			5		
Marlborough	192	23	Danton	Samuel			3		1	1				1			6		
Marlborough	192	24	Maynard	Ephraim	1		2		1	1	1			1			7		
Marlborough	192	25	Hapgood	Thomas		2	1							1			5		
Marlborough	192	26	Hapgood	Joseph	1	2			1	3	1		1				9		
Marlborough	192	27	Hapgood	Mary									1		2		3		
Marlborough	192	28	Peirce	John	1			1	1	3			1				7		
Marlborough	192	29	Willkins	Levi	2	1		1		2	2		1				9		
Marlborough	192	30	Wilkins	David	2	1		1		3	2		1				10		
Marlborough	192	31	Jewell	Silas 3rd			2			1		1					4		
Marlborough	192	32	Cranston	Lydia				1				1		1			3		
Marlborough	192	33	Wilkins	Edward	1			1		1	2	2	1				8		
Marlborough	192	34	Wilkins	Jonas	2		1			2	1	1	1				8		
Marlborough	192	35	Dunn	Lovewell		2		1					1				4		
Marlborough	192	36	Moore	Bezaleel					1				1	1			3		
Marlborough	192	37	Jewell	Silas					1				1				2		
Marlborough	192	38	Jewell	Silas Jr		1	2		2		1			1			7		
Marlborough	192	39	Jewell	Jacob	1	1		1		3	1		1				8		
Marlborough	192	40	Maynard	Levina				1			1			2			4		
Marlborough	192	41	Hunter	Robert			2		1			1	1				5		
Marlborough	193	1	Pratt	Mary						1			1				2		
Marlborough	193	2	Hunter	David	3				1	1	1		1				7		
Marlborough	193	3	Taylor	David	1					1		1					3		
Marlborough	193	4	Whitcomb	Zelotes	2			1					1				4		
Marlborough	193	5	Witt	Josiah			1		2				2				5		
Marlborough	193	6	Whitcomb	Timothy	1			1	1	1			2	1			7		
Marlborough	193	7	Felton	Archelaus	1	1			1				1				4		
Marlborough	193	8	Newton	Micah			1	1	1				1				4		
Marlborough	193	9	Gould	Benjamin					1				1				2		
Marlborough	193	10	Hunting	Samuel			1		1			1		1			3		
Marlborough	193	11	Eager	Uriah	1				1				1				3		
Marlborough	193	12	Eager	Moses	3		1	1		1			2				8		
Marlborough	193	13	Bread	Ephraim				1				1	1				3		
Marlborough	193	14	Toflin	Thomas				1		1				2			4		
Marlborough	193	15	How	Josiah	1		2		1	1			1	2			8		
Marlborough	193	16	How	John		1		1		1	4	3		2			12		

78

TOWN	PG#	LN#	HEADS OF HOUSEHOLD LAST NAME	FIRST NAME	FREE WHITE MALES under 10	10 to 16	16 to 26	26 to 45	45 and over	FREE WHITE FEMALES under 10	10 to 16	16 to 26	26 to 45	45 and over	TOTAL ALL OTHER	TOTAL SLAVES	TOTALS	DISTRICT/ TOWNSHIP	NOTES
Marlborough	193	17	Brigham	Zedidiah		1		1		4			1				7		
Marlborough	193	18	Brigham	Elizabeth						1		1		1			3		
Marlborough	193	19	Brigham	Daniel	4	2		1		1	1	1	1				11		
Marlborough	193	20	How	John	1		1	1	1	1		2	1	1			9		
Marlborough	193	21	Perrigo	John		1	1						1				3		
Marlborough	193	22	Stow	Heman	1		2		1	1	1	2		1			9		
Marlborough	193	23	How	John 3rd		1		1					1				3		
Marlborough	193	24	Witt	Samuel	3	1	1	1		1			2				9		
Marlborough	193	25	Williams	Stephen				1				1					2		
Marlborough	193	26	Hayden	Josiah	2			1		1			1				5		
Marlborough	193	27	Parmenter	Eliab	1			1		1			1				4		
Marlborough	193	28	Weeks	John	1			2		3	1		1				8		
Marlborough	193	29	Hayden	Nahum		1			1		1			1			4		
Marlborough	193	30	Clark	Benjamin		1	1		1	1	1			1			6		
Marlborough	193	31	Eames	Ebenezer	2	1		1	2	1		1	1				9		
Marlborough	193	32	Temple	Isaac			1			1			1				3		
Marlborough	193	33	Weeks	Jonathan	2	1	1		1	1	1	2		2			11		
Marlborough	193	34	Potter	Ephraim		1		1				1					3		
Marlborough	193	35	Wiswall	Oliver				1					1				2		
Marlborough	193	36	Potter	Stephen	1			1		2	1		1				6		
Marlborough	193	37	Baker	John	1	1			1	2	1		1				7		
Marlborough	193	38	Russell	Nathaniel P.	1	1			1	1	1			2			7		
Marlborough	193	39	Darling	Jonas	3	1	1				1			2			9		
Marlborough	193	40	Hager	William			2		1				1	1			5		
Marlborough	193	41	Hager	Abigail		1						1	2	1			5		
Marlborough	193	42	Arnold	Winslow	2			1		1			1				5		
Marlborough	193	43	Munroe	David	1	1	1		3				2	1			9		
Marlborough	194	1	Munroe	Lois	2			1				1					4		
Marlborough	194	2	Sherman	Moses	3			1		1			1				6		
Marlborough	194	3	Bill	Elizabeth										2			2		
Marlborough	194	4	Darling	Daniel	1			1		1			1				4		
Marlborough	194	5	Rice	Jabez Jr				1									1		
Marlborough	194	6	Morse	Stephen	3			3		2		2	1	1			12		
Marlborough	194	7	Stow	Samuel				1					1				2		
Marlborough	194	8	Williams	Joseph		2		2			1	2		1			8		
Marlborough	194	9	Warren	Thaddeus		1	1		1	2	1	2		1			9		
Marlborough	194	10	Bruce	Osaoah	3	1	1		1	2	1		1				10		
Marlborough	194	11	Barns	Benjamin				1					1				2		
Marlborough	194	12	Barns	Mary Widow									1				1		
Marlborough	194	13	Stow	Abraham	2	1		1	1	2	1		1				9		
Marlborough	194	14	Foster	Nathan	2			1		1			1				5		
Marlborough	194	15	Stow	Josiah				1					1				2		
Marlborough	194	16	Stow	Jabez Jr			1	1		2			1				5		
Marlborough	194	17	Arnold	Joseph	1	1		1		3		1	1				8		
Marlborough	194	18	Brigham	John G.	2	1	1		1	1			1				7		
Marlborough	194	19	Brigham	Sarah								1		1			2		
Marlborough	194	20	Shawman	Micah	1		2	2		1		2	1				9		
Marlborough	194	21	Temple	Jonas		1		2		1	1	2		1			8		
Marlborough	194	22	Temple	Moses	2			1		1			1				5		
Marlborough	194	23	Arnold	Persis								1		1			2		
Marlborough	194	24	Arnold	John	1			1		1			1				4		
Marlborough	194	25	Temple	John Jr		1		1	1					1			4		
Marlborough	194	26	Harrington	John	1		2		1			3		2			9		
Marlborough	194	27	Biglow	Gershom Jr	2	1			2	1		2		2			10		
Marlborough	194	28	Biglow	Ephraim			1			2		1					4		
Marlborough	194	29	Temple	Silas		1	1			3		1	1				7		
Marlborough	194	30	Moses	Nanna								1	1				2		
Marlborough	194	31	Barnard	Francis	2			1		1			1				5		
Marlborough	194	32	Morse	William		2		1		1				1			5		
Marlborough	194	33	Newton	Adonijah				1			1		1				3		
Marlborough	194	34	Barns	Jacob	1		1	2		1		1		1			7		
Marlborough	194	35	Maynard	John	3		1	1				2	1				8		
Marlborough	194	36	Ames	Stephen		1	1	1			1	1	2				7		
Marlborough	194	37	Townsend	Joseph			1		1		1		1	2			6		
Marlborough	194	38	Temple	John	2		2		1	2	2	1		1			11		
Marlborough	194	39	Dadman	Elijah	3			1		1	2	1	1				9		
Marlborough	194	40	Newton	William			2	1						2			5		
Marlborough	195	1	Sewell	Ephraim	2	1	1	1		2			1				8		
Marlborough	195	2	Felton	William	1			1					1		1		5		
Marlborough	195	3	Straten	Moses			1			1			1				3		

TOWN	PG#	LN#	LAST NAME	FIRST NAME	under 10	10 to 16	16 to 26	26 to 45	45 and over	under 10	10 to 16	16 to 26	26 to 45	45 and over	TOTAL ALL OTHER	TOTAL SLAVES	TOTALS	DISTRICT/ TOWNSHIP	NOTES
			HEADS OF HOUSEHOLD		FREE WHITE MALES					FREE WHITE FEMALES									
Medford	99	1	Abbott	Saml	1		1		1			1					4		
Medford	99	2	Adams	Nathan	1	1		1		2		2	1				8		
Medford	99	3	Andries	Eliza	3							1			5		9		
Medford	99	4	Anthony	Jona											1		1		
Medford	99	5	Bradbury	Wm	1			1		2			1				5		
Medford	99	6	Bacon	Jona	1			1				1	1				4		
Medford	99	7	Blanchard	Hezh				2				1	1		1		5		
Medford	99	8	Buckman	Wm		1		1		1	2						5		
Medford	99	9	Bannister	Jno'	2			1		2			1				6		
Medford	99	10	Butterfield	Fra'							1	1	1				3		
Medford	99	11	Blanchard	Andr'	2	1		1		1	1		1				7		
Medford	99	12	Bradshaw	Tho'	1			1					1				3		
Medford	99	13	Burage	Jno'				1		1			1				3		
Medford	99	14	Brown	Saml			1			1			1				3		
Medford	99	15	Blanchard	Caleb	1	1	2	1		4	1	1	1				12		
Medford	99	16	Barton	Wm				1		1			1				3		
Medford	99	17	Buckman	Leonard		1		1					1	1			4		
Medford	99	18	Buckman	Spencer	1			1		1		1					4		
Medford	99	19	Buckman	David				1					1	1			3		
Medford	99	20	Brooks	John		2		1		1	2						6		
Medford	99	21	Brooks	Caleb		1		2			2	1	2				8		
Medford	99	22	Brooks	Caleb Jr				1		1		1					3		
Medford	99	23	Brooks	Caleb 3rd				1									1		
Medford	99	24	Brooks	Jona'	2			1		1			1	1			6		
Medford	99	25	Brooks	Peter C.	4			1		1			1	1	1		9		
Medford	99	26	Brooks	Mary				1					1	1			3		
Medford	99	27	Brooks	Abigl										1			1		
Medford	99	28	Bosquet	Jno' L.				1		1			1				3		
Medford	99	29	Blanchard	Rebecca						1				1			2		
Medford	99	30	Blanchard	Rebecca Jr.	2	1				1			1				5		
Medford	99	31	Blanchard	Tabatha									1				1		
Medford	99	32	Blanchard	Sylvas	2		3	1		1		1	1				9		
Medford	99	33	Buel	Saml		1	1						2				4		
Medford	99	34	Billings	Marah								1		1			2		
Medford	99	35	Burns	Fra'		1		1		1			1				4		
Medford	99	36	Buffy	Mary										1			1		
Medford	99	37	Bishop	Jno'	1	1		1	1	1	3	1					9		
Medford	99	38	Bishop	Abijh						1			1	1			3		
Medford	99	39	Coverly	Saml		2	1	2	1					1			7		
Medford	99	40	Cutter	Jno'	3			1		1			1				6		
Medford	99	41	Cutter	Danl'	1	1		1					1				4		
Medford	99	42	Crowel	Aaron	1		3	1		2			1				8		
Medford	99	43	Collings	Jno'	1			2		1			1				5		
Medford	99	44	Convers	James	1	1		1				1		1			5		
Medford	99	45	Caldwell	Saml	1	1							1				3		
Medford	99	46	McCloud	Jno'				1		2				1			4		
Medford	99	47	McClester	Phillip				1									1		
Medford	99	48	Carlton	Jno'		1	1	1	1	1		2		1			8		
Medford	100	1	Conners	Peter	1			1		1		1					4		
Medford	100	2	Clisby	Jos'			4										4		
Medford	100	3	Dexter	Timo'	3			1		1	1		1				7		
Medford	100	4	Dexter	Paul		1		1						1			3		
Medford	100	5	Dixon	Josiah		1				1	1		1				4		
Medford	100	6	Dixon	Hannah									1				1		
Medford	100	7	Dunham	Jona'	1		1	1					1				4		
Medford	100	8	Earl	Wm	1			1		3		1		1			7		
Medford	100	9	Fitch	Jno' B.	1	1		1		3			1		1		8		
Medford	100	10	Farrington	Dan'		1		1		2		1	1				6		
Medford	100	11	Francis	Convers	1	1		2		2		1	1				8		
Medford	100	12	Francis	Eliza										1			1		
Medford	100	13	Francis	Jane										1			1		
Medford	100	14	Fulton	Sarah								1	2	1			4		
Medford	100	15	Fowl	John	3	2		1						1			7		
Medford	100	16	Fowl	Henry				1						1			2		
Medford	100	17	Frost	Rufus		1	1						1				3		
Medford	100	18	Floyd	Benja		1		1		1	1			1			5		
Medford	100	19	Floyd	Benja Jr	2			1		1	2		1				7		
Medford	100	20	Floyd	Isaac				1		1			1	1			4		
Medford	100	21	Floyd	James	2			1						1			4		
Medford	100	22	Foster	Jno'				1						1			2		
Medford	100	23	Greenleaf	Gardner						1			1				2		
Medford	100	24	Greenleaf	Gardner Jr				1		3			1				5		
Medford	100	25	Greenleaf	Jona'		2		1					1				4		
Medford	100	26	Greenleaf	Isaac			1	1		3	2	2		1			10		
Medford	100	27	Gleason	Jacob	1		1	1		1			1				5		
Medford	100	28	Gleason	Joshua	1			1		1			1				4		
Medford	100	29	Gates	Edm' T.		2	2		1	4	1	2		1			13		
Medford	100	30	Gyer	Fredk	1			1		3			1	2			8		
Medford	100	31	Green	Wm				1					1				2		

TOWN	PG#	LN#	LAST NAME	FIRST NAME	FREE WHITE MALES					FREE WHITE FEMALES					TOTAL ALL OTHER	TOTAL SLAVES	TOTALS	DISTRICT/ TOWNSHIP	NOTES
					under 10	10 to 16	16 to 26	26 to 45	45 and over	under 10	10 to 16	16 to 26	26 to 45	45 and over					
Medford	100	32	Gray	Wm	3	1	1	1	1		1	1	2				11		
Medford	100	33	Hewes	Tho'			1			1		1	2		1		6		
Medford	100	34	Hall	Saml'	2		1			1	2		1	1			8		
Medford	100	35	Hall	Willis				1		1		1	1				4		
Medford	100	36	Hall	Jno'	3		1			1	1		1				7		
Medford	100	37	Hall	Fra'	1		1		1	1	2		1				7		
Medford	100	38	Hall	Eben		1	2		1		1	2	1		1		9		
Medford	100	39	Hall	Eben Jr		1	2	2				2					7		
Medford	100	40	Hall	Eben 3rd			1	1		1	1	2					6		
Medford	100	41	Hall	James	1		1				1						3		
Medford	100	42	Hall	Benja'		1		1		1		1	2		1		7		
Medford	100	43	Hall	Benja' Jr		1	1	1		1	1	1	1		1		8		
Medford	100	44	Hall	Fitch	1			1		2			1		1		6		
Medford	100	45	Hall	Epm		1		1		1	1	2			1		7		
Medford	100	46	Hall	Andr'	2		1	1		3	1	1	1				10		
Medford	101	1	Hall	Rich		1	2	1				1		2			7		
Medford	101	2	Hall	Nath			1			2	1		2				6		
Medford	101	3	Hall	Step'			1	1						2			4		
Medford	101	4	Hall	Jane										1			1		
Medford	101	5	Hall	Jos' P.	1		1	1		1		1	1				6		
Medford	101	6	Harrington	Jona'			1					1					2		
Medford	101	7	Haines	Tho'			1			2		1					4		
Medford	101	8	Hadley	Tho'	2	1		1		1			1				6		
Medford	101	9	Hadley	Danl'		1				1		1					3		
Medford	101	10	Hadley	Rich		1				1		1					3		
Medford	101	11	Hadley	Saml		2		1		1			1				5		
Medford	101	12	Headley	Saml Jr	3		1			1		1					6		
Medford	101	13	Hadley	Huldah								1					1		
Medford	101	14	Hawley	Noah	3	1		1		2	1	1					9		
Medford	101	15	Ingraham	Duncan		1			1			1		1			4		
Medford	101	16	Johnson	Hannah	2							1					3		
Medford	101	17	Jones	Jno' C.	1	1	1		1	4	1		1	2			12		
Medford	101	18	Kidder	Saml	3	1		1		2	1		1				9		
Medford	101	19	Kidder	James	1		1			1		1					4		
Medford	101	20	Kidder	Joanne								2	1				3		
Medford	101	21	Knight	Rebecca						1		1					2		
Medford	101	22	Learned	Tho'	3		1			1		1					6		
Medford	101	23	Leathe	Jno'				3				1			1		5		
Medford	101	24	Manning	Sarah								1					1		
Medford	101	25	Mead	Nath	1			1				1					3		
Medford	101	26	Mead	Jno'	2	1		1		1			1				6		
Medford	101	27	Newhall	Saml			1			1		1					3		
Medford	101	28	Osgood	David	1			1		2	1		1				6		
Medford	101	29	Pratt	Jos	1			1					1				3		
Medford	101	30	Pratt	Isaac	2		1			2			1				6		
Medford	101	31	Pratt	Benja'		1		1		2			1				5		
Medford	101	32	Pratt	Timo'			1			1			1				3		
Medford	101	33	Pritchard	Lucy	1								1				2		
Medford	101	34	Porter	Jona'	2		1		2	2		2	1				10		
Medford	101	35	Parker	Farwell	1		4			1		1					7		
Medford	101	36	Polly	Josiah	1	1		1	1			1					5		
Medford	101	37	Porter	Rufus		1				2		1					4		
Medford	101	38	Peirce	Abner	2			2	1	1	1	1					8		
Medford	101	39	Peirce	Jos'		1						1					2		
Medford	101	40	Prince	James	1			1		1	1	1	1		1		7		
Medford	101	41	Putnam	Eleazer	1			1					1				3		
Medford	101	42	Putnam	Henry		1											1		
Medford	101	43	Patten	Mary								1	1				2		
Medford	101	44	Polly	Sampson											4		4		
Medford	101	45	Reed	Benjm	1		2	1		2	1	1		1			9		
Medford	102	1	Rand	Jos	3	1		1		2	1		1				9		
Medford	102	2	Rand	Mary								1		1			2		
Medford	102	3	Richardson	Jedun		1		1		2		1	1				6		
Medford	102	4	Rowson	Wm			2			7	23	12	3	1			48		
Medford	102	5	Raynard	James	3			1		2			1				7		
Medford	102	6	Symonds	Danl'	2			1		1			1				5		
Medford	102	7	Symonds	Jude					1	1	2	1					5		
Medford	102	8	Symonds	Eben	2		1		1	1	2		1				8		
Medford	102	9	Symonds	Joshua		1			1	1	2		1				6		
Medford	102	10	Savel	Tho'					1				1				2		
Medford	102	11	Savel	Tho' Jr			1					1					2		
Medford	102	12	Smith	Jos'		1	1	1					1				4		
Medford	102	13	Symmes	Jno'	4	2	1	1		1	1	1					11		
Medford	102	14	Symmes	Josiah					1								1		
Medford	102	15	Symmes	Timo'		1	1					2					4		
Medford	102	16	Symmes	Danl'		2											2		
Medford	102	17	Shed	Zachh	2			1		2		1	1				7		
Medford	102	18	Swan	Saml		3	2		1	1	2	2					11		
Medford	102	19	Shelbeck				1				1	2					5		

TOWN	PG#	LN#	LAST NAME	FIRST NAME	under 10	10 to 16	16 to 26	26 to 45	45 and over	under 10	10 to 16	16 to 26	26 to 45	45 and over	TOTAL ALL OTHER	TOTAL SLAVES	TOTALS	DISTRICT/ TOWNSHIP	NOTES
Medford	102	20	Teal	Saml			1		1			1		1			4		
Medford	102	21	Teal	Benja		1		1		2	2		1				7		
Medford	102	22	Teal	Gershom	3	1	1	1		3	1	2	1				13		
Medford	102	23	Tufts	Peter	1	1	1		1	2	1	2	1				10		
Medford	102	24	Tufts	Jona'	4	1		1				1		1			8		
Medford	102	25	Tufts	Jos'	1		1			1		1					4		
Medford	102	26	Tufts	Cha'				1									1		
Medford	102	27	Tufts	Isaac			1		1			2		1			5		
Medford	102	28	Tufts	James		1	1		1	2	2	2		1			10		
Medford	102	29	Tufts	Gershom	2	1		1		4			1				9		
Medford	102	30	Tufts	Benja'				1					1				2		
Medford	102	31	Tufts	Benja' Jr	2		1	1			1		1				6		
Medford	102	32	Tufts	Hutch			1		1			2		1			5		
Medford	102	33	Tufts	Hutch Jr	1			1		1			1				4		
Medford	102	34	Tufts	Tabitha									1				1		
Medford	102	35	Tufts	Saml'				1		1		1					3		
Medford	102	36	Tufts	Saml' Jr		1	2	1		1		1	1				7		
Medford	102	37	Tufts	Saml' 3rd	2				1	2	1			1			7		
Medford	102	38	Tufts	Jacob	3		1	1		1			1				7		
Medford	102	39	Tufts	Nath		1			1	1				1			4		
Medford	102	40	Tufts	Mary										1			1		
Medford	102	41	Tufts	Eben'		1			1				1	1			4		
Medford	102	42	Tufts	Jos'	2		1					1					4		
Medford	102	43	Tufts	Eliza						1				1			2		
Medford	103	1	Turner	*	1			1			1						3		
Medford	103	2	Tysick	Jos'				1		3				1			5		
Medford	103	3	Tuttle	Mary	1								1				2		
Medford	103	4	Thompson	Saml			1	1		1	1		2	1			7		
Medford	103	5	Townsend	Jethro			2	1		1							4		
Medford	103	6	Toleman	Nath'	1			1			1						3		
Medford	103	7	Thoring	James				1			1						2		
Medford	103	8	Usher	Susan						1			1				2		
Medford	103	9	Williams	Eben		1	1	1					1				4		
Medford	103	10	Williams	Gershom	1			1		1			1				4		
Medford	103	11	Watts	Nath'	1	1			1	2				1			6		
Medford	103	12	Watts	Nath' Jr				1			1						2		
Medford	103	13	Watts	Nathan	1			1		3	2		1				8		
Medford	103	14	Wait	Fra'	1	1		1		1		2					6		
Medford	103	15	Wait	Jacob		2			1					1			4		
Medford	103	16	Winship	Moses				1					1				2		
Medford	103	17	Wilson	Miles				1		2		1					4		
Medford	103	18	Waller	Jno'	4	1		1					1				7		
Medford	103	19	Wetherton	Henry	1			1		2		1	1				6		
Medford	103	20	Wheelwright	Jos'	1			3		1			1				6		
Medford	103	21	Wright	John			2		1	2	1			1			7		
Medford	103	22	Weston	Esther										1			1		
Medford	103	23	Weston	Wymond				1				1	2				4		
Medford	103	24	Wyman	Joseph	2	1	1	1			1		1	1			8		
Medford	103	25	Wyman	James		1		1	1				1	1			5		
Medford	103	26	Wealer	Jona'	1			1		1		1					4		
Medford	103	27	Wyer	Danl'	2			2					1				5		
Medford	103	28	Wyer	David	1			1		1			1				4		
Medford	103	29	Wiley	John	1				1	2	1		4		4		13		
Medford	103	30	Willis	David				1					1				2		
Medford	103	31	Warren	Isaac	1	1			1				2				5		
Medford	103	32	Warren	Silas	1		1	1					1				4		
Medford	103	33	Wade	John	1		1		1	2	1		1				7		

82

TOWN	PG#	LN#	HEADS OF HOUSEHOLD		FREE WHITE MALES					FREE WHITE FEMALES					TOTAL ALL OTHER	TOTAL SLAVES	TOTALS	DISTRICT/ TOWNSHIP	NOTES
			LAST NAME	FIRST NAME	under 10	10 to 16	16 to 26	26 to 45	45 and over	under 10	10 to 16	16 to 26	26 to 45	45 and over					
Natick	245	1	Alden	Wm	3	2		1						4			10		
Natick	245	2	Atkins	John	1	2	1	1	1			2	1	1			10		
Natick	245	3	Bigelow	Isaac	1		1			1		1					4		
Natick	245	4	Broad	Hezekh	1			1	1	1		1	1	1			7		
Natick	245	5	Bacon	Richd Jr.	1			1					1				3		
Natick	245	6	Bacon	Ezra				1						1			2		
Natick	245	7	Bacon	Mehitable	2					2		1	1				6		
Natick	245	8	Bacon	Richd	1				1	1		1		1			5		
Natick	245	9	Bacon	Jona		1		1		2		1					5		
Natick	245	10	Broad	Thos		1	2	2	2			1		1			9		
Natick	245	11	Broad	Moses	2			1	1	1			1				6		
Natick	245	12	Bacon	Henry		1				2				2	1		6		
Natick	245	13	Bailey	Eliphalet	3				1	1	1		1				7		
Natick	245	14	Boden	Wm		1			2	1		1		1			6		
Natick	245	15	Bryant	Jona	2		1		1	2				1			7		
Natick	245	16	Badger	John				1						1			2		
Natick	245	17	Bacon	David	2	2		1		2	2		1				10		
Natick	245	18	Bacon	Elijah	1		1	2	1	2		1	1	1	2		12		
Natick	245	19	Bacon	John	2			1		1			1				5		
Natick	245	20	Bacon	Asa	1			1		3	1		1				7		
Natick	245	21	Bane	Wm				1									1		
Natick	245	22	Badger	Stephen			1		1			1	1				4		
Natick	246	1	Brown	Wm		1	1		1			1	1	2			7		
Natick	246	2	Bacon	Oliver				1					1				2		
Natick	246	3	Bacon	John	3			1		1			1				6		
Natick	246	4	Bigelow	Wm		1			1	2	1	2		1			8		
Natick	246	5	Carter	Joshua	1	1			1	3			1				7		
Natick	246	6	Coollidge	Isaac					1		2			1			4		
Natick	246	7	Childs	Josiah		1	1	1		2		1	1				7		
Natick	246	8	Coggen	Mary									2				2		
Natick	246	9	Coolidge	Asa			2			1		1		1			5		
Natick	246	10	Coolidge	John	2			1		1	2		1				7		
Natick	246	11	Cobb	Nathl											4		4		
Natick	246	12	Chon	John											7		7		
Natick	246	13	Dune	Jona		1			1	2		1		1			6		
Natick	246	14	Duntin	Isaac			1	1									2		
Natick	246	15	Drewry	Saml		1			1	1				1			4		
Natick	246	16	Drewry	Asa		1			1	1		1		1			5		
Natick	246	17	Drewry	Elijah	3			1		1			1				6		
Natick	246	18	Draper	Enoch		1	1	1		3			1				7		
Natick	246	19	Dana	Tabatha	1				1				1	1			4		
Natick	246	20	Dana	David		1	1					3					5		
Natick	246	21	Easter	Elijah Jr	2			1		1			1				5		
Natick	246	22	Easter	Elijah				1				1		1			3		
Natick	246	23	Fisk	Moses	1	1	2		1		1		1				7		
Natick	246	24	Fisk	Asa	1			1		2	1		1				6		
Natick	246	25	Farns	Wm	1	1			1		1	2		1			7		
Natick	246	26	Frail	David	1		2		1			1		1			6		
Natick	246	27	Fitch	John	2			2		2	2		1	1			10		
Natick	246	28	Goodnough	Elisha	2			1	1	2	1		1	1			9		
Natick	246	29	Gay	Joseph					1		1	2		1			5		
Natick	246	30	Golden	Eleazer		1			1	1		1	1				5		
Natick	246	31	Green	Newport											4		4		
Natick	246	32	Haynes	Daniel	3		1	1		1		1	2	1			10		
Natick	246	33	Hall	David		1			2	1			2	2			8		
Natick	246	34	Hammond	Edward	5		1	1	1	2	2	2	2	1			17		
Natick	246	35	Haven	David	1	1	1		1			2		1			7		
Natick	246	36	Haynes	Nathan	1			2		1			2				6		
Natick	246	37	Janneson	Lott	1	1	1		1			2		1			7		
Natick	246	38	Jennings	Ethel	3	1		1	1		2		1	1			10		
Natick	246	39	Jonah	Jacob											5		5		
Natick	246	40	Kingsbury	Elipht	4			1	1				1	1			8		
Natick	246	41	Kimball	Ebenr	1		1						1				3		
Natick	246	42	Locker	Isaac		5			1		1	2		1			10		
Natick	246	43	Lucus	Henry			1						1				2		
Natick	246	44	Lucus	Abrm			1							1			2		
Natick	246	45	Lowton	Saml	1			1		1		1					4		
Natick	246	46	Morse	Adam	1	2	1	1		3	1		1				10		
Natick	247	1	Morse	Saml	2	2	3		1	2		1	1	2			14		
Natick	247	2	Morse	Elisha	1		1		1	1	1	1		1			6		
Natick	247	3	Man	John	2	1	1	1		2	1		1				9		
Natick	247	4	Morse	Henry	3	2	1	1		2	1		1				11		
Natick	247	5	Morse	Wm	1			2		2		2	1				8		
Natick	247	6	Moore	David	2		4	1	1	1		2	1				12		
Natick	247	7	Morse	Daniel					1				1				2		
Natick	247	8	Morse	Gershom		1						1					2		
Natick	247	9	Newhall	Ebenr		1		2		3	1		1				8		
Natick	247	10	Pratt	Silas	1			1		3			1				6		
Natick	247	11	Perrey	Louis					1				1				2		

TOWN	PG#	LN#	LAST NAME	FIRST NAME	FREE WHITE MALES					FREE WHITE FEMALES					TOTAL ALL OTHER	TOTAL SLAVES	TOTALS	DISTRICT/ TOWNSHIP	NOTES
					under 10	10 to 16	16 to 26	26 to 45	45 and over	under 10	10 to 16	16 to 26	26 to 45	45 and over					
Natick	247	12	Perry	Abial Jr		1	1	1		2			1						
Natick	247	13	Perry	Abial		1			1				1				3		
Natick	247	14	Perry	Saml Jr.	4			1				1	1				7		
Natick	247	15	Perry	Elijah	1	1	1	1				1	1				6		
Natick	247	16	Prat	Jacob	1			1		1			1				4		
Natick	247	17	Perry	Saml		1	1		1			2			1		6		
Natick	247	18	Price	Jonas		1			1				1				4		
Natick	247	19	Rice	David		1		1		2	1	1	1				7		
Natick	247	20	Rice	Jona				1		4	2		1				8		
Natick	247	21	Rice	James		1		1				1	1	1			5		
Natick	247	22	Rockwood	Elisha		1	1						1				3		
Natick	247	23	Russell	Joel					1				1	1			3		
Natick	247	24	Rice	John	3			2		1		2					8		
Natick	247	25	Smith	Timothy				1						2			3		
Natick	247	26	Smith	Henry	1			1		1			1				4		
Natick	247	27	Smith	Timothy Jr.			1						1				2		
Natick	247	28	Sawing	Thos	2		1		1	2	2		1				9		
Natick	247	29	Sawing	Moses	1	1		1		3			2				8		
Natick	247	30	Sawing	Ezekiel	2			1		2	1		1				7		
Natick	247	31	Stratten	James	1			1		1		1					4		
Natick	247	32	Stratten	Elijah	1	1		1		3	1		1				8		
Natick	247	33	Stratten	Saml	1		1	1			1	1		1			7		
Natick	247	34	Sparrowhawk	Beriah			1	1				1		1			4		
Natick	247	35	Stone	Wm	1	1	1			3	1	3		1			11		
Natick	247	36	Sawing	John				1	1		2		1				5		
Natick	247	37	Stratten	Daniel	2				1	2	1			1			7		
Natick	247	38	Stone	Saml				1	1	1		1					3		
Natick	247	39	Sawing	Fracs	2	1		1		1				1			6		
Natick	247	40	Stratten	Abijah		1	1		1			2		1			6		
Natick	247	41	Travis	Daniel	3			1	1				1	2			8		
Natick	247	42	Travis	David		1			1					2			4		
Natick	247	43	Whitney	Jason			2		1		1	1		1			6		
Natick	247	44	Ward	Daniel	1		1						1				3		
Natick	247	45	Walker	Josiah			1			1	1	1					4		
Natick	247	1	Washman	Saml	2	1	1		1	2	1			3			11		
Natick	248	2	Whitney	El*	1			1		2			1				5		
Natick	248	3	Wait	John			1			2		1					4		

TOWN	PG#	LN#	LAST NAME	FIRST NAME	M under 10	M 10 to 16	M 16 to 26	M 26 to 45	M 45 and over	F under 10	F 10 to 16	F 16 to 26	F 26 to 45	F 45 and over	TOTAL ALL OTHER	TOTAL SLAVES	TOTALS	DISTRICT/ TOWNSHIP	NOTES
Newton	117	1	Adams	Roger	1	1	1		1		4	3		1			12		
Newton	117	2	Adams	Smith	2	2	1	1		4			1				11		
Newton	117	3	Adams	Jacob			1			1				1			3		
Newton	117	4	Adams	Joseph		1			1				1				3		
Newton	117	5	Allen	Michael	1			1					1				3		
Newton	117	6	Alden	Paul		1	2			3			1				7		
Newton	117	7	Blake	Joseph		2	3	1			1	3	3	1			14		
Newton	117	8	Brown	Molly										1			1		
Newton	117	9	Bartlett	Joshua	2			1		1			1				5		
Newton	117	10	Beal	Thomas			1	1						1			3		
Newton	117	11	Beal	William	2			1		1	2		1				7		
Newton	117	12	Brown	Ebenezer	1			1		1			1				4		
Newton	117	13	Blandon	Jonas	2	2		1		1		1	1				8		
Newton	117	14	Blandon	Phinehas				1					1				2		
Newton	117	15	Blandon	Abigail	2					1		1	1	1			6		
Newton	117	16	Bartlett	Luke		2			1	1			1				5		
Newton	118	1	Benny	Jonathan	2		1		1				1	2			7		
Newton	118	2	Barney	Solomon			2	2		1	1	1					7		
Newton	118	3	Bull	Milissent			1			1			1	1			4		
Newton	118	4	Bartlett	Elisha	2	1		1		1				2			7		
Newton	118	5	Bullough	Abigail	3		1			4		3		2			13		
Newton	118	6	Bacon	Phinehas	2		1					1	1				5		
Newton	118	7	Bartlett	David			1	1				1	1				4		
Newton	118	8	Cutter	Richard	3	1		1		1	2	1	1				10		
Newton	118	9	Cheney	David	1	1		1			1	1	1				6		
Newton	118	10	Coollege	Isaac			1			4			1				6		
Newton	118	11	Cutter	Nathaniel	1		1					1					3		
Newton	118	12	Cushing	Thomas			1	3				1			2		7		
Newton	118	13	Curtis	Obadiah	1		1		1			1	1	1			6		
Newton	118	14	Corey	David		1	1	2		1			1				6		
Newton	118	15	Child	Daniel	1	2	1		1	2		1	1				9		
Newton	118	16	Craft	Henry		1	1			1			1				4		
Newton	118	17	Cook	Jona				1			1	2		1			5		
Newton	118	18	Cushing	Edward		1	2			3	1	1		1			9		
Newton	118	19	Clark	Norman	2	2		1	1	3		1	2	1			13		
Newton	118	20	Clark	Daniel		1		1	1	2			1				6		
Newton	118	21	Craft	Joseph	1	1			2	2		1		1			8		
Newton	118	22	Collins	Mathias		1				2		1					5		
Newton	118	23	Curtis	Solomon	4	1	4	2		2		1	1				15		
Newton	118	24	Crane	Stephen	2			1		3			1	1			8		
Newton	118	25	Cook	Benjamin	1			2		2	1		1				7		
Newton	118	26	Cheney	William	1				1	1			1	1			5		
Newton	118	27	Cheney	Ebenezer	1	1		1			1		1				5		
Newton	118	28	Cheney	Aaron		1			1					1			3		
Newton	118	29	Durant	Thomas	2			1		2		2					7		
Newton	118	30	Durant	Peter	1			1					1				3		
Newton	119	1	Durell	David	2			1		1			1				5		
Newton	119	2	Daniels	Osemus	1		1			1			1				4		
Newton	119	3	Durell	John	1			1		2			1				5		
Newton	119	4	Dix	Samuel		1	1	1	1			2					6		
Newton	119	5	Downing	John			2		1	1				1			4		
Newton	119	6	Eustis	Thomas		1	1		1		1	1	1	1			7		
Newton	119	7	Eustis	Thomas Jr	2		2	1		2	2		1				10		
Newton	119	8	Fuller	Joseph Jr			1						1				2		
Newton	119	9	Fuller	Joseph	4	1			2	2		1	1				12		
Newton	119	10	Fuller	David		1			1	2	1		1				6		
Newton	119	11	Fuller	Joshua		1	2		1	1	1			2			8		
Newton	119	12	Fuller	Nathan			2		1	1	1		1				6		
Newton	119	13	Fuller	Silas	2	1	2	1		1			1				8		
Newton	119	14	Flagg	Joshua		1	1		1			1					4		
Newton	119	15	Fuller	Edward		1	1		1			1		1			5		
Newton	119	16	Fuller	Amariah				1					1				2		
Newton	119	17	Fuller	Sarah				1						1			2		
Newton	119	18	Fuller	Josiah			1	1				1		1			4		
Newton	119	19	Fuller	Nathl	1				1	2	1		1				6		
Newton	119	20	Greenough	William	2			1		2	2	1	2				10		
Newton	119	21	Grafton	Joseph	2			1		3			1	1			8		
Newton	119	22	Greggs	William	1			1		2			1	1			6		
Newton	119	23	Greenwood	Miles	1		1	1		2	2	1	1				9		
Newton	119	24	Grimes	James				1									1		
Newton	119	25	Hammond	Joshua	1	1	3			1		2					8		
Newton	119	26	Hovey	George		1						1					2		
Newton	119	27	Hyde	William	1			1					1				3		
Newton	119	28	Hyde	Amos		2		1		1		1	1				6		
Newton	119	29	Hyde	Daniel		1		1	1	1	1	2					6		
Newton	120	1	Homer	Jonathan		1	3	1	1	1		1	1	1	1		11		
Newton	120	2	Hyde	Samuel	1	1	1					2	1				6		
Newton	120	3	Hyde	Jonathan	2	1		1		1	1		1				7		
Newton	120	4	Hammond	Thomas	1	1	1		1	3		1	1				9		

TOWN	PG#	LN#	LAST NAME	FIRST NAME	FWM under 10	FWM 10 to 16	FWM 16 to 26	FWM 26 to 45	FWM 45 and over	FWF under 10	FWF 10 to 16	FWF 16 to 26	FWF 26 to 45	FWF 45 and over	TOTAL ALL OTHER	TOTAL SLAVES	TOTALS	DISTRICT/ TOWNSHIP	NOTES
Newton	120	5	Hammond	William			2		1	2	2	2		1			10		
Newton	120	6	Hammond	Benjm	1				1			2	1				5		
Newton	120	7	Hammond	Benjm Jr	2		1	1		2			1				7		
Newton	120	8	Hyde	Elisha	2			1		2			1				6		
Newton	120	9	Hyde	Thaddeus	1	2		1			1		1				6		
Newton	120	10	Hyde	John	1	1	2	2		1			1	1			9		
Newton	120	11	Harbach	Thomas				1					1				2		
Newton	120	12	Hall	Eward	2	2		1		1	1		1				8		
Newton	120	13	Hyde	Enoch				1		1			1				3		
Newton	120	14	Hyde	Benjm				1					1	1			3		
Newton	120	15	Hastings	Thomas	1		2		1	1	1	2	1	1			10		
Newton	120	16	Hastings	Samuel				1					1	1			3		
Newton	120	17	Hull	William		1		1		2	3	4	1		1		13		
Newton	120	18	Hyde	Ephraim				1		1			1				3		
Newton	120	19	Hastings	Thoams Jr	1			1		2			1	1			6		
Newton	120	20	Hastings	John				1		3	1		1				6		
Newton	120	21	Hastings	Daniel	2	1		1		2	1	2		1			10		
Newton	120	22	Hunter	Solomon	3		1			1	2		1				8		
Newton	120	23	Hall	Solomon	3	1		1		1			2				8		
Newton	120	24	Hall	Samuel	2	2		1		1	1		1				8		
Newton	120	25	Hovey	Thomas	1			1			1	1		1			5		
Newton	120	26	Hooker	*ibeon	1	1	1		1	3		1	1				9		
Newton	120	27	Hoogs	William			2	2	1	1	1	2		1			10		
Newton	120	28	Hoogs	William Jr	1		2			3			1				7		
Newton	121	1	Jackson	Edward	1		2		2	1	1	3	1				11		
Newton	121	2	Jackson	Daniel	2			1		1	1		1				6		
Newton	121	3	Jackson	Oliver	2		1	1		2				2			8		
Newton	121	4	Jones	Mijah	2	1		1		3	1		1				9		
Newton	121	5	Jackson	Simon	1	1	1	1		1	1	2					8		
Newton	121	6	Jackson	Joshua		1		1		1		1		1			5		
Newton	121	7	Jackson	Samuel		1		1				1		1			4		
Newton	121	8	Ingraham	Margaret						1		2		1			4		
Newton	121	9	Jackson	Joshua Jr		1		1					1				3		
Newton	121	10	Jarvis	Caleb				1		1		3	1				6		
Newton	121	11	Jennison	Phinehas	2			1					1				4		
Newton	121	12	Jennison	Elias	1			1		2			1	1			6		
Newton	121	13	Jackson	Oliver				1				1	1	1			4		
Newton	121	14	Jennison	Phinehas Jr	1		1		1			1		1			5		
Newton	121	15	Jackson	Michael		1	1		1			1		1			5		
Newton	121	16	Jackson	Michael Jr	2			1		1			1				5		
Newton	121	17	Jackson	Timo	2	1	1	1			1			1			7		
Newton	121	18	Jackson	Joseph				1					1	1			3		
Newton	121	19	Jackson	Joseph Jr	2			1					1				4		
Newton	121	20	Knapp	Lydia									1				1		
Newton	121	21	King	John	4			1			2		1				8		
Newton	121	22	King	Henry	3	1		1	1	1	1	1	2				11		
Newton	121	23	King	Noah			1	1		3			1				6		
Newton	121	24	Kimball	Richard				1					1				2		
Newton	121	25	Kimball	Richard Jr	1			1		2			1				5		
Newton	121	26	King	Ebenezer		1	1	1					1		1		5		
Newton	121	27	King	John		1		1		1		1	1	1			5		
Newton	121	28	Kenrick	John	1	1	1		1			1		1			6		
Newton	122	1	Kenrick	Caleb		1	1	1		1			1	1			6		
Newton	122	2	Kenrick	John Jr		2	1		1	1	1	2	1	1			10		
Newton	122	3	Lenox	Cornelius											1		1		
Newton	122	4	Learnard	Jonas	3			1		1	1		1				7		
Newton	122	5	Livermore	John	1	2		1		4	1		1				10		
Newton	122	6	Murdock	Saml	1		1	1		1	2	1	1				8		
Newton	122	7	Murdock	Elisha	1			1				1					2		
Newton	122	8	Murdock	Esther									1				1		
Newton	122	9	Murdock	Jonathan				1		2			1				4		
Newton	122	10	Munroe	Nathan	1								1				3		
Newton	122	11	Mathews	John			2		1			1	1	1			5		
Newton	122	12	Mallard	James	1			1		1			1				4		
Newton	122	13	Moore	Reuben	1	2		1		3		1	1				9		
Newton	122	14	Munroe	Oliver				1				1		1			3		
Newton	122	15	Marshall	Catharine		1		1					1	1			4		
Newton	122	16	Merrick	Abigail									1	1			2		
Newton	122	17	Murdock	Robert	3	1		1					2				7		
Newton	122	18	Morse	James											4		4		
Newton	122	19	Mitchell	Edward				1		3	1		1				6		
Newton	122	20	Mills	Luke		1		1			1	2		1			6		
Newton	122	21	Mills	Luke Jr	1			1					1				3		
Newton	122	22	Nutting	Samuel	1	1		1	1	2		2		2			10		
Newton	122	23	Norcross	Nathaniel	1	1		1		3	2	1	1				10		
Newton	122	24	Neal	William				1				1	1				3		
Newton	122	25	Parker	Joseph	1	1	1	1	1		1	2	1	1			10		
Newton	122	26	Park	Amasa	1	1		1		1	1			3			8		
Newton	122	27	Pratt	Thomas	2		1	1		1			2	1			8		

TOWN	PG#	LN#	LAST NAME	FIRST NAME	FWM under 10	FWM 10 to 16	FWM 16 to 26	FWM 26 to 45	FWM 45 and over	FWF under 10	FWF 10 to 16	FWF 16 to 26	FWF 26 to 45	FWF 45 and over	TOTAL ALL OTHER	TOTAL SLAVES	TOTALS	DISTRICT/ TOWNSHIP	NOTES
Newton	122	28	Pigeon	Elizabeth	2	1	1			3	1	1	1				10		
Newton	122	29	Pigeon	Jane					1			1		1	1		4		
Newton	123	1	Park	Joshua	2	2	1		1	2		1	1				10		
Newton	123	2	Parker	Jonathan		1	1	1			1		2				6		
Newton	123	3	Parker	Samuel		1	1		1			1		1			5		
Newton	123	4	Palmer	Thomas		2			2			2		1			7		
Newton	123	5	Park	Nathan	2			1				1					4		
Newton	123	6	Park	Cornelius	1			1	1	1				1			4		
Newton	123	7	Pike	Hannah	1								1				2		
Newton	123	8	Pigeon	John	2			1		3	1		1				8		
Newton	123	9	Porter	Amasa	1			1		3			1		1		7		
Newton	123	10	Prentice	Robert			2		1	2	1		2				8		
Newton	123	11	Robbins	Silas					1				1	1	1		3		
Newton	123	12	Robbins	Eliphalet					1				1				2		
Newton	123	13	Richards	Aaron	1	1	1		1	1		1	1				7		
Newton	123	14	Richardson	Jeremiah		1	1		1			2		1			6		
Newton	123	15	Richards	Thaddeus	1		1	1		2		1	1	1			8		
Newton	123	16	Richards	James		1	2		1	1	2		1				8		
Newton	123	17	Richards	Daniel		1	3	1			2		1	1			9		
Newton	123	18	Richards	Solomon	1	1	1		2			1	1	1			8		
Newton	123	19	Richardson	Samuel	1				1			1		1			4		
Newton	123	20	Richardson	Benjm	4		1	1				1		1			8		
Newton	123	21	Ross	Silas			3			1		1		1			6		
Newton	123	22	Rogers	John	1	1		1					1				4		
Newton	123	23	Rogers	John Jr	3		2		1	2			1				9		
Newton	123	24	Richardson	David	1		2	1		1		1	1				7		
Newton	123	25	Richardson	Ebenz	1	1	1	1		2		1					7		
Newton	123	26	Reed	Josiah				1					1				2		
Newton	123	27	Rogers	Caleb	1	1		1					1				4		
Newton	124	1	Smith	Enoch	2	1		1		2			1				7		
Newton	124	2	Seavern	Elisha		1	1	1						1			4		
Newton	124	3	Stimpson	Samuel	1	1	2	2				1	1	1			9		
Newton	124	4	Seavern	Richard			1					1					2		
Newton	124	5	Stone	John			1	1				2		1			5		
Newton	124	6	Stone	James		2	1	1		1		3	2				10		
Newton	124	7	Stone	David				1		1			1	1			4		
Newton	124	8	Stone	Moses	3	1		1		2		1	1				9		
Newton	124	9	Seaverns	Abijah	1		7	2		2		1	1				14		
Newton	124	10	Stone	Jonas		1			1	1				2			5		
Newton	124	11	Stone	Jonas Jr		1			1	1				2			5		
Newton	124	12	Stone	Timothy		2	1	1		1		1					6		
Newton	124	13	Stearns	Luther	8	10	2	1		1	1	3	1				27		
Newton	124	14	Sanger	Nathan			1			2		1					4		
Newton	124	15	Starr	Ebenezer	1			1		2		1					5		
Newton	124	16	Tolman	Thomas				1					1				2		
Newton	124	17	Tower	Jonathan	2			1		1		1					5		
Newton	124	18	Twing	Nicholas	3	1		1		2		1					8		
Newton	124	19	Twing	John		1	2		1				3	2			9		
Newton	124	20	Twing	John Jr	4		2	1		1		2					10		
Newton	124	21	Thayer	Eleazer	1			1		2			1				5		
Newton	124	22	Twing	James	3			1		1	1	1	1	1			9		
Newton	124	23	Trowbridge	Edmund	2				1			1	1				5		
Newton	124	24	Trowbridge	Saml	2	1			1	2		1	1				8		
Newton	124	25	Ward	Joseph	2	1	1		1			2	1				10		
Newton	124	26	Ward	Samuel	3	1	1	1		1		1	1		1		10		
Newton	124	27	White	Eleazer	2	1		1	1	3		1	1				10		
Newton	125	1	Whitney	Thaddeus		1			1	2		1		1			6		
Newton	125	2	Whitney	Timo	1		1		1	1			1				5		
Newton	125	3	Whitney	Moses				1					1				2		
Newton	125	4	Wilson	Moses				2			1						3		
Newton	125	5	Wiswell	Jeremiah		1		2					1				4		
Newton	125	6	Wiswell	Jeremiah Jr	4	2		1				1	1				9		
Newton	125	7	Wiswell	Elizabeth	1					4			1				6		
Newton	125	8	Wood	Ryal				1				1		1			3		
Newton	125	9	White	Loas	1			1		2	1		1				6		
Newton	125	10	Winch	Ebenezer	3	1			1	1		1	2				9		
Newton	125	11	Wentworth	Isaac				1				2		1	3		7		
Newton	125	12	Whitmore	Jona W.		1	1	1		2			1				6		
Newton	125	13	Winchester	Amos		1	1		1	1	1	1					6		
Newton	125	14	Ward	John		1		1				1		1			4		
Newton	125	15	Woodward	Ebenezer		1		1				2	1				5		
Newton	125	16	Woodward	John				1				1	1				3		
Newton	125	17	Ware	John		2	5		1	3	1	2					15		
Newton	125	18	Ware	Azariah	1		2	2		1		1	1				8		
Newton	125	19	Ware	Walter	1		2					1	1		1		6		
Newton	125	20	Woodcock	Nathan	3			1		1				1			6		
Newton	125	21	Whitney	Amasa	1			1		4	1		1				8		
Newton	125	22	Welsh	Michael		1	1		1				1				4		
Newton	125	23	Winchester	Ichabod	1					1			1				4		

TOWN	PG#	LN#	LAST NAME	FIRST NAME	FREE WHITE MALES					FREE WHITE FEMALES					TOTAL ALL OTHER	TOTAL SLAVES	TOTALS	DISTRICT/TOWNSHIP	NOTES
					under 10	10 to 16	16 to 26	26 to 45	45 and over	under 10	10 to 16	16 to 26	26 to 45	45 and over					
Pepperell	30	1	Adams	James	2			1		1			1				5		
Pepperell	30	2	Adams	Joseph	1	1			1					1			4		
Pepperell	30	3	Ames	Elijah	1	1	1		1				2	1			7		
Pepperell	30	4	Blood	Timo	1		1			1		1					4		
Pepperell	30	5	Bancroft	End		1		1	1			1		1			5		
Pepperell	30	6	Bancroft	Jona		1		1				1					3		
Pepperell	30	7	Bancroft	Thos			1		1	1	1		1				5		
Pepperell	30	8	Birde	Wm	1	1		1		1	1		1				6		
Pepperell	30	9	Blood	David		1		1				2		1			5		
Pepperell	30	10	Blood	Isaac	2	2	1	1		1	1	1	1				10		
Pepperell	30	11	Blood	Moses			2		1		1			2			6		
Pepperell	30	12	Blood	John		2		1		1		1	1				6		
Pepperell	30	13	Blood	Edm		1		1	1		1		1				5		
Pepperell	30	14	Blood	Abigail									2				2		
Pepperell	30	15	Blood	Robert			1						1				2		
Pepperell	30	16	Blood	Wm	1	1		1		1			1				5		
Pepperell	30	17	Boynton	Abijah		1	2				1		1				6		
Pepperell	30	18	Boynton	Abijah Jr			1				1						2		
Pepperell	30	19	Blood	Joshua			3	1			1		1				6		
Pepperell	30	20	Barron	Jona		1		1	1			1	1				5		
Pepperell	30	21	Bailey	Abrm	2				1			1	1				5		
Pepperell	30	22	Butterfield	Daniel	1			1		3	1	1	1				8		
Pepperell	30	23	Baldwin	David			1	1	1	2	2		1				8		
Pepperell	30	24	Buttrick	Francis	2	3			1	1			1				8		
Pepperell	30	25	Brooks	Jonas	2	1		1		3			1		1		9		
Pepperell	30	26	Bowers	John			1		1				2				4		
Pepperell	30	27	Boynton	Isaac		1	3	1					1				6		
Pepperell	30	28	Blood	Jona		3			1	1		1	1				7		
Pepperell	30	29	Blood	David Jr		1						1					2		
Pepperell	30	30	Blood	Saml	3		1		1	1	1		1				8		
Pepperell	30	31	Bowers	Azubah						2		1					3		
Pepperell	30	32	Barker	Leml					1		1		1				3		
Pepperell	30	33	Campbell	Jonas	2			1		2			1				6		
Pepperell	30	34	Conant	Shebuel		1		1				1	1				4		
Pepperell	30	35	Chase	Jacob	1	2		1		1			1				6		
Pepperell	30	36	Crawford	John			1		1	1		2		1			6		
Pepperell	30	37	Clark	John	2			1					1				4		
Pepperell	30	38	Eliott	Jerh				1	1		1	1	1				5		
Pepperell	30	39	Eliott	David	4			1		2		1					8		
Pepperell	30	40	Emerford	Joseph S.				1				1		1			3		
Pepperell	30	41	Eliott	Sarah			1			1		2		1			5		
Pepperell	30	42	Fitch	Jonas			1		1		1		1				4		
Pepperell	30	43	Fisk	Daniel		1	1		1		1						4		
Pepperell	30	44	Fisk	Micah	1												1		
Pepperell	30	45	Farrar	Joseph	3												3		
Pepperell	31	1	Farrar	Saml	2		2						1				5		
Pepperell	31	2	Fletcher	John				1	1				1				3		
Pepperell	31	3	Green	Simon	1		1		1		2		1				6		
Pepperell	31	4	Green	Jona		1		1		2	1		1				6		
Pepperell	31	5	Green	John				1		1		1	2		1		6		
Pepperell	31	6	Gibson	Simon				1					1				2		
Pepperell	31	7	Gibson	Joseph	1		1			1		1					4		
Pepperell	31	8	Green	James				1			1	1	1				4		
Pepperell	31	9	Getchel	Josh	1	1	1		1	3	1	2		1			11		
Pepperell	31	10	Hutchinson	Nathl		2	2		1		1	2		1			9		
Pepperell	31	11	Hutchinson	Wm		2	1		1		1	2		1			8		
Pepperell	31	12	Hutchinson	Joseph				1				1					2		
Pepperell	31	13	Harrington	Loa	2	1			1	1	2		1				8		
Pepperell	31	14	Hale	Saml			1	1			2						4		
Pepperell	31	15	Hosley	Joshua		1	1		1	2			1				6		
Pepperell	31	16	Hosley	John		1		1		2	1		1				6		
Pepperell	31	17	Hosley	Stephen	1	1		1		1		1	1				6		
Pepperell	31	18	Hosley	Timo				1			2		1				4		
Pepperell	31	19	Hildreth	James	1	1	1		1	1	1	3		2			11		
Pepperell	31	20	Heald	Joseph		1			1		1		1				4		
Pepperell	31	21	Heald	Eleazer	1		1	1		3	1		1				8		
Pepperell	31	22	Hall	Benja	2		2	1			1		1				7		
Pepperell	31	23	Hildreth	James Jr				1		1		1					3		
Pepperell	31	24	Jewett	David			2		1		1	2		1			7		
Pepperell	31	25	Jewett	Zeah				1				1					2		
Pepperell	31	26	Jewett	Edmd	2	1		1		1	1		1				7		
Pepperell	31	27	Jewett	Nehh Jr	1			1		2	1		1				6		
Pepperell	31	28	Jewett	Nehh			1		1			1		2			5		
Pepperell	31	29	Jewett	Caleb	2		1		1		1	2		1			8		
Pepperell	31	30	Kemp	D.B.	3	1			1	1	1		1				8		
Pepperell	31	31	Kemp	Jonas	2				1	1			2				6		
Pepperell	31	32	Lakin	Nathl		1	1		1		1		1				5		
Pepperell	31	33	Lakin	James					1		1	1		1			4		
Pepperell	31	34	Lakin	Nathl Jr	1			2			2	2		1			8		

TOWN	PG#	LN#	LAST NAME	FIRST NAME	FREE WHITE MALES					FREE WHITE FEMALES					TOTAL ALL OTHER	TOTAL SLAVES	TOTALS	DISTRICT/ TOWNSHIP	NOTES
					under 10	10 to 16	16 to 26	26 to 45	45 and over	under 10	10 to 16	16 to 26	26 to 45	45 and over					
Pepperell	31	35	Lakin	Nathl 3rd				1		2	1		1				5		
Pepperell	31	36	Laurence	Thos					1					1			2		
Pepperell	31	37	Laurence	M. Thos.	2	2		1		2			1	1			9		
Pepperell	31	38	Laurence	Ephm	1	1		2			2			1			7		
Pepperell	31	39	Laurence	Benja		2		1			1			1			5		
Pepperell	31	40	Laurence	Jesse	1		1					1					3		
Pepperell	31	41	Laurence	Abm	2		1					1					4		
Pepperell	31	42	Laurence	Elizabeth										1			1		
Pepperell	31	43	Laurence	Thos 3rd	1		1			2	2	1					7		
Pepperell	31	44	Landel	James	1		3	1		2		1		2			10		
Pepperell	31	45	Laurence	Josh		1	2	1		2		1		1			8		
Pepperell	31	46	Laurence	Thos Jr	1	1	1				1	1		1			6		
Pepperell	31	47	Laurence	David				1		4			1				6		
Pepperell	31	48	Laurence	Joseph	1	3	1	1	1				1	2			10		
Pepperell	32	1	Laurence	Peter		1		1				1		1			4		
Pepperell	32	2	Lovjoy	Wc						1			1	1			3		
Pepperell	32	3	Lakin	Robn	3	2		1				1		1			8		
Pepperell	32	4	Nutting	Simeon	1		2	1				1	1	1			7		
Pepperell	32	5	Nutting	John				1				1	1	1			4		
Pepperell	32	6	Nutting	John Jr	1		1	2		3	1	1					9		
Pepperell	32	7	Newhall	Oliver	1		1	1		1		1		1			6		
Pepperell	32	8	Nutting	Benja		1	1	1				1	2	1			7		
Pepperell	32	9	Nutting	Ebenr	1	1		1		1		1					5		
Pepperell	32	10	Nutting	Levi			1	1		1		1	1				5		
Pepperell	32	11	Parker	Edmund				1				1		1			3		
Pepperell	32	12	Parker	Abijah				1			1	1		1			4		
Pepperell	32	13	Parker	Jonas	3		1	1		2	1		1	1			10		
Pepperell	32	14	Parker	James	2		1	1		2	1		1				8		
Pepperell	32	15	Parker	Asa			1			3			1				5		
Pepperell	32	16	Pratt	Robert	1	1		1		1		1	1				6		
Pepperell	32	17	Parker	Abijah Jr	1			1		1			1				4		
Pepperell	32	18	Parker	Caleb	1			1		1		1	1	1			6		
Pepperell	32	19	Parker	John	1		2			1			1				5		
Pepperell	32	20	Perham	Ezekiel				1					1	1			3		
Pepperell	32	21	Perham	John	1		1			2			1				5		
Pepperell	32	22	Prescott	Abigail								1	1		1		3		
Pepperell	32	23	Pierce	Ephm	1		1	1		2		2		1			8		
Pepperell	32	24	Parker	Abijah		1	1			1		1	1				5		
Pepperell	32	25	Parker	Abijah Jr	3	1	1	1		1	3		1				11		
Pepperell	32	26	Pierce	Edward	1	1	1						1				4		
Pepperell	32	27	Powers	Hannah									1	1			2		
Pepperell	32	28	Parker	Nathl	1	1	2		1	3	1			1			10		
Pepperell	32	29	Parker	Jona									1				1		
Pepperell	32	30	Powers	Wm	1		1	1					1				4		
Pepperell	32	31	Shattuck	James				1				1		1			3		
Pepperell	32	32	Shattuck	Thos				1				1		1			3		
Pepperell	32	33	Shattuck	Reuben		1	3	1				1		1			7		
Pepperell	32	34	Shattuck	Joseph		1	1	1		1		1		1			6		
Pepperell	32	35	Shattuck	Moses	3	1		1		2	2	2		1			12		
Pepperell	32	36	Shattuck	Saml				1				1		1			3		
Pepperell	32	37	Shattuck	Philip		2		1				1					4		
Pepperell	32	38	Shattuck	Jona				1						1			2		
Pepperell	32	39	Shattuck	Jona Jr			2	1					1	1			5		
Pepperell	32	40	Shattuck	John				1						1			2		
Pepperell	32	41	Shed	David		1		1						1			3		
Pepperell	32	42	Shed	David Jr	1		1					1					3		
Pepperell	32	43	Shattuck	Jesse	3			1		1			1				6		
Pepperell	32	44	Stevens	Simon	3		1	1				1		1			7		
Pepperell	32	45	Stevens	Joseph	1	2							1				4		
Pepperell	32	46	Shed	Willard		1	1						1				3		
Pepperell	32	47	Shattuck	Abijah			1			1			1				3		
Pepperell	32	48	Shattuck	Abijah	1		1	1		2			1				6		
Pepperell	32	49	Shepard	Francis	1	1		1		1	1		1				7		
Pepperell	33	1	Shepard	Jona			2	1						1			4		
Pepperell	33	2	Shattuck	Jona 3rd	1			1		2			1	1			6		
Pepperell	33	3	Spaulding	Josiah	1			1		2			1				5		
Pepperell	33	4	Shattuck	James Jr		1		1		1	1		1				5		
Pepperell	33	5	Shed	Daniel				1			1			1			3		
Pepperell	33	6	Shepley	John	1			1		2		1			1		6		
Pepperell	33	7	Spaulding	Thos	1		1	1				1		1			5		
Pepperell	33	8	Shepley	Sarah								1		1			2		
Pepperell	33	9	Shattuck	Emerson	2	1		1		2			1	1			8		
Pepperell	33	10	Shattuck	Nathl	2			1		2			1				7		
Pepperell	33	11	Scott	Aaron			1	1	1			2		1			6		
Pepperell	33	12	Shattuck	Reuben Jr	1		1	1				1					4		
Pepperell	33	13	Spaulding	Abel	3	1	1	1	2	1			1	1			11		
Pepperell	33	14	Tarbell	James			1	1				1		1			4		
Pepperell	33	15	Tarbell	Wm		1	2	1				1	1	1			7		
Pepperell	33	16	Tarbell	David				1						1			2		

TOWN	PG#	LN#	LAST NAME	FIRST NAME	FREE WHITE MALES					FREE WHITE FEMALES					TOTAL ALL OTHER	TOTAL SLAVES	TOTALS	DISTRICT/ TOWNSHIP	NOTES
					under 10	10 to 16	16 to 26	26 to 45	45 and over	under 10	10 to 16	16 to 26	26 to 45	45 and over					
Pepperell	33	17	Tarbell	David Jr	1			1		1			1				4		
Pepperell	33	18	Tucker	Benja	2			1					1	1			5		
Pepperell	33	19	Trobridge	Thos	1			1		3	1		1				7		
Pepperell	33	20	Tarbell	Sewall				1					1				2		
Pepperell	33	21	Shattuck	Jerh					1	1	1	2		1			6		
Pepperell	33	22	Spaulding	Leml			1		1	1		1		1			5		
Pepperell	33	23	Shattuck	Oliver			1							1			2		
Pepperell	33	24	Shattuck	David				1	1					1			3		
Pepperell	33	25	Shattuck	Elijah		1	2		1		1	1		1			7		
Pepperell	33	26	Shattuck	Ebenr	3	1		1			2	1	1				9		
Pepperell	33	27	Shed	Esther	1		2				1			1			5		
Pepperell	33	28	Shattuck	Asa	1	1	1	1		2		1	1	1			9		
Pepperell	33	29	Shattuck	Israel	1	2		1		3		1	1				9		
Pepperell	33	30	Shattuck	Junia				1		2			1				4		
Pepperell	33	31	Sartill	Nathl		1		1				1	1				4		
Pepperell	33	32	Varnum	Jonas					1					1			2		
Pepperell	33	33	Varnum	John		1	1	1		1	1		1				6		
Pepperell	33	34	Varnum	Spaulding			1					1					2		
Pepperell	33	35	Walton	John	5		1	1					1				8		
Pepperell	33	36	Williams	Tho	2	1		1		2			1				7		
Pepperell	33	37	Williams	Isaac					1					1			2		
Pepperell	33	38	Williams	Isaac Jr	1	1		1			1		1				5		
Pepperell	33	39	Williams	Jonah	1		1	1		5	1	1	1				11		
Pepperell	33	40	Woodard	Benja					1					1			2		
Pepperell	33	41	Wright	Saml				2		2	2		1	1			8		
Pepperell	33	42	Wright	Edmund				1		1	1	1	1				5		
Pepperell	33	43	Wright	Josiah	2	2			1	2	2			1			10		
Pepperell	33	44	Wright	David			2		1	1			1	1			6		
Pepperell	33	45	Wright	Noah	2	3		1					1				7		
Pepperell	33	46	Woods	Stephen	1			1		1			1				4		
Pepperell	33	47	Scott	Eunice						1				1			2		
Pepperell	33	48	Wood	Aaron		1	2				1	1		1			6		
Pepperell	33	49	Whiting	Benja		1	3	1				1		1			7		
Pepperell	33	50	Wright	Abel	2		2		1	2	1			1			9		
Pepperell	34	1	Woods	Henry					1					2			3		
Pepperell	34	2	Woods	Isaac					1			2		1			4		
Pepperell	34	3	Woods	James	1			1		1		1					4		
Pepperell	34	4	Warren	Joseph			2		1		1			1			5		
Pepperell	34	5	Woods	Levi	3		1		1	1	2	2		1			11		
Pepperell	34	6	White	David				1	1	4			1	1			8		
Pepperell	34	7	White	Josh			1	1				2		1			5		
Pepperell	34	8	Wheeler	Benja			2	1						1			4		
Pepperell	34	9	Warner	Joseph		1	1	1				2		1			6		
Pepperell	34	10	Woods	Isaac Jr				1					1				2		
Pepperell	34	11	Woods	Thos	1			1		3			1				6		
Pepperell	34	12	Woods	Leml		1		1						1			3		
Pepperell	34	13	Montague	Seth				1									1		
Pepperell	34	14	Manning	Peter	2			1		2	1		1				7		
Pepperell	34	15	Menihan	Robert	1			1		3			1				6		
Pepperell	34	16	Shattuck	Amaziah	1			1				1					3		
Pepperell	34	17	Bullard	John Rev	1	2	1	1		2	1	1		1			10		
Pepperell	34	18	Parker	Levi	3	1		1		1				1			7		
Pepperell	34	19	Wright	Wc B						2		1	1				4		
Pepperell	34	20	Williams	Benja	1			1					1				3		
Pepperell	34	21	Lovjoy	Jesse	1			1		3	1		1				7		
Pepperell	34	22	Smith	David				1		2		1		1			5		
Pepperell	34	23	Wright	Natha	1	1	1		1	1			1				6		
Pepperell	34	24	Conant	Rachel								1		1			2		
Pepperell	34	25	Conant	Josiah	1	1		1		1			1				5		
Pepperell	34	26	Hosley	Tho			1					1					2		
Pepperell	34	27	Phillis	*											5		5		

TOWN	PG#	LN#	LAST NAME	FIRST NAME	FREE WHITE MALES under 10	10 to 16	16 to 26	26 to 45	45 and over	FREE WHITE FEMALES under 10	10 to 16	16 to 26	26 to 45	45 and over	TOTAL ALL OTHER	TOTAL SLAVES	TOTALS	DISTRICT/ TOWNSHIP	NOTES
Reading	127	1	Abbot	Ebenezer	1	3		1		3		1					9		
Reading	127	2	Atwell	Joseph		1	1		1		1	1		1			6		
Reading	127	3	Bancroft	James			1		1				1	1	1		5		
Reading	127	4	Bancroft	Joseph					1				1	1			3		
Reading	127	5	Bancroft	Timothy	3			1		2			1				7		
Reading	127	6	Brown	John		1		1					1				3		
Reading	127	7	Brown	Jeremiah	2		2	1			1	1	1	1			9		
Reading	127	8	Brown	Benjamin				1						2	1		4		
Reading	127	9	Bordman	Amos	2	1	3	1		1	2	2		1			13		
Reading	127	10	Burdet	Joseph		1		1			1			1			4		
Reading	127	11	Bryant	Jeremiah		1		1						1			3		
Reading	128	1	Bryant	Jeremiah Jr		1	1	1			1		1				5		
Reading	128	2	Bryant	Timothy		1		1				1		1			4		
Reading	128	3	Bryant	Nathan	2	1	1			1		1					6		
Reading	128	4	Batt	William	1	1	1					1					4		
Reading	128	5	Burnop	Abigail	1							2		2			5		
Reading	128	6	Bancroft	Jonathan			1					1	1				3		
Reading	128	7	Brown	Jepththap			1					1	1				3		
Reading	128	8	Bouttell	James		1	1		1	1	1	1		3			9		
Reading	128	9	Bouttell	James Jr			1			1		1					3		
Reading	129	1	B*t	Edward	2		1			2	1		1				7		
Reading	129	2	Burnap	Joseph				1						1			2		
Reading	129	3	Burnap	James				1						2			3		
Reading	129	4	Bachelor	Simeon	1	3		1		2	1		1				9		
Reading	129	5	Buxton	Stephen	1	1	1		1	1	1		1	1			8		
Reading	129	6	Buxton	Ebenezer	3	2		1		3	1		1				11		
Reading	129	7	Bachelor	Joseph	2			1		1	1		1				6		
Reading	129	8	Bachelor	Jonathan				1						1			2		
Reading	129	9	Bachelor	Nathaniel		1		1				1	1				4		
Reading	129	10	Bachelor	John	2	1		1		2	1		1				8		
Reading	129	11	Bachelor	John	2			1		2			1	1			7		
Reading	129	12	Beard	William		1	1			1	1			3			8		
Reading	129	13	Beard	Cleveland				1						2			3		
Reading	129	14	Bancroft	Joseph Jr			1	1		3	1		1	1			8		
Reading	129	15	Bancroft	Nehemiah	1			1		2			2				6		
Reading	129	16	Baldwin	Jonathan Jr				1				1					2		
Reading	129	17	Beors	William	2	1		1		1	2		1				8		
Reading	129	18	Bailey	Jesse	1			1				1	2				5		
Reading	129	19	Bryant	Thomas			1	1		1			1				4		
Reading	129	20	Bodger	Benjamin	1		1	1			1		1				5		
Reading	129	21	Burdet	Aaron			2	1		1			1				5		
Reading	129	22	Burdet	James			1						1				2		
Reading	129	23	Baldwin	Jonathan		1			1		1			1			4		
Reading	129	24	Burnap	John					1		1	1		1			4		
Reading	129	25	Buxton	Widow										1			1		
Reading	129	26	Brown	Nathaniel				1					1				2		
Reading	129	27	Bordman	Aaron		1	2	1					1	1			6		
Reading	129	28	Bordman	Ivery				1					1				2		
Reading	129	29	Case	Humphra	2	1	1		1		1	1		1			8		
Reading	129	30	Cobb	Mallatia	2	1			1	3	1		1				9		
Reading	129	31	Carter	Thomas	2	2	1	1		2	1		1				10		
Reading	129	32	Chute	Daniel		1	1						1				3		
Reading	129	33	Cowdrey	Nathaniel				1					1				2		
Reading	129	34	Cowdrey	Nathaniel Jr	1	1		1		2	1	1	1				8		
Reading	129	35	Cowdrey	Aaron	1			1					1				3		
Reading	129	36	Cordis	Joseph	2		2	2		1	2	2			1		12		
Reading	129	37	Clement	Thomas	2		1	1	1		1	2		1	1		10		
Reading	129	38	Chaney	Jacob			1					1					2		
Reading	130	1	Carter	Elijah	4			1		1			1				7		
Reading	130	2	Damon	John	1		1	1		1		1	1	3			9		
Reading	130	3	Damon	Daniel Jr	2	3		1		2			1	1			10		
Reading	130	4	Damon	Aaron	3	1		1		1	1		1				8		
Reading	130	5	Damon	Joseph	1	1		1		2			1		1		7		
Reading	130	6	Damon	Ebenezer			1		1			1		1			4		
Reading	130	7	Damon	Ebenezer Jr		1	1		1	2	1			2			8		
Reading	130	8	Damon	Daniel				1						2			3		
Reading	130	9	Damon	Ezra				1						1			2		
Reading	130	10	Damon	Amos	2	2		1					1	1			7		
Reading	130	11	Dix	John	1	1	1	1				1	1				6		
Reading	130	12	Damon	Joshua	3			1		1	2		1				8		
Reading	130	13	Damon	Edmund	2	1		1		3	2		1				10		
Reading	130	14	Eaton	Nathaniel	3	1		1		2		1	1				9		
Reading	130	15	Eaton	Hannah					1		1	2		1			5		
Reading	130	16	Eaton	Thomas		1	2	1				1		2			7		
Reading	130	17	Eaton	Samuel	3	1	1		1		1		1	2			10		
Reading	130	18	Eaton	Timothy				1				1	1	1			4		
Reading	130	19	Emerson	John				1					2	1			4		
Reading	130	20	Emerson	John Jr	1	1	1	1		1		2	2	1			10		
Reading	130	21	Emerson	Daniel	3	2		1			1		1				8		

TOWN	PG#	LN#	LAST NAME	FIRST NAME	FREE WHITE MALES					FREE WHITE FEMALES					TOTAL ALL OTHER	TOTAL SLAVES	TOTALS	DISTRICT/ TOWNSHIP	NOTES
					under 10	10 to 16	16 to 26	26 to 45	45 and over	under 10	10 to 16	16 to 26	26 to 45	45 and over					
Reading	130	22	Emerson	David	2	1	1	1			1	1	1				8		
Reading	130	23	Emerson	Ebenezer					1		1			2			4		
Reading	130	24	Emerson	Ebenezer	1			1			2		1				5		
Reading	130	25	Eaton	Osgood	2		2	1			1		1				7		
Reading	130	26	Eaton	Ebenezer		1	1		1		1			1			5		
Reading	130	27	Emerson	Joseph			1	1	1				1	2			6		
Reading	130	28	Eads	Anna								1		1			2		
Reading	130	29	Emerson	James	2	1		1	1	2			1				8		
Reading	130	30	Emerson	Benjamin	1		2		1	1	2	1		1			9		
Reading	130	31	Emerson	Thomas				1						1			2		
Reading	130	32	Emerson	Thomas Jr	2	2	1	1		1	2	1	1				11		
Reading	130	33	Eaton	Lille		1	1	1	1			2	2	1			9		
Reading	130	34	Eaton	Lille Jr				1		1	1						3		
Reading	130	35	Eaton	Nathan		1	2		1	3				1			8		
Reading	130	36	Eaton	Elizabeth										1			1		
Reading	131	1	Evens	Samuel	1	1	2	1		2	1	1	1				10		
Reading	131	2	Evens	Thomas	2	2	2		1			1		1			9		
Reading	131	3	Eaton	Reuben			1	1	1		1	1	1				6		
Reading	131	4	Eaton	Jacob	1		1			1		1	1				5		
Reading	131	5	Emerson	Charles		2	2						2				6		
Reading	131	6	Emerson	Jonathan	2			1					1				4		
Reading	131	7	Foster	Abigail										2			2		
Reading	131	8	Foster	Jonathan				1		1	2		1				5		
Reading	131	9	Flint	John				1					1				2		
Reading	131	10	Flint	George				1					1				2		
Reading	131	11	Flint	George Jr	1	1		1			1		1				5		
Reading	131	12	Flint	William		1	1	1	1		1		1				6		
Reading	131	13	Flint	William Jr	3		1			2		2	1				9		
Reading	131	14	Flint	Adam	1			1	3	1	1	1	1	2			11		
Reading	131	15	Flint	Ebenezer	2	1	1		1	1				1			7		
Reading	131	16	Flint	Eleazer		1		1					1	1			4		
Reading	131	17	Flint	Daniel	2	1	2	1		3	2	1	1				13		
Reading	131	18	Flint	Daniel Jr	2			1		3		1					7		
Reading	131	19	Flint	Benjamin		1	1		1			2		1			6		
Reading	131	20	Fry	Mary	1	1			2	3			2	2			11		
Reading	131	21	Foster	Abraham	1			1		2			1	1			6		
Reading	131	22	Foster	Mary	2	2	1			1	1	1	1	1			10		
Reading	131	23	Flint	John Jr	2	1		1		3		1	1				9		
Reading	131	24	Fowler	Lowel		1		1			1		1				4		
Reading	131	25	Flint	Eleazer Jr	2			1		2			1				6		
Reading	131	26	Flint	Hezekiah	1	1		1	1	1	1		1				6		
Reading	131	27	Foster	William	1		1		1	1	1			1			6		
Reading	131	28	Flagg	Theodias	1			1		1		1					4		
Reading	131	29	Flint	Kindel	1			1		2		1	1				6		
Reading	131	30	Flint	Levy		1	1		1	2	1		1				7		
Reading	131	31	Freeman	Peter											3		3		
Reading	131	32	Freeman	Dors											2		2		
Reading	131	33	Freeman	*											4		4		
Reading	131	34	Freeman	Jonah											2		2		
Reading	132	1	Green	Caleb			2	1		1			1				5		
Reading	132	2	Gould	Joseph					1					1			2		
Reading	132	3	Gould	John	1	2		1		3			1				8		
Reading	132	4	Gould	James	3		1	1		1	1		1	1			9		
Reading	132	5	Gould	Daniel		1	1				1	1	1				5		
Reading	132	6	Green	Nathan		1		1		1	1		1	1			6		
Reading	132	7	Green	Daniel		1			1	2			2				6		
Reading	132	8	Green	Reuben		2		1		2		1	1				7		
Reading	132	9	Green	Thomas				1					2	1			4		
Reading	132	10	Green	Jeremiah		1	2	1		4	2	1	1				12		
Reading	132	11	Green	Aaron		2		1		2		2	1				8		
Reading	132	12	Goodwin	John				1						1			2		
Reading	132	13	Goodwin	John Jr	2			1		1	1		1	1			7		
Reading	132	14	Graves	Daniel	2	1	1	1	1	2	2	1	1	1			13		
Reading	132	15	Green	Sarah		1				1			1				3		
Reading	132	16	Hay	Daniel				1					1				2		
Reading	132	17	Herrick	Mortin				1		3	1		1				6		
Reading	132	18	Hill	Joseph				1		1		1					3		
Reading	132	19	Hill	Asa			2	1				1	1				5		
Reading	132	20	Hopkins	Joseph	1		1	1				2					5		
Reading	132	21	Hawks	Adam		1	1			1		1					4		
Reading	132	22	Hartshorn	James	1	2	1		1		1	2		1			9		
Reading	132	23	Hartshorn	Jeremiah	1	1		1					1	1			5		
Reading	132	24	Hay	John				1	1		1		1				4		
Reading	132	25	Hartshorn	John	1	1			1	1	2	1	1	2			10		
Reading	132	26	Hartshorn	Timothy		1	2		1			1		1			6		
Reading	132	27	Holt	Joseph	1		2		1	2	1	1	1	1			10		
Reading	132	28	Haywood	William	2			1	1	3	2	1	1	1			12		
Reading	132	29	Haywood	John		1			1	1	1		1				5		
Reading	132	30	Haywood	Jabez	1	2	1	1			1	2		2			10		

TOWN	PG#	LN#	LAST NAME	FIRST NAME	FREE WHITE MALES					FREE WHITE FEMALES					TOTAL ALL OTHER	TOTAL SLAVES	TOTALS	DISTRICT/ TOWNSHIP	NOTES
					under 10	10 to 16	16 to 26	26 to 45	45 and over	under 10	10 to 16	16 to 26	26 to 45	45 and over					
Reading	132	31	Herrick	Mary							1		1				2		
Reading	132	32	Hay	Jonathan	2			1		2			1				6		
Reading	132	33	Hale	Stephen			1	1				2		1			5		
Reading	132	34	Hovey	Darius	1			1		1	1	1					5		
Reading	132	35	Hadley	Sarah	1								2				3		
Reading	133	1	Hart	Joseph		1		1					1				3		
Reading	133	2	Hart	Daniel	3			1		1		1					6		
Reading	133	3	Jeffrey	Joseph					1		1		1				3		
Reading	133	4	Jeffrey	Joseph Jr				1				1					2		
Reading	133	5	Johnson	William		1	1		1			1		1			5		
Reading	133	6	Johnson	William Jr	2			1				1					4		
Reading	133	7	Johnson	John	2	1		1			2		1				7		
Reading	133	8	Kenney	Jethro	1		1					1					3		
Reading	133	9	Lambert	William	1			1					1				3		
Reading	133	10	Lewis	William		1						1					2		
Reading	133	11	Lewis	Charles		1				1		1					3		
Reading	133	12	Legros	Samuel	1	1						1					3		
Reading	133	13	Larrebee	Samuel		3						1					4		
Reading	133	14	Mackintone	Archelas		1	1			3		1	1				7		
Reading	133	15	Mackintone	Hezekiah	1	1	2		1	2	1			1			9		
Reading	133	16	Mackintone	Benjamin	2	2		1		1	2			1			9		
Reading	133	17	Mackintone	Solomon	1			1	1	1				1			4		
Reading	133	18	Mason	Nathan		1		1			1		1				4		
Reading	133	19	Mackintone	Ebenezer	1			1	1	3	1	1	1				9		
Reading	133	20	Mackintone	Ephraim		1		1					1				3		
Reading	133	21	Mackintone	John	3	1		1					1	1			7		
Reading	133	22	Nichols	Jesse	2	1		1		1			1				6		
Reading	133	23	N*s	Daniel	1	1			1				1				4		
Reading	133	24	Nichols	James Jr	3			1					1				5		
Reading	133	25	Newhall	Reuben	2			1			1	1					5		
Reading	133	26	Nichols	Simon	1	1	1		1		1	3		1			9		
Reading	133	27	Nichols	James	1		2	1			1			1			6		
Reading	133	28	Newhall	James	2			1		1			1				5		
Reading	133	29	Nichols	Reuben		1	1		1		1			1			5		
Reading	133	30	Nichols	Jeremiah			2	1		2	1	1	1				8		
Reading	133	31	Nichols	John			1	1					1	1			4		
Reading	133	32	Nichols	John Jr		1		1		2	1		1	1			7		
Reading	134	1	Nichols	Simon Jr	1		1					1		1			4		
Reading	134	2	Nichols	Hay			1					1					2		
Reading	134	3	Newhall	Olive						1	1	1	1				4		
Reading	134	4	Nelson	John	2			1		1	1			1			6		
Reading	134	5	Nichols	Edmund	1	2		1		2			1				7		
Reading	134	6	Osgood	Joshua			1	1		3		1	1	1			8		
Reading	134	7	Oliver	William	2		1	1		1	1	1					7		
Reading	134	8	Parker	William	3			1	1				1	1			7		
Reading	134	9	Parker	Daniel Jr	1	2	1		1		1			1			7		
Reading	134	10	Parker	Daniel					1					2			3		
Reading	134	11	Parker	Isaac	2	1	1		1		1						6		
Reading	134	12	Parker	Asa			2		1		1	1		1			6		
Reading	134	13	Parker	Asa Jr	2			1		1			1				5		
Reading	134	14	Parker	Simeon	1				1				1				3		
Reading	134	15	Pratt	Isaac		1	1		1		1	2		1			7		
Reading	134	16	Pratt	Benjamin	1	1	1	1		3				1			8		
Reading	134	17	Pratt	Daniel			1		1			1	1				4		
Reading	134	18	Parker	David	1	1	2		2			2		2			10		
Reading	134	19	Parker	Eliab	1			1					1				3		
Reading	134	20	Pratt	Ephraim	4	2			1	1			1	1			9		
Reading	134	21	Putnam	Henry	1	1	3	1	1	2		2	1				12		
Reading	134	22	Parker	Joseph		1		1				2					4		
Reading	134	23	Pool	Thomas		1	2	1		1	1						6		
Reading	134	24	Pratt	William			2						1				3		
Reading	134	25	Peters	Benjamin	1			1	1		1		1				5		
Reading	134	26	Pool	Elizabeth										1			1		
Reading	134	27	Parker	Thomas		1			1		1	1		1			5		
Reading	134	28	Parker	Phinehas		1			1			1		1			4		
Reading	134	29	Parker	Amos	2		1	1		2		1	1	1			9		
Reading	134	30	Prentop	Caleb Rev	3		2		1	3	1	1	1	1	1		14		
Reading	134	31	Parker	Nathan	2	1	4		2		3	1	1				14		
Reading	134	32	Parker	William Jr		1	1	1		2			2				7		
Reading	134	33	Parker	Aaron	2	1		1				1	1				6		
Reading	134	34	Parker	Jonas	1	1			1	1	2		1				7		
Reading	135	1	Parker	Samuel			1	1		3		1					6		
Reading	135	2	Pratt	David	2			1		2		1	1				7		
Reading	135	3	Pratt	Amos	1			1		2			1				5		
Reading	135	4	Parker	Ephraim			1	1					1	1			4		
Reading	135	5	Parker	Ephraim Jr				1						1			2		
Reading	135	6	Pool	Jonathan	1		2		1		1	1		2			8		
Reading	135	7	Pool	Timothy				1			1	1	1				4		
Reading	135	8	Parker	Benjamin	1		1	1		3		1	2	1			10		

TOWN	PG#	LN#	HEADS OF HOUSEHOLD		FREE WHITE MALES					FREE WHITE FEMALES					TOTAL ALL OTHER	TOTAL SLAVES	TOTALS	DISTRICT/ TOWNSHIP	NOTES
			LAST NAME	FIRST NAME	under 10	10 to 16	16 to 26	26 to 45	45 and over	under 10	10 to 16	16 to 26	26 to 45	45 and over					
Reading	135	9	Pratt	Jonathan	1			1					1				3		
Reading	135	10	Roop	Oliver	3	1	2	1		2	1		1				11		
Reading	135	11	Parker	Moly	2					1			1				4		
Reading	135	12	Peters	Ezra			1			1		1					3		
Reading	135	13	Roop	John	1		2						1				4		
Reading	135	14	Roop	Jesse			1						1				2		
Reading	135	15	Peters	Samuel	3			1					2				6		
Reading	135	16	Rold	Daniel	1		1						2				4		
Reading	135	17	Richardson	Harburt	3	1		1		2			1	1			9		
Reading	135	18	Richardson	Jethro		1	1		1	1	2	2	1				8		
Reading	135	19	Rayner	John	2		1	1	1	1			1	1			8		
Reading	135	20	Richardson	Asa	1	1		1		2			1				6		
Reading	135	21	Rolf	Stephen		1	2	1						1			5		
Reading	135	22	Russel	Timothy					1				1		2		4		
Reading	135	23	Richardson	Edward	1		2						1				4		
Reading	135	24	Russel	Stephen			1			1	1						3		
Reading	135	25	Reed	Hannah						1	1		1				3		
Reading	135	26	Reed	Berzellai		1	1						1				3		
Reading	135	27	Sawyer	William		1	1						1				3		
Reading	135	28	Sawyer	Thomas		2	1	1		2	1		1				8		
Reading	135	29	Shilden	Nathaniel		1			2	1	1	1	1	1			8		
Reading	135	30	Shilden	Russel	2	1	1		1			1	1				7		
Reading	135	31	Swain	John	1	2	5	2	2	2	1	2	1				18		
Reading	135	32	Swain	Oliver	4			1				1		1			7		
Reading	135	33	Stone	Eliab Rev	1	1		1	1			1		1	1		7		
Reading	135	34	Stone	Eliab Jr	2		1	1		2	1		1	1			9		
Reading	136	1	Slack	John	2			1					1	1			5		
Reading	136	2	Swain	Thomas Jr			1						1	1			3		
Reading	136	3	Symonds	Thomas		1	1		1	1		1	1	1			7		
Reading	136	4	Smith	David			4	1	1	1			1	1			9		
Reading	136	5	Smith	Noah		1							1				2		
Reading	136	6	Stimpson	Thomas				1									1		
Reading	136	7	Stimpson	Thomas Jr	3			1					1				5		
Reading	136	8	Sweetser	Daniel	2		1	1		2			2	1			9		
Reading	136	9	Sweetser	John		1	1	1	1	1		1	2	1			9		
Reading	136	10	Stowel	Eli*	1	2			1					1			5		
Reading	136	11	Sweetser	Paul	1		3		1	2	2		1				10		
Reading	136	12	Smith	Mary										1			1		
Reading	136	13	Sweetser	Mary										2			2		
Reading	136	14	Sweet	Phinehas		1	1	1		2			1	1			7		
Reading	136	15	Stimpson	William	1			1						2			4		
Reading	136	16	Stimpson	William Jr	3			1	1	1			2				8		
Reading	136	17	Swain	Benjamin	2		1	1					2				6		
Reading	136	18	Sweetser	Cornelius	1	1	1		1			1		1			6		
Reading	136	19	Swain	Thomas			1					1		1			3		
Reading	136	20	Sanburn	Peter Rev			1			1		2					4		
Reading	136	21	Souker	Enoch			1						1				2		
Reading	136	22	Swain	Hannah								1		1			2		
Reading	136	23	Sweetser	Thomas	3	1		1					1	1			7		
Reading	136	24	Sweetser	Ezra	2		1					1	1				5		
Reading	136	25	Sweetser	Moses	2			1					2				5		
Reading	136	26	Smith	John	2		1	1		1			1				6		
Reading	136	27	Smith	James					1			1		1			3		
Reading	136	28	Smith	Jonathan	1			1		1		1	1	1			6		
Reading	136	29	Swain	John Jr	1		1					1		1			4		
Reading	136	30	Smith	Joseph	2	1		1		1			1				6		
Reading	136	31	Sweetser	Timothy			1			1			2				4		
Reading	136	32	Temple	William	1		1	1				1		2			6		
Reading	136	33	Temple	John	1			1				1		1			4		
Reading	136	34	Temple	John Jr	2		2	1		2	1	1					9		
Reading	136	35	Temple	Jonathan	1			1		3			1				6		
Reading	137	1	Temple	Richard	1			1					1				3		
Reading	137	2	Temple	Jabez	1			1		3	2			1			8		
Reading	137	3	Temple	Daniel	1	1	1	1		2			2	1			9		
Reading	137	4	Tay	Nathaniel	1	1		1					1				4		
Reading	137	5	Taylor	James	1			1			1	3		1			7		
Reading	137	6	Taylor	Joseph				1			1		1				3		
Reading	137	7	Upton	Daniel	1	1		1		2			1	2			8		
Reading	137	8	Upton	Benjamin		3	1		1				2	1			8		
Reading	137	9	Upton	Amos		1	1	1	1	1				1			5		
Reading	137	10	Upton	Hezekiah		1	1	1				1		1			5		
Reading	137	11	Upton	Nathaniel	1	2	1		1	3		1	1				10		
Reading	137	12	Upton	David	1	1	1	1					1	2			7		
Reading	137	13	Upton	David Jr	1				1	2		1	1		1		7		
Reading	137	14	Upham	Tammey		1							1				2		
Reading	137	15	Upton	Elijah				1						1			2		
Reading	137	16	Upton	Jabez				1						1			2		
Reading	137	17	Upton	Benjamin Jr		1		1				1	1	1			5		
Reading	137	18	Vinton	John			1	1				1					3		
Reading	137	19	Vinton	John Jr	1			1		2	1		1				6		

94

TOWN	PG#	LN#	LAST NAME	FIRST NAME	FREE WHITE MALES					FREE WHITE FEMALES					TOTAL ALL OTHER	TOTAL SLAVES	TOTALS	DISTRICT/ TOWNSHIP	NOTES
					under 10	10 to 16	16 to 26	26 to 45	45 and over	under 10	10 to 16	16 to 26	26 to 45	45 and over					
Reading	137	20	Willy	John	1	2	5			1		2					11		
Reading	137	21	Whitridge	William				1				1		1			3		
Reading	137	22	Whitridge	William Jr	2			1		1			1	1			6		
Reading	137	23	Wakefield	Timothy		2	1	1		1			1	1			7		
Reading	137	24	Weston	James	1	1			1	1	2		1				7		
Reading	137	25	Weston	James Jr	2	1		1		3			1				8		
Reading	137	26	Weston	James 3rd	2			1		1			1				5		
Reading	137	27	Weston	James 4th				1		1		1					3		
Reading	137	28	Weston	John		1	1		1		1		1	1			6		
Reading	137	29	Weston	John Jr	2			1					1				4		
Reading	137	30	Weston	Abijah	1			1		2			1	1			6		
Reading	137	31	Weston	Jabez	2			1		2			1	1			7		
Reading	137	32	Weston	Jonathan	1		3	1			1		1				7		
Reading	137	33	Weston	Samuel	4			1			1		1				7		
Reading	137	34	Wiley	James		1	2		1	2				1			7		
Reading	137	35	Walton	Benjamin		1	1		2			1		2			7		
Reading	138	1	Williams	William	1	1	1	1		1	1		1				7		
Reading	138	2	Wiley	Eli	1		1			1		1					4		
Reading	138	3	Walton	Oliver	4			1	1	2	1	2	1	2			14		
Reading	138	4	Walton	Timothy		1			1			2		1			5		
Reading	138	5	Wiley	Nathaniel					1					1			2		
Reading	138	6	Wiley	Nathaniel Jr	3	1	2	1		1	1	2	1	1			13		
Reading	138	7	Weston	Ephraim	2	1		1		1			1				6		
Reading	138	8	Winn	Jeremiah	1		1			1		1					4		
Reading	138	9	Wiley	Edmund	2			1		3		1	1				8		
Reading	138	10	Woodward	John G				1		2			1				4		
Reading	138	11	Wiley	Samuel	2		2	1					1				6		
Reading	138	12	Williams	William Jr	1		1					1					3		
Reading	138	13	Young	Benjamin	1	1		1		1	2		1				7		

TOWN	PG#	LN#	LAST NAME	FIRST NAME	FREE WHITE MALES					FREE WHITE FEMALES					TOTAL ALL OTHER	TOTAL SLAVES	TOTALS	DISTRICT/ TOWNSHIP	NOTES
					under 10	10 to 16	16 to 26	26 to 45	45 and over	under 10	10 to 16	16 to 26	26 to 45	45 and over					
Sherburn	248	1	Adams	James			1			1			1				3		
Sherburn	248	2	Adams	Wm	2		1				1		1				5		
Sherburn	248	3	Babcock	Moses	2		1			1		1					5		
Sherburn	248	4	Bullard	Saml				1				1		1			3		
Sherburn	248	5	Bullard	James		1		1		1			1				4		
Sherburn	248	6	Blodget	Saml				1						1			2		
Sherburn	248	7	Badger	John	3			1		2			1				7		
Sherburn	248	8	Bullard	Galam	1			1		1			1				4		
Sherburn	248	9	Bullard	Moses			2						1				3		
Sherburn	248	10	Babcock	Malaca				1		2				1			4		
Sherburn	248	11	Babcock	Ebenz	1		1			2	2	1					7		
Sherburn	248	12	Bullard	Peter Jr	1			1					1				3		
Sherburn	248	13	Brown	Elijah			2	1						1			4		
Sherburn	248	14	Brick	Daniel	1			1		5			1				8		
Sherburn	248	15	Bigelow	Convers	2	2	1		1	2		2	1				11		
Sherburn	248	16	Barber	Elisha				1			1		1	1			3		
Sherburn	248	17	Barber	Elisha Jr	1					1	2	1	1				6		
Sherburn	248	18	Barber	Oliver	2	1		1		2			2				8		
Sherburn	248	19	Brick	Jona	1	1	1				1			3			7		
Sherburn	248	20	Brick	Thos	2		1	1						1			5		
Sherburn	248	21	Brick	John			1	1						1			3		
Sherburn	248	22	Bullard	Peter	1	1		1				1		1			5		
Sherburn	249	1	Bullard	John			1			1			1				3		
Sherburn	249	2	Bullard	Benjm	1	1	1						2				5		
Sherburn	249	3	Brickford	James			1	1		1		1	1				5		
Sherburn	249	4	Clark	Mical	3	1		1		1		1					7		
Sherburn	249	5	Coolidge	Wm			1			1	1	1					4		
Sherburn	249	6	Chamberlin	Moses			1						1				2		
Sherburn	249	7	Clarck	Wm	1	1		1			1	1	1				6		
Sherburn	249	8	Clark	Sama		1	1	1				1		1			5		
Sherburn	249	9	Coolidge	Daniel	2	1		1		3	2	1	1	1			12		
Sherburn	249	10	Cushings	Isaac		1	1	1				1	1				5		
Sherburn	249	11	Cushings	Asa		1	3	1		2		1	1				9		
Sherburn	249	12	Crackbone	Joseph	2	1		1		2	1		1				8		
Sherburn	249	13	Clark	Daniel				1						1			2		
Sherburn	249	14	Clark	John	4			1		1	1		1				8		
Sherburn	249	15	Clark	Asa	1			2		2			1	1			7		
Sherburn	249	16	Coolidge	Joseph	1	1	1					1	1	1			7		
Sherburn	249	17	Downs	Elezer				1						1			2		
Sherburn	249	18	Downs	Joseph	1	1		1		2			1				6		
Sherburn	249	19	Downs	Elezer Jr	1	1			1	1	1			1			6		
Sherburn	249	20	Death	Marget	1									2			5		
Sherburn	249	21	Daniels	Timothy		1	1		1	1	1	1		1			7		
Sherburn	249	22	Death	Henry	1		2		1	2	1	1		1			9		
Sherburn	249	23	Ellis	Bethael	1	1		1		1			1				5		
Sherburn	249	24	Frost	John	2			1		2				1			6		
Sherburn	249	25	Foster	Eli		1		1			1		1				4		
Sherburn	249	26	Fisk	John				1			1		1				3		
Sherburn	249	27	Freeman	Lewis											5		5		
Sherburn	249	28	Gay	Abigail	2						1						3		
Sherburn	249	29	Grout	Elias	1		1	1		1			1				5		
Sherburn	249	30	Gardner	Aaron		1		1		1	1		1	1			6		
Sherburn	249	31	Greenwood	Jonas				1				2	1				4		
Sherburn	249	32	Greenwood	Jonas Jr	1		1					1					3		
Sherburn	249	33	Greenwood	Reuben	1			1		1			1				4		
Sherburn	249	34	Grout	Belea	1			1					2				4		
Sherburn	249	35	Golden	John	1			1	1				1				5		
Sherburn	249	36	Grant	Hannah		1			1	1		1		1			5		
Sherburn	249	37	Horton	Benjm		1		1	1	2	2		1	1			9		
Sherburn	249	38	Haynes	Martin				1			1		1				3		
Sherburn	249	39	Holbrook	Mical				1				2	1	1			5		
Sherburn	249	40	Holbrook	Elliot			1			1		1					3		
Sherburn	249	41	Hill	John	2	1		1		1			1				6		
Sherburn	249	42	Haven	Gideon				1						1			2		
Sherburn	249	43	Hill	Timothy				1		1				1			3		
Sherburn	249	44	Hill	Timothy Jr	2			1		1			1				5		
Sherburn	250	1	Holbrook	Thos				1	1	2		1	1	1			7		
Sherburn	250	2	Holbrook	Joseph	1	1		1		1			1	1			6		
Sherburn	250	3	Holbrook	Nathl				1				1		1			3		
Sherburn	250	4	Holbrook	Jona			1					1	1	1			4		
Sherburn	250	5	Hill	James	1	1		1	1				2	1			8		
Sherburn	250	6	Hart	Wm		1	1							2			5		
Sherburn	250	7	Holbrook	James	3	2	1			1	1		1				9		
Sherburn	250	8	Hill	James Jr		1	2	1					1				5		
Sherburn	250	9	Hart	Willard			1			2			1				4		
Sherburn	250	10	Haws	Daniel	4		1	1		2	1		1				10		
Sherburn	250	11	Holbrook	Joshua	1		1	1		1			1				5		
Sherburn	250	12	Jay	Jona			1	1	1	1		1	1	1			7		
Sherburn	250	13	Johnson	Nathan	2		1		1			1					5		

96

TOWN	PG#	LN#	LAST NAME	FIRST NAME	M under 10	M 10-16	M 16-26	M 26-45	M 45 & over	F under 10	F 10-16	F 16-26	F 26-45	F 45 & over	TOTAL ALL OTHER	TOTAL SLAVES	TOTALS	DISTRICT/TOWNSHIP	NOTES
Sherburn	250	14	Kolton	Wm					1	1		1		1			4		
Sherburn	250	15	Kimbal	Thos	1		1	1		3			1				7		
Sherburn	250	16	Kimbal	John		1	1			1			1				4		
Sherburn	250	17	Kimbal	Benjm		1		1	1			1	1				5		
Sherburn	250	18	Leland	Adam		1			1			1		1			4		
Sherburn	250	19	Leland	Jona			2		1	2	1		1				7		
Sherburn	250	20	Leland	Jonas	1			1		1			1				4		
Sherburn	250	21	Leland	Hinsy	2	2		1		1	1		1				8		
Sherburn	250	22	Leland	Mical	2	1			1		1	1	1				7		
Sherburn	250	23	Leland	Eli	1			1				1					3		
Sherburn	250	24	Leland	John	2			1			1		1				5		
Sherburn	250	25	Leland	Asa					1			1	1				3		
Sherburn	250	26	Leland	Wm	2			1					1				4		
Sherburn	250	27	Leland	Saml		1	1	1		1			1				5		
Sherburn	250	28	Leland	Balak		1	1	1					1				4		
Sherburn	250	29	Leland	Joseph			1		1	2			2				6		
Sherburn	250	30	Leland	Hoptes			1	1	1				1				4		
Sherburn	250	31	Leland	Moses		2			1		1	1		3			8		
Sherburn	250	32	Leland	Aaron	1		1		1	1	1			1			6		
Sherburn	250	33	Learned	Saml		1		1		3			1				6		
Sherburn	250	34	Morse	Hezekh	3		1			1	1		1				7		
Sherburn	250	35	Morse	Jona				1						1			2		
Sherburn	250	36	Marshall	James				1						2			3		
Sherburn	250	37	Morse	Levi				1				1		1			3		
Sherburn	250	38	Morse	Hezekh	2			1		1			1	1			6		
Sherburn	250	39	Morse	Moses			1						2	1			4		
Sherburn	250	40	Morse	Jason	1			1				1		1			4		
Sherburn	250	41	Morse	Saml			1			3			1				5		
Sherburn	250	42	Newhall	Thos	2	1		1		3			1	1			9		
Sherburn	251	1	Perry	West	1			1		2			1				5		
Sherburn	251	2	Perry	Moses				1				1	1	1			4		
Sherburn	251	3	Perry	Moses Jr			1	1		1		3					6		
Sherburn	251	4	Perry	Moses 3rd		2	1	1		2			1				7		
Sherburn	251	5	Perry	Tiler		1	1	1		3		1	1				8		
Sherburn	251	6	Perry	Daniel	2			1		1		1					5		
Sherburn	251	7	Phipps	Jedeh	1			1		1		1		1			5		
Sherburn	251	8	Phipps	John	2			1		1		1					5		
Sherburn	251	9	Pratt	Jacob				1				1		1			3		
Sherburn	251	10	Pratt	Ebenz	1	1		1				1					5		
Sherburn	251	11	Pond	Aplos		1		1				1					3		
Sherburn	251	12	Prentice	Stephen	2			1				1					4		
Sherburn	251	13	Pond	Theodore			1					1					2		
Sherburn	251	14	Pratt	Henry	3	2		1				1					7		
Sherburn	251	15	Russell	Jona			1	1			1	2		1			6		
Sherburn	251	16	Stratton	Abijah	1	1	1					1					4		
Sherburn	251	17	Sanger	John			2		1	1	1		1				6		
Sherburn	251	18	Stratton	Nathan			1		1				1				3		
Sherburn	251	19	Stratton	Nathan Jr	3			1			2	1	1				8		
Sherburn	251	20	Stone	Silas	5	1			1	1	2	1	1				12		
Sherburn	251	21	Sparrowhawk	Jacob	1		1		1				1				4		
Sherburn	251	22	Sanger	Asa		3			1	2	1		1				8		
Sherburn	251	23	Sanger	David			1			1		1					3		
Sherburn	251	24	Sanger	Calven				1					1				2		
Sherburn	251	25	Sanger	Samll			1		1			3		1			6		
Sherburn	251	26	Sparrowhawk	Timth			2		1	1	1			1			6		
Sherburn	251	27	Tucker	Wm		2			1		1	1		1			6		
Sherburn	251	28	Twitchell	Peter	2	1	1	1		1		1	1				8		
Sherburn	251	29	Twitchell	John	1	1		1	1	1		1	1				8		
Sherburn	251	30	Whitney	Daniel	1				1		1			1			4		
Sherburn	251	31	Whitney	Aaron	1		1		1		1		1				5		
Sherburn	251	32	Wyeth	Tapley				1		1	1			1			4		
Sherburn	251	33	Westbury	Edward		1			1			3		1			6		
Sherburn	251	34	Whitney	Joseph	2	1			1	2	1		1				8		
Sherburn	251	35	Whitney	John			1		1			1	1				4		
Sherburn	251	36	Whitney	Susanna		1	1			2		1					5		
Sherburn	251	37	Ware	Alpha			1			1		1					3		
Sherburn	251	38	Ware	Benjm		1	1		1		1			2			6		
Sherburn	251	39	Ware	Joseph		1	1		1		1			2			6		

TOWN	PG#	LN#	LAST NAME	FIRST NAME	under 10	10 to 16	16 to 26	26 to 45	45 and over	under 10	10 to 16	16 to 26	26 to 45	45 and over	TOTAL ALL OTHER	TOTAL SLAVES	TOTALS	DISTRICT/ TOWNSHIP	NOTES
			HEADS OF HOUSEHOLD		FREE WHITE MALES					FREE WHITE FEMALES									
Shirley	213	1	Adams	Jonas	1			1		2	1		1				6		
Shirley	213	2	Atherton	Jona	1			1		3			1	1			7		
Shirley	213	3	Alexander	Wm				1					1				2		
Shirley	213	4	Adams	Nathan	1	1		1		2	1		1				7		
Shirley	213	5	Adams	Joseph	1			1		1			1				4		
Shirley	213	6	Bolton	Wm			1		1			1		1			4		
Shirley	213	7	Bolton	Timothy	1			1		1			1				4		
Shirley	213	8	Burrage	Ephraim			1	1				1		1			4		
Shirley	213	9	Blood	Josiah				1						1			2		
Shirley	213	10	Brooks	Sewell	1		1						1				3		
Shirley	213	11	Baker	Jonas	2			1		2			1				6		
Shirley	213	12	Bartlett	Wm				1		4	2		1				8		
Shirley	213	13	Brown	Joseph Dea.	1		1		2	1	1	1		2			9		
Shirley	213	14	Bartlett	Silence Wid.										2			2		
Shirley	213	15	Brown	Daniel G.		1		1		1		1	1	1			6		
Shirley	213	16	Conant	Levi		1							1				2		
Shirley	213	17	Conant	Wm	1		1			1			1				4		
Shirley	213	18	Chase	Moody		1	1		1			2		1			6		
Shirley	213	19	Chase	Samuel		1	1	1		1		1					5		
Shirley	213	20	Chaplin	Jeremiah			2	1	1			1	1	1			7		
Shirley	213	21	Chandler	Henry			2			1		1		1			5		
Shirley	213	22	Cooper	Saml				1		1			1				3		
Shirley	213	23	Day	Nathl	1	1	1		1	1	1	1		1			8		
Shirley	213	24	Dwight	John		1	2		1			3	2	1			10		
Shirley	214	1	Dickinson	James		1	1	2				1					5		
Shirley	214	2	Davis	John	2	1	1	1		4	1	1	1	1			13		
Shirley	214	3	Darby	Calvin		1		1				1	1				4		
Shirley	214	4	Dodge	Elisha	1		1	1		1			1				5		
Shirley	214	5	Davis	Saml			1						1				2		
Shirley	214	6	Dunn	Andrew		1	1						1		1		4		
Shirley	214	7	Egerton	John		3		1		1	1	1		2			9		
Shirley	214	8	Egerton	Leonard	1			1		1			1				4		
Shirley	214	9	Frost	Seripter	2			1		2	1		1				7		
Shirley	214	10	Farnsworth	Jona				1		2			1				4		
Shirley	214	11	Farnsworth	Levi	2			1					1				4		
Shirley	214	12	Farnsworth	Flint	1			1	1	1			1	1			6		
Shirley	214	13	Farnsworth	Jesse	2	1		1				1	1				6		
Shirley	214	14	Farnsworth	John	2			1		2		1					6		
Shirley	214	15	Farrar	George	2		1	1		3	1		1				9		
Shirley	214	16	Gleason	Wm	1			1					1				3		
Shirley	214	17	Gowin	Ebenzr				1				1	1				3		
Shirley	214	18	Gowin	Wm	3			1		1		1	1				7		
Shirley	214	19	Holden	Asa Capt.			1		1			1		1			4		
Shirley	214	20	Holden	Nathl	1	1		1		1			1				5		
Shirley	214	21	Heald	John Dea				1			1	1	1				4		
Shirley	214	22	Heald	John Jr	1		1	1				1					4		
Shirley	214	23	Holden	Simon				1					2				3		
Shirley	214	24	Holden	Simon Jr		1		1		1			2				5		
Shirley	214	25	Hartwell	Amasa		1	1	1			1	2		1			7		
Shirley	214	26	Holden	Amos		1	1		1	1							4		
Shirley	214	27	Hartwell	Jonathan	3	1	1		1	2			1	1			10		
Shirley	214	28	Hall	Josiah				1			1			1			3		
Shirley	214	29	Hartwell	Reuben	2			1		2	2		1				8		
Shirley	214	30	Hazen	Saml Capt.		1			1	1	1	1		1			6		
Shirley	214	31	Hazen	Saml Jr Capt.	2			1		1			1				5		
Shirley	214	32	Hazen	Thomas			1			1		1	1				4		
Shirley	214	33	Harrington	Simeon				1				1	1				3		
Shirley	214	34	Holden	Philemon				1		1		1	1				4		
Shirley	214	35	Hartwell	Benjm Doct.	2			1		1	2	1	1				8		
Shirley	214	36	Holden	Phinehas			1			3			1				5		
Shirley	214	37	Harrington	Thaddeus				1									1		
Shirley	214	38	Holden	Elizabeth Wid.	2						1		1				4		
Shirley	214	39	Hazard	Thomas											6		6		
Shirley	214	40	Harris	Francis	1			1		1	1		1				5		
Shirley	214	41	Jenerson	Moses	1	2			1	1	1	1		1			8		
Shirley	214	42	Jones	Saml	2	1	1		1			1		1			7		
Shirley	214	43	Kelsey	John Capt.		1	2		1		1	2	1	1			9		
Shirley	214	44	Kelsey	John Jr	1			1					1				3		
Shirley	214	45	Kendall	Enosh	4	1		1		1			1	1			9		
Shirley	214	46	Kilburn	Daniel				1		1			1				3		
Shirley	214	47	Longley	Joshua Esq		2	1		1		1	1		2			8		
Shirley	214	48	Little	Wa*	1	3	3		1		1	2		1			12		
Shirley	214	49	Livermore	Daniel		1		1				1					3		
Shirley	214	50	Livermore	Jonas	3	1	1	1					1				7		
Shirley	215	1	Laughton	Oliver	1			1		2			1				5		
Shirley	215	2	Lock	Bezeleel	1			1					1				3		
Shirley	215	3	Longley	Wm		1	2		1					1			5		
Shirley	215	4	Longley	Israel				2	1	1			2				6		
Shirley	215	5	Longley	Abel			2										2		

TOWN	PG#	LN#	HEADS OF HOUSEHOLD LAST NAME	FIRST NAME	FREE WHITE MALES under 10	10 to 16	16 to 26	26 to 45	45 and over	FREE WHITE FEMALES under 10	10 to 16	16 to 26	26 to 45	45 and over	TOTAL ALL OTHER	TOTAL SLAVES	TOTALS	DISTRICT/ TOWNSHIP	NOTES
Shirley	215	6	Little	Elizabeth Wid.										2			2		
Shirley	215	7	Longley	Asa	2	1		1		1	2		1				8		
Shirley	215	8	Longley	Joseph	2	1		1		2	1	1					8		
Shirley	215	9	Longley	Ivery			1			1		1	1				4		
Shirley	215	10	Longley	Stephen	1	1	1						1				4		
Shirley	215	11	McKenzie	Bho*				1						1			2		
Shirley	215	12	Moore	Abel	3		1	1		2			1				8		
Shirley	215	13	McLeod	Sarah Wid.							1	2		2			5		
Shirley	215	14	Patterson	Hezekiah		1		1					1	1			4		
Shirley	215	15	Page	Phinehas	1	1	2		1				1	1			7		
Shirley	215	16	Parker	Jonas	1	1	1			1			1				5		
Shirley	215	17	Parker	James		1	1	2	1			1	1	1			8		
Shirley	215	18	Phelps	Timothy				1			1			1			3		
Shirley	215	19	Phelps	John			1			1			1				3		
Shirley	215	20	Phelps	Jacob			1			1		1					3		
Shirley	215	21	Pratt	Ebenzr				1		1				1			3		
Shirley	215	22	Pratt	Hannah	1					1			1	1			4		
Shirley	215	23	Proctor	Wm				1			1	1					4		
Shirley	215	24	Pays	Oliver	3	1		1	1	1			1	1			9		
Shirley	215	25	Pays	Jonas		1	3		1	4	2	2		1			14		
Shirley	215	26	Parker	John		1		1		1				1			4		
Shirley	215	27	Peabody	Thomas	3	1		1		2			1				8		
Shirley	215	28	Ritter	Moses				1		1				1			3		
Shirley	215	29	Robbins	John		1	1	1		1		1					5		
Shirley	215	30	Russell	Solomon		1		1		2	1			2			7		
Shirley	215	31	Richardson	Jeremiah			1			1			1				3		
Shirley	215	32	Stimpson	Stephen	1	1	2		1	2	1	1		1			10		
Shirley	215	33	Smith	Mary Wid.								1		1			2		
Shirley	215	34	Sanderson	David	2			1		2			1				6		
Shirley	215	35	Smith	Nathan Capt.				1			1			1			3		
Shirley	215	36	Smith	Salvinas Capt.				1					1	1			3		
Shirley	215	37	Smith	Salvinas Jr	1			1		1			1				4		
Shirley	215	38	Whitney	Thomas Esq	1		1	1					1	1			5		
Shirley	215	39	Warren	Ephraim		1		1		1				1			4		
Shirley	215	40	Willard	Israel	1			1	1	1	1	2	1	1			9		
Shirley	215	41	Willard	Nathan			5	4	8			7	21	4			49		
Shirley	215	42	Walker	John	1	1	1	1	1	3			1				9		
Shirley	215	43	Woodbury	Benjm				1						1			2		
Shirley	215	44	Wodd	Aaron		1	1	1				1	1				5		
Shirley	215	45	Williams	Wm	2	1	1	1		2	1		1				9		
Shirley	215	46	Warren	John		1				2			1				4		
Shirley	215	47	Warren	Wm		1		1		1							3		
Shirley	215	48	Wilds	Ivery		1	2	1	3			5	7	6			25		

TOWN	PG#	LN#	LAST NAME	FIRST NAME	FREE WHITE MALES					FREE WHITE FEMALES					TOTAL ALL OTHER	TOTAL SLAVES	TOTALS	DISTRICT/ TOWNSHIP	NOTES
					under 10	10 to 16	16 to 26	26 to 45	45 and over	under 10	10 to 16	16 to 26	26 to 45	45 and over					
Stoneham	138	1	Bryant	Joseph					1					2			3		
Stoneham	138	2	Bryant	Joseph Jr	1			1				1			1		5		
Stoneham	138	3	Bryant	Elias	1	1		2		2	1	1	1				9		
Stoneham	138	4	Bryant	Ebenezer	2			1		1	1		1				6		
Stoneham	138	5	Bucknam	Edward			1	1	1	3			1				7		
Stoneham	138	6	Bucknam	John		1	1	1	1	1		2					7		
Stoneham	138	7	Bucknam	Ebenezer	2				1			1		1			5		
Stoneham	138	8	Brown	Ephraim			1		2			1		1			5		
Stoneham	138	9	Bucknam	Nathan				1					1				2		
Stoneham	138	10	Cutter	Jacob				1					1				2		
Stoneham	138	11	Crocker	James	2			1					1				4		
Stoneham	138	12	Dolten	Joseph	2		1	1		1		1		1			7		
Stoneham	138	13	Geary	John				1					1				2		
Stoneham	138	14	Geary	John Jr	2			1			1		1				5		
Stoneham	138	15	Geary	David	2	1	1		1	1		2	1				9		
Stoneham	138	16	Geary	Benjamin	2	1		1		3	1		1				9		
Stoneham	138	17	Geary	Johanna	1								1				2		
Stoneham	138	18	Green	Daniel	2	2			1	1			1				7		
Stoneham	139	1	Green	Josiah			1		1	1		1					4		
Stoneham	139	2	Green	Josiah Jr	1	1		1		2	1		1				7		
Stoneham	139	3	Green	Thomas	3		1	1		1	1	1	1	1			10		
Stoneham	139	4	Green	Jonathan		2		1				2	1				6		
Stoneham	139	5	Green	John				1					2				3		
Stoneham	139	6	Gould	Abraham			1		1		1	1	1				5		
Stoneham	139	7	Gould	Jacob			1	2					1				4		
Stoneham	139	8	Gould	David			1	1			1		1				4		
Stoneham	139	9	Gould	Daniel		1	1	1		2	1		1	2	1		10		
Stoneham	139	10	Green	Sarah		1							1		1		3		
Stoneham	139	11	Gould	Thomas	4			1		2			1				8		
Stoneham	139	12	Hay	Peter			2		1			1		2			6		
Stoneham	139	13	Hay	Peter Jr			1				1	1					3		
Stoneham	139	14	Hay	David	1	1			1		1		1		1		6		
Stoneham	139	15	Hill	James	1				1	1		2		1			6		
Stoneham	139	16	Hill	James Jr	3	1	1		1	3	1		1				11		
Stoneham	139	17	Holden	William	2			1		1			1				5		
Stoneham	139	18	Hardy	Antony			1	1	1	3			1	1			8		
Stoneham	139	19	Lyonds	Jebez	2			1					1				4		
Stoneham	139	20	Lyonds	Stephen	1	1		1					1				4		
Stoneham	139	21	Mathers	Timothy				1					1				2		
Stoneham	139	22	Mathers	Timothy Jr	2			2		2		1					7		
Stoneham	139	23	Noble	John	1			1		4	1		1				8		
Stoneham	139	24	Poland	John	1			1		1			1				4		
Stoneham	139	25	Pearce	Ephraim	2	1	1		1	1	2		1				9		
Stoneham	139	26	Pain	Daniel				1					2				3		
Stoneham	139	27	Richardson	Caleb	1		3	1	1			1		1			8		
Stoneham	139	28	Richardson	Elijah		1	1		1	1			1				5		
Stoneham	139	29	Richardson	Oliver				1					2				3		
Stoneham	139	30	Richardson	Oliver Jr	1		1			1		1					4		
Stoneham	139	31	Richardson	Thadeous	1	2	2	1	1		1	1	1	1			11		
Stoneham	139	32	Richardson	Mallechy	1			1		2			1				5		
Stoneham	139	33	Richardson	Charly		1		1				1	1				5		
Stoneham	139	34	Richardson	Benjamin		1		1			1						4		
Stoneham	139	35	Row	William A	1	1	1	1		2	1		1				8		
Stoneham	139	36	Stephens	John H	1	1		1		3			1				7		
Stoneham	139	37	Sprague	Samuel				1			1		1				3		
Stoneham	140	1	Wi*	Mathew			1			2			1				4		
Stoneham	140	2	Vinton	Thomas			1	1					1				3		
Stoneham	140	3	Vinton	Timothy				1			1		1				3		
Stoneham	140	4	Vinton	Ezra	2	2		1		2		3	1				11		
Stoneham	140	5	Wiley	Phinehas	1	1	1	1		3	2	1	1				11		
Stoneham	140	6	Willy	Nathan	3	1	2	1	1	2	2		3				15		
Stoneham	140	7	Wright	Timothy			1	1	1			1		1			5		
Stoneham	140	8	Wright	John	1		2			2		1					6		
Stoneham	140	9	Wright	Timothy Jr	1			1		1		1					4		
Stoneham	140	10	Willy	James		1			1				1	1			4		

TOWN	PG#	LN#	LAST NAME	FIRST NAME	FREE WHITE MALES					FREE WHITE FEMALES					TOTAL ALL OTHER	TOTAL SLAVES	TOTALS	DISTRICT/ TOWNSHIP	NOTES
					under 10	10 to 16	16 to 26	26 to 45	45 and over	under 10	10 to 16	16 to 26	26 to 45	45 and over					
Stow	195	1	Walcutt	William	1				1	2			1				5		
Stow	195	2	Walcutt	Silas	1		1						1				3		
Stow	195	3	Whitcomb	Silas				1		3			1	1			6		
Stow	195	4	Whitcomb	Simeon	1		1	1					1				4		
Stow	195	5	Whitcomb	Oliver			1			1		1					3		
Stow	195	6	Walcutt	Frederick		1		1					1				3		
Stow	195	7	Walcutt	John	1		1	1		1		1					5		
Stow	195	8	Rand	David	1		1		1	2	2	1	1				9		
Stow	195	9	Hale	Charles	1		2		1	3	1	2	1				11		
Stow	195	10	Hale	Bezeleel					1				1				2		
Stow	195	11	Hale	Bezeleel Jr	1	2		1		1	1	1	1				8		
Stow	195	12	Hale	Jonas		1			1					1			3		
Stow	195	13	Hale	Ephraim				1	1	3			1	1			7		
Stow	195	14	Witherbee	Ephraim		2	1	1		1		2	1				8		
Stow	195	15	Abbot	Jeremiah			1			1			1	1			4		
Stow	195	16	Gates	Isaac Jr	2			1				1	1				5		
Stow	195	17	Rogers	Abraham F.	2	1		1		2	1		1				8		
Stow	195	18	Gates	Oliver		1	1		1			1		1			5		
Stow	195	19	Witherbee	Jonas			2						1				3		
Stow	195	20	Condee	Nathaniel	1				1	1	2		1				6		
Stow	195	21	Gates	John	1	1	1		1	2	1		1				8		
Stow	195	22	Brown	Jabez					1			1	1				3		
Stow	196	1	Carter	Abijah	2	2		1		3			1				9		
Stow	196	2	Gates	Israel	1		2	1	1	1	2	2	1	1			12		
Stow	196	3	Gates	Ezekiel	4	2		1		1	1		1				10		
Stow	196	4	Gates	Caleb			1		1			1		1			4		
Stow	196	5	Gates	Mary									3				3		
Stow	196	6	Walcutt	Jonathan	2		1	1		1			1		1		7		
Stow	196	7	Brigham	Timothy				1					1				2		
Stow	196	8	Taylor	William			1			4	1		1				7		
Stow	196	9	Taylor	Paul	1			1		3	1						6		
Stow	196	10	Gates	Levi	1	1	1			1	1		1				6		
Stow	196	11	McLeod	William L	1		1					1					3		
Stow	196	12	Gates	Samuel			1	1			1		1				4		
Stow	196	13	Whitney	Abraham				1					1				2		
Stow	196	14	Whitney	Abraham Jr	2	1			2	1	1	1	1				9		
Stow	196	15	Brown	Isaac				1		1	1		1				4		
Stow	196	16	Whitcomb	William		1		1		1			1				4		
Stow	196	17	Whitcomb	Abraham	1	1	1	1		1		1					6		
Stow	196	18	Stone	Stephen				1					1				2		
Stow	196	19	Stow	Ichabod	3	1	2	1		1		1	1				10		
Stow	196	20	Brown	Jishua		1	1	1					1				4		
Stow	196	21	Gates	Charles		1	1					1					3		
Stow	196	22	Hastings	John	3		1	1		1			1	1			8		
Stow	196	23	Ray	Abraham	2			1					1				4		
Stow	196	24	Ray	Abner		1		1				1					3		
Stow	196	25	Euleth	Daniel	3			2		2	1	1	1	1			11		
Stow	196	26	Maynard	Jabez	1	1		1				1	1				5		
Stow	196	27	Gates	Thomas	1			1		2	1	1	1				7		
Stow	196	28	Whitcomb	Hezekiah	2	1		1		3			1	1			9		
Stow	196	29	Werthinton	Samuel	3	1			1	1	2	1		1			10		
Stow	196	30	Jewell	William	1				1		1	1	1				5		
Stow	196	31	Davidson	George	2		1	1		1			1				6		
Stow	196	32	Gates	Ebenezer	1	1		1		2		1	1	1			8		
Stow	196	33	Jenney	Eliphelet			2		1				3	1			7		
Stow	196	34	Sawyer	Caleb	1			1		2	1		1				6		
Stow	196	35	Whitney	Hezekiah		1		1	1	2	1		2	1			9		
Stow	196	36	Whitney	Elias				1					1				2		
Stow	196	37	Green	Oliver											5		5		
Stow	196	38	Davidson	John				1					1				2		
Stow	196	39	Davidson	John Jr	2			1		1			1				5		
Stow	196	40	Wheeler	Levi			1	1		1	1	1					5		
Stow	196	41	Oaks	John	2			1		1		1					5		
Stow	196	42	Maxwell	William				1					1				2		
Stow	196	43	Maxwell	George	2		1						1				4		
Stow	196	44	Coolledg	Augusts	2	2		1		2	1		1				9		
Stow	197	1	Forbush	Abraham	1	2	2					2	1	1			10		
Stow	197	2	Whitney	Lemuel				1						1			2		
Stow	197	3	Patch	John	1	2	1		1	2		3	1				11		
Stow	197	4	Whitney	Daniel	4	2	3		1		1	2	1				14		
Stow	197	5	Whit	Dorothy									1				1		
Stow	197	6	Carriel	Sarah									1				1		
Stow	197	7	Brooks	Nathan	2	1	1	1		2	2		1				10		
Stow	197	8	Whitney	Jacob	2	3	1	1		1		1	1	1			11		
Stow	197	9	Searjents	Nathaniel		1	1		1			1	1	1			6		
Stow	197	10	Robbins	Martha									1	1			2		
Stow	197	11	Rice	Mallethias				1					1				2		
Stow	197	12	Puffer	Mary		1	2	1					1				5		
Stow	197	13	Conant	John	2	2		1		2		1	1	1			10		

TOWN	PG#	LN#	LAST NAME	FIRST NAME	FREE WHITE MALES					FREE WHITE FEMALES					TOTAL ALL OTHER	TOTAL SLAVES	TOTALS	DISTRICT/ TOWNSHIP	NOTES
					under 10	10 to 16	16 to 26	26 to 45	45 and over	under 10	10 to 16	16 to 26	26 to 45	45 and over					
Stow	197	14	Gibson	Stephen					1					1			2		
Stow	197	15	Gibson	Arrington	2	2	1	1				1	1				8		
Stow	197	16	Brooks	Luke		1		2	1		1	1		1			7		
Stow	197	17	Randell	Josiah		1	1		1	2	2		1				8		
Stow	197	18	Osbourn	Samuel					1				1				2		
Stow	197	19	Osbourn	David	1		1	2		1		1					6		
Stow	197	20	Taylor	Abel		1		1	1			1	1	1			6		
Stow	197	21	Brown	Josiah		1	3		1	1	1	1	1	2			11		
Stow	197	22	Marble	John	1	1	1		1	1		1	1	2			9		
Stow	197	23	Conant	Daniel	1	1	1		1		1	1		1			7		
Stow	197	24	Blood	Oliver				1	1			1	1				4		
Stow	197	25	Smith	Benjamin			2		1			1		1			5		
Stow	197	26	Brown	Benjamin	2				1	1			1				5		
Stow	197	27	Hapgood	Samuel	2		1	1		2				1			7		
Stow	197	28	Wood	Jonathan			2	1		2	2		1				8		
Stow	197	29	Duffer	Jonathan			3	1	1	1	2	1		1			10		
Stow	197	30	Wood	Joseph			2	1		1		2		1			7		
Stow	197	31	Taylor	Abigail				1						2			3		
Stow	197	32	Hapgood	Daniel	1	1	2		1	2			1				8		
Stow	197	33	Trask	John	2			1		1			1				5		
Stow	197	34	Jewell	Samuel	1	1			1	1			1				5		
Stow	197	35	Eames	John		1		1				1		1			4		
Stow	197	36	Goodenow	Samuel		1		1				1		1			4		
Stow	197	37	Goodenow	Thaddeus	1			1				1					3		
Stow	197	38	Bayley	Elizabeth				1						1			2		
Stow	197	39	Conant	Josiah	1	1		1		1			1				5		
Stow	197	40	Goodenow	Eliab	2	1		1		1	1		1				7		
Stow	197	41	Randell	Abraham	1	2	2		1			1	1	1			9		
Stow	197	42	Gates	Mary										2			2		
Stow	197	43	Gates	Oliver Jr		1	1		1	1				1			5		
Stow	198	1	Whitman	Charles					1					2			3		
Stow	198	2	Whitman	Charles Jr			1	1		1	1	1					5		
Stow	198	3	Whitman	Thomas	1	1	2		1	1		2		1			9		
Stow	198	4	Osbourn	James	2	2		1		1							6		
Stow	198	5	Brooks	Amos			1	1		2		1	1				6		
Stow	198	6	Hayden	David	1			2					1				4		
Stow	198	7	Munroe	Benjamin		1	1	1		1		1		1			5		
Stow	198	8	Randell	Silas	1	1	4		1		1	1	1	1			11		
Stow	198	9	Rand	Lucy										1			1		
Stow	198	10	Rand	Ephraim		1								1			2		
Stow	198	11	Gates	Jacob			1			1		1					3		
Stow	198	12	Gates	Mary Jr	2					1	1	2	1				7		
Stow	198	13	Gates	Nathan	2			1		1		1					5		
Stow	198	14	Brown	Desire		1				2			1				4		
Stow	198	15	Swift	Luther	1		1					1					3		
Stow	198	16	Smith	Nahum	2			1		1		1	1				6		
Stow	198	17	Hapgood	Jonathan					1			1		1			3		
Stow	198	18	Whitman	Joseph			1	1		1	1	1					5		
Stow	198	19	Rice	Solomon			1	1		2			1				5		
Stow	198	20	Wakefield	Mary									1				1		
Stow	198	21	Gates	Elisha			1					2		1			4		
Stow	198	22	Rand	Oliver	1			1		1			1				4		
Stow	198	23	Burges	Thomas	2			1		1			1				5		
Stow	198	24	Warren	Huldy									1				1		
Stow	198	25	Perlin	Isaac	1		1	1				2					5		
Stow	198	26	Putman	Asa	4			1		1	1		1				8		
Stow	198	27	Williams	Robert		2	4	1						1			8		
Stow	198	28	Moses	Anna	1					1				1			3		
Stow	198	29	Howard	Peter			1			1		2					4		
Stow	198	30	Putman	Nathan		2	1		1	1	1	1		2			9		
Stow	198	31	Houghton	Abigail										2			2		
Stow	198	32	Hastings	Jonas	2	1			1	2			1				7		
Stow	198	33	Gates	Elisha Jr	1		1	1		2		1					6		
Stow	198	34	Warren	Abijah	2		1		1	2	3	1		1			11		
Stow	198	35	Rice	Buckminster	2			1				1	1				5		
Stow	198	36	Newell	Jonathan	2				1			2	1		1		7		
Stow	198	37	Tower	Augustus	1		1	1		2		1	1	1			8		
Stow	198	38	Wheeler	Ephraim		1		1		1		1		1			4		
Stow	198	39	Russell	Ephraim	1	1			1	2		2	2		1		10		
Stow	198	40	Conant	Peter	3	2	2		1	2		1	1				12		
Stow	198	41	Conant	Sarah										1			1		
Stow	198	42	Brown	Benjamin Jr	1		1			2			2				6		
Stow	199	1	Euleth	Francis		1		2	1			1		1			6		
Stow	199	2	Dubbleday	Elizabeth		1						1	1	2	1		6		
Stow	199	3	Soper	Jacob	1		1	1		2	1	1					7		
Stow	199	4	Wood	Daniel			1			1			1				3		
Stow	199	5	Robbins	Israel	1			1		2			1				5		
Stow	199	6	Witherbee	Judah	2		1		1	2		2	1	1			10		

TOWN	PG#	LN#		HEADS OF HOUSEHOLD	FREE WHITE MALES					FREE WHITE FEMALES					TOTAL ALL OTHER	TOTAL SLAVES	TOTALS	DISTRICT/ TOWNSHIP	NOTES
			LAST NAME	FIRST NAME	under 10	10 to 16	16 to 26	26 to 45	45 and over	under 10	10 to 16	16 to 26	26 to 45	45 and over					
Sudbury	57	1	Rice	Benjamin	2				1	1	1	1		1			7		
Sudbury	57	2	Willard	John			1	1					1	1			4		
Sudbury	57	3	Tayler	John	1		1	1		1			1				5		
Sudbury	57	4	Robinson	Paul	1		1			1			1				4		
Sudbury	57	5	Barker	Ephraim	3	2		1		1			1	1			9		
Sudbury	57	6	Goodnow	Levi	2	1		1		1			1				6		
Sudbury	57	7	Goodnow	Joseph		1			1			1		1			4		
Sudbury	57	8	Goodnow	Jotham	2	2		1		2		1	1				9		
Sudbury	57	9	Bogie	Rowand			1	1	1		1		1	1			6		
Sudbury	57	10	Graves	Jonathan			1	1		1	1		1	1			6		
Sudbury	57	11	Carter	Ephraim				1		2				1			4		
Sudbury	57	12	Goodnow	Asher	1	1		1					1				4		
Sudbury	58	1	Goodnow	Silas		1		1	1			1	1	1			6		
Sudbury	58	2	Reed	Abel	2	1		1		2	1		1				8		
Sudbury	58	3	Reed	Isaac	1		1	1		2		1	1				7		
Sudbury	58	4	Moore	Isaac	2			1			1		1	1			6		
Sudbury	58	5	Hunt	William	1		1	1		2			1	1			7		
Sudbury	58	6	Hunt	Haman	3	1		1		1			1				7		
Sudbury	58	7	Bacon	Elijah	1		1	1					1				4		
Sudbury	58	8	Eaton	Reuben	1			1		2			1				5		
Sudbury	58	9	Mone	Joel	1	1					1		1				4		
Sudbury	58	10	Brown	Hopestill	1	1		1		1			1				5		
Sudbury	59	1	Hunt	Jonas	4			1	1	1	1	1		1			10		
Sudbury	59	2	How	Elizabeth						1				1			2		
Sudbury	59	3	Holdin	Thos	1		1					1	1				4		
Sudbury	59	4	Gibbs	Asahel	1	1		2		1			1				6		
Sudbury	59	5	Goodnow	John Jr	2	2		1		2			1				8		
Sudbury	59	6	Goodnow	Sarah			1	1					1	1			4		
Sudbury	59	7	Child	Saml	1			1		2			1				5		
Sudbury	59	8	Burbank	Ebenezer				1						1			2		
Sudbury	59	9	Richardson	Josiah	2		1	1	1	1			1	1			8		
Sudbury	59	10	Rice	Nahum				1		2		1					4		
Sudbury	59	11	Brigham	Jesse		2	1	1		2			1				7		
Sudbury	59	12	Cutlar	Asher		1	1	1	1			2		1			7		
Sudbury	59	13	Cutlar	Roland	2			1					1				4		
Sudbury	59	14	Cutler	Joseph	1	1		1		3	2	1	1	1			11		
Sudbury	59	15	Sawin	Benjm	2	2		1		1		2		1			9		
Sudbury	59	16	Lock	Nathan	1		2						1				4		
Sudbury	59	17	Brown	William Jr			2					1					3		
Sudbury	59	18	Thompson	James	2		1	1		1			2				7		
Sudbury	59	19	Brown	Elinor	1		1							1			3		
Sudbury	59	20	Brown	Jonas	2			1	1	1			1				6		
Sudbury	59	21	Holdin	Jonas	1			1	1	1			1	1			6		
Sudbury	59	22	Holdin	Jonas Jr		1	2	1		3	2		1				10		
Sudbury	59	23	Brown	Caleb	3			1		2	1		1				8		
Sudbury	59	24	Brown	William	2	3		1				1	1				8		
Sudbury	59	25	Brown	John	3			1		1	3		1				9		
Sudbury	59	26	Brown	Samuel	2		1		1	1	1		1	1			8		
Sudbury	59	27	Nixon	John	2			1	1			1		1			6		
Sudbury	59	28	How	David Jr	1	1		1		3	1		1				8		
Sudbury	59	29	Gibbs	Isaac	2		1	1		1			1				6		
Sudbury	59	30	Gibbs	Gill	1			1				1					3		
Sudbury	59	31	Gibbs	Ruth	1		1				1	2		1			6		
Sudbury	59	32	Goodnow	Ephraim				1					1	1			3		
Sudbury	59	33	Bryant	Nathaniel				1						1			2		
Sudbury	59	34	Stone	Moses	2	1	1	1					2	2			9		
Sudbury	59	35	Moore	Jonathan	1	2		1	1			1		1			7		
Sudbury	59	36	Dalrymple	Thos				1						1			2		
Sudbury	59	37	Dutton	Abigail	1	1				1			1				4		
Sudbury	59	38	Parmenter	Jedediah	1		1	1	1	1	1	1		1			8		
Sudbury	60	1	Parmenter	Abel	1	1		1		1			1				5		
Sudbury	60	2	Parmenter	Micah				1						1			2		
Sudbury	60	3	Parmenter	Levi				1		2			1				4		
Sudbury	60	4	Parmenter	Israel	2	2		1		1	1	2	1				10		
Sudbury	60	5	Parmenter	Uriah			1		2			3		1			7		
Sudbury	60	6	How	David Jr				1						1			2		
Sudbury	60	7	How	Joseph	2	1	1	1		1	2		1				9		
Sudbury	60	8	How	Adam			2	1		2	1	1	1	1			9		
Sudbury	60	9	Knight	Samuel			1	1	2					1			5		
Sudbury	60	10	Knight	Joel				1		3		1					5		
Sudbury	60	11	Wheeler	Israel Jr	1		1	1		1			1				5		
Sudbury	60	12	Walker	Thomas				1						1			2		
Sudbury	60	13	Walker	Abner			1	1		1			1				4		
Sudbury	60	14	Walker	Paul	3			1		2			1				7		
Sudbury	60	15	Fairbanks	Jonathn	2	1			2	2	1	1	1				10		
Sudbury	60	16	Hayden	William	2	2		2	1	3			1	1			12		
Sudbury	60	17	Moore	John		1	1	1		1	1		1				6		
Sudbury	60	18	Hayden	Ephraim	1	1		1	1	3	2		1	1			11		
Sudbury	60	19	Trull	David	1			1		2			4				8		

103

TOWN	PG#	LN#	LAST NAME	FIRST NAME	FREE WHITE MALES under 10	10 to 16	16 to 26	26 to 45	45 and over	FREE WHITE FEMALES under 10	10 to 16	16 to 26	26 to 45	45 and over	TOTAL ALL OTHER	TOTAL SLAVES	TOTALS	DISTRICT/ TOWNSHIP	NOTES
Sudbury	60	20	Dudley	Benjm	2			1		2			1	1			7		
Sudbury	60	21	Moore	Olive			1					1	1				3		
Sudbury	60	22	Lincoln	Isaac			2		1		1	1		1			6		
Sudbury	60	23	Haynes	Peter			1		1		1	1		1			5		
Sudbury	60	24	Moore	Reuben			1	2				1	1				5		
Sudbury	60	25	Symonds	John	2				1	2			1				6		
Sudbury	60	26	Reed	Joseph Jr			1			2		1	1	1			6		
Sudbury	60	27	Green	John					1		1		1				3		
Sudbury	60	28	Bennet	Sarah										1			1		
Sudbury	60	29	Stevens	Benjm			1	1		1		1					4		
Sudbury	60	30	Johnson	Aaron				1					1				2		
Sudbury	60	31	Kidder	Ashbel			1			1	1	1					4		
Sudbury	60	32	Robinson	Jona			1		1				1	1			4		
Sudbury	60	33	Pollard	John			1						1	1			3		
Sudbury	60	34	Wier	Isaac		2		1					1				4		
Sudbury	60	35	Dix	James	1			1	1			1		1			5		
Sudbury	60	36	Goodnow	John	1			2				2	1	1			8		
Sudbury	61	1	Richardson	Gideon	2	1		1		3	1		1				9		
Sudbury	61	2	Mathews	James			1			1		1					3		
Sudbury	61	3	Rice	Reuben	3	3	1	2	1	1		1	1				13		
Sudbury	61	4	Biglow	Jacob		1	1		1			2		1			6		
Sudbury	61	5	Rice	William		2		1		2			2				7		
Sudbury	61	6	Vorce	Reuben				1					1				2		
Sudbury	61	7	Tower	Silas	2	1		1		3	2		1				10		
Sudbury	61	8	Tower	Abel	1	1	1	1		2	1	1	2				10		
Sudbury	61	9	Goodnow	Luther		1		2		1		1		1			6		
Sudbury	61	10	Moore	Timothy	2			1		1	1		1	1			7		
Sudbury	61	11	Scott	Jacob	2			1				1					4		
Sudbury	61	12	Smith	Israel		1		1			1		1	2			6		
Sudbury	61	13	Smith	Jedediah	1	1	1	1			1			1			6		
Sudbury	61	14	Haynes	Charles		1		1		1				1			4		
Sudbury	61	15	Haynes	Luke	3			1				1					5		
Sudbury	61	16	Carter	James		1		1		3	2		1	1			9		
Sudbury	61	17	Carter	Priscilla								1		1			2		
Sudbury	61	18	Clark	John		1		1	1	1		1					5		
Sudbury	61	19	Plympton	Ebenz	4	1		1		2	2	1	2				13		
Sudbury	61	20	Wheeler	Israel	1	2			1		1	2		1			8		
Sudbury	61	21	Wheeler	Asahel	1			1	1	1	1	1		1			7		
Sudbury	61	22	Jones	Samuel	2	1	2	1		1			1				8		
Sudbury	61	23	Jones	Elijah		1						1					2		
Sudbury	61	24	Moore	William	2		1		1	3			1				8		
Sudbury	61	25	Osborn	Obediah	1			1				1					3		
Sudbury	61	26	Parmenter	James	1	1	1		1	2	1	1		3			11		
Sudbury	61	27	Parmenter	Ebenezer	1	1		1		1	1	1	1	1			8		
Sudbury	61	28	Loring	Nathan			1	1		1		1	1	1			6		
Sudbury	61	29	Bent	Anna		2							1	1			4		
Sudbury	61	30	Noyes	Peter	1			1						2			4		
Sudbury	61	31	Hunt	William 3rd	1		1						1				3		
Sudbury	61	32	Wheeler	Abel	1		1						1				3		
Sudbury	61	33	Maynard	John	2			2	1		1		1				7		
Sudbury	61	34	Osborn	Daniel	1	2			1	1	1			2			8		
Sudbury	61	35	Brigham	John			3		1	1	4			1			10		
Sudbury	61	36	Gleazon	Samuel	2	2			1			1		1			7		
Sudbury	61	37	Goodnow	Abigail		1	1					1		1			4		
Sudbury	62	1	Willis	Sarah			1					1		1			3		
Sudbury	62	2	Will	Asahel	2			1			1	1					5		
Sudbury	62	3	Parmenter	Deliverance		1		1		1				1			4		
Sudbury	62	4	Perry	John	1		1		1	1	1		1	1			7		
Sudbury	62	5	Loring	Ezekiel H.	1			1		2		1					5		
Sudbury	62	6	Moore	Ephraim	1	1	1		1	1			1	1			7		
Sudbury	62	7	Knight	Asahel		1			1					1			3		
Sudbury	62	8	Lovering	Jonas	1			1		1				1			4		
Sudbury	62	9	Carr	Anna									1				2		
Sudbury	62	10	Carr	Thomas	2	1	1		1		1	2		1			9		
Sudbury	62	11	Carr	John	1			1		1			1				4		
Sudbury	62	12	Willis	Abel	2	1		1	1	2			1				8		
Sudbury	62	13	Rice	Jonathan		2		1						1			4		
Sudbury	62	14	Ruffer	Daniel		2		1		1		1		1			6		
Sudbury	62	15	Cutting	Abel	1	1		1		2	1	1		1			8		
Sudbury	62	16	Willis	Elisabeth		1	1						1	1			4		
Sudbury	62	17	Willis	Hopestill	1				1	2				1			5		
Sudbury	62	18	Willis	Jedediah	1	1		1		1	1	1					6		
Sudbury	62	19	Maynard	Zachariah				1			1			1			3		
Sudbury	62	20	Maynard	Gideon	2	1	1		1			1	1				7		
Sudbury	62	21	Willis	Jesse	2	1		1	1	1	1	1		1			9		
Sudbury	62	22	Willis	Jesse Jr	2			1		2	1		1				7		
Sudbury	62	23	Noyes	Oliver		2		1			1			1			5		
Sudbury	62	24	Noyes	Asahel	2			1					1	1			5		
Sudbury	62	25	Mosman	Silas		2		1		4			1	1			9		

TOWN	PG#	LN#	LAST NAME	FIRST NAME	M under 10	M 10 to 16	M 16 to 26	M 26 to 45	M 45 and over	F under 10	F 10 to 16	F 16 to 26	F 26 to 45	F 45 and over	TOTAL ALL OTHER	TOTAL SLAVES	TOTALS	DISTRICT/ TOWNSHIP	NOTES
Sudbury	62	26	Haywood	John				1				1		2			4		
Sudbury	62	27	Balcom	James	1			1			1						3		
Sudbury	62	28	Balcom	John	1	2		1		1	1	2	1				9		
Sudbury	62	29	Johnson	Hezekiah	1	1		1			2		1				6		
Sudbury	62	30	Bowker	Daniel	1		3	1	1	1		2		1			10		
Sudbury	62	31	Mosman	Moses	1		2		2	1		2		1			9		
Sudbury	62	32	Ruffer	Silas	3	2		1		2	1		1				10		
Sudbury	62	33	Haynes	James					1					1			2		
Sudbury	62	34	Maynard	Moses Jr				1		3	1		1				6		
Sudbury	62	35	Brown	Abel	1			1		2	1		1				6		
Sudbury	62	36	Ruffer	Samuel	4	1	1	1	1		3		1	1			13		
Sudbury	62	37	Hunt	William Jr	1	1	2		1	1	2			1			9		
Sudbury	63	1	Smith	Abel	1	1	1	1	1	3	2	1	1				12		
Sudbury	63	2	Wheeler	Caleb	2	1		1		4	2	3	1				14		
Sudbury	63	3	Robins	Eunice							1	1		1			3		
Sudbury	63	4	Weighton	John				1									1		
Sudbury	63	5	Ruffer	Samuel Jr	3			1		2	1		1	2			9		
Sudbury	63	6	Bent	Jonathan	1	2	1	1		2	1	1	1				10		
Sudbury	63	7	Conant	Silas				1				1		2			4		
Sudbury	63	8	Conant	Amos	2			1					1				4		
Sudbury	63	9	Haynes	Jason	2		1	1	1		1	2		1			9		
Sudbury	63	10	Haynes	Joshua				1				1		1			3		
Sudbury	63	11	Haynes	John	3	1		1			1		1				7		
Sudbury	63	12	Brown	Hopestill	2	1		1	1	1	1		1	1			9		
Sudbury	63	13	Dakin	Joseph	2	1		1	1	1	1		1				8		
Sudbury	63	14	Dakin	Samuel			1	1			2	1	1				6		
Sudbury	63	15	Maynard	Moses		2	2	1			1	1	1				8		
Sudbury	63	16	Ruffer	James Jr		1		2		1		2		1			7		
Sudbury	63	17	Haynes	Moses			2	1			1		1				5		
Sudbury	63	18	Haynes	Israel			2	1		2	1	1		1			8		
Sudbury	63	19	Ruffer	Phinehas		1		1	1			1		1			5		
Sudbury	63	20	Dakin	Samuel Jr	1			1		1			1				4		
Sudbury	63	21	Ruffer	James	2		1		1	1		1		1			7		
Sudbury	63	22	Smith	Daniel N.		1	2			2		1					6		
Sudbury	63	23	Ruffer	Isaac		1		1				1		1			4		
Sudbury	63	24	Ruffer	Asahel		1	1			2		1					5		
Sudbury	63	25	Wheeler	Loring	1			1				1					3		
Sudbury	63	26	Maynard	Samuel			1			2		1		1			5		
Sudbury	63	27	Brigham	Abijah	1		1	1				2		1			7		
Sudbury	63	28	Rice	Ithemer	1	1	2		1	2	1		1				9		
Sudbury	63	29	Balcom	Jonas	2	1	1	1	1	1	1	1	1	1			11		
Sudbury	63	30	Balcom	Joel	1	1		1		2			1				6		
Sudbury	63	31	Balcom	Asahel			1	1					1	2			5		
Sudbury	63	32	Smith	William	1		1	1		1	1		1				6		
Sudbury	63	33	Smith	Jonathan		3		1				1		2			7		
Sudbury	63	34	Brigham	Joseph	1			2		2			1				6		
Sudbury	63	35	Dorman	Mary										1			1		
Sudbury	63	36	Brigham	Samuel			1	1		1	1	2		1			7		
Sudbury	63	37	Smith	Asahel			1	1				1		1			4		
Sudbury	65	1	Smith	Henry			1	2	2		1	1	1				8		
Sudbury	65	2	Maynard	Joshua		2	1	1					1	1			6		
Sudbury	65	3	Shirtliff	Joseph	1			1		1	1		1				5		
Sudbury	65	4	Wheeler	William	3	1	1	1		1			1				8		
Sudbury	65	5	Ives	William	1			1		2			1				5		
Sudbury	65	6	Maynard	Asa				1			1		1				3		
Sudbury	65	7	Hunt	Isaac Jr				1		2			1				4		
Sudbury	65	8	Bussy	Isaiah	1		1						1				3		
Sudbury	65	9	Parmenter	William	2	1		1		2			1				7		
Sudbury	65	10	Parmenter	Hepzibah										1			1		

TOWN	PG#	LN#	LAST NAME	FIRST NAME	FREE WHITE MALES					FREE WHITE FEMALES					TOTAL ALL OTHER	TOTAL SLAVES	TOTALS	DISTRICT/ TOWNSHIP	NOTES
					under 10	10 to 16	16 to 26	26 to 45	45 and over	under 10	10 to 16	16 to 26	26 to 45	45 and over					
Tewksbury	49	1	Ames	Ezekiel	1		1						1				3		
Tewksbury	49	2	Brown	Wm Jr	1			1		1	2		2				7		
Tewksbury	49	3	Brown	Wm			1	2		1	1	1	1		1		8		
Tewksbury	49	4	Brown	Joseph	1			1		2			1	1			6		
Tewksbury	49	5	Brown	Saml			1	1	1	1	1	1					6		
Tewksbury	49	6	Brown	Jonathan		1	2	1	1	1		1		1			8		
Tewksbury	49	7	Balchader	John T	1			1		2		1					5		
Tewksbury	49	8	Baldwin	Joshua B				1			1		1				3		
Tewksbury	49	9	Baldwin	Davies	1	1		1		2			1				6		
Tewksbury	49	10	Burt	Thos	2			1		1		1	1				6		
Tewksbury	49	11	Baldwin	John T	2			1		1			1				5		
Tewksbury	49	12	Bailey	John T	3	2			1	3	2			1			12		
Tewksbury	49	13	Bailey	Timothy		1		1	1				3	1			7		
Tewksbury	49	14	Bailey	Nathan Jr		1	1	1					1				4		
Tewksbury	49	15	Bookman	Edward				1		2			1				4		
Tewksbury	49	16	Bookman	Jona	2	1		1		2			1				7		
Tewksbury	49	17	Barton	R Silas T	2			1				1	1				5		
Tewksbury	49	18	Beard	Eben	1	2		1	2	1	1		1				9		
Tewksbury	49	19	Beard	Reuben	2			2		1			1				6		
Tewksbury	50	1	Ball	John	2				1	2		1					6		
Tewksbury	50	2	Clark	Thomas		1	3		1	1				1	2		9		
Tewksbury	50	3	Clark	Thos Jr	2	1		1		3			1				8		
Tewksbury	50	4	Carter	David	1	1	1	1		3		1	1				9		
Tewksbury	50	5	Clark	Natha	1			1		3	1		2				8		
Tewksbury	50	6	Chapman	John	1			1		3		1					6		
Tewksbury	50	7	Clark	John	1			1		2			1	2			7		
Tewksbury	50	8	Clark	Joseph	1			1		2		1					5		
Tewksbury	50	9	Clark	Peter		1		1		1				1			4		
Tewksbury	50	10	Clark	Samll	1			1		1			1				4		
Tewksbury	50	11	Clark	Zeph*			1			3			1				5		
Tewksbury	50	12	Chandler	Wm			1	1		2			1				5		
Tewksbury	50	13	Carter	Adino				1						2			3		
Tewksbury	50	14	Chandler	Thos			1	1				1		1			4		
Tewksbury	50	15	Dutton	Timo			1	1					1	1			4		
Tewksbury	50	16	Danforth	Samll				1				1					2		
Tewksbury	50	17	Dana	Samll	2	1		1						1			5		
Tewksbury	50	18	Dunttin	Andrew	1			1		2			1				5		
Tewksbury	50	19	French	John		1		1	1				1	1			5		
Tewksbury	50	20	French	Thos				1				1	1	1			4		
Tewksbury	50	21	Frost	John			1							1			2		
Tewksbury	50	22	French	Nehemi	3		1		1	1	1		1				8		
Tewksbury	50	23	French	Joseph			1	1					1				3		
Tewksbury	50	24	French	Solomon		1		1		1		1					4		
Tewksbury	50	25	French	Joseph Jr	3	2		1		2	1		1				10		
Tewksbury	50	26	French	Solomon Jr		1		1		1			1	1			5		
Tewksbury	50	27	French	Aaron		2	1		1	1	1	2		1			9		
Tewksbury	50	28	French	Joel		1	1		1	1	1		1				6		
Tewksbury	50	29	Frost	Joseph	2				1	3		2	1	1			10		
Tewksbury	50	30	Frost	Zephani	1		1	1		3	1		1				8		
Tewksbury	50	31	Frost	Joseph Jr	1			1	1	2			1				6		
Tewksbury	50	32	Frost	Jonathan		1		1			1			1			4		
Tewksbury	50	33	Frost	Jonath Jr	3	1	1							1			6		
Tewksbury	50	34	Frost	Ephm			1	1									2		
Tewksbury	50	35	Frost	Benja		1		1						1			3		
Tewksbury	50	36	Frost	Abiel			2						1				3		
Tewksbury	50	37	Foster	Sarah			1			1	1		1				4		
Tewksbury	51	1	Foster	Amos	2	1		1		1	1	1					7		
Tewksbury	51	2	Foster	Jona			1	1		1		2	1				6		
Tewksbury	51	3	Farmer	Peter				1				1	1				3		
Tewksbury	51	4	Farmer	Lafe	2	1		1		3			1				8		
Tewksbury	51	5	Farmer	Silas	1		1	1		1			1				5		
Tewksbury	51	6	Foster	Isaac			1	1					1				3		
Tewksbury	51	7	Foster	Wm		1		1		1	1	1	1				6		
Tewksbury	51	8	Foster	Joseph	1			1		2		1					5		
Tewksbury	51	9	Flint	Eben				1		1			1				3		
Tewksbury	51	10	Foster	James			1	1				1		1			4		
Tewksbury	51	11	Griffin	Shamll		1	1	1				2	1	2			8		
Tewksbury	51	12	Griffin	Uriah		2		1				1	2	1			7		
Tewksbury	51	13	Gray	Jonathan	2	2		1		2	1		1				9		
Tewksbury	51	14	Gray	John	2		1			1			1				5		
Tewksbury	51	15	Hall	John				1		1		1		1			4		
Tewksbury	51	16	Hardy	Peter		2	1	1		1	1	1	1				8		
Tewksbury	51	17	Hunt	John		1		1	2	1	2	1	1				9		
Tewksbury	51	18	Hunt	Timothy	2	2	1	1					1				7		
Tewksbury	51	19	Hunt	Jona	2			1		1			1				5		
Tewksbury	51	20	Hunt	Solomon	1			1	1	2			3	1			9		
Tewksbury	51	21	Hunt	Noah	1			1					1				3		
Tewksbury	51	22	Hunt	Eben			1	1				1	1				5		
Tewksbury	51	23	Hardy	Wm	1	1	2	1			1		1				7		

106

TOWN	PG#	LN#	LAST NAME	FIRST NAME	FREE WHITE MALES					FREE WHITE FEMALES					TOTAL ALL OTHER	TOTAL SLAVES	TOTALS	DISTRICT/ TOWNSHIP	NOTES
					under 10	10 to 16	16 to 26	26 to 45	45 and over	under 10	10 to 16	16 to 26	26 to 45	45 and over					
Tewksbury	51	24	Hunt	John Jr			1	1		3	1	1		1			8		
Tewksbury	51	25	Hardy	Nathll		2	1		1	1		2	1				8		
Tewksbury	51	26	Hosmer	Amos	3			1		2			1				7		
Tewksbury	51	27	Jaquith	John	3		3	1		1	1	2	2				13		
Tewksbury	51	28	Kittridge	Jon		1			1	2			1	1			6		
Tewksbury	51	29	Kelley	James	2			1					1				4		
Tewksbury	51	30	Kittridge	Thos				1		1			1	1			4		
Tewksbury	51	31	Kittridge	Jeremiah	1	1		1		2			1				6		
Tewksbury	51	32	Kittridge	Simeon		1			1		2			1			5		
Tewksbury	51	33	Kittridge	Nathan Jr	1	1		1				1	1				5		
Tewksbury	51	34	Kittridge	Eben				1			1			1			3		
Tewksbury	52	1	Kittridge	Francis Jr	1	1	2		2	2	1	1					10		
Tewksbury	52	2	Kidder	Jeremiah Jr	1		1	1		1	2		1				7		
Tewksbury	52	3	Kidder	Jerem				1					1				2		
Tewksbury	52	4	Kidder	Lemual				1		2			1	1			5		
Tewksbury	52	5	Kendal	Ezra				1			1		1	1			4		
Tewksbury	52	6	Kendal	Ezra Jr	3	1		1		1			1				7		
Tewksbury	52	7	Kittridge	Benja		3	3				1		1	1			10		
Tewksbury	52	8	Mears	Aaron	2			1					1				4		
Tewksbury	52	9	Mears	Isaac	1		1			1		1					4		
Tewksbury	52	10	Lewiston	Daniel	2			1				3	2				8		
Tewksbury	52	11	Lewiston	Asa	1	1		1		1		1	1				6		
Tewksbury	52	12	Glode	Samll L		1	1						1				4		
Tewksbury	52	13	Marshal	Joel	1		2		1	2	2			1			9		
Tewksbury	52	14	Marshal	Daniel	2	1			1	1		1	2		1		9		
Tewksbury	52	15	Manning	Hannah		1						1	1	1			4		
Tewksbury	52	16	Mace	Furtam	1			1		1			1	1			5		
Tewksbury	52	17	Mears	Samll	1				1					1			3		
Tewksbury	52	18	Manning	Samll			3		1	2		2	1				9		
Tewksbury	52	19	Maning	Elizabeth	1	1		1	1	3			1	1			9		
Tewksbury	52	20	Marshal	Jacob	1	1	1	1		3	1	1	1				10		
Tewksbury	52	21	Mears	Russel	1			1				1					3		
Tewksbury	52	22	Mace	Benja	2	1	1			2	1	1	1				10		
Tewksbury	52	23	Merrit	David Jr	1			1		1			1				4		
Tewksbury	52	24	Merrit	David				1						1			2		
Tewksbury	52	25	Matthews	John			1						1				2		
Tewksbury	52	26	Morton	Amos	2	1		1				1	1	1			7		
Tewksbury	52	27	Needham	John	3		1	1		3	3		1				12		
Tewksbury	52	28	Persons	Wm	4			1				1	1				7		
Tewksbury	52	29	Rogers	Timo			2		1	1		2	1	1			8		
Tewksbury	52	30	Rogers	Philip P	1			1		2	1		1				6		
Tewksbury	52	31	Rogers	David	1	1	1	1				1	1	1			7		
Tewksbury	52	32	Rogers	Zadoch			2					1	1	1			5		
Tewksbury	52	33	Rea	Percie R	1	1		1		1	3	2					9		
Tewksbury	53	1	Shad	Joseph	2	1		2	1	1		2		1			10		
Tewksbury	53	2	Shad	Jona Jr	2	1	1	1		2	1		1				9		
Tewksbury	53	3	Stickney	Abran			1	1		1		1			1		5		
Tewksbury	53	4	Stickney	Eleazer			2		1	1			1	1			6		
Tewksbury	53	5	Symmon	Wm	2		2	2		2	3	2		2			15		
Tewksbury	53	6	Spaulding	John			1	1				1		1	1		5		
Tewksbury	53	7	Saunders	Benja	1	2		1		3	2		1				10		
Tewksbury	53	8	Saunders	Amos	3			1		1			1	1			7		
Tewksbury	53	9	Saunders	Timo	2			1		3			1	1			8		
Tewksbury	53	10	Staton	Benja				1		1	1		1				4		
Tewksbury	53	11	Saunders	Samll				1		1		1					3		
Tewksbury	53	12	Shad	Jacob			1	1	1	1	1		2				7		
Tewksbury	53	13	Swain	Walter	1			1		1			1				4		
Tewksbury	53	14	Shad	Joel	1	2		1		1		2	1				8		
Tewksbury	53	15	Stickney	Amos	2			1		1			1				5		
Tewksbury	53	16	Scarlet	Molly		1	1					1		1			4		
Tewksbury	53	17	Tuell	Jesse	2		1	1		1		1		1			7		
Tewksbury	53	18	Thorndike	Paul		1	2				2			1			7		
Tewksbury	53	19	Thorndike	Hezeh	2	2		1		2		1	1	1			10		
Tewksbury	53	20	Tucker	David	3			1	1	1			1	2			9		
Tewksbury	53	21	Thompson	Samll	3			1		2			1				7		
Tewksbury	53	22	Woodward	Joseph	2	2		1		1		2	1		2		11		
Tewksbury	53	23	Wooster	Samll	2	1	1	1	2	2	3		1	1			14		
Tewksbury	53	24	Wooster	Eldad	4	1		1				1	1	1			9		
Tewksbury	53	25	Wood	Eben				1						1			2		
Tewksbury	53	26	Wood	Thos	1	1	2		1	2	2		1				10		
Tewksbury	53	27	Wood	Edward			1			1	1			1			4		
Tewksbury	53	28	Whitemore	Isaac	2	1				1		1		1			6		
Tewksbury	53	29	Wood	Joseph			1				1						2		

TOWN	PG#	LN#	LAST NAME	FIRST NAME	FREE WHITE MALES					FREE WHITE FEMALES					TOTAL ALL OTHER	TOTAL SLAVES	TOTALS	DISTRICT/ TOWNSHIP	NOTES
					under 10	10 to 16	16 to 26	26 to 45	45 and over	under 10	10 to 16	16 to 26	26 to 45	45 and over					
Townsend	25	1	Adams	Anhelat			1	1	1			1					4		
Townsend	25	2	Adams	Peter	1		1	1		1		1					5		
Townsend	25	3	Adams	Daniel		1	2		1		2		1				7		
Townsend	25	4	Adams	Abner	1	1			1			1	1				5		
Townsend	25	5	Adams	Joseph	1	1		1		3		1	1	1			9		
Townsend	25	6	Allen	James			1					1					2		
Townsend	25	7	Adams	Elipht	2			1		1		1		1			6		
Townsend	25	8	Archaball	Willm			1						1				2		
Townsend	25	9	Brooks	Elit			1				1		1	1			4		
Townsend	25	10	Brooks	Saml	2	2		1		1			1				7		
Townsend	25	11	Ball	Noah		1	1			2		1		1			6		
Townsend	25	12	Ball	Jerh		1	1			1		1	1	2			7		
Townsend	25	13	Brown	Sarah									1				1		
Townsend	25	14	Bowers	Sarah		1	1				1	1		1			5		
Townsend	25	15	Butterfield	Peter	2	2	1		1			1		1			8		
Townsend	25	16	Baldwin	Asa	1	1		1			1		1				5		
Townsend	25	17	Bunge	Jonah Jr	2	1			1	3	1		1				9		
Townsend	25	18	Baldwin	Jonas		1			1			2	1				5		
Townsend	25	19	Blood	Joseph	1		1			1		1					4		
Townsend	25	20	Bruce	Stephen	1		1	1	1			1					5		
Townsend	25	21	Blodget	Jacob			2		1	2				2			7		
Townsend	25	22	Boutwell	John					1		1		1				3		
Townsend	25	23	Bailey	Jona	1			1		2	1		1				6		
Townsend	25	24	Bailey	Nathl	1		1		1	2			2	1			8		
Townsend	26	1	*	Ezekiel	2	1	1		1	2	2						9		
Townsend	26	2	Bacheldor	Jacob			1										1		
Townsend	26	3	Ball	Ebenz	3	2			1	1		1	1	1			10		
Townsend	26	4	Butters	Joel		1		1		3			1				6		
Townsend	26	5	Blood	Ezra	1			1		1			1				4		
Townsend	26	6	Bailey	Saml		1						1					2		
Townsend	26	7	Butterfield	Francis			1						1				2		
Townsend	26	8	Bunge	Moses	2			1		2			1				6		
Townsend	26	9	Conant	Nathn	1		1		1	2	1	1	1				8		
Townsend	26	10	Jewett	John	2		1	1		1		1					6		
Townsend	26	11	Conant	Melley		1				1	1		1				4		
Townsend	26	12	Conant	John	2			1		1		1					5		
Townsend	26	13	Conant	Sarah	1		4				2	1		1			9		
Townsend	26	14	Campbell	John	1	2			1	2	1	1					8		
Townsend	26	15	Campbell	Wm J.	1	1	1		1	1	1	1	1				8		
Townsend	26	16	Dix	Benja	3			1		1			1				6		
Townsend	26	17	Davis	Josiah	1	1		1	2	2	1	2	1				11		
Townsend	26	18	Davis	Eleazer		1	1	1	1					1			5		
Townsend	26	19	Dix	Jona	1	1		1		1		1		1			6		
Townsend	26	20	Dix	Jona Jr	1			1		1			1				4		
Townsend	26	21	Emery	John	3		2		2	2	2		1	1			13		
Townsend	26	22	Batcheldor	Nathl	1	1			1					1			4		
Townsend	26	23	Davis	Timo	2	1		1		1			1				6		
Townsend	26	24	Flagg	Elijah	1				1	2	2		1				7		
Townsend	26	25	Fesendon	Timo	3			1		2			1				7		
Townsend	26	26	Foster	Leonard	2	1		1		4	1		1				10		
Townsend	26	27	Farmer	Jonas	2	2	2		1			1		1			9		
Townsend	26	28	Farrar	Thos		1	1		1	1	2	2		1			9		
Townsend	26	29	Farrar	Isaac			1		1					1			3		
Townsend	26	30	Farrar	Thos Jr	1		1					1					3		
Townsend	26	31	Fesendon	Aaron		1	1	1	1			2		1			7		
Townsend	26	32	Fesendon	Aaron Jr			1	1				1					3		
Townsend	26	33	Flint	John		1		1	1	1	2			1			7		
Townsend	26	34	Foster	Jona	1	1			1	1				1			5		
Townsend	26	35	Graham	David				1									1		
Townsend	26	36	Graham	Saml	2			2		1			1	2			8		
Townsend	26	37	Giles	Ebenz Jr		1	1	1		1			1				5		
Townsend	26	38	Giles	John	4	2		1	1				1	1			10		
Townsend	26	39	Gaset	Reuben	1	2	1		1	2	1	1		1			10		
Townsend	26	40	Green	Solo	4	2		1		1			1				9		
Townsend	26	41	Giles	James Jr	2		4	1			1		1				9		
Townsend	26	42	Gaset	Ruthie								1		1			2		
Townsend	26	43	Gaset	Loten	1			1		1			1				4		
Townsend	26	44	Gowing	Eliab	1			1		2			1		1		6		
Townsend	27	1	Hart	Daniel			1						2				3		
Townsend	27	2	Hobert	Benja	2			1		1	1		1				6		
Townsend	27	3	Holt	Mary	1					2	1		1	2			7		
Townsend	27	4	Heald	Asa	2	1	2		1	4	1			1			12		
Townsend	27	5	Kildreth	Zach	1	1	2		1		3	1	1				10		
Townsend	27	6	Hill	Adam	1		1					1					3		
Townsend	27	7	Hartwell	Saml	1	1	1	1		2	1		1	1			9		
Townsend	27	8	Hodgman	John L.	4			1		1			1				8		
Townsend	27	9	Hosley	Saml	1	1		1	1	2			1				7		
Townsend	27	10	Jefts	Henry	2	2		1		1			1				7		
Townsend	27	11	Jenkins	Leml			1	1					1				3		

TOWN	PG#	LN#	HEADS OF HOUSEHOLD LAST NAME	FIRST NAME	FREE WHITE MALES under 10	10 to 16	16 to 26	26 to 45	45 and over	FREE WHITE FEMALES under 10	10 to 16	16 to 26	26 to 45	45 and over	TOTAL ALL OTHER	TOTAL SLAVES	TOTALS	DISTRICT/ TOWNSHIP	NOTES
Townsend	27	12	Jenkins	Saml	2	1		1		2			2	1			9		
Townsend	27	13	Jewett	Solo	1	1		1		2			1				6		
Townsend	27	14	Keep	Jonas	1	2	1		1	1	2	2		1			11		
Townsend	27	15	Ketridge	Ingals	1		1	1			1		1				5		
Townsend	27	16	Keyes	Abel		1	1		1				1				4		
Townsend	27	17	Kidder	Isaac	2	1	1		1	1	1			2			9		
Townsend	27	18	Lamson	Ephm	3			1		1	1		1				7		
Townsend	27	19	Lewis	Isaac	1	2		1		3	1		1				9		
Townsend	27	20	Lewis	Seth	2			1		1			1				5		
Townsend	27	21	Lawrence	Silas	1			1		1			1				4		
Townsend	27	22	Lawrence	Saml				1					1				2		
Townsend	27	23	Livingston	Wm	3			1		1	1		1				7		
Townsend	27	24	Mulliken	Isaac	1			1				1	1				4		
Townsend	27	25	Manning	Saml		1		1		1			1				4		
Townsend	27	26	Manning	Wm	2	1		1		1			1				6		
Townsend	27	27	Mulliken	Amos				1					1				2		
Townsend	27	28	Spaulding	Benja	1	1		1		2	1	1	1				8		
Townsend	27	29	Proctor	Oliver		2		1				1	1				5		
Townsend	27	30	Petts	Leml		1		1					2				4		
Townsend	27	31	Pratt	Benl		1		1		4	1		1				8		
Townsend	27	32	Peirce	Jona			1	1				1	1				4		
Townsend	27	33	Parker	Wm	3			1					1				5		
Townsend	27	34	Putnam	Andrew				1	1	1			1				4		
Townsend	27	35	Turner	Simon		1		1		1	1		1				5		
Townsend	27	36	Petts	Leml Jr	3		1		1	1	1		1				8		
Townsend	27	37	Petts	John	1		1			1		1					4		
Townsend	27	38	Peirce	Solo	3	1		1		1	1		1				8		
Townsend	27	39	Richardson	Simeon	1	2	1		1	3				2			10		
Townsend	27	40	Richardson	Josiah	1	2			1	1	2			1			8		
Townsend	27	41	Rumerell	Wi*	1					1			2	1			5		
Townsend	27	42	Rumerell	Joseph	2	1		1		1			1	1			7		
Townsend	27	43	Richardson	Herh				1				3		1			5		
Townsend	27	44	Richardson	Herh Jr			1						1				2		
Townsend	27	45	Richardson	Zach	1			1					1				3		
Townsend	28	1	Sarles	*		2		2		1			1	1			7		
Townsend	28	2	Sarles	Saml	3	1		1		1	2		1				9		
Townsend	28	3	Santell	Simeon			4	1		2	2			2			10		
Townsend	28	4	Shriver	Daniel						1					1		2		
Townsend	28	5	Sarles	James	1			1		3			1				6		
Townsend	28	6	Sherwin	H* P.	2		1	1		3			1				8		
Townsend	28	7	Shinvin	Levi		2						1					3		
Townsend	28	8	Sanders	James	1		2	1		1			1				7		
Townsend	28	9	Spaulding	Benja Jr	2			1		1	1		1				6		
Townsend	28	10	Sparrowhawk	Saml	1	2		1		2	1		2				9		
Townsend	28	11	Shattuck	Solo	3	1		1		2	1		2				10		
Townsend	28	12	Stone	Ebenz	1			1	1	2	2		1				8		
Townsend	28	13	Spaulding	Jona	1	1		1				1		1			5		
Townsend	28	14	Stevens	Solo		1			1					1			3		
Townsend	28	15	Stevens	Solo Jr	2	1		1					1				5		
Townsend	28	16	Sever	Thos			1		1			2		2			6		
Townsend	28	17	Sever	Thos Jr		1		1					1				3		
Townsend	28	18	Sylvester	Caleb	2	3	1		1	1		2		1			11		
Townsend	28	19	Seales	Nathn		1	1		1		1		1				5		
Townsend	28	20	Sartell	Ephm			1			2			1				4		
Townsend	28	21	Sanders	Solo	3		1		1		1	1		1			8		
Townsend	28	22	Stone	Peter	1	3			1	3			1				9		
Townsend	28	23	Sloan	James	3	1	1		2	1				1			9		
Townsend	28	24	Simons	James		1						1		1 1			4		
Townsend	28	25	Spaulding	Joel			1			1			1				3		
Townsend	28	26	Stevens	Jona		1		1				2		1			5		
Townsend	28	27	Sanders	Jonas			1				1		2				4		
Townsend	28	28	Spaulding	Eleazer						1			1				2		
Townsend	28	29	Spaulding	Thos	1			1		1			1				4		
Townsend	28	30	Spaulding	Jesse			1			2			1				4		
Townsend	28	31	Sanders	Jacob	2	2			1		1	3		2			11		
Townsend	28	32	Stone	Saml			1		1	1	2	2	1				8		
Townsend	28	33	Shattuck	Zach			1	1					1	1			4		
Townsend	28	34	Shattuck	Noah	1		2			1			1				5		
Townsend	28	35	Seales	Natha	1			1		1	2	1		1			7		
Townsend	28	36	Sherwin	John	1	1	1	1		2			1				7		
Townsend	28	37	Stickney	Joseph	1			1		2			1				5		
Townsend	28	38	Sanders	Wm	1		1			1			1				4		
Townsend	28	39	Stevens	John		2		1		1			1				5		
Townsend	28	40	Taylor	Robert	2	2		1		2			1				8		
Townsend	28	41	Walker	Silas					1				1				2		
Townsend	28	42	Wilson	Thos	1			1				1					3		
Townsend	28	43	Sanders	Perly						1		1					2		
Townsend	28	44	Blood	Jona	1					1		1					4		
Townsend	28	45	Waugh	John				1					1				2		

TOWN	PG#	LN#	LAST NAME	FIRST NAME	FREE WHITE MALES					FREE WHITE FEMALES					TOTAL ALL OTHER	TOTAL SLAVES	TOTALS	DISTRICT/ TOWNSHIP	NOTES
					under 10	10 to 16	16 to 26	26 to 45	45 and over	under 10	10 to 16	16 to 26	26 to 45	45 and over					
Townsend	28	46	Palmer	David Rev	1		1				1	1					4		
Townsend	29	1	Walker	Isaac Jr	1	2	1			3			1				8		
Townsend	29	2	Simons	James Jr				1					1				2		
Townsend	29	3	Wilder	Isaac		2	1		1	1	1	1		1			8		
Townsend	29	4	Verde	George	3			1					1				5		
Townsend	29	5	Sherwin	Salome	1			1		1			1				4		
Townsend	29	6	Giles	Isaac	1			1		3			1				6		
Townsend	29	7	Putney	Joseph					1					1			2		
Townsend	29	8	Turner	Luther	1			1		1	2		1				6		
Townsend	29	9	Warren	Aaron	1		1					1	1				4		
Townsend	29	10	Wyer	Richard		1			1	1				2			5		
Townsend	29	11	Warren	Ephm					1	1		1		1			4		
Townsend	29	12	Warren	Moses	1	1	2	2		3	1	1	1				12		
Townsend	29	13	Wallis	Isaac	1		1	1	1	1		1		1			7		
Townsend	29	14	Wesson	Wm	1				1	1	1	1		1			6		
Townsend	29	15	Walker	Joseph	1			1		2			1				5		
Townsend	29	16	Warner	Joseph	1			1					1				3		
Townsend	29	17	Wilson	James	1		1		1	1			1				5		
Townsend	29	18	Wallis	Wm	3	1		1		1			1				7		
Townsend	29	19	Whitney	Asa	3			1		3			1				8		
Townsend	29	20	Whitney	Levi					1					1			2		
Townsend	29	21	Wright	Washn	1		1			1		1					4		
Townsend	29	22	Waugh	John	2	2		1	1	2	1		1	1			11		
Townsend	29	23	Wheeler	Solo	2			1		3			1				7		
Townsend	29	24	Wallis	Jona	1				1	1							3		
Townsend	29	25	Wallis	Joseph	1		1					1					3		
Townsend	29	26	Wallis	Benja				1		1			1				3		
Townsend	29	27	Wallis	Jona Jr			1	1		1			1				4		
Townsend	29	28	Warner	Richard	4			1		1			1				7		
Townsend	29	29	Wood	Benja					1	1			1	1			4		
Townsend	29	30	Wheeler	Benja			1				1						2		
Townsend	29	31	Win	Hezh	2			1		3			1				7		
Townsend	29	32	Wallis	Mary		1		1				3		1			6		
Townsend	29	33	Wyman	Zebn					1					1			2		
Townsend	29	34	Weatherbee	Jacob	1	1		1		3	1		1				8		
Townsend	29	35	Sherwin	Zemry			1	1		3		2	1				8		
Townsend	29	36	Holt	Jona	1		1						1				3		
Townsend	29	37	Sarles	Azubah	1					1			1				3		
Townsend	29	38	Green	Simeon	1			1					1	1			4		
Townsend	29	39	Tarbox	Daniel				1				1		1			3		
Townsend	29	40	Giles	James				1				1		1			3		
Townsend	29	41	Sarles	Uriah			1						1				2		
Townsend	29	42	Spaulding	Sarah										2			2		
Townsend	29	43	Boutwell	Silas		1				1		1					3		
Townsend	29	44	Warner	Saml		1						1					2		

TOWN	PG#	LN#	HEADS OF HOUSEHOLD		FREE WHITE MALES					FREE WHITE FEMALES					TOTAL ALL OTHER	TOTAL SLAVES	TOTALS	DISTRICT/ TOWNSHIP	NOTES
			LAST NAME	FIRST NAME	under 10	10 to 16	16 to 26	26 to 45	45 and over	under 10	10 to 16	16 to 26	26 to 45	45 and over					
Tyngsborough	40	1	Barker	Moses	1			1						1			3		
Tyngsborough	40	2	Butterfield	Reuben			1	1		3		1		1			7		
Tyngsborough	40	3	Barker	Ezra				1		3			1				5		
Tyngsborough	40	4	Butterfield	James	2	1		1		2			1				7		
Tyngsborough	40	5	Butterfield	Abner R	2			1		3			1				7		
Tyngsborough	40	6	Butterfield	Asa	2	1	7	1		1	1	2	1	1			17		
Tyngsborough	40	7	Butterfield	Joseph	1	2		1					1				5		
Tyngsborough	40	8	Bloghet	Nehem			1	1					1				3		
Tyngsborough	40	9	Blood	Joseph		1		1		3			2	1			8		
Tyngsborough	40	10	Bootman	Thos	4			1			1		1				7		
Tyngsborough	40	11	Burroughs	Joseph	1			1		2			2				6		
Tyngsborough	40	12	Brown	Elisha				1					1				2		
Tyngsborough	40	13	Coburn	Abiel		1	1	1				1		1			5		
Tyngsborough	40	14	Coburn	John Jr	2			1		4			1				8		
Tyngsborough	40	15	Coburn	John		1		1						1			3		
Tyngsborough	40	16	Coburn	Oliver	2			1		1			1				5		
Tyngsborough	40	17	Cummings	John	1		4	1				2		1			9		
Tyngsborough	40	18	Coburn	Nathl	3		1	1		1		2	1				9		
Tyngsborough	40	19	Coburn	Caleb				1			1	1		1			4		
Tyngsborough	40	20	Coburn	Moses	1			1		2			1				5		
Tyngsborough	40	21	Barkin	Sy*	1												1		
Tyngsborough	40	22	*eng	Luther				1		2			1				4		
Tyngsborough	40	23	Car*	Jonas	1		1			1			1				4		
Tyngsborough	41	1	Abbot	Nathl	1			1		1	2		1				6		
Tyngsborough	41	2	Brindley	Nathl		2	1		1			1		1			6		
Tyngsborough	41	3	Bancroft	Eben	2				1	3	1		1				8		
Tyngsborough	41	4	Bancroft	Jona	1		2		1	1	1	1		1			8		
Tyngsborough	42	1	Blodget	William	1	1		1		1	1		1				6		
Tyngsborough	42	2	Blodget	Thaddeus	4			1		1	1	1					8		
Tyngsborough	42	3	Blodget	Ezra	1	1		1		4	1	1	1				10		
Tyngsborough	42	4	Davis	Thaddeus	3			1		1			1				6		
Tyngsborough	42	5	Dandley	John	3			1		1			1				6		
Tyngsborough	42	6	Dalton	John	2	2		1					1				6		
Tyngsborough	42	7	Dunn	Edward		1		1					1				3		
Tyngsborough	42	8	Dunn	Robert				1					1				2		
Tyngsborough	42	9	Daken	Levi	1	1	2		1			1	1	1			8		
Tyngsborough	42	10	Danforth	Josiah	3	1	2	1				2	1				10		
Tyngsborough	42	11	Dix	Joseph	1	2			1	2			1		1		8		
Tyngsborough	42	12	Durant	Jacob				1					1				2		
Tyngsborough	42	13	Dow	Samll	2	1	1		1	3	1		1				10		
Tyngsborough	42	14	Epes	Benja	1	1	4		1		2	2		1			12		
Tyngsborough	42	15	Farwell	John		1	1	2		4	2	1	1				12		
Tyngsborough	42	16	Fletcher	Jacob			1	1					1				3		
Tyngsborough	42	17	Ford	John	1			1					1				3		
Tyngsborough	42	18	Fletcher	William	1	1		1		2			1				6		
Tyngsborough	42	19	Fletcher	Elijah	1		1						1				3		
Tyngsborough	42	20	Fletcher	Mercy		1						1	3	1			6		
Tyngsborough	42	21	Flint	Charles	2	1		1		2	1	1	2	1	1		12		
Tyngsborough	42	22	Farwell	Nathan	3			2			1	2	1		2		11		
Tyngsborough	42	23	Fredric	George	2			1		2	1		1				7		
Tyngsborough	42	24	Farwell	Henry	3			1		2			1				7		
Tyngsborough	42	25	Farmer	Jeremiah		1		1	1				1				4		
Tyngsborough	42	26	Gilson	Solomon	2	2		1		1	2		1				9		
Tyngsborough	42	27	Gilson	Jeremiah	1			1		2	2		1				7		
Tyngsborough	42	28	Gilson	Levi	2			1		1		1					5		
Tyngsborough	42	29	Gilson	Peter				1		2			1				4		
Tyngsborough	42	30	Gould	David				1						1			2		
Tyngsborough	42	31	Gould	Noah	2			1		3	1		1				8		
Tyngsborough	42	32	Glynn	Isaac	3	1		1		2	1		1				9		
Tyngsborough	42	33	Holden	Nathl			2		1				1	1			5		
Tyngsborough	42	34	Gould	Reuben	2			1		2			1				6		
Tyngsborough	42	35	Holden	John	3			1		2	1		1				8		
Tyngsborough	42	36	Howard	Jona	1		1	1					1				4		
Tyngsborough	42	37	Hildreth	Hezeh		1		1			1	1	1				5		
Tyngsborough	42	38	Han*	Jonathan				1					1		5		7		
Tyngsborough	42	39	Hayson	John	3				1	1			1				6		
Tyngsborough	42	40	Holden	Nathll Jr				1		1			1				3		
Tyngsborough	42	41	Jaques	Daniel	1			1		1			1				4		
Tyngsborough	42	42	Jaques	Nehem				1						1			2		
Tyngsborough	42	43	Ingals	Joseph		1	1		1		1	1		2			7		
Tyngsborough	42	44	Ingals	Nathl		1		1		2	2		1				7		
Tyngsborough	43	1	*	*	2		2	1	1	1		1		1			9		Illegible
Tyngsborough	43	2	L	*					1					1			2		Illegible
Tyngsborough	43	3	Littlehale	Abram	1	1		1		2	1		1				7		
Tyngsborough	43	4	Littlehale	Roger	2			1		4			1	1			9		
Tyngsborough	43	5	Lawrance	Lemuel	2			1		1			1				5		
Tyngsborough	43	6	Merril	John	1				1				1				3		
Tyngsborough	43	7	Melvin	Reuben	3		1	1		2		1	1				9		
Tyngsborough	43	8	Nutting	David	1			1		1			1				4		
Tyngsborough	43	9	Perham	John		1	1		2	3		1	1				9		

TOWN	PG#	LN#	LAST NAME	FIRST NAME	FREE WHITE MALES					FREE WHITE FEMALES					TOTAL ALL OTHER	TOTAL SLAVES	TOTALS	DISTRICT/ TOWNSHIP	NOTES
					under 10	10 to 16	16 to 26	26 to 45	45 and over	under 10	10 to 16	16 to 26	26 to 45	45 and over					
Tyngsborough	43	10	Perham	Peter		1			1				1				3		
Tyngsborough	43	11	Perham	Elijah		1		1		2			1				5		
Tyngsborough	43	12	Perham	Jonathan		2	3		1	2	2	1	1				12		
Tyngsborough	43	13	Perham	Willm	1	1		1		2	1		1				7		
Tyngsborough	43	14	Perham	Joseph	1			1				2	1				5		
Tyngsborough	43	15	Pike	Isaac			1		1				1	1			4		
Tyngsborough	43	16	Parker	Aaron	2			1		1	1	1					6		
Tyngsborough	43	17	Parker	Elijah	3	2		1		2	1		1				10		
Tyngsborough	43	18	Pitts	John					1			2		2	3		8		
Tyngsborough	43	19	Pear	William	2				1	2	1		1				7		
Tyngsborough	43	20	Swan	Benja			1		1				1	1			4		
Tyngsborough	43	21	Spalding	Joel		1		1		1	1		1				5		
Tyngsborough	43	22	Spalding	Jonah	1			1		3			1				6		
Tyngsborough	43	23	Scrivner	Matthew	2	2	1		1	1	3		1	1			12		
Tyngsborough	43	24	Stewart	Robert			1		1		1			1			4		
Tyngsborough	43	25	Sawyer	David	1	1		1		3	1	1	1				9		
Tyngsborough	43	26	Smith	Aaron	1		3	1		2	1	1					9		
Tyngsborough	43	27	Thompson	Nathan	1				1			2		1			5		
Tyngsborough	43	28	Thompson	Ezra		1		1	1	2	1		1	1			8		
Tyngsborough	43	29	Thompson	Asa			1		1	1	1		1				5		
Tyngsborough	43	30	Upton	Joseph			1						1	1			3		
Tyngsborough	43	31	Underwood	Asa	3				1			1					5		
Tyngsborough	43	32	Woodward	Jona			1		1					1			3		
Tyngsborough	43	33	Woodward	John	2	1		1		1			1				6		
Tyngsborough	43	34	Wooster	Samll		1			1		1		1				4		
Tyngsborough	43	35	Wooster	Francis	2	1	1		1		1	2	1				9		
Tyngsborough	43	36	Wooster	Jonath	1			1		3			1				6		
Tyngsborough	43	37	Wilson	John	2	1	2	1		2	1		1				10		
Tyngsborough	43	38	Whitney	James	3	1				2			1				7		
Tyngsborough	43	39	Sherburne	Samll	1			1		2			1				5		
Tyngsborough	43	40	White	Mark				1					1				2		

TOWN	PG#	LN#	LAST NAME	FIRST NAME	under 10	10 to 16	16 to 26	26 to 45	45 and over	under 10	10 to 16	16 to 26	26 to 45	45 and over	TOTAL ALL OTHER	TOTAL SLAVES	TOTALS	DISTRICT/ TOWNSHIP	NOTES
			HEADS OF HOUSEHOLD		FREE WHITE MALES					FREE WHITE FEMALES									
Waltham	112	1	Allen	James	3				1	1			1				6		
Waltham	112	2	Adams	William					1					2			3		
Waltham	112	3	Brown	Nathaniel			2	1		1		1					5		
Waltham	112	4	Brown	Amos Jr	2			1		1		1					5		
Waltham	112	5	Bemis	Josiah	3	2	1		1	2	1	1	1				12		
Waltham	112	6	Bright	John	2	2	2		1	2		1	1				11		
Waltham	112	7	B*	Benjm			1	1	1		1	1		1			6		
Waltham	112	8	Barnes	Samuel		1		1	1	2	1	1	1	1			9		
Waltham	112	9	Brown	Joseph					1					1			2		
Waltham	112	10	Brigham	Saml	1	1		1				1					4		
Waltham	112	11	Bemis	Abraham					1					1			2		
Waltham	112	12	Bemis	Abraham Jr	2		1	1	1			2					8		
Waltham	112	13	Bridge	Mary		1		1					1	1			4		
Waltham	112	14	Bridge	William			1			4	1		1				7		
Waltham	112	15	Baldwin	Isaac		1	2			1		1					5		
Waltham	113	1	Brown	*		1	1		1		1		1	1			6		
Waltham	113	2	Barnard	Hannah		1								2			3		
Waltham	113	3	Brown	Jonas			1	1		2			2	1			7		
Waltham	113	4	Bemis	Isaac	3	1	5		1		1		2				13		
Waltham	113	5	Biglow	Thomas	2		2	2		2		1	1				10		
Waltham	113	6	Boles	John		2	4		1	1	2	1			1		12		
Waltham	113	7	Buchanan	James	1			1		1		1	1				5		
Waltham	113	8	Cushing	Jacob		1		1				3	1				6		
Waltham	113	9	Clark	Sarah	1	2		1				2		1			7		
Waltham	113	10	Colling	Abigail	1		1			1	1		1				5		
Waltham	113	11	Clark	John	1		5	1		2	1	1	1	1			13		
Waltham	113	12	Coolledge	Jonas	3	2	1	1		3	1	1	1	1			14		
Waltham	113	13	Cushing	Warham	2	1	3		2	4			1				13		
Waltham	113	14	Child	Isaac	1			1	1	2			1				6		
Waltham	113	15	Child	Abijah	1		1		1			1	1	1			6		
Waltham	113	16	Child	Josiah	1	1		1					1				4		
Waltham	113	17	Den	Elizabeth						1		2	1				4		
Waltham	113	18	Den	Joel	1	1	1		1				2		1		7		
Waltham	113	19	Foley	John		2			1	1			1				5		
Waltham	113	20	Fisk	Samuel			3		1			1	1				6		
Waltham	113	21	Fisk	Francis		1	1	1		1	1	1					6		
Waltham	113	22	Flagg	Solomon		1	4	1		1		1	1				9		
Waltham	113	23	Fisher	Abraham	2			1		1		1					5		
Waltham	113	24	Flagg	Bezayeel		1		1				1					3		
Waltham	113	25	Flagg	Bezatesel Jr	2		1	1		2			1				7		
Waltham	113	26	Flagg	Timothy			1	1					1				3		
Waltham	113	27	Fisher	Jonathan		1	1	1				1	1				5		
Waltham	113	28	Fisher	Elijah	1	1	1	1				1	1				6		
Waltham	113	29	Fuller	Lydia								1					1		
Waltham	113	30	Fisher	William	3	2			1	1		1	1				9		
Waltham	114	1	Gale	Alpheus	1	1	2	1		2	1		1				9		
Waltham	114	2	Gale	Jacob			1			1			1				3		
Waltham	114	3	Goodwin	Ruth									1				1		
Waltham	114	4	Green	Benjm				1			1			2			4		
Waltham	114	5	Green	Jonas		1	1			1		1	1				5		
Waltham	114	6	Garfield	Esther	1							1		2			4		
Waltham	114	7	Hastings	Elephalet					1		1		1	1			4		
Waltham	114	8	Hastings	Elephalet Jr			1			1		1					3		
Waltham	114	9	Hammond	Jacob			1					1					2		
Waltham	114	10	Harrington	Joel				1		4			1				6		
Waltham	114	11	Hastings	Josiah			1	1			1						3		
Waltham	114	12	Hastings	Samuel	2			1		1		1					5		
Waltham	114	13	Hammond	Jonathan	3		1	1		2	1	1	1				10		
Waltham	114	14	Hammond	Ephraim	1	1	1		1	1	2	2	1				10		
Waltham	114	15	Harrington	Saml				1		2		1	1	1			6		
Waltham	114	16	Harrington	Samuel Jr	1	1					1	2		1			7		
Waltham	114	17	Harrington	Benjm	2	1		1		1			1				6		
Waltham	114	18	Hagar	Joseph	1	1	1	1		2	1		1				8		
Waltham	114	19	Hagar	L*		1							1				2		
Waltham	114	20	Kimball	Harry	2	2		1		1	2	1					9		
Waltham	114	21	Livermore	Nathl	2	1	4	1			1	2		1			12		
Waltham	114	22	Livermore	Abijah	1	1	1	1	2	2	1		2				11		
Waltham	114	23	Livermore	Phinehas	1	1	2		1			3	1				9		
Waltham	114	24	Lyman	Theodore	2	1	2	2	1			6	2				16		
Waltham	114	25	Livermore	Moses			1			1		1	1				4		
Waltham	114	26	Lawrence	Benjamin	1		1	1	2	2	1	1		1			10		
Waltham	114	27	Morse	Luther	1			1		2			1				5		
Waltham	114	28	Mead	Stephen	2		1	1		1			1				6		
Waltham	114	29	Morse	Levi			1	3		2			1				7		
Waltham	115	1	Mead	Jacob	1			1					1				3		
Waltham	115	2	Miller	Thomas			1			3			1				5		
Waltham	115	3	Mead	Moses	1	1	1		1	3		1	1	1			10		
Waltham	115	4	Macomber	Zabidee	3		1	1		1		1					7		
Waltham	115	5	Wiswell	Moore &		2	9					5	1				17		

113

TOWN	PG#	LN#	HEADS OF HOUSEHOLD		FREE WHITE MALES					FREE WHITE FEMALES					TOTAL ALL OTHER	TOTAL SLAVES	TOTALS	DISTRICT/ TOWNSHIP	NOTES
			LAST NAME	FIRST NAME	under 10	10 to 16	16 to 26	26 to 45	45 and over	under 10	10 to 16	16 to 26	26 to 45	45 and over					
Waltham	115	6	Nison	Joseph	3		4	1		2	1	2					13		
Waltham	115	7	Nutting	Samuel					1	1		1		1			4		
Waltham	115	8	Paine	William			1					1	3				5		
Waltham	115	9	Parkhurst	Sarah	2				1					1			4		
Waltham	115	10	Pierce	Samuel			1	2	2	1	1	1		1			9		
Waltham	115	11	Pierce	William	3	1		1		1		1					7		
Waltham	115	12	Piper	Filly M.	1			1		3	1		1	1			8		
Waltham	115	13	Pierce	Ephraim			1	1		2	1	1	1				7		
Waltham	115	14	Pierce	Abraham		1	1		2	1				1			6		
Waltham	115	15	Pierce	Isaac	2		1		1			1		1			6		
Waltham	115	16	Poriet	Sally	1		1							1			3		
Waltham	115	17	Sanderson	John			1	2	1			3	1	1			9		
Waltham	115	18	Smith	Amos	2	2	1	1		2	1						10		
Waltham	115	19	Smith	Elijah	4	2	1	1		1		1	1				11		
Waltham	115	20	Smith	Jonas				1					1				2		
Waltham	115	21	Stearns	Daniel	1			1				1	1				4		
Waltham	115	22	Stearns	Joseph				1				1					2		
Waltham	115	23	Sanderson	Jonathan	3	2		1		2	1		1				10		
Waltham	115	24	Stearns	David	2	3	4	2				1	1				13		
Waltham	115	25	Sanderson	Abner		1	1		1	1	1		2				7		
Waltham	115	26	Smith	Nathan	2	1	1	1		3	1	1	1				11		
Waltham	115	27	Stearns	Juda			1	1		3	2		1				8		
Waltham	115	28	Stearns	Ismael	1			1		1			1	1			5		
Waltham	115	29	Sanderson	Nathan	4	1	1		1	2	1	1					11		
Waltham	115	30	Sanderson	Mary									2				2		
Waltham	115	31	Sanderson	Josiah	1		1	1	1			2	1				7		
Waltham	116	1	Stearns	Silas			2	1				1		1			5		
Waltham	116	2	Stearns	Jonathan	3	2	1		1	1	1	2	1				12		
Waltham	116	3	Stearns	Joshua	1				1	3	2	2		1			10		
Waltham	116	4	Smith	Elijah Jr		1		1				1					3		
Waltham	116	5	Stearns	Samuel		1	1		1			3		1			7		
Waltham	116	6	Stearns	Thomas	1			1					1				3		
Waltham	116	7	Stearns	John	3		1	1		2	1	1					9		
Waltham	116	8	Stearns	Samuel Jr	1			1					1				3		
Waltham	116	9	Smith	Thomas	2	1	1		1	3		2		1			11		
Waltham	116	10	Shed	Zacheus	2	1	1		1	3	1			1			10		
Waltham	116	11	Smith	David	1	1	3		1	2	1	2					11		
Waltham	116	12	Twist	Timothy	2			1					1				4		
Waltham	116	13	Townsend	David		2	4	2	1		3	3		2			17		
Waltham	116	14	Upham	Nathan		1		1		1		1					4		
Waltham	116	15	Viles	John	3				1	3	1		1				9		
Waltham	116	16	Viles	Irena	1		1	1		2	1	1					7		
Waltham	116	17	Wellington	William Jr			1	1		1	1	1					5		
Waltham	116	18	Welsh	William	1	1		1				1	1				5		
Waltham	116	19	Wolcott	Edward K	1		1		1	1	1		1		1		7		
Waltham	116	20	Warren	Peter	4	1	2		1	2	1	1	1				13		
Waltham	116	21	Wellington	William	1	2		1	1	1		2		1	1		10		
Waltham	116	22	Wellington	Abraham	1			1		1		1					4		
Waltham	116	23	Whitney	Josiah		1		1	1			1	1				5		
Waltham	116	24	Weston	Zachariah		1	3		1	1	1	1	1				9		

TOWN	PG#	LN#	LAST NAME	FIRST NAME	FREE WHITE MALES under 10	10 to 16	16 to 26	26 to 45	45 and over	FREE WHITE FEMALES under 10	10 to 16	16 to 26	26 to 45	45 and over	TOTAL ALL OTHER	TOTAL SLAVES	TOTALS	DISTRICT/ TOWNSHIP	NOTES
Watertown	231	1	Annas	Thos'	2	2	2	1		1	1		1				10		
Watertown	231	2	Alden	Jona	2		2			2	2						8		
Watertown	231	3	Aspinwall	Palnopha				1				1	1				3		
Watertown	231	4	Barnard	Daniel	2	1	1	1	1	3			3	1			13		
Watertown	231	5	Bright	Nathan			1	1				1		1			4		
Watertown	231	6	Bright	Moses	2			1		2			2				7		
Watertown	231	7	Bright	Francis	1			1		1		1					4		
Watertown	231	8	Bemis	Seth	3		3	2				1	1	1			11		
Watertown	231	9	Bemis	Luke	1		3	1				2	1				8		
Watertown	231	10	Barry	Willm					2	2				1			5		
Watertown	231	11	Bond	Amos			3		1			5		1			10		
Watertown	231	12	Bond	Daniel				1		2			1	1			5		
Watertown	231	13	Bemis	Nathl	1	2	3	1					2				9		
Watertown	231	14	Bond	Charles	3		3	1		1	1		1				10		
Watertown	231	15	Bridge	Jeremiah	1			1		2			1				5		
Watertown	231	16	Bond	Wm	1	1	1	1	1	2	1		1	1			10		
Watertown	231	17	Brown	Adam	1	1			1				3	1			7		
Watertown	231	18	Bright	Rachel						1	1						2		
Watertown	231	19	Bright	Joseph	2	3	1	1		2	1	1	1				12		
Watertown	231	20	Bond	Leonard				4					1	2			7		
Watertown	231	21	Bird	Jona		2	1		1	1	2		1				8		
Watertown	231	22	Benjamin	Saml				1	2				1				4		
Watertown	231	23	Barnard	James	3	1	1	1		3		1	1				11		
Watertown	231	24	Bond	Susannah		1	1			1	1	1					5		
Watertown	231	25	Blackman	Andrew	2			1		2			1				6		
Watertown	231	26	Blaver	Wm				1						1			2		
Watertown	231	27	Blay	Thos H.				1		3			1	1			6		
Watertown	231	28	Babcock	Saml	1	1				2	1		1				7		
Watertown	231	29	Clark	Peter			1	1		1		1	1				5		
Watertown	231	30	Clark	Richard				1			1			1			3		
Watertown	231	31	Clark	Thos		2	1	1		3	1		1	1			10		
Watertown	231	32	Cheaney	Sollomon	1		2			1		1					5		
Watertown	231	33	Cole	Thadius				5		3	1		1				10		
Watertown	231	34	Craft	Abner	1			1		1			1	1			5		
Watertown	231	35	Conwell	Daniel		1	2		1					2			6		
Watertown	231	36	Coollidge	John			1			2							3		
Watertown	231	37	Coollidge	Nathl		1			1				1				3		
Watertown	231	38	Coollidge	Joshua	3	3	2	1		1	1		1				12		
Watertown	232	1	Coollidge	Eunis						3			2				5		
Watertown	232	2	Coollidge	Moses		2	2		1	2	1	1					9		
Watertown	232	3	Cheaney	Wm				1		1		2					4		
Watertown	232	4	Cheaney	Ebenz		1			1	1		1					4		
Watertown	232	5	Cheaney	Moses	2		1		1	2	1	1					8		
Watertown	232	6	Coollidge	Daniel	1		1	1		1	1			1			6		
Watertown	232	7	Coollidge	Saml	2	2		1		2	1	1	1	1			11		
Watertown	232	8	Cook	Stephen		2			1	2		1	1	1			8		
Watertown	232	9	Cook	Israel	1	2		1		2		2					8		
Watertown	232	10	Davis	Aaron	1					2		1					5		
Watertown	232	11	Dana	Isaac			2	1		3			1	1			8		
Watertown	232	12	Draper	John		1	1	1	1					1			5		
Watertown	232	13	Dana	Aaron	2	1	1	1			1	1					7		
Watertown	232	14	Durant	John	2		1	1		1		1	1				7		
Watertown	232	15	Everet	Aaron	3	1	2	1		1		1					9		
Watertown	232	16	Elliott	Richd R.		1		1		1	1		1				5		
Watertown	232	17	Fowle	Jeremiah	1	1	2	1		1		1	2				10		
Watertown	232	18	Fullar	Joshua	1		1					1		1			4		
Watertown	232	19	Faulkner	Francis		1	1	2				2					6		
Watertown	232	20	Fowle	John	2		3	1		2	2	1	1		1		13		
Watertown	232	21	Fowle	Edmund	3	2			1	1	2		1				10		
Watertown	232	22	Fessenden	George	2		1	2		1		1					7		
Watertown	232	23	Ferrington	Wm				1		2			1				4		
Watertown	232	24	Gardner	Joseph			1	1	1				2	2			7		
Watertown	232	25	Gerrey	John	1	1			1	3	1		1				8		
Watertown	232	26	Gardner	Benjm	1		1			1			1				4		
Watertown	232	27	Gay	Wm	3	1		1		2	1		1				9		
Watertown	232	28	Godard	Abigail										2			2		
Watertown	232	29	Grant	Christopher		1				1		1		1			4		
Watertown	232	30	Grant	Joshua	2		1	2			1	1	1				8		
Watertown	232	31	Groves	Stephen	1		1					1					3		
Watertown	232	32	Harrington	Peter		2	2		1	3	1			1			10		
Watertown	232	33	Hager	David	2			1		1			1				5		
Watertown	232	34	Hager	Moses				1					1				2		
Watertown	232	35	Hide	Enoch		1	1			1	1		1	1			6		
Watertown	232	36	Harris	Stephen	1					2				1			4		
Watertown	233	1	Harod	John		1			1	4				1			7		
Watertown	233	2	Hastings	Benjm Jr	2	2		1	1	3			1				10		
Watertown	233	3	Holland	Wm	2			1	1			1					5		
Watertown	233	4	Harris	Stephen Jr	2			1		1			1				5		
Watertown	233	5	Harris	Lydia				1					1				2		

TOWN	PG#	LN#	LAST NAME	FIRST NAME	FREE WHITE MALES					FREE WHITE FEMALES					TOTAL ALL OTHER	TOTAL SLAVES	TOTALS	DISTRICT/ TOWNSHIP	NOTES
					under 10	10 to 16	16 to 26	26 to 45	45 and over	under 10	10 to 16	16 to 26	26 to 45	45 and over					
Watertown	233	6	Holt	Saml		3		1		1			1				6		
Watertown	233	7	Hunt	Ruth						1				4			5		
Watertown	233	8	Hunnewell	Walter			1					1		1			3		
Watertown	233	9	Hunt	Wm	2	1	3		1	2		3	2		1		15		
Watertown	233	10	Jones	Joseph		1		1		1		1		1			5		
Watertown	233	11	Knight	Christham	2			1			1	1					5		
Watertown	233	12	Kelley	John			1			2			1				4		
Watertown	233	13	Kent	Ebenz	1			1	1	2	2	2		1			10		
Watertown	233	14	Laith	Wm		1		1				1					3		
Watertown	233	15	Laith	Jedediah	1	1		1				1	1				5		
Watertown	233	16	Livemore	Amos		1	3	1			1		1				7		
Watertown	233	17	Livemore	Amos Jr	1			1		2	1		1				6		
Watertown	233	18	Learned	Elijah	1			1					1				3		
Watertown	233	19	Learned	Saml			1	1			2		2	1			7		
Watertown	233	20	Learned	Paul	1	1	1	1						1			5		
Watertown	233	21	Learned	Sarah	1					3			1				5		
Watertown	233	22	Livemore	David	1		3	1		1		1					7		
Watertown	233	23	Laffan	Robert			2	1				1		1	1		6		
Watertown	233	24	Leath	Ebenz	1			1		1		1	1				5		
Watertown	233	25	Lowd	Edward	1			1		1		1					4		
Watertown	233	26	Levett	Josiah				1									1		
Watertown	233	27	Mixter	Josiah	1		1	1			1	2		1			7		
Watertown	233	28	Moredoe	Artimas	1		1	1		1	1	1					6		
Watertown	233	29	Mitcham	John	3	1		1		1	1		1				8		
Watertown	233	30	Norton	Jeremiah			1					1					2		
Watertown	233	31	Norcross	Elijah		1	1			2		1					5		
Watertown	233	32	Norcross	Joseph	2	1	1		1			1		1			7		
Watertown	233	33	Nuting	Charles	1	2			1	2		1					7		
Watertown	233	34	Newhall	Artimas	2	1						1					4		
Watertown	233	35	Patch	Ellis	2	1			1	2			1				7		
Watertown	233	36	Prentice	Benjm			1	1						2			4		
Watertown	233	37	Prentice	Hannah	1			1				1		1			4		
Watertown	233	38	Potts	Wm	1		1					1					3		
Watertown	233	39	Prentice	Thos				1					1				2		
Watertown	233	40	Patten	Thos		1	1	2	1	1				1			7		
Watertown	233	41	Pierce	Joseph	2		4	1				1	1				9		
Watertown	234	1	Robbins	James	2	1	3		1	1	3	1	1				13		
Watertown	234	2	Remington	John	1		1	1	1	1		3					7		
Watertown	234	3	Russell	Hubbard	1	1		1	1				1				5		
Watertown	234	4	Richardson	Fisher			1			2		1					4		
Watertown	234	5	Spring	Marshall	2		1		1				3	2			9		
Watertown	234	6	Stearns	David			1			2	1	2	1				7		
Watertown	234	7	Stone	Wm	1	1	1		1	4	2	1	1				12		
Watertown	234	8	Stone	Jona	2	2	4		1	2	1	1	1	1			15		
Watertown	234	9	Stone	Abijah		1			1	5	2			3			12		
Watertown	234	10	Stone	Moses	2	2	2		1	1	2			1			11		
Watertown	234	11	Stone	Nathl	2	1	1	1		2	1						9		
Watertown	234	12	Sawing	Daniel	1			1					1				3		
Watertown	234	13	Stone	David		1	2						1	1			5		
Watertown	234	14	Smith	Jubel	2			1		2			1				6		
Watertown	234	15	Sanger	Abraham			1			1		1					3		
Watertown	234	16	Seger	Ebenz	1				1	2	3	2	1				10		
Watertown	234	17	Sparrowhead	Blake	2	1		1		2	1	1		1			9		
Watertown	234	18	Soden	Saml	1	1		1			1			1			5		
Watertown	234	19	Sanderson	Josiah	1	1		1		1	1	1		1			7		
Watertown	234	20	Stimpson	John	1			1		1			1				4		
Watertown	234	21	Sanger	Daniel	2		3	1		1	1	1					9		
Watertown	234	22	Sanders	Robert			1			1				1			3		
Watertown	234	23	Studson	Ebenz				1					1				2		
Watertown	234	24	Sanger	David		1		2			1			1			5		
Watertown	234	25	Sanger	Abigail										1			1		
Watertown	234	26	Sanger	Richard			1			2			1				4		
Watertown	234	27	Sanger	John	1					2	1		1				6		
Watertown	234	28	Simonds	James		1		1		1	1	1	1	1			7		
Watertown	234	29	Stearns	George	4		1	1		1		1		1			9		
Watertown	234	30	Spear	Francis	1			1		1		1		1			5		
Watertown	234	31	Stimpson	John	1				1	1			1				4		
Watertown	234	32	Souldier	John T.	3			1		1	1		1				7		
Watertown	234	33	Tuttle	Stephen	2			1		3			1				7		
Watertown	234	34	Tainter	Benjm	2	2			1	2	1		1				9		
Watertown	234	35	Twist	Elias	1	1	1	1		2			1				7		
Watertown	234	36	Thompson	Wm	3		1		1	1	1		2				9		
Watertown	234	37	Tucker	John	3	2		1		2	2		1				11		
Watertown	234	38	Villey	Daniel	2			1		2			1				6		
Watertown	234	39	Vinal	John	2			1		2		1	1				7		
Watertown	234	40	Vole	Ebenz	2			2		3			1				8		
Watertown	234	41	Whitney	Saml		1			1					2			4		
Watertown	234	42	Whitney	Daniel	1		2		1		2	2		2			10		
Watertown	234	43	Whitney	Jona	1		1		1			1		1			5		

TOWN	PG#	LN#	HEADS OF HOUSEHOLD		FREE WHITE MALES					FREE WHITE FEMALES					TOTAL ALL OTHER	TOTAL SLAVES	TOTALS	DISTRICT/ TOWNSHIP	NOTES
			LAST NAME	FIRST NAME	under 10	10 to 16	16 to 26	26 to 45	45 and over	under 10	10 to 16	16 to 26	26 to 45	45 and over					
Watertown	235	1	Whitney	Jona Jr	3			1		1		1					6		
Watertown	235	2	Wilkins	John	1			1		3			1				6		
Watertown	235	3	Warren	Eliphalet				1					1				4		
Watertown	235	4	Willington	Thos	1				2					5			8		
Watertown	235	5	Willington	Edmund	2			1		2			1				6		
Watertown	235	6	White	Andrew					1					1			2		
Watertown	235	7	White	Andrew Jr	2			1		2			1				6		
Watertown	235	8	Warren	Moses	1		1	1		2			1				6		
Watertown	235	9	Warren	Charles	3		1			2			1				7		
Watertown	235	10	Whitney	Abrm		1			1	2				1			5		
Watertown	235	11	Whitney	Ezekl	1		1		1					1			4		
Watertown	235	12	Whitney	Francis					1								1		
Watertown	235	13	Whitney	Moses			1			1			1				3		
Watertown	235	14	Whitney	Ezekl	3		1			2			1				7		
Watertown	235	15	White	Jonas		2	3	2	1			4		1			13		
Watertown	235	16	Winchester	Wm	1	1		2		3			1				8		
Watertown	235	17	Winship	Thos		1		1		2			2				6		
Watertown	235	18	White	Saml	3	1				1				1			7		
Watertown	235	19	Whitney	Nathl R.	3	3	2	1		1		2	2				14		
Watertown	235	20	White	Saml		1			1	1							3		
Watertown	235	21	White	Moses	3		2		1	1	1	1	1	1			11		
Watertown	235	22	Whiting	Samuel				1		2	1		1				5		
Watertown	235	23	Woods	Jonas	1			2			1	1	1				6		
Watertown	235	24	Willington	Joel	2				1	2			2	1			8		
Watertown	235	25	Wild	Nathl		1	2	1	1		1	2	2	1			11		
Watertown	235	26	Willington	Saml		1	2		2		2	3	1	1			12		

117

TOWN	PG#	LN#	HEADS OF HOUSEHOLD		FREE WHITE MALES					FREE WHITE FEMALES					TOTAL ALL OTHER	TOTAL SLAVES	TOTALS	DISTRICT/ TOWNSHIP	NOTES
			LAST NAME	FIRST NAME	under 10	10 to 16	16 to 26	26 to 45	45 and over	under 10	10 to 16	16 to 26	26 to 45	45 and over					
Westford	179	1	Abbott	Jacob	1			1		1	1		1				5		
Westford	179	2	Abbott	John			2		1		1			1			5		
Westford	179	3	Abbott	Joel	2		1	1		1	1		1	2			9		
Westford	179	4	Adams	Tho'	2	2	2		1	1			1				9		
Westford	179	5	Adams	Ruth			2				1			1			4		
Westford	179	6	Andrews	Wm	2			1		2			1				6		
Westford	179	7	Blood	Amaziah		1	1		1	2		1		1			7		
Westford	179	8	Blood	Aaron					1			2		1			4		
Westford	179	9	Blood	Eleazer					1				1				2		
Westford	179	10	Boynton	Josiah			2		1		1	2		1			7		
Westford	179	11	Boynton	Josiah Jr	2	1		1			1		1				6		
Westford	179	12	Boynton	Abel	1		2		1	1	1	3		1			10		
Westford	179	13	Brooks	Lois								1		1			2		
Westford	179	14	Brooks	Lydia									1	1			2		
Westford	179	15	Blake	Caleb	1	4	1	1		1		1	1		1		11		
Westford	179	16	Bixby	Asa		1		2						1			4		
Westford	179	17	Bixby	Asa Jr	1			1	1	2			1				6		
Westford	179	18	Blodget	Jonas		3		1		3	1		1				9		
Westford	179	19	Bignal	Saml	1			1		2			1				5		
Westford	179	20	Butters	John			1		1	2				1			5		
Westford	179	21	Butters	Jed'			1		1					1			3		
Westford	179	22	Boynton	Luther	2			1		2	1		1				7		
Westford	180	1	Chandler	Wm	1	1			1	2	1			1			7		
Westford	180	2	Chandler	Silas		1			1					1			3		
Westford	180	3	Cummings	Isaac	1				1			1		1			4		
Westford	180	4	Cummings	John			1	1					1				3		
Westford	180	5	Cummings	Timo'	1	1	1		1	2	1	3		1			11		
Westford	180	6	Cummings	Wilson	1			1		1			1				4		
Westford	180	7	Cummings	Tho'		1			1					1			3		
Westford	180	8	Cummings	Jos'					1				1				2		
Westford	180	9	Cummings	Jos' Jr	1	1		1		1			1				5		
Westford	180	10	Clatter	Jacob		1		1		1			1				4		
Westford	180	11	Cogswell	Jona'	1			1					1				3		
Westford	180	12	Carver	Jona			1		1			1		1			4		
Westford	180	13	Carver	Benja'				1		1				2			4		
Westford	180	14	Carver	Jona' Jr		1			1			1		1			4		
Westford	180	15	Crosfield	John			1			2		1					4		
Westford	180	16	Chamberlin	James			1			1		1					4		
Westford	180	17	Craft	Saml	2			1		1				1			5		
Westford	180	18	Cory	Abel	1	1	1		1	1				1			6		
Westford	180	19	Davis	Ann	2					2	2	1	1				8		
Westford	180	20	Dudley	John	1			1					1				3		
Westford	180	21	Day	Isaac	2	1	1					1					5		
Westford	180	22	Dutton	Benja'	1	1			1				1	1			5		
Westford	180	23	Dutton	David					1					1			2		
Westford	180	24	Dutton	Tho'	1			1					1				3		
Westford	180	25	Dutton	Jos'					1			2		1			4		
Westford	180	26	Estabrook	Joel		1			1	1	1	1		1			6		
Westford	180	27	Estabrook	Benja'			1		1		1	1		1			5		
Westford	180	28	Evelith	Timmi			1	2			1	2	1				7		
Westford	180	29	Evelith	John	1				1					1			3		
Westford	180	30	Fletcher	David					1			1		1			3		
Westford	180	31	Fletcher	David Jr		1			1					1			3		
Westford	180	32	Fletcher	Oliver					1			2		1			4		
Westford	180	33	Fletcher	Andri'		2		1		3	1		1				8		
Westford	180	34	Fletcher	Tho'					1					1			2		
Westford	180	35	Fletcher	Tho' Jr	1		1	1		2	1		1				7		
Westford	180	36	Fletcher	Paletiah		1	2	1				2		1			7		
Westford	180	37	Fletcher	Willard	1	1	1		1	1	1			1			7		
Westford	180	38	Fletcher	Amos		1	2		1	1		1		1			7		
Westford	180	39	Fletcher	Jona'					1					1			2		
Westford	180	40	Fletcher	Jos'	2	1	1	1		2		1	1				9		
Westford	180	41	Fletcher	Seth		1	1		1			2		1			6		
Westford	180	42	Fletcher	Saml'	1	1			1	3	2	2	1				11		
Westford	181	1	Fletcher	Samson	1	2			1	1	1		1				7		
Westford	181	2	Fletcher	Jona' Jr			1	1	1					1			4		
Westford	181	3	Fletcher	Simeon	2			1	1			1		1			6		
Westford	181	4	Fletcher	Eliza'				1				2		1			4		
Westford	181	5	Foster	Saml'		1		1		1	1		1	1			6		
Westford	181	6	Foster	Jos'	2	1		1		2			1				7		
Westford	181	7	Gould	Reuben					1					1			2		
Westford	181	8	Goodhue	Imla			1										1		
Westford	181	9	Goodhue	Esther									2	1			3		
Westford	181	10	Goodhue	John	1			1		3			1				6		
Westford	181	11	Goodhue	Danl		1	2		1		1	1		1			7		
Westford	181	12	Green	Benja'	2		1	1		1			1				6		
Westford	181	13	Green	Danl	2		1		1	2	2	1		1			10		
Westford	181	14	Green	Calvin	1			1					1				3		
Westford	181	15	Griffin	Mathis			1		1			1		1			4		

118

TOWN	PG#	LN#	HEADS OF HOUSEHOLD		FREE WHITE MALES					FREE WHITE FEMALES					TOTAL ALL OTHER	TOTAL SLAVES	TOTALS	DISTRICT/ TOWNSHIP	NOTES
			LAST NAME	FIRST NAME	under 10	10 to 16	16 to 26	26 to 45	45 and over	under 10	10 to 16	16 to 26	26 to 45	45 and over					
Westford	181	16	Gould	Mary			1							2			3		
Westford	181	17	Hunt	Simeon	3	1		1					1				6		
Westford	181	18	Holt	Elisha				1		2				1			4		
Westford	181	19	Hall	Willis			1	2		2	2			1			8		
Westford	181	20	Hale	Eph'		1	2	1						1			5		
Westford	181	21	Hastens	Saml	1			1					1				3		
Westford	181	22	Hinkley	Ebenz	1	4		1	1		1	1		1			10		
Westford	181	23	Hamlin	Eleazr		2	4	1				1	1				9		
Westford	181	24	Hildrith	Amaziah				1		2			1				4		
Westford	181	25	Hildrith	Pheebe				1				1	1				3		
Westford	181	26	Hildrith	Isaiah		1		1			1		1				4		
Westford	181	27	Hildrith	Mary	2					1		1		1			5		
Westford	181	28	Hildrith	Jonas	2			1		2			1				6		
Westford	181	29	Hildrith	Levi			1						1				2		
Westford	181	30	Hildrith	Amos			1	1				1	1	1			5		
Westford	181	31	Hildrith	Ruth										1			1		
Westford	181	32	Hildrith	John			2	1		1		2		2			8		
Westford	181	33	Hildrith	John Jr	2			1		1	1	1					6		
Westford	181	34	Hildrith	Jerem'	1			1		2	1		1	1			7		
Westford	181	35	Hildrith	Oliver	1		1	1		1	3	1		1			9		
Westford	181	36	Hildrith	Seth	1		1			1		1					4		
Westford	181	37	Hildrith	Lucy								2		1			3		
Westford	181	38	Hildrith	Benja'	1			1		3			1				6		
Westford	181	39	Hildrith	Peter			1						1				2		
Westford	181	40	Hildrith	Wm		1		1			1			1			4		
Westford	181	41	Hildrith	Nath	1			1		1			1				4		
Westford	181	42	Hildrith	Simeon	2			1					1				4		
Westford	181	43	Hildrith	Jona'	3			1		2		2	1	1			10		
Westford	181	44	Hutchens	Tho'			1			2			1				4		
Westford	181	45	Jackson	Phillip											3		3		
Westford	182	1	Johnson	Sarah									1				1		
Westford	182	2	Johnson	Jona'	4			1		1			1				7		
Westford	182	3	Jenkins	Edw'				1			1			1			3		
Westford	182	4	Keyes	May			1					1	1				3		
Westford	182	5	Kneeland	Martha	2						1		1				4		
Westford	182	6	Keyes	Isachar		2	1	1					1	1			6		
Westford	182	7	Keyes	James			1						1				2		
Westford	182	8	Keyes	Joseph	1	1	3	1		2			2	1			11		
Westford	182	9	Kent	Abner				1					1	1			3		
Westford	182	10	Kent	Elisha		1							1				2		
Westford	182	11	King	Roger		1	1	1					1	2			6		
Westford	182	12	Keyes	Mary															Enumeration blank
Westford	182	13	Kidder	James	1		1						1				3		
Westford	182	14	Kidder	Mary								1	1				2		
Westford	182	15	Kemp	Jonas		1		1						1			3		
Westford	182	16	Kemp	Simeon				1		4				1			6		
Westford	182	17	Keyes	Jona	2	1		1	1	4	1		1	1			12		
Westford	182	18	Leighton	Isaiah	1			1		1	1		1				5		
Westford	182	19	Leighton	Reuben	2	1		1		2		1	1				8		
Westford	182	20	Leighton	Fra'			1	1					1	2			5		
Westford	182	21	Leighton	John	1			1		1	1		1				5		
Westford	182	22	Lancy	Saml	3	2		1		1	1		1				9		
Westford	182	23	Learned	Isaac		2			1	2	1			1			7		
Westford	182	24	Lawrence	James	1			1		2			1				5		
Westford	182	25	Mears	Wm	2			1		2	1	1	1				8		
Westford	182	26	Miat	Henry				1						1			2		
Westford	182	27	Minot	John				1						1			2		
Westford	182	28	Minot	Jesse	5	2		1				1	1				10		
Westford	182	29	Nutting	Tho'	4	2		1		1	2		1				11		
Westford	182	30	Nutting	Danl	2				1			2		1			6		
Westford	182	31	Nichols	Wm		1		1		1	1	1					5		
Westford	182	32	Nichols	Steph'	1			1					1				3		
Westford	182	33	Nichols	Mich'			1	1						1			3		
Westford	182	34	Osgood	Benja'		2	3	1		2	2	1		1			12		
Westford	182	35	Parker	Isaac				1		1				1			3		
Westford	182	36	Parker	Saml S.			1			2		1					4		
Westford	182	37	Parker	Benja'	2	1		1		2	1	1					8		
Westford	182	38	Parker	David	3	1	1	1		1	1			1			9		
Westford	182	39	Parker	Joshua		1		1						1			3		
Westford	182	40	Parker	Aaron	2	1		1		1			1	2			8		
Westford	182	41	Patch	David		1							1				2		
Westford	182	42	Patch	Isaac									1	1			2		
Westford	182	43	Patch	Isaac Jr	1	2		1		3			1	1			9		
Westford	182	44	Pierce	Jona		2			1			3		2			8		
Westford	182	45	Patten	Isaac	4	2	1	1		2		1	1	1			13		
Westford	182	46	Perry	Obadiah	2			1		1	1			1			6		
Westford	182	47	Procter	Cha'			1	1		2				1			5		
Westford	183	1	Procter	Phin				1									1		
Westford	183	2	Procter	Pheeb								1	1				2		
Westford	183	3	Procter	Mary			1				1	1		1			4		

TOWN	PG#	LN#	LAST NAME	FIRST NAME	FREE WHITE MALES					FREE WHITE FEMALES					TOTAL ALL OTHER	TOTAL SLAVES	TOTALS	DISTRICT/ TOWNSHIP	NOTES
					under 10	10 to 16	16 to 26	26 to 45	45 and over	under 10	10 to 16	16 to 26	26 to 45	45 and over					
Westford	183	4	Pratt	Isaac		1	1			1		1					4		
Westford	183	5	Prescott	Isaiah	1	1		1		4			1				8		
Westford	183	6	Prescott	Timo'					1		1	2		1			5		
Westford	183	7	Prescott	Amos				1		3	1	1					6		
Westford	183	8	Prescott	John	1	1	4		1		1	1		1			10		
Westford	183	9	Prescott	Jonas				3	1				2				6		
Westford	183	10	Prescott	Ebenz		1	2		1	2	1	1		1			9		
Westford	183	11	Prescott	Ebenz Jr			1					1					2		
Westford	183	12	Prescott	Joseph			2		1		1	1		1			6		
Westford	183	13	Prescott	Abra'	1	1		1	1	1		2					7		
Westford	183	14	Prescott	James		1	2	1		3		1	1				9		
Westford	183	15	Richardson	Silas	1	1		1		1		1	1				6		
Westford	183	16	Richardson	Saml		1	1	2				1	1				6		
Westford	183	17	Richardson	Abijah		1	1	1			2		1				6		
Westford	183	18	Richardson	Lydia									1	1			2		
Westford	183	19	Richardson	Jona'		1		1		4	1		1	1			9		
Westford	183	20	Richardson	Tho'		1	2		1			1		1			5		
Westford	183	21	Raymond	Danl		1			1		2			1			5		
Westford	183	22	Raymond	John	3	1		1		2	1		1	1			10		
Westford	183	23	Robbinson	John			2		1			1		1			5		
Westford	183	24	Reed	Joshua				1						1			2		
Westford	183	25	Reed	Zach'	1	1	1	1		1		1	1				7		
Westford	183	26	Reed	Saml'	1			1		2			1				5		
Westford	183	27	Reed	Saml' Jr	2		2	1		3	2		1				11		
Westford	183	28	Reed	Hannah									1	1			2		
Westford	183	29	Reed	Wm	1	1			1	2	1		1	1			8		
Westford	183	30	Reed	Amos	4			1		1			1	1			9		
Westford	183	31	Reed	Eleaz'	2	1		1		1			1				6		
Westford	183	32	Reed	Leon'		2			1			2		1			6		
Westford	183	33	Reed	Tho'	2		1		1	3		2					9		
Westford	183	34	Reed	Abijah		1	2	1		3	1		1				9		
Westford	183	35	Reed	Willard	1		2		1	1	1	1		1			8		
Westford	183	36	Reed	Willard Jr			1					1					2		
Westford	183	37	Reed	Silas	3		2		1	1	2	1		1			11		
Westford	183	38	Reed	Abel	1			1		2			1				5		
Westford	183	39	Robbins	Benja'	3	1		1		1	1	1	1	1			10		
Westford	183	40	Robbins	Jacob			1		1			1		1			4		
Westford	183	41	Snow	Levi'	2	1	1	1		1	1	1		1			9		
Westford	183	42	Snow	James	1			1		1			1				4		
Westford	183	43	Sloan	John					1					1			2		
Westford	183	44	Smith	Tho'	1	1	1		1		2	1		1			8		
Westford	183	45	Sheppard	Chri'					1			1		1			3		
Westford	183	46	Saunderson	Wm	1	1			1					1			4		
Westford	184	1	Spaulding	Sola'	2	2			1	1	1			1			8		
Westford	184	2	Stevens	Bill W.	2			1		1			1				5		
Westford	184	3	Stoddard	Ann										1			1		
Westford	184	4	Spaulding	Phillip				1						1			2		
Westford	184	5	Simmes	Tho'		1		1		2			1				5		
Westford	184	6	Tidd	John	3	1			1			1		1			7		
Westford	184	7	Tarble	Saml				1		1			1	1			4		
Westford	184	8	Tarble	Abijah	2	1	1	1			1		1				7		
Westford	184	9	Wright	Zach'		2	1		1		1			1			6		
Westford	184	10	Wright	Zach' Jr				1		1			1				3		
Westford	184	11	Wright	Amos		2			1			2		2			7		
Westford	184	12	Wright	John			1		1				1	1			4		
Westford	184	13	Wright	Reuben	3	1		1		2				1			8		
Westford	184	14	Wright	Abijah		1	1			1		1		2			6		
Westford	184	15	Wright	Nathan	5	1		1					1				8		
Westford	184	16	Wright	Jos'		2			1			2		1			6		
Westford	184	17	Wright	Asa	2	1		1		2	1		1				8		
Westford	184	18	Wright	James		1			1	1		1		1			5		
Westford	184	19	Wright	Abel	2		1	1		1			1	1			7		
Westford	184	20	Wright	John T.	1	1	1			1		1					5		
Westford	184	21	Wright	Eleazer	3			1		1			1				6		
Westford	184	22	Wright	Saml		1		1		1	1	2		1			7		
Westford	184	23	Wright	Levi'	2			1		1			1				5		
Westford	184	24	Wendal	Jacob	1	1		1			1		1				5		
Westford	184	25	Wilson	Isaac	2			1		3			1				7		
Westford	184	26	Wilkins	Robert	2			1		1			1				5		
Westford	184	27	Wood	Saml	2			1		3	1		1				8		
Westford	184	28	Whiting	Wm	2	1		1					1				5		
Westford	184	29	White	Aaron		1						1					2		
Westford	184	30	White	Abel		1								1			2		

TOWN	PG#	LN#	LAST NAME	FIRST NAME	FREE WHITE MALES under 10	10 to 16	16 to 26	26 to 45	45 and over	FREE WHITE FEMALES under 10	10 to 16	16 to 26	26 to 45	45 and over	TOTAL ALL OTHER	TOTAL SLAVES	TOTALS	DISTRICT/ TOWNSHIP	NOTES
Weston	105	1	Allen	Nathaniel		1			2	1			1	2			7		
Weston	105	2	Allen	Priscilla	2					1		2					5		
Weston	105	1	Alexander	Giles			1		1	1		3	1		2		9		
Weston	106	2	Bond	Henry				1					2				3		
Weston	106	3	Bancroft	Amos			1	1		1		1					4		
Weston	106	4	Budge	Elizabeth							1		1		1		3		
Weston	106	5	Biglow	Josiah				1					1				2		
Weston	106	6	Biglow	Alpheus	1	2		1		3	1						9		
Weston	106	7	Biglow	Lucy			1			1	1	1	1	1			6		
Weston	106	8	Barrett	Hannah							1		2		3		6		
Weston	106	9	Brackett	David	1	1			1	2	1		1	1			8		
Weston	106	10	Brackett	Ebenezer	2	1	1			3	1	1	1				11		
Weston	106	11	Ballad	Ebenezer	2			1		2	1		1				7		
Weston	106	12	Bogle	William	1		1	1	1				1	1			6		
Weston	106	13	Billings	Jonas	4			1		2	1		1				9		
Weston	106	14	Bemis	Nathl		1		1					1				3		
Weston	106	15	Bemis	Lot	2			1		1			1				5		
Weston	106	16	Brown	Thomas	1		1	1		1			1				5		
Weston	106	17	Bemis	Daniel	3	1		1		2	2		1				10		
Weston	106	18	Boyles	Daniel				1		3			1				5		
Weston	107	1	Cox	Joseph	2			1		1			1				5		
Weston	107	2	Cotting	John	1	1	1					1	1	1			6		
Weston	107	3	Calef	Robert	1		2		1			1	1	2			8		
Weston	107	4	Child	Nathan				1						1			2		
Weston	107	5	Child	Jonathan			2		1			1	3	1			8		
Weston	107	6	Cuff	Venus											2		2		
Weston	107	7	Cheney	Jesse	1		1		1				1				4		
Weston	107	8	Child	Edward		1	1		1	1		1					5		
Weston	107	9	Conant	Oliver	1	2	2		1	1	1	2	1	1			12		
Weston	107	10	Cobb	Samuel	4	1	1		1	2	1		1				11		
Weston	107	11	Coburn	Lois	2	1				1	1	1	1				7		
Weston	107	12	Dudley	John	1	1	1		1			1	1				6		
Weston	107	13	Davis	Jonathan	1				1		1	1		1			5		
Weston	107	14	Furbush	Elisha	2			1					1				4		
Weston	107	15	Fiske	Samuel	1	1			2			2		1			7		
Weston	107	16	Fiske	Jonathan			1		1				1				3		
Weston	107	17	Fiske	Nathan	2	1		1		1	1		1				7		
Weston	107	18	Fiske	Ebenezer	1			1		2		1					5		
Weston	107	19	Fiske	Jacob	2		1	1		1		1	1				7		
Weston	107	20	Flagg	John		1	1		1			2	1				6		
Weston	107	21	Flagg	Isaac					1	1	1		1				4		
Weston	107	22	Fiske	Abijah	2	1			1	1	1		1				7		
Weston	107	23	Fuller	Moses	2	1			1	1	1			1			7		
Weston	107	24	Gould	Isaac	2				1	1				1			5		
Weston	107	25	Garfield	Damarus			1							1			2		
Weston	107	26	Green	Samuel		1		1		2			2	1			7		
Weston	107	27	Garfield	Joseph	2	2		1		3			1	1			10		
Weston	107	28	Greenleaf	Enoch					1					1			2		
Weston	107	29	Gregory	Uriah	1	1	1		1			2		1			7		
Weston	107	30	Gregory	Silas			1			1		1					3		
Weston	107	31	Goodhue	Jeremy			2		1		1			1			5		
Weston	107	32	Gleason	Amos	2			1					1	1			5		
Weston	108	1	Hager	Nathan	1		4		1	2	1	1					10		
Weston	108	2	Harrington	Abraham	2	2	1		1	1	1	1	1	1			11		
Weston	108	3	Hobbs	Matthew			2		1	1			1	1			6		
Weston	108	4	Hobbs	Isaac		1	1		1					1			4		
Weston	108	5	Hobbs	Ebenezer	2	1	3		1	3	1	1	1				13		
Weston	108	6	Hobbs	Isaac Jr	4		2	1			1	1					9		
Weston	108	7	Hews	Abraham	2	1	2		1		1	1	1				9		
Weston	108	8	Hews	Abraham Jr	3			1		1		1					6		
Weston	108	9	Hagar	Phinehas	3	2		1		2	1		1	1			11		
Weston	108	10	Hubbard	Anna								1		1			2		
Weston	108	11	Harrington	Charles			1	1		1		1	1	1			6		
Weston	108	12	Hobbs	Amos		1	1	1		1		1					5		
Weston	108	13	Heyward	Caleb	2	1	1	1		1			1				7		
Weston	108	14	Harrington	Joel	2	1		1		1			1				6		
Weston	108	15	Harrington	Jonas		1			3				1	1			6		
Weston	108	16	Heyward	Josiah	1			1		1	1		1				5		
Weston	108	17	Hobbs	Nathan				1					1				2		
Weston	108	18	Hobbs	Nathan Jr	4	1	1	2			1	1	1				11		
Weston	108	19	Hastings	Josiah Jr	1	3	1	1		3		1	1				11		
Weston	108	20	Harrington	Solomon		1		1		2			1				5		
Weston	108	21	Harrington	Stephen					1		1		1	1			4		
Weston	108	22	Harrington	Enoch			1	1					1	1			4		
Weston	108	23	Harrington	Loas		1							1				2		
Weston	108	24	Jones	Solomon		1			1					1			3		
Weston	108	25	Jones	Isaac		1	1	1		1		1	2	2			10		
Weston	108	26	Jones	Amos	4				1	1	1	1	1				9		
Weston	108	27	Jones	Sarah								1		1			2		

TOWN	PG#	LN#	HEADS OF HOUSEHOLD		FREE WHITE MALES					FREE WHITE FEMALES					TOTAL ALL OTHER	TOTAL SLAVES	TOTALS	DISTRICT/ TOWNSHIP	NOTES
			LAST NAME	FIRST NAME	under 10	10 to 16	16 to 26	26 to 45	45 and over	under 10	10 to 16	16 to 26	26 to 45	45 and over					
Weston	108	28	Jones	James	1				1	2				1			5		
Weston	108	29	Johnson	Abiathur	2			2		2			1	1			8		
Weston	108	30	Kendal	Samuel	1	1	2		2	1	1	1	1				10		
Weston	108	31	Kingsbury	Elijah	1			2		2	1		1				7		
Weston	108	32	Lamson	Isaac	1		1	1			1		1				5		
Weston	108	33	Lamson	Elizabeth	2						1		1	1			5		
Weston	109	1	Lawrence	Joseph				1		1		1					3		
Weston	109	2	Lamson	Amos			1	1			1			1			4		
Weston	109	3	Livemore	Ephraim	2			1		3	1			1			8		
Weston	109	4	Livemore	Samuel	1			2	1		1		1	1			7		
Weston	109	5	Lawrence	William Jr	3			1	1			1					6		
Weston	109	6	Lamson	John	3			1		2		1	1				8		
Weston	109	7	Lovewell	Samuel		1		1		2			1				5		
Weston	109	8	Lovewell	Joseph				1					1				2		
Weston	109	9	Leadbetter	Increase		1	1	1	1			1		1			6		
Weston	109	10	Pierce	Benj															Enumeration blank
Weston	109	11	Melo	Cato											2		2		
Weston	109	12	Mosman	Micah			1			2			1				4		
Weston	109	13	Marshall	Thomas		1	1	1	2	1	2	2	2	2			14		
Weston	109	14	Morse	Beniah	3			1		2			1				7		
Weston	109	15	Pierce	Benjamin	2			1		2	1	1	1				8		
Weston	109	16	Parker	Joseph	1		1	1		3			1				7		
Weston	109	17	Pierce	Jacob	1			1		1			1				4		
Weston	109	18	Philemon	Pegg											1		1		
Weston	109	19	Pierce	Amos	2	2		1		1	1		1				8		
Weston	109	20	Pierce	Thaddeus	3			1		2			1				7		
Weston	109	21	Pratt	Paul		1		1		3	2	1		1			9		
Weston	109	22	Pierce	Abel	3	1		1		1	2			1			9		
Weston	109	23	Pierce	Joshua		1	1		1	1	1		1				6		
Weston	109	24	Russell	Joseph	2	1	1	1	1		1	2		1	1		11		
Weston	109	25	Russell	Abner	2	1		1					1	1			6		
Weston	109	26	Rand	Thomas			3		1			2		1			7		
Weston	109	27	Rand	Daniel	2	1		1		1			1				6		
Weston	109	28	Rand	Benjamin	2	2		1		2	1		1				9		
Weston	109	29	Russell	Samuel	2			1					1				4		
Weston	109	30	Roberts	Joseph	2	1		1	1				1				6		
Weston	109	31	Smith	Nathan	1			1					1				3		
Weston	110	1	Samson	John		1	1		1		1		1	1			6		
Weston	110	2	Sanderson	Abijah	1	1		1		2	1	1	1				8		
Weston	110	3	Smith	Joel	2	1	1		1			2	2				9		
Weston	110	4	Smith	John	1			1					1				3		
Weston	110	5	Stone	Joseph	1			1		2			1	1			6		
Weston	110	6	Stearns	Jepthah		1	1				1		1				4		
Weston	110	7	Starr	Josiah		1	1	1					1				4		
Weston	110	8	Starr	Abigail		1					1		2				4		
Weston	110	9	Stimson	James		1		1		1			1				4		
Weston	110	10	Stearns	Charles	3		1	2		1			1	1			9		
Weston	110	11	Stack	John	2	1		1		2	2	1	1				11		
Weston	110	12	Steoman	Hannah	1			1		1			1				4		
Weston	110	13	Seaverns	Josiah		1	1		1	1		2		1	1		8		
Weston	110	14	Stearns	Silas	1			1			1		1				4		
Weston	110	15	Sanderson	Jonas		1		1					1	1			4		
Weston	110	16	Sanderson	Jonas Jr			1	1		1		1					4		
Weston	110	17	Seaverns	Joseph	1		1		1	3	1		1	1			9		
Weston	110	18	Stratton	Elisha	3	1			1	1	1	1		1			9		
Weston	110	19	Stratton	Isaac	3	1			1	3	1						9		
Weston	110	20	Stratton	John		1	1	1	1	1			1				6		
Weston	110	21	Stratton	Daniel	1	1	1		1	3		2		1			10		
Weston	110	22	Sanderson	Abraham			1	1			3			1			6		
Weston	110	23	Smith	Samuel	3		1	1		2			1				8		
Weston	110	24	Stearns	Nathan	2			1		2			1				6		
Weston	110	25	Smith	James				1			2		1				4		
Weston	110	26	Sanderson	Abraham Jr		1		1		3	1		1				7		
Weston	110	27	Spring	Amasa				1		1			1				3		
Weston	110	28	Stearns	*	1	1		1		3			1				7		
Weston	110	29	Sanderson	Jacob	2			1		3			1				7		
Weston	110	30	Train	Nahum	3		1	1	1	2	1	1	1				12		
Weston	110	31	Train	Enoch	1	1		2		1	1			1			7		
Weston	110	32	Train	Samuel Jr	3	1	2		1				1	1			9		
Weston	110	33	Train	Arthur	1	1			1	1				1			5		
Weston	110	34	Townsend	Tho. H.				1	1	2	1	1	1		1		8		
Weston	111	1	Travis	Elijah	1			1		2	1	1	1				7		
Weston	111	2	Upham	Lydia		2						1		1			5		
Weston	111	3	Upham	Martha		1							1	1			3		
Weston	111	4	Warren	Jona	1	1			1		1	1		1			6		
Weston	111	5	Warren	Nathan	2	1		1		3	1	1	1				10		
Weston	111	6	Warren	Micah	1				1				1				3		
Weston	111	7	Ward	Artemas	1	2	1	1		4			1	1			12		
Weston	111	8	Wyman	Hezekiah			3		1				1	1			6		
Weston	111	9	Warren	John		1			1		1	1	1	2			7		

TOWN	PG#	LN#	LAST NAME	FIRST NAME	FREE WHITE MALES					FREE WHITE FEMALES					TOTAL ALL OTHER	TOTAL SLAVES	TOTALS	DISTRICT/ TOWNSHIP	NOTES
					under 10	10 to 16	16 to 26	26 to 45	45 and over	under 10	10 to 16	16 to 26	26 to 45	45 and over					
Weston	111	10	Warren	Jedediah	1		1			1			2				5		
Weston	111	11	Way*	Nero											2		2		
Weston	111	12	Whittemore	Aaron	1	1	1				1	1					5		
Weston	111	13	Whittemore	Israel				1						1			2		
Weston	111	14	Ward	Lucy						1	1		1				3		
Weston	111	15	Whitney	Abijah	2	2	1			2		1	1	1			10		
Weston	111	16	Wentworth	Elijah		1			1	2		1		1			6		

TOWN	PG#	LN#	HEADS OF HOUSEHOLD		FREE WHITE MALES					FREE WHITE FEMALES					TOTAL ALL OTHER	TOTAL SLAVES	TOTALS	DISTRICT/ TOWNSHIP	NOTES
			LAST NAME	FIRST NAME	under 10	10 to 16	16 to 26	26 to 45	45 and over	under 10	10 to 16	16 to 26	26 to 45	45 and over					
Wilmington	140	1	Alexander	John	3	1	2	1	1	1		1		1			11		
Wilmington	140	2	Ba*	Timothy		1			1			2		1			5		
Wilmington	140	3	Bell	John	2	3	2		1	3			1				12		
Wilmington	140	4	Blanchard	William	2		3		2			1		1			9		
Wilmington	140	5	Brown	Jabez			2		1		1			1			5		
Wilmington	140	6	Burt	Jacob	1		2					1					4		
Wilmington	140	7	Bea*	Edward	2	1		1	1	2	1		1				9		
Wilmington	140	8	Burt	Brown	2	2		1		2			1	1			9		
Wilmington	140	9	Buck	Ephraim				1						2			3		
Wilmington	140	10	Buck	Nathan	3			1		2			1				7		
Wilmington	140	11	Butter	James		1		1					1				3		
Wilmington	140	12	Beard	Jonathan	1	2		1		1	1	1	1				8		
Wilmington	140	13	Butter	William				1						3			4		
Wilmington	140	14	Butter	William Jr	3	1		1		2			1				8		
Wilmington	140	15	Bouttell	Jonathan			2	1			1		1				5		
Wilmington	140	16	Beard	Nathan		1		1					1				3		
Wilmington	140	17	Buck	Samuel	1	1		1		3	2		1	1			10		
Wilmington	140	18	Butter	Reuben	1	1	2	1					1				6		
Wilmington	140	19	Buck	Reuben	3	1		1		2	1	1	1				10		
Wilmington	141	1	Buxton	John				1		1	1			1			4		
Wilmington	141	2	Beard	Jacob		1		1		1	2		1				6		
Wilmington	141	3	Bachelor	Nathaniel		1		1		1		1					4		
Wilmington	141	4	Buck	Ephraim Jr	2	2		1		1			1				7		
Wilmington	141	5	Buck	Zebediah	1			1		1		1					4		
Wilmington	141	6	Butter	James Jr	2		1			4	1		1				9		
Wilmington	141	7	Butter	Ruth	1			3		1		1	1				7		
Wilmington	141	8	Bouttell	Jonathan Jr	2			1					1				4		
Wilmington	141	9	Beard	Abel	3	2		1					1				7		
Wilmington	141	10	Carter	Jonathan	4	2	1	1					1				9		
Wilmington	141	11	Carter	Joel	3		1		1	2	1	2		1			11		
Wilmington	141	12	Carter	Benjamin	2	1		1		2			1				7		
Wilmington	141	13	Carter	John				1		3			1				5		
Wilmington	141	14	Carter	Jonathan Jr	2	1		1					1				5		
Wilmington	141	15	Carter	Eleazer		2		1					1	2			6		
Wilmington	141	16	Carter	Ezra		1		1		1	4						7		
Wilmington	141	17	Carter	Ebenezer Jr	1		1			1		1					4		
Wilmington	141	18	Corneal	Peter				1				1	1				3		
Wilmington	141	19	Carter	Timothy	2	2		1		3		1	1				10		
Wilmington	141	20	Carter	Nathan				1					1				2		
Wilmington	141	21	Carter	Nathan Jr	2	1	3	1		3	2	2	1	1			16		
Wilmington	141	22	Carter	Moses	2		1						1	1			5		
Wilmington	141	23	Carter	Joel Jr	2		1					1					4		
Wilmington	141	24	Carter	Ebenezer	1			1					1				3		
Wilmington	141	25	Coburn	Titus											7		7		
Wilmington	141	26	Corneal	James	1		1			1		1					4		
Wilmington	141	27	Durnin	Abigail		1							1				2		
Wilmington	141	28	Deon	Samuel		1		1				1	1				4		
Wilmington	141	29	Eams	John	2		2	1		2			2				9		
Wilmington	141	30	Eams	Samuel		1	1	1				1	1	1			6		
Wilmington	141	31	Eams	Jonathan		3	1	1		1			1				7		
Wilmington	141	32	Eams	Jonathan Jr	1		1	2		2		1					7		
Wilmington	141	33	Eams	Caleb		1		1				1	1				4		
Wilmington	141	34	Eams	Caleb Jr	2		1			1		1					5		
Wilmington	141	35	Eams	John Jr	3	1		1		1			1				7		
Wilmington	141	36	Emerson	Aaron	1	1	1	1		1		1					6		
Wilmington	141	37	Eams	William	2			1		2			1				6		
Wilmington	142	1	Evens	B*						1							1		
Wilmington	142	2	Ford	Cad*		2		1	1	1	1		1				7		
Wilmington	142	3	Flagg	John	2			1		2			1				6		
Wilmington	142	4	Foster	Samuel		1	2	1		1	1		1				7		
Wilmington	142	5	Foster	John				1		2			1				4		
Wilmington	142	6	Foster	Ebenezer		1		1		1			1				5		
Wilmington	142	7	Gowing	Daniel				1		1			1				3		
Wilmington	142	8	Gowing	Daniel Jr	3	1		1		1	1	1	1				9		
Wilmington	142	9	Gowing	Jabez	3			1		2		2					8		
Wilmington	142	10	Gowing	John				1	1				1	1			4		
Wilmington	142	11	Gowing	John Jr		2		1		4	2	1	1				12		
Wilmington	142	12	Griffin	Ebenezer				1		4		1					6		
Wilmington	142	13	Griffin	James				1					1				2		
Wilmington	142	14	Gout	John	1	1		1		1	1		1				6		
Wilmington	142	15	Gowing	Joseph	2			1		1	1		1				6		
Wilmington	142	16	Harnden	Joshua				1				1	3	1			6		
Wilmington	142	17	Harnden	John		1	2	1	1	1		1	1	1			9		
Wilmington	142	18	Harnden	Benjaman		1	2		1			1	1	1			7		
Wilmington	142	19	Hopkins	Samuel				1		1			1				3		
Wilmington	142	20	Hopkins	Samuel Jr		1	1	1		1			1				5		
Wilmington	142	21	Holt	Asa	3			1					1				5		
Wilmington	142	22	Harnden	Benjamin Jr															Name crossed out
Wilmington	142	23	Harnden	Samuel	1		1			1			1				4		
Wilmington	142	24	Honden	Joshua Jr	2		1			1			1				5		

TOWN	PG#	LN#	LAST NAME	FIRST NAME	FREE WHITE MALES					FREE WHITE FEMALES					TOTAL ALL OTHER	TOTAL SLAVES	TOTALS	DISTRICT/ TOWNSHIP	NOTES
					under 10	10 to 16	16 to 26	26 to 45	45 and over	under 10	10 to 16	16 to 26	26 to 45	45 and over					
Wilmington	142	25	Harnden	John Jr	1			1				1					3		
Wilmington	142	26	Harnden	Augustus	1		1					1					3		
Wilmington	142	27	Jones	Abel			1			1		1					3		
Wilmington	142	28	Jaqueth	John	1		1		1	1		1					5		
Wilmington	142	29	Jaques	Samuel	2	10	2	1		2	1	2	1	2			23		
Wilmington	142	30	Jones	Russel	5	1	1		1		2	2	1				13		
Wilmington	142	31	Jaquith	David			2		1	1				2			6		
Wilmington	142	32	Jaquith	Samuel															Name crossed out
Wilmington	142	33	Jaquith	John Jr	2	1	1				1	1		1			7		
Wilmington	142	34	Jones	David	1	1		1		1	1		1				6		
Wilmington	143	1	Jaquith	James	1		1		2	1		1		2			8		
Wilmington	143	2	Jaquith	Joshua	1		1	1					1				4		
Wilmington	143	3	Jaquith	Jonathan		2					1						3		
Wilmington	143	4	Jaquith	Ebenezer				1					1				2		
Wilmington	143	5	Jenkens	Joseph				1					1				2		
Wilmington	143	6	Jenkens	Joel	1	1		1		1	1		1				6		
Wilmington	143	7	Jaquith	Anna		2	2				1	2		1			8		
Wilmington	143	8	Jones	Abial		1				1		1					3		
Wilmington	143	9	Jones	Willard	1			1		1			1				4		
Wilmington	143	10	Kendel	Elizabeth	2			1				1		1			5		
Wilmington	143	11	Morriel	Nathaniel	2	2	2	1		2	1		1				11		
Wilmington	143	12	Morriel	Doratha									2	1			3		
Wilmington	143	13	Meers	Zebediah	1			1		2			1				5		
Wilmington	143	14	Nichols	Jonathan			2	1			1		1				5		
Wilmington	143	15	P*	John				1					1				2		
Wilmington	143	16	Parker	Thomas		1			1	1	1	1	1				6		
Wilmington	143	17	Parker	Joseph				2					2	1			5		
Wilmington	143	18	Pearson	Aaron	2		1	1		1		2					7		
Wilmington	143	19	Parker	Samuel				1					1				2		
Wilmington	143	20	Pearson	Isaac															Name crossed out
Wilmington	143	21	Pearson	Moses	4	3	1		1	1			1				11		
Wilmington	143	22	Peabody	Joseph			1					1					2		
Wilmington	143	23	Pence	Isaac	1	1	2		1	3		1		1			10		
Wilmington	143	24	Ru*nd	Re* Freegrace	1		1	1		1		1					5		
Wilmington	143	25	Richardson	Jude	1	1		1					1				4		
Wilmington	143	26	Richardson	Lowammer	4			1		1			1				7		
Wilmington	143	27	Stanly	Elijah		1		1					1				3		
Wilmington	143	28	Stanly	Abraham	4			1					1				6		
Wilmington	143	29	Stanly	Jonathan				1			1		1				3		
Wilmington	143	30	Thompson	Benjamen				1			1		1				3		
Wilmington	144	1	Thompson	Ebenezer				1		1	1	1	1				5		
Wilmington	144	2	Tw*	James		1		1						2			4		
Wilmington	144	3	Thompson	Benjamen Jr	3	1	1	1		1	1		1				9		
Wilmington	144	4	Upton	Thomas R			2		1		2	1	1				7		
Wilmington	144	5	Upton	Jethro			1	1		1		1					4		
Wilmington	144	6	Upton	Raul	1	2			1	2				1			7		
Wilmington	144	7	Walker	Timothy			2	1	1					1			5		
Wilmington	144	8	Wyman	Catharine						1	1						2		
Wilmington	144	9	Whitney	Samson	2			1		1			1	1			6		
Wilmington	144	10	Whitney	Elda			20	13		1		1	1				36		

125

TOWN	PG#	LN#	HEADS OF HOUSEHOLD		FREE WHITE MALES					FREE WHITE FEMALES					TOTAL ALL OTHER	TOTAL SLAVES	TOTALS	DISTRICT/ TOWNSHIP	NOTES
			LAST NAME	FIRST NAME	under 10	10 to 16	16 to 26	26 to 45	45 and over	under 10	10 to 16	16 to 26	26 to 45	45 and over					
Woburn	148	1	Baldwin	Leaming	1		3	1	1	1	1	1			1		10		
Woburn	148	2	Brooks	Joseph	4	1		1		1			1	1			9		
Woburn	148	3	Butters	Joshua					1					1			2		
Woburn	148	4	Beers	Joseph W	3	2		1		1			1				8		
Woburn	148	5	Bond	Joseph	1	2	1	1			1		1	1			8		
Woburn	148	6	Brooks	Nathaniel		1	1	2				1		1			6		
Woburn	148	7	Brown	Josiah	1			1	1	2	1			1			7		
Woburn	148	8	Brown	Joseph			1	1	1		1		1	2			7		
Woburn	148	9	Brown	Edward		2		1			2		1				6		
Woburn	148	10	Bruce	John					2								2		
Woburn	148	11	Bruce	John Jr.		1		1	1	1	1			1			5		
Woburn	148	12	Bruce	James			1						1				2		
Woburn	148	13	Clapp	Jeremiah		1		3		1	1		1				7		
Woburn	148	14	Carter	Josiah							1		1	1			3		
Woburn	148	15	Coggin	Jacob			1		1	1	1		1				5		
Woburn	148	16	Convers	Jesse	1			1					1				3		
Woburn	148	17	Convers	Josiah			2	1					1				4		
Woburn	148	18	Convers	Josiah Jr	1	2		1		1	1	1	1				8		
Woburn	148	19	Convers	Jeremiah	2			1		3			1				7		
Woburn	148	20	Convers	Mary		1							2	1			4		
Woburn	148	21	Convers	John	1		1	1		1			1				5		
Woburn	148	22	Convers	Benjamin	1	2			1		1			1			6		
Woburn	149	1	Convers	James	2		1		1			1					5		
Woburn	149	2	Cummings	Stephen	2	1		1		1			1	1			7		
Woburn	149	3	Cox	William	1	1	1	1	1	1		1	1	1			9		
Woburn	149	4	Cummings	Ebenezer	3	2	2		1	1	1	3		1			14		
Woburn	149	5	Clapp	Elisha		1						1					2		
Woburn	149	6	Dean	Lemuel	1		1	1		1	2	1					7		
Woburn	149	7	Dexter	David	2				1				2				5		
Woburn	149	8	Eames	Jacob	1	1	3		1	1			1				8		
Woburn	149	9	Eames	John	1	3	1		1	1	1	2		1			11		
Woburn	149	10	Eaton	Lille				1				1	1	1			4		
Woburn	149	11	Edgell	Benjamin	1		2		2	1		2		1			9		
Woburn	149	12	Eaton	Jonathan Jr		1	1	1		1	1		1				6		
Woburn	149	13	Eaton	Jonathan	1				1			1		1			4		
Woburn	149	14	Eaton	Thomas	1		1			1		1					4		
Woburn	149	15	Eaton	Lot	5	1		1		1			1				9		
Woburn	149	16	Emerson	William	2			1					1				4		
Woburn	149	17	Eames	James H	1			1					1				3		
Woburn	149	18	Evans	Sarah		1		1					1	1			4		
Woburn	149	19	Evans	Asaph	1		1			2		1					5		
Woburn	149	20	Eaton	Joseph		1		1		2	2		1				7		
Woburn	149	21	Fowle	Benjamin		1	2		1					1			5		
Woburn	149	22	Fowle	Josiah				1			1			1			3		
Woburn	149	23	Fowle	Jane	1	1	1					1	1				5		
Woburn	149	24	Fowle	Samuel			1				1		1	1			4		
Woburn	149	25	Fowle	Joseph	1		1	1		1		2	1				7		
Woburn	149	26	Fowle	Bridgett										1			1		
Woburn	149	27	Fox	William	2			1		1			1				5		
Woburn	149	28	Fox	Thomas					1					1			2		
Woburn	149	29	Flagg	John		1	1		1		1			1			5		
Woburn	149	30	Flagg	Hiram	4			1			1	1	1				8		
Woburn	149	31	Fowle	John	2	1	1	1		2	1	1	1				10		
Woburn	149	32	Fowle	Bill	3		1	1		2	2		1				10		
Woburn	149	33	Ferrel	Mitchel			1			1			1				3		
Woburn	149	34	Holden	Asa	2			1					1				4		
Woburn	149	35	Hadley	David	1				1		1			1			4		
Woburn	149	36	Hastings	John		1			1	3	3		1		1		10		
Woburn	149	37	Hadley	Ebenezer	1	3			1	1				1			7		
Woburn	149	38	Holden	Thomas	2			1	1	1			1				6		
Woburn	149	39	Harrington	Nathaniel	2		1	1		3	1	1	1				10		
Woburn	149	40	Hunt	William C		1		1				1	1				4		
Woburn	149	41	Hadley	David	3			1		1							5		
Woburn	149	42	Hadley	Daniel	1		1					1					3		
Woburn	150	1	Johnson	Francis		2	1		1	1		2		1			8		
Woburn	150	2	Johnson	Frederick	1	2		1		1			1				6		
Woburn	150	3	Johnson	Susann										1			1		
Woburn	150	4	Johnson	Anna								1		1			2		
Woburn	150	5	Johnson	Isaac				1						1			2		
Woburn	150	6	Johnson	Reuben		2	1		1	1			2	1			8		
Woburn	150	7	Johnson	Josiah			2		1				2	1			6		
Woburn	150	8	Johnson	David			1		1					1			3		
Woburn	150	9	Johnson	Jesse				1		2			1				4		
Woburn	150	10	Jordan	John	1			1		1			1				4		
Woburn	150	11	Kimbal	Ezra			2	1					1				4		
Woburn	150	12	Kendell	Obediah				1					1				2		
Woburn	150	13	Kendell	Obediah Jr	1	2		1			2	1	1				8		
Woburn	150	14	Lawrence	Joseph						1	1		1		1	1	5		
Woburn	150	15	Lawrence	Ebenezer		1	2			1	2			1			7		

126

| TOWN | PG# | LN# | HEADS OF HOUSEHOLD | | FREE WHITE MALES | | | | | FREE WHITE FEMALES | | | | | TOTAL ALL OTHER | TOTAL SLAVES | TOTALS | DISTRICT/ TOWNSHIP | NOTES |
			LAST NAME	FIRST NAME	under 10	10 to 16	16 to 26	26 to 45	45 and over	under 10	10 to 16	16 to 26	26 to 45	45 and over					
Woburn	150	16	Lawrence	Rachel									1	1			2		
Woburn	150	17	Leathe	Elijah		2			1		1			1			5		
Woburn	150	18	Leathe	Elijah Jr	2	1			1	1		1	1				7		
Woburn	150	19	Lock	James	1		1	1		1	1	1		1			7		
Woburn	150	20	Leathe	James		1		1					1				3		
Woburn	150	21	Lock	Josiah	2	2	2		1	1		1	1				10		
Woburn	150	22	Leathe	Jacob				1		1			1				3		
Woburn	150	23	Miller	Job					1				2	1	2		6		
Woburn	150	24	Munro	Jonas	2			1		1			2				6		
Woburn	150	25	Nichols	William		1	1			1		1					4		
Woburn	150	26	Parker	Ichabod	1		1	1		1	1		1	1			7		
Woburn	150	27	Parker	Josiah	1		2		1	2		2	1				9		
Woburn	150	28	Parker	Benjamin		1			1	4	2		2				10		
Woburn	150	29	Parker	Edmund	2	1		1		2	1		1				8		
Woburn	150	30	Parker	Nathaniel			4	1		3	1	2					11		
Woburn	150	31	Pierce	Abigail									2	1			3		
Woburn	150	32	Pierce	Jacob	1	1	1	2				2	1		3		11		
Woburn	150	33	Pierce	Abel	2	1		1		1			1				6		
Woburn	150	34	Pierce	Nathan	3	1		1		2			1				8		
Woburn	150	35	Plympton	Sylvanus	2			1		1	1		1				6		
Woburn	151	1	Pollard	John	1			1		1		1	1				5		
Woburn	151	2	Poole	Thomas	1			1		1			1				4		
Woburn	151	3	Pierce	Samuel	1	1	1	2		1							7		
Woburn	151	4	Reed	Daniel			1	1				1	1				4		
Woburn	151	5	Reed	Daniel Jr	1			1		2			1				5		
Woburn	151	6	Reed	Ebenezer		1		1				1	1				4		
Woburn	151	7	Reed	Joshua	1		1	1		1		1	1				6		
Woburn	151	8	Reed	Joshua Jr	3			1					1				5		
Woburn	151	9	Richardson	Abel		1	2	1					1				5		
Woburn	151	10	Richardson	Abel 3rd	3			1					1				5		
Woburn	151	11	Richardson	James	4	1	1		1	1	1		1				10		
Woburn	151	12	Richardson	Joseph		2		1				1					4		
Woburn	151	13	Richardson	Barnabas				1									1		
Woburn	151	14	Richardson	Barnabas Jr	1	1		1		1	1		1				6		
Woburn	151	15	Richardson	Joseph Jr	1			1		1		1					4		
Woburn	151	16	Richardson	Bartholomew				1					1	1			3		
Woburn	151	17	Richardson	Bartholomew Jr	1	1	1		1	1		2		1			8		
Woburn	151	18	Richardson	Bartholomew 3rd	1		1	1		1			1				5		
Woburn	151	19	Richardson	J*	1			1		1							4		
Woburn	151	20	Richardson	Edward		1	1		1		1			1			5		
Woburn	151	21	Richardson	Zadock		1	1	1				1		1			5		
Woburn	151	22	Richardson	Eleazer	1			1				1		1			4		
Woburn	151	23	Richardson	Zadock Jr	1			1		1			1				4		
Woburn	151	24	Richardson	Ethan	3			1		1			1	1			7		
Woburn	151	25	Richardson	Samuel		1		1		1	1		1				5		
Woburn	151	26	Richardson	Stephen	1			1		3		1	1				7		
Woburn	151	27	Richardson	Jese				1		1				1			3		
Woburn	151	28	Richardson	Jese Jr			1			1		1					3		
Woburn	151	29	Richardson	Jedu*				1			1	2		1			5		
Woburn	151	30	Richardson	Thomas		1		1		1		1					4		
Woburn	151	31	Russell	Bill		4	1	1				1	1				8		
Woburn	151	32	Reed	Jacob					1					2			3		
Woburn	151	33	Reed	Isacc	3	3	1	1				1		1			10		
Woburn	151	34	Richardson	Calvin			1					1					2		
Woburn	151	35	Richardson	Zachariah				1						2			3		
Woburn	151	36	Richardson	Zachariah Jr		1		1		1			1	1			5		
Woburn	151	37	Richardson	Jese	1	2	1	1		3	1		1				10		
Woburn	151	38	Richardson	Nathan		1						1		1			4		
Woburn	151	39	Richardson	Abel Jr	2	1	2		1	1	1		1				9		
Woburn	151	40	Richardson	Mary			1			1				1			3		
Woburn	151	41	Richardson	Rebekah	1			1		1			1	1			5		
Woburn	151	42	Richardson	Jerusha		1	1					1					4		
Woburn	151	43	Richardson	Josiah		1	1	1					1				5		
Woburn	152	1	Richardson	Josiah Jr				1									1		
Woburn	152	2	Richardson	Jacob	1	2	2	1		1	1		1	1			10		
Woburn	152	3	Richardson	Jethro			2			1			1				4		
Woburn	152	4	Richardson	Samuel T		1					1						2		
Woburn	152	5	Richardson	Reuben				1				1					3		
Woburn	152	6	Richardson	Richard	1		1			1		1					4		
Woburn	152	7	Richardson	Peter			1	1				1	1				5		
Woburn	152	8	Smith	Benjamin		2		1					1	1			5		
Woburn	152	9	Scotts	John				1				1		1			3		
Woburn	152	10	Steel	James	1	2		1		1	1	1	1				7		
Woburn	152	11	Smith	Elias	1			1		2			1				5		
Woburn	152	12	Swan	Caleb	1		2		1	2	1	1					8		
Woburn	152	13	Simonds	Benjamin	2	1	4		1				1	1			10		
Woburn	152	14	Simonds	Nathan		1		1	1	1			1	2			8		
Woburn	152	15	Symmes	Zachariah			1	1					1	1			4		
Woburn	152	16	Symmes	Samuel	1	2	2		1								8		

127

TOWN	PG#	LN#	LAST NAME	FIRST NAME	FREE WHITE MALES					FREE WHITE FEMALES					TOTAL ALL OTHER	TOTAL SLAVES	TOTALS	DISTRICT/ TOWNSHIP	NOTES
					under 10	10 to 16	16 to 26	26 to 45	45 and over	under 10	10 to 16	16 to 26	26 to 45	45 and over					
Woburn	152	17	Symmes	William		1		1		1		1					4		
Woburn	152	18	Sargeant	Samuel	3	1		1		1		1					7		
Woburn	152	19	Snow	Ruth								1		1			2		
Woburn	152	20	Skinner	Mary	1								1				2		
Woburn	152	21	Tay	William	1		1		1			2		3			8		
Woburn	152	22	Tay	Joshua	1		1	1	1	1		1	1	1			8		
Woburn	152	23	Tylor	Jonathan	3		1	1		3	1	2	3				14		
Woburn	152	24	Tay	Samuel		1	2		1			1					6		
Woburn	152	25	Tay	John	3	1		1		1		1					7		
Woburn	152	26	Thompson	Samuel		1			1	1		1	1				5		
Woburn	152	27	Thompson	Jonathan	1	1	1	1		3			1				8		
Woburn	152	28	Thompson	Hiram				1		1		1		1			4		
Woburn	152	29	Thompson	Jaber	1			1					1				3		
Woburn	152	30	Thompson	Abijah		1	2	1	1	2			1				8		
Woburn	152	31	Thompson	Abijah Jr	3			1		1	1		1				7		
Woburn	152	32	Thompson	Leonard	2	1		1		1	1		1				7		
Woburn	152	33	Tidd	Jonathan	1	1		1			1		1				5		
Woburn	152	34	Tidd	Samuel	1	2		1			1		1				6		
Woburn	152	35	Tottingham	Elisha				3						5			8		
Woburn	152	36	Tay	Comfort	2					2			1				5		
Woburn	152	37	Wade	Ebenezer			2	1					1				4		
Woburn	152	38	Wade	Nathaniel	1		1	1		2			1				6		
Woburn	152	39	Wood	Seth		1	1	1	3			1	1	2			10		
Woburn	152	40	Wood	Sylvann	1	1			1	1			1				5		
Woburn	152	41	Wright	Josiah		1	2	1	1			1		1			7		
Woburn	152	42	Wyman	Samuel E	3			2		2			2				9		
Woburn	153	1	Wyman	Benjamin	2		1	1		2	1		1				8		
Woburn	153	2	Wyman	Daniel	2		1		1	2	2	1	1		1		11		
Woburn	153	3	Wyman	Eunice			1			1	1		1				4		
Woburn	153	4	Wyman	Jesse			1			3			1				5		
Woburn	153	5	Wyman	Joshua		1	1	1	1				1				5		
Woburn	153	6	Wyman	Joshua Jr	1	1	2			1		1					6		
Woburn	153	7	Wyman	Jonathan	4	1		1		1			1				8		
Woburn	153	8	Wyman	Paul		1		1				1	1				4		
Woburn	153	9	Wyman	Zebadiah			2					2					4		
Woburn	153	10	Wright	Philemon	2	1	1	1		2	1		1	1			10		
Woburn	153	11	Wright	James				1									1		
Woburn	153	12	Winship	Joel	3			1					1				5		
Woburn	153	13	Wyman	Nathan				1					1				2		
Woburn	153	14	Wyman	Nathan Jr	1	1	1		1	1	1	1	1				8		
Woburn	153	15	Wyman	David	3	3	2		1	1		1	1	3			15		
Woburn	153	16	Wyman	James	1		1					1					3		
Woburn	153	17	Wheeler	Benjamin	1		1	1					1				5		
Woburn	153	18	Walker	Abel	1	1		1		3		1					7		
Woburn	153	19	Wyer	Abigail									1				1		
Woburn	153	20	Wyman	Nathaniel	1	1	2			1		2					7		
Woburn	153	21	Young	William		1			1			2		1			5		

TOWN	PG#	LN#	LAST NAME	FIRST NAME	M under 10	M 10 to 16	M 16 to 26	M 26 to 45	M 45 and over	F under 10	F 10 to 16	F 16 to 26	F 26 to 45	F 45 and over	TOTAL ALL OTHER	TOTAL SLAVES	TOTALS	DISTRICT/ TOWNSHIP	NOTES
Tyngsborough	43	1	*	*	2		2	1	1	1	1		1				9		Illegible
Townsend	26	1	*	Ezekiel	2	1		1		1	2	2					9		
Ashby	37	48	*	John		1											1		
Concord	7	1	*	Joseph				1			2						3		
Concord	7	20	*	Stephen									1	1			2		
Tyngsborough	40	22	*eng	Luther			1			2		1					4		
Cambridge	220	1	A*	James	2		2	2		2		3					11		
Lincoln	14	1	Abbot	Abiel	1			1		1			1				4		
Billerica	173	2	Abbot	David			2	1					1				4		
Reading	127	1	Abbot	Ebenezer	1	3		1		3		1					9		
Billerica	173	3	Abbot	James	3	1	3	2		2		1	1	1			14		
Stow	195	15	Abbot	Jeremiah		1						1	1	1			4		
Lincoln	13	39	Abbot	Joseph	2	1	1		1	2			1	1			9		
Billerica	173	4	Abbot	Joshua		1		1					1	1			4		
Billerica	173	1	Abbot	Nathan		1		1		1	2		1				6		
Tyngsborough	41	1	Abbot	Nathl	1			1		1	2		1				6		
Lincoln	13	37	Abbot	Nehemiah	1	1			1		1			1			5		
East Sudbury	67	16	Abbott	Amos	1			1		1			1				4		
Dracut	44	15	Abbott	Daniel	1		1	2		1			1	1			7		
Dracut	49	2	Abbott	David		1	1			1		1		1			5		
East Sudbury	65	3	Abbott	Ephraim		1		1	1	1		3		1			8		
Bedford	161	2	Abbott	Henry		1											1		
Westford	179	1	Abbott	Jacob	1			1		1	1		1				5		
Westford	179	3	Abbott	Joel	2		1	1		1	1		1	2			9		
Ashby	34	1	Abbott	John	2	1		1		3	1	1	1				10		
Westford	179	2	Abbott	John			2		1			1		1			5		
Ashby	34	2	Abbott	Jonh	3			1		2	1		1				8		
Chelmsford	166	1	Abbott	Joseph			1			2		1					4		
Framingham	70	2	Abbott	Josiah		1						2		1			4		
Bedford	161	1	Abbott	Moses	2			1						1			4		
Bedford	161	3	Abbott	Moses Jr	2	1		1		1		1	1	1			8		
Medford	99	1	Abbott	Saml	1		1	1					1				4		
Dracut	44	25	Abbott	Solomon	1	1		1		4	1		1				9		
Burlington	154	1	Abbott	William		1			1					2			4		
Burlington	154	2	Abbott	William Jr			1				1		1				3		
Charlestown	79	5	Abraham	Eliza'										2			2		
Charlestown	79	6	Abraham	Jos'				1						1			2		
Chelmsford	166	7	Adams	Abel		1	2			1		1					5		
Townsend	25	4	Adams	Abner	1	1			1			1	1				5		
Acton	16	22	Adams	Ammi F			1			3		1	1				6		
Lincoln	12	8	Adams	Andrew			1						1				2		
Townsend	25	1	Adams	Anhelat		1	1	1				1					4		
Hopkinton	240	6	Adams	Asa Jr		1		1		3			1				6		
Chelmsford	166	6	Adams	Benja		1	1	1				1	1				5		
East Sudbury	65	1	Adams	Benjamin			2	1		3	2	2	1				11		
Hopkinton	240	3	Adams	Benjm	1		1	1		2	3		1				9		
Lincoln	14	4	Adams	Buckley		1	1					2	1				5		
Cambridge	220	5	Adams	Daniel	1		1	1		2		1	1				7		
Townsend	25	3	Adams	Daniel		1	2		1		2		1				7		
Townsend	25	7	Adams	Elipht	2			1		1		1		1			6		
Hopkinton	240	2	Adams	Elisha		1	2		1	2		1	1				8		
Hollistown	236	4	Adams	Ezekiel				1					1				2		
Lexington	156	3	Adams	George				1					1				2		
Cambridge	220	6	Adams	Hanah									1	1			2		
Chelmsford	166	11	Adams	Isaac	1	1		1		1		1					5		
Newton	117	3	Adams	Jacob		1				1				1			3		
Lincoln	12	7	Adams	James		1		1				2		1			5		
Pepperell	30	1	Adams	James	2			1		1			1				5		
Sherburn	248	1	Adams	James		1					1		1				3		
Acton	16	21	Adams	John				1					1	1			3		
Cambridge	220	3	Adams	John	2		1			2	1	1	2	1			11		
Chelmsford	166	10	Adams	John				1		1			1				3		
Groton	207	2	Adams	John		1		1					1				3		
Lincoln	15	6	Adams	John				1						1	1		3		
Acton	16	10	Adams	John Jr		1	2	1		1		1	1				7		
Groton	207	3	Adams	John Jr		1						1					2		
Hollistown	236	2	Adams	Jona	1		1	1		1	1		1				6		
Lincoln	15	7	Adams	Jonas		1		1				2	2				6		
Shirley	213	1	Adams	Jonas	1			1		2	1		1				6		
Charlestown	79	2	Adams	Jos'			3	1					1	1			6		
Chelmsford	166	5	Adams	Joseph	2	1		1					1	1			6		
Lincoln	12	5	Adams	Joseph		2	1	1				2	1	1			8		
Littleton	202	47	Adams	Joseph	1		1	1		4			1				8		
Newton	117	4	Adams	Joseph		1							1	1			3		
Pepperell	30	2	Adams	Joseph	1	1		1						1			4		
Shirley	213	5	Adams	Joseph	1			1		1			1				4		
Townsend	25	5	Adams	Joseph	1	1		1		3		1	1	1			9		
Lexington	156	2	Adams	Katharine								1		1			2		
Hollistown	236	3	Adams	Levi				1					1				2		
Acton	18	27	Adams	Moses	1		2		1	1	2	2	1	1			11		

129

TOWN	PG#	LN#	LAST NAME	FIRST NAME	FREE WHITE MALES under 10	10 to 16	16 to 26	26 to 45	45 and over	FREE WHITE FEMALES under 10	10 to 16	16 to 26	26 to 45	45 and over	TOTAL ALL OTHER	TOTAL SLAVES	TOTALS	DISTRICT/ TOWNSHIP	NOTES
Hopkinton	240	1	Adams	Moses			1	1		2		2	1	2	1		10		
Groton	206	2	Adams	Natha		1			1								2		
Medford	99	2	Adams	Nathan	1	1		1		2		2	1				8		
Shirley	213	4	Adams	Nathan	1	1		1		2	1	1					7		
Charlestown	79	3	Adams	Nathn	3	1		1				2	1				8		
Charlestown	79	4	Adams	Nathn Jr			2	1					1				4		
Chelmsford	166	8	Adams	Olive		1							1	1			3		
Townsend	25	2	Adams	Peter	1		1	1		1			1				5		
Newton	117	1	Adams	Roger	1	1	1		1	4	3		1				12		
Westford	179	5	Adams	Ruth		2						1		1			4		
Chelmsford	166	12	Adams	Saml				1		1	2			1			5		
Chelmsford	166	4	Adams	Saml Jr		1	1		1	2		1		1			7		
Chelmsford	166	9	Adams	Sarah										1			1		
East Sudbury	65	2	Adams	Seth	2			1	1				1	1			6		
Newton	117	2	Adams	Smith	2	2	1	1		4			1				11		
Framingham	74	13	Adams	Stephen		2						1					3		
Westford	179	4	Adams	Tho'	2	2	2		1	1			1				9		
Carlisle	21	25	Adams	Timothy	2	2	1	1		2			1				9		
Hollistown	236	1	Adams	Timothy	2	1		1		1	1		1				7		
Waltham	112	2	Adams	William				1						2			3		
Charlestown	79	1	Adams	Wm		1	1			1	1		1				5		
Chelmsford	166	3	Adams	Wm	3			1		2	1		2				9		
Sherburn	248	2	Adams	Wm	2			1			1		1				5		
Dracut	45	37	Aiken	Solomon	3			1		1	1		1				7		
Lexington	156	1	Ainger	John	2	1		1		1		1					6		
Framingham	70	1	Ainger	Joseph	2	1		1		2			1	1			8		
Watertown	231	2	Alden	Jona	2		2			2	2						8		
Newton	117	6	Alden	Paul			1	2		3			1				7		
Natick	245	1	Alden	Wm	3	2		1					4				10		
Burlington	154	3	Alexander	Giles		2		1				1	1	1			6		
Weston	105	1	Alexander	Giles		1		1		1		3	1		2		9		
Wilmington	140	1	Alexander	John	3	1	2	1	1	1		1		1			11		
Shirley	213	3	Alexander	Wm			1						1				2		
Cambridge	220	2	Allen	Abijah			1	3		1	1						6		
Ashby	37	43	Allen	Benja	1		3						1				5		
East Sudbury	69	15	Allen	Deborah									1	1			2		
Concord	4	32	Allen	George				1				2	1				4		
Townsend	25	6	Allen	James			1					1					2		
Waltham	112	1	Allen	James	3			1		1			1				6		
Billerica	173	6	Allen	Jerem'	3	1	1		1		1	1	1				9		
East Sudbury	65	4	Allen	John		1	1						1				3		
Malden	93	2	Allen	John		1						1					2		
Billerica	173	5	Allen	Mala'		2		1		2			1				6		
Newton	117	5	Allen	Michael	1		1						1				3		
Weston	105	1	Allen	Nathaniel		1			2	1		1	2				7		
Weston	105	2	Allen	Priscilla	2					1	2						5		
Charlestown	79	11	Allen	Saml			1					1	1				3		
Littleton	204	14	Allen	Zadock		1		1		1		1					4		
Groton	207	1	Allin	Joseph		1	2	1	1			2		2			9		
Malden	93	1	Ally	John		1											1		
Groton	206	1	Ames	Amos					1	1	1		1				4		
Groton	207	5	Ames	Berkley	1		2	1				1					5		
Pepperell	30	3	Ames	Elijah	1	1	1		1			2		1			7		
Tewksbury	49	1	Ames	Ezekiel	1		1					1					3		
Marlborough	188	41	Ames	Moses		1		1		1	1		1				5		
Chelmsford	166	2	Ames	Nathan		1	2	1		2			2				8		
Groton	207	4	Ames	Peter	1			1				1					3		
Charlestown	79	12	Ames	Robt		1											1		
Marlborough	194	36	Ames	Stephen		1	1	1				1	1	2			7		
Billerica	173	7	Amory	Nath'															
Framingham	78	12	Amsdel	Joseph	1		1			1		1					4		
Carlisle	23	6	Anderson	Nehemiah		2				1	1						5		
Charlestown	79	14	Ando	Tho'	1			1				1		1			4		
Carlisle	23	7	Andrews	Edmund				1		1	1		1				4		
Hopkinton	240	4	Andrews	Joshua				1					1				2		
Carlisle	23	8	Andrews	Solomon			1						1				2		
Hopkinton	240	5	Andrews	Wm	1			1				1	1				4		
Westford	179	6	Andrews	Wm	2		1			2			1				6		
Medford	99	3	Andries	Eliza	3								1		5		9		
Charlestown	79	13	Ango	John	3			1		2			1				7		
Watertown	231	1	Annas	Thos'	2	2	2	1		1	1		1				10		
Medford	99	4	Anthony	Jona											1		1		
Townsend	25	8	Archaball	Willm			1						1				2		
Charlestown	79	7	Armstead	James	1		1			1		1					4		
Marlborough	194	24	Arnold	John	1			1		1			1				4		
Marlborough	194	17	Arnold	Joseph	1	1		1		3		1	1				8		
Marlborough	194	23	Arnold	Persis								1		1			2		
Framingham	70	3	Arnold	William		1			1			2		1			5		
Marlborough	188	19	Arnold	William	3		1	1		1			1	1			8		

TOWN	PG#	LN#	LAST NAME	FIRST NAME	FREE WHITE MALES under 10	10 to 16	16 to 26	26 to 45	45 and over	FREE WHITE FEMALES under 10	10 to 16	16 to 26	26 to 45	45 and over	TOTAL ALL OTHER	TOTAL SLAVES	TOTALS	DISTRICT/ TOWNSHIP	NOTES
Marlborough	193	42	Arnold	Winslow	2			1		1			1				5		
Cambridge	220	4	Aspenwall	Saml			1			3	1	1	1				7		
Watertown	231	3	Aspinwall	Palnopha				1				1	1				3		
Shirley	213	2	Atherton	Jona	1			1		3			1	1			7		
Natick	245	2	Atkins	John	1	2	1	1	1			2	1	1			10		
Reading	127	2	Atwell	Joseph		1	1		1		1	1		1			6		
Dracut	46	31	Austin	David		1	1		2	1	1	1		1			8		
Dracut	46	32	Austin	David Jr		1							1				2		
Charlestown	79	9	Austin	Ebenz			1		1				1				3		
Charlestown	79	8	Austin	John		1			1				1	1			4		
Dracut	45	16	Austin	Lewis	3	1	1		1	1	4		1				12		
Charlestown	79	10	Austin	Nath			2	1	1		1			3			8		
Dracut	46	30	Austin	Solomon	1			1		2	1	1	1				8		
Dracut	48	20	Austin	William	1	1	1	1		2		1					8		
Waltham	112	7	B*	Benjm			1	1	1		1	1		1			6		
Reading	129	1	B*t	Edward	2			1		2	1		1				7		
Wilmington	140	2	Ba*	Timothy		1			1			2		1			5		
Charlestown	81	38	Babb	Jos'				1		3		1					5		
Sherburn	248	11	Babcock	Ebenz	1		1			2	2	1					7		
Sherburn	248	10	Babcock	Malaca				1		2				1			4		
Sherburn	248	3	Babcock	Moses	2			1		1		1					5		
Watertown	231	28	Babcock	Saml	1	1		1		2	1		1				7		
Lincoln	12	19	Babcock	Seth	4			1		3	1		1				10		
Hopkinton	240	18	Bachelder	Benjm				1		3			2	1			7		
Hopkinton	240	12	Bachelder	Thos			1					1					2		
Townsend	26	2	Bacheldor	Jacob			1										1		
Reading	129	10	Bachelor	John	2	1		1		2	1		1				8		
Reading	129	11	Bachelor	John	2			1		2			1	1			7		
Reading	129	8	Bachelor	Jonathan				1						1			2		
Reading	129	7	Bachelor	Joseph	2			1		1	1		1				6		
Reading	129	9	Bachelor	Nathaniel		1		1				1	1				4		
Wilmington	141	3	Bachelor	Nathaniel		1		1		1		1					4		
Boxborough	199	5	Bachelor	Nehemiah	1	1		1		1		1		1			6		
Reading	129	4	Bachelor	Simeon	1	3		1		2	1		1				9		
Cambridge	220	35	Backer	Benjn		1	1	1				1		1			5		
Bedford	161	5	Bacon	Benjamin				1						1			2		
Bedford	161	6	Bacon	Benjamin Jr	1	1		1		2		1	1				7		
Sudbury	58	7	Bacon	Elijah	1		1	1					1				4		
Bedford	161	9	Bacon	Flagg	1		3	1		3		1					9		
Billerica	174	13	Bacon	John	1	1		1			1	1	1				6		
Medford	99	6	Bacon	Jona	1			1					1	1			4		
Bedford	161	7	Bacon	Jonah & Joseph F	3			1					1	1			6		
Billerica	174	16	Bacon	Jonas	3	1		1		2	1		1				9		
Cambridge	220	34	Bacon	Norman				1		2			1	1			5		
Newton	118	6	Bacon	Phinehas	2		1					1	1				5		
Bedford	161	8	Bacon	Solomon		1		1					1				3		
Bedford	161	4	Bacon	Thompson	3	3		1		2			1				10		
Malden	93	17	Bacon	Wm	1			1				1					3		
Natick	245	20	Bacon	Asa	1			1		3	1		1				7		
Natick	245	17	Bacon	David	2	2		1		2	2		1				10		
Natick	245	18	Bacon	Elijah	1		1	2	1	2		1	1	1	2		12		
Natick	245	6	Bacon	Ezra				1					1				2		
Natick	245	12	Bacon	Henry		1				2			2		1		6		
Natick	245	19	Bacon	John	2			1		1			1				5		
Natick	246	3	Bacon	John	3			1		1			1				6		
Natick	245	9	Bacon	Jona		1		1		2		1					5		
Natick	245	7	Bacon	Mehitable	2					2		1	1				6		
Natick	246	2	Bacon	Oliver				1					1				2		
Natick	245	8	Bacon	Richd	1			1		1		1		1			5		
Natick	245	5	Bacon	Richd Jr.	1		1						1				3		
Natick	245	16	Badger	John				1					1				2		
Sherburn	248	7	Badger	John	3			1		2			1				7		
Natick	245	22	Badger	Stephen			1			1			1	1			4		
Ashby	34	4	Badlam	Stephen	1			1		2	1	1	1	1			8		
Pepperell	30	21	Bailey	Abrm	2			1				1	1				5		
Charlestown	81	39	Bailey	Danl	2	1		1				1					5		
Concord	6	18	Bailey	David			1			2		1					4		
Natick	245	13	Bailey	Eliphalet	3		1	1		1	1		1				7		
Reading	129	18	Bailey	Jesse	1		1					1	2				5		
Groton	208	20	Bailey	John	1		1						1				3		
Tewksbury	49	12	Bailey	John T	3	2			1	3	2		1				12		
Townsend	25	23	Bailey	Jona	1			1		2	1	1					6		
Charlestown	81	19	Bailey	Kendal			2	1									3		
Dracut	46	39	Bailey	Moses	1	1		1		3	1		1				8		
Tewksbury	49	14	Bailey	Nathan Jr		1	1	1						1			4		
Townsend	25	24	Bailey	Nathl	1		1		1	2			2	1			8		
Townsend	26	6	Bailey	Saml			1					1					2		
Tewksbury	49	13	Bailey	Timothy		1		1	1				3	1			7		
Ashby	34	7	Bain	*	3		3	2		1			2				11		
Lincoln	13	18	Baker	Amos	3	1		1			2		1	1			9		

TOWN	PG#	LN#	LAST NAME	FIRST NAME	FREE WHITE MALES					FREE WHITE FEMALES					TOTAL ALL OTHER	TOTAL SLAVES	TOTALS	DISTRICT/ TOWNSHIP	NOTES
					under 10	10 to 16	16 to 26	26 to 45	45 and over	under 10	10 to 16	16 to 26	26 to 45	45 and over					
Lincoln	15	23	Baker	Amos Jr	1		1						1				3		
Concord	4	7	Baker	Daniel	1		1						1				3		
Littleton	201	18	Baker	Edward	1		1		1	2		1	1				7		
Littleton	203	10	Baker	Ezra	2				1	2	2		1				8		
Lincoln	14	38	Baker	Jacob		2			1	2	1			1			7		
Concord	9	5	Baker	James			1		1	1	1			1			5		
Marlborough	193	37	Baker	John	1	1			1	2	1			1			7		
Shirley	213	11	Baker	Jonas	2				1	2			1				6		
Lincoln	13	17	Baker	Nathaniel		1			1			1	1	2			6		
Billerica	174	15	Balch	Tho'					1					1			2		
Tewksbury	49	7	Balchader	John T	1				1	2		1					5		
Sudbury	63	31	Balcom	Asahel			1	1					1	2			5		
Sudbury	62	27	Balcom	James	1				1				1				3		
Sudbury	63	30	Balcom	Joel	1	1		1		2			1				6		
Sudbury	62	28	Balcom	John	1	2			1	1	1	2	1				9		
Sudbury	63	29	Balcom	Jonas	2	1	1	1	1	1	1	1	1	1			11		
Townsend	25	16	Baldwin	Asa	1	1		1			1		1				5		
Billerica	174	18	Baldwin	Benja'					1	2	2			1			6		
Chelmsford	168	4	Baldwin	Cyrus			1	1		1		1					4		
Chelmsford	168	16	Baldwin	David	1			1		3			1				6		
East Sudbury	65	6	Baldwin	David	2	2		2		1	1	2	1				11		
Pepperell	30	23	Baldwin	David		1	1	1		2	2		1				8		
Tewksbury	49	9	Baldwin	Davies	1	1		1		2			1				6		
Burlington	154	9	Baldwin	Isaac	3	2		1				1	1				8		
Waltham	112	15	Baldwin	Isaac		1	2			1			1				5		
Billerica	174	20	Baldwin	Joel		1	1	1					1				4		
Billerica	174	19	Baldwin	John					1					1			2		
Malden	93	11	Baldwin	John	1		1						1				3		
Tewksbury	49	11	Baldwin	John T	2			1		1			1				5		
Townsend	25	18	Baldwin	Jonas		1			1			2	1				5		
Reading	129	23	Baldwin	Jonathan		1			1	1				1			4		
Reading	129	16	Baldwin	Jonathan Jr			1						1				2		
Tewksbury	49	8	Baldwin	Joshua B					1			1	1				3		
Woburn	148	1	Baldwin	Leaming	1		3	1	1	1	1	1			1		10		
Billerica	174	17	Baldwin	Nahum	1			1		1	2		1				6		
Billerica	174	21	Baldwin	Reuben	2	1		1		3			1				8		
Billerica	174	25	Baldwin	Wm	2	1	1	1				1	1				9		
Framingham	68	9	Baley	Joseph	3	1		1		2			1	1			9		Stamped pg# was x'd out
Littleton	202	24	Baley	Joseph	3			1		1		1					6		
Marlborough	189	15	Baley	Samuel		1			1	1				1			4		
Concord	10	28	Ball	Abner			2					2					4		
Hopkinton	240	16	Ball	Abram				2		1				2			5		
Concord	10	27	Ball	Benjamin	1			1						1			3		
Townsend	26	3	Ball	Ebenz	3	2			1	1		1	1	1			10		
Townsend	25	12	Ball	Jerh			1	1		1		1	1	2			7		
Tewksbury	50	1	Ball	John	2			1		2		1					6		
Concord	10	20	Ball	Lydia									1	1			2		
Townsend	25	11	Ball	Noah			1	1		2		1		1			6		
Concord	10	21	Ball	Reuben	2	1		1		1			1				6		
Weston	106	11	Ballad	Ebenezer	2		1			2	1		1				7		
Framingham	68	13	Ballard	Samuel	1			1		3	2		1				8		Stamped pg# was x'd out
Framingham	68	12	Ballard	William			5		2	1	2			1			11		Stamped pg# was x'd out
Weston	106	3	Bancroft	Amos			1	1		1		1					4		
Tyngsborough	41	3	Bancroft	Eben	2			1		3	1		1				8		
Pepperell	30	5	Bancroft	End		1		1	1			1	1				5		
Charlestown	79	19	Bancroft	James		3		1		1	1						6		
Reading	127	3	Bancroft	James			1		1			1	1	1	1		5		
Pepperell	30	6	Bancroft	Jona		1		1					1				3		
Tyngsborough	41	4	Bancroft	Jona	1		2		1	1	1	1		1			8		
Reading	128	6	Bancroft	Jonathan			1						1	1			3		
Reading	127	4	Bancroft	Joseph			1						1	1			3		
Reading	129	14	Bancroft	Joseph Jr			1	1		3	1		1	1			8		
Reading	129	15	Bancroft	Nehemiah	1			1		2			2				6		
Groton	208	14	Bancroft	Saml	3	1		1		1			1				7		
Groton	206	14	Bancroft	Sarah Wid.		1											1		
Pepperell	30	7	Bancroft	Thos			1	1		1	1		1				5		
Reading	127	5	Bancroft	Timothy	3			1		2			1				7		
Groton	206	7	Bancroft	Wm	1	2	1	1	1	4		1	1				13		
Natick	245	21	Bane	Wm				1									1		
Framingham	70	9	Banister	Berzellia		1			1	1	1						5		
Malden	93	13	Banks	Wm				1					1				2		
Medford	99	9	Bannister	Jno'	2			1		2			1				6		
Dracut	47	9	Banon	Samll				1		2	1	1	1				6		
Billerica	173	8	Banres	Isaac	1	2			1	1		1		2			8		
Lincoln	13	14	Bapson	Theodore	1		3	1		1		1	1				8		
Sherburn	248	16	Barber	Elisha					1			1	1				3		
Sherburn	248	17	Barber	Elisha Jr	1			1		2		1					6		
Marlborough	190	8	Barber	Ephraim			1		2		1		1				5		
Sherburn	248	18	Barber	Oliver	2	1		1		2			2				8		
Acton	16	9	Barber	Robert				1			1		1	1			4		

TOWN	PG#	LN#	LAST NAME	FIRST NAME	FREE WHITE MALES					FREE WHITE FEMALES					TOTAL ALL OTHER	TOTAL SLAVES	TOTALS	DISTRICT/ TOWNSHIP	NOTES
					under 10	10 to 16	16 to 26	26 to 45	45 and over	under 10	10 to 16	16 to 26	26 to 45	45 and over					
Dracut	45	8	Barker	Andrew				1		3		1					5		
Chelmsford	168	22	Barker	Asa	3		1	1					1				6		
Charlestown	81	9	Barker	David	1	1	1	1				1		1	2		8		
Acton	16	11	Barker	Ebenezer				1		2			1	1			5		
Charlestown	81	22	Barker	Eliza	1					3	1	3	1				9		
Sudbury	57	5	Barker	Ephraim	3	2		1		1			1	1			9		
Tyngsborough	40	3	Barker	Ezra				1		3			1				5		
Acton	18	25	Barker	Francis				1			1		1				3		
Dracut	46	16	Barker	Isaac	3			1		1			1				6		
Acton	18	1	Barker	Joseph				1			1		1				3		
Acton	16	8	Barker	Joseph Jr		1	2	1		2			1				7		
Charlestown	81	10	Barker	Josi'	2	1		1		1	1	1	1				8		
Pepperell	30	32	Barker	Leml				1			1		1				3		
Chelmsford	168	21	Barker	Mary							1		1				2		
Tyngsborough	40	1	Barker	Moses	1			1					1				3		
Dracut	49	12	Barker	Richard				1					1				2		
Acton	18	37	Barker	Samuel				1					1				2		
Dracut	48	15	Barker	Timothy				1					2				3		
Dracut	48	16	Barker	Timothy Jr			1	1				1	1				4		
Tyngsborough	40	21	Barkin	Sy*	1												1		
Watertown	231	4	Barnard	Daniel	2	1	1	1	1	3			3	1			13		
Acton	18	24	Barnard	David	1		2			3	1		1				8		
Marlborough	194	31	Barnard	Francis	2		1			1			1				5		
Waltham	113	2	Barnard	Hannah		1								2			3		
Watertown	231	23	Barnard	James	3	1	1	1		3		1	1				11		
Marlborough	191	23	Barnard	Stephen	1			1					1				3		
Marlborough	191	21	Barnard	William	2	1		1		2	1		3	1			11		
Dracut	48	5	Barnes	Benejah	3	2	1	1		1			1	1			10		
Carlisle	20	19	Barnes	Elias	3		1		1	3			1				9		
Concord	7	33	Barnes	Josiah	3	2			1		2			1			9		
Malden	93	28	Barnes	Robt				1				3		1			5		
Waltham	112	8	Barnes	Samuel		1	1	1		2	1	1	1	1			9		
Newton	118	2	Barney	Solomon			2	2		1	1	1					7		
Concord	10	32	Barns	Benjamin	2			1		2			1				7		
Marlborough	194	11	Barns	Benjamin				1					1				2		
Marlborough	187	1	Barns	Edward	1		1	1		2	1	1	1				8		
Marlborough	194	34	Barns	Jacob	1		1	2		1		1		1			7		
Hopkinton	240	15	Barns	Joseph	1	1		1		1	1		1				6		
Marlborough	191	1	Barns	Lovewell	4	1		1		1	1		1				9		
Marlborough	192	2	Barns	Mary								1	1				2		
Marlborough	194	12	Barns	Mary Widow									1				1		
Marlborough	191	2	Barns	Sarah							1		1				2		
Marlborough	192	10	Barns	Solomon				1					1				2		
Marlborough	187	22	Barns	Stephen	2			1		1	1		1				6		
Marlborough	192	11	Barns	William	4		1	1		2	1	1	1				11		
Ashby	34	8	Barr	Robt. W.	1			1	1	2		1					6		
Charlestown	81	25	Barrell	Jos'	1		2	4	2	1		2	2	1			15		
Hopkinton	240	23	Barret	Ames			1	1		2				1			5		
Chelmsford	168	6	Barret	Joel				1			1			1			3		
Malden	93	24	Barret	Mary		1	1				1	1		1	2		7		
Ashby	34	11	Barrett	Benja			1						1				2		
Ashby	34	12	Barrett	Benja Jr	1	1	1	1		2		1	1				8		
Carlisle	21	13	Barrett	Benjamin	1	1	1	1		2	2		1				9		
Weston	106	8	Barrett	Hannah							1		2		3		6		
Concord	6	7	Barrett	Humphrey		1	1	1	1	1	1	1					7		
Concord	3	8	Barrett	James	2	1	2	1	1	1		2	2	2			14		
Concord	11	4	Barrett	John		3	2		1	3	1		1	1			12		
Ashby	34	9	Barrett	Jona		2	1	1				1		1			6		
Malden	93	21	Barrett	Jona'			1			1		1					3		
Ashby	34	13	Barrett	Jonas	1	2	1	1	1	2	1	1	1				11		
Malden	93	15	Barrett	Jos'	1		1		1	3	1		1				8		
Carlisle	21	16	Barrett	Joseph				1					1				2		
Concord	3	12	Barrett	Mary									2				2		
Concord	11	11	Barrett	Nathan	2	1		2			1	1	1	1			9		
Concord	3	11	Barrett	Peter	2	2	3		1		1	2	1	1			13		
Concord	3	13	Barrett	Samuel			2	1					1	1			5		
Billerica	174	23	Barrett	Steph'			2	1		3		1	1				8		
Concord	6	15	Barrett	Stephen			1			1		2					4		
Concord	7	19	Barrett	Stephen	1	1	1		2			3	1	1			10		
Concord	7	28	Barrett	Thomas				1			1	2	1				5		
Ashby	34	10	Barrett	Zebn	1	1		1		1	1	1					6		
Billerica	174	27	Barron	Isaac			1	1			2	1	1				6		
Pepperell	30	20	Barron	Jona		1		1	1				1	1			5		
Chelmsford	168	8	Barron	Jona'	1	1		3		2		2				1	10		
Chelmsford	168	7	Barron	Oliver				1					1				2		
Concord	10	31	Barron	Oliver				1					1				2		
Dracut	44	34	Barron	Saml				1		2	1	1	1				6		
Watertown	231	10	Barry	Willm			2	2		2			1				5		
Newton	118	7	Bartlett	David			1		1			1	1				4		

133

TOWN	PG#	LN#	HEADS OF HOUSEHOLD LAST NAME	FIRST NAME	FREE WHITE MALES under 10	10 to 16	16 to 26	26 to 45	45 and over	FREE WHITE FEMALES under 10	10 to 16	16 to 26	26 to 45	45 and over	TOTAL ALL OTHER	TOTAL SLAVES	TOTALS	DISTRICT/ TOWNSHIP	NOTES
Cambridge	220	23	Bartlett	Eben	1			1						1			3		
Newton	118	4	Bartlett	Elisha	2	1		1		1				2			7		
Charlestown	81	21	Bartlett	Geo'	2		2	2		3	1		2				12		
Cambridge	220	24	Bartlett	Joseph		1	3	1					1	1			7		
Newton	117	9	Bartlett	Joshua	2			1		1			1				5		
Charlestown	81	18	Bartlett	Josiah	5	1		2				2	1	2			13		
Newton	117	16	Bartlett	Luke		2		1				1		1			5		
Cambridge	220	30	Bartlett	Saml			3	1		2		2	3	1			12		
Shirley	213	14	Bartlett	Silence Wid.										2			2		
Shirley	213	12	Bartlett	Wm				1		4	2		1				8		
Marlborough	189	10	Bartley	Jonas		1	2	1		1		2		1			8		
Tewksbury	49	17	Barton	R Silas T	2			1					1	1			5		
Medford	99	16	Barton	Wm				1		1				1			3		
Charlestown	81	26	Bassett	Mary	2					1			1	1			5		
Townsend	26	22	Batcheldor	Nathl	1	1		1						1			4		
Billerica	173	9	Batchelor	Jos'			1						1				2		
Billerica	174	24	Batchelor	Jos' Jr	2	2	1	1				1	1				8		
Chelmsford	167	4	Bateman	Jno'		1		2		4		2	2	1			12		
Concord	4	24	Bateman	Jonas		1		1		1				1			4		
Cambridge	220	22	Bates	Joseph		2		1				2		1			6		
Reading	128	4	Batt	William	1	1	1						1				4		
Stow	197	38	Bayley	Elizabeth				1						1			2		
Wilmington	140	7	Bea*	Edward	2	1		1		2	1		1	1			9		
Newton	117	10	Beal	Thomas			1	1						1			3		
Newton	117	11	Beal	William	2			1		1	2		1				7		
Hollistown	236	18	Beals	Elizth									3				3		
Cambridge	220	7	Beals	Thon			1		2	1	1	1					6		
Wilmington	141	9	Beard	Abel	3	2		1					1				7		
Billerica	174	2	Beard	Benja'				1		1				2			4		
Billerica	174	3	Beard	Benja' Jr		1		1					1				3		
Reading	129	13	Beard	Cleveland				1						2			3		
Tewksbury	49	18	Beard	Eben	1	2		1	2	1			1	1			9		
Billerica	173	22	Beard	Isaac				1					1	1			3		
Billerica	173	23	Beard	Isaac Jr	1		1			3				1			6		
Littleton	204	18	Beard	Ithamer	1	1	2	1		1				1			7		
Wilmington	141	2	Beard	Jacob		1		1		1	2			1			6		
Wilmington	140	12	Beard	Jonathan	1	2		1		1	1	1	1				8		
Billerica	174	1	Beard	Mary	1								1	1			3		
Wilmington	140	16	Beard	Nathan		1		1						1			3		
Tewksbury	49	19	Beard	Reuben	2		2			1				1			6		
Reading	129	12	Beard	William		1	1	1		1	1			3			8		
Malden	93	27	Becham	John				1				1		2			4		
Woburn	148	4	Beers	Joseph W	3	2		1		1			1				8		
Framingham	70	11	Belcher	Ezra	2			1		2			1				6		
Framingham	70	10	Belcher	Jacob	1			1			1	1	1				5		
Framingham	70	16	Belcher	John	2	1		1					1				5		Stamped pg# was x'd out
Framingham	70	12	Belcher	Joseph	2	1		1		1	1		1				7		
Framingham	70	6	Belknap	Abraham			1	1		1		1	1	1			5		
Framingham	70	8	Belknap	Daniel				1			1						2		
Framingham	70	13	Belknap	Enoch				1		1			1				3		
Framingham	70	4	Belknap	Jeremiah				1				2		1			4		
Framingham	70	5	Belknap	Jesse	1	1		1		4			1				8		
Framingham	70	7	Belknap	Luther				1					1				2		
Cambridge	220	21	Bell	Daniel		1	1			1			1	1			5		
Malden	93	8	Bell	Eliza'									1				1		
Wilmington	140	3	Bell	John	2	3	2		1	3				1			12		
Charlestown	81	30	Bell	Wm	1			1		1				1			4		
Cambridge	220	8	Belnap	Jason	1			1						1			3		
Cambridge	220	9	Belnap	Joseph		1			1			2					4		
Waltham	112	11	Bemis	Abraham				1						1			2		
Waltham	112	12	Bemis	Abraham Jr	2		1	1	1			2		1			8		
Lincoln	14	39	Bemis	Amos	1			1		3			1				6		
Weston	106	17	Bemis	Daniel	3	1		1		2	2		1				10		
Waltham	113	4	Bemis	Isaac	3	1	5		1		1		2				13		
Lincoln	15	21	Bemis	Joel	2			1		2	1		1				7		
Lincoln	14	18	Bemis	Jonas	3			1		2			1				7		
Waltham	112	5	Bemis	Josiah	3	2	1	1		2		1	1	1			12		
Weston	106	15	Bemis	Lot	2			1				1					5		
Watertown	231	9	Bemis	Luke	1		3	1					2	1			8		
Watertown	231	13	Bemis	Nathl	1	2	3	1					2				9		
Weston	106	14	Bemis	Nathl		1			1				1				3		
Watertown	231	8	Bemis	Seth	3		3	2				1	1	1			11		
Marlborough	187	18	Bender	Peter		1	1	1	1		1	1		1			7		
Framingham	78	13	Benj	Holdin	1			1		1				1			4		
Watertown	231	22	Benjamin	Saml			1	2						1			4		
Lexington	156	14	Benjamin	William	3			1		2			2	1			7		
Framingham	70	17	Bennet	Joseph	1	1	2			1		2	2				11		
Ashby	34	5	Bennet	Phinehas				1						1			2		
Sudbury	60	28	Bennet	Sarah									1				1		
Groton	208	18	Bennett	Ebenzr	2	1		1		1			1				6		

TOWN	PG#	LN#	LAST NAME	FIRST NAME	M <10	M 10-16	M 16-26	M 26-45	M 45+	F <10	F 10-16	F 16-26	F 26-45	F 45+	TOTAL ALL OTHER	TOTAL SLAVES	TOTALS	DISTRICT/ TOWNSHIP	NOTES
Charlestown	81	37	Bennett	Fra'			1										1		
Groton	208	9	Bennett	James				1					1				2		
Groton	208	17	Bennett	Jona		1	1			1							3		
Groton	208	10	Bennett	Thomas	2	1	1		1		1	1	1				8		
Groton	206	3	Bennett	Wm			1			2			1				4		
Concord	9	33	Benney	Elizabeth							2		1				3		
Newton	118	1	Benny	Jonathan	2		1		1			1		2			7		
Framingham	68	17	Benson	Abel											8		8		Stamped pg# was x'd out
Marlborough	189	39	Benson	Lydia									1				1		
Sudbury	61	29	Bent	Anna		2						1	1				4		
Marlborough	188	28	Bent	Jabez		1		1				1		2			5		
Framingham	70	14	Bent	John				1					1				2		
Sudbury	63	6	Bent	Jonathan	1	2	1	1		2	1	1	1				10		
Framingham	70	16	Bent	Matthias				1		1	1		1	1			5		
Marlborough	188	27	Bent	Peter			1	1				1					3		
East Sudbury	67	24	Bent	Rufus		1		1					1				3		
East Sudbury	65	9	Bent	William	3	2	1	1			1		2				10		
Framingham	70	15	Bent	John Jr		1		1				2	1		1		6		
Groton	208	22	Benteroth	Wm			1			1			1				3		
Reading	129	17	Beors	William	2	1		1		1	2		1				8		
Lincoln	14	11	Bernis	Phinehas	2			1		2			1				6		
Burlington	154	7	Berry	James		1	1	1		1	1		1				6		
East Sudbury	65	12	Berry	John				2					1				3		
Cambridge	220	16	Bettleship	Levis			2	2					1		1		6		
Chelmsford	168	18	Betty	John	1	1	1					1	1				5		
East Sudbury	66	28	Bevis	William				1					1				2		
Groton	206	4	Bigelow	Aaron			1	1		1			1				4		
Cambridge	220	26	Bigelow	Abel	1	1		1		3		2					8		
Sherburn	248	15	Bigelow	Convers	2	2	1		1	2		2	1				11		
Hollistown	236	16	Bigelow	Ephm	1	1	1	1		1			1				6		
Natick	245	3	Bigelow	Isaac	1		1			1		1					4		
Groton	206	15	Bigelow	Timothy Esq	3		1	2		1		3	1				11		
Natick	246	4	Bigelow	Wm		1		1		2	1	1	1				8		
Weston	106	6	Biglow	Alpheus	1	2		1		3	1		1				9		
Framingham	68	6	Biglow	Asaph				1			1	2	1				5		Stamped pg# was x'd out
Framingham	68	16	Biglow	Daniel	1	2		1		1	1		1				7		Stamped pg# was x'd out
Marlborough	194	28	Biglow	Ephraim				1			2		1				4		
Marlborough	190	24	Biglow	Gershom Jr	2			1		3	1		1				8		
Marlborough	194	27	Biglow	Gershom Jr	2	1			2	1		2		2			10		
Marlborough	190	34	Biglow	Ivory	1	2		1		1		3	1				9		
Sudbury	61	4	Biglow	Jacob		1	1	1				2	1				6		
Weston	106	5	Biglow	Josiah				1					1				2		
Weston	106	7	Biglow	Lucy			1			1	1	1	1	1			6		
Waltham	113	5	Biglow	Thomas	2		2	2		2		1	1				10		
Marlborough	189	28	Biglow	William	3	2		1		1			1				8		
Westford	179	19	Bignal	Saml	1			1		2			1				5		
Hopkinton	240	28	Bigsby	Abijah			1			1							3		
Hopkinton	240	25	Bigsby	Peletiah	1		1	1	1			1	1				6		
Marlborough	194	3	Bill	Elizabeth									2				2		
Acton	18	31	Billings	Ephraim	1	1		1		2			1				6		
Acton	18	30	Billings	James		1	1	1		1			1	1			6		
Weston	106	13	Billings	Jonas	4			1		2	1		1				9		
Lincoln	13	15	Billings	Jonathan B	1		1	1				1		1			5		
Lincoln	13	20	Billings	Joseph		1		1		1			1				4		
Lincoln	14	35	Billings	Joseph Jr	1	1		1		2	2		1				8		
Medford	99	34	Billings	Marah								1		1			2		
Lincoln	13	21	Billings	Nathan	1		2	1				1	1	1			7		
Lincoln	13	16	Billings	Timothy	1	1		1						1			4		
Charlestown	81	35	Bird	Comfort									1				1		
Watertown	231	21	Bird	Jona		2	1	1			1	2		1			8		
Charlestown	81	36	Bird	Jos'	3			1			1	1					6		
Pepperell	30	8	Birde	Wm	1	1		1		1	1		1				6		
Medford	99	38	Bishop	Abijh							1		1	1			3		
Medford	99	37	Bishop	Jno'	1	1		1	1		1	3	1				9		
Charlestown	81	34	Bispham	Wm	1			1		3			1				6		
Westford	179	16	Bixby	Asa			1		2				1				4		
Westford	179	17	Bixby	Asa Jr	1			1		1	2		1				6		
Framingham	68	11	Bixby	Sarah	1		1				1	2	1				6		Stamped pg# was x'd out
Cambridge	220	20	Blackington	Edward		1						1					2		
Cambridge	220	19	Blackington	Israel			1						2				3		
Cambridge	220	18	Blackington	Wm	1		1			2			1				5		
Watertown	231	25	Blackman	Andrew	2		1			2			1				6		
Charlestown	81	13	Blair	Jno'				1					1				2		
Chelmsford	168	19	Blaizdel	Aaron	3	1		1		2			1				8		
Chelmsford	168	17	Blaizdel	Henry	2			1		2	1		1				7		
Westford	179	15	Blake	Caleb	1	4		1		1		1	1	1	1		11		
Newton	117	7	Blake	Joseph			2	3	1		1	3	3	1			14		
Cambridge	220	15	Blake	Oliver			1						1				2		
Littleton	205	2	Blanchard	Abigail	1	1	3			2		1	1				9		
Medford	99	11	Blanchard	Andr'	2	1		1		1	1		1				7		

TOWN	PG#	LN#	LAST NAME	FIRST NAME	M under 10	M 10 to 16	M 16 to 26	M 26 to 45	M 45 and over	F under 10	F 10 to 16	F 16 to 26	F 26 to 45	F 45 and over	TOTAL ALL OTHER	TOTAL SLAVES	TOTALS	DISTRICT/ TOWNSHIP	NOTES
Burlington	154	4	Blanchard	Benjamin	2		1	1		1	1	1	1				8		
Dracut	49	5	Blanchard	Caleb	2	2		1		2			1	1			9		
Medford	99	15	Blanchard	Caleb	1	1	2	1		4	1	1	1				12		
Burlington	154	6	Blanchard	David	2				1	1	1	1	1				7		
Medford	99	7	Blanchard	Hezh					2			1	1		1		5		
Charlestown	81	2	Blanchard	Hezk	3	2		1		3			1				10		
Charlestown	81	1	Blanchard	Joshua	4		1						1				6		
Chelmsford	167	2	Blanchard	Joshua	1	1		1		2		1	1				7		
Burlington	154	5	Blanchard	Josiah	1			1		2			1				5		
Groton	208	12	Blanchard	Nathl	2			1			1		1	1			6		
Medford	99	29	Blanchard	Rebecca							1			1			2		
Medford	99	30	Blanchard	Rebecca Jr.	2	1					1		1				5		
Dracut	49	6	Blanchard	Saml				1						1			2		
Charlestown	79	23	Blanchard	Simon	1		2	2		3			1	1			10		
Malden	93	18	Blanchard	Sylvanus		2		1					1	1			5		
Medford	99	32	Blanchard	Sylvas	2		3	1		1			1	1			9		
Medford	99	31	Blanchard	Tabatha									1				1		
Wilmington	140	4	Blanchard	William	2		3		2			1		1			9		
Billerica	174	10	Blanchard	Fra'			1					1					2		
Billerica	174	8	Blanchard	Isaac	2	1		1		1	2		1				8		
Billerica	174	7	Blanchard	Jerem'	2	1		1					1				5		
Billerica	174	9	Blanchard	Joseph		1			1	3				1			6		
Billerica	174	5	Blanchard	Saml'					1	1			1	1			4		
Billerica	174	6	Blanchard	Saml' Jr	2	2			1			1	4	1			11		
Newton	117	15	Blandon	Abigail	2					1		1	1	1			6		
Newton	117	13	Blandon	Jonas	2	2		1		1		1	1				8		
Newton	117	14	Blandon	Phinehas			1						1				2		
Malden	93	29	Blany	Andros	1		1					1					3		
Malden	93	30	Blany	Benja'			1		1					1			3		
Malden	93	31	Blany	Benja' Jr			1			1		1					3		
Carlisle	21	4	Blasdel	William	2	1		1		2	1		1	1			9		
Watertown	231	26	Blaver	Wm			1						1				2		
Watertown	231	27	Blay	Thos H.			1			3			1	1			6		
Cambridge	220	37	Bliss	Eli	3		1		2	1			2				9		
Cambridge	220	32	Bliss	Theordore				1					1				2		
Tyngsborough	42	3	Blodget	Ezra	1	1		1		4	1	1					10		
Townsend	25	21	Blodget	Jacob			2		1		2			2			7		
Westford	179	18	Blodget	Jonas		3		1		3	1		1				9		
Malden	93	14	Blodget	Phins	1			1		2			1				5		
Sherburn	248	6	Blodget	Saml				1						1			2		
Chelmsford	168	1	Blodget	Simeon				1						1			2		
Chelmsford	168	2	Blodget	Simeon Jr			1	1					1				3		
Tyngsborough	42	2	Blodget	Thaddeus	4			1		1	1	1					8		
Tyngsborough	42	1	Blodget	William	1	1		1		1	1		1				6		
Bedford	161	12	Blodgett	Aaron	1			1		1		1					4		
Lexington	156	4	Blodgett	Isaac		1		1		1	1		1	1			6		
Lexington	156	5	Blodgett	Isaac Jr		1	1					1					3		
Lexington	156	15	Blodgett	James	2	1		1		3		1					9		
Dunstable	216	1	Blodgett	Josiah			2		1		1			1			5		
Lexington	156	9	Blodgett	Nathan	4		1		1	1		1	1				9		
Dunstable	216	2	Blodgett	Zebulon	1	1			1	1		1	1	1			7		
Tyngsborough	40	8	Bloghet	Nehem			1	1					1				3		
Westford	179	8	Blood	Aaron				1				2		1			4		
Pepperell	30	14	Blood	Abigail										2			2		
Dracut	45	3	Blood	Abraham	1	1	1	1	1			1	4	1			11		
Westford	179	7	Blood	Amaziah		1	1		1	2		1		1			7		
Dunstable	216	7	Blood	Caleb					1	1	2	2	1				7		
Groton	206	6	Blood	Caleb		1	1			1	1	2		1			8		
Dunstable	216	8	Blood	Caleb Jr			2			1			1				4		
Carlisle	22	33	Blood	David		1	1		1			1		1			5		
Pepperell	30	9	Blood	David			1		1			2		1			5		
Pepperell	30	29	Blood	David Jr			1					1					2		
Groton	208	15	Blood	Eben	1			1		2			1				5		
Pepperell	30	13	Blood	Edm		1		1	1	1			1				5		
Westford	179	9	Blood	Eleazer				1					1				2		
Townsend	26	5	Blood	Ezra	1			1		1			1				4		
Carlisle	23	12	Blood	Frederick			1			2		1	1				5		
Dunstable	216	9	Blood	Henry	1	1	1	1		1		1	1				7		
Groton	208	5	Blood	Henry	2			1		3			1				7		
Pepperell	30	10	Blood	Isaac	2	2	1	1		1	1	1	1				10		
Concord	10	35	Blood	James	2			1		1			1	1			6		
Groton	208	2	Blood	James			1		1				1	2			5		
Pepperell	30	12	Blood	John		2		1		1		1	1				6		
Pepperell	30	28	Blood	Jona		3	1			1		1		1			7		
Townsend	28	44	Blood	Jona	1		1			1		1					4		
Groton	208	11	Blood	Jona	3	1		1		1			1				7		
Carlisle	22	2	Blood	Jonas			1							1			2		
Groton	206	8	Blood	Jonas			1		1			1		1			4		
Carlisle	23	13	Blood	Jonathan			3	2	1			2		1			9		

TOWN	PG#	LN#	LAST NAME	FIRST NAME	FREE WHITE MALES					FREE WHITE FEMALES					TOTAL ALL OTHER	TOTAL SLAVES	TOTALS	DISTRICT/ TOWNSHIP	NOTES
					under 10	10 to 16	16 to 26	26 to 45	45 and over	under 10	10 to 16	16 to 26	26 to 45	45 and over					
Townsend	25	19	Blood	Joseph	1		1			1		1					4		
Tyngsborough	40	9	Blood	Joseph		1		1		3			2	1			8		
Pepperell	30	19	Blood	Joshua			3		1			1		1			6		
Shirley	213	9	Blood	Josiah				1					1				2		
Concord	11	1	Blood	Jotham				1		2		1					4		
Groton	208	3	Blood	Levi			1	1		1		1		1			5		
Pepperell	30	11	Blood	Moses			2		1		1			2			6		
Groton	208	4	Blood	Oliver					1					1			2		
Stow	197	24	Blood	Oliver				1					1	1			4		
Groton	206	10	Blood	Oliver 3rd			2						1				4		
Groton	206	5	Blood	Oliver Jr			1		1	2				1			5		
Dunstable	216	6	Blood	Peter	3		1		1	1	1	1	1				9		
Carlisle	23	15	Blood	Phinehas	2		1							2			6		
Pepperell	30	15	Blood	Robert				1						1			2		
Groton	208	13	Blood	Royal	3	1		1				1		1			7		
Pepperell	30	30	Blood	Saml	3		1		1	1	1			1			8		
Carlisle	23	16	Blood	Sarah										1			1		
Groton	208	6	Blood	Shattuck					1					1			2		
Groton	208	7	Blood	Shattuck Jr		1		1					1				3		
Dunstable	216	5	Blood	Silas	3	1			1	1			1	1			8		
Carlisle	23	9	Blood	Stephen			1			1		1	1				4		
Groton	206	11	Blood	Thomas			1					1					2		
Pepperell	30	4	Blood	Timo	1		1			1		1					4		
Concord	10	34	Blood	Timothy			1					1					2		
Concord	10	33	Blood	Willard				1				1					2		
Groton	208	19	Blood	Wm	1			1	1	1		1					5		
Pepperell	30	16	Blood	Wm	1	1			1	1				1			5		
Carlisle	23	14	Blood	Zebulon			1	1				1					3		
Cambridge	220	14	Boardman	Aaron				1		1	2	1	1				6		
Cambridge	220	29	Boardman	Richard				1		1	1	1					4		
Cambridge	220	13	Boardman	William	1			1		1			1				4		
Natick	245	14	Boden	Wm		1			2	1		1		1			6		
Charlestown	81	33	Bodge	Henry	1		1			1			1				4		
Charlestown	79	15	Bodge	Nath		1	1						1				3		
Reading	129	20	Bodger	Benjamin	1		1	1				1	1				5		
Sudbury	57	9	Bogie	Rowand			1	1	1	1			1	1			6		
Weston	106	12	Bogle	William	1		1	1	1				1	1			6		
Waltham	113	6	Boles	John		2	4		1		1	2	1		1		12		
Shirley	213	7	Bolton	Timothy	1			1		1			1				4		
Shirley	213	6	Bolton	Wm			1		1				1	1			4		
Hollistown	236	7	Bond	Aaron				1			1			1			3		
Hollistown	236	8	Bond	Aaron Jr	2		1	1		1	2	1					8		
Watertown	231	11	Bond	Amos			3		1				5	1			10		
Watertown	231	14	Bond	Charles	3		3	1		1	1		1				10		
Watertown	231	12	Bond	Daniel				1		2			1	1			5		
Weston	106	2	Bond	Henry				1						2			3		
Marlborough	188	38	Bond	John	1	1				2							6		
Billerica	174	4	Bond	Jona'	1	1	1	1					1	1			6		
Woburn	148	5	Bond	Joseph	1	2	1				1		1	1			8		
Watertown	231	20	Bond	Leonard				4					1	2			7		
Concord	5	30	Bond	Martha										1			1		
East Sudbury	65	11	Bond	Nathan	1			1		4			1				7		
East Sudbury	65	10	Bond	Phinehas				1	1				1				3		
Watertown	231	24	Bond	Susannah		1	1					1	1	1			5		
Charlestown	81	32	Bond	Wm		2			1	1	1			1			6		
Watertown	231	16	Bond	Wm	1	1	1	1	1	2	1		1	1			10		
Cambridge	220	27	Bonner	George	1			1		2	1						5		
Tewksbury	49	15	Bookman	Edward				1		2			1				4		
Tewksbury	49	16	Bookman	Jona	2	1		1		2			1				7		
Charlestown	79	20	Bootman	Jno'				1									1		
Tyngsborough	40	10	Bootman	Thos	4			1		1			1				7		
Reading	129	27	Bordman	Aaron		1	2	1					1	1			6		
Reading	127	9	Bordman	Amos	2	1	3		1	1	2	2		1			13		
Reading	129	28	Bordman	Ivery			1						1				2		
Medford	99	28	Bosquet	Jno' L.			1			1		1					3		
Charlestown	81	4	Boston	Peter	1			1					1				3		
Reading	128	8	Bouttell	James		1	1		1	1		1		3			9		
Reading	128	9	Bouttell	James Jr				1		1		1					3		
Wilmington	140	15	Bouttell	Jonathan			2		1	1				1			5		
Wilmington	141	8	Bouttell	Jonathan Jr	2			1					1				4		
Townsend	25	22	Boutwell	John				1				1		1			3		
Townsend	29	43	Boutwell	Silas			1			1			1				3		
Billerica	173	19	Bowars	Benja'	3	2	1		1			1	1	1			10		
Billerica	173	18	Bowars	Jon'		1	1	1					1	1			5		
Billerica	173	21	Bowars	Jona' Jr			1	1			1	1	1	1			6		
Chelmsford	167	3	Bowars	Luke	2	1		1		2			1				7		
Chelmsford	168	5	Bowars	Phillip	1			1					1				3		
Billerica	173	20	Bowars	Saml	1	3	2		1	2	2	1					13		
Billerica	173	17	Bowars	Wm		1			1					1			3		

TOWN	PG#	LN#	LAST NAME	FIRST NAME	FREE WHITE MALES					FREE WHITE FEMALES					TOTAL ALL OTHER	TOTAL SLAVES	TOTALS	DISTRICT/ TOWNSHIP	NOTES
					under 10	10 to 16	16 to 26	26 to 45	45 and over	under 10	10 to 16	16 to 26	26 to 45	45 and over					
Chelmsford	168	3	Bowars	Wm			2		1	1				1			5		
Dracut	47	32	Bowen	John	2		1	1		2	1	1		1			9		
Concord	6	22	Bowen	William	1	1	1	1				1					5		
Groton	208	8	Bowern	Isaac			1	1		1		1		1			5		
Pepperell	30	31	Bowers	Azubah						2		1					3		
Pepperell	30	26	Bowers	John			1		1					2			4		
Littleton	202	25	Bowers	Lucy	2					1	1	1					5		
Townsend	25	14	Bowers	Sarah		1	1					1	1	1			5		
Hopkinton	240	10	Bowker	Abiether	1		1	1		1	1		1	1			7		
Hopkinton	240	11	Bowker	Asa	1		2	1		2			1	5			12		
Sudbury	62	30	Bowker	Daniel	1		3	1	1	1		2		1			10		
Hopkinton	240	9	Bowker	John	2	2		1		1		1	1				8		
Hopkinton	240	8	Bowker	Uriah	1	1	1	1		1			3				8		
Billerica	174	12	Bowman	Abel		2	1	1		1	1	2	1				9		
Concord	8	9	Bowman	Edmond				1						1			2		
Lexington	156	11	Bowman	Francis	1	1		1		1		1					5		
Marlborough	189	37	Boyd	William		1	2		1			2		2			8		
Weston	106	18	Boyles	Daniel			1			3			1				5		
Charlestown	81	40	Boylston	Richd			1	2			1	1	1				6		
Westford	179	12	Boynton	Abel	1		2		1	1	1	3		1			10		
Pepperell	30	17	Boynton	Abijah		1	2		1			1		1			6		
Pepperell	30	18	Boynton	Abijah Jr			1					1					2		
Groton	208	16	Boynton	Calvin	2		1	1		1		1					6		
Pepperell	30	27	Boynton	Isaac		1	3	1						1			6		
Westford	179	10	Boynton	Josiah			2		1		1	2		1			7		
Westford	179	11	Boynton	Josiah Jr	2	1			1			1	1				6		
Westford	179	22	Boynton	Luther	2			1		2	1		1				7		
Groton	208	1	Br*er	James Esq	1	1	2		1			1	1	1			8		
Acton	18	35	Brabook	Benjamin		1		1				1		1			4		
Acton	19	7	Brabook	Joseph		1			1	1				1			4		
Littleton	202	23	Bracket	Samuel	2	1	1		1	2			1				8		
East Sudbury	65	8	Bracket	William	2	2		1		2	1		1				9		
Weston	106	9	Brackett	David	1	1			1	1		1	1	1			8		
Weston	106	10	Brackett	Ebenezer	2	1	1		1	3	1	1	1				11		
East Sudbury	69	3	Brackett	John	2	1		1		2			1				7		
Framingham	74	3	Brackett	Solomon	2			1		2			1				6		
Malden	93	4	Bradbury	Cha'	1		1			1		1					4		
Medford	99	5	Bradbury	Wm	1			1		2			1				5		
Malden	93	3	Bradbury	Wymond			2		1			2		1			6		
Charlestown	81	16	Bradish	Catha'										2			2		
Cambridge	220	25	Bradish	William	1			1		1		4		1			8		
Dracut	44	3	Bradley	Amos			1	2			1	1	1				6		
Dracut	44	2	Bradley	Amos Jr	5	1	1	1		1	2		1				12		
Dracut	44	6	Bradley	Isaac		1		1	1		2	1		1			7		
Dracut	44	7	Bradley	Isaac Jr	1	1	1	1		1			2				7		
Dracut	44	5	Bradley	Joseph	1			1		2			1	1			6		
Dracut	44	4	Bradley	Joshua	3		1	1		2			1	1			9		
Charlestown	81	3	Bradshaw	Lois							1			1			2		
Charlestown	81	29	Bradshaw	Tho'	1	1		1		2			1				6		
Medford	99	12	Bradshaw	Tho'	1				1					1			3		
Billerica	174	22	Bradstreet	Elijah	2			1		4		1	1				9		
Charlestown	79	22	Bradstreet	Saml		1		1		1		2	1		2		8		
Billerica	174	11	Bratten	Mary								1		1			2		
Cambridge	220	31	Brattle	Thos	1	2			1			2					6		
Charlestown	81	27	Brazier	Abigl								1	1				2		
Charlestown	79	21	Brazier	Tho'	2			1					1				4		
Marlborough	193	13	Bread	Ephraim				1				1		1			3		
Charlestown	79	18	Breed	Ebenz			2		2	1	1	1					8		
Concord	3	5	Breed	John C	1			1					1				3		
Malden	93	5	Breed	Nathan	1			1		2			1				5		
Malden	93	7	Breeden	John			1			2		1					4		
Charlestown	81	12	Breelat	Jno'	1		1						1				3		
Framingham	68	2	Brewer	David	3	2	3		1	1			1	1			12		Stamped pg# was x'd out
Framingham	74	6	Brewer	Jason			1			2	2		1				6		
Malden	93	6	Briant	John			1				1		1				3		
Hollistown	236	12	Briant	Jona	1		1					1					3		
Charlestown	81	20	Briant	Timo'	1			1		1			1				4		
Sherburn	248	14	Brick	Daniel	1			1		5			1				8		
Sherburn	248	21	Brick	John			1	1						1			3		
Hollistown	236	15	Brick	Jona				1		1			1				3		
Sherburn	248	19	Brick	Jona	1	1	1				1			3			7		
Sherburn	248	20	Brick	Thos	2		1	1					1				5		
Sherburn	249	3	Brickford	James			1	1		1		1	1				5		
Hollistown	236	13	Bridge	Benjm			1	1					1				3		
Chelmsford	167	7	Bridge	Ebenz			1	1				3	1				6		
Watertown	231	15	Bridge	Jeremiah	1			1		2			1				5		
Chelmsford	168	20	Bridge	Joanna								2	1			3		
Lexington	156	6	Bridge	John			1			1							2		
Lexington	156	7	Bridge	Jonas	3		1	1		2	2		1	1	1		12		
Lexington	156	10	Bridge	Jonathan	1	1		1		1	2		1	1			8		

TOWN	PG#	LN#	HEADS OF HOUSEHOLD		FREE WHITE MALES					FREE WHITE FEMALES					TOTAL ALL OTHER	TOTAL SLAVES	TOTALS	DISTRICT/ TOWNSHIP	NOTES
			LAST NAME	FIRST NAME	under 10	10 to 16	16 to 26	26 to 45	45 and over	under 10	10 to 16	16 to 26	26 to 45	45 and over					
East Sudbury	67	7	Bridge	Josiah		1	1	2	1			2		1			8		
Charlestown	79	16	Bridge	Mary										1			1		
Waltham	112	13	Bridge	Mary		1		1					1	1			4		
Charlestown	81	28	Bridge	Mathew	1		3		1		1	2	1				9		
Hollistown	236	21	Bridge	Nathan	1		1				1						3		
Billerica	174	26	Bridge	Saml	2	1	1	1			1	1	1				8		
Waltham	112	14	Bridge	William			1			4	1		1				7		
Chelmsford	168	15	Bridge	Wm	1		3		1			1		1			7		
Billerica	174	28	Bridge for Lela	Saml			46	40	3								89		
Charlestown	79	17	Brigden	Micah			1			1			1	1			4		
Hopkinton	240	21	Briggs	Philip	1	1	1		1					1			5		
Marlborough	190	6	Brigham	Aaron	1			1		1	2		1				6		
Sudbury	63	27	Brigham	Abijah	1		1	1	1			2		1			7		
Marlborough	188	32	Brigham	Abner	2			1		1		1	1				6		
Marlborough	190	12	Brigham	Asa			1	1						2			4		
Marlborough	189	36	Brigham	Ashbel S.	1			1					1				3		
Marlborough	190	35	Brigham	Caleb			2		1				1				4		
Marlborough	193	19	Brigham	Daniel	4	2		1		1	1	1	1				11		
Marlborough	193	18	Brigham	Elizabeth						1		1		1			3		
Marlborough	192	1	Brigham	Ephraim	3	1		2		1		2					9		
Marlborough	190	15	Brigham	Fortunalus	2	1		1		1	1	1	2	2			11		
Marlborough	190	14	Brigham	Ithamer	3	2	1	1		1			1				9		
Marlborough	191	13	Brigham	Ivory				1				1					2		
Sudbury	59	11	Brigham	Jesse		2	1	1		2			1				7		
Sudbury	61	35	Brigham	John			3		1	1	4			1			10		
Marlborough	194	18	Brigham	John G.	2	1	1		1	1			1				7		
Marlborough	188	40	Brigham	Joseph					1		1	1					3		
Sudbury	63	34	Brigham	Joseph	1			2		2			1				6		
Marlborough	187	15	Brigham	Joseph Jr	1		2	1		3		2					9		
Marlborough	188	8	Brigham	Jotham	2	1		1		1	1		1				7		
Marlborough	190	13	Brigham	Lewis		1			1	2			1				5		
Marlborough	188	33	Brigham	Mary				1						1			2		
Marlborough	189	11	Brigham	Mattathias R.			1	1					1				3		
Marlborough	189	12	Brigham	Noah					1		1			1			3		
Marlborough	188	31	Brigham	Paul	3	2		1			1		1				8		
Waltham	112	10	Brigham	Saml	1	1		1				1					4		
Sudbury	63	36	Brigham	Samuel			1		1	1	1	2		1			7		
Marlborough	194	19	Brigham	Sarah								1		1			2		
Marlborough	191	12	Brigham	Solomon	1			1	2	5			2				11		
Stow	196	7	Brigham	Timothy					1					1			2		
Marlborough	188	39	Brigham	Warren		1		1		1		1	1	1			6		
Marlborough	193	17	Brigham	Zedidiah		1		1		4			1				7		
Watertown	231	7	Bright	Francis	1			1		1		1					4		
Waltham	112	6	Bright	John	2	2	2		1	2			1	1			11		
Watertown	231	19	Bright	Joseph	2	3	1	1		2	1	1	1				12		
Watertown	231	6	Bright	Moses	2			1		2			2				7		
Watertown	231	5	Bright	Nathan			1	1					1	1			4		
Watertown	231	18	Bright	Rachel							1	1					2		
Hopkinton	240	14	Brigsby	Joel	3			1					2				6		
Tyngsborough	41	2	Brindley	Nathl		2	1		1			1		1			6		
Charlestown	81	17	Brinkley	Jno'	1			1		2			1				5		
Malden	93	22	Brintnal	Rebecca										1			1		
Natick	245	4	Broad	Hezekh	1			1	1	1		1	1	1			7		
Natick	245	11	Broad	Moses	2			1	1	1			1				6		
Natick	245	10	Broad	Thos		1	2	2	2			1		1			9		
Billerica	174	14	Bromfield	John					1	1	2	1	1				6		
Concord	10	26	Brook	Asa	2		2		1	1	1	1	1				9		
Lincoln	15	22	Brook	Timothy		1			2			1		1			5		
Lincoln	15	24	Brook	Timothy Jr			1	1					1				3		
Lincoln	13	23	Brook	Daniel	2	1	1	1		2	1	1	1				10		
Concord	10	25	Brook	Samuel		1		1	1		1		1	1			6		
Lincoln	13	32	Brooks	Aaron			1	1	1			1					4		
Concord	10	24	Brooks	Abel		1		1		1			1				4		
Medford	99	27	Brooks	Abigl										1			1		
Stow	198	5	Brooks	Amos			1	1		2			1	1			6		
Medford	99	21	Brooks	Caleb			1		2			2	1	2			8		
Medford	99	23	Brooks	Caleb 3rd				1									1		
Medford	99	22	Brooks	Caleb Jr				1		1			1				3		
Boxborough	200	6	Brooks	Calvin	1			1		1			2				5		
Acton	16	25	Brooks	Daniel		1			1				1	1			4		
Concord	4	27	Brooks	Ebenezer		1							1				2		
Lincoln	15	25	Brooks	Eleazer		1	1		1				2	2			7		
Townsend	25	9	Brooks	Elit		1					1		1	1			4		
Lincoln	13	26	Brooks	Hannah									1	1			2		
Lincoln	13	22	Brooks	John					1				1	1			3		
Medford	99	20	Brooks	John		2		1			1	2					6		
Medford	99	24	Brooks	Jona'	2			1		1			1	1			6		
Acton	16	24	Brooks	Jonas		1		1	1			1	1	2			7		
Pepperell	30	25	Brooks	Jonas	2	1		1		3			1		1		9		

TOWN	PG#	LN#	LAST NAME	FIRST NAME	FREE WHITE MALES under 10	10 to 16	16 to 26	26 to 45	45 and over	FREE WHITE FEMALES under 10	10 to 16	16 to 26	26 to 45	45 and over	TOTAL ALL OTHER	TOTAL SLAVES	TOTALS	DISTRICT/TOWNSHIP	NOTES
Acton	17	3	Brooks	Joseph			1	1	1			1	1	1			6		
Woburn	148	2	Brooks	Joseph	4	1		1		1			1	1			9		
Lincoln	13	25	Brooks	Joshua	1	2	2		1	3	1	1	1				12		
Lincoln	13	29	Brooks	Levi	3		1	1		1	1		2	1			10		
Westford	179	13	Brooks	Lois								1		1			2		
Stow	197	16	Brooks	Luke		1		2	1		1	1		1			7		
Westford	179	14	Brooks	Lydia									1	1			2		
Medford	99	26	Brooks	Mary			1					1		1			3		
Littleton	203	18	Brooks	Matthew	1	1	1		2			3		2			10		
Acton	19	5	Brooks	Nathan	2			1					1				4		
Stow	197	7	Brooks	Nathan	2	1	1	1		2	2		1				10		
Woburn	148	6	Brooks	Nathaniel		1	1	2				1		1			6		
Lincoln	13	24	Brooks	Noah	1	1	1					1	1				6		
Acton	18	28	Brooks	Paul			2	1					1	1			5		
Medford	99	25	Brooks	Peter C.	4			1		1			1	1	1		9		
Charlestown	81	24	Brooks	Pomp											5		5		
Townsend	25	10	Brooks	Saml	2	2		1		1			1				7		
Acton	19	4	Brooks	Seth			2		1		1	1		1			6		
Shirley	213	10	Brooks	Sewell	1		1						1				3		
Concord	4	22	Brooks	Susanna		1				3	1		1				6		
Charlestown	81	23	Brooks	Tho'	1	3	1	1	1	2	2	1	1				13		
Waltham	113	1	Brown	*		1	1		1		1		1	1			6		
Littleton	203	25	Brown	Abel			1				1		1				3		
Sudbury	62	35	Brown	Abel	1		1			2	1		1				6		
Concord	4	6	Brown	Abel	1	1		1		3			1				7		
Concord	3	6	Brown	Abel Jr	2			1		3	1		1				8		
Lincoln	12	10	Brown	Abjah				1						1			2		
Watertown	231	17	Brown	Adam	1	1		1				3	1				7		
Waltham	112	4	Brown	Amos Jr	2			1		1			1				5		
Framingham	68	3	Brown	Andrew			2	1				1		1			5		Stamped pg# was x'd out
Lexington	156	8	Brown	Benjamin				1			1		1	1			4		
Reading	127	8	Brown	Benjamin				1					2	1	1		4		
Stow	197	26	Brown	Benjamin	2			1	1				1				5		
Stow	198	42	Brown	Benjamin Jr	1		1			2			2				6		
Sudbury	59	23	Brown	Caleb	3			1		2	1		1				8		
Concord	11	2	Brown	Charles		1		1	1	1	1		1				6		
Acton	16	30	Brown	Daniel				1					1				2		
Ashby	34	6	Brown	Daniel	1	2		1		2			1	1			8		
Cambridge	220	33	Brown	Daniel			1	1			1	3					6		
Lincoln	13	38	Brown	Daniel		1		1	1			1		1			5		
Shirley	213	15	Brown	Daniel G.			1		1	1		1	1	1			6		
Concord	4	9	Brown	David		1	1	1	1			2	2	2			10		
Marlborough	190	20	Brown	Delivarance	1			1	1				1	1			5		
Stow	198	14	Brown	Desire		1				2			1				4		
Framingham	68	4	Brown	Ebenezer	3			1		2	1		1				8		Stamped pg# was x'd out
Newton	117	12	Brown	Ebenezer	1			1		1			1				4		
Cambridge	220	36	Brown	Ebenr		1	1	1		2	1	1	1				8		
Bedford	161	10	Brown	Edward			1			1		1					3		
Boxborough	199	26	Brown	Edward				1					1				2		
Woburn	148	9	Brown	Edward		2		1		2			1				6		
Sherburn	248	13	Brown	Elijah		2		1						1			4		
Sudbury	59	19	Brown	Elinor	1									1			3		
Tyngsborough	40	12	Brown	Elisha			1						1				2		
Concord	6	2	Brown	Ephraim	1			1		4	1		1				8		
Lincoln	14	16	Brown	Ephraim	1	2	1	1		2		1	1				9		
Stoneham	138	8	Brown	Ephraim			1		2			1		1			5		
Hollistown	236	14	Brown	Ezra	2		1	1		1	1		1				7		
Charlestown	81	7	Brown	Farwel			1					1					2		
Lincoln	14	17	Brown	Hannah		1	3					1		2			7		
Sudbury	58	10	Brown	Hopestill	1	1		1		1		1					5		
Sudbury	63	12	Brown	Hopestill	2	1		1	1	1	1		1	1			9		
Marlborough	191	35	Brown	Isaac	2			1		1		1	1				6		
Stow	196	15	Brown	Isaac				1		1	1			1			4		
Stow	195	22	Brown	Jabez				1			1		1				3		
Wilmington	140	5	Brown	Jabez		2		1		1			1				5		
Concord	7	6	Brown	Jacob		1		1	1				1				4		
Concord	3	17	Brown	James		1	3	2				1		1			8		
Lexington	156	12	Brown	James	1	1	2	1		1	1		1				8		
Lexington	156	13	Brown	James Jr			1	1		1			1	1			5		
Reading	128	7	Brown	Jepththap				1				1		1			3		
Reading	127	7	Brown	Jeremiah	2		2	1			1	1	1	1			8		
Concord	6	20	Brown	Jesse					1			2		1			4		
Stow	196	20	Brown	Jishua		1	1	1						1			4		
Billerica	173	11	Brown	John		3	1		1		1		1	1			8		
Cambridge	220	28	Brown	John			1	1		2			1				5		
Carlisle	21	28	Brown	John	3			1		3			1				8		
Reading	127	6	Brown	John		1		1					1				3		
Sudbury	59	25	Brown	John	3			1		1	3		1				9		
Sudbury	59	20	Brown	Jonas	2		1	1		1			1				6		
Waltham	113	3	Brown	Jonas			1	1		2			2	1			7		

TOWN	PG#	LN#	LAST NAME	FIRST NAME	M under 10	M 10 to 16	M 16 to 26	M 26 to 45	M 45 and over	F under 10	F 10 to 16	F 16 to 26	F 26 to 45	F 45 and over	TOTAL ALL OTHER	TOTAL SLAVES	TOTALS	DISTRICT/TOWNSHIP	NOTES
Tewksbury	49	6	Brown	Jonathan		1	2	1	1	1		1		1			8		
Charlestown	81	5	Brown	Jos'			2		1					1			4		
Acton	18	3	Brown	Joseph	4	1	1		1	1		1	1				10		
Tewksbury	49	4	Brown	Joseph	1			1		2		1	1				6		
Waltham	112	9	Brown	Joseph				1						1			2		
Woburn	148	8	Brown	Joseph			1	1	1		1		1	2			7		
Shirley	213	13	Brown	Joseph Dea.	1		1		2	1	1	1		2			9		
Stow	197	21	Brown	Josiah		1	3		1	1	1	1	1	2			11		
Woburn	148	7	Brown	Josiah	1		1		1	2	1			1			7		
Billerica	173	13	Brown	Mary									1	1			2		
Newton	117	8	Brown	Molly										1			1		
Billerica	173	10	Brown	Nath'			1						1	2			4		
Billerica	173	14	Brown	Nath' Jr			1						3				4		
Bedford	161	13	Brown	Nathan				1				1		1			3		
Bedford	161	11	Brown	Nathaniel		1	1			1			1				4		
Reading	129	26	Brown	Nathaniel			1						1				2		
Waltham	112	3	Brown	Nathaniel		2	1			1		1					5		
Billerica	174	29	Brown	Nathl Jr			1							2			3		
Charlestown	81	6	Brown	Nich'	1			1		2		1					5		
Dracut	45	10	Brown	Osgood	2			1		1		1					5		
Concord	8	27	Brown	Paul				1									1		
East Sudbury	69	7	Brown	Rebeckah						1		1					2		
Concord	6	29	Brown	Reuben	1	2	2	1	1			1		2			10		
Concord	9	13	Brown	Roger		1	3		2	1	2			1			10		
Chelmsford	167	6	Brown	Saml		1		1		1		1					4		
Medford	99	14	Brown	Saml			1			1		1					3		
Tewksbury	49	5	Brown	Saml			1	1	1	1	1	1					6		
Billerica	173	12	Brown	Saml'	1	1				3							6		
Carlisle	22	20	Brown	Samuel		1	1					1					3		
Concord	7	16	Brown	Samuel	2	3		1	1		1	2		3			13		
Marlborough	189	2	Brown	Samuel	2			1		1	1		1				6		
Sudbury	59	26	Brown	Samuel	2		1		1	1	1		1	1			8		
Lincoln	14	15	Brown	Sarah									1	2			3		
Townsend	25	13	Brown	Sarah										1			1		
Littleton	205	3	Brown	Stephen	3		1	1					1				6		
Billerica	173	15	Brown	Tho'	2	2		1				1		1			7		
Charlestown	81	8	Brown	Tho'				1					1				2		
Billerica	173	16	Brown	Tho' Jr	3	1		1		1	1		1				8		
Weston	106	16	Brown	Thomas	1		1	1		1			1				5		
Dracut	45	12	Brown	Timothy	1			1				1		1			4		
Acton	19	18	Brown	Timothy	1	1		1		1	1	1					6		
East Sudbury	67	8	Brown	William				1		1		2					4		
Sudbury	59	24	Brown	William	2	3		1				1	1				8		
Sudbury	59	17	Brown	William Jr			2					1					3		
Natick	246	1	Brown	Wm		1	1		1			1	1	2			7		
Tewksbury	49	3	Brown	Wm			1	2		1	1	1	1		1		8		
Tewksbury	49	2	Brown	Wm Jr	1			1		1	2		2				7		
Ashby	34	3	Brown	Zach		1	1	1		2	1	1	1				8		
Concord	4	14	Brown	Zachariah	2		1					1					4		
Marlborough	191	5	Bruce	Daniel	2	1		1		3	1		1				9		
Hopkinton	240	13	Bruce	Elisha	1			1						1			3		
Marlborough	188	26	Bruce	James				1			1			1			3		
Woburn	148	12	Bruce	James			1						1				2		
Woburn	148	10	Bruce	John				2									2		
Woburn	148	11	Bruce	John Jr.		1		1		1	1		1				5		
Groton	208	21	Bruce	Jonas			1			1		1					3		
Marlborough	191	41	Bruce	Jonathan	4	1		1		2			1				9		
Marlborough	191	24	Bruce	Moses	1		1						1				3		
Marlborough	191	18	Bruce	Nathaniel		1	1						1	1			4		
Marlborough	194	10	Bruce	Osaoah	3	1	1	1		2	1		1				10		
Townsend	25	20	Bruce	Stephen	1		1	1				1	1				5		
Marlborough	191	17	Bruce	William				1		1		1		1			4		
Marlborough	191	16	Bruce	Zeduthun			1			1			1				3		
Stoneham	138	4	Bryant	Ebenezer	2			1		1	1		1				6		
Stoneham	138	3	Bryant	Elias	1	1		2		2	1	1	1				9		
Reading	127	11	Bryant	Jeremiah		1		1						1			3		
Reading	128	1	Bryant	Jeremiah Jr		1	1	1				1		1			5		
East Sudbury	65	7	Bryant	Joel	1		1	1		1			1	2			7		
Natick	245	15	Bryant	Jona	2		1		1	2			1				7		
Stoneham	138	1	Bryant	Joseph				1						2			3		
Stoneham	138	2	Bryant	Joseph Jr	1			1			1		1		1		5		
Reading	128	3	Bryant	Nathan	2	1		1		1	1						6		
Sudbury	59	33	Bryant	Nathaniel				1						1			2		
Concord	3	7	Bryant	Reuben	1		1	1				1	1				5		
Reading	129	19	Bryant	Thomas		1	1			1			1				4		
Reading	128	2	Bryant	Timothy		1		1					1	1			4		
Waltham	113	7	Buchanan	James	1			1		1			1	1			5		
Wilmington	140	9	Buck	Ephraim					1					2			3		
Wilmington	141	4	Buck	Ephraim Jr	2	2		1		1			1				7		

TOWN	PG#	LN#	LAST NAME	FIRST NAME	FREE WHITE MALES under 10	10 to 16	16 to 26	26 to 45	45 and over	FREE WHITE FEMALES under 10	10 to 16	16 to 26	26 to 45	45 and over	TOTAL ALL OTHER	TOTAL SLAVES	TOTALS	DISTRICT/ TOWNSHIP	NOTES
Wilmington	140	10	Buck	Nathan	3				1	2			1				7		
Wilmington	140	19	Buck	Reuben	3	1		1		2	1	1	1				10		
Wilmington	140	17	Buck	Samuel	1	1		1		3	2		1	1			10		
Wilmington	141	5	Buck	Zebediah	1			1		1		1					4		
Hopkinton	240	22	Buckler	Thos			1	1		1		1					4		
Malden	93	10	Buckman	Aaron	1	2	1		1	1	1	1		1			9		
Malden	93	9	Buckman	Benja'		1	1	1			1		2				6		
Medford	99	19	Buckman	David				1				1		1			3		
Malden	93	26	Buckman	Elisha			1			1			1				3		
Cambridge	220	17	Buckman	Jacob	2			1					1				4		
Medford	99	17	Buckman	Leonard		1		1					1	1			4		
Medford	99	18	Buckman	Spencer	1			1		1		1					4		
Medford	99	8	Buckman	Wm		1		1		1	2						5		
Framingham	71	1	Buckminster	Dawson		2	2	1	1	3	2	3	1	1			16		
Framingham	78	4	Buckminster	Joseph		1					1						2		
Framingham	68	1	Buckminster	Tho	1	2	1		1	2	2	1	1		1		12		Stamped pg# was x'd out
Stoneham	138	7	Buckman	Ebenezer	2			1				1	1				5		
Stoneham	138	5	Buckman	Edward			1	1	1	3		1					7		
Stoneham	138	6	Buckman	John		1	1	1	1	1		2					7		
Stoneham	138	9	Buckman	Nathan			1					1					2		
Charlestown	81	31	Bucknam	Saml		1		1		3		1					6		
Weston	106	4	Budge	Elizabeth							1		1	1	1		3		
Medford	99	33	Buel	Saml			1	1			2						4		
Medford	99	36	Buffy	Mary									1				1		
Malden	93	16	Bulfinch	Jno'				1									1		
Littleton	201	3	Bulkely	Charles				1					1				2		
Littleton	201	2	Bulkely	Joseph	2			1		1			1				5		
Newton	118	3	Bull	Milissent				1		1			1	1			4		
Framingham	68	14	Bullard	Aaron	2	1		1					1				4		Stamped pg# was x'd out
Hollistown	236	10	Bullard	Asa		1	1		1			1		1			5		
Hollistown	236	11	Bullard	Benjm			1		1			1					3		
Hopkinton	240	26	Bullard	Benjm				1		1	1			1			4		
Sherburn	249	2	Bullard	Benjm	1	1	1						2				5		
Hopkinton	240	7	Bullard	Daniel	1			1		1			1				4		
Hollistown	236	20	Bullard	Ebenz	1	1		1		1			1				5		
Framingham	68	7	Bullard	Eli	1			1		2	2						6		Stamped pg# was x'd out
Sherburn	248	8	Bullard	Galam	1			1		1			1				4		
Framingham	66	10	Bullard	Henry	1			1					1				3		Stamped pg# was x'd out
Hollistown	236	5	Bullard	Henry		1		1		1			1				4		
Hollistown	236	19	Bullard	Hezekh		1	2	1					1				5		
Hollistown	236	23	Bullard	Isaac				1				1		1			3		
Hollistown	236	17	Bullard	Isaac Jr			1	1			1		1				4		
Sherburn	248	5	Bullard	James		1		1		1			1				4		
Hollistown	236	24	Bullard	Joel	1		2			1		2					6		
Sherburn	249	1	Bullard	John			1			1			1				3		
Pepperell	34	17	Bullard	John Rev	1	2	1	1		2	1	1	1				10		
Sherburn	248	9	Bullard	Moses			2					1					3		
Hollistown	236	6	Bullard	Nathan		1	1		1				2	1			6		
Sherburn	248	22	Bullard	Peter	1	1			1				1	1			5		
Sherburn	248	12	Bullard	Peter Jr	1			1					1				3		
Sherburn	248	4	Bullard	Saml					1			1		1			3		
Hollistown	236	22	Bullard	Samll				2	1			1		2			6		
Hollistown	236	9	Bullard	Walter	3	1		1		2			1				8		
Newton	118	5	Bullough	Abigail	3		1			4		3		2			13		
Townsend	25	17	Bunge	Jonah Jr	2	1	1			3	1		1				9		
Townsend	26	8	Bunge	Moses	2			1		2			1				6		
Medford	99	13	Burage	Jno'				1		1				1			3		
Sudbury	59	8	Burbank	Ebenezer				1						1			2		
Charlestown	81	41	Burbank	Elisha			1			2		1					4		
East Sudbury	68	31	Burbanks	Thos				1		2	1		1				5		
Reading	129	21	Burdet	Aaron			2	1		1			1				5		
Reading	129	22	Burdet	James			1						1				2		
Reading	127	10	Burdet	Joseph		1		1		1				1			4		
Malden	93	20	Burdit	Hannah										1			1		
Charlestown	81	14	Burdit	Jno	1			1					1				3		
Malden	93	12	Burdit	Nathan				1		1		1	1	1			4		
Charlestown	81	15	Burdit	Saml			1						1				2		
Malden	93	19	Burdit	Saml	2	1	2	1		1	1		1				9		
Malden	93	25	Burdit	Tho'	1			1					1	1			4		
Malden	93	23	Burdit	Tho' Jr		1											1		
Boxborough	200	4	Burges	Levi	1		1			1		1					4		
Acton	19	39	Burges	Solomon	2	1		1				1	1	1			7		
Stow	198	23	Burges	Thomas	2			1		1			1				5		
Groton	206	13	Burgess	John	1			1	1	4			1	1			9		
Charlestown	81	11	Burket	Wm	2		1			2		1					6		
Hopkinton	240	17	Burlingham	Benjm					1					1			2		
Framingham	68	10	Burnam	Job		1			1				1	1			4		Stamped pg# was x'd out
Framingham	68	15	Burnam	Joshua		1			1	1			1	1			5		Stamped pg# was x'd out
Hopkinton	240	27	Burnam	Josiah	2	1	1		1				2	2			9		
Hopkinton	240	20	Burnam	Zadock	2	2			1	1	1		1				8		

TOWN	PG#	LN#	LAST NAME	FIRST NAME	under 10	10 to 16	16 to 26	26 to 45	45 and over	under 10	10 to 16	16 to 26	26 to 45	45 and over	TOTAL ALL OTHER	TOTAL SLAVES	TOTALS	DISTRICT/ TOWNSHIP	NOTES
Reading	129	3	Burnap	James					1					2			3		
Reading	129	24	Burnap	John					1		1	1		1			4		
Reading	129	2	Burnap	Joseph					1					1			2		
Reading	128	5	Burnop	Abigail	1								2	2			5		
Medford	99	35	Burns	Fra'			1		1		1		1				4		
Hopkinton	240	19	Burnup	Isaac	1	1	1	1	1	1	2			2			10		
Shirley	213	8	Burrage	Ephraim				1	1			1		1			4		
Tyngsborough	40	11	Burroughs	Joseph	1			1		2			2				6		
Wilmington	140	8	Burt	Brown	2	2		1		2			1	1			9		
Wilmington	140	6	Burt	Jacob	1		2						1				4		
Tewksbury	49	10	Burt	Thos	2			1		1			1	1			6		
Burlington	154	8	Burton	Rebekah		1							1	1			3		
Cambridge	220	38	Bush	Levi	4		7	1		3	2	1					18		
Sudbury	65	8	Bussy	Isaiah	1		1						1				3		
Hopkinton	240	24	Butlar	Aaron	2			1		1	1		1	1			7		
Wilmington	140	11	Butter	James		1			1				1				3		
Wilmington	141	6	Butter	James Jr	2		1			4	1		1				9		
East Sudbury	67	30	Butter	Joseph			1		1	1	2	1	1				7		
East Sudbury	69	17	Butter	Micah M		1							1				3		
Wilmington	140	18	Butter	Reuben	1	1	2	1					1				6		
Wilmington	141	7	Butter	Ruth	1			3		1		1		1			7		
East Sudbury	67	28	Butter	Thomas	1		2		1	1		1	1				7		
Wilmington	140	13	Butter	William				1						3			4		
Wilmington	140	14	Butter	William Jr	3	1		1		2			1				8		
Tyngsborough	40	5	Butterfield	Abner R	2			1		3			1				7		
Tyngsborough	40	6	Butterfield	Asa	2	1	7	1		1	1	2	1	1			17		
Chelmsford	168	24	Butterfield	Benja'				1				1		1			3		
Chelmsford	167	1	Butterfield	Benja Jr	2	2	1	1		1		2	1				10		
Pepperell	30	22	Butterfield	Daniel	1			1		3		1	1	1			8		
Cambridge	220	10	Butterfield	Deborah	1			2				1		1			5		
Medford	99	10	Butterfield	Fra'						1	1	1					3		
Townsend	26	7	Butterfield	Francis			1						1				2		
Tyngsborough	40	4	Butterfield	James	2	1		1		2			1				7		
Cambridge	220	12	Butterfield	John		1			1	3			1				6		
Chelmsford	167	8	Butterfield	John		1		1	1	2		1	1	1			8		
Chelmsford	168	23	Butterfield	John Jr		1		1		2			1				5		
Tyngsborough	40	7	Butterfield	Joseph	1	2		1					1				5		
Dunstable	216	3	Butterfield	Leonard Capt.	1		1	1	1	1		2	1	1			9		
Townsend	25	15	Butterfield	Peter	2	2	1		1			1		1			8		
Dunstable	216	4	Butterfield	Phillip Capt.	2	2	1	2		2		2	1				12		
Tyngsborough	40	2	Butterfield	Reuben		1		1		3		1		1			7		
Cambridge	220	11	Butterfield	Saml	2	1	1		1	2	1		1				9		
Chelmsford	167	5	Butterick	Charles			1					1					2		
Westford	179	21	Butters	Jed'			1	1					1				3		
Townsend	26	4	Butters	Joel		1		1		3		1					6		
Westford	179	20	Butters	John		1		1		2			1				5		
Woburn	148	3	Butters	Joshua				1					1				2		
Groton	206	9	Buttrick	Benjm				1		1			1				3		
Concord	11	5	Buttrick	David	1	1		1		2	1		2				8		
Concord	7	36	Buttrick	Eli	3			1	1	2		1					8		
Pepperell	30	24	Buttrick	Francis	2	3		1		1				1			8		
Concord	7	37	Buttrick	John	1	1		1		1		1	2				7		
Concord	7	38	Buttrick	Jonas	2		2	2		1	1	2	2				12		
Concord	11	7	Buttrick	Joseph			1	1		1			1				4		
Concord	7	35	Buttrick	Nathan			1	1					1				3		
Concord	11	8	Buttrick	Samuel	2		1	2		2		1	2	1			11		
Concord	11	9	Buttrick	Samuel Jr	3		1	2		2		1	1				10		
Groton	206	12	Buttrick	Tilly			1	1		2	2						6		
Dracut	45	22	Buttrick	Willard			1	1		1	1						4		
Reading	129	6	Buxton	Ebenezer	3	2		1		3	1		1				11		
Wilmington	141	1	Buxton	John				1		1	1			1			4		
Reading	129	5	Buxton	Stephen	1	1	1		1	1	1		1	1			8		
Reading	129	25	Buxton	Widow									1				1		
Chelmsford	168	9	Byan	Benja'			1					1					2		
Chelmsford	168	11	Byan	John			1	1				1		1			4		
Chelmsford	168	14	Byan	Lucy	1	2					1	2		1			7		
Chelmsford	168	13	Byan	Sarah									1				1		
Chelmsford	168	12	Byan	Solo'	1			1		3			1				6		
Chelmsford	168	10	Byan	Wm	1			1					1				3		
Charlestown	82	4	Calder	Eliz'						1				1			2		
Charlestown	82	5	Calder	Geo'				1			1	1		2			5		
Charlestown	82	6	Calder	Robt	3		1	1		2	1		2				10		
Charlestown	82	17	Calder	Wm			1	1					2	1			5		
Lexington	157	2	Caldwell	John		1		1					1				3		
Marlborough	188	1	Caldwell	John	1	1		1					1				4		
Burlington	154	12	Caldwell	Joseph	2	1		2					1				6		
Charlestown	82	13	Caldwell	Saml	2			1		1	1	1					6		
Medford	99	45	Caldwell	Saml	1			1					1				3		
Burlington	154	11	Caldwell	Sarah	1							1	1				3		

143

TOWN	PG#	LN#	LAST NAME	FIRST NAME	FREE WHITE MALES under 10	10 to 16	16 to 26	26 to 45	45 and over	FREE WHITE FEMALES under 10	10 to 16	16 to 26	26 to 45	45 and over	TOTAL ALL OTHER	TOTAL SLAVES	TOTALS	DISTRICT/ TOWNSHIP	NOTES
Lexington	157	1	Caldwell	Thomas I			1	1		2			1				5		
Weston	107	3	Calef	Robert	1		2		1		1	1		2			8		
Charlestown	82	34	Call	James				1						2			3		
Malden	93	39	Call	John		1		1		1	1		1				5		
Charlestown	82	19	Call	Jona'			2	2					1				5		
Boxborough	199	3	Cameron	Hugh				1					1				2		
Framingham	78	3	Campbell	Daniel	2	1		1		3	1		1				9		
Townsend	26	14	Campbell	John	1	2			1		2	1	1				8		
Pepperell	30	33	Campbell	Jonas	2			1		2			1				6		
Townsend	26	15	Campbell	Wm J.	1	1	1		1	1	1	1	1				8		
Boxborough	201	2	Canada	John					2					2			4		
Groton	208	28	Capel	John	1	1	1	1		4	2		1				11		
Cambridge	222	16	Capen	Benjn	2	2			1	1			2				8		
Cambridge	222	18	Capen	Jona	1		1			1			1				4		
Tyngsborough	40	23	Car*	Jonas	1		1			1			1				4		
Concord	7	5	Cargill	Reuben		1	1			1		1	1				5		
Marlborough	190	28	Carley	Job				1						2			3		
Marlborough	190	25	Carley	Joseph	1			1						1			3		
Marlborough	190	26	Carley	Sarah										1			1		
Marlborough	190	19	Carley	Silas				1		2	1	1		1			6		
Groton	208	26	Carlisle	Levi		1	1			1		1					4		
Billerica	174	30	Carlton	Amos		1		1		2			1				5		
Charlestown	82	46	Carlton	Isaac	2		9	2					2				15		
Charlestown	82	28	Carlton	Jno'		1		1					1				3		
Medford	99	48	Carlton	Jno'		1	1	1	1	1		2		1			8		
Billerica	174	31	Carlton	John		1		1		1	1			1			4		
Billerica	174	32	Carlton	John Jr	1			1		1			1				4		
Groton	208	25	Carlton	Solomon	1	1	1						1				4		
Sudbury	62	9	Carr	Anna									1	1			2		
Marlborough	191	25	Carr	Ephraim	1		1			1			1	1			5		
Sudbury	62	11	Carr	John	1			1		1				1			4		
Sudbury	62	10	Carr	Thomas	2	1	1		1			1	2	1			9		
Billerica	174	34	Carr	Walter	3			1						1			5		
Charlestown	82	44	Carrel	Peggy	1								1				2		
Stow	197	6	Carriel	Sarah										1			1		
Charlestown	83	1	Carrol	Tho'			1						1				2		
Hollistown	236	27	Carroll	Elijah	2		1			2			1				6		
Stow	196	1	Carter	Abijah	2	2		1		3				1			9		
Tewksbury	50	13	Carter	Adino				1						2			3		
Lincoln	14	31	Carter	Benjamin	1		1	1		3			1				7		
Wilmington	141	12	Carter	Benjamin	2	1		1		2			1				7		
Hopkinton	240	38	Carter	Daniel		1		1	1	1	1	1					6		
Charlestown	82	1	Carter	Danl	2			1		1			1				5		
Tewksbury	50	4	Carter	David	1	1	1	1		3			1	1			9		
Wilmington	141	24	Carter	Ebenezer	1			1					1				3		
Wilmington	141	17	Carter	Ebenezer Jr	1		1			1		1					4		
Wilmington	141	15	Carter	Eleazer		2		1					1	2			6		
Reading	130	1	Carter	Elijah	4			1		1			1				7		
Sudbury	57	11	Carter	Ephraim				1		2				1			4		
Wilmington	141	16	Carter	Ezra		1		1			1	4					7		
Burlington	154	16	Carter	James	1	2	1	1		2	1	1	1				10		
Sudbury	61	16	Carter	James		1		1		3	2		1	1			9		
Wilmington	141	11	Carter	Joel	3		1	1		2	1	2	1				11		
Wilmington	141	23	Carter	Joel Jr	2			1					1				4		
Charlestown	81	45	Carter	John		1	1	1					1	2			6		
Wilmington	141	13	Carter	John				1		3			1				5		
Charlestown	82	3	Carter	John Jr				1		1			1				3		
Burlington	154	19	Carter	Jonas	1		1	1		1	2	1	1				8		
East Sudbury	67	25	Carter	Jonathan				1		2	1		1				5		
Wilmington	141	10	Carter	Jonathan	4	2	1	1					1				9		
Wilmington	141	14	Carter	Jonathan Jr	2	1		1					1				5		
Burlington	154	18	Carter	Joshua		2	1	1		1			1				6		
Natick	246	5	Carter	Joshua	1	1		1		3			1				7		
Woburn	148	14	Carter	Josiah						1		1	1				3		
Dunstable	216	18	Carter	Michal	1			1		3			1				6		
Wilmington	141	22	Carter	Moses	2			1				1	1				5		
Wilmington	141	20	Carter	Nathan				1					1				2		
Wilmington	141	21	Carter	Nathan Jr	2	1	3		1	3	2	2	1				16		
Sudbury	61	17	Carter	Priscilla									1	1			2		
Charlestown	82	32	Carter	Richd	1	1	2	1					1				6		
Charlestown	82	2	Carter	Saml	1				1	1		1	1				5		
Reading	129	31	Carter	Thomas	2	2	1	1		2	1		1				10		
Wilmington	141	19	Carter	Timothy	2	2		1		3			1	1			10		
Burlington	154	17	Carter	William	1		3	1					1	1			7		
Charlestown	82	47	Carterett	Richd	1			1					1				3		
Charlestown	82	22	Carterett	Saml		1							1				2		
Westford	180	13	Carver	Benja'					1				1	2			4		
Westford	180	12	Carver	Jona			1		1				1	1			4		
Westford	180	14	Carver	Jona' Jr		1			1				1	1			4		

TOWN	PG#	LN#	LAST NAME	FIRST NAME	FREE WHITE MALES					FREE WHITE FEMALES					TOTAL ALL OTHER	TOTAL SLAVES	TOTALS	DISTRICT/ TOWNSHIP	NOTES
					under 10	10 to 16	16 to 26	26 to 45	45 and over	under 10	10 to 16	16 to 26	26 to 45	45 and over					
Charlestown	82	14	Carver	Reuben	1			1		1	1		1				5		
Ashby	34	15	Carver	Thos	1			1					1				3		
Ashby	34	17	Carver	Thos Jr			1		1		1			2			5		
Charlestown	82	42	Cary	Han'				1					1				2		
Charlestown	81	44	Cary	Saml	1			1			1						3		
Charlestown	82	43	Cary	Saml															Enumeration blank
Concord	11	23	Case	Huldy									1				1		
Reading	129	29	Case	Humphra	2	1	1		1		1	1		1			8		
Concord	11	25	Case												1		1		
Bedford	161	16	Catowell	John	3			1		1			1				6		
Burlington	154	10	Center	Bill				1					1				2		
Charlestown	82	26	Center	Cotton	1		1	1		4			2				9		
Charlestown	82	27	Center	Roland	1			1					1				3		
Charlestown	81	43	Center	Saml	1		1	1		1		1	1				6		
Charlestown	82	31	Chadwick	Benja'	2	1	3					1					7		
Charlestown	82	45	Chadwick	John	2			1		1		1	1				6		
Acton	18	10	Chaffin	David				1					1				2		
Acton	19	32	Chaffin	Joseph	1	1		1		1		1	1				6		
Acton	18	11	Chaffin	Sarah		1					1		1				3		
Acton	18	26	Chaffin	Simon	1			1		3	1		1				7		
Acton	16	15	Chaffin	Stephen	1			1			1		1				4		
Hollistown	236	31	Chamberlain	Enoch		1	1		1	3	1		1				8		
Hollistown	236	34	Chamberlain	Jason	2	1	1		1	2			2	2			11		
Hopkinton	240	33	Chamberlain	John						1			1				2		
Acton	19	8	Chamberlain	Joseph	1	1		1		2	1		1				7		
Hopkinton	240	34	Chamberlain	Moses	1			1		2			1				5		
Hopkinton	240	37	Chamberlain	Nathl				1		2			1				4		
Bedford	161	15	Chamberlain	Phincas			2	1		2		1	1				7		
Hopkinton	240	32	Chamberland	Ebenz			1			2			1				4		
Chelmsford	168	37	Chamberlin	Aaron		1			1	1		1	1				5		
Chelmsford	168	38	Chamberlin	Aaron	2	1	1		1	2	2			1			10		
Chelmsford	168	36	Chamberlin	Benja'				1			1		1				3		
Ashby	35	13	Chamberlin	Ephm				1					1				2		
Chelmsford	168	40	Chamberlin	Issac	1	1	1	1		1			1	2			8		
Chelmsford	168	35	Chamberlin	Jacob	1		2	1		3	1		1				9		
Westford	180	16	Chamberlin	James		1				2		1					4		
Chelmsford	168	34	Chamberlin	Jos'	1	1		1					1				4		
Sherburn	249	6	Chamberlin	Moses			1					1					2		
Chelmsford	168	33	Chamberlin	Phins			2		1	1			1				5		
Chelmsford	168	32	Chamberlin	Roger	2			1					1				4		
Chelmsford	168	39	Chamberlin	Saml				1					1				2		
Ashby	35	8	Chamberlin	Thos	3	1		1		2		1	1				9		
Chelmsford	168	31	Chambers	Jos'	1				1	2			1				5		
Cambridge	222	20	Champaney	Isaac				1		2	1		1				5		
Groton	208	30	Champney	Francis	3			1		2	1		1				8		
Cambridge	222	13	Champney	Nathl	2	1		1		1		1	1				7		
Dunstable	216	17	Chancy	John	1	1	1		1	1		1					6		
Shirley	213	21	Chandler	Henry		2				1		1		1			5		
Lexington	156	17	Chandler	John				1					1				2		
Lexington	156	18	Chandler	John Jr	3	3		1		3		1					11		
Concord	7	17	Chandler	Joseph		1		1		1	1		1		1		6		
Lexington	156	20	Chandler	Joseph		1	1			2		1	1				6		
Cambridge	222	2	Chandler	Lois			1					1	1				3		
Lexington	156	19	Chandler	Nathan	1	1		1			1		1				5		
Chelmsford	168	25	Chandler	Roger	2			1					1				4		
Westford	180	2	Chandler	Silas		1			1				1				3		
Tewksbury	50	14	Chandler	Thos			1	1			1		1				4		
Tewksbury	50	12	Chandler	Wm			1	1		2			1				5		
Westford	180	1	Chandler	Wm	1	1		1		2	1		1				7		
Reading	129	38	Chaney	Jacob		1						1					2		
Groton	208	37	Chaplin	Daniel Revd	1	1	2		1	1	3	1	1				11		
Groton	208	29	Chaplin	Jeremiah				1		4	1		1		1		8		
Shirley	213	20	Chaplin	Jeremiah			2	1			1	1	1				7		
Tewksbury	50	6	Chapman	John	1			1		3		1					6		
Littleton	201	20	Chase	Francis									1				1		
Pepperell	30	35	Chase	Jacob	1	2		1		1			1				6		
Shirley	213	18	Chase	Moody		1	1		1			2		1			6		
Groton	208	27	Chase	Moses	2			1			1	1					5		
Shirley	213	19	Chase	Samuel		1	1	1		1		1					5		
Cambridge	222	3	Chatburn	Sarah	1			1				1		1			4		
Watertown	232	4	Cheaney	Ebenz		1			1		1		1				4		
Watertown	232	5	Cheaney	Moses	2		1		1	2	1	1					8		
Watertown	231	32	Cheaney	Sollomon	1		2				1		1				5		
Watertown	232	3	Cheaney	Wm				1		1		2					4		
Hopkinton	240	35	Cheany	Wm		1		1					1				3		
Dracut	49	4	Cheever	Ezehl		1		1		1	1		1				5		
Dracut	48	28	Cheever	John	1			1		3	1						6		
Malden	93	32	Cheever	Jos'	2			1		1	1	3		1			9		
Dracut	46	9	Cheever	Moses	4		1				1	1	1				8		
Dracut	49	8	Cheever	Solomon		1				1		1		1			4		

TOWN	PG#	LN#	LAST NAME	FIRST NAME	FREE WHITE MALES under 10	10 to 16	16 to 26	26 to 45	45 and over	FREE WHITE FEMALES under 10	10 to 16	16 to 26	26 to 45	45 and over	TOTAL ALL OTHER	TOTAL SLAVES	TOTALS	DISTRICT/ TOWNSHIP	NOTES
Newton	118	28	Cheney	Aaron		1			1					1			3		
Newton	118	9	Cheney	David	1	1			1		1	1		1			6		
Newton	118	27	Cheney	Ebenezer	1	1		1			1		1				5		
Weston	107	7	Cheney	Jesse	1		1		1				1				4		
Newton	118	26	Cheney	William	1				1	1			1	1			5		
Boxborough	200	42	Chester	Prince											5		5		
Cambridge	222	8	Chickering	Joseph		1											1		
Waltham	113	15	Child	Abijah	1			1				1	1	1			6		
Lincoln	15	20	Child	Anna								1	1				2		
Newton	118	15	Child	Daniel	1	2	1		1	2			1	1			9		
Weston	107	8	Child	Edward		1	1	1		1			1				5		
Lincoln	15	14	Child	Elijah			1						1	1			3		
Lincoln	15	19	Child	Elisha	2			1		1				1			5		
Waltham	113	14	Child	Isaac	1			1	1	2			1				6		
Weston	107	5	Child	Jonathan		2		1		1	3		1				8		
Lincoln	15	15	Child	Joshua		1	1		1	1	1	1					6		
Waltham	113	16	Child	Josiah	1	1								1			4		
Weston	107	4	Child	Nathan			1						1				2		
Charlestown	82	18	Child	Saml	4			1		2		1	1				9		
Sudbury	59	7	Child	Saml	1			1		2			1				5		
Framingham	71	5	Childs	Abel	2	2	1	1		3	1		1				11		
Lexington	156	16	Childs	Abijah		1		1						1			3		
Groton	208	35	Childs	Abraham Capt.	1			1			2	1		1			6		
Framingham	71	4	Childs	Josiah				1		1				1			3		
Natick	246	7	Childs	Josiah		1	1	1		2		1	1				7		
Cambridge	221	1	Childs	Phinias			1			2			1				4		
Cambridge	222	9	Childs	Saml	1	1	1		1	1			1				6		
Malden	93	35	Chittendon	Clavin		1		1			1			1			4		
Malden	93	36	Chittendon	Isaac	1			1						1			3		
Charlestown	82	15	Choat	John		2		1		2		1	1				7		
Charlestown	82	41	Choate	Saml	3			1		1		1	1				7		
Natick	246	12	Chon	John											7		7		
Charlestown	82	23	Christy	Tho'			1			2		1					4		
Charlestown	82	29	Chubb	Tho'	2			1						1			4		
Framingham	74	8	Churchill	Mary										1			1		
Reading	129	32	Chute	Daniel		1	1						1				3		
Hopkinton	240	45	Claflan	Aaron	1		1		1	1	1						5		
Hopkinton	241	1	Claflan	Isaac		1	1	1		1		1	1				6		
Hollistown	236	30	Clafland	Wm	1			1		2			1				5		
Framingham	75	6	Claflin	Asa	3			1				1	1				6		
Framingham	75	4	Claflin	Cornelius		1		1	1	3	1						7		
Framingham	75	5	Claflin	Daniel				1					2				3		
Hopkinton	240	36	Clafton	Amaziah			2					1	1				4		
Hollistown	236	28	Clafton	John	1	1	1		1	1		1		1			7		
Woburn	149	5	Clapp	Elisha		1							1				2		
Charlestown	82	12	Clapp	Gates		1	1						1				3		
Woburn	148	13	Clapp	Jeremiah		1		3		1	1		1				7		
Concord	5	23	Clapp	Salma		1						1					2		
Hopkinton	240	30	Clapton	Caleb			1		1			1					3		
Hopkinton	240	31	Clapton	Elisha	1			1	1			1					4		
Hollistown	236	26	Clarck	Nathan				1					1				2		
Sherburn	249	7	Clarck	Wm	1	1		1		1	1	1					6		
Malden	93	34	Clarenbone	Tho'			1										1		
Hollistown	236	32	Clark	Abijah	2		1						1				4		
Sherburn	249	15	Clark	Asa	1			2		2			1	1			7		
Cambridge	220	42	Clark	Ballard	1	1				1		1					4		
Concord	2	3	Clark	Benjamin		1		1					1				3		
Marlborough	193	30	Clark	Benjamin		1	1	1		1	1						6		
Concord	11	12	Clark	Benjamin Jr		2		1		1	1	2	1				8		
Cambridge	222	7	Clark	Charles	2		3	1	1	1		1	1				10		
Newton	118	20	Clark	Daniel		1		1	1	2			1				6		
Sherburn	249	13	Clark	Daniel				1						1			2		
Hopkinton	241	2	Clark	Isaac	2	2		2		1	1		2	1			11		
Pepperell	30	37	Clark	John	2		1						1				4		
Sherburn	249	14	Clark	John	4			1		1	1		1				8		
Sudbury	61	18	Clark	John		1	1	1		1			1				5		
Tewksbury	50	7	Clark	John	1			1		2			1	2			7		
Waltham	113	11	Clark	John	1		5	1		2	1	1	1	1			13		
Framingham	74	7	Clark	Jonas				1		1			1		1		4		
Lexington	156	23	Clark	Jonas				2			2	1	1				6		
Tewksbury	50	8	Clark	Joseph	1			1		2		1					5		
Sherburn	249	4	Clark	Mical	3	1		1		1		1					7		
Hollistown	236	29	Clark	Naham	1	2		1		1	1	1	1				8		
Tewksbury	50	5	Clark	Natha	1			1		3	1		2				8		
Newton	118	19	Clark	Norman	2	2		1	1	3		1	2	1			13		
Hopkinton	240	29	Clark	Peter	1	1	1		1					1			6		
Tewksbury	50	9	Clark	Peter		1		1		1				1			4		
Watertown	231	29	Clark	Peter			1	1		1		1	1				5		
Watertown	231	30	Clark	Richard				1			1			1			3		

TOWN	PG#	LN#	LAST NAME	FIRST NAME	M under 10	M 10 to 16	M 16 to 26	M 26 to 45	M 45 and over	F under 10	F 10 to 16	F 16 to 26	F 26 to 45	F 45 and over	TOTAL ALL OTHER	TOTAL SLAVES	TOTALS	DISTRICT/ TOWNSHIP	NOTES
Sherburn	249	8	Clark	Sama		1	1		1			1		1			5		
Tewksbury	50	10	Clark	Samll	1			1		1			1				4		
Hopkinton	241	4	Clark	Sarah			1				1	1	1				4		
Waltham	113	9	Clark	Sarah	1	2		1				2	1				7		
Tewksbury	50	2	Clark	Thomas		1	3		1	1			1	1	2		9		
Watertown	231	31	Clark	Thos		2	1	1		3	1		1	1			10		
Tewksbury	50	3	Clark	Thos Jr	2	1		1		3			1				8		
Dracut	46	35	Clark	Timothy	2			1					1				4		
East Sudbury	65	17	Clark	William			1			1			1				3		
Tewksbury	50	11	Clark	Zeph*			1			3			1				5		
Westford	180	10	Clatter	Jacob		1		1		1			1				4		
Framingham	74	6	Clayes	Elijah	2			1		3			1				7		Stamped pg# was x'd out
Framingham	71	3	Clayes	James		1	1	1					1				4		
Framingham	75	2	Clayes	Josiah	2			1		2	1		1				7		
Framingham	75	9	Clayes	Peter	3	1		1		1	4	2	1				13		
Charlestown	82	30	Clement	Elijah			1					1					2		
Reading	129	37	Clement	Thomas	2		1	1	1		1	2		1	1		10		
Dracut	47	23	Clements	Moses	3	1		1		2	2		1				10		
Hopkinton	241	5	Clemmons	John				1				1	1				3		
Hopkinton	240	43	Clemons	John Jr	1			1		1		1					4		
Medford	100	2	Clisby	Jos'			4										4		
Dracut	48	22	Clough	Abigal		1	1						1				3		
Dracut	47	7	Clough	William		1		1				1	1				4		
Reading	129	30	Cobb	Mallatia	2	1		1		3	1		1				9		
Natick	246	11	Cobb	Nathl											4		4		
Weston	107	10	Cobb	Samuel	4	1	1	1		2	1		1				11		
Hollistown	236	33	Cobbett	Nathan	2			1		2	2		1				8		
Littleton	205	8	Cobleigh	John	2			1				1					4		
Littleton	205	9	Cobleigh	Mary									1				1		
Littleton	205	6	Cobleigh	Nathaniel	1		1			2			1				5		
Littleton	205	7	Cobleigh	Rachel	2			1					1	1			5		
Tyngsborough	40	13	Coburn	Abiel		1	1		1				1	1			5		
Tyngsborough	40	19	Coburn	Caleb				1			1	1	1				4		
Dracut	44	29	Coburn	Elijah		2	1	1					1				5		
Dracut	44	21	Coburn	Ephm		1	1	1				2					5		
Dracut	44	18	Coburn	Ezra				1					1				2		
Chelmsford	168	27	Coburn	Henry		1	1	1	1		1		2				7		
Dracut	47	13	Coburn	Hezeh		2		1					1		4		7		
Dracut	48	36	Coburn	Isaac			2			1		1					4		
Dracut	47	17	Coburn	Jabeth	1	1	1		1	1		2	3	1			11		
Dracut	47	25	Coburn	Jacob			2	1		1		1	1				6		
Dracut	45	27	Coburn	Jeptha	1	1		1				1	2	1			7		
Dracut	46	10	Coburn	Job		1			1	1			1				4		
Tyngsborough	40	15	Coburn	John			1	1					1				3		
Tyngsborough	40	14	Coburn	John Jr	2			1		4			1				8		
Dracut	47	26	Coburn	Jonas				1					1				2		
Dracut	47	29	Coburn	Jonas Jr	1	1		1		3	2		1				9		
Dracut	44	39	Coburn	Kezia		1							1				2		
Weston	107	11	Coburn	Lois	2	1				1	1	1	1				7		
Dracut	45	15	Coburn	Mary		1	1			1	1		1				5		
Dracut	45	13	Coburn	Mary Jr						1	1		1				3		
Dracut	45	20	Coburn	Micah	1								1				2		
Tyngsborough	40	20	Coburn	Moses	1		1			2			1				5		
Dracut	45	14	Coburn	Moses B.	1	2		1		1	1		1				7		
Tyngsborough	40	18	Coburn	Nathl	3		1	1		1		2	1				9		
Tyngsborough	40	16	Coburn	Oliver	2			1		1			1				5		
Dracut	47	19	Coburn	Peter				1					1				2		
Dracut	47	20	Coburn	Peter Jr	2	2		1		1	1	1	1				9		
Dracut	47	27	Coburn	Saul	3	1		1		1			1				7		
Dracut	44	37	Coburn	Simeon				1			1	1		1			4		
Dracut	44	36	Coburn	Simon	1	1		1		1			1				5		
Dracut	47	28	Coburn	Thaddeus		2		1		1				2			6		
Dracut	45	2	Coburn	Thomas			2		1			2	1				7		
Dracut	45	11	Coburn	Timo		1		1		1			1	1			5		
Wilmington	141	25	Coburn	Titus											7		7		
Dracut	46	11	Coburn	Uriah		1		1		1	1		1				5		
Dracut	45	6	Coburn	Willard		1		1				2	1				5		
Dracut	45	7	Coburn	Willard Jr	2			1		3			1				7		
Charlestown	82	35	Cockran	Mary		1	1	1				1	1				5		
Lincoln	13	12	Codman	John	3			1		2	1	2	3		1		13		
Natick	246	8	Coggen	Mary									2				2		
Woburn	148	15	Coggin	Jacob			1		1		1	1		1			5		
Concord	6	17	Coggswell	Emerson	1			1		2	2	1	1				9		
Concord	6	19	Coggswell	James				1		2			1				4		
Littleton	202	21	Cogswell	Jeremiah			2		1	1	2	2		1			9		
Westford	180	11	Cogswell	Jona'	1			1					1				3		
Marlborough	188	5	Cogswell	William	2	1	1		1	3	1	4		1			14		
Dracut	44	19	Cohen	J* W	1			1	1	1			1				6		
Concord	8	20	Colburn	James		1		1					1	1			4		
Lincoln	14	20	Colburn	Joseph	2			1		1				2			6		

147

TOWN	PG#	LN#	LAST NAME	FIRST NAME	FREE WHITE MALES					FREE WHITE FEMALES					TOTAL ALL OTHER	TOTAL SLAVES	TOTALS	DISTRICT/ TOWNSHIP	NOTES
					under 10	10 to 16	16 to 26	26 to 45	45 and over	under 10	10 to 16	16 to 26	26 to 45	45 and over					
Lincoln	14	27	Colburn	Joseph	4	1		1		2	2		1				11		
Billerica	174	36	Colburn	Phins	1		1			1		1					4		
Lincoln	15	5	Cole	Abraham	1	1		1		2		1	1				7		
Framingham	75	8	Cole	Anesimus	1		1		1	4		1	1				9		
Cambridge	221	10	Cole	Caleb	2			2		1			1				6		
Charlestown	82	7	Cole	Cha'		1			1	1		2					5		
Acton	16	6	Cole	John	2	1	1		1					1			6		
Acton	16	7	Cole	Joseph	2			1					1				4		
Watertown	231	33	Cole	Thadius				5		3	1		1				10		
Malden	93	38	Coleman	Dorothy										1			1		
Waltham	113	10	Colling	Abigail	1		1				1	1		1			5		
Medford	99	43	Collings	Jno'	1			2		1			1				5		
Newton	118	22	Collins	Mathias		1				2		1		1			5		
Lincoln	13	31	Collwell	William	1	2			1	2	1			1			8		
Ashby	34	16	Colman	Benja	1	2	3		1		1	1		1			10		
Lincoln	14	8	Colowin	Joseph	1	1	1	1		1	1	1	1	1			9		
Cambridge	222	6	Colstone	John		1		1				1	1				4		
Hopkinton	240	41	Comey	John	1			1			1		1	1			5		
Concord	10	4	Conant	Abel		1		1				1	1				4		
Sudbury	63	8	Conant	Amos	2			1					1				4		
Concord	9	20	Conant	Andrew		1	1	2	1			1		1			7		
Stow	197	23	Conant	Daniel	1	1	1		1	1	1		1				7		
Concord	9	14	Conant	Ezra				1				3	1				5		
Stow	197	13	Conant	John	2	2		1		2		1	1	1			10		
Townsend	26	12	Conant	John	2			1		1		1					5		
Pepperell	34	25	Conant	Josiah	1	1			1	1				1			5		
Stow	197	39	Conant	Josiah	1	1			1	1			1				5		
Shirley	213	16	Conant	Levi			1					1					2		
Concord	9	15	Conant	Lot	2			1			1		1				5		
Townsend	26	11	Conant	Melley		1				1	1	1					4		
Townsend	26	9	Conant	Nathn	1		1		1	2	1	1	1				8		
Weston	107	9	Conant	Oliver	1	2	2		1	1	1	2	1	1			12		
Stow	198	40	Conant	Peter	3	2	2		1	2	1		1				12		
Pepperell	34	24	Conant	Rachel								1		1			2		
Charlestown	81	42	Conant	Saml				1				1	1				3		
Acton	18	13	Conant	Samuel P	2	1		1		2			1				7		
Stow	198	41	Conant	Sarah									1				1		
Townsend	26	13	Conant	Sarah	1		4				2	1					9		
Pepperell	30	34	Conant	Shebuel		1		1					1	1			4		
Sudbury	63	7	Conant	Silas				1			1			2			4		
Shirley	213	17	Conant	Wm	1			1		1			1				4		
Concord	8	22	Conant	Eli			1	1		1	1						4		
Concord	7	29	Conantt	Abel		1		1		1			1				4		
Stow	195	20	Condee	Nathaniel	1			1		1	2		1				6		
Concord	5	10	Condy	Mary						1	1	2	1				5		
Medford	100	1	Conners	Peter	1			1			1		1				4		
Malden	93	33	Connery	Jno'		1		1			1		1	1			5		
Woburn	148	22	Convers	Benjamin	1	2			1		1			1			6		
Medford	99	44	Convers	James	1	1			1			1		1			5		
Woburn	149	1	Convers	James	2		1		1			1					5		
Woburn	148	19	Convers	Jeremiah	2			1		3			1				7		
Woburn	148	16	Convers	Jesse	1			1					1				3		
Woburn	148	21	Convers	John	1		1	1		1			1				5		
Bedford	161	14	Convers	Joseph		1	1	1	1			2		1			7		
Woburn	148	17	Convers	Josiah			2	1					1				4		
Woburn	148	18	Convers	Josiah Jr	1	2		1		1	1	1	1				8		
Woburn	148	20	Convers	Mary			1						2	1			4		
Watertown	231	35	Conwell	Daniel		1	2	1						2			6		
Marlborough	188	15	Cook	Ananias		2		1		2	3		1				9		
Newton	118	25	Cook	Benjamin	1			2		2	1		1				7		
Cambridge	220	43	Cook	Betsy			1	1						2			4		
Cambridge	221	5	Cook	Ephm		1	4	1		1	2		1				10		
Charlestown	82	40	Cook	Isaac	2			1		1		1	1				6		
Watertown	232	9	Cook	Israel	1	2		1		2		2					8		
Newton	118	17	Cook	Jona					1		1	2		1			5		
Cambridge	220	39	Cook	Mary	3	1				4		1	3	1			13		
Groton	208	34	Cook	Peter			1			1		1					3		
Groton	208	24	Cook	Samuel	2							1	1				5		
Billerica	174	33	Cook	Sears	1	1	1		1			3		1			8		
Watertown	232	8	Cook	Stephen		2			1	2		1	1	1			8		
Cambridge	222	12	Cook	Thos				1					1				2		
Cambridge	222	17	Cook	William		1	1	1					1				5		
Charlestown	82	21	Cook	Wm				1		1			1				3		
Boxborough	200	17	Cooledg	Henry				1									1		
Boxborough	200	18	Cooledg	James D.	3	2		1		1	1		1				9		
Natick	246	9	Coolidge	Asa			2			1		1		1			5		
Cambridge	222	15	Coolidge	Caleb	2			1		1			1				5		
Cambridge	222	19	Coolidge	Caleb Jr	1			1					1				3		
Sherburn	249	9	Coolidge	Daniel	2	1			1	3	2	1	1	1			12		

TOWN	PG#	LN#	LAST NAME	FIRST NAME	FREE WHITE MALES					FREE WHITE FEMALES					TOTAL ALL OTHER	TOTAL SLAVES	TOTALS	DISTRICT/ TOWNSHIP	NOTES
					under 10	10 to 16	16 to 26	26 to 45	45 and over	under 10	10 to 16	16 to 26	26 to 45	45 and over					
Framingham	75	7	Coolidge	Joel	3		1	1		1	2	1	1				10		
Natick	246	10	Coolidge	John	2				1	1	2		1				7		
Sherburn	249	16	Coolidge	Joseph	1	1	1	1				1	1	1			7		
Sherburn	249	5	Coolidge	Wm			1			1	1	1					4		
Stow	196	44	Coolledg	Augusts	2	2		1		2	1		1				9		
Waltham	113	12	Coolledge	Jonas	3	2	1	1		3	1	1	1	1			14		
Newton	118	10	Coollege	Isaac				1		4			1				6		
Watertown	232	6	Coollidge	Daniel	1		1	1		1	1			1			6		
Watertown	232	1	Coollidge	Eunis						3			2				5		
Natick	246	6	Coollidge	Isaac					1	2			1				4		
Watertown	231	36	Coollidge	John			1			2							3		
Watertown	231	38	Coollidge	Joshua	3	3	2	1		1	1		1				12		
Watertown	232	2	Coollidge	Moses		2	2		1	2	1	1					9		
Watertown	231	37	Coollidge	Nathl		1			1				1				3		
Watertown	232	7	Coollidge	Saml	2	2			1	2	1	1	1	1			11		
Shirley	213	22	Cooper	Saml			1		1	1			1				3		
Groton	208	23	Cooper	Simon			1		1				1				3		
Reading	129	36	Cordis	Joseph	2			2	2	1	2	2			1		12		
Newton	118	14	Corey	David		1	1	2			1		1				6		
Wilmington	141	26	Corneal	James	1			1			1		1				4		
Wilmington	141	18	Corneal	Peter				1				1		1			3		
Lincoln	12	15	Cornwall	Thomas			1			1		1		1			4		
Chelmsford	168	30	Cornwell	Foster											6		6		
Westford	180	18	Cory	Abel	1	1	1		1	1				1			6		
Groton	208	31	Cory	Elisha	2	1	1		1		1			1			7		
Marlborough	187	14	Cory	Enoch				1		1			1				3		
Chelmsford	168	28	Cory	Ezra				1		2			1				4		
East Sudbury	66	2	Cory	Isaac	2		2		1	1	1	1		1			9		
Hopkinton	240	40	Cory	Jona			1	1				1	1				4		
Groton	208	33	Cory	Nathan	1		1		1	1	3	1		1			9		
Groton	208	36	Cory	Saml	2				1			1	1				5		
Charlestown	82	8	Coster	John D.		1		1	3				1				6		
Marlborough	187	17	Cotting	Amos	5	1		1	1			1	2				11		
Weston	107	2	Cotting	John	1	1	1				1	1	1				6		
Medford	99	39	Coverly	Saml		2	1	2	1					1			7		
Reading	129	35	Cowdrey	Aaron	1			1				1					3		
Reading	129	33	Cowdrey	Nathaniel				1					1				2		
Reading	129	34	Cowdrey	Nathaniel Jr	1	1		1		2	1	1	1				8		
Littleton	203	37	Cowing	Anna	1					1	1		1				4		
Marlborough	191	27	Cox	Elisha	4		1						1				6		
Weston	107	1	Cox	Joseph	2			1		1			1				5		
Cambridge	222	1	Cox	Saml	2		3	4		1		1					11		
Charlestown	82	11	Cox	Saml		1			1			1		1			4		
Charlestown	82	24	Cox	Tho'			1			2		1		1			5		
Malden	93	40	Cox	Unite	2	3			1	2		1		1			10		
Cambridge	222	4	Cox	Walter		1	2	1		2		1					7		
Woburn	149	3	Cox	William	1	1	1	1	1	1	1	1	1				9		
Boxborough	201	1	Coy	John W.					1				1				2		
Hollistown	236	36	Cozens	Isaac	2			1		2	2		1	1	1		10		
Sherburn	249	12	Crackbone	Joseph	2	1		1		2	1		1				8		
Watertown	231	34	Craft	Abner	1				1	1			1	1			5		
Newton	118	16	Craft	Henry		1	1			1			1				4		
Newton	118	21	Craft	Joseph	1	1			2	2		1		1			8		
Westford	180	17	Craft	Saml	2				1	1				1			5		
Cambridge	222	14	Crafts	Joseph	1		2			1		1					5		
Cambridge	221	2	Crafts	Saml	1			1		1			1				4		
Billerica	175	3	Cragg	Tho'		1	1	1		2	2	1	1				9		
Billerica	175	4	Cragin	Aaron	1		1	1		1	1		1				6		
Billerica	175	5	Cragin	Silas	1	1	2				1	2					7		
Cambridge	222	11	Craige	Andrew		1		1		1		1	1	1			6		
Malden	93	37	Crane	John	3	1	1		1	1	1			2			10		
Newton	118	24	Crane	Stephen	2					3			1	1			8		
Marlborough	191	15	Cranston	Joel			2	2		1			1	1			7		
Marlborough	192	32	Cranston	Lydia			1					1		1			3		
Pepperell	30	36	Crawford	John		1		1		1		2		1			6		
Stoneham	138	11	Crocker	James	2			1					1				4		
Hopkinton	240	39	Crook	Eleazer				1					1				2		
Hopkinton	241	3	Crooks	Abrm	1				1		4		2	2	2		12		
Carlisle	21	5	Crosby	Benjamin		1	1		1			1	1	1			6		
Concord	5	26	Crosby	Elizabeth									1				1		
Billerica	174	41	Crosby	Eph'				1					1				2		
Billerica	174	42	Crosby	Eph' Jr	3		1	1		2			1				8		
Billerica	174	44	Crosby	Hez'		1		1		1		1	1				5		
Billerica	174	45	Crosby	Jerem'		1	1			1	1		1				5		
Billerica	174	43	Crosby	John		1		1									1		
Chelmsford	168	29	Crosby	John			1			1	3	1	1				7		
Dracut	47	30	Crosby	Jona				1					1				2		
Dracut	47	31	Crosby	Jona Jr		1	2		1	1			1				6		
Billerica	174	37	Crosby	Josiah			1		1			1		1			4		

149

TOWN	PG#	LN#	LAST NAME	FIRST NAME	FREE WHITE MALES					FREE WHITE FEMALES					TOTAL ALL OTHER	TOTAL SLAVES	TOTALS	DISTRICT/ TOWNSHIP	NOTES
					under 10	10 to 16	16 to 26	26 to 45	45 and over	under 10	10 to 16	16 to 26	26 to 45	45 and over					
Billerica	174	40	Crosby	Josiah		3	1		1					2			7		
Littleton	204	17	Crosby	Michael	2			1		3			1				7		
Chelmsford	168	26	Crosby	Nathan					1					1			2		
Billerica	174	38	Crosby	Oliver	1	1			1		1	1		1			6		
Billerica	175	1	Crosby	Seth					1			1		1			3		
Billerica	175	2	Crosby	Seth Jr				1		2			1				4		
Cambridge	221	19	Crosby	Simeon	4			1					1				6		
Billerica	174	39	Crosby	Timo'	1			1		2			1				5		
Westford	180	15	Crosfield	John			1			2			1				4		
Charlestown	82	33	Cross	Danl	1			1				1					3		
Boxborough	200	36	Crouch	Amos	2			1		1			1				5		
Boxborough	200	33	Crouch	John				1					1				2		
Boxborough	200	34	Crouch	John Jr	2			1		1			1				5		
Boxborough	200	41	Crouch	Jonathan	2	1	1		1	1	1			1			8		
Boxborough	200	40	Crouch	Timothy	3		1		1	2				1			8		
Medford	99	42	Crowel	Aaron	1		3	1		2			1				8		
Weston	107	6	Cuff	Venus											2		2		
Groton	208	32	Culter	Jemima Wid									1				1		
Woburn	149	4	Cummings	Ebenezer	3	2	2		1	1	1	3		1			14		
Billerica	174	35	Cummings	Henry				1		1		1	1				4		
Westford	180	3	Cummings	Isaac	1			1				1		1			4		
Dunstable	216	12	Cummings	James	1			1		3	1	1	1				8		
Dunstable	216	15	Cummings	Jeremiah	2	1		1		2			1				8		
Tyngsborough	40	17	Cummings	John	1		4	1				2		1			9		
Westford	180	4	Cummings	John		1	1						1				3		
Westford	180	8	Cummings	Jos'				1					1				2		
Westford	180	9	Cummings	Jos' Jr	1	1		1		1			1				5		
Dunstable	216	14	Cummings	Joshiah Capt.			1			1	1		1				4		
Dunstable	216	13	Cummings	Nathl		3		1					1		1		6		
Dunstable	216	16	Cummings	Nathl Jr			1					1					2		
Dunstable	216	10	Cummings	Oliver Capt.				1		1			1				3		
Dracut	47	21	Cummings	Samll		1		1					1				3		
Dunstable	216	11	Cummings	Simeon		1		1	1	2	2		1				8		
Woburn	149	2	Cummings	Stephen	2	1		1		1			1	1			7		
Westford	180	7	Cummings	Tho'		1		1					1				3		
Westford	180	5	Cummings	Timo'	1	1	1		1	2	1	3		1			11		
Westford	180	6	Cummings	Wilson	1			1		1			1				4		
Hopkinton	240	42	Cunningham	Joseph	2	2		1		1			1				7		
Marlborough	189	14	Cunningham	Simeon	2			1		2			1				6		
Cambridge	222	10	Cunningham	Wm	1		1			2		1					5		
Concord	4	11	Curtis	John	2			1		1	1		1				6		
Concord	5	4	Curtis	Jonathan	3			1		1			1				6		
Newton	118	13	Curtis	Obadiah	1		1		1		1	1	1				6		
Newton	118	23	Curtis	Solomon	4	1	4	2		2		1	1				15		
Charlestown	82	25	Curtis	Steph	2			1		1			1				5		
East Sudbury	65	13	Curtis	William		1	1				1			1			4		
Newton	118	18	Cushing	Edward			1	2		3	1	1	1				9		
Waltham	113	8	Cushing	Jacob		1			1				3	1			6		
Newton	118	12	Cushing	Thomas			1	3					1		2		7		
Waltham	113	13	Cushing	Warham	2	1	3		2	4			1				13		
Sherburn	249	11	Cushings	Asa		1	3	1		2	1		1				9		
Sherburn	249	10	Cushings	Isaac		1	1			1			1				5		
East Sudbury	69	8	Cutlar	Abel	1	2	3	1		3			1	3			14		
Sudbury	59	12	Cutlar	Asher		1	1	1	1			2		1			7		
Sudbury	59	13	Cutlar	Roland	2			1					1				4		
Sudbury	59	14	Cutler	Joseph	1	1		1		3	2	1	1	1			11		
Burlington	154	14	Cutler	Nathaniel				1						1			2		
Lexington	156	22	Cutler	Nathaniel	1	1		1		1	1						5		
Burlington	154	15	Cutler	Nathaniel Jr		1	3	1					1				6		
Burlington	154	13	Cutler	Samuel	2		1	1		1	1		1				7		
Lexington	156	21	Cutler	Thomas	1	1	2		1	1	1		1				8		
Ashby	37	36	Cutler	Thos	1	1		1		2			1				6		
Cambridge	221	7	Cutter	Aaron	1			1		3	1		1				7		
Charlestown	82	20	Cutter	Ammi	1		1		1	2	2		1				8		
Cambridge	221	13	Cutter	Amos				2						1			3		
Charlestown	82	39	Cutter	Benja'		1		1			1		1		1		5		
Cambridge	221	4	Cutter	Charles	1	1		1					1				4		
Medford	99	41	Cutter	Danl'	1	1			1				1				4		
Hopkinton	240	44	Cutter	David	1			1	1	1	1	1	1				7		
Charlestown	82	36	Cutter	Ebenz	2			1		1			1				5		
Hollistown	236	35	Cutter	Ebenz		1		1			1		1				4		
Hollistown	236	37	Cutter	Elihu	1	1		1			1						4		
Hollistown	236	25	Cutter	Elizth			1				1		1				3		
Cambridge	221	8	Cutter	Ephraim	3			1		2			1				7		
Cambridge	221	9	Cutter	Frances		2	1	5	1	2	1	1	1				14		
Cambridge	221	6	Cutter	Gersham				1					1				2		
Charlestown	82	9	Cutter	Gershom	1	1	1	1				1					5		
Cambridge	221	16	Cutter	Hannah	2	1				1	1	1	1				7		
Charlestown	82	37	Cutter	Isaac	1	2		1		1	1		1				7		

150

TOWN	PG#	LN#	HEADS OF HOUSEHOLD		FREE WHITE MALES					FREE WHITE FEMALES					TOTAL ALL OTHER	TOTAL SLAVES	TOTALS	DISTRICT/ TOWNSHIP	NOTES
			LAST NAME	FIRST NAME	under 10	10 to 16	16 to 26	26 to 45	45 and over	under 10	10 to 16	16 to 26	26 to 45	45 and over					
Stoneham	138	10	Cutter	Jacob					1					1			2		
Cambridge	220	41	Cutter	James	3	1		1		2		1	1				9		
Medford	99	40	Cutter	Jno'	3			1		1			1				6		
Cambridge	221	17	Cutter	John		1	1			1			1				4		
Cambridge	221	11	Cutter	Jona	2			1		1			1	1			6		
Charlestown	82	10	Cutter	Jos'	1			1	1	1	2		1				7		
Cambridge	221	15	Cutter	Lucy									1				1		
Cambridge	222	5	Cutter	Mary						2	1		1	1			5		
Newton	118	11	Cutter	Nathaniel	1		1					1					3		
Cambridge	221	3	Cutter	Nehemiah	3	2		1		2	2		1				11		
Newton	118	8	Cutter	Richard	3	1		1		1	2	1	1				10		
Charlestown	82	38	Cutter	Saml	2	1		1		3	1			1			9		
Cambridge	221	14	Cutter	Stephen		1		1		1	1			1			5		
Concord	3	14	Cutter	Thomas	1			1		1				1			4		
Cambridge	220	40	Cutter	Washington			1	1		1							3		
Cambridge	221	18	Cutter	William			1	1		1			1	1			5		
Cambridge	221	12	Cutter	William Jr	2	2	1	1			2		1				9		
Sudbury	62	15	Cutting	Abel	1	1		1		2	1		1	1			8		
Framingham	75	3	Cutting	Daniel				1		1	3			1			6		
East Sudbury	65	14	Cutting	Elisha	2	1		1		2		2	1	2			11		
East Sudbury	65	15	Cutting	John		3	1	1		2			1				8		
East Sudbury	65	16	Cutting	Robert	1			1				1	1				4		
Framingham	71	2	Cutting	Samuel				1		1	1	2	2				7		
Acton	17	39	Cutting	William		2		1			2			2			7		
Marlborough	194	39	Dadman	Elijah	3			1		1	2	1	1				9		
Malden	93	44	Dager	Jno'				1						1			2		
Malden	93	43	Dager	Jos'			1			2			1				4		
Tyngsborough	42	9	Daken	Levi	1	1	2	1				1	1	1			8		
Sudbury	63	13	Dakin	Joseph	2	1		1		1	1		1	1			8		
Concord	7	27	Dakin	Samuel		1	2	1				1		1			6		
Sudbury	63	14	Dakin	Samuel		1		1				2	1	1			6		
Concord	7	34	Dakin	Samuel Jr	1		2	1		1			1	1			7		
Sudbury	63	20	Dakin	Samuel Jr	1			1		1			1				4		
Billerica	175	17	Dale	Jos'		2	1		1	1	1						6		
Framingham	75	17	Dalrymple	James	1	2	1	1		2	1		1				9		
Sudbury	59	36	Dalrymple	Thos				1					1				2		
Tyngsborough	42	6	Dalton	John	2	2		1					1				6		
Charlestown	83	2	Dammon	Wm			1										1		
Reading	130	4	Damon	Aaron	3	1		1		1	1		1				8		
Reading	130	10	Damon	Amos	2	2		1					1	1			7		
Ashby	35	6	Damon	Benja	1	2	1	1		3	1		1				10		
Reading	130	8	Damon	Daniel				1						2			3		
Reading	130	3	Damon	Daniel Jr	2	3		1		2			1	1			10		
Ashby	35	3	Damon	David				1					1				2		
Reading	130	6	Damon	Ebenezer		1		1				1		1			4		
Reading	130	7	Damon	Ebenezer Jr	1	1		1		2	1			2			8		
Reading	130	13	Damon	Edmund	2	1		1		3	2		1				10		
Reading	130	9	Damon	Ezra				1					1				2		
East Sudbury	66	5	Damon	Isaac	1		1		1	2		1	1	1			8		
Ashby	35	5	Damon	Jacob		2		1				1		1			5		
Ashby	35	1	Damon	Jacob								1	1				2		
Ashby	35	2	Damon	Jacob Jr			1			2			1				4		
Reading	130	2	Damon	John	1		1	1		1		1	1	3			9		
Ashby	35	24	Damon	Joseph				1				1	1	1			4		
Reading	130	5	Damon	Joseph	1	1		1		2			1		1		7		
Ashby	35	7	Damon	Joseph Jr	2			1		3			1				7		
Reading	130	12	Damon	Joshua	3			1		1	2		1				8		
East Sudbury	66	3	Damon	Thomas	2	1		2	1	2			2	3			13		
East Sudbury	66	4	Damon	William	1		1	1				1	1				5		
Watertown	232	13	Dana	Aaron	2	1	1	1				1	1				7		
Cambridge	222	35	Dana	Caleb	3			1		3	1		1				9		
Natick	246	20	Dana	David		1	1						3				5		
Cambridge	222	25	Dana	Francis		3	1	2		1	3	1	1	1	2		15		
Cambridge	222	33	Dana	Henry	2			1		2	1	1					7		
Watertown	232	11	Dana	Isaac		2	1			3			1	1			8		
Cambridge	222	34	Dana	James	1		1						1				3		
Cambridge	222	26	Dana	Joseph	1		1			3		1	1				7		
Groton	208	44	Dana	Saml Esq	1		1	1		1	1		1		1		7		
Tewksbury	50	17	Dana	Samll	2	1		1					1				5		
Cambridge	222	32	Dana	Stephen	1		2	1		2	1		1				8		
Natick	246	19	Dana	Tabatha	1			1				1	1				4		
Tyngsborough	42	5	Dandley	John	3		1			1			1				6		
Dracut	44	33	Dane	Joseph	1	1		1				1	1	1			6		
East Sudbury	69	14	Dane	Susannah									1	1			2		
Chelmsford	169	4	Dane	Wm	3	1		1		2			1				8		
Billerica	175	13	Danforth	Benja'		1		1					1				3		
Billerica	175	14	Danforth	Eliz'	1	1							1	2			5		
Cambridge	222	23	Danforth	Elizabeth										4			4		
Billerica	175	10	Danforth	Jan*	1	1							1	1			4		

TOWN	PG#	LN#	LAST NAME	FIRST NAME	FREE WHITE MALES					FREE WHITE FEMALES					TOTAL ALL OTHER	TOTAL SLAVES	TOTALS	DISTRICT/ TOWNSHIP	NOTES
					under 10	10 to 16	16 to 26	26 to 45	45 and over	under 10	10 to 16	16 to 26	26 to 45	45 and over					
Billerica	175	12	Danforth	John	2	1		1		1	1						6		
Billerica	175	11	Danforth	Jos'	1			1		3	1	1	1				8		
Tyngsborough	42	10	Danforth	Josiah	3	1	2	1				2	1				10		
Tewksbury	50	16	Danforth	Samll				1				1					2		
Hollistown	236	39	Daniels	Amonasa	1			1				1					3		
Hollistown	236	40	Daniels	Daniel				1				1		1			3		
Hollistown	236	41	Daniels	Elisha	1	1		1				1					4		
Framingham	76	4	Daniels	Israel	1			1		1	1	1					5		
Hollistown	236	38	Daniels	Japhet				1				1		1			3		
Hollistown	237	1	Daniels	Jesse	1	1		1	1				2				6		
Charlestown	83	8	Daniels	John			1	1		1		1					4		
Hollistown	237	2	Daniels	John		1		1						1			3		
Hopkinton	241	6	Daniels	Obediah		1		1				1					3		
Newton	119	2	Daniels	Osemus	1			1		1		1					4		
Hollistown	237	3	Daniels	Perry	1		1					1					3		
Hollistown	236	42	Daniels	Saml				1						1			2		
Hopkinton	241	11	Daniels	Simeon		1		1		3			1				6		
Sherburn	249	21	Daniels	Timothy		1	1		1	1	1	1		1			7		
Marlborough	192	23	Danton	Samuel			3	1		1			1				6		
Shirley	214	3	Darby	Calvin		1		1				1	1				4		
Marlborough	194	4	Darling	Daniel	1			1		1			1				4		
Framingham	75	13	Darling	Job			1	1						1			3		
Marlborough	193	39	Darling	Jonas	3	1	1				1			2			9		
Charlestown	83	3	Davidson	Geo'	1			1		1	1	1					5		
Stow	196	31	Davidson	George	2		1		1	1			1				6		
Stow	196	38	Davidson	John				1						1			2		
Stow	196	39	Davidson	John Jr	2			1		1			1				5		
Dracut	46	27	Davies	Moses	2	2		1		2			1				8		
Watertown	232	10	Davis	Aaron	1			1		2		1					5		
Concord	7	9	Davis	Abel		2		1	1	3	1	1	1				10		
Groton	209	1	Davis	Abel	2		1	1					1				5		
Chelmsford	169	1	Davis	Abijah	1		5	1		4			1				12		
Framingham	78	9	Davis	Amos	2			1		1	1	1					7		
Westford	180	19	Davis	Ann	2					2	2	1	1				8		
Billerica	175	15	Davis	Benja'	1	2			1	3	1	2		1			11		
Acton	19	21	Davis	Daniel			3	1		2	2		1				9		
Acton	19	16	Davis	David	3			1		1		1					6		
Groton	208	42	Davis	David			1	1		1		1		1			5		
Concord	7	13	Davis	Dorothy				1				1	1				3		
Dracut	47	6	Davis	Eben				1				1	1				3		
Townsend	26	18	Davis	Eleazer		1	1	1	1					1			5		
Bedford	161	20	Davis	Eleazer				1				1	1	1			4		
Bedford	161	19	Davis	Eleazer Jr			1			1	1	1					4		
Acton	19	14	Davis	Elijah	2	1			2	2			1	1			9		
Acton	19	34	Davis	Ephraim	2		1	1		2			1	1			8		
Acton	19	11	Davis	James			1		1	6	2	1	1				12		
Cambridge	222	27	Davis	John		1		1		2			1	1			7		
Shirley	214	2	Davis	John	2	1	1	1		4	1	1	1				13		
Cambridge	222	28	Davis	John Jr	1		3					1					5		
Chelmsford	169	2	Davis	Johnson	1			1		1			1				4		
Acton	19	17	Davis	Jonathan	1		1		1		4	3	1	1			14		
Weston	107	13	Davis	Jonathan	1			1			1	1		1			5		
Littleton	202	43	Davis	Jonathan				1						1			2		
Ashby	35	9	Davis	Joseph			2	3	1	1		1		1			9		
Chelmsford	168	42	Davis	Joshua	1			1		1			1				4		
Groton	208	39	Davis	Joshua	1				1	2	2	1					7		
Townsend	26	17	Davis	Josiah	1	1		1	2	2	1	2	1				11		
Chelmsford	168	41	Davis	Moses				1			2			1			4		
Concord	5	8	Davis	Nathaniel	2		1	1		2	1	1	1				9		
Boxborough	199	22	Davis	Oliver T.	1	1		1		3	1		1				8		
Lexington	157	5	Davis	Peter	2	1	3	1		1			1				9		
Shirley	214	5	Davis	Saml				1					1				2		
Acton	17	24	Davis	Sarah	1					1			1				3		
Acton	18	33	Davis	Stephen	2			1		2			1	1			7		
Bedford	161	18	Davis	Thaddeus	1	1	1		1	2	1	2	1				10		
Tyngsborough	42	4	Davis	Thaddeus	3			1		1			1				6		
Dracut	47	5	Davis	Timo	1	1		1		1	1	3		1			9		
Townsend	26	23	Davis	Timo	2	1		1		1			1				6		
Billerica	175	16	Davis	Timo'	1	1		1		2		2	2				9		
Westford	180	21	Day	Isaac	2	1	1					1					5		
Groton	208	43	Day	Moses			1					1					2		
Shirley	213	23	Day	Nathl	1	1	1		1	1	1	1	1				8		
Hopkinton	241	7	Day	Uriah	2			1		1			1				5		
Burlington	154	20	Dean	Jesse		1	2		1			1	1	1			7		
Woburn	149	6	Dean	Lemuel	1		1	1			1	2	1				7		
Charlestown	83	12	Dean	Mary								1					1		
Bedford	161	17	Dean	Thaddeus	2				1	3	1		1				8		
Burlington	154	21	Dean	Thomas		1		2			1		2	1			7		
Sherburn	249	22	Death	Henry	1		2		1	2	1	1		1			9		

TOWN	PG#	LN#	LAST NAME	FIRST NAME	FREE WHITE MALES					FREE WHITE FEMALES					TOTAL ALL OTHER	TOTAL SLAVES	TOTALS	DISTRICT/ TOWNSHIP	NOTES
					under 10	10 to 16	16 to 26	26 to 45	45 and over	under 10	10 to 16	16 to 26	26 to 45	45 and over					
Hollistown	237	4	Death	John	2		1			1		1					5		
Sherburn	249	20	Death	Marget	1		1		1				2				5		
Hollistown	237	5	Death	Rachel										1			1		
Framingham	71	6	Dedman	Jonathan			1	1				1	2	1			6		
Framingham	71	9	Dedman	Joseph	3			1		2		1					7		
Framingham	75	15	Dedman	Martha			1					2	1	1			5		
Framingham	75	14	Dedman	Nathan		1	1		1	1	3		1				8		
Framingham	71	7	Dedman	Timothy	2			1				1		1			6		
Cambridge	222	24	Deforis	Stephen	1	1		1			2		1				6		
Waltham	113	17	Den	Elizabeth						1		2	1				4		
Waltham	113	18	Den	Joel	1	1	1		1				2		1		7		
Hopkinton	241	10	Dench	Gilbert		2	1		1	1	2		1				8		
Wilmington	141	28	Deon	Samuel			1		1			1		1			4		
Concord	7	4	Derby	Eunice									2				2		
Concord	9	8	Derby	Joseph		1			1			2		2			6		
Concord	9	9	Derby	Robert				1						1			2		
Lincoln	13	11	Derby	Samuel	2			1		4	1		1				9		
Charlestown	83	5	Devens	Richd	1				2		1	1	1				6		
Cambridge	222	31	Dewing	Jabez	1	1	1	1	1	1	1	1					8		
Hopkinton	241	8	Dewing	John	1			1		2	1		1				6		
Marlborough	192	17	Dexter	Charles	2		1					1					4		
Woburn	149	7	Dexter	David	2			1					2				5		
Charlestown	83	11	Dexter	Geo' B.		1											1		
Acton	18	22	Dexter	John		1	1		1			2	1				6		
Billerica	175	18	Dexter	John		2											2		
Marlborough	188	3	Dexter	Mary		1				1			1	1			4		
Charlestown	83	10	Dexter	Nathan	1		1		1	2	3		1				9		
Medford	100	4	Dexter	Paul		1		1					1				3		
Malden	93	42	Dexter	Rich'	2		1	1		2	1	1	1				9		
Charlestown	83	18	Dexter	Saml	1		1				1	1	2				6		
Medford	100	3	Dexter	Timo'	3			1		1	1		1				7		
Malden	93	41	Dexter	Wm		1			1	1		2		1			6		
Cambridge	222	30	Dickenson	Gilbert				1		1	1	1					4		
Cambridge	222	29	Dickenson	Henry				1		1					1		3		
Cambridge	222	21	Dickinson	Edward			1						2				3		
Cambridge	222	22	Dickinson	Isiah	1			1		2			1				5		
Shirley	214	1	Dickinson	James		1	1	2				1					5		
Hopkinton	241	9	Dickman	John	2	2	2	1	2	2	2		1	1			13		
Charlestown	83	21	Dickson	Aaron	1		1	1				1					4		
Charlestown	83	7	Dickson	John	1	1			1			1		1			5		
Charlestown	83	22	Dickson	Jona'	1				1					1			3		
Groton	208	38	Dickson	Walter	1		2	1		3		1	2	1			11		
Charlestown	83	19	Dickson	Wm				1					1				2		
Charlestown	83	20	Dickson	Wm Jr	1			1		2			1				5		
Dracut	45	9	Didson	Seth	1				2	1			1	1			6		
Billerica	175	7	Dike	John		2		1		1			1				5		
Malden	94	3	Dimond	Hall				1					1			3	5		
Charlestown	83	15	Direr	Ann		1		1				1	1				4		
Ashby	35	4	Ditson	Thos				1		1			1				3		
Townsend	26	16	Dix	Benja	3		1			1			1				6		
Littleton	202	40	Dix	Benjamin	2	3	1					1	1				8		
Sudbury	60	35	Dix	James	1		1	1				1		1			5		
Littleton	201	25	Dix	John	1		1	2		1			1	1			7		
Reading	130	11	Dix	John	1	1	1		1			1		1			6		
Townsend	26	19	Dix	Jona	1	1		1		1		1	1				6		
Townsend	26	20	Dix	Jona Jr	1		1			1		1					4		
Bedford	161	21	Dix	Jonathan	2		1						1				4		
Tyngsborough	42	11	Dix	Joseph	1	2		1		2			1	1	1		8		
Newton	119	4	Dix	Samuel		1	1	1	1			2					6		
Medford	100	6	Dixon	Hannah									1				1		
Medford	100	5	Dixon	Josiah		1		1		1			1				4		
Hollistown	237	6	Dixon	Timothy	3		1	1		2			3	2			12		
Dracut	45	24	Doak	William		1		1		1	1		1				5		
Shirley	214	4	Dodge	Elisha	1		1	1		1			1				5		
Groton	208	40	Dodge	Saml	5	1	1	1	1	1		1	1	1			13		
Charlestown	83	24	Dodge	Tho'		2		1		1		1					5		
Groton	208	41	Dolbt	Frederick				1					1				2		
Acton	17	40	Dole	Joseph				1					1				2		
Acton	17	25	Dole	Joseph Jr	1			1		2			1				5		
Littleton	204	8	Dole	Lemuel	1			1		3	1		1				7		
Charlestown	83	6	Dolliver	Peter		2	1				1	4	1				9		
Stoneham	138	12	Dolten	Joseph	2		1	1		1		1		1			7		
Sudbury	63	35	Dorman	Mary									1				1		
Framingham	74	2	Dorothy	Martha									1				1		
Tyngsborough	42	13	Dow	Samll	2	1	1		1	3	1		1				10		
Newton	119	5	Downing	John			2			1			1				4		
Lexington	157	4	Downing	Susanna	2					1		1					4		
Sherburn	249	17	Downs	Elezer				1					1				2		
Sherburn	249	19	Downs	Elezer Jr	1	1			1	1	1		1				6		

153

TOWN	PG#	LN#	LAST NAME	FIRST NAME	FREE WHITE MALES under 10	10 to 16	16 to 26	26 to 45	45 and over	FREE WHITE FEMALES under 10	10 to 16	16 to 26	26 to 45	45 and over	TOTAL ALL OTHER	TOTAL SLAVES	TOTALS	DISTRICT/ TOWNSHIP	NOTES
Sherburn	249	18	Downs	Joseph	1	1		1		2			1				6		
Charlestown	83	4	Dowse	Ann								1	2				3		
Billerica	175	20	Dowse	Benja'	1		1		1	2	2	1					8		
Billerica	175	19	Dowse	Jos'		1		1		3		2	1		1		9		
Natick	246	18	Draper	Enoch		1	1	1		3			1				7		
Watertown	232	12	Draper	John		1	1	1	1				1				5		
Boxborough	199	25	Draper	Triphena	1		1					2		1			5		
Framingham	75	11	Drewing	Thomas	3			1				2	1				7		
Natick	246	16	Drewry	Asa		1			1	1		1		1			5		
Framingham	75	10	Drewry	Caleb		2	3	1				1		1			8		
Natick	246	17	Drewry	Elijah	3			1		1			1				6		
Framingham	78	6	Drewry	Lydia	1					1	2		1				5		
Natick	246	15	Drewry	Saml		1		1		1				1			4		
East Sudbury	67	23	Drummond	Rebecka	1									1			2		
Stow	199	2	Dubbleday	Elizabeth		1						1	1	2	1		6		
Lincoln	14	24	Dudley	Benjamin	1			1					1	1			4		
East Sudbury	66	8	Dudley	Benjm	2		1		1	1			1	1			7		
Sudbury	60	20	Dudley	Benjm	2			1		2			1	1			7		
East Sudbury	66	10	Dudley	Daniel	3	2		1		1			1				8		
Acton	18	7	Dudley	Ephraim				1					1	1			3		
Framingham	75	12	Dudley	John	3			1	1	1			1	1			8		
Westford	180	20	Dudley	John	1			1					1				3		
Weston	107	12	Dudley	John	1	1	1	1		1			1				6		
Acton	16	18	Dudley	Joseph	1			1		1			1				4		
East Sudbury	66	6	Dudley	Joseph	3		1	1	1	1			1	1			9		
Lexington	157	3	Dudley	Nathan	1		1		1	2	1		2				8		
Acton	18	32	Dudley	Paul	2		1	1		1			1				6		
East Sudbury	66	7	Dudley	William				1			1						2		
East Sudbury	66	9	Dudley	William Jr	1			1		1			1				4		
Stow	197	29	Duffer	Jonathan		3	1	1		1	2	1		1			10		
Concord	11	30	Dugan	Thomas											4		4		
Natick	246	13	Dune	Jona		1		1		2		1		1			6		
Medford	100	7	Dunham	Jona'	1		1		1				1				4		
Charlestown	83	23	Dunham	Sarah									1				1		
Charlestown	83	14	Dunkley	Isaac	1			1					1				3		
Charlestown	83	13	Dunkley	John	1			1		2			1				5		
Shirley	214	6	Dunn	Andrew			1	1					1		1		4		
Tyngsborough	42	7	Dunn	Edward		1		1					1				3		
Chelmsford	169	7	Dunn	James	1	2		1		2	1	2	1				10		
Chelmsford	169	5	Dunn	John		1	1	1					1	2			6		
Framingham	75	16	Dunn	John	1			1		1			1	1			5		
Chelmsford	169	6	Dunn	John Jr	2			1				1					4		
Marlborough	192	35	Dunn	Lovewell		2		1					1				4		
Chelmsford	169	8	Dunn	Mary	1					1			1	1			4		
Tyngsborough	42	8	Dunn	Robert				1					1				2		
Natick	246	14	Duntin	Isaac				1	1								2		
Tewksbury	50	18	Dunttin	Andrew	1			1		2			1				5		
Charlestown	83	16	Dupee	Ellias				1		1			1				4		
Acton	17	9	Durant	Henry		1		1		1		1					4		
Littleton	202	45	Durant	Henry	1	1			1					1			4		
Tyngsborough	42	12	Durant	Jacob				1						1			2		
Watertown	232	14	Durant	John	2		1	1		1		1	1				7		
Carlisle	20	17	Durant	Jonas			1		1	3			1				6		
Concord	4	30	Durant	Keturah									1				1		
Dracut	44	14	Durant	Nathan			1	1				1					3		
Newton	118	30	Durant	Peter	1			1					1				3		
Carlisle	22	28	Durant	Reuben	1	1	2	1					1				6		
Dracut	44	16	Durant	Saml		1			1	1			1				4		
Newton	118	29	Durant	Thomas	2			1		2		2					7		
Carlisle	21	30	Durant	Willard	1			1		2			1				5		
Billerica	175	6	Durel	Ann			1			1			1				3		
Newton	119	1	Durell	David	2			1		1			1				5		
Newton	119	3	Durell	John	1			1		2			1				5		
Billerica	175	21	Duren	John	4			1					1				6		
Billerica	175	8	Duren	Reuben		1	1		1	1				1			5		
Billerica	175	9	Duren	Reuben Jr	1		2	1					1				5		
Wilmington	141	27	Durnin	Abigail		1							1				2		
Carlisle	21	27	Dutten	Nathaniel	4		1						1				6		
Sudbury	59	37	Dutton	Abigail	1	1				1			1				4		
Westford	180	22	Dutton	Benja'	1	1			1				1	1			5		
Westford	180	23	Dutton	David				1						1			2		
Carlisle	22	17	Dutton	Hannah								2		1			3		
Littleton	202	4	Dutton	James	1			1			1			1			4		
Chelmsford	169	3	Dutton	John			1						2	2			5		
Westford	180	25	Dutton	Jos'				1			2		1				4		
Westford	180	24	Dutton	Tho'	1			1					1				3		
Tewksbury	50	15	Dutton	Timo				1	1				1	1			4		
Shirley	213	24	Dwight	John		1	2		1			3	2	1			10		

TOWN	PG#	LN#	LAST NAME	FIRST NAME	M under 10	M 10 to 16	M 16 to 26	M 26 to 45	M 45 and over	F under 10	F 10 to 16	F 16 to 26	F 26 to 45	F 45 and over	TOTAL ALL OTHER	TOTAL SLAVES	TOTALS	DISTRICT/ TOWNSHIP	NOTES
Malden	93	46	Dyer	James	1		1			1	1	1					5		
Malden	93	45	Dyer	Jno'	1			1		1	1		1				5		
Malden	94	1	Dyer	Jos'	3		1			1			1	1			7		
Malden	94	2	Dyer	Naomi										1			1		
Reading	130	28	Eads	Anna								1		1			2		
Marlborough	193	12	Eager	Moses	3		1	1		1		2					8		
Marlborough	193	11	Eager	Uriah	1				1					1			3		
Hollistown	237	11	Eames	Aaron		1		1		1		1	1				5		
Framingham	77	6	Eames	Alexander			1					1					2		
Hopkinton	241	12	Eames	Asa	1	1		1		1	1		1				6		
Hollistown	237	7	Eames	Daniel		1	1	1				2		2			7		
Hopkinton	241	13	Eames	David	1	1		1		1	1		1				6		
Marlborough	193	31	Eames	Ebenezer	2	1		1	2	1		1	1				9		
Hollistown	237	12	Eames	Ezra		1		1	1	2	3	1	1				10		
Framingham	66	4	Eames	Henry	1	1			1	2	1	1					7		Stamped pg# was x'd out
Hollistown	237	9	Eames	Hopsil	1		1		1	1	1		1				6		
Woburn	149	8	Eames	Jacob	1	1	3		1	1			1				8		
Woburn	149	17	Eames	James H	1		1						1				3		
Hopkinton	241	14	Eames	Jessa	1	1		1		2			1				6		
Framingham	66	5	Eames	John			1		1		1	1		1			5		Stamped pg# was x'd out
Stow	197	35	Eames	John			1		1			1		1			4		
Woburn	149	9	Eames	John	1	3	1			1	1	2	1				11		
Framingham	66	7	Eames	Moses	3			1		3	2		1				10		Stamped pg# was x'd out
Framingham	66	6	Eames	Nathaniel	1	2			1		1	1	1	1			8		Stamped pg# was x'd out
Framingham	70	15	Eames	Phinehas	2		1	1		2			1				7		Stamped pg# was x'd out
Hollistown	237	10	Eames	Reuben		1		1	1	1		2		1			7		
Framingham	71	14	Eames	Timothy	1		1	1					1				4		
Hollistown	237	8	Eames	Wm		1	1					1					3		
Wilmington	141	33	Eams	Caleb		1		1			1		1				4		
Wilmington	141	34	Eams	Caleb Jr	2		1			1		1					5		
Wilmington	141	29	Eams	John	2			2	1	2			2				9		
Wilmington	141	35	Eams	John Jr	3	1			1		1			1			7		
Wilmington	141	31	Eams	Jonathan		3	1		1	1				1			7		
Wilmington	141	32	Eams	Jonathan Jr	1		1	2		2		1					7		
Wilmington	141	30	Eams	Samuel		1	1	1				1	1	1			6		
Wilmington	141	37	Eams	William	2		1			2		1					6		
Medford	100	8	Earl	Wm	1		1			3		1		1			7		
Natick	246	22	Easter	Elijah				1			1		1				3		
Natick	246	21	Easter	Elijah Jr	2		1			1			1				5		
Cambridge	222	38	Easterbrooks	Eliakim	3		1			1		1					6		
Cambridge	223	1	Easterbrooks	John			3										3		
Cambridge	222	37	Easterbrooks	Nehemiah				1		1							2		
Lincoln	12	13	Easty	Ebenezer		2						1					3		
Billerica	175	22	Easty	Ebenz'			1						1	1			3		
Ashby	35	10	Eaton	Benja	3	1		1		1		1	1				8		
Charlestown	83	36	Eaton	Benja'	1	1	1			1		1					5		
Groton	209	2	Eaton	Calvin			1			3			1				5		
Framingham	71	16	Eaton	Ebenezer		1	1		1	1	2	2		1			9		
Reading	130	26	Eaton	Ebenezer		1	1		1		1			1			5		
Charlestown	83	35	Eaton	Edm'	1		1			2			1				5		
Reading	130	36	Eaton	Elizabeth									1				1		
Reading	130	15	Eaton	Hannah				1			1	2		1			5		
Reading	131	4	Eaton	Jacob	1		1			1		1	1				5		
Framingham	71	15	Eaton	John	2	1	3	1	1	1	1	1	1	1			13		
Framingham	66	3	Eaton	Jonas	1	1	1	1					1				6		Stamped pg# was x'd out
Groton	209	4	Eaton	Jonas				1						1			2		
Groton	209	5	Eaton	Jonas Jr	2		1			2			1				6		
Woburn	149	13	Eaton	Jonathan	1			1				1		1			4		
Woburn	149	12	Eaton	Jonathan Jr		1	1	1		1	1		1				6		
Ashby	35	11	Eaton	Joseph	2			1		1		1	1				6		
Woburn	149	20	Eaton	Joseph		1	1			2	2		1				7		
Reading	130	33	Eaton	Lille		1	1	1	1			2	2	1			9		
Woburn	149	10	Eaton	Lille			1					1	1	1			4		
Reading	130	34	Eaton	Lille Jr			1					1	1				3		
Woburn	149	15	Eaton	Lot	5	1		1		1			1				9		
Framingham	71	17	Eaton	Luther	2	1		1		1			1				6		
Framingham	71	13	Eaton	Nathan	1	1	1	1		1			2				7		
Reading	130	35	Eaton	Nathan		1	2		1	3				1			8		
Reading	130	14	Eaton	Nathaniel	3	1		1		2	1		1				9		
Framingham	71	12	Eaton	Noah				1					1				2		
Reading	130	25	Eaton	Osgood	2		2	1				1	1				7		
Lexington	157	6	Eaton	Rebekah						1	1			2			4		
Reading	131	3	Eaton	Reuben		1	1	1				1	1	1			6		
Sudbury	58	8	Eaton	Reuben	1		1			2			1				5		
Reading	130	17	Eaton	Samuel	3	1	1						1	2			10		
Malden	94	6	Eaton	Sarah									1	1			2		
Framingham	68	5	Eaton	Silas		1	1		1	3	1		1				8		Stamped pg# was x'd out
Reading	130	16	Eaton	Thomas		1	2	1				1		2			7		
Woburn	149	14	Eaton	Thomas	1		1			1		1					4		
Reading	130	18	Eaton	Timothy					1			1	1				4		

TOWN	PG#	LN#	LAST NAME	FIRST NAME	FREE WHITE MALES					FREE WHITE FEMALES					TOTAL ALL OTHER	TOTAL SLAVES	TOTALS	DISTRICT/ TOWNSHIP	NOTES
					under 10	10 to 16	16 to 26	26 to 45	45 and over	under 10	10 to 16	16 to 26	26 to 45	45 and over					
Groton	209	3	Edes	Isaiah	1	1			1	2			2				7		
Charlestown	83	26	Edes	Peter	1	1		1		1	3		1				8		
Charlestown	83	27	Edes	Saml				1						1			2		
Charlestown	83	28	Edes	Tho'	3	1		1		2			1				8		
Framingham	71	11	Edgel	Aaron	1			1		2			1				5		
Framingham	71	10	Edgel	Simon				1						1			2		
Woburn	149	11	Edgell	Benjamin	1		2		2	1		2		1			9		
Charlestown	83	31	Edmands	David	1		1		1		2	1		1			7		
Charlestown	83	32	Edmands	David Jr	1		1			1		1					4		
Charlestown	83	33	Edmands	James		1	1	1					1	1			5		
Charlestown	83	29	Edmands	John			1		1			1		1			4		
Malden	94	4	Edmands	John	2		1	1		2	1	1					8		
Charlestown	83	30	Edmands	John Jr	2	1	2					1					6		
Charlestown	83	34	Edmands	Tho'			1	1				1					3		
Framingham	71	8	Edmunds	Jonathan			1	2						2			5		
Acton	19	3	Edward	John		1	2	2		3		1	2	2			13		
Ashby	35	12	Edwards	Abram	1	2	2	1		2	1		2	1			12		
Framingham	66	1	Edwards	Benj		1		1				1		1			4		Stamped pg# was x'd out
Shirley	214	7	Egerton	John			3		1	1	1	1		2			9		
Shirley	214	8	Egerton	Leonard	1			1		1		1					4		
Dunstable	216	20	Eldridge	Micah Doct.	1		1			1		1					4		
Pepperell	30	39	Eliott	David	4			1		2			1				8		
Pepperell	30	38	Eliott	Jerh			1	1			1	1	1				5		
Pepperell	30	41	Eliott	Sarah		1				1		2		1			5		
Dracut	47	10	Ellingswood	Robert		1		1		3		1		1			7		
Charlestown	83	37	Elliot	Tho'		1		1		2	2		1	1			8		
Watertown	232	16	Elliott	Richd R.		1		1		1	1	1					5		
Cambridge	223	3	Ellis	Andrew			1	1			1						3		
Sherburn	249	23	Ellis	Bethael	1	1		1		1			1				5		
Littleton	202	50	Elsworth	Edward			1	1					1				3		
Pepperell	30	40	Emerford	Joseph S.			1					1	1				3		
Wilmington	141	36	Emerson	Aaron	1	1	1		1	1			1				6		
Chelmsford	169	11	Emerson	Asa				1			1		1				3		
Acton	19	36	Emerson	Augustus		1	1						1				3		
Reading	130	30	Emerson	Benjamin	1		2		1	1	2	1		1			9		
Reading	131	5	Emerson	Charles			2	2					2				6		
Reading	130	21	Emerson	Daniel	3	2		1			1		1				8		
Reading	130	22	Emerson	David	2	1	1	1		1	1	1					8		
Reading	130	23	Emerson	Ebenezer				1		1				2			4		
Reading	130	24	Emerson	Ebenezer	1			1		2			1				5		
Cambridge	222	36	Emerson	Elias	3	1	1	1		1	1		1				9		
Reading	130	29	Emerson	James	2	1		1	1	2			1				8		
Reading	130	19	Emerson	John				1				2	1				4		
Reading	130	20	Emerson	John Jr	1	1	1	1		1	2	2		1			10		
Reading	131	6	Emerson	Jonathan	2			1					1				4		
Cambridge	223	2	Emerson	Joseph			1										1		
Reading	130	27	Emerson	Joseph			1	1	1				1	2			6		
Dunstable	216	19	Emerson	Mary Wid		2					1	2	1				6		
Chelmsford	169	12	Emerson	Owen	2	1		1		1		1		2			8		
Chelmsford	169	10	Emerson	Saml	2			1					1				4		
Reading	130	31	Emerson	Thomas				1						1			2		
Reading	130	32	Emerson	Thomas Jr	2	2	1	1		1	2	1	1				11		
Woburn	149	16	Emerson	William	2			1					1				4		
Malden	94	7	Emerson	Wm	2	2			1	1	1	1		1			9		
Townsend	26	21	Emery	John	3		2		2	2	2		1	1			13		
Lincoln	15	8	Emes	Ephraim	1	1		1					1				4		
Cambridge	223	5	English	John		1	2						1				4		
Cambridge	223	4	English	Thos	1	1	1	2	1	1		1	2				10		
Charlestown	83	25	English	Wm		1											1		
Tyngsborough	42	14	Epes	Benja	1	1	4		1		2	2		1			12		
Westford	180	27	Estabrook	Benja'		1			1		1	1		1			5		
Lexington	157	7	Estabrook	Benjamin		1	2	1		1		1		1	1		8		
Lexington	157	8	Estabrook	Benjamin Jr	1	1		1		1			1				5		
Westford	180	26	Estabrook	Joel		1			1	1	1	1		1			6		
Concord	11	18	Estabrook	John		1			1	2			1				5		
Chelmsford	169	9	Estabrook	Moses			2	1		1			1				5		
Lexington	157	9	Estabrook	Nehemiah	1			1			2		1				5		
Concord	7	12	Estabrook	Robert		1			2			1	1	2			7		
Lincoln	15	10	Estey	John	1	1		1		2			1				6		
Charlestown	83	38	Ethridge	Saml		2	2	2		2	2		1				11		
Acton	17	28	Eule	Asahel	2		1	1					1				5		
Stow	196	25	Euleth	Daniel	3			2		2	1	1	1				11		
Stow	199	1	Euleth	Francis		1	2		1			1		1			6		
Newton	119	6	Eustis	Thomas		1	1		1		1	1	1	1			7		
Newton	119	7	Eustis	Thomas Jr	2		2	1		2	2		1				10		
Woburn	149	19	Evans	Asaph	1		1			2			1				5		
Woburn	149	18	Evans	Sarah		1		1					1	1			4		
Westford	180	29	Evelith	John	1			1					1				3		
Westford	180	28	Evelith	Timmi			1	2			1	2	1				7		
Wilmington	142	1	Evens	B*						1							1		

TOWN	PG#	LN#	HEADS OF HOUSEHOLD LAST NAME	FIRST NAME	FREE WHITE MALES under 10	10 to 16	16 to 26	26 to 45	45 and over	FREE WHITE FEMALES under 10	10 to 16	16 to 26	26 to 45	45 and over	TOTAL ALL OTHER	TOTAL SLAVES	TOTALS	DISTRICT/ TOWNSHIP	NOTES
Reading	131	1	Evens	Samuel	1	1	2	1		2	1	1	1				10		
Framingham	74	14	Evens	Sherebiah	1			1					1				3		
Reading	131	2	Evens	Thomas	2	2			1			1		1			9		
Watertown	232	15	Everet	Aaron	3	1	2	1		1		1					9		
Malden	94	5	Everet	Epm	1		1						1		1		4		
Framingham	66	8	Everett	Jesse			1	2	1	1	1		1				7		Stamped pg# was x'd out
Littleton	202	11	Fagon	Mentus											1		1		
Hopkinton	241	18	Fairbanks	Adam	3			1		2	1		1				8		
Hollistown	237	17	Fairbanks	Adams	3			1		2		1					7		
Hollistown	237	21	Fairbanks	John	3	2	1	1			1	1	1				10		
Sudbury	60	15	Fairbanks	Jonathn	2	1			2	2	1	1	1				10		
Framingham	74	4	Fairbanks	Joshua	3		1	2	1	1	1	2	1	1			13		Stamped pg# was x'd out
Hollistown	237	19	Fairbanks	Reuben				1		1			1				3		
Cambridge	223	34	Fairweather	Thos			1		1		1	1	1				5		
Groton	209	19	Faran	Ebenzr				1									1		
Hopkinton	241	22	Farland	Joseph				1		2	1		1				5		
Charlestown	84	15	Farley	John		1				1	1						3		
Billerica	175	23	Farmer	Edw'		1		1	1				1				4		
Billerica	175	25	Farmer	Edw' 3rd	1	1	1	1		2			1				7		
Billerica	175	24	Farmer	Edw' Jr	1		1		1				1				4		
Tyngsborough	42	25	Farmer	Jeremiah		1		1	1				1				4		
Groton	209	34	Farmer	Jessa				1		1		1					3		
Billerica	175	26	Farmer	John	1		1		1	1		1		1			6		
Chelmsford	169	17	Farmer	John	1	2		1		2			1				7		
Chelmsford	169	18	Farmer	Jonas				1					1				2		
Townsend	26	27	Farmer	Jonas	2	2	2	1				1	1				9		
Billerica	175	40	Farmer	Jotham	2		1			1		1					5		
Tewksbury	51	4	Farmer	Lafe	2	1		1		3			1				8		
Billerica	175	27	Farmer	Mary								1	1				2		
Littleton	201	12	Farmer	Nathaniel			1		1				1	1			4		
Billerica	175	28	Farmer	Oliver		1		1	1				1				4		
Billerica	175	29	Farmer	Oliver Jr	2	1		1		2			2				8		
Tewksbury	51	3	Farmer	Peter				1			1		1				3		
Tewksbury	51	5	Farmer	Silas	1		1	1		1		1					5		
Chelmsford	169	16	Farmer	Simeon		1		1									2		
Natick	246	25	Farns	Wm	1	1			1	1	2		1				7		
Groton	209	18	Farnsworth	Aaron	2			1		1	1		1				6		
Groton	209	23	Farnsworth	Amos Dea.	2	2		1		1		1	1				8		
Groton	209	10	Farnsworth	Betty Wid.		2	3			1	2		1				9		
Littleton	203	17	Farnsworth	Edmond	1	1		1		1			2				6		
Charlestown	84	19	Farnsworth	Elias	2								1				4		
Shirley	214	12	Farnsworth	Flint	1			1	1	1			1	1			6		
Groton	209	11	Farnsworth	Isaac Dea.				1									1		
Shirley	214	13	Farnsworth	Jesse	2	1		1				1	1				6		
Groton	209	15	Farnsworth	John	4		1	1	1	2	1		1				11		
Shirley	214	14	Farnsworth	John	2			1		2		1					6		
Shirley	214	10	Farnsworth	Jona				1		2			1				4		
Groton	209	22	Farnsworth	Jonas	1	1	1		1	2		2		1			9		
Shirley	214	11	Farnsworth	Levi	2			1					1				4		
Groton	209	20	Farnsworth	Lydia Wid.									1				1		
Charlestown	84	12	Farnsworth	Marcy	2	1							1				4		
Groton	209	12	Farnsworth	Oliver				1				1	1				3		
Groton	209	25	Farnsworth	Saml	1	1		1		2							5		
Groton	209	17	Farnsworth	Samson Capt.	2			1					1				4		
Ashby	35	23	Farr	Wm	1	1		1		1	1	1	1				7		
Concord	7	25	Farrar	Ephraim	4	2		1		1			1				9		
Shirley	214	15	Farrar	George	2		1	1		3	1		1				9		
Townsend	26	29	Farrar	Isaac		1		1					1				3		
Concord	7	26	Farrar	Jacob	3	1		1	1	1			1				8		
Chelmsford	169	19	Farrar	Jonas		1		1					1				3		
Pepperell	30	45	Farrar	Joseph	3												3		
Chelmsford	169	24	Farrar	Nath'			2					1					3		
Lincoln	12	2	Farrar	Nehemiah	1			1		4	1		2				9		
Concord	7	23	Farrar	Reuben	1			1		3			1				6		
Pepperell	31	1	Farrar	Saml	2		2						1				5		
Lincoln	12	17	Farrar	Samuel		1	2	1	1		1	1		2			9		
Groton	209	8	Farrar	Stephen		1	1	1	1	2		2					8		
Townsend	26	28	Farrar	Thos		1	1		1	1	2	2		1			9		
Townsend	26	30	Farrar	Thos Jr	1		1					1					3		
Concord	7	24	Farrar	Timothy				1	1				1				3		
Lincoln	12	3	Farrar	Zebediah		1			1				1				3		
Cambridge	223	32	Farrer	Samll			1										1		
Medford	100	10	Farrington	Dan'		1		1		2		1	1				6		
Burlington	154	23	Farrington	Mathw				1		1			1				3		
Cambridge	223	22	Farthingham	Charles	1		1		4	1		1					8		
Cambridge	223	21	Farthingham	Willm			3	1			1		1				6		
Dunstable	217	6	Farwell	Ebenz				1					2				3		
Tyngsborough	42	24	Farwell	Henry	3			1		2			1				7		
Groton	209	13	Farwell	Henry Capt.	1			1	1				2				5		
Groton	209	7	Farwell	Henry Jr			2		1					1			4		

TOWN	PG#	LN#	LAST NAME	FIRST NAME	FREE WHITE MALES under 10	10 to 16	16 to 26	26 to 45	45 and over	FREE WHITE FEMALES under 10	10 to 16	16 to 26	26 to 45	45 and over	TOTAL ALL OTHER	TOTAL SLAVES	TOTALS	DISTRICT/ TOWNSHIP	NOTES
Charlestown	84	14	Farwell	James			1						1				2		
Tyngsborough	42	15	Farwell	John		1	1	2		4	2	1	1				12		
Tyngsborough	42	22	Farwell	Nathan	3			2			1	2	1		2		11		
Groton	209	27	Farwell	Wm				1					1	1			3		
Lexington	157	17	Fassett	Abiel	1	1	1	1				1					5		
Acton	17	18	Faulkner	Aaron			1					2	1	1			5		
Malden	94	9	Faulkner	Benja'	1		1	2		3		1					8		
Malden	94	8	Faulkner	David	1			1		2			1				5		
Acton	16	33	Faulkner	Francis		1	2	1	1				1	1	1		8		
Watertown	232	19	Faulkner	Francis		1	1	2				2					6		
Acton	17	19	Faulkner	Nathaniel			1		1		1	1	1				5		
Acton	16	34	Faulkner	Obedience										1			1		
Concord	6	30	Fay	Jonathan			1		1	1		1	3		1	1	9		
Marlborough	190	3	Fay	Josiah	2	1		1		3			1				8		
Marlborough	191	10	Fay	Micijah				1									1		
Hopkinton	241	23	Fay	Nathan	3		3	1		1							8		
Framingham	74	1	Fay	Ruben	2			1			1	1	1				6		Stamped pg# was x'd out
Charlestown	84	9	Fayerweather	David			1						1		2		4		
Marlborough	193	7	Felton	Archelaus	1	1		1					1				4		
Marlborough	189	16	Felton	Joel	3	1	1	1	1		1		2				10		
Marlborough	191	19	Felton	Silas			1					1					2		
Marlborough	189	23	Felton	Stephen	2	1	1		1			2		2			9		
Marlborough	195	2	Felton	William	1			1		1			1		1		5		
Charlestown	84	13	Ferguson	Wm			1					1					2		
Woburn	149	33	Ferrel	Mitchel				1		1			1				3		
Watertown	232	23	Ferrington	Wm				1		2			1				4		
Townsend	26	31	Fesendon	Aaron		1	1	1				2	1				7		
Townsend	26	32	Fesendon	Aaron Jr		1	1					1					3		
Charlestown	83	42	Fesendon	Eliza'								1		1			2		
Townsend	26	25	Fesendon	Timo	3			1		2			1				7		
Watertown	232	22	Fessenden	George	2		1	2		1		1					7		
Cambridge	223	18	Fessenden	Icabud	3	1		1					1	1			7		
Lexington	157	11	Fessendon	Nathan	1			1			1		1				4		
Lexington	157	10	Fessendon	Thomas	1		2		1		1	2		1			8		
Charlestown	84	11	Fezendon	John			1										1		
Cambridge	223	39	Fillebrown	Edward				1		1	1	1		1			5		
Cambridge	223	29	Fillebrown	James	1	1		3				1		1			7		
Cambridge	223	31	Fillebrown	James Jr	1		1			2			1				5		
Charlestown	83	44	Fillebrown	John			1				1	1					3		
Charlestown	84	10	Fillebrown	Tho'				1						1			2		
Framingham	74	15	Fish	John	2	1	1		1		1	2		1			9		
Groton	209	24	Fish	John	2	1	1		1	2	3			1			11		
Groton	209	6	Fish	Jonathan				3				1	1				5		
Framingham	74	5	Fish	Micah	1	1	1	1				1	1				6		Stamped pg# was x'd out
Framingham	78	2	Fish	Moses	1		2	1		1	3		1	1			10		
Framingham	78	1	Fish	Richard	1	1	1		1		2		1				7		
Waltham	113	23	Fisher	Abraham	2			1		1		1					5		
Waltham	113	28	Fisher	Elijah	1	1	1	1				1	1				6		
Waltham	113	27	Fisher	Jonathan		1	1	1				1	1				5		
Hollistown	237	16	Fisher	Lewis		1		1		1		1					4		
Waltham	113	30	Fisher	William	3	2			1	1		1	1				9		
Hopkinton	241	15	Fisk	Abial			1	1	1	1		1		1			5		
Hollistown	237	22	Fisk	Asa	1		3	1		1				1			7		
Natick	246	24	Fisk	Asa	1			1		2	1		1				6		
Pepperell	30	43	Fisk	Daniel		1	1	1				1					4		
Hollistown	237	13	Fisk	David			2	1	1		1		1	1			7		
Lexington	157	12	Fisk	David				1						1			2		
Lexington	157	14	Fisk	David 3rd	3	1		1		2	2		1	1			11		
Lexington	157	13	Fisk	David Jr		1	1	1			1		1				5		
Lincoln	14	26	Fisk	Elijah		1	1				2	1					5		
Waltham	113	21	Fisk	Francis		1	1	1		1	1	1					6		
Hollistown	237	14	Fisk	John	1			1					1				3		
Sherburn	249	26	Fisk	John				1			1		1				3		
Lexington	157	15	Fisk	Joseph		1		1	1			1	1				5		
Lexington	157	16	Fisk	Joseph Jr	2	1		1		1		1	1				7		
Hollistown	237	18	Fisk	Levi	2			1		2			1				6		
Pepperell	30	44	Fisk	Micah	1												1		
Natick	246	23	Fisk	Moses	1	1	2	1			1		1				7		
Hollistown	237	15	Fisk	Nathan	2			1					1				4		
Lincoln	13	8	Fisk	Phinehas		1		1			2		1				5		
Waltham	113	20	Fisk	Samuel		3		1				1		1			6		
Cambridge	223	6	Fisk	Thaddeus		1		1		3	1	1	1				8		
Weston	107	22	Fiske	Abijah	2	1		1		1	1		1				7		
Weston	107	18	Fiske	Ebenezer	1			1		2		1					5		
Weston	107	19	Fiske	Jacob	2		1	1		1			1	1			7		
Weston	107	16	Fiske	Jonathan		1	1						1				3		
Weston	107	17	Fiske	Nathan	2	1				1		1	1				7		
Weston	107	15	Fiske	Samuel	1	1			2			2		1			7		
Bedford	162	3	Fitch	David				1					1	1			3		
Bedford	162	6	Fitch	David Jr		1					1						2		

| TOWN | PG# | LN# | HEADS OF HOUSEHOLD | | FREE WHITE MALES | | | | | FREE WHITE FEMALES | | | | | TOTAL ALL OTHER | TOTAL SLAVES | TOTALS | DISTRICT/ TOWNSHIP | NOTES |
			LAST NAME	FIRST NAME	under 10	10 to 16	16 to 26	26 to 45	45 and over	under 10	10 to 16	16 to 26	26 to 45	45 and over					
Hopkinton	241	16	Fitch	Hannah		1	1				1	2		1			6		
Bedford	162	4	Fitch	Jeremiah		1	1		1			1		1			5		
Medford	100	9	Fitch	Jno' B.	1	1		1		3			1		1		8		
Natick	246	27	Fitch	John	2			2		2	2		1	1			10		
Pepperell	30	42	Fitch	Jonas		1		1			1			1			4		
Bedford	162	1	Fitch	Matthew		1		2					1	3	1		8		
Bedford	162	2	Fitch	Moses	1		1		1	1	1		1				6		
Acton	17	4	Fitch	Noah	2			1					1				4		
Bedford	162	5	Fitch	Thaddeus	2				1			2	1	1			7		
Groton	209	14	Fitch	Zacht Capt.		1	2		1			1	1	2			8		
Lincoln	14	13	Flag	Silas	2	1		1					1				5		
Waltham	113	25	Flagg	Bezatesel Jr	2		1	1		2			1				7		
Waltham	113	24	Flagg	Bezayeel		1		1				1					3		
Littleton	202	29	Flagg	Daniel		1	1			2		1					5		
Townsend	26	24	Flagg	Elijah	1				1	2	2		1				7		
Burlington	154	22	Flagg	Goliah		1		1		2			1				5		
Woburn	149	30	Flagg	Hiram	4			1		1	1	1					8		
Weston	107	21	Flagg	Isaac				1		1	1		1				4		
East Sudbury	66	11	Flagg	John	2	1		2		3	1	1	1				11		
Weston	107	20	Flagg	John		1	1		1		2		1				6		
Wilmington	142	3	Flagg	John	2			1		2		1					6		
Woburn	149	29	Flagg	John		1	1		1	1			1				5		
Framingham	74	16	Flagg	Jonathan	1		1			1	1		1				5		
Newton	119	14	Flagg	Joshua		1	1		1			1					4		
Waltham	113	22	Flagg	Solomon		1	4	1		1		1	1				9		
Reading	131	28	Flagg	Theodias	1			1		1		1					4		
Waltham	113	26	Flagg	Timothy			1	1						1			3		
Ashby	35	15	Flagg	Wm		1		1						1			3		
Hopkinton	241	21	Flagg	Wm		1	1		1			1		1			5		
Ashby	35	22	Flagge	Allen	1			1		1	1						4		
Cambridge	223	30	Flagsawyer	Samll			2	2				1					5		
Ashby	35	14	Flant	Edmund	1	1		1		2	1	1					7		
Boxborough	199	23	Fletcher	Abel	1	1	1		1	1	1		1				7		
Westford	180	38	Fletcher	Amos		1	2		1	1		1		1			7		
Chelmsford	169	26	Fletcher	Andr'			1										1		
Westford	180	33	Fletcher	Andri'		2		1		3	1		1				8		
Chelmsford	169	34	Fletcher	Benja		1		1		1	1		1				5		
Chelmsford	169	35	Fletcher	Benja' Jr		1	1			1	1	1					5		
Groton	209	21	Fletcher	David	1		2	1		1			1	1			7		
Westford	180	30	Fletcher	David				1			1		1				3		
Westford	180	31	Fletcher	David Jr		1		1					1				3		
Boxborough	199	15	Fletcher	Eleazer		1		1					1				3		
Boxborough	199	16	Fletcher	Eleazer Jr	2	1		1		1		1					6		
Tyngsborough	42	19	Fletcher	Elijah	1		1					1					3		
Westford	181	4	Fletcher	Eliza'			1				2		1				4		
Groton	209	30	Fletcher	Ezekiel		1		1			3						5		
Groton	209	31	Fletcher	Ezekiel Jr	3		1		1	1		1					7		
Tyngsborough	42	16	Fletcher	Jacob		1		1					1				3		
Acton	18	29	Fletcher	James	1	1		1		1		1					5		
Ashby	35	16	Fletcher	James				1		1	2	2		1			7		
Pepperell	31	2	Fletcher	John			1	1					1				3		
Westford	180	39	Fletcher	Jona'				1					1				2		
Dunstable	216	22	Fletcher	Jona Capt.		1	1			1	1		1				6		
Westford	181	2	Fletcher	Jona' Jr		1	1	1					1				4		
Ashby	35	17	Fletcher	Jonas			1			1			1				3		
Westford	180	40	Fletcher	Jos'	2	1	1	1		2		1	1				9		
Chelmsford	169	29	Fletcher	Joseph	3		1			1			1				6		
Dunstable	216	23	Fletcher	Joseph	1		1		1	1	1	1					7		
Littleton	202	19	Fletcher	Joseph		1	3	1		2	1		1				9		
Chelmsford	169	30	Fletcher	Josiah				1									1		
Chelmsford	169	31	Fletcher	Josiah Jr	2		1	1				1	2				7		
Chelmsford	169	27	Fletcher	Levi'	2			1		2			1	1			7		
Groton	209	33	Fletcher	Lyman			1						1				2		
Tyngsborough	42	20	Fletcher	Mercy		1						1	3	1			6		
Dunstable	217	2	Fletcher	Nathl Capt.		1	1						2				4		
Chelmsford	169	32	Fletcher	Nehson'	1			1		2			1				5		
Groton	209	28	Fletcher	Oliver				1		1			1				3		
Westford	180	32	Fletcher	Oliver				1				2		1			4		
Westford	180	36	Fletcher	Paletiah		1	2	1				2		1			7		
Groton	209	26	Fletcher	Peletiah	4	1		1		1	2	1	1				11		
Acton	17	7	Fletcher	Peter		1		1					1				3		
Dunstable	217	1	Fletcher	Phinehas		1	1	1		3	1	2	1	1			11		
Groton	209	29	Fletcher	Sador	1			1		2			1				5		
Chelmsford	169	36	Fletcher	Saml				1					1				2		
Dunstable	217	3	Fletcher	Saml	1			1		1		1	1				5		
Westford	180	42	Fletcher	Saml'	1	1			1	3	2	2	1				11		
Westford	181	1	Fletcher	Samson	1	2		1		1	1		1				7		
Littleton	204	13	Fletcher	Samuel	2			1					1				4		
Westford	180	41	Fletcher	Seth		1	1		1			2		1			6		

| | | | HEADS OF HOUSEHOLD | | FREE WHITE MALES | | | | | FREE WHITE FEMALES | | | | | | | | | |
TOWN	PG#	LN#	LAST NAME	FIRST NAME	under 10	10 to 16	16 to 26	26 to 45	45 and over	under 10	10 to 16	16 to 26	26 to 45	45 and over	TOTAL ALL OTHER	TOTAL SLAVES	TOTALS	DISTRICT/TOWNSHIP	NOTES
Westford	181	3	Fletcher	Simeon	2			1	1		1		1				6		
Chelmsford	169	37	Fletcher	Solomon			1						1				2		
Chelmsford	169	28	Fletcher	Susan									1	1			2		
Westford	180	34	Fletcher	Tho'				1						1			2		
Westford	180	35	Fletcher	Tho' Jr	1		1	1		2	1		1				7		
Dunstable	216	21	Fletcher	Thomas		1			1			2		1			5		
Westford	180	37	Fletcher	Willard	1	1		1	1	1	1		1				7		
Tyngsborough	42	18	Fletcher	William	1	1		1		2			1				6		
Chelmsford	169	33	Fletcher	Wm		1	1		1	1			1				5		
Groton	209	32	Fletcher	Zryling	1			1		1							3		
Concord	6	1	Flint	Abishai	1	1		2		2		1	1				8		
Reading	131	14	Flint	Adam	1			1	3	1	1	1	1	2			11		
Carlisle	22	24	Flint	Amos	3	1	1		1	1	1	2	1				11		
Reading	131	19	Flint	Benjamin		1	1		1			2		1			6		
Tyngsborough	42	21	Flint	Charles	2	1		1		2	1	1	2	1	1		12		
Reading	131	17	Flint	Daniel	2	1	2	1		3	2	1	1				13		
Reading	131	18	Flint	Daniel Jr	2			1		3			1				7		
Tewksbury	51	9	Flint	Eben			1			1			1				3		
Reading	131	15	Flint	Ebenezer	2	1	1		1	1				1			7		
Concord	8	13	Flint	Edward	1	1	2		1	1	2	2		2			12		
Reading	131	16	Flint	Eleazer			1		1				1	1			4		
Reading	131	25	Flint	Eleazer Jr	2			1		2			1				6		
Groton	209	9	Flint	Elisha	2			1		1			1				5		
Lincoln	14	23	Flint	Ephraim		2		1		1	2	2					8		
Reading	131	10	Flint	George			1						1				2		
Reading	131	11	Flint	George Jr	1	1		1		1			1				5		
Carlisle	21	1	Flint	Henry	2	1			1			1	2	1			8		
Reading	131	26	Flint	Hezekiah	1	1			1	1	1		1				6		
Reading	131	9	Flint	John								1		1			2		
Townsend	26	33	Flint	John		1		1	1		1	2		1			7		
Reading	131	23	Flint	John Jr	2	1		1		3		1	1				9		
Littleton	204	7	Flint	Josiah		1							1				2		
Reading	131	29	Flint	Kindel	1			1		2		1	1				6		
Reading	131	30	Flint	Levy		1	1		1	2	1		1				7		
Concord	11	6	Flint	Mary	1					2			1				4		
Dracut	45	29	Flint	Nehemiah		1		1		1	3						6		
Littleton	204	9	Flint	Willard	1	1		1					1				4		
Reading	131	12	Flint	William		1	1	1			1		1				6		
Reading	131	13	Flint	William Jr	3			1		2	2		1				9		
Medford	100	18	Floyd	Benja		1			1	1	1		1				5		
Medford	100	19	Floyd	Benja Jr	2			1		1	2	1					7		
Medford	100	20	Floyd	Isaac			1		1		1		1				4		
Medford	100	21	Floyd	James	2			1					1				4		
Malden	94	11	Floyd	Jos'	1	2			1	2		1	1	1			9		
Cambridge	223	28	Fluker	Mima							1	1	1	1			4		
Waltham	113	19	Foley	John		2		1		1			1				5		
Malden	94	10	Forbes	Cha'				1									1		
Stow	197	1	Forbush	Abraham	1	2	2		1	2	1		1				10		
Wilmington	142	2	Ford	Cad*		2		1	1	1	1		1				7		
Chelmsford	169	25	Ford	John			3	1	1	1		1	1				8		
Tyngsborough	42	17	Ford	John	1			1				1					3		
Cambridge	223	35	Fortner	Nathl			1			1		1					3		
Charlestown	83	43	Fosdick	David	1	2		1		2	1	3	1				11		
Reading	131	7	Foster	Abigail										2			2		
Reading	131	21	Foster	Abraham	1			1		2		1	1				6		
Ashby	35	19	Foster	Abram	2			1		1	2	1	1				8		
Tewksbury	51	1	Foster	Amos				1		1	1	1					7		
Cambridge	223	33	Foster	Bassender	1	2	2	2	1	1	1		1	1			12		
Carlisle	22	16	Foster	Benjamin	1	1		1		4	1		1				9		
Ashby	35	18	Foster	David	1			1		2			1				5		
Wilmington	142	6	Foster	Ebenezer		1	1		1		1			1			5		
Littleton	201	21	Foster	Edmond	3	2			1	2	2		2				12		
Sherburn	249	25	Foster	Eli		1		1			1		1				4		
Hollistown	237	23	Foster	Isaac	1	1		1		2			2				7		
Tewksbury	51	6	Foster	Isaac			1	1					1				3		
Chelmsford	169	13	Foster	Isaiah				1									1		
Charlestown	84	16	Foster	Jacob	1	3	5	2		3	1	1	1				17		
Chelmsford	169	14	Foster	Jacob				1	1	1	1		1				5		
Hopkinton	241	17	Foster	James	2	1			1	3			1				8		
Tewksbury	51	10	Foster	James			1	1		1				1			4		
Carlisle	21	24	Foster	Jane									1				1		
Medford	100	22	Foster	Jno'			1						1				2		
Ashby	35	20	Foster	John	3	1	1		1	2		1		1			10		
Boxborough	199	18	Foster	John		2			1	1			1				5		
Cambridge	223	36	Foster	John	2	2		1		3		1	1				10		
Carlisle	21	9	Foster	John	2			1		2			1				6		
Wilmington	142	5	Foster	John			1			2		1					4		
Ashby	35	21	Foster	Jona			1		1				1				3		
Tewksbury	51	2	Foster	Jona			1	1		1		2		1			6		

160

TOWN	PG#	LN#	LAST NAME	FIRST NAME	FWM under 10	FWM 10 to 16	FWM 16 to 26	FWM 26 to 45	FWM 45 and over	FWF under 10	FWF 10 to 16	FWF 16 to 26	FWF 26 to 45	FWF 45 and over	TOTAL ALL OTHER	TOTAL SLAVES	TOTALS	DISTRICT/ TOWNSHIP	NOTES
Townsend	26	34	Foster	Jona	1	1			1	1			1				5		
Reading	131	8	Foster	Jonathan					1		1	2		1			5		
Westford	181	6	Foster	Jos'	2	1		1		2			1				7		
Tewksbury	51	8	Foster	Joseph	1			1		2		1					5		
Townsend	26	26	Foster	Leonard	2	1		1		4	1		1				10		
Chelmsford	169	22	Foster	Mary	1		1						1	1			4		
Reading	131	22	Foster	Mary	2	2	1			1	1	1	1	1			10		
Marlborough	194	14	Foster	Nathan	2			1		1			1				5		
Cambridge	223	14	Foster	Noah	1			1						1			3		
Westford	181	5	Foster	Saml'		1		1		1	1		1	1			6		
Wilmington	142	4	Foster	Samuel		1	2		1	1	1			1			7		
Tewksbury	50	37	Foster	Sarah			1			1	1		1				4		
Carlisle	22	15	Foster	Smith	2			1		1	1	1					6		
Lincoln	14	21	Foster	Solomon		1	1						1	1			4		
Charlestown	83	41	Foster	Tho'	2			3		2			1				8		
Billerica	175	30	Foster	Timo'					1		1	2	2	1			7		
Reading	131	27	Foster	William	1		1			1	1		1	1			6		
Tewksbury	51	7	Foster	Wm		1		1		1	1	1	1				6		
Medford	100	16	Fowl	Henry				1						1			2		
Medford	100	15	Fowl	John	3	2		1						1			7		
Cambridge	223	17	Fowl	Martha										1			1		
Woburn	149	21	Fowle	Benjamin		1	2	1						1			5		
Woburn	149	32	Fowle	Bill	3		1	1		2	2		1				10		
Woburn	149	26	Fowle	Bridgett										1			1		
Watertown	232	21	Fowle	Edmund	3	2		1		1	2		1				10		
Woburn	149	23	Fowle	Jane	1	1	1					1	1				5		
Watertown	232	17	Fowle	Jeremiah	1	1	2	1		1	1	2		1			10		
Watertown	232	20	Fowle	John	2		3	1		2	2	1	1		1		13		
Woburn	149	31	Fowle	John	2	1	1	1		2	1	1	1				10		
Woburn	149	25	Fowle	Joseph	1		1	1		1		2	1				7		
Woburn	149	22	Fowle	Josiah				1			1		1				3		
Burlington	154	24	Fowle	Samuel	1	2			1	1	1	1		1			8		
Woburn	149	24	Fowle	Samuel				1			1		1	1			4		
Reading	131	24	Fowler	Lowel		1		1		1		1					4		
Dracut	46	36	Fox	Abijah	1		1		1	2	1	1		1			8		
Charlestown	83	40	Fox	Ann									1				1		
Dracut	48	4	Fox	Daniel			1			2		1					4		
Dracut	48	3	Fox	David		2	3	1			1	2		1			10		
Dracut	47	36	Fox	Eliphalet	1		3	1		2	2			2			11		
Dracut	46	37	Fox	Joel	1	3		1		2			1				8		
Charlestown	83	39	Fox	John	2	1		1					1				5		
Dracut	47	34	Fox	Josiah		2		1		2	2		1				8		
Boxborough	199	20	Fox	Peter				1					1				2		
Dracut	47	35	Fox	Peter		1				1		1					3		
Woburn	149	28	Fox	Thomas				1					1				2		
Woburn	149	27	Fox	William	2			1		1			1				5		
Cambridge	223	16	Foxcraft	John				2				2	1				5		
Natick	246	26	Frail	David	1		2			1			1	1			6		
Hopkinton	241	20	Frail	Joseph		1			1	2	2		1				7		
Hopkinton	241	19	Frail	Saml	1	1		1		1	1		1				6		
Hollistown	237	20	Frail	Sarah									2				2		
Medford	100	11	Francis	Convers	1	1		2		2		1	1				8		
Medford	100	12	Francis	Eliza									1				1		
Medford	100	13	Francis	Jane									1				1		
Tyngsborough	42	23	Fredric	George	2			1		2	1		1				7		
Hopkinton	241	25	Freeland	Abrm		1		1		1			1				4		
Chelmsford	169	23	Freeland	John			1		1				1				3		
Hopkinton	241	26	Freeland	Thos	1	1		1			1	2	1	1			8		
Hopkinton	241	24	Freeland	Wm	1	2	1		1	1	1		1				8		
Reading	131	33	Freeman	*											4		4		
Concord	11	27	Freeman	Brister											4		4		
Reading	131	32	Freeman	Dors											2		2		
Littleton	204	1	Freeman	Jacob											3		3		
Reading	131	34	Freeman	Jonah											2		2		
Sherburn	249	27	Freeman	Lewis											5		5		
Reading	131	31	Freeman	Peter											3		3		
Cambridge	223	40	Freeman	Ruth										1	1		2		
Tewksbury	50	27	French	Aaron		2	1		1	1	1	2		1			9		
Dunstable	217	4	French	Ebenz		1	1		1			1		1			5		
Billerica	175	32	French	Isaac	1	1	1		1	1		1		1			7		
Billerica	175	34	French	Isaac 3rd	1	1	1			1		1					5		
Billerica	175	33	French	Isaac Jr	1	3			1	1	1	1		1			9		
Billerica	175	35	French	Jesse				1						1			2		
Tewksbury	50	28	French	Joel		1	1		1	1	1		1				6		
Tewksbury	50	19	French	John		1		1	1				1	1			5		
Billerica	175	37	French	Jonas				1					1				2		
Dunstable	217	5	French	Jonas	1	1	1						2				6		
Tewksbury	50	23	French	Joseph					1	1			1				3		
Tewksbury	50	25	French	Joseph Jr	3	2		1		2	1		1				10		

161

TOWN	PG#	LN#	LAST NAME	FIRST NAME	FREE WHITE MALES					FREE WHITE FEMALES					TOTAL ALL OTHER	TOTAL SLAVES	TOTALS	DISTRICT/ TOWNSHIP	NOTES
					under 10	10 to 16	16 to 26	26 to 45	45 and over	under 10	10 to 16	16 to 26	26 to 45	45 and over					
Concord	7	3	French	Nathaniel	2		2	1		3	2		1				11		
Tewksbury	50	22	French	Nehemi	3		1		1	1	1		1				8		
Billerica	175	36	French	Seth	1			1		1			1				4		
Tewksbury	50	24	French	Solomon			1		1		1		1				4		
Tewksbury	50	26	French	Solomon Jr		1		1		1			1	1			5		
Tewksbury	50	20	French	Thos				1				1	1	1			4		
Dracut	46	8	Friend	Isaac	1			1		2			1				5		
Billerica	175	38	Friend	Reuben	4	1		1		2			1				9		
Tewksbury	50	36	Frost	Abiel				2					1				3		
Cambridge	223	12	Frost	Amos	3	2		1	1	2		1	1	1			12		
Chelmsford	169	21	Frost	Asa	2		3	1		2			1				9		
Tewksbury	50	35	Frost	Benja		1			1				1				3		
Cambridge	223	20	Frost	Cooper	2			1		2			1				6		
Cambridge	223	26	Frost	David			1	1					1				3		
Chelmsford	169	20	Frost	Ebenz				1					1				2		
Framingham	74	3	Frost	Elisha	3	1		1		2	1	1	1				10		Stamped pg# was x'd out
Cambridge	223	9	Frost	Ephhm	2		2	1		2		1	2				11		
Tewksbury	50	34	Frost	Ephm			1	1									2		
Cambridge	223	24	Frost	Gideon				1				1	2				4		
Cambridge	223	15	Frost	James		1		1			1	2		1			6		
Cambridge	223	27	Frost	James				2			1						3		
Cambridge	223	10	Frost	John	3		1	1		2	1	1	1				10		
Cambridge	223	19	Frost	John	2			1		2	1	2		1			9		
Sherburn	249	24	Frost	John	2			1		2			1				6		
Tewksbury	50	21	Frost	John			1						1				2		
Tewksbury	50	33	Frost	Jonath Jr	3		1	1					1				6		
Tewksbury	50	32	Frost	Jonathan		1		1		1			1				4		
Tewksbury	50	29	Frost	Joseph	2			1		3		2	1	1			10		
Tewksbury	50	31	Frost	Joseph Jr	1		1	1		2			1				6		
Charlestown	84	18	Frost	Marg'	1						1						2		
Charlestown	84	17	Frost	Mary									1				1		
Cambridge	223	38	Frost	Nepton											3		3		
Medford	100	17	Frost	Rufus		1	1						1				3		
Framingham	74	2	Frost	Samuel		1			1	2	2		1	1			8		Stamped pg# was x'd out
Cambridge	223	7	Frost	Sarah		2				2			1	2			7		
Cambridge	223	8	Frost	Sarah	1									3			4		
Shirley	214	9	Frost	Seripter	2			1		2	1		1				7		
Cambridge	223	11	Frost	Seth	1	2		1		2	1	1	1				9		
Groton	209	16	Frost	Solomon	2	1		1			1		1				6		
Cambridge	223	13	Frost	Stephen	1		1		1	1	3	2		1			10		
Cambridge	223	23	Frost	Walter	2	2	2	1		1	2			1			11		
Cambridge	223	25	Frost	Willm			1					1					2		
Billerica	175	31	Frost	Wm	2	1		1		2			1				7		
Tewksbury	50	30	Frost	Zephani	1		1	1		3	1		1				8		
Charlestown	84	3	Frothingham	Benja'		1	3		1		1		1	1			8		
Charlestown	84	4	Frothingham	Benja' Jr			1										1		
Charlestown	84	8	Frothingham	Debor'									1				1		
Charlestown	84	2	Frothingham	Jabez			1					2	1				4		
Charlestown	84	6	Frothingham	James				1					1				2		
Charlestown	84	7	Frothingham	James Jr		1	1	1		3	1		1				8		
Charlestown	84	1	Frothingham	Richd		3	3		1	2	1			2			12		
Charlestown	84	5	Frothingham	Tho'		2		1									3		
Reading	131	20	Fry	Mary	1	1			2	3			2	2			11		
Dracut	48	6	Frye	Jedidiah	1			1				1					3		
Dracut	45	26	Frye	Timothy			2		1	1		2		1			7		
Watertown	232	18	Fullar	Joshua	1			1					1	1			4		
Newton	119	16	Fuller	Amariah				1					1				2		
Newton	119	10	Fuller	David		1			1		2	1		1			6		
Littleton	204	32	Fuller	Ebenezer W.	2			1					1				4		
Cambridge	223	37	Fuller	Ebenz	1			1		2			1				5		
Newton	119	15	Fuller	Edward		1	1		1				1				5		
Newton	119	9	Fuller	Joseph	4	1			2	2			1	1			12		
Newton	119	8	Fuller	Joseph Jr			1						1				2		
Newton	119	11	Fuller	Joshua		1	2		1		1	1		2			8		
Newton	119	18	Fuller	Josiah			1	1					1	1			4		
Waltham	113	29	Fuller	Lydia									1				1		
Weston	107	23	Fuller	Moses	2	1			1	1	1			1			7		
Newton	119	12	Fuller	Nathan			2		1		1	1		1			6		
Newton	119	19	Fuller	Nathl	1				1	2	1		1				6		
Newton	119	17	Fuller	Sarah				1					1				2		
Billerica	175	39	Fuller	Silas				1				1		1			3		
Newton	119	13	Fuller	Silas	2		1	2		1			1				8		
Medford	100	14	Fulton	Sarah								1	2	1			4		
Acton	17	12	Furbush	David				1		2			1				4		
Weston	107	14	Furbush	Elisha	2			1					1				4		
Acton	17	6	Furbush	Ephraim	2		1	1	1	2	2		1				10		
Chelmsford	169	15	Furbush	Silas	1		1			1		1					4		
Acton	17	13	Furbush	Simeon	1			1					1				3		
Charlestown	84	38	Gage	Ebenz	2	1	1	1					1	1			7		
Lincoln	15	9	Gage	Lydia	1								1	1			3		

TOWN	PG#	LN#	LAST NAME	FIRST NAME	FREE WHITE MALES under 10	10 to 16	16 to 26	26 to 45	45 and over	FREE WHITE FEMALES under 10	10 to 16	16 to 26	26 to 45	45 and over	TOTAL ALL OTHER	TOTAL SLAVES	TOTALS	DISTRICT/ TOWNSHIP	NOTES
Waltham	114	1	Gale	Alpheus	1	1	2	1		2	1		1				9		
Waltham	114	2	Gale	Jacob				1		1			1				3		
Framingham	75	1	Gallett	John	1			1		1			1				4		
Framingham	68	18	Gallett	Peter					1				2				3		Stamped pg# was x'd out
Cambridge	224	6	Gammage	Wm	1	3	1		1	2	2	1	1				12		
Cambridge	224	5	Gannett	Caleb		1	2		1	1	1	1	1				8		
Groton	209	36	Gap	Thomas	2			1					1				4		
Charlestown	85	1	Gardner	*	1			1		1		1					4		
Sherburn	249	30	Gardner	Aaron		1			1	1	1		1	1			6		
Littleton	203	20	Gardner	Bela			1						1				2		
Watertown	232	26	Gardner	Benjm	1		1			1			1				4		
Charlestown	85	4	Gardner	Edw'	1		1		1			2		2			7		
Cambridge	224	16	Gardner	Jethro											3		3		
Charlestown	85	3	Gardner	John			1		1		4	1	1				8		
Charlestown	85	2	Gardner	John Jr	2			1					1	1			5		
Watertown	232	24	Gardner	Joseph			1	1	1				2	2			7		
Charlestown	84	46	Gardner	Martha									1				2		
Groton	210	8	Gardner	Mary Ann Wid.	1		2			2	1	3	1				10		
Cambridge	224	15	Gardner	Richd	1		3	1			2	3					10		
Charlestown	85	5	Gardner	Saml			1	1		1	1		1				5		
Dracut	47	8	Gardner	Samll			1		1	2		1		2			7		
Groton	210	5	Gardner	Thomas Maj.	4		2	1		2		1	1		1		12		
Cambridge	224	14	Gardner	Thos		1	3	1	1	2		2	1				11		
Weston	107	25	Garfield	Damarus			1						1				2		
Lincoln	14	25	Garfield	Elisha			1	1					1				3		
Lincoln	13	9	Garfield	Enock			1			1		1					3		
Waltham	114	6	Garfield	Esther	1							1		2			4		
Weston	107	27	Garfield	Joseph	2	2		1		3			1	1			10		
Lincoln	12	1	Garfield	Thadeus	3	1			1	1			1				7		
Townsend	26	43	Gaset	Loten	1			1		1			1				4		
Townsend	26	39	Gaset	Reuben	1	2	1		1	2	1	1		1			10		
Townsend	26	42	Gaset	Ruthie								1		1			2		
Marlborough	189	1	Gassett	John		1			1				1				3		
Ashby	35	32	Gates	Abrm	2			1	1	2	1			1			7		
Stow	196	4	Gates	Caleb			1		1			1		1			4		
Stow	196	21	Gates	Charles		1	1					1					3		
Stow	196	32	Gates	Ebenezer	1	1		1		2		1	1	1			8		
Medford	100	29	Gates	Edm' T.		2	2		1	4	1	2		1			13		
Stow	198	21	Gates	Elisha				1				2		1			4		
Stow	198	33	Gates	Elisha Jr	1		1	1		2		1					6		
Marlborough	190	5	Gates	Elizabeth						1		1	1				3		
Stow	196	3	Gates	Ezekiel	4	2		1		1	1	1					10		
Stow	195	16	Gates	Isaac Jr	2			1			1	1					5		
Stow	196	2	Gates	Israel	1		2	1	1	1	2	2	1	1			12		
Stow	198	11	Gates	Jacob			1			1		1					3		
Stow	195	21	Gates	John	1	1	1		1	2	1			1			8		
Stow	196	10	Gates	Levi	1		1	1		1	1			1			6		
Stow	196	5	Gates	Mary										3			3		
Stow	197	42	Gates	Mary										?			2		
Stow	198	12	Gates	Mary Jr	2					1	1	2		1			7		
Stow	198	13	Gates	Nathan	2			1		1		1					5		
Stow	195	18	Gates	Oliver		1	1					1		1			5		
Stow	197	43	Gates	Oliver Jr	1	1	1			1				1			5		
Ashby	37	22	Gates	Paul		1		1					1				3		
Stow	196	12	Gates	Samuel			1	1			1			1			4		
Stow	196	27	Gates	Thomas	1			1		2	1	1	1				7		
Marlborough	189	30	Gates	William	1		2	1		1	2		1				8		
Sherburn	249	28	Gay	Abigail	2							1					3		
Natick	246	29	Gay	Joseph				1			1	2		1			5		
Watertown	232	27	Gay	Wm	3	1		1		2	1		1				9		
Stoneham	138	16	Geary	Benjamin	2	1		1		3	1		1				9		
Stoneham	138	15	Geary	David	2	1	1		1			2	1				9		
Stoneham	138	17	Geary	Johanna	1								1				2		
Stoneham	138	13	Geary	John				1						1			2		
Stoneham	138	14	Geary	John Jr	2			1			1		1				5		
Charlestown	84	34	George	Wm			1										1		
Watertown	232	25	Gerrey	John	1	1		1		3	1		1				8		
Cambridge	224	7	Gerry	Elbridge	3		2	1		4	1	2	3				16		
Cambridge	224	2	Gervis	Leonard	2	1	5		2		1	4	2	1			18		
Cambridge	224	4	Gervis	Nathl			3	1	1	2		2	1				10		
Pepperell	31	9	Getchel	Josh	1	1	1		1	3	1	2		1			11		
Charlestown	84	33	Getty	James	1	1		1		1			1				5		
Marlborough	188	20	Gibbon	Samuel	3		1	1		2			2				9		
Sudbury	59	4	Gibbs	Asahel	1	1		2		1			1				6		
Sudbury	59	30	Gibbs	Gill	1			1				1					3		
Sudbury	59	29	Gibbs	Isaac	2		1	1		1			1				6		
Hopkinton	241	27	Gibbs	Jacob				1					1				2		
Charlestown	84	35	Gibbs	James		1	1			2	1						7		
Framingham	74	9	Gibbs	Jonathan				1		1				1			3		Stamped pg# was x'd out
Framingham	74	7	Gibbs	Phinehas	2	1	1	1	1	3	2	1	1	1			14		Stamped pg# was x'd out

TOWN	PG#	LN#	LAST NAME	FIRST NAME	FREE WHITE MALES					FREE WHITE FEMALES					TOTAL ALL OTHER	TOTAL SLAVES	TOTALS	DISTRICT/ TOWNSHIP	NOTES
					under 10	10 to 16	16 to 26	26 to 45	45 and over	under 10	10 to 16	16 to 26	26 to 45	45 and over					
Sudbury	59	31	Gibbs	Ruth	1		1				1	2		1			6		
Hopkinton	241	41	Gibbs	Saml		1	1			1			1				4		
Hopkinton	241	28	Gibbs	Wm	3		2	1	1	2		1	2	1			13		
Ashby	35	33	Gibson	Abrm	1	1		1		2	1	1	1				8		
Stow	197	15	Gibson	Arrington	2	2	1	1				1	1				8		
Charlestown	84	28	Gibson	Asa	2		1						1				4		
Ashby	35	35	Gibson	Ephrm		1								1			2		
Ashby	35	36	Gibson	Israel	1			1					1				3		
Hopkinton	241	35	Gibson	James			1		1	2			1	1			6		
Pepperell	31	7	Gibson	Joseph	1		1			1			1				4		
Ashby	36	3	Gibson	Silas		1	1	1		2	1		1				7		
Pepperell	31	6	Gibson	Simon					1					1			2		
Ashby	35	34	Gibson	Stephen	1		1		1					1			4		
Stow	197	14	Gibson	Stephen				1						1			2		
Acton	18	12	Gilbert	Jude		2		1	1					1			5		
Dracut	48	7	Gilcrest	John	3			1				2	1	1			8		
Townsend	26	37	Giles	Ebenz Jr		1	1	1		1			1				5		
Townsend	29	6	Giles	Isaac	1			1		3			1				6		
Townsend	29	40	Giles	James				1			1		1				3		
Townsend	26	41	Giles	James Jr	2		4	1			1		1				9		
Townsend	26	38	Giles	John	4	2		1	1				1	1			10		
Hollistown	237	24	Giles	Paul	1	1	2	1		2	1	1	1				10		
Malden	94	26	Gill	Joshua					1				1	1			3		
Concord	6	9	Gill	Silas			1			3	1		1				6		
Groton	209	40	Gillson	Amasa					1					1			2		
Groton	209	38	Gillson	Asa	2		1			1			1				5		
Groton	209	43	Gillson	Jonas	3			1		1			1	1			7		
Groton	209	39	Gillson	Nathl	1		1			2			1	1			6		
Groton	209	37	Gillson	Nehemiah		2		2		1		1		2			8		
Groton	209	44	Gillson	Nehh Jr	3	1		1		1			1	1			8		
Groton	210	7	Gillson	Peter	2	1		1		1	1		1				7		
Groton	209	42	Gillson	Simeon	1	2		1		3	1		1				9		
Groton	209	41	Gillson	Simon	2			1		3			1				7		
Charlestown	84	36	Gilman	Jona'		1		1					1				3		
Chelmsford	170	2	Gilson	Ichab'			1			1			1				3		
Tyngsborough	42	27	Gilson	Jeremiah	1			1		2	2		1				7		
Hopkinton	241	34	Gilson	John		2		2		2	2		1				9		
Tyngsborough	42	28	Gilson	Levi	2			1		1		1					5		
Tyngsborough	42	29	Gilson	Peter				1		2			1				4		
Tyngsborough	42	26	Gilson	Solomon	2	2		1		1	2		1				9		
Weston	107	32	Gleason	Amos	2			1					1	1			5		
East Sudbury	67	17	Gleason	Edward		1		1			1	3	1		1		8		
East Sudbury	66	14	Gleason	Isaac			1						1				2		
Medford	100	27	Gleason	Jacob	1		1	1		1			1				5		
Marlborough	189	31	Gleason	James	1	1		1		3			1				7		
Framingham	66	13	Gleason	John	1		1		1	1	1		1				6		Stamped pg# was x'd out
Marlborough	192	8	Gleason	John					1		1		1				3		
Marlborough	192	9	Gleason	John Jr		1	1	1		2			1				6		
Bedford	162	7	Gleason	Jonas		2	1		1		2	1	1				8		
Framingham	70	9	Gleason	Jonathan				1	1				2				4		Stamped pg# was x'd out
Billerica	175	41	Gleason	Jos'	2			1					1				4		
Marlborough	189	32	Gleason	Joseph					1				1	1			3		
Medford	100	28	Gleason	Joshua	1			1		1			1				4		
East Sudbury	66	16	Gleason	Luther	1			1		1			1				4		
East Sudbury	66	15	Gleason	Nathan	1			1		3			1				6		
East Sudbury	66	17	Gleason	Reuben		2				2		1		1			6		
Burlington	154	27	Gleason	Thomas				1		1				1			3		
Billerica	175	42	Gleason	Wm					1			1		1			3		
Shirley	214	16	Gleason	Wm	1			1					1				3		
Billerica	175	43	Gleason	Wm Jr		1		1		1			1				4		
Marlborough	191	7	Gleason	Zacheus		1		1					1				3		
Sudbury	61	36	Gleazon	Samuel	2	2			1			1	1				7		
Chelmsford	170	1	Glinn	John	3			1		1			1				6		
Chelmsford	169	38	Gload	John			1				2	1		1			5		
Chelmsford	169	39	Gload	Wm			1			2			1				4		
Tewksbury	52	12	Glode	Samll L		1	1	1					1				4		
Tyngsborough	42	32	Glynn	Isaac	3	1				2	1		1	1			9		
Watertown	232	28	Godard	Abigail									2				2		
Hopkinton	241	40	Godard	Edward		1		1		1	2		1				6		
Hopkinton	241	37	Godard	Saml	2		1	1		2	1	1					8		
Cambridge	224	3	Godard	Thos		1	1		1	1				1			5		
Charlestown	85	9	Goddard	Benja'				1					1				2		
Charlestown	85	10	Goddard	Nath'				1					1				2		
Framingham	74	8	Goddard	Ruth			1						1	3			5		Stamped pg# was x'd out
Charlestown	85	8	Goddard	Step'		1		1		1	2						5		
Cambridge	224	8	Godden	Jona	1	2	1	1		3	2		1				11		
Hopkinton	241	38	Godfry	Saml	1		1			2			1				5		
Hopkinton	241	30	Gody	John	1		1	2	1	2	3		1				11		
Hopkinton	241	31	Gody	Joseph				1					1				2		
Acton	19	29	Gold	Benjamin				3					2				5		

164

TOWN	PG#	LN#	LAST NAME	FIRST NAME	FREE WHITE MALES					FREE WHITE FEMALES					TOTAL ALL OTHER	TOTAL SLAVES	TOTALS	DISTRICT/ TOWNSHIP	NOTES
					under 10	10 to 16	16 to 26	26 to 45	45 and over	under 10	10 to 16	16 to 26	26 to 45	45 and over					
Natick	246	30	Golden	Eleazer		1			1	1		1	1				5		
Hopkinton	241	33	Golden	John	2	1	1	1	1	1	1	1	1				10		
Sherburn	249	35	Golden	John	1			1	1			1		1			5		
Marlborough	189	33	Goodell	Abner	1	1	2	1		3	1	1	1	1			12		
Lincoln	13	13	Goodenough	Isaac			5	1				1	1				8		
Stow	197	40	Goodenow	Eliab	2	1		1		1	1		1				7		
Marlborough	191	26	Goodenow	Jonathan					2					2			4		
Stow	197	36	Goodenow	Samuel			1					1		1			4		
Stow	197	37	Goodenow	Thaddeus	1			1				1					3		
Westford	181	11	Goodhue	Danl		1	2		1		1	1		1			7		
Westford	181	9	Goodhue	Esther								2		1			3		
Westford	181	8	Goodhue	Imla			1										1		
Weston	107	31	Goodhue	Jeremy			2		1		1			1			5		
Westford	181	10	Goodhue	John	1			1		3			1				6		
Dracut	45	28	Goodhue	Moses		1	1	1				2	1				6		
Dracut	45	23	Goodhue	Zach	1			1	1	1		2	2	1			8		
Natick	246	28	Goodnough	Elisha	2			1	1	2	1		1	1			9		
Sudbury	61	37	Goodnow	Abigail		1	1				1						4		
East Sudbury	66	20	Goodnow	Asahel	3			1		2	1		1				8		
Sudbury	57	12	Goodnow	Asher	1	1		1				1					4		
Framingham	78	7	Goodnow	Ephraim	1	1		1		2			1				6		
Sudbury	59	32	Goodnow	Ephraim				1				1	1				3		
Sudbury	60	36	Goodnow	John	1		2		1			2	1	1			8		
Sudbury	59	5	Goodnow	John Jr	2	2		1		2			1				8		
Framingham	66	14	Goodnow	Jonathan	3			1		2			1				7		Stamped pg# was x'd out
Sudbury	57	7	Goodnow	Joseph		1			1		1		1				4		
Sudbury	57	8	Goodnow	Jotham	2	2		1		2		1	1				9		
Sudbury	57	6	Goodnow	Levi	2	1		1		1			1				6		
Sudbury	61	9	Goodnow	Luther		1		2		1		1		1			6		
East Sudbury	66	19	Goodnow	Micah	1			1	1	1	1			1			6		
Sudbury	59	6	Goodnow	Sarah		1	1						1	1			4		
Sudbury	58	1	Goodnow	Silas		1		1	1		1	1	1				6		
Bedford	162	8	Goodridge	William	1			1		2			1	1			6		
Charlestown	84	21	Goodwin	Benja				1		1				1			3		
Charlestown	84	24	Goodwin	David			2		1					1			4		
Charlestown	84	25	Goodwin	David Jr	3	1	1	1		1			1	1			9		
Charlestown	84	20	Goodwin	Edw'			1		1				1				3		
Charlestown	84	27	Goodwin	Edw' Jr		1	2					2					5		
Charlestown	84	26	Goodwin	John	2	1	2	1		1			1				8		
Reading	132	12	Goodwin	John				1						1			2		
Reading	132	13	Goodwin	John Jr	2			1		1	1		1	1			7		
Burlington	154	26	Goodwin	Reuel		1	1	1		1			1				5		
Waltham	114	3	Goodwin	Ruth									1				1		
Charlestown	84	23	Goodwin	Saml				1					1				2		
Billerica	176	1	Goodwin	Tho'	2			1		2	1		1				7		
Burlington	154	25	Goodwin	Thomas	1			1						1			3		
Bedford	162	9	Goodwin	Uriah	3			1		3			1				8		
Charlestown	84	22	Goodwin	Wm		1		1				1		1			4		
Cambridge	224	11	Gookin	Edmund	1	1	1	1		2			1				7		
Cambridge	224	10	Gookin	Esquise	2		1	1		2			1				7		
Charlestown	85	6	Gorham	Nath	2			1		1		1	1				6		
Charlestown	85	7	Gorham	Rebecca								1		1			2		
Hopkinton	241	39	Gossett	Seth			3		1			1					5		
Stoneham	139	6	Gould	Abraham		1		1				1	1	1			5		
Chelmsford	170	4	Gould	Benja'	1			1		3	2		1				8		
Marlborough	193	9	Gould	Benjamin				1						1			2		
Reading	132	5	Gould	Daniel			1	1				1	1	1			5		
Stoneham	139	9	Gould	Daniel		1	1	1		2	1		1	2	1		10		
Stoneham	139	8	Gould	David			1	1				1		1			4		
Tyngsborough	42	30	Gould	David			1						1				2		
Chelmsford	170	3	Gould	Ebenz	1								1				3		
Cambridge	224	1	Gould	Elizabeth	1	1	1			1	2	1	1				8		
Weston	107	24	Gould	Isaac	2			1		1				1			5		
Stoneham	139	7	Gould	Jacob			1	2					1				4		
East Sudbury	66	18	Gould	James		1				1		1		2			5		
Reading	132	4	Gould	James	3		1	1		1	1		1	1			9		
Charlestown	84	37	Gould	Joanna								1					1		
Charlestown	85	11	Gould	John			1			1			1				3		
Reading	132	3	Gould	John	1	2		1		3			1				8		
Reading	132	2	Gould	Joseph				1						1			2		
Westford	181	16	Gould	Mary		1								2			3		
Tyngsborough	42	31	Gould	Noah	2			1		3	1		1				8		
Tyngsborough	42	34	Gould	Reuben	2			1		2			1				6		
Westford	181	7	Gould	Reuben				1						1			2		
Stoneham	139	11	Gould	Thomas	4			1		2			1				8		
Wilmington	142	14	Gout	John	1	1			1	1	1		1				6		
Lincoln	14	9	Gove	Nathaniel	1	1	1		1	1	2	1		1			9		
Lincoln	14	10	Gove	Nathaniel Jr	1		1			1		1					4		
Shirley	214	17	Gowin	Ebenzr				1				1	1				3		
Shirley	214	18	Gowin	Wm	3			1		1	1		1				7		

TOWN	PG#	LN#	LAST NAME	FIRST NAME	FREE WHITE MALES under 10	10 to 16	16 to 26	26 to 45	45 and over	FREE WHITE FEMALES under 10	10 to 16	16 to 26	26 to 45	45 and over	TOTAL ALL OTHER	TOTAL SLAVES	TOTALS	DISTRICT/TOWNSHIP	NOTES
Wilmington	142	7	Gowing	Daniel					1	1			1				3		
Wilmington	142	8	Gowing	Daniel Jr	3	1			1	1	1	1	1				9		
Townsend	26	44	Gowing	Eliab	1			1		2			1		1		6		
Wilmington	142	9	Gowing	Jabez	3			1			2	2					8		
Wilmington	142	10	Gowing	John			1	1				1	1				4		
Wilmington	142	11	Gowing	John Jr		2		1		4	2	1	1	1			12		
Wilmington	142	15	Gowing	Joseph	2			1		1	1		1				6		
Newton	119	21	Grafton	Joseph	2			1		3			1	1			8		
Groton	210	2	Gragg	Joseph	2	1		1		2			1				7		
Groton	210	1	Gragg	Thomas		1			1			1		2			5		
Townsend	26	35	Graham	David					1								1		
Boxborough	200	19	Graham	Reuben		1		1				1					3		
Townsend	26	36	Graham	Saml	2			2		1			1	2			8		
Watertown	232	29	Grant	Christopher		1		1		1			1				4		
Sherburn	249	36	Grant	Hannah		1		1		1		1	1				5		
Watertown	232	30	Grant	Joshua	2		1	2				1	1	1			8		
Reading	132	14	Graves	Daniel	2	1	1	1	1	2	1	1	1				13		
Groton	210	10	Graves	Hannah Wid.								1	1				2		
Groton	210	9	Graves	John			1										1		
Sudbury	57	10	Graves	Jonathan			1	1		1	1		1	1			6		
Hopkinton	241	36	Graves	Nathan	2			1				1		1			5		
Groton	209	35	Graves	Peter		2		1		1		1		1			6		
Charlestown	84	41	Gray	Benja'	4			1		1	1		1				8		
Tewksbury	51	14	Gray	John	2		1			1		1					5		
Tewksbury	51	13	Gray	Jonathan	2	2		1		2	1		1				9		
Medford	100	32	Gray	Wm	3	1	1	1	1		1	1	2				11		
Malden	94	17	Green	Aaron	1	1		1				2					5		
Reading	132	11	Green	Aaron			2	1		2		2	1				8		
Carlisle	22	32	Green	Amos			1					1					2		
Carlisle	22	35	Green	Asa			1					1					2		
Malden	94	16	Green	Barnard	2			1			1	1		1			6		
Charlestown	84	42	Green	Benja'	3			1		1			1				6		
Westford	181	12	Green	Benja'	2		1	1		1			1				6		
Waltham	114	4	Green	Benjm				1			1			2			4		
Reading	132	1	Green	Caleb			2	1		1			1				5		
Westford	181	14	Green	Calvin	1			1					1				3		
Charlestown	84	32	Green	Charlotte								1					1		
Hollistown	237	25	Green	Close	1				1	1	1	2	1				7		
Reading	132	7	Green	Daniel		1		1		2			2				6		
Stoneham	138	18	Green	Daniel	2	2		1		1			1				7		
Westford	181	13	Green	Danl	2		1	1		2	2	1	1				10		
Groton	210	4	Green	David			1										1		
Groton	210	3	Green	Eleazr	2	1		1		1			1				6		
Malden	94	21	Green	Eliza'									1	1			2		
Malden	94	18	Green	Ezra	1			1		1		1					4		
Charlestown	84	31	Green	Fra'		1			1	3	2	1	1				9		
Charlestown	84	43	Green	James	1	1		1			1	1	1				6		
Malden	94	19	Green	James					1				1	1			3		
Pepperell	31	8	Green	James					1			1	1	1			4		
Reading	132	10	Green	Jeremiah		1	2	1		4	2	1	1				12		
Carlisle	22	37	Green	Jesse	2			1					1				4		
Carlisle	22	23	Green	John			1						1				2		
Charlestown	84	30	Green	John				1						1			2		
Malden	94	12	Green	John				1	1				1				3		
Pepperell	31	5	Green	John				1		1		1	2		1		6		
Stoneham	139	5	Green	John				1					2				3		
Sudbury	60	27	Green	John				1		1		1	1				3		
Pepperell	31	4	Green	Jona		1		1		2		1					6		
Groton	210	6	Green	Jonas	1	1	1		1	1	2		1				8		
Malden	94	22	Green	Jonas		1		1			1		1				4		
Waltham	114	5	Green	Jonas			1	1		1		1	1				5		
Stoneham	139	4	Green	Jonathan		2		1				2	1				6		
Groton	210	11	Green	Joshua			1										1		
Stoneham	139	1	Green	Josiah			1		1	1		1					4		
Stoneham	139	2	Green	Josiah Jr	1	1		1		2	1		1				7		
Carlisle	22	4	Green	Leonard	2			1		1	1	1	1	1			8		
Malden	94	14	Green	Lois							1			1			2		
Carlisle	22	36	Green	Nathan			1		1			1	1	1			5		
Reading	132	6	Green	Nathan		1		1		1	1		1	1			6		
Natick	246	31	Green	Newport											4		4		
Stow	196	37	Green	Oliver											5		5		
Malden	94	23	Green	Phins		1		1				1		1			4		
Malden	94	24	Green	Phins Jr		1		1		2	1	1					6		
Concord	10	29	Green	Reuben	3			1					1				5		
Reading	132	8	Green	Reuben		2		1		2			1	1			7		
Malden	94	25	Green	Saml		1	2		1				1		1	1	7		
Carlisle	21	34	Green	Samuel			1	1	1				2	1			6		
Weston	107	26	Green	Samuel		1		1		2			2	1			7		
Reading	132	15	Green	Sarah			1			1			1				3		

TOWN	PG#	LN#	LAST NAME	FIRST NAME	FREE WHITE MALES					FREE WHITE FEMALES					TOTAL ALL OTHER	TOTAL SLAVES	TOTALS	DISTRICT/ TOWNSHIP	NOTES
					under 10	10 to 16	16 to 26	26 to 45	45 and over	under 10	10 to 16	16 to 26	26 to 45	45 and over					
Stoneham	139	10	Green	Sarah		1							1		1		3		
Townsend	29	38	Green	Simeon	1			1					1	1			4		
Pepperell	31	3	Green	Simon	1		1	1				2	1				6		
Townsend	26	40	Green	Solo	4	2		1		1			1				9		
Reading	132	9	Green	Thomas				1					2	1			4		
Stoneham	139	3	Green	Thomas	3		1	1		1	1	1	1	1			10		
Charlestown	84	44	Green	Wm	1	1		1				1					4		
Malden	94	20	Green	Wm	1					1		1	1				5		
Carlisle	22	34	Green	Zacheus		1	2	2	1			1	2				9		
Medford	100	31	Green	Wm				1					1				2		
Ashby	35	30	Greene	Isaac	1			1			2		1				5		
Ashby	35	31	Greene	Wm	2	1		1		3		1	1				9		
Weston	107	28	Greenleaf	Enoch				1					1				2		
Medford	100	23	Greenleaf	Gardner				1				1					2		
Medford	100	24	Greenleaf	Gardner Jr			1			3			1				5		
Medford	100	26	Greenleaf	Isaac		1		1		3	2	2	1				10		
Medford	100	25	Greenleaf	Jona'		2		1				1					4		
Newton	119	20	Greenough	William	2			1		2	2	1	2				10		
Framingham	66	9	Greenwood	Abel	1	1	3		2	3	1	2	1	1			15		Stamped pg# was x'd out
Framingham	66	11	Greenwood	James	1	1		1		2				3			8		Stamped pg# was x'd out
Sherburn	249	31	Greenwood	Jonas				1				2	1				4		
Sherburn	249	32	Greenwood	Jonas Jr	1		1					1					3		
Newton	119	23	Greenwood	Miles	1		1	1		2	2	1	1				9		
Hopkinton	241	32	Greenwood	Moses	3	2		1					2				8		
Cambridge	224	9	Greenwood	Nevin			1										1		
Sherburn	249	33	Greenwood	Reuben	1		1			1			1				4		
Framingham	70	17	Greenwood	William			1						1	1			3		Stamped pg# was x'd out
Newton	119	22	Greggs	William	1			1		2			1	1			6		
Framingham	66	12	Gregory	Daniel		1		1		1			1				4		Stamped pg# was x'd out
Ashby	35	28	Gregory	Isaac				1		1			1				3		
Ashby	35	29	Gregory	Josiah			1			2			1				4		
Concord	5	5	Gregory	Marshall			1			1		1					3		
Weston	107	30	Gregory	Silas			1			1		1					3		
Weston	107	29	Gregory	Uriah	1	1	1		1			2		1			7		
East Sudbury	69	2	Griffin	Daniel		1		1		2		1	1				6		
Wilmington	142	12	Griffin	Ebenezer			1			4		1					6		
Wilmington	142	13	Griffin	James				1						1			2		
Westford	181	15	Griffin	Mathis		1		1				1		1			4		
East Sudbury	66	13	Griffin	Samuel		1	1	1		1		1	1	1			7		
Tewksbury	51	11	Griffin	Shamll		1	1	1				2	1	2			8		
Tewksbury	51	12	Griffin	Uriah		2		1		1		2	1				7		
Charlestown	84	29	Griffith	James	1			2			2		2		1		8		
Cambridge	224	13	Griggs	Moses	1	2	3	1			1	2	1				11		
Cambridge	224	12	Griggs	Nathl			1	1					1				3		
Newton	119	24	Grimes	James				1									1		
Littleton	201	5	Grimes	William		1	1	1				1	1				5		
Sherburn	249	34	Grout	Belea	1			1					2				4		
Sherburn	249	29	Grout	Elias	1		1	1		1			1				5		
East Sudbury	66	21	Grout	Silas		1	1		1	3			1				7		
Charlestown	84	40	Grover	Ebenz			1						1				2		
Malden	94	13	Grover	Hanh										1			1		
Malden	94	27	Grover	Martha										1			1		
Malden	94	15	Grover	Peter			1	1									2		
Charlestown	84	39	Grover	Simon			2					1	1				4		
Watertown	232	31	Groves	Stephen	1		1						1				3		
Hopkinton	241	29	Guild	Wm			1			2			1				4		
Marlborough	187	8	Guliker	Jane							1	1		1			3		
Medford	100	30	Gyer	Fredk	1			1		3		1	2				8		
Concord	7	18	Ha*well	David		1		1		1			1				4		
Lexington	157	35	Hadley	Benjamin	2			1		3			1				7		
Woburn	149	42	Hadley	Daniel	1		1						1				3		
Medford	101	9	Hadley	Danl'			1					1	1				3		
Woburn	149	35	Hadley	David	1			1		1			1				4		
Woburn	149	41	Hadley	David	3		1			1							5		
Woburn	149	37	Hadley	Ebenezer	1	3		1		1			1				7		
Medford	101	13	Hadley	Huldah									1				1		
Concord	3	9	Hadley	Joseph		1		1				1	1				4		
Charlestown	85	19	Hadley	Moses	2		1		1	1		1		1			7		
Medford	101	10	Hadley	Rich			1			1		1					3		
Medford	101	11	Hadley	Saml		2		1				1		1			5		
Concord	7	2	Hadley	Samuel				1		2	1	1	1				6		
Reading	132	35	Hadley	Sarah	1							2					3		
Bedford	162	15	Hadley	Simon	4		1			2			1	1			9		
Medford	101	8	Hadley	Tho'	2	1		1		1			1				6		
Charlestown	85	31	Hagar	Joel	2		1	1				1	1				6		
Waltham	114	18	Hagar	Joseph	1	1	1	1		2		1	1				8		
Waltham	114	19	Hagar	L*			1							1			2		
Weston	108	9	Hagar	Phinehas	3	2		1		2	1		1	1			11		
Marlborough	193	41	Hager	Abigail		1						1	2	1			5		
Watertown	232	33	Hager	David	2		1			1			1				5		

TOWN	PG#	LN#	LAST NAME	FIRST NAME	FREE WHITE MALES					FREE WHITE FEMALES					TOTAL ALL OTHER	TOTAL SLAVES	TOTALS	DISTRICT/ TOWNSHIP	NOTES
					under 10	10 to 16	16 to 26	26 to 45	45 and over	under 10	10 to 16	16 to 26	26 to 45	45 and over					
Framingham	72	5	Hager	Ephraim	3			1		2			1				7		
Acton	19	28	Hager	Joseph				1					1				2		
Watertown	232	34	Hager	Moses				1					1				2		
Weston	108	1	Hager	Nathan	1		4	1		2	1	1					10		
Marlborough	193	40	Hager	William			2		1			1	1				5		
Charlestown	85	23	Hailey	Charles	1		1					1					3		
Charlestown	85	22	Hailey	Danl				1					1				2		
Medford	101	7	Haines	Tho'				1		2			1				4		
Stow	195	10	Hale	Bezeleel				1					1				2		
Stow	195	11	Hale	Bezeleel Jr	1	2		1		1	1	1	1				8		
Stow	195	9	Hale	Charles	1		2	1		3	1	2	1				11		
Westford	181	20	Hale	Eph'		1	2	1					1				5		
Stow	195	13	Hale	Ephraim			1	1		3			1	1			7		
Stow	195	12	Hale	Jonas		1		1					1				3		
Chelmsford	170	6	Hale	Moses			2	1		3	1		1				8		
Pepperell	31	14	Hale	Saml			1	1				2					4		
Reading	132	33	Hale	Stephen			1	1				2		1			5		
Medford	100	46	Hall	Andr'	2		1	1		3	1	1	1				10		
Dracut	49	13	Hall	Asa	4	1		1		1	1		1	1			10		
Pepperell	31	22	Hall	Benja	2		2	1			1		1				7		
Medford	100	42	Hall	Benja'			1		1		1		1	2	1		7		
Medford	100	43	Hall	Benja' Jr			1	1	1		1	1	1	1	1		8		
Malden	94	45	Hall	Chri			1										1		
Natick	246	33	Hall	David			1		2	1		2	2				8		
Medford	100	38	Hall	Eben		1	2		1			1	2	1	1		9		
Medford	100	40	Hall	Eben 3rd			1	1		1	1	2					6		
Medford	100	39	Hall	Eben Jr		1	2	2				2					7		
Cambridge	224	38	Hall	Ebenz	3	1		1		1	2		1				9		
Charlestown	85	34	Hall	Ebenz			1										1		
Medford	100	45	Hall	Epm		1		1			1	1	2		1		7		
Newton	120	12	Hall	Eward	2	2			1		1	1		1			8		
Medford	100	44	Hall	Fitch	1			1			2		1		1		6		
Medford	100	37	Hall	Fra'	1		1	1		1			1				7		
Groton	210	17	Hall	Isaiah			2	1			2		1				6		
Medford	100	41	Hall	James	1		1					1					3		
Medford	101	4	Hall	Jane									1				1		
Medford	100	36	Hall	Jno'	3			1		1	1		1				7		
Ashby	35	45	Hall	John	4			1		2			1				8		
Tewksbury	51	15	Hall	John				1			1	1	1				4		
Charlestown	86	1	Hall	Jona'	4			1		2			2				9		
Medford	101	5	Hall	Jos' P.	1		1	1		1		1	1				6		
Shirley	214	28	Hall	Josiah				1			1			1			3		
Medford	101	2	Hall	Nath			1			2	1		2				6		
Marlborough	188	37	Hall	Paul	1	1		1	1			1	1	1			7		
Medford	101	1	Hall	Rich		1	2		1			1		2			7		
Dracut	48	18	Hall	Richard			3			1	1	1					6		
Hopkinton	241	42	Hall	Saml				1				1		1			3		
Medford	100	34	Hall	Saml'	2			1		1	2		1	1			8		
Newton	120	24	Hall	Samuel	2	2			1	1	1		1				8		
Newton	120	23	Hall	Solomon	3	1		1		1			2				8		
Medford	101	3	Hall	Step'			1		1				2				4		
Cambridge	224	23	Hall	Thos	1	1	1	1		2	3	1	1				11		
Dracut	47	12	Hall	Timothy	1			1		2	1		1				6		
Medford	100	35	Hall	Willis				1		1		1	1				4		
Westford	181	19	Hall	Willis			1	2		2	2			1			8		
Dracut	47	18	Ham*	John	1		1	1				1	1				5		
Dracut	44	17	Hamblet	Jona	2	1		1				1	1				6		
Westford	181	23	Hamlin	Eleazr		2	4	1				1	1				9		
Newton	120	6	Hammond	Benjm	1			1				2	1				5		
Newton	120	7	Hammond	Benjm Jr	2		1	1		2			1				7		
Natick	246	34	Hammond	Edward	5		1	1	1	2	2	2	2	1			17		
Waltham	114	14	Hammond	Ephraim	1	1	1	1		1	2	2	1				10		
Waltham	114	9	Hammond	Jacob				1				1					2		
Waltham	114	13	Hammond	Jonathan	3		1	1		2	1	1	1				10		
Newton	119	25	Hammond	Joshua	1	1	3			1		2					8		
Newton	120	4	Hammond	Thomas	1	1	1		1	3		1	1				9		
Newton	120	5	Hammond	William			2	1		2	2	2	1				10		
Tyngsborough	42	38	Han*	Jonathan				1				1			5		7		
Charlestown	86	10	Hancock	John	1		1			1		1					4		
Cambridge	225	1	Hancock	Mary		1				1		2					4		
Framingham	76	3	Hancock	Nathan	1	1	1		1		1	2					7		
Acton	18	23	Handley	Amos	3			1		1		1					6		
Acton	18	20	Handley	Charles	2	1		1		3	2	1	1				11		
Acton	19	26	Handley	John	1	1		1		1			1				5		
Concord	3	16	Handley	John	1				1				1	1			4		
Dracut	47	11	Hanich	Israel				1					1				2		
Framingham	76	2	Hanker	Cato									1		2		3		
Concord	8	21	Hannon	Henry				1		2			1				4		
Acton	16	35	Hapgood	Abraham	2	1	1		1	2		2		1			10		

168

TOWN	PG#	LN#	LAST NAME	FIRST NAME	FREE WHITE MALES					FREE WHITE FEMALES					TOTAL ALL OTHER	TOTAL SLAVES	TOTALS	DISTRICT/ TOWNSHIP	NOTES
					under 10	10 to 16	16 to 26	26 to 45	45 and over	under 10	10 to 16	16 to 26	26 to 45	45 and over					
Stow	197	32	Hapgood	Daniel	1	1	2		1	2			1				8		
Acton	17	1	Hapgood	Ephraim		2	1		1	4	1	1	1	1			12		
Marlborough	191	36	Hapgood	John		1	2		1	3	2		1				10		
Marlborough	191	38	Hapgood	Jonathan	1	1	1	1		2	2		1	1			10		
Stow	198	17	Hapgood	Jonathan				1				1		1			3		
Marlborough	192	26	Hapgood	Joseph	1	2			1	3	1		1				9		
Marlborough	192	27	Hapgood	Mary										1	2		3		
Stow	197	27	Hapgood	Samuel	2		1	1				2		1			7		
Marlborough	192	25	Hapgood	Thomas		2	1		1					1			5		
Newton	120	11	Harbach	Thomas					1					1			2		
Charlestown	85	30	Harden	Wm			1			1			1				3		
Littleton	204	16	Harding	Jesse		1		1						1			3		
Stoneham	139	18	Hardy	Antony			1	1	1	3			1	1			8		
Concord	4	25	Hardy	Ebenzer	1	1	1	2		3	2		1	1			12		
Hollistown	237	30	Hardy	Fairbush	3			1							1		5		
Dunstable	217	7	Hardy	Moses		1		1			2		1				5		
Tewksbury	51	25	Hardy	Nathll		2	1		1	1		2	1				8		
Tewksbury	51	16	Hardy	Peter		2	1		1	1	1	1		1			8		
Marlborough	191	37	Hardy	Rachel						1				1			2		
Hopkinton	241	45	Hardy	Seth				1						1			2		
Tewksbury	51	23	Hardy	Wm	1	1	2	1				1		1			7		
Lincoln	14	5	Harrington	Daniel	2			1		1			1				5		
Concord	6	11	Harley	John			2					1					3		
Charlestown	85	20	Harley	Solomon	3		1						1				5		
Cambridge	224	34	Harlow	Asaph		1		1		3		1	1				7		
Wilmington	142	26	Harnden	Augustus	1		1					1					3		
Wilmington	142	18	Harnden	Benjaman		1	2		1	1	1		1				7		
Wilmington	142	22	Harnden	Benjamin Jr															Name crossed out
Malden	95	4	Harnden	Eben	1	1			1	1	1	1		2			8		
Malden	95	3	Harnden	Jno'				1						1			2		
Wilmington	142	17	Harnden	John		1	2	1	1	1	1	1		1			9		
Wilmington	142	25	Harnden	John Jr	1			1					1				3		
Wilmington	142	16	Harnden	Joshua			1	1				3		1			6		
Wilmington	142	23	Harnden	Samuel	1		1			1			1				4		
Watertown	233	1	Harod	John		1			1	4				1			7		
Acton	18	8	Harras	John				1		1		1					3		
Acton	18	39	Harras	Joseph	1			1		1		1	1	1			6		
Lexington	157	20	Harrington	Abijah			1						1				2		
Weston	108	2	Harrington	Abraham	2	2	1		1	1	1	1	1	1			11		
Waltham	114	17	Harrington	Benjm	2	1			1	1			1				6		
Cambridge	224	35	Harrington	Benjn	1			1		2	1		1				6		
Lexington	157	34	Harrington	Charles	1			1		2	1		1				6		
Weston	108	11	Harrington	Charles			1	1		1		1	1	1			6		
Lexington	157	23	Harrington	Daniel				1				2		1			4		
Lexington	157	36	Harrington	Ebenezer	1	2		1		2	1		1	1			9		
Concord	8	26	Harrington	Edward	2			1					2	1			6		
Weston	108	22	Harrington	Enoch			1	1					1	1			4		
Lexington	157	21	Harrington	Isaac	1			1	1	1			1	2			7		
Lexington	157	24	Harrington	Jeremiah				1						1			2		
Waltham	114	10	Harrington	Joel					1	4			1				6		
Weston	108	14	Harrington	Joel	2	1		1		1			1				6		
Marlborough	194	26	Harrington	John	1		2		1			3		2			9		
Medford	101	6	Harrington	Jona'			1						1				2		
Weston	108	15	Harrington	Jonas		1			3				1	1			6		
Lexington	157	18	Harrington	Jonathan				1									1		
Lexington	157	19	Harrington	Jonathan Jr	3		1	1				2		1			8		
Lexington	157	30	Harrington	Joseph	3			2		1			1				7		
Lexington	157	26	Harrington	Levi	2	1		1		2	1		1				8		
Pepperell	31	13	Harrington	Loa	2	1			1	1	2			1			8		
Weston	108	23	Harrington	Loas		1								1			2		
Lexington	157	25	Harrington	Moses	2	2			1			1		1			7		
Woburn	149	39	Harrington	Nathaniel	2		1	1		3	1	1	1				10		
Lexington	157	31	Harrington	Peter	1			1		1		1					4		
Watertown	232	32	Harrington	Peter		2	2		1	3	1			1			10		
Waltham	114	15	Harrington	Saml					1	2		1	1	1			6		
Lexington	157	29	Harrington	Samuel	2			1		4	1		1				9		
Waltham	114	16	Harrington	Samuel Jr	1	1			1			1	2	1			7		
Shirley	214	33	Harrington	Simeon				1				1	1				3		
Lexington	157	32	Harrington	Solomon	3	1	1						1				6		
Weston	108	20	Harrington	Solomon		1		1		2			1				5		
Weston	108	21	Harrington	Stephen					1		1		1	1			4		
Shirley	214	37	Harrington	Thaddeus				1									1		
Chelmsford	170	5	Harrington	Wm	1			1		1			1				4		
East Sudbury	69	19	Harris	Amos	1		1					1		1			4		
Shirley	214	40	Harris	Francis	1			1		1	1		1				5		
Charlestown	85	12	Harris	John		1	1	1					1				4		
Charlestown	86	8	Harris	John Jr	3	1		1		1			1				7		
Concord	11	19	Harris	Jonathan				1		1			1	1			4		
Charlestown	85	14	Harris	Josiah		1	1					1					3		
Watertown	233	5	Harris	Lydia									1	1			2		

169

TOWN	PG#	LN#	LAST NAME	FIRST NAME	FREE WHITE MALES					FREE WHITE FEMALES					TOTAL ALL OTHER	TOTAL SLAVES	TOTALS	DISTRICT/ TOWNSHIP	NOTES
					under 10	10 to 16	16 to 26	26 to 45	45 and over	under 10	10 to 16	16 to 26	26 to 45	45 and over					
Littleton	204	2	Harris	Noah			1		1				1	1			4		
Dracut	46	23	Harris	Peter	1	1		1		2		1					6		
Charlestown	85	13	Harris	Sarah									1				1		
Dracut	46	24	Harris	Simon	2			1		2	1		1				7		
Watertown	232	36	Harris	Stephen	1				2				1				4		
Watertown	233	4	Harris	Stephen Jr	2			1		1			1				5		
Charlestown	86	7	Harris	Tho'	1		2		1	1	2	2		1			10		
Charlestown	85	28	Harrison	Wm	1	1		1		2		2	1				8		
Hollistown	237	31	Harrod	John	1	1			1		1	1		1			6		
Malden	94	43	Hart	Asa	3			1					1				5		
Reading	133	2	Hart	Daniel	3			1		1			1				6		
Townsend	27	1	Hart	Daniel				1					2				3		
Sherburn	250	9	Hart	Willard			1			2			1				4		
Sherburn	250	6	Hart	Wm		1	1		1					2			5		
Reading	133	1	Hart	Joseph			1		1					1			3		
Reading	132	22	Hartshorn	James	1	2	1		1		1	2		1			9		
Reading	132	23	Hartshorn	Jeremiah	1	1							1	1			5		
Reading	132	25	Hartshorn	John	1	1			1	1	2	1	1	2			10		
Concord	6	23	Hartshorn	Martha										1			1		
Reading	132	26	Hartshorn	Timothy		1	2		1			1		1			6		
Shirley	214	25	Hartwell	Amasa		1	1	1		1	2			1			7		
Carlisle	22	7	Hartwell	Asa	1			1					1	1			4		
Shirley	214	35	Hartwell	Benjm Doct.	2			1		1	2	1	1				8		
Littleton	201	11	Hartwell	Daniel	1		1	1			2		1				6		
Carlisle	22	6	Hartwell	David	1	1		1	1				2				6		
Lincoln	13	28	Hartwell	John	1	1		1	1	1	2	2		2	1		12		
Littleton	202	41	Hartwell	John	3				1	1	2	2	1	1			11		
Littleton	205	11	Hartwell	John Jr	2	1	1		1	2			1				9		
Shirley	214	27	Hartwell	Jonathan	3	1	1		1			1	1				10		
Bedford	162	13	Hartwell	Joseph		1			1				2				4		
Shirley	214	29	Hartwell	Reuben	2			1		2	2		1				8		
Groton	210	23	Hartwell	Saml				1		1			1				3		
Townsend	27	7	Hartwell	Saml	1	1	1		1	2	1		1	1			9		
Bedford	162	12	Hartwell	Samuel			1	1		1	1	1					5		
Lincoln	13	30	Hartwell	Samuel		2	2		1			2	1	1			9		
Littleton	201	6	Hartwell	Simon	2			1		2			2				7		
Lexington	157	22	Hartwell	Stephen		1			1			1	1				4		
Littleton	202	5	Hartwell	Thomas	3	1		1		2	1	1	1				10		
Ashby	36	39	Hartwell	Timo	3			1		1			1				6		
Bedford	162	14	Hartwell	William	3		1	1				1	1				7		
Dracut	48	12	Harvey	Benja		1				1			1				3		
Dracut	46	25	Harvey	James				1		1	2	2	1	1			8		
Dracut	48	17	Harvey	John D	2	1			1	3	1		1				9		
Dracut	48	9	Harvey	Joseph	1			1		2			1				5		
Chelmsford	170	18	Harwood	John	1	1	2		1	1	1	2		1			10		
Littleton	201	14	Harwood	Joseph	1	2			1	2		1		1			8		
Cambridge	225	16	Haryd	Dudly	1			1	1			1	1				5		
Charlestown	85	25	Haskel	Jerem		1			2	1				1			5		
Littleton	202	42	Haskell	Solomon		1			1		1	1		1			5		
Malden	95	7	Haskins	Robt				1		1	1	1					4		
Malden	95	1	Haskins	Wm	1			1		2			1				5		
Dracut	45	25	Hasseltine	James		1		1						1			3		
Dracut	45	34	Hasseltine	Peter	1	2			1	2			2				9		
Westford	181	21	Hastens	Saml	1			1					1				3		
Watertown	233	2	Hastings	Benjm Jr	2	2		1	1	3			1				10		
Newton	120	21	Hastings	Daniel	2	1			1	2	1	2		1			10		
Cambridge	225	19	Hastings	Edward		1	1		1	2			1	1			7		
Waltham	114	7	Hastings	Elephalet					1		1		1	1			4		
Waltham	114	8	Hastings	Elephalet Jr			1			1			1				3		
Lexington	157	27	Hastings	Isaac	2	2	1	1			1	2	1				10		
Boxborough	200	11	Hastings	John	1		1						1				3		
Newton	120	20	Hastings	John				1		3	1			1			6		
Stow	196	22	Hastings	John	3		1	1				1	1				8		
Woburn	149	36	Hastings	John		1			1	3	3			1	1		10		
Stow	198	32	Hastings	Jonas	2	1		1		2			1				7		
Waltham	114	11	Hastings	Josiah			1	1				1					3		
Weston	108	19	Hastings	Josiah Jr	1	3	1	1		3			1	1			11		
Cambridge	224	28	Hastings	Lydia									4	1			6		
Cambridge	225	14	Hastings	Reuben	1			2	1		1	1					8		
Cambridge	224	30	Hastings	Saml				3			1	1					5		
Lexington	157	28	Hastings	Samuel				1		1	1		1				4		
Lincoln	13	36	Hastings	Samuel	3	1	1	1		2	2	2	2				14		
Newton	120	16	Hastings	Samuel					1			1	1				3		
Waltham	114	12	Hastings	Samuel	2			1		1			1				5		
Newton	120	19	Hastings	Thoams Jr	1			1		2		1	1				6		
Newton	120	15	Hastings	Thomas	1		2		1	1	1	2	1	1			10		
Framingham	72	13	Hastings	William	1			1		1			1				4		
Malden	94	46	Hatch	Lou'									1				1		
Malden	95	2	Hatch	Nalar		1	1		1			1		2			6		
Framingham	66	16	Haven	Abner	4		3	2		1	2		1				13		Stamped pg# was x'd out

TOWN	PG#	LN#	LAST NAME	FIRST NAME	M under 10	M 10 to 16	M 16 to 26	M 26 to 45	M 45 and over	F under 10	F 10 to 16	F 16 to 26	F 26 to 45	F 45 and over	TOTAL ALL OTHER	TOTAL SLAVES	TOTALS	DISTRICT/ TOWNSHIP	NOTES
Framingham	76	5	Haven	Benj	1	1	1		1		1	2	2	2			11		
Framingham	66	15	Haven	David				1		1				1			3		Stamped pg# was x'd out
Natick	246	35	Haven	David	1	1	1		1			2		1			7		
Sherburn	249	42	Haven	Gideon					1					1			2		
Hopkinton	241	44	Haven	Isaac	1	1	1		1					1			5		
Hollistown	237	28	Haven	Jessa		1		1			2		1				5		
Framingham	74	15	Haven	Jesse			1					2					3		Stamped pg# was x'd out
Framingham	76	6	Haven	Jesse	1	1	1		1	3	1		2				10		
Hopkinton	242	15	Haven	John		2		1	1		1						5		
Hopkinton	242	11	Haven	Jotham	3		1	1		2			1				8		
Framingham	74	17	Haven	Luther			1					1					2		
Hollistown	237	29	Haven	Luther			1			2		1					4		
Framingham	74	14	Haven	Moses	1	1		1		4			1				8		Stamped pg# was x'd out
Hopkinton	241	43	Haven	Moses				1					1				2		
Hopkinton	242	1	Haven	Sedde		1		1	1	1			1				4		
Framingham	73	2	Haven	Timothy		2		1		3	2		1				9		
East Sudbury	68	15	Hawes	Jeremiah		1		1				1	1				4		
Charlestown	85	27	Hawkins	Nath'		2	2	1	1		1			1			8		
Reading	132	21	Hawks	Adam		1	1				1		1				4		
Medford	101	14	Hawley	Noah	3	1		1		2	1		1				9		
Sherburn	250	10	Haws	Daniel	4		1	1		2	1		1				10		
Charlestown	85	37	Hay	Ann		1					1			1			3		
Reading	132	16	Hay	Daniel			1					1					2		
Stoneham	139	14	Hay	David	1	1			1		1			1	1		6		
Charlestown	85	35	Hay	John			1										1		
Malden	95	5	Hay	John	2			1					1				4		
Reading	132	24	Hay	John				1	1	1		1					4		
Reading	132	32	Hay	Jonathan	2			1		2			1				6		
Stoneham	139	12	Hay	Peter			2		1			1		2			6		
Stoneham	139	13	Hay	Peter Jr			1				1	1					3		
Charlestown	85	36	Hay	Wm	2			1			1		1				5		
Stow	198	6	Hayden	David	1			2						1			4		
Hopkinton	242	4	Hayden	Elisha				1		1		1					3		
Sudbury	60	18	Hayden	Ephraim	1	1		1	1	3	2		1	1			11		
Cambridge	224	33	Hayden	John	1	4	2			1	1	1					10		
Charlestown	85	42	Hayden	John				1				1		2			4		
Hopkinton	242	6	Hayden	John		1			1	4			1				7		
Hopkinton	242	7	Hayden	John Jr				1		3			1				5		
Marlborough	193	26	Hayden	Josiah	2			1		1			1				5		
Marlborough	193	29	Hayden	Nahum		1			1		1		1				4		
Sudbury	60	16	Hayden	William	2	2		2	1	3			1	1			12		
Hopkinton	242	5	Hayden	Wm		1			1			1	1				4		
Cambridge	225	3	Hayles	Tabor	2			1		2	1						6		
Sudbury	61	14	Haynes	Charles		1		1	1					1			4		
Natick	246	32	Haynes	Daniel	3		1	1		1	1	2	1				10		
Sudbury	63	18	Haynes	Israel		2		1		2	1	1		1			8		
Sudbury	62	33	Haynes	James				1						1			2		
Sudbury	63	9	Haynes	Jason	2		1	1		1	2		1				9		
Sudbury	63	11	Haynes	John	3	1		1			1		1				7		
Cambridge	224	27	Haynes	Joseph			1					1					2		
Sudbury	63	10	Haynes	Joshua				1			1		1				3		
Sudbury	61	15	Haynes	Luke	3			1				1					5		
Sherburn	249	38	Haynes	Martin		1				1		1					3		
Sudbury	63	17	Haynes	Moses		2		1			1		1				5		
Natick	246	36	Haynes	Nathan	1		2			1			2				6		
Sudbury	60	23	Haynes	Peter		1		1			1	1		1			5		
East Sudbury	66	26	Haynes	Samiel			1	1		2		1	1				7		
Tyngsborough	42	39	Hayson	John	3			1		1		1					6		
Acton	17	22	Hayward	Benjamin		2	1		1	3	1	1		1			10		
Acton	16	14	Hayward	John		2		1				1		1			5		
Concord	10	10	Hayward	John	3			1		2	2	1					9		
Acton	16	20	Hayward	John Jr	2		1	1		1	2		1				8		
Concord	10	9	Hayward	Joseph		1		1						1			3		
Boxborough	199	4	Hayward	Paul		1	2		1	1	1	1		1			8		
Boxborough	200	38	Hayward	Paul Jr	3			1		1			1				6		
Acton	17	32	Hayward	samuel	3	1			1	1		1	1				8		
Acton	16	19	Hayward	Simeon			1			1	2		1				6		
Acton	17	23	Hayward	Stephen		1	1	1		1		1	1				6		
Reading	132	30	Haywood	Jabez	1	2	1	1			1	2		2			10		
Reading	132	29	Haywood	John		1			1	1	1		1				5		
Sudbury	62	26	Haywood	John				1			1		2				4		
Bedford	162	18	Haywood	Mather		2						3					5		
Reading	132	28	Haywood	William	2	1		1	1	3		1	1				12		
Shirley	214	39	Hazard	Thomas											6		6		
Shirley	214	30	Hazen	Saml Capt.		1			1	1	1	1		1			6		
Shirley	214	31	Hazen	Saml Jr Capt.	2			1		1			1				5		
Shirley	214	32	Hazen	Thomas			1			1		1	1				4		
Charlestown	85	29	Hazwell	Robert	1		1	1			3					1	7		
Medford	101	12	Headley	Saml Jr	3			1			1		1				6		
Townsend	27	4	Heald	Asa	2	1	2		1	4	1			1			12		

TOWN	PG#	LN#	LAST NAME	FIRST NAME	M under 10	M 10 to 16	M 16 to 26	M 26 to 45	M 45 and over	F under 10	F 10 to 16	F 16 to 26	F 26 to 45	F 45 and over	TOTAL ALL OTHER	TOTAL SLAVES	TOTALS	DISTRICT/ TOWNSHIP	NOTES
Carlisle	22	13	Heald	Eleazer	3			1		1	1		1				7		
Pepperell	31	21	Heald	Eleazer	1		1	1		3	1		1				8		
Carlisle	22	12	Heald	Gershum					1					1			2		
Carlisle	20	1	Heald	Israel					1		1	1	1				4		
Acton	19	19	Heald	John	1				1				1				3		
Carlisle	20	10	Heald	John	1	1	1	1	1	1		3		1			10		
Shirley	214	21	Heald	John Dea					1		1	1	1				4		
Shirley	214	22	Heald	John Jr	1		1	1				1					4		
Carlisle	22	5	Heald	Jonathan		1	1	1			2		1				6		
Pepperell	31	20	Heald	Joseph		1			1		1			1			4		
Carlisle	21	35	Heald	Samuel			1	1			3		1				6		
Carlisle	22	3	Heald	Silas	1	1		1			1		1	1			6		
Carlisle	22	9	Heald	Thomas	4			1		2	1		1				9		
Carlisle	20	2	Heald	Timothy	2	1		1		1	1		1				7		
East Sudbury	66	24	Heard	David	2	1		1		1	1	1					8		
East Sudbury	66	25	Heard	Richard	2	1		1		1	1	1					8		
East Sudbury	66	22	Heard	Thomas	1	1		1		1	1	2		1			8		
East Sudbury	66	23	Heard	Zeuheriah	2	2		1			1		1				7		
Billerica	176	2	Heardman	Tho'	1			1		1			1				4		
Burlington	154	31	Heath	James	2		1					1					4		
Cambridge	225	7	Hedge	Levi				1									1		
Framingham	72	1	Hemenway	Abijah	1	2		1				2	1				7		
Framingham	72	7	Hemenway	Benjm S	2	1		1				2		1	1		8		
Hollistown	237	27	Hemenway	Daniel	2		1	1			1	1	1				7		
Framingham	74	12	Hemenway	Danl		1	1		1				1				4		Stamped pg# was x'd out
Framingham	72	8	Hemenway	Ebenezer		1	4		1			1	1	2			10		
Malden	94	29	Hemenway	Israel	1			1		1			1				4		
Framingham	72	2	Hemenway	Jacob	1		2		1	3		2	1	1			11		
Framingham	74	13	Hemenway	John	1		1		1		1	1		2			7		Stamped pg# was x'd out
Framingham	72	9	Hemenway	Josiah	3		1						1				5		
Framingham	74	16	Hemenway	Rebecka	1	1		1		1		1		1			5		Stamped pg# was x'd out
Framingham	72	3	Hemenway	Saml			1	1					1				3		
Groton	210	12	Hemenway	Saml	2	2	1		1		1	1		1			9		
Framingham	74	12	Hemenway	Susannah		1							1				2		
Charlestown	86	3	Henderson	Mary									1				1		
Charlestown	85	21	Henly	Cath'	1		1				2	1	1				6		
Cambridge	225	5	Henry	Jona	3		1	1		2		2					9		
East Sudbury	67	22	Herington	Elisha			1				1		1				3		
Reading	132	31	Herrick	Mary							1		1				2		
Reading	132	17	Herrick	Mortin				1	1	3	1		1				6		
Malden	94	28	Hersey	John	1			1				1	1				4		
Charlestown	85	24	Hersy	Wm				1		1	1		1				4		
Framingham	74	11	Hervey	John	2			2		2	1	1	1				9		Stamped pg# was x'd out
Littleton	202	13	Herwood	Vilet											4		4		
Hollistown	237	26	Hescock	Moses	1			1		4			1				7		
Medford	100	33	Hewes	Tho'				1				1	2		1		6		
Weston	108	7	Hews	Abraham	2	1	2		1			1	1	1			9		
Weston	108	8	Hews	Abraham Jr	3			1			1		1				6		
Charlestown	86	13	Heyden	Danl			1										1		
Weston	108	13	Heyward	Caleb	2	1	1	1		1			1				7		
Weston	108	16	Heyward	Josiah	1			1		1	1		1				5		
Concord	6	31	Heywood	Abiel				1			1		1				3		
Concord	6	32	Heywood	Asa			1	1			2	1					5		
Acton	19	35	Heywood	Calven	2			1		2			1	1			7		
Concord	9	18	Heywood	Cyrus				1				1					2		
Concord	9	10	Heywood	Edward	1				1			1					3		
Concord	9	21	Heywood	Ephraim				1				1					2		
Concord	4	4	Heywood	Jonas					1		1	1		2			5		
Concord	4	5	Heywood	Jonas Jr	1		1	1			2		1				6		
Concord	6	35	Heywood	Jonathan			2					1		1			4		
Chelmsford	170	16	Heywood	Jos'	1	1	1	1		3	2	1	1				11		
Concord	9	16	Heywood	Josiah				1					1				2		
Concord	9	17	Heywood	Reuben	3		1	1					1				6		
Chelmsford	170	17	Heywood	Sarah									1				1		
Concord	4	2	Heywood	William	1		3	1		2	1	1	1				10		
Concord	3	18	Hibrett	Jonathan	3	1	3	3	1	2	1	1	1	2			18		
Billerica	176	3	Hickle	Wm	1			1		1			1				4		
Watertown	232	35	Hide	Enoch		1	1		1	1			1	1			6		
Dracut	44	12	Hildren	Micah			2			1				1			4		
Tyngsborough	42	37	Hildreth	Hezeh		1		1			1	1	1				5		
Dracut	48	11	Hildreth	Israel	2		1	1	1	1	1	2	1				11		
Dracut	45	36	Hildreth	James	1		1						1				3		
Pepperell	31	19	Hildreth	James	1	1	1		1	1		1	3	2			11		
Pepperell	31	23	Hildreth	James Jr			1			1			1				3		
Dracut	44	30	Hildreth	John				1						1			2		
Dracut	45	35	Hildreth	Josiah	1		1	1				1		4			8		
Dracut	45	38	Hildreth	Josiah Jr	2			1		2		1					6		
Dracut	44	11	Hildreth	William	1	1		1		1	1	1	2				8		
Westford	181	24	Hildrith	Amaziah			1			2			1				4		
Westford	181	30	Hildrith	Amos		1		1			1	1	1				5		

TOWN	PG#	LN#	HEADS OF HOUSEHOLD LAST NAME	FIRST NAME	FREE WHITE MALES under 10	10 to 16	16 to 26	26 to 45	45 and over	FREE WHITE FEMALES under 10	10 to 16	16 to 26	26 to 45	45 and over	TOTAL ALL OTHER	TOTAL SLAVES	TOTALS	DISTRICT/ TOWNSHIP	NOTES
Westford	181	38	Hildrith	Benja'	1			1		3			1				6		
Westford	181	26	Hildrith	Isaiah		1		1			1		1				4		
Westford	181	34	Hildrith	Jerem'	1			1		2		1	1	1			7		
Westford	181	32	Hildrith	John			2	1		1		2		2			8		
Westford	181	33	Hildrith	John Jr	2			1		1	1		1				6		
Westford	181	43	Hildrith	Jona'	3			1		2		2	1	1			10		
Westford	181	28	Hildrith	Jonas	2			1		2			1				6		
Westford	181	29	Hildrith	Levi			1					1					2		
Westford	181	37	Hildrith	Lucy								2		1			3		
Westford	181	27	Hildrith	Mary	2							1	1	1			5		
Westford	181	41	Hildrith	Nath	1		1			1			1				4		
Westford	181	35	Hildrith	Oliver	1		1	1		1	3	1		1			9		
Westford	181	39	Hildrith	Peter				1					1				2		
Westford	181	25	Hildrith	Pheebe				1					1	1			3		
Westford	181	31	Hildrith	Ruth										1			1		
Westford	181	36	Hildrith	Seth	1		1			1		1					4		
Westford	181	42	Hildrith	Simeon	2			1						1			4		
Charlestown	86	4	Hildrith	Tho'			1			1			1				3		
Westford	181	40	Hildrith	Wm		1		1		1				1			4		
Cambridge	225	8	Hill	Aaron	1	2	1	1		3	2	1	2				13		
Framingham	72	11	Hill	Aaron				1		1	1		1				4		
Cambridge	224	21	Hill	Abrm				1						1			2		
Townsend	27	6	Hill	Adam	1		1						1				3		
Billerica	176	14	Hill	Alph'	1	1		1		1	1		1				6		
Reading	132	19	Hill	Asa		2	1					1	1				5		
Malden	94	39	Hill	Benja'				1									1		
Cambridge	225	11	Hill	Benjn Jr	1	1		1					1				4		
Ashby	35	38	Hill	Betty							2		1				3		
Malden	94	40	Hill	Cha'	1		1	1		2	3	1					9		
Malden	94	41	Hill	Cha' Jr		1				1		1			1		4		
Cambridge	224	17	Hill	David	1		1					1	1				4		
Cambridge	224	18	Hill	Dorcas			1					1	1				3		
Hollistown	237	32	Hill	Ebenz				1							1		2		
Cambridge	225	13	Hill	Edward				1		2			1				4		
Cambridge	224	22	Hill	James		1		1		1	1	1					5		
Charlestown	85	33	Hill	James				1									1		
Sherburn	250	5	Hill	James	1	1		1	1	1			2	1			8		
Stoneham	139	15	Hill	James	1			1	1	1		2					6		
Sherburn	250	8	Hill	James Jr		1	2	1					1				5		
Stoneham	139	16	Hill	James Jr	3	1	1		1	3	1		1				11		
Billerica	176	11	Hill	Job	4		1		1	1	1	1	1				10		
Billerica	176	7	Hill	John				1									1		
Sherburn	249	41	Hill	John	2		1			1			1				6		
Billerica	176	8	Hill	John Jr			1					1					2		
Billerica	176	10	Hill	Jona'		1	1	1				1		2			6		
Framingham	72	10	Hill	Jonathan		2		1		2	1		1				7		
Cambridge	224	29	Hill	Joseph	1			1		3		1					6		
Reading	132	18	Hill	Joseph				1			1		1				3		
Bedford	162	11	Hill	Josiah	3		1	1		2	1		1				9		
Billerica	176	4	Hill	Lot			1			2			1				4		
Cambridge	224	36	Hill	Lydia	1							1	1	1			4		
Billerica	176	9	Hill	Mary				1						1			2		
Cambridge	224	24	Hill	Mathew	1		1							1			3		
Hollistown	237	34	Hill	Moses	1		1						1				3		
Billerica	176	13	Hill	Noah			1					1					2		
Billerica	176	5	Hill	Peter		1	1	1	1	1		1		1			7		
Hollistown	237	33	Hill	Rachel	1							1	1				3		
Ashby	35	39	Hill	Ralph		2	1		1	4		1	1				10		
Cambridge	224	37	Hill	Sarah										1			1		
Billerica	176	12	Hill	Thad'	1			1		1			1				4		
Charlestown	85	46	Hill	Tho'			1										1		
Malden	94	38	Hill	Tho'	1			1			1		1	1			5		
Sherburn	249	43	Hill	Timothy				1		1				1			3		
Sherburn	249	44	Hill	Timothy Jr	2			1		1			1				5		
Billerica	176	6	Hill	Wm	1	2			1	2	1		1				8		
Cambridge	224	19	Hill	Wm		1	2		1		1	3	1	1			10		
Cambridge	224	20	Hill	Wm Jr	2			1		1		1	1				6		
Cambridge	224	26	Hill	Zachr	3	1				1		1	1				8		
Cambridge	225	12	Hill	Benjn		1	1	1		1				1			5		
Westford	181	22	Hinkley	Ebenz	1	4		1	1	1	1			1			10		
Hopkinton	242	13	Hitchcock	Thos		1		1		2							4		
Malden	94	47	Hitchens	James	1			1		2		1					5		
Littleton	201	19	Hoar	Abel				1		3			1				5		
Concord	4	23	Hoar	Daniel	4			1			1	1	1				8		
Littleton	201	17	Hoar	Heber	2		2			2			1				7		
Concord	5	18	Hoar	Jonathan	1		1	1			1		1	1			6		
Lincoln	14	2	Hoar	Leonard	3	1		2		3			1	3			13		
Concord	6	25	Hoar	Mary						1		1	1				3		
Littleton	201	16	Hoar	Oliver	4			1	1	1			1	1			9		

Table header — HEADS OF HOUSEHOLD; FREE WHITE MALES: under 10 / 10 to 16 / 16 to 26 / 26 to 45 / 45 and over; FREE WHITE FEMALES: under 10 / 10 to 16 / 16 to 26 / 26 to 45 / 45 and over.

TOWN	PG#	LN#	LAST NAME	FIRST NAME	M <10	M 10-16	M 16-26	M 26-45	M 45+	F <10	F 10-16	F 16-26	F 26-45	F 45+	TOTAL ALL OTHER	TOTAL SLAVES	TOTALS	DISTRICT/TOWNSHIP	NOTES
Littleton	204	28	Hoar	Paul	1	2			1			2		1			7		
Littleton	202	6	Hoar	Peter		1		1		2			1				5		
Lincoln	14	29	Hoar	Samuel		3	1	1	1	2		1		1			10		
Littleton	204	29	Hoar	Samuel Jr	2		2		2		1	1		1			9		
Chelmsford	170	7	Hoar	Silas	1				1	2			1				5		
Groton	210	18	Hobart	Jeremiah					1				1				2		
Groton	210	20	Hobart	Josiah	1			1	1	2		1					6		
Groton	210	19	Hobart	Nathl	3			1		2	2		1				9		
Weston	108	12	Hobbs	Amos		1	1	1		1		1					5		
Weston	108	5	Hobbs	Ebenezer	2	1	3	1		3	1	1	1				13		
Weston	108	4	Hobbs	Isaac		1	1		1				1				4		
Weston	108	6	Hobbs	Isaac Jr	4		2	1			1		1				9		
Weston	108	3	Hobbs	Matthew			2		1	1		1		1			6		
Weston	108	17	Hobbs	Nathan					1				1				2		
Weston	108	18	Hobbs	Nathan Jr	4	1	1	2			1	1	1				11		
Townsend	27	2	Hobert	Benja	2			1		1	1		1				6		
Carlisle	23	17	Hodgman	Abijah		1	2		1	2	1	1	1				9		
Chelmsford	170	14	Hodgman	Asa	1			1		3	3		1				9		
Carlisle	23	3	Hodgman	John	4	1	1		1	1			1				9		
Carlisle	23	18	Hodgman	John		1		1		3		1					6		
Townsend	27	8	Hodgman	John L.	4			1		1			1				8		
Chelmsford	170	15	Hodgman	Josiah					1				1	1			3		
Carlisle	23	19	Hodgman	Thomas	1			1		2	1		1				6		
Ashby	35	44	Hodgmon	Benja		1		1		1	2	1		1			7		
Ashby	35	37	Hodgmon	Benja Jr		1		1		1		1					4		
Ashby	35	42	Hodgmon	Jonas				1		4			1				6		
Ashby	35	25	Hodgmon	Willard	1			1					1				3		
Sherburn	249	40	Holbrook	Elliot			1			1		1					3		
Sherburn	250	7	Holbrook	James	3	2	1			1	1		1				9		
Cambridge	225	18	Holbrook	John	2	2		1		1	1		1				8		
Sherburn	250	4	Holbrook	Jona			1				1		1	1			4		
Sherburn	250	2	Holbrook	Joseph	1	1			1	1		1					6		
Sherburn	250	11	Holbrook	Joshua	1		1	1			1		1				5		
Sherburn	249	39	Holbrook	Mical				1			2	1	1				5		
Sherburn	250	3	Holbrook	Nathl				1			1			1			3		
Sherburn	250	1	Holbrook	Thos			1	1		2	1	1	1				7		
Shirley	214	26	Holden	Amos		1	1	1		1							4		
Woburn	149	34	Holden	Asa	2			1					1				4		
Shirley	214	19	Holden	Asa Capt.		1		1			1		1				4		
Concord	10	2	Holden	Daniel		1	1	1	1		1	1		1			7		
Shirley	214	38	Holden	Elizabeth Wid.	2					1			1				4		
Concord	9	4	Holden	Hannah									1				1		
Charlestown	85	18	Holden	John	2			1		1	1		1				6		
Tyngsborough	42	35	Holden	John	3			1		2	1		1				8		
Groton	210	24	Holden	Mabel Wid.				1		1				1			3		
Shirley	214	20	Holden	Nathl	1	1		1		1			1				5		
Tyngsborough	42	33	Holden	Nathl		2		1				1		1			5		
Tyngsborough	42	40	Holden	Nathll Jr			1				1						3		
Charlestown	85	43	Holden	Nehm				1			1		1				3		
Charlestown	85	44	Holden	Nehm Jr	2			1		2		1					6		
Charlestown	85	17	Holden	Oliver	4	1	3	1		2		2	1				14		
Shirley	214	34	Holden	Philemon				1				1	1	1			4		
Littleton	202	16	Holden	Phinehas	1		2	1		2		1			1		7		
Shirley	214	36	Holden	Phinehas			1			3		1					5		
Charlestown	86	2	Holden	Richd															Enumeration blank
Charlestown	86	14	Holden	Richd	1			1		2			1				5		
Shirley	214	23	Holden	Simon				1						2			3		
Shirley	214	24	Holden	Simon Jr		1		1		1				2			5		
Malden	95	6	Holden	Tho'	3		1						1				5		
Woburn	149	38	Holden	Thomas	2			1	1	1			1				6		
Stoneham	139	17	Holden	William	2			1		1			1				5		
Sudbury	59	21	Holdin	Jonas	1			1	1	1			1	1			6		
Sudbury	59	22	Holdin	Jonas Jr		1	2	1		3	2		1				10		
Sudbury	59	3	Holdin	Thos	1		1					1	1				4		
Dracut	47	3	Holl	Ephraim		1			1		1			1			4		
Dracut	47	4	Holl	Phinehas		1							1				2		
Watertown	233	3	Holland	Wm	2			1	1				1				5		
Lincoln	14	37	Hollowell	Benjamin	1			1		3			1				6		
Wilmington	142	21	Holt	Asa	3			1					1				5		
Westford	181	18	Holt	Elisha				1		2				1			4		
Townsend	29	36	Holt	Jona	1		1					1					3		
Reading	132	27	Holt	Joseph	1		2		1	2	1	1	1	1			10		
Townsend	27	3	Holt	Mary	1					2	1			2			7		
Watertown	233	6	Holt	Saml		3		1		1			1				6		
Boxborough	200	8	Holt	Thomas		1		1		1			1				4		
Cambridge	225	17	Holten	Benjn	1		1					1					3		
Boxborough	200	43	Holten	Phinehas	3			1		1		1					7		
Marlborough	188	36	Holyoke	Sarah	1							2		1			4		
Hopkinton	242	2	Homer	John			1		1	4	2	2	1				11		
Newton	120	1	Homer	Jonathan		1	3	1	1	1		1	1		1		11		

TOWN	PG#	LN#	LAST NAME	FIRST NAME	FREE WHITE MALES under 10	10 to 16	16 to 26	26 to 45	45 and over	FREE WHITE FEMALES under 10	10 to 16	16 to 26	26 to 45	45 and over	TOTAL ALL OTHER	TOTAL SLAVES	TOTALS	DISTRICT/TOWNSHIP	NOTES
Hopkinton	242	16	Homer	Mitchel		1	1		2					1			5		
Burlington	154	28	Homer	Robert		1		1					1	1			4		
Hopkinton	242	3	Homes	Francis			1	1		1	1		1				5		
Hopkinton	242	14	Homes	John Jr	2	1	2		1	1	1	2		1			11		
Wilmington	142	24	Honden	Joshua Jr	2			1		1			1				5		
Newton	120	27	Hoogs	William			2	2	1	1	1	2		1			10		
Newton	120	28	Hoogs	William Jr	1		2			3			1				7		
Newton	120	26	Hooker	*ibeon	1	1	1		1	3		1	1				9		
Charlestown	86	12	Hooker	James		1	1	1		2			1				6		
Charlestown	85	15	Hooper	Joshua	1			1		2		1		1			6		
Charlestown	85	16	Hooper	Tho'				1		2			1				4		
Littleton	201	26	Hoping	Thomas	2	1		1		3			1				8		
Groton	210	16	Hopkins	Ebenzr	3		1	1		1		1	1				8		
Burlington	154	29	Hopkins	Jesse				1			1		1				3		
Reading	132	20	Hopkins	Joseph	1		1	1				2					5		
Wilmington	142	19	Hopkins	Samuel				1			1		1				3		
Wilmington	142	20	Hopkins	Samuel Jr	1	1	1			1		1					5		
Charlestown	86	5	Hoppen	Hannah										1			1		
Charlestown	85	26	Hoppen	Nich'				1						1			2		
Sherburn	249	37	Horton	Benjm		1		1	1	2	2		1	1			9		
Pepperell	31	16	Hosley	John		1		1		2	1		1				6		
Pepperell	31	15	Hosley	Joshua		1	1		1	2			1				6		
Townsend	27	9	Hosley	Saml	1	1		1	1	2			1				7		
Pepperell	31	17	Hosley	Stephen	1	1		1			1		1	1			6		
Pepperell	34	26	Hosley	Tho			1					1					2		
Pepperell	31	18	Hosley	Timo				1				2	1				4		
Concord	7	39	Hosmer	Abigail						1			1				2		
Concord	10	13	Hosmer	Amos		2	1		1	1	1	2		1			9		
Tewksbury	51	26	Hosmer	Amos	3			1		2			1				7		
Concord	8	34	Hosmer	Benjamin				1						1			2		
Concord	9	2	Hosmer	Bethiah										2			2		
Concord	8	31	Hosmer	Cyrus	2	1	1	1		2	1		1				9		
Concord	9	11	Hosmer	Daniel				1			2	1	1	1			6		
Concord	9	7	Hosmer	David				1					1				2		
Concord	4	26	Hosmer	Elijah		1	1		1	1	1			2			7		
Acton	17	37	Hosmer	Ephraim	2		1	1	1				1	1			7		
Concord	10	18	Hosmer	Israel		1	1					1	1	1			5		
Concord	9	26	Hosmer	Jesse	2	1		1		2	3			1			10		
Bedford	162	16	Hosmer	John	3	1	1	1		2	2		1				11		
Concord	9	3	Hosmer	John	3	1	2		1	2	1	1	1	1			13		
Acton	17	34	Hosmer	Jonathan	1		3	1	1	1		2		1	1		11		
Concord	8	30	Hosmer	Joseph			2		1				1	1			5		
Acton	17	36	Hosmer	Nathan				1		1			1				3		
Acton	17	38	Hosmer	Samuel	2			1		3	1		1				8		
Concord	9	34	Hosmer	Silas	3	1		1					1				6		
Acton	17	35	Hosmer	Stephen		1	1	1				3		1			7		
Concord	9	32	Hosmer	Stephen		1		1						1			3		
Concord	3	1	Hosner	Nathan			1	1				1					3		
Framingham	72	4	Hoton	John			2	1		4			1				8		
Stow	198	31	Houghton	Abigail										2			2		
Ashby	35	40	Houghton	Elijah				1						1			2		
Ashby	35	41	Houghton	Elijah Jr	1			1		1	1	1	1				6		
Acton	17	21	Houghton	Joseph				1						1			2		
Acton	17	20	Houghton	Oliver	1			1		1			1				4		
Charlestown	86	11	Houghton	Oliver	1		1			1		1					4		
Reading	132	34	Hovey	Darius	1			1			1	1	1				5		
Cambridge	225	21	Hovey	Ebenz		1	1	1		1		1					5		
Newton	119	26	Hovey	George			1					1					2		
Dracut	44	9	Hovey	Henry A		1		1		4	1		1				8		
Cambridge	225	20	Hovey	James	1	1		1		1				1			5		
Cambridge	224	31	Hovey	Josiah			2			1			1				4		
Cambridge	224	39	Hovey	Moses	1			1			2			1			5		
Cambridge	224	32	Hovey	Phineas		1				3		1	1				6		
Dracut	44	8	Hovey	Saml		2	1						1				4		
Dracut	44	10	Hovey	Thom		4	2	1				1		1			9		
Newton	120	25	Hovey	Thomas	1			1			1	1		1			5		
Cambridge	225	15	Hovey	Thos	2	1	1	1		1	1	1					8		
Malden	94	44	Hovy	Nathan		1											1		
Marlborough	188	12	How	Aaron	2			1		1			1				5		
Marlborough	190	32	How	Aaron				1						1			2		
Marlborough	189	26	How	Abraham	2	1		1		1		1		1			7		
Sudbury	60	8	How	Adam		2	1			2	1	1	1				9		
Marlborough	190	22	How	Archelas	3		1			1	1		1				7		
Marlborough	191	39	How	Azlemas	2	2	2		1	1		2	1	1			12		
Marlborough	189	25	How	Benjamin	3	1			1	1		1	1				8		
Sudbury	59	28	How	David Jr	1	1		1		3	1		1				8		
Sudbury	60	6	How	David Jr				1						1			2		
Marlborough	189	29	How	Eleazer	2			1				1	1	1			6		
Marlborough	190	10	How	Elizabeth										1			1		
Sudbury	59	2	How	Elizabeth							1			1			2		

175

TOWN	PG#	LN#	LAST NAME	FIRST NAME	FREE WHITE MALES					FREE WHITE FEMALES					TOTAL ALL OTHER	TOTAL SLAVES	TOTALS	DISTRICT/ TOWNSHIP	NOTES
					under 10	10 to 16	16 to 26	26 to 45	45 and over	under 10	10 to 16	16 to 26	26 to 45	45 and over					
Marlborough	190	9	How	Ephraim	2		2		1	1	1		1				8		
Framingham	72	6	How	Ezekiel		2	1		1	1	1	3	1				10		
Marlborough	190	33	How	Fortunalus	3	2		1		2			1				9		
Framingham	76	1	How	Francis	3	2	1		1				1				8		
Marlborough	187	4	How	Francis	1		2		1	2	2		1				9		
Marlborough	187	5	How	Francis Jr			1						1				2		
Marlborough	190	23	How	Gilbert			1						1				2		
Cambridge	225	9	How	Hannah				1		2			2				5		
Framingham	72	12	How	Isaac	1	2		1		1	1		1				7		
Marlborough	193	16	How	John			1		1	1	4	3		2			12		
Marlborough	193	20	How	John	1		1	1	1	1		2	1	1			9		
Marlborough	193	23	How	John 3rd		1		1					1				3		
Marlborough	190	21	How	John Jr	2	2		1		2	1		1				9		
Marlborough	192	16	How	Jonah	1			1		4			1				7		
Marlborough	192	4	How	Joseph		1			1				1		1		4		
Sudbury	60	7	How	Joseph	2	1	1	1		1	2		1				9		
Marlborough	192	5	How	Joseph 3rd		1						1					2		
Marlborough	188	24	How	Joseph Jr	1			1					1				3		
Marlborough	193	15	How	Josiah	1		2		1	1	1		2				8		
Marlborough	190	31	How	Levi	1		1	1					1				4		
Marlborough	188	10	How	Lovewell	1	2			1				1				5		
Marlborough	188	34	How	Luther			1										1		
Marlborough	190	11	How	Mary									3				3		
Hopkinton	242	18	How	Nehemiah	1			1			2	2					6		
Marlborough	190	29	How	Noah				1			1		1				3		
Framingham	66	18	How	Pearly		4	1	1		1	1	1			1		10		Stamped pg# was x'd out
Hopkinton	242	17	How	Phineas		2	1	1		1	1		1				7		
Marlborough	190	16	How	Phinehas			1			1	1		1				5		
Marlborough	189	3	How	Samuel	1		1		1			2		1			6		
Marlborough	188	11	How	Simon		1		1	1	2		2	1				8		
Marlborough	190	17	How	Sylvanus	2			1		1			1				5		
Marlborough	187	3	How	Thomas				1					1				2		
East Sudbury	69	6	How	Willard			1					1					2		
Marlborough	192	12	How	William	1	1		1				1	1				5		
Marlborough	190	30	How	Winslow	1			1		2			1				5		
Cambridge	225	4	How	Nancy								3					3		
Hopkinton	242	9	How	Nathan	1		1		2		1	1					6		
Hopkinton	242	10	Howard	Alexr			1			1		1					3		
Malden	94	36	Howard	Amos				1		2			1				4		
Malden	94	37	Howard	Amos Jr	2	1		1		2	2		1				9		
Cambridge	224	40	Howard	Charles	1			1		2		1					5		
Ashby	35	43	Howard	Daniel	2		1		1	2	2	1	1				12		
Burlington	154	30	Howard	Ebenez			1						1				2		
Malden	94	33	Howard	Eunice							1						1		
Malden	94	35	Howard	Ezra				1		1	2		1				5		
Malden	94	31	Howard	Jabez	1			1		2			1				5		
Chelmsford	170	12	Howard	Jacob	1		1	1					1				4		
Hopkinton	242	8	Howard	Jason	2			1					1				4		
Malden	94	30	Howard	John	1	1		1		1	1		1				6		
Tyngsborough	42	36	Howard	Jona	1		1	1				1					4		
Malden	94	34	Howard	Jos'	1	1		1		1			2				6		
Hopkinton	242	12	Howard	Joshua	1			1		3	2		2				9		
Chelmsford	170	11	Howard	Nath'			1			1		1					3		
Stow	198	29	Howard	Peter			1			1		2					4		
Chelmsford	170	10	Howard	Saml		1		1				1		1			4		
Charlestown	85	32	Howard	Tho' C.			2										2		
Chelmsford	170	13	Howard	Willard		1		1					2				4		
Malden	94	32	Howard	Wm			1					1	1				3		
Littleton	202	15	Howell	Jesse	1		1	1		1		1					5		
Concord	5	7	Hubard	Ebenezer			1	1					1				3		
Cambridge	225	10	Hubard	Wm	1			1		3	1		1				7		
Weston	108	10	Hubbard	Anna								1		1			2		
Groton	210	13	Hubbard	Nathan				1					1				2		
Concord	8	14	Hubbard	Thomas		1		1				1		1			4		
Groton	210	14	Hubbard	Thomas		1	1	1		1	1		1				6		
Concord	8	15	Hubbard	Thomas Jr	3			1		1	1		1				7		
Groton	210	15	Hubbard	Thos Jr	1		1	1		1			1				5		
Marlborough	189	6	Hudson	Elijah				1					1				2		
Marlborough	189	7	Hudson	Francis			1					1					2		
Marlborough	191	6	Hudson	Stephen	1			1		3			1				6		
Newton	120	17	Hull	William		1		1		2	3	4	1		1		13		
Littleton	203	9	Humfries	John		1		1			2	2		1			7		
Littleton	203	19	Humfries	Richard				1				1		1			3		
Cambridge	225	6	Hunnawell	Elizath	2			1		2			1	1			5		
Cambridge	225	2	Hunnawell	Eunos		2	1					2	1	1			7		
Watertown	233	8	Hunnewell	Walter			1					1	1				3		
Charlestown	86	6	Hunniwell	Wm	2		1	1		1			1				6		
Tewksbury	51	22	Hunt	Eben			1	1		1			1	1			5		
Sudbury	58	6	Hunt	Haman	3	1		1		1			1				7		
Concord	8	23	Hunt	Hannah									1				1		

TOWN	PG#	LN#	LAST NAME	FIRST NAME	FREE WHITE MALES under 10	10 to 16	16 to 26	26 to 45	45 and over	FREE WHITE FEMALES under 10	10 to 16	16 to 26	26 to 45	45 and over	TOTAL ALL OTHER	TOTAL SLAVES	TOTALS	DISTRICT/ TOWNSHIP	NOTES
Sudbury	65	7	Hunt	Isaac Jr				1		2			1				4		
Dracut	44	38	Hunt	Israel	4			1			1		1				7		
Littleton	201	13	Hunt	Jane										1			1		
Concord	4	29	Hunt	Jeremiah				1				2	1				4		
Acton	17	17	Hunt	John		1	2	1	1			1		1			7		
Framingham	66	17	Hunt	John	3			1	1	1	2		1				8		Stamped pg# was x'd out
Tewksbury	51	17	Hunt	John		1	1	2		1	2	1	1				9		
Tewksbury	51	24	Hunt	John Jr			1	1		3	1	1		1			8		
Tewksbury	51	19	Hunt	Jona	2			1		1			1				5		
Charlestown	85	45	Hunt	Jona'	2			1		1				1			5		
Sudbury	59	1	Hunt	Jonas	4			1	1	1	1	1	1				10		
Lexington	157	33	Hunt	Jonathan		1	2	1		1		1					6		
Concord	6	24	Hunt	Joseph		1		1			1		1				4		
Carlisle	21	14	Hunt	Joshua	2			1		1		1	1				6		
Concord	11	10	Hunt	Nehemiah	2			1		2	1	1	1	1			9		
Tewksbury	51	21	Hunt	Noah	1			1					1				3		
Littleton	201	1	Hunt	Peter			1	1					1				3		
Concord	4	8	Hunt	Reuben		4		1	1	1	2	3	1				13		
Watertown	233	7	Hunt	Ruth						1			4				5		
Cambridge	224	25	Hunt	Saml	2		1			1		1					5		
Chelmsford	170	8	Hunt	Saml			1					1					2		
Lincoln	12	11	Hunt	Samuel		1		1					2				4		
Westford	181	17	Hunt	Simeon	3	1		1				1					6		
Acton	17	8	Hunt	Simon	1			1				1	1	1			5		
Charlestown	85	41	Hunt	Simon			1										1		
Tewksbury	51	20	Hunt	Solomon	1		1	1		2			3	1			9		
Concord	5	17	Hunt	Thadeus			2					1	2				6		
Malden	94	42	Hunt	Tho'		1		1		1			1				4		
Tewksbury	51	18	Hunt	Timothy	2	2	1	1				1					7		
Sudbury	58	5	Hunt	William	1			1	1	2			1	1			7		
Sudbury	61	31	Hunt	William 3rd	1		1					1					3		
Woburn	149	40	Hunt	William C		1		1				1	1				4		
Sudbury	62	37	Hunt	William Jr	1	1	2		1	1	2			1			9		
Watertown	233	9	Hunt	Wm	2	1	3		1	2		3	2		1		15		
Marlborough	193	2	Hunter	David	3			1	1	1	1		1				7		
Marlborough	192	41	Hunter	Robert			2		1			1	1				5		
Newton	120	22	Hunter	Solomon	3			1		1	2		1				8		
Chelmsford	170	9	Hunting	Nathan	1		2	1		4			1				9		
Marlborough	193	10	Hunting	Samuel			1		1			1		1			4		
Charlestown	85	38	Hurd	Benja'				1				1	1				3		
Charlestown	85	39	Hurd	Benja' Jr	1	3	2		1	2		4		1			14		
Concord	5	25	Hurd	Isaac		1	1	1			1	2	2		1		9		
Charlestown	85	40	Hurd	Jos'		1	1		1	1		2		1			7		
Westford	181	44	Hutchens	Tho'				1		2			1				4		
Bedford	162	10	Hutchinson	Benjamin			1		1					2			4		
Bedford	162	17	Hutchinson	James			1			1			1				3		
Charlestown	86	15	Hutchinson	John	1	1	2		1		1	1		1			8		
Pepperell	31	12	Hutchinson	Joseph				1				1					2		
Carlisle	20	13	Hutchinson	Nathaniel		1	2		1	1			1	1			7		
Carlisle	20	12	Hutchinson	Nathaniel Jr	1	1		1		2	1		1				7		
Pepperell	31	10	Hutchinson	Nathl		2	2		1		1	2		1			9		
Carlisle	20	18	Hutchinson	Thomas	4			1	1				2	1			9		
Pepperell	31	11	Hutchinson	Wm		2	1		1		1	2		1			8		
Concord	4	19	Hutton	Nathaniel				1				1	2				4		
Groton	210	21	Huzen	Benjm		1	1		1					1			4		
Groton	210	22	Huzen	David		2	1		1	1		1					6		
Newton	119	28	Hyde	Amos			2		1	1		1		1			6		
Newton	120	14	Hyde	Benjm				1				1	1				3		
Newton	119	29	Hyde	Daniel			1		1	1	1	2					6		
Newton	120	8	Hyde	Elisha	2			1		2			1				6		
Newton	120	13	Hyde	Enoch				1		1			1				3		
Newton	120	18	Hyde	Ephraim				1		1				1			3		
Charlestown	86	9	Hyde	Fredr'		2	1				1		1				5		
Newton	120	10	Hyde	John	1	1	2	2		1			1	1			9		
Newton	120	3	Hyde	Jonathan	2	1		1		1	1		1				7		
Newton	120	2	Hyde	Samuel	1	1	1					2		1			6		
Newton	120	9	Hyde	Thaddeus	1	2		1			1		1				6		
Newton	119	27	Hyde	William	1			1					1				3		
Carlisle	21	22	Ingals	James	2			1		1			1				5		
Tyngsborough	42	43	Ingals	Joseph		1	1		1		1	1		2			7		
Tyngsborough	42	44	Ingals	Nathl		1			1	2	2		1				7		
Dunstable	217	8	Ingoll	John	1			1		1		1	1	1			7		
Littleton	202	46	Ingols	Daniel	1	1			1	2		2		1			8		
Concord	11	28	Ingraham	Cato											4		4		
Medford	101	15	Ingraham	Duncan		1			1			1		1			4		
Newton	121	8	Ingraham	Margaret						1		2		1			4		
Hopkinton	242	20	Ingram	Nathan				1		1			1				3		
Charlestown	86	18	Ireland	Jona'	2	1			1	2	1	1	1				9		
Charlestown	86	17	Ireland	Saml		1			1		1			1			4		
Charlestown	86	16	Ireland	Tho'					1	1			1	1			4		

TOWN	PG#	LN#	LAST NAME	FIRST NAME	FREE WHITE MALES					FREE WHITE FEMALES					TOTAL ALL OTHER	TOTAL SLAVES	TOTALS	DISTRICT/ TOWNSHIP	NOTES
					under 10	10 to 16	16 to 26	26 to 45	45 and over	under 10	10 to 16	16 to 26	26 to 45	45 and over					
Sudbury	65	5	Ives	William	1			1		2			1				5		
Charlestown	86	22	Jack	David	1	2	1		1	1		1		1			8		
Newton	121	2	Jackson	Daniel	2			1		1	1	1					6		
Newton	121	1	Jackson	Edward	1		2		2	1		1	3	1			11		
Malden	95	11	Jackson	Isaac		1											1		
Newton	121	18	Jackson	Joseph				1					1	1			3		
Newton	121	19	Jackson	Joseph Jr	2			1					1				4		
Newton	121	6	Jackson	Joshua		1		1		1		1		1			5		
Newton	121	9	Jackson	Joshua Jr		1		1						1			3		
Newton	121	15	Jackson	Michael		1	1		1			1		1			5		
Newton	121	16	Jackson	Michael Jr	2			1		1			1				5		
Newton	121	3	Jackson	Oliver	2			1	1	2				2			8		
Newton	121	13	Jackson	Oliver				1				1	1	1			4		
Westford	181	45	Jackson	Phillip											3		3		
Charlestown	86	30	Jackson	Saml	1			1	1	1			1				5		
Newton	121	7	Jackson	Samuel			1		1			1		1			4		
Newton	121	5	Jackson	Simon	1	1	1	1		1	1	2					8		
Newton	121	17	Jackson	Timo	2	1	1	1			1			1			7		
Littleton	202	36	Jacobs	Braddock	1			1		3			1				6		
Carlisle	22	25	Jacobs	John	2			1		2	2		1				8		
Carlisle	21	23	Jamison	Matthew				1						1			2		
Natick	246	37	Janneson	Lott	1	1	1		1				2	1			7		
Tyngsborough	42	41	Jaques	Daniel	1			1		1			1				4		
Billerica	176	17	Jaques	Jos'		1			1			1	1	1			5		
Billerica	176	18	Jaques	Jos' Jr	1			1		1			1	1			5		
Tyngsborough	42	42	Jaques	Nehem				1						1			2		
Charlestown	86	21	Jaques	Saml		1											1		
Wilmington	142	29	Jaques	Samuel	2	10	2	1		2	1	2	1	2			23		
Billerica	176	19	Jaques	Timo'				1						1			2		
Wilmington	142	28	Jaqueth	John	1		1		1	1		1					5		
Ashby	36	1	Jaquith	Alford		1			1	1	1			1			5		
Burlington	154	36	Jaquith	Andrew			1			1			1				3		
Wilmington	143	7	Jaquith	Anna		2	2					1	2	1			8		
Groton	210	25	Jaquith	Benjm				1			1			1			3		
Wilmington	142	31	Jaquith	David		2		1		1				2			6		
Wilmington	143	4	Jaquith	Ebenezer				1						1			2		
Wilmington	143	1	Jaquith	James	1		1	2		1		1		2			8		
Ashby	35	48	Jaquith	John		1	1		1	1	1			1			6		
Tewksbury	51	27	Jaquith	John	3		3	1		1	1	2	2				13		
Wilmington	142	33	Jaquith	John Jr	2	1	1				1	1		1			7		
Wilmington	143	3	Jaquith	Jonathan		2						1					3		
Wilmington	143	2	Jaquith	Joshua	1		1	1					1				4		
Wilmington	142	32	Jaquith	Samuel															Name crossed out
Newton	121	10	Jarvis	Caleb				1		1			3	1			6		
Concord	3	2	Jarvis	Francis	1		1	1		2			1	1			7		
Charlestown	86	32	Jarvis	James				1		2				1			4		
Sherburn	250	12	Jay	Jona		1	1	1		1	1		1	1			7		
Reading	133	3	Jeffrey	Joseph				1			1			1			3		
Reading	133	4	Jeffrey	Joseph Jr			1					1					2		
Billerica	176	15	Jeffs	Henry				1			1			1			3		
Billerica	176	16	Jeffs	Mary								2	1				3		
Townsend	27	10	Jefts	Henry	2	2		1		1			1				7		
Shirley	214	41	Jenerson	Moses	1	2			1	1	1	1		1			8		
Wilmington	143	6	Jenkens	Joel	1	1		1		1	1		1				6		
Wilmington	143	5	Jenkens	Joseph				1						1			2		
Malden	95	9	Jenkins	Abigl										1			1		
Westford	182	3	Jenkins	Edw'				1					1	1			3		
Charlestown	86	31	Jenkins	Israel		1	1	1					2				5		
Malden	95	8	Jenkins	Jno'				1				1		1			3		
Townsend	27	11	Jenkins	Leml			1	1					1				3		
Townsend	27	12	Jenkins	Saml	2	1		1		2			2	1			9		
East Sudbury	66	27	Jenkison	Abraham			1		1	1	1		1	1			6		
Cambridge	225	22	Jenks	Samll		1	2	1						1			5		
Cambridge	225	24	Jenks	Wm	1	1	1					1	1				5		
Hollistown	237	39	Jennens	Daniel				1		1		1	1				4		
Hollistown	237	38	Jennens	Isaac	1			1		3		1	1				7		
Stow	196	33	Jenney	Eliphelet		2		1					3	1			7		
Natick	246	38	Jennings	Ethel	3	1		1	1	1		2		1			10		
Hopkinton	242	21	Jennings	Noses	1			1		1		1	1	1			6		
Littleton	205	1	Jennings	Stephen		1		1		1	1	1		1			6		
Newton	121	12	Jennison	Elias	1			1		2			1	1			6		
Newton	121	11	Jennison	Phinehas	2			1					1				4		
Newton	121	14	Jennison	Phinehas Jr	1		1		1				1	1			5		
Charlestown	86	26	Jepson	John				1					1	1			3		
Marlborough	192	39	Jewell	Jacob	1	1		1		3	1		1				8		
Stow	197	34	Jewell	Samuel	1	1			1	1			1				5		
Marlborough	192	37	Jewell	Silas				1					1				2		
Marlborough	192	31	Jewell	Silas 3rd			2			1		1					4		
Marlborough	192	38	Jewell	Silas Jr		1	2	2		1				1			7		
Stow	196	30	Jewell	William	1			1			1	1		1			5		
Littleton	203	1	Jewett	Aquilla		1		1			1			1			4		

178

TOWN	PG#	LN#	LAST NAME	FIRST NAME	FREE WHITE MALES under 10	10 to 16	16 to 26	26 to 45	45 and over	FREE WHITE FEMALES under 10	10 to 16	16 to 26	26 to 45	45 and over	TOTAL ALL OTHER	TOTAL SLAVES	TOTALS	DISTRICT/ TOWNSHIP	NOTES
Pepperell	31	29	Jewett	Caleb	2		1		1		1	2		1			8		
Pepperell	31	24	Jewett	David			2		1		1	2		1			7		
Pepperell	31	26	Jewett	Edmd	2	1		1		1	1	1					7		
Littleton	203	2	Jewett	Israel H.			1			1		1					3		
Townsend	26	10	Jewett	John	2		1	1		1		1					6		
Dunstable	217	10	Jewett	Joseph				1		1	1		1				4		
Littleton	204	27	Jewett	Joseph	2			1		1			1				5		
Groton	210	27	Jewett	Joshua A.				1					1				3		
Littleton	204	10	Jewett	Lucy								1	1				2		
Pepperell	31	28	Jewett	Nehh		1		1				1		2			5		
Pepperell	31	27	Jewett	Nehh Jr	1		1			2	1	1					6		
Townsend	27	13	Jewett	Solo	1	1	1			2		1					6		
Pepperell	31	25	Jewett	Zeah			1						1				2		
Sudbury	60	30	Johnson	Aaron				1					1				2		
Lexington	157	37	Johnson	Ab*son			4	1		2		1					8		
Burlington	154	38	Johnson	Abiathar				1					1				2		
Weston	108	29	Johnson	Abiathur	2			2		2			1	1			8		
Burlington	154	37	Johnson	Abijah				1		2		1	1				5		
Framingham	76	7	Johnson	Amos	2		1			3	2	1					9		
Woburn	150	4	Johnson	Anna								1		1			2		
Chelmsford	170	20	Johnson	David			1										1		
Woburn	150	8	Johnson	David			1	1					1				3		
East Sudbury	66	31	Johnson	Ebenezer	1	1	2		1		1		1				7		
Charlestown	86	29	Johnson	Edmd	2		1			2		1					6		
Chelmsford	170	19	Johnson	Ezra			1										1		
Woburn	150	1	Johnson	Francis		2	1		1	1		2		1			8		
Woburn	150	2	Johnson	Frederick	1	2		1		1			1				6		
Groton	210	28	Johnson	George			1										1		
Medford	101	16	Johnson	Hannah	2								1				3		
Sudbury	62	29	Johnson	Hezekiah	1	1		1			2		1				6		
Woburn	150	5	Johnson	Isaac				1					1				2		
Billerica	176	20	Johnson	James			1			4		1	1				7		
Woburn	150	9	Johnson	Jesse			1			2		1					4		
Charlestown	86	33	Johnson	John			1						1				2		
Groton	210	26	Johnson	John	2	1		1			1		1				6		
Reading	133	7	Johnson	John	2	1		1			2		1				7		
Westford	182	2	Johnson	Jona'	4			1		1			1				7		
Charlestown	86	20	Johnson	Jos'				1					1				2		
Woburn	150	7	Johnson	Josiah		2						2		1			6		
Burlington	154	34	Johnson	Jotham	2		1		1	1	2			2			9		
Hollistown	237	36	Johnson	Levi			1						1				2		
Sherburn	250	13	Johnson	Nathan	2		1					1					5		
Hollistown	237	35	Johnson	Nathl	3	1	1	1		1	1		1				9		
East Sudbury	66	30	Johnson	Peter	1		2		1	1	1	2		1			9		
Burlington	154	32	Johnson	Rebekah			1	1					1				3		
Hopkinton	242	23	Johnson	Reuben			2	1	1	1		1					6		
Woburn	150	6	Johnson	Reuben		2	1		1	1		2		1			8		
Charlestown	86	28	Johnson	Saml			1			1			1				3		
Westford	182	1	Johnson	Sarah										1			1		
Dunstable	217	9	Johnson	Silas	2	1		1		1		1	1				7		
Woburn	150	3	Johnson	Susann									1				1		
Hopkinton	242	26	Johnson	Syvannus	1		1			4		1					7		
Charlestown	86	27	Johnson	Tho'			1				1	1					3		
Malden	95	10	Johnson	Tho'		1	1										2		
Burlington	154	33	Johnson	William				1			1	1					3		
East Sudbury	66	29	Johnson	William		2				1	1	1					5		
Littleton	204	3	Johnson	William	4	2		1	1	2		1	1	1			13		
Reading	133	5	Johnson	William		1	1	1				1	1				5		
Reading	133	6	Johnson	William Jr	2		1					1					4		
Ashby	36	2	Johnson	Wm	1		1	1		3			1				7		
Natick	246	39	Jonah	Jacob											5		5		
Acton	17	15	Jones	Aaron	2	2	1		1	3	1	1	1				12		
Wilmington	142	27	Jones	Abel		1				1		1					3		
Wilmington	143	8	Jones	Abial		1				1		1					3		
Burlington	154	35	Jones	Abigail										1	1		2		
Concord	8	3	Jones	Abigail										3			3		
Weston	108	26	Jones	Amos	4			1		1	1	1	1				9		
Concord	4	31	Jones	Asa		1						1					2		
Ashby	35	47	Jones	Daniel		1	1					1					3		
Framingham	72	15	Jones	Daniel	2	1		1		3			1				8		
Dracut	46	33	Jones	David				1					1				2		
Hollistown	237	37	Jones	David				1					1				2		
Wilmington	142	34	Jones	David	1	1		1		1	1		1				6		
Dracut	46	34	Jones	David Jr		1						1					2		
Charlestown	86	23	Jones	Ebenz	1		1				1	2					5		
Lincoln	12	9	Jones	Eli		1		1		3	3	2	1		1		12		
Sudbury	61	23	Jones	Elijah			1						1				2		
Concord	6	4	Jones	Elisha		1	2	1				2		2			8		
Hopkinton	242	25	Jones	Elisha	2			1		2			1				6		
Concord	5	31	Jones	Ephraim		1			1	2		1	2				7		

TOWN	PG#	LN#	LAST NAME	FIRST NAME	FREE WHITE MALES					FREE WHITE FEMALES					TOTAL ALL OTHER	TOTAL SLAVES	TOTALS	DISTRICT/ TOWNSHIP	NOTES
					under 10	10 to 16	16 to 26	26 to 45	45 and over	under 10	10 to 16	16 to 26	26 to 45	45 and over					
Concord	8	16	Jones	Farwell				1	2	2	1	1	1	1			9		
Acton	18	15	Jones	Hannah		1					1			1			3		
Dracut	45	30	Jones	Hugh				1						1			2		
Hopkinton	242	19	Jones	Isaac		1		1		2	1		1				6		
Weston	108	25	Jones	Isaac		1	1	1	1	1		1	2	2			10		
Lincoln	15	12	Jones	Jacob			1						1				2		
Weston	108	28	Jones	James	1			1		2				1			5		
Bedford	162	20	Jones	James C	2	1		1	1		1		1	1			8		
Medford	101	17	Jones	Jno' C.	1	1	1		1	4	1		1	2			12		
Ashby	35	46	Jones	John				1					1				2		
Framingham	72	14	Jones	John	2	2		1				1					6		
Hopkinton	242	24	Jones	John	1	1	1	1		3	2	1	1				11		
Watertown	233	10	Jones	Joseph			1	1		1		1		1			5		
Concord	5	12	Jones	Joshua			4	1		1			1	1			8		
Concord	4	1	Jones	Mary		1	1				1	1		2			6		
Hopkinton	242	22	Jones	Mary		1					1	1		1			4		
Newton	121	4	Jones	Mijah	2	1				3	1		1	1			9		
Dracut	45	33	Jones	Nathl	1	1	1		1	1	1	1	1				8		
Framingham	78	17	Jones	Nathl A.				1		1		2		1			5		
Acton	17	16	Jones	Oliver		1	1	1				3		1			7		
Dracut	45	31	Jones	Oliver	2	1		1		2	1		1				8		
Charlestown	86	24	Jones	Peter			4	1		3		1	1				10		
Concord	7	21	Jones	Peter		1		1		1	2	1			1		7		
Concord	10	3	Jones	Redit	2		1	1	1	1	1		1				8		
Wilmington	142	30	Jones	Russel	5	1	1		1			2	2	1			13		
Charlestown	86	34	Jones	Ruth									1				1		
Shirley	214	42	Jones	Saml	2	1	1	1					1	1			7		
Cambridge	225	23	Jones	Samll	1			1		1			1				4		
Acton	17	14	Jones	Samuel				1					2				3		
Concord	8	24	Jones	Samuel		1	3		1		2			1			8		
Sudbury	61	22	Jones	Samuel	2	1	2	1		1			1				8		
Concord	6	6	Jones	Samuel Jr		1		1				1	2				5		
Weston	108	27	Jones	Sarah								1		1			2		
Lincoln	13	19	Jones	Silas	2			1		1			1				5		
Dracut	47	38	Jones	Solomon			1		1	1		1					4		
Weston	108	24	Jones	Solomon		1		1						1			3		
Concord	6	12	Jones	Stephen		1		1				2	2	1			7		
Bedford	162	19	Jones	Timothy	1	1	1		1	1	2	2		2			11		
Wilmington	143	9	Jones	Willard	1			1		1			1				4		
Concord	6	16	Jones	William	1	1	1	1				2					6		
Dracut	45	32	Jones	Zebediah	1		1		1	2	1			1			7		
Cambridge	225	25	Jonneson	Timothy L.	2	1		1		2			2				8		
Woburn	150	10	Jordan	John	1			1		1		1					4		
Charlestown	86	25	Joy	Benja			1			1		1					3		
East Sudbury	69	20	Joy	Reuben			1			2		1					4		
Townsend	27	14	Keep	Jonas	1	2	1	1		1	2	2		1			11		
Charlestown	86	36	Keith	Timo'		3				1			2				6		
Tewksbury	51	29	Kelley	James	2		1							1			4		
Watertown	233	12	Kelley	John			1			2				1			4		
Littleton	201	24	Kelley	Nathan	2		1			1				1			5		
Framingham	70	5	Kellogg	David	2	1		1			2	2		2	1		11		Stamped pg# was x'd out
Dracut	49	9	Kelly	George				1					1				2		
Dracut	48	25	Kelly	George Jr	3		1				1						5		
Dracut	49	10	Kelly	John	1		1			2				1			5		
Shirley	214	43	Kelsey	John Capt.		1	2	1		1	2	1	1				9		
Shirley	214	44	Kelsey	John Jr	1		1						1				3		
Groton	210	31	Kemp	Capt. Levi		1	2	1		2	1	2		1			10		
Pepperell	31	30	Kemp	D.B.	3	1		1		1	1			1			8		
Groton	210	32	Kemp	Ephraim	1	1	1	1		1	1						6		
Carlisle	21	10	Kemp	James	1			1		2	1		1				6		
Groton	210	33	Kemp	John	1			1		1			1				4		
Pepperell	31	31	Kemp	Jonas	2			1		1				2			6		
Westford	182	15	Kemp	Jonas		1		1						1			3		
Groton	210	29	Kemp	Saml				1						1			2		
Groton	210	30	Kemp	Saml Jr		2	1	1		1		2		1			8		
Westford	182	16	Kemp	Simeon				1		4				1			6		
Tewksbury	52	5	Kendal	Ezra				1			1		1	1			4		
Tewksbury	52	6	Kendal	Ezra Jr	3	1		1		1				1			7		
Charlestown	86	42	Kendal	Isaac		1							1	1			3		
Framingham	76	8	Kendal	Jemima			2								1		3		
Billerica	176	26	Kendal	Jos'	1	1	1	1		3		1	1				9		
Billerica	176	25	Kendal	Reuben				1									1		
Weston	108	30	Kendal	Samuel	1	1	2		2	1	1	1	1				10		
Ashby	36	41	Kendall	Asa				1					2				3		
Ashby	36	42	Kendall	Asa Jr	4	1		1		2	1		1				10		
Ashby	36	44	Kendall	Benja	1	2	1			1		1					6		
Burlington	154	43	Kendall	Daniel			1						1				2		
Dunstable	217	14	Kendall	Edward				1						1			2		
Shirley	214	45	Kendall	Enosh	4	1		1		1		1	1				9		
Cambridge	225	29	Kendall	Jabez		1		1			1	1	1				6		

TOWN	PG#	LN#	LAST NAME	FIRST NAME	M under 10	M 10 to 16	M 16 to 26	M 26 to 45	M 45 and over	F under 10	F 10 to 16	F 16 to 26	F 26 to 45	F 45 and over	TOTAL ALL OTHER	TOTAL SLAVES	TOTALS	DISTRICT/ TOWNSHIP	NOTES
Dunstable	217	12	Kendall	Jacob				1						1			2		
Burlington	154	39	Kendall	John	1	1		1		3	1	1	1				9		
Dunstable	217	11	Kendall	John				1				1	1				3		
Framingham	72	16	Kendall	John	1		2	1		2	2		1	1			10		Stamped pg# was x'd out
Dunstable	217	18	Kendall	Jonas	1	1		1		1			2	1			7		
Ashby	36	45	Kendall	Joseph	1		2					1					4		
Burlington	154	41	Kendall	Joshua				1					1				2		
Cambridge	225	27	Kendall	Joshua	2	1	1	1				2	1	1			10		
Dunstable	217	16	Kendall	Josiah				1		1			1				3		
Framingham	72	17	Kendall	Nathan		2		1		2	1		1				7		Stamped pg# was x'd out
Ashby	36	40	Kendall	Oliver			2	1		2			1				6		
Lexington	157	38	Kendall	Oliver				1					1				2		
Ashby	36	43	Kendall	Pierpoint	1		2	1		1			1	1			7		
Dunstable	217	13	Kendall	Temple				1	1			1		1			4		
Dunstable	217	17	Kendall	Temple Jr	2	1		1		2			1	1			8		
Burlington	154	42	Kendall	William		1						1					2		
Dunstable	217	15	Kendall	Zebed* Dea.	2	2	2	1			1		1				9		
Wilmington	143	10	Kendel	Elizabeth	2			1				1		1			5		
Woburn	150	12	Kendell	Obediah				1					1				2		
Woburn	150	13	Kendell	Obediah Jr	1	2		1		2	1	1					8		
Reading	133	8	Kenney	Jethro	1		1						1				3		
Hopkinton	242	29	Kenny	Asa				1		1				1			3		
Hopkinton	242	28	Kenny	Wm				1		1		1		2			5		
Newton	122	1	Kenrick	Caleb		1	1	1		1		1		1			6		
Newton	121	28	Kenrick	John	1	1	1	1				1		1			6		
Newton	122	2	Kenrick	John Jr		2	1		1	1	1	2	1				10		
Westford	182	9	Kent	Abner				1				1		1			3		
Watertown	233	13	Kent	Ebenz	1			1	1	2	2		1				10		
Westford	182	10	Kent	Elisha		1						1					2		
Charlestown	86	44	Kent	Mary										1			1		
Charlestown	86	45	Kent	Saml	4	2		1			1			1			9		
Cambridge	225	32	Kerr	Wm	1		1			1		1					4		
Townsend	27	15	Ketridge	Ingals	1		1	1			1	1					5		
Charlestown	86	40	Kettell	Andr'				1			1	2		1			5		
Charlestown	86	39	Kettell	John				1				2					3		
Concord	4	15	Kettell	John				1	1					1			3		
Charlestown	86	41	Kettell	Jona'		1		1		2	1		1				6		
Townsend	27	16	Keyes	Abel		1	1	1					1				4		
Chelmsford	170	21	Keyes	David	1			1		2			1				5		
Westford	182	6	Keyes	Isachar		2	1	1				1		1			6		
Westford	182	7	Keyes	James		1						1					2		
Westford	182	17	Keyes	Jona	2	1		1	1	4	1		1	1			12		
Westford	182	8	Keyes	Joseph	1	1	3		1	2		2		1			11		
Westford	182	12	Keyes	Mary															Enumeration blank
Westford	182	4	Keyes	May		1						1		1			3		
Littleton	204	30	Keyes	Solomon		1	1			2			1				5		
Charlestown	86	46	Keys	John				1									1		
Groton	210	34	Keyzer	Jona	1	1			1	1	1	1		1			7		
Concord	11	17	Kibby	Elizabeth									1				1		
Carlisle	21	21	Kidder	Amos				1				2		2			5		
Sudbury	60	31	Kidder	Ashbel			1			1	1	1					4		
Billerica	176	23	Kidder	Eph' Jr			1	1		1	1	1					5		
Billerica	176	22	Kidder	Ephrm		1		1					1				3		
Littleton	203	26	Kidder	Francis	3	1	2	2	1		2	1	1		1		14		
Charlestown	86	37	Kidder	Isaac				1					2				3		
Townsend	27	17	Kidder	Isaac	2	1	1	1		1	1		2				9		
Chelmsford	170	23	Kidder	Jacob	1			1		1			1				4		
Medford	101	19	Kidder	James	1		1			1		1					4		
Westford	182	13	Kidder	James	1		1					1					3		
Tewksbury	52	3	Kidder	Jerem				1					1				2		
Tewksbury	52	2	Kidder	Jeremiah Jr	1		1	1		1	2	1					7		
Medford	101	20	Kidder	Joanne								2		1			3		
Billerica	176	21	Kidder	John	2	2	1	1					1	1			8		
Boxborough	199	21	Kidder	John	1			1		2		1		1			6		
Charlestown	86	38	Kidder	John	1	2			1	1	1			1			7		
Tewksbury	52	4	Kidder	Lemual				1		2			1	1			5		
Cambridge	225	30	Kidder	Mary						1		1		1			3		
Westford	182	14	Kidder	Mary									1	1			2		
Medford	101	18	Kidder	Saml	3	1			1	2	1		1				9		
Cambridge	225	28	Kidder	Samll	2	1			1	3		2	3	2			14		
Shirley	214	46	Kilburn	Daniel			1			1		1					3		
Hollistown	237	42	Kilburn	John	1			1		1		2	1				6		
Hollistown	237	41	Kilburn	Josiah				1		2			1				4		
Townsend	27	5	Kildreth	Zach	1	1	2		1	3	1	1					10		
Sherburn	250	17	Kimbal	Benjm		1		1	1			1	1				5		
Chelmsford	170	22	Kimbal	Dema*	2			1		2	1		1				7		
Woburn	150	11	Kimbal	Ezra			2	1				1					4		
Sherburn	250	16	Kimbal	John		1	1			1			1				4		
Burlington	154	40	Kimbal	Reuben		1			2			1		1			5		
Dracut	49	3	Kimbal	Samll	1	1			1	3			1				7		

181

TOWN	PG#	LN#	LAST NAME	FIRST NAME	FREE WHITE MALES					FREE WHITE FEMALES					TOTAL ALL OTHER	TOTAL SLAVES	TOTALS	DISTRICT/ TOWNSHIP	NOTES
					under 10	10 to 16	16 to 26	26 to 45	45 and over	under 10	10 to 16	16 to 26	26 to 45	45 and over					
Sherburn	250	15	Kimbal	Thos	1		1	1		3			1				7		
Littleton	203	32	Kimball	Daniel	1	1	3		1	3	1		1				11		
Natick	246	41	Kimball	Ebenr	1		1					1					3		
Waltham	114	20	Kimball	Harry	2	2		1		1	2	1					9		
Newton	121	24	Kimball	Richard				1					1				2		
Newton	121	25	Kimball	Richard Jr	1			1		2			1				5		
Carlisle	23	10	Kimbell	William	1		1			1		1					4		
Newton	121	26	King	Ebenezer		1	1	1					1		1		5		
Newton	121	22	King	Henry	3	1		1	1	1	1	1	2				11		
Ashby	36	38	King	James				1		1			1				3		
Newton	121	21	King	John	4			1			2		1				8		
Newton	121	27	King	John		1			1		1	1	1	1			5		
Cambridge	225	26	King	Lemuel	2			1		1			1				5		
Newton	121	23	King	Noah			1	1		3			1				6		
Westford	182	11	King	Roger		1	1	1				1		2			6		
Weston	108	31	Kingsbury	Elijah	1				2	2	1		1				7		
Natick	246	40	Kingsbury	Elipht	4			1	1				1	1			8		
Hopkinton	242	27	Kinsman	Aaron	1			1	1	1			1				4		
Charlestown	86	43	Kinsman	Wm				1					1				2		
Framingham	76	9	Kitteridge	John B.				1							1		2		
Billerica	176	24	Kitteridge	Nehem'		1	3		1		1	2		1			9		
Tewksbury	52	7	Kittridge	Benja		3	3		1		1		1	1			10		
Tewksbury	51	34	Kittridge	Eben				1			1		1				3		
Tewksbury	52	1	Kittridge	Francis Jr	1	1	2		2	2	1	1					10		
Tewksbury	51	31	Kittridge	Jeremiah	1	1		1		2			1				6		
Tewksbury	51	28	Kittridge	Jon		1			1	2			1	1			6		
Tewksbury	51	33	Kittridge	Nathan Jr	1	1		1			1		1				5		
Tewksbury	51	32	Kittridge	Simeon		1			1		2			1			5		
Tewksbury	51	30	Kittridge	Thos				1	1	1		1		1			4		
Newton	121	20	Knapp	Lydia									1				1		
Cambridge	225	31	Kneeland	Elizath				1		1	3		1				6		
Westford	182	5	Kneeland	Martha	2						1		1				4		
Sudbury	62	7	Knight	Asahel		1		1					1				3		
Watertown	233	11	Knight	Christham	2			1		1	1						5		
Sudbury	60	10	Knight	Joel			1			3	1						5		
Concord	6	5	Knight	Jonathan	1	2		1		2			3				9		
Charlestown	86	35	Knight	Mary									1				1		
Malden	95	14	Knight	Mary									1				1		
Medford	101	21	Knight	Rebecca						1			1				2		
Sudbury	60	9	Knight	Samuel		1	1	2					1				5		
Hollistown	237	40	Knolton	Elias	2	1		1		1			1				6		
Malden	95	13	Knowah	Ann	2					1			1				4		
Malden	95	12	Knowah	Jona'				1					1				2		
Framingham	64	16	Knowlton	Isaiah	1			1						2			4		Stamped pg# was x'd out
Framingham	78	11	Knowlton	Nathan				1		3	2		1				7		
Sherburn	250	14	Kolton	Wm				1		1		1		1			4		
Tyngsborough	43	2	L	*				1					1				2		Illegible
Malden	95	17	Ladd	Wm	2			1		1	1		4		2		11		
Watertown	233	23	Laffan	Robert			2	1			1		1	1	1		6		
Watertown	233	15	Laith	Jedediah	1	1		1			1		1				5		
Watertown	233	14	Laith	Wm		1		1			1						3		
Groton	211	10	Lakin	David	1	2	1		1	1	1	1		1			9		
Pepperell	31	33	Lakin	James				1		1	1		1				4		
Groton	211	6	Lakin	Lemuel		1											1		
Groton	211	7	Lakin	Levi	1		1		1	1	2		1				7		
Pepperell	31	32	Lakin	Nathl		1	1		1				1				5		
Pepperell	31	35	Lakin	Nathl 3rd				1		2	1		1				5		
Pepperell	31	34	Lakin	Nathl Jr	1			2		2	2		1				8		
Pepperell	32	3	Lakin	Robn	3	2		1			1		1				8		
Hollistown	237	43	Laland	Oliver	4			1		1			1				7		
Reading	133	9	Lambert	William	1			1					1				3		
Framingham	76	11	Lamle	David	2	1		1			1	1	1				7		
Groton	210	42	Lampson	Amos				1					1				2		
Weston	109	2	Lamson	Amos		1	1			1			1				4		
Charlestown	87	17	Lamson	Caleb				1		2			1				4		
Weston	108	33	Lamson	Elizabeth	2						1	1	1				5		
Townsend	27	18	Lamson	Ephm	3			1		1	1	1					7		
Weston	108	32	Lamson	Isaac	1		1	1			1		1				5		
Charlestown	87	18	Lamson	Iza'				1					1				2		
Acton	19	22	Lamson	John				1				2		1			4		
Weston	109	6	Lamson	John	3			1		2		1	1				8		
Acton	19	23	Lamson	Nathan			1			3		1					5		
Westford	182	22	Lancy	Saml	3	2		1		1	1		1				9		
Pepperell	31	44	Landel	James	1		3		1	2		1		2			10		
Bedford	162	26	Lane	David	2	1		1		1	1	1					7		
Cambridge	225	34	Lane	Ebenz	1			1		1	1						4		
Bedford	162	29	Lane	Elizabeth								1		1			2		
Charlestown	87	3	Lane	Geo'			4	2		2	1	2	4		1		16		
Bedford	162	25	Lane	James				1									1		
Cambridge	226	3	Lane	John	1	4	2		1	1				1			10		

TOWN	PG#	LN#	LAST NAME	FIRST NAME	FREE WHITE MALES under 10	10 to 16	16 to 26	26 to 45	45 and over	FREE WHITE FEMALES under 10	10 to 16	16 to 26	26 to 45	45 and over	TOTAL ALL OTHER	TOTAL SLAVES	TOTALS	DISTRICT/ TOWNSHIP	NOTES
Bedford	162	24	Lane	Jonathan	1	1	1	1		2	1	1	1				9		
Bedford	162	28	Lane	Luke	3			1		1			1				6		
Bedford	162	22	Lane	Samuel	1		1		1			2		1			6		
Bedford	162	23	Lane	Samuel Jr	1				1	1	1	1		1			6		
Bedford	162	27	Lane	Solomon	1	1		1			1	1	1				6		
Bedford	162	21	Lane	Stephen		1		1			1			1			4		
Charlestown	87	19	Lanson	Jos'	3			1		1			1				6		
Charlestown	87	13	Larkin	Eben	2		1			2		1	2				8		
Charlestown	87	14	Larkin	Isaac	1		1			1		2					5		
Charlestown	87	11	Larkin	John					1		1		2	1	1		6		
Charlestown	87	12	Larkin	Mary	1		1				2		1				5		
Charlestown	86	47	Larkin	Saml		2		1				1		1			5		
Charlestown	87	4	Larrabee	Jona'	2	1		1		2			1				7		
Reading	133	13	Larrebee	Samuel			3						1				4		
Shirley	215	1	Laughton	Oliver	1		1			2			1				5		
Pepperell	31	41	Laurence	Abm	2		1						1				4		
Ashby	37	7	Laurence	Benja	2		1					1	1				5		
Pepperell	31	39	Laurence	Benja		2		1			1			1			5		
Ashby	37	2	Laurence	Charles			2	1				1	1	1			6		
Pepperell	31	47	Laurence	David				1		4			1				6		
Ashby	37	4	Laurence	El*				1		1		1		1			4		
Pepperell	31	42	Laurence	Elizabeth									1				1		
Pepperell	31	38	Laurence	Ephm	1	1		2		2			1				7		
Ashby	37	1	Laurence	Isaac		1		1		1		1					4		
Ashby	37	10	Laurence	Jacob	2			1		1	1		1				6		
Pepperell	31	40	Laurence	Jesse	1		1						1				3		
Ashby	37	5	Laurence	John		1	1	1		1		4	1				9		
Ashby	37	6	Laurence	Jona Jr	1			1		2	2	1	1				8		
Ashby	37	12	Laurence	Jonas		1	1	1				1		1			5		
Pepperell	31	48	Laurence	Joseph	1	3	1	1	1			1		2			10		
Ashby	36	47	Laurence	Josh	1			1		2			1				5		
Pepperell	31	45	Laurence	Josh		1	2	1				2	1	1			8		
Pepperell	31	37	Laurence	M. Thos.	2	2		1		2			1	1			9		
Ashby	37	8	Laurence	Oliver				1		1			1				3		
Pepperell	32	1	Laurence	Peter		1		1			1		1				4		
Ashby	37	3	Laurence	Reuben	1			1		2			1				5		
Ashby	37	11	Laurence	Thos	2		1	1		1			1				6		
Pepperell	31	36	Laurence	Thos					1				1				2		
Pepperell	31	43	Laurence	Thos 3rd	1			1		2	2		1				7		
Pepperell	31	46	Laurence	Thos Jr	1	1	1	1			1		1				6		
Lincoln	14	33	Laurence	William	2	2		1		2	2		1				10		
Acton	18	16	Law	Danforth		1		1					1				3		
Concord	7	30	Law	David	1			2					1				4		
Acton	16	3	Law	Stephen			2	1	1	1	3		1				9		
Acton	16	4	Law	Stephen Jr	2		1	1		1	1		1				7		
Acton	16	26	Law	Thomas				1		4			1				6		\
Groton	211	12	Lawrance	Abel	1		1			1		1		1			5		
Groton	211	14	Lawrance	Asa Capt.				1					1				2		
Groton	210	43	Lawrance	Asa Jr	2		1	1		1			1				6		
Groton	211	3	Lawrance	Benjm				1					1				2		
Groton	211	8	Lawrance	Ephraim	3	1		1		2			1				8		
Groton	210	41	Lawrance	Isaac	1	2		1		1		2	1				8		
Groton	210	38	Lawrance	Joel	2			1		2			1				6		
Groton	211	5	Lawrance	John		1	1		2	2	1		1				8		
Groton	211	15	Lawrance	John 3rd	1		1					1					3		
Groton	211	9	Lawrance	John Jr	3			1					1				5		
Groton	210	35	Lawrance	Jona				1						2			3		
Tyngsborough	43	5	Lawrance	Lemuel	2			1		1			1				5		
Groton	211	2	Lawrance	Roland	2			1		3	1		1				8		
Groton	211	4	Lawrance	Salmon	2	1		1		2			1				7		
Groton	210	36	Lawrance	Saml Esq	1	1	2	1	1	2	1		2	1			12		
Groton	211	13	Lawrance	Wm			1	1		1		1	1				5		
Littleton	203	13	Lawrence	Abijah	1		1	1		1		1					5		
Waltham	114	26	Lawrence	Benjamin	1		1	1	2	2	1	1	1				10		
Littleton	202	22	Lawrence	David	1		1	1		1		2		1			7		
Woburn	150	15	Lawrence	Ebenezer		1	2			1	2		1				7		
Charlestown	87	5	Lawrence	Isaac	1		1	1		1		1					5		
Dunstable	217	19	Lawrence	Isaac				1					1				2		
Westford	182	24	Lawrence	James	1			1		2			1				5		
Concord	11	3	Lawrence	John				1		2	1		2	1			7		
Lexington	158	3	Lawrence	Jonathan		1				1	1	1					4		
Burlington	155	1	Lawrence	Jonathn	2			1		1			1				6		
Weston	109	1	Lawrence	Joseph				1		1		1					3		
Woburn	150	14	Lawrence	Joseph						1	1		1		1	1	5		
Lincoln	15	11	Lawrence	Love		1				2		1	1				5		
Lexington	158	2	Lawrence	Phinehas	1		1			2	1	1					6		
Woburn	150	16	Lawrence	Rachel								1	1				2		
Townsend	27	22	Lawrence	Saml					1				1				2		
Lexington	158	4	Lawrence	Sarah									2	1			3		

TOWN	PG#	LN#	LAST NAME	FIRST NAME	FREE WHITE MALES under 10	10 to 16	16 to 26	26 to 45	45 and over	FREE WHITE FEMALES under 10	10 to 16	16 to 26	26 to 45	45 and over	TOTAL ALL OTHER	TOTAL SLAVES	TOTALS	DISTRICT/ TOWNSHIP	NOTES
Townsend	27	21	Lawrence	Silas	1			1		1			1				4		
Boxborough	199	14	Lawrence	Thomas		2		1			2			1			6		
Weston	109	5	Lawrence	William Jr	3			1	1			1					6		
Weston	109	9	Leadbetter	Increase		1	1	1	1			1		1			6		
Hopkinton	242	31	Leaky	Simeon		1	1			1		1					4		
Malden	95	16	Lear	John	1			1		1	1		1				5		
Malden	95	15	Lear	Peter	1			1		3			1				6		
Newton	122	4	Learnard	Jonas	3			1		1	1		1				7		
Framingham	76	12	Learnard	Sarah					1					1			2		
Cambridge	226	5	Learned	Aaron				1		2		1					4		
Watertown	233	18	Learned	Elijah	1			1					1				3		
Westford	182	23	Learned	Isaac		2		1		2	1		1				7		
Cambridge	226	9	Learned	Josiah	1	1	1	1			1		1				6		
Watertown	233	20	Learned	Paul	1	1	1	1					1				5		
Cambridge	226	11	Learned	Saml				1					1				2		
Sherburn	250	33	Learned	Saml		1		1		3			1				6		
Watertown	233	19	Learned	Saml		1	1				2		2	1			7		
Watertown	233	21	Learned	Sarah	1					3			1				5		
Malden	95	18	Learned	Tho			1										1		
Medford	101	22	Learned	Tho'	3			1		1			1				6		
Cambridge	226	4	Learned	Thos		1			1			1		1			4		
Watertown	233	24	Leath	Ebenz	1			1				1	1	1			5		
Woburn	150	17	Leathe	Elijah		2			1		1			1			5		
Woburn	150	18	Leathe	Elijah Jr	2	1			1	1		1	1				7		
Woburn	150	22	Leathe	Jacob			1			1			1				3		
Woburn	150	20	Leathe	James		1		1					1				3		
Medford	101	23	Leathe	Jno'					3				1		1		5		
Malden	95	19	Leatherly	Saml		2			1		1	1		1			6		
Charlestown	87	6	Leathers	Benja	1			1					1				3		
Concord	10	14	Lee	Betty									1				1		
Concord	10	6	Lee	Isaac	2	1		1		2		1	1	1			9		
Cambridge	226	7	Lee	Jane	1			1	1	1	1	1	1				7		
Concord	6	14	Lee	Jonas		1	1		1	2	1		1				7		
Cambridge	226	8	Lee	Joseph			1		2	2			1				6		
Concord	8	29	Lee	Lucy		2	1			1	1		1		1		7		
Cambridge	226	13	Lee	Mark											3		3		
Ashby	37	13	Lees	Jonas	1	3		1				1	1				7		
Reading	133	12	Legros	Samuel	1		1						1				3		
Westford	182	20	Leighton	Fra'			1		1			1		2			5		
Westford	182	18	Leighton	Isaiah	1			1		1	1		1				5		
Westford	182	21	Leighton	John	1			1		1	1		1				5		
Westford	182	19	Leighton	Reuben	2	1		1		2		1	1				8		
Sherburn	250	32	Leland	Aaron	1		1		1	1	1			1			6		
Hollistown	238	5	Leland	Abner	2		2		1			1		1			7		
Sherburn	250	18	Leland	Adam		1			1			1		1			4		
Hollistown	238	2	Leland	Asa		1	1		1			1		1			5		
Sherburn	250	25	Leland	Asa					1				1	1			3		
Hollistown	238	15	Leland	Asapher					1					1			2		
Hollistown	238	11	Leland	Asapher Jr	2		1	1		1	2		1				8		
Sherburn	250	28	Leland	Balak		1	1	1					1				4		
Hollistown	238	10	Leland	Daniel	1	1	2		1	1		3		1			10		
Hollistown	238	19	Leland	Daniel	1		2		1		2	1		1			8		
Sherburn	250	23	Leland	Eli	1			1					1				3		
Hollistown	238	13	Leland	Henry		1			1				1				3		
Sherburn	250	21	Leland	Hinsy	2	2		1		1	1		1				8		
Sherburn	250	30	Leland	Hoptes			1	1	1				1				4		
Hollistown	238	18	Leland	Jeremh	1		1		1	1	1	1	1				7		
Sherburn	250	24	Leland	John	2			1				1		1			5		
Sherburn	250	19	Leland	Jona			2		1	2	1		1				7		
Sherburn	250	20	Leland	Jonas	1			1		1			1				4		
Sherburn	250	29	Leland	Joseph			1		1	2			2				6		
Sherburn	250	22	Leland	Mical	2	1			1		1	1	1				7		
Sherburn	250	31	Leland	Moses		2			1	1	1		3				8		
Hollistown	238	14	Leland	Parley			1			1			1				3		
Sherburn	250	27	Leland	Saml		1	1	1		1			1				5		
Hollistown	238	12	Leland	Timothy			1		1		1			1			4		
Sherburn	250	26	Leland	Wm	2			1					1				4		
Charlestown	87	15	Leman	Danl			1					1					2		
Charlestown	87	16	Leman	Eliz'							1	1	1				3		
Newton	122	3	Lenox	Cornelius											1		1		
Groton	211	11	Lepcar	Wm		2			1				1				4		
Watertown	233	26	Levett	Josiah					1								1		
Reading	133	11	Lewis	Charles			1			1		1					3		
Charlestown	87	7	Lewis	Debo'								1					1		
Groton	211	1	Lewis	Ebenzr	5	2			1	1	1			1			11		
Groton	210	40	Lewis	Eunice Wid.							1		1				2		
Townsend	27	19	Lewis	Isaac	1	2		1		3	1		1				9		
Charlestown	87	8	Lewis	James	2						2		1				6		
Groton	210	44	Lewis	James Capt.				1					2				3		

TOWN	PG#	LN#	LAST NAME	FIRST NAME	FREE WHITE MALES under 10	10 to 16	16 to 26	26 to 45	45 and over	FREE WHITE FEMALES under 10	10 to 16	16 to 26	26 to 45	45 and over	TOTAL ALL OTHER	TOTAL SLAVES	TOTALS	DISTRICT/ TOWNSHIP	NOTES
Groton	210	45	Lewis	James Jr Capt.	3	3	1	1					1	1			10		
Billerica	176	27	Lewis	John				1					1				2		
Groton	210	39	Lewis	Reuben	1	1		1				1	1				5		
Hollistown	238	9	Lewis	Samll				1					1				2		
Townsend	27	20	Lewis	Seth	2			1		1			1				5		
Reading	133	10	Lewis	William			1					1					2		
Chelmsford	170	26	Lewis	Wm	1	1		1				1		1			5		
Tewksbury	52	11	Lewiston	Asa	1	1		1		1		1	1				6		
Tewksbury	52	10	Lewiston	Daniel	2			1			3		2				8		
Charlestown	87	10	Lewiston	James			1			2	1						4		
Billerica	176	31	Lewiston	John			1						1				2		
Chelmsford	170	24	Lewiston	Seth	1	2	1		1	1				1			7		
Chelmsford	170	25	Lewiston	Seth Jr			1										1		
Billerica	176	30	Lewiston	Tho'				1					1				2		
Billerica	176	29	Lewiston	Wm	2		1	1		2			1				7		
Cambridge	226	10	Linch	John	1			1		2			1				5		
Hollistown	238	8	Lincoln	Asa	2		1	1			1		1				6		
Charlestown	87	9	Lincoln	Hezl			1										1		
Sudbury	60	22	Lincoln	Isaac			2		1	1	1		1				6		
Littleton	202	33	Lindley	James											2		2		
Acton	16	16	Linfield	Nathaniel				1		1			1				3		
Acton	16	23	Linfield	Nathaniel Jr			2						1				3		
Littleton	203	38	Litchfield	Andrew	1			1		1							3		
Carlisle	21	11	Litchfield	Paul	1	1	3		1					2			8		
Littleton	203	39	Litchfield	Penelope						1	1		1				3		
Shirley	215	6	Little	Elizabeth Wid.										2			2		
Shirley	214	48	Little	Wa*	1	3	3		1	1	2		1				12		
Framingham	76	10	Littlefield	Asa		1	1			2		1		1			6		
Hollistown	238	17	Littlefield	Ephm			2		1	1	1		1				6		
Hopkinton	242	34	Littlefield	Jeremh		1			1	1	1		1				5		
Hollistown	237	44	Littlefield	John				1			1		1				3		
Hollistown	237	45	Littlefield	John Jr	2			1		2			1				6		
Hollistown	238	16	Littlefield	Jotham	1			1				1	1				4		
Hopkinton	242	33	Littlefield	Pelletiah			1			1		1					3		
Hollistown	238	6	Littlefield	Simeon				1			1		1				3		
Tyngsborough	43	3	Littlehale	Abram	1	1		1		2	1		1				7		
Dracut	44	20	Littlehale	James		1	2		1			1		1			6		
Tyngsborough	43	4	Littlehale	Roger	2			1		4			1	1			9		
Cambridge	226	12	Livanos	Jona	1	2			1	3	1			1			9		
Watertown	233	16	Livemore	Amos		1	3		1		1		1				7		
Watertown	233	17	Livemore	Amos Jr	1			1		2	1		1				6		
Watertown	233	22	Livemore	David	1		3	1		1		1					7		
Weston	109	3	Livemore	Ephraim	2			1		3	1			1			8		
Weston	109	4	Livemore	Samuel	1		2	1		1		1	1				7		
Waltham	114	22	Livermore	Abijah	1	1	1	1	2	2	1			2			11		
Shirley	214	49	Livermore	Daniel		1		1				1					3		
Newton	122	5	Livermore	John	1	2		1		4	1		1				10		
Shirley	214	50	Livermore	Jonas	3	1	1	1					1				7		
East Sudbury	69	16	Livermore	Joseph				1				1		1			3		
Waltham	114	25	Livermore	Moses			1			1		1	1				4		
Waltham	114	21	Livermore	Nathl	2	1	4	1			1	2		1			12		
Waltham	114	23	Livermore	Phinehas	1	1	2		1			3		1			9		
Townsend	27	23	Livingston	Wm	3			1		1	1		1				7		
Lexington	158	5	Lock	Amos	2	1			1				1				5		
Lexington	158	8	Lock	Asa B	3		1	1				2					7		
Lexington	158	9	Lock	Benjamin	2			1		2			1				6		
Cambridge	225	39	Lock	Benjm	3			1		1	1		1	1			8		
Shirley	215	2	Lock	Bezeleel	1			1					1				3		
Cambridge	226	1	Lock	Francis	2	1	2		1		1		2				9		
Woburn	150	19	Lock	James	1		1	1		1	1	1		1			7		
Charlestown	87	1	Lock	Jona'	2	1	1		1	1		2		1			9		
Lexington	158	6	Lock	Jonas		1	2	1		1	1		1				7		
Acton	18	34	Lock	Joseph	1	1			1	1	1		1				6		
Cambridge	225	37	Lock	Joseph	2		2		1	1				1			7		
Cambridge	226	2	Lock	Joseph			2	1									3		
Woburn	150	21	Lock	Josiah	2	2	2		1	1			1	1			10		
Lexington	158	11	Lock	Mehitabel								1	1	1			3		
Sudbury	59	16	Lock	Nathan	1		2						1				4		
Cambridge	225	40	Lock	Nathn			1			2		1					4		
Lexington	158	10	Lock	Reuben	1	1			1			1		1			5		
Cambridge	225	33	Lock	Saml	1	3	2	1	1	1		1		1			11		
Cambridge	226	6	Lock	Saml Jr	1		1					1					4		
Lexington	158	7	Lock	Samuel				1									1		
Lexington	158	1	Lock	Thomas		2		1		3		2	1				9		
Cambridge	225	38	Lock	Wm		1		1			1		1				4		
Ashby	36	46	Locke	David		1	1		1	1				1			5		
Ashby	37	9	Locke	John	1			1		1		1					4		
Ashby	37	14	Locke	Jonas		1	1			1	1	1	3	1			9		
Natick	246	42	Locker	Isaac			5		1		1	2		1			10		

185

TOWN	PG#	LN#	LAST NAME	FIRST NAME	FREE WHITE MALES under 10	10 to 16	16 to 26	26 to 45	45 and over	FREE WHITE FEMALES under 10	10 to 16	16 to 26	26 to 45	45 and over	TOTAL ALL OTHER	TOTAL SLAVES	TOTALS	DISTRICT/ TOWNSHIP	NOTES
East Sudbury	66	36	Loker	Alpheus			1	1		1		1	1				5		
East Sudbury	66	32	Loker	Bulah				1					1	1			3		
East Sudbury	66	34	Loker	Ebenezer	2			1				1		1			5		
East Sudbury	69	5	Loker	Ephraim			1			3		1					5		
East Sudbury	66	35	Loker	Isaac	2			1		1			1				5		
East Sudbury	66	33	Loker	John				1					1				2		
East Sudbury	67	1	Loker	Paul			1			1			1				3		
East Sudbury	69	4	Loker	Stephen	3				1	2	2		1				9		
Charlestown	87	2	Long	Benja'	3		1						1				5		
Shirley	215	5	Longley	Abel			2										2		
Littleton	201	10	Longley	Anna										1			1		
Shirley	215	7	Longley	Asa	2	1		1		1	2		1				8		
Shirley	215	4	Longley	Israel			2	1		1			2				6		
Shirley	215	9	Longley	Ivery			1			1		1	1				4		
Shirley	215	8	Longley	Joseph	2	1		1		2	1		1				8		
Shirley	214	47	Longley	Joshua Esq		2	1		1		1	1		2			8		
Shirley	215	10	Longley	Stephen	1	1	1						1				4		
Shirley	215	3	Longley	Wm		1	2	1						1			5		
Cambridge	225	36	Lopas	Kathm										2			2		
Groton	210	37	Loreing	John	1		1	1		1		1	1				6		
Sudbury	62	5	Loring	Ezekiel H.	1			1		2		1					5		
Concord	3	4	Loring	Henry	1			3				1	1				6		
Marlborough	189	40	Loring	John	2	1		1		2	2		1				9		
Lexington	158	13	Loring	Jonathan	2			1		1	2		1				7		
Lexington	158	12	Loring	Joseph	1		1	1			1			1			5		
Hopkinton	242	30	Loring	Nathan	1		1	1				1					4		
Sudbury	61	28	Loring	Nathan			1	1		1		1	1	1			6		
Marlborough	188	17	Loring	William	1		1			1	4		1				9		
Cambridge	225	35	Loseing	David	2			1		1			1	1			6		
Billerica	176	28	Love	Wm					1					1			2		
Acton	19	12	Lovejoy	Samuel			1			2			1				4		
Framingham	76	13	Lovering	Amos	1		1			1		1					4		
Hollistown	238	3	Lovering	Craft				1						1			2		
Hollistown	238	1	Lovering	Eli*		1	1						1	1			4		
Hollistown	238	7	Lovering	Elias			1						1				2		
Burlington	155	2	Lovering	John	1			1		1			1				4		
Sudbury	62	8	Lovering	Jonas	1			1		1				1			4		
Hollistown	238	4	Lovering	Wm			1						1	1			3		
Weston	109	8	Lovewell	Joseph				1						1			2		
Weston	109	7	Lovewell	Samuel		1		1		2			1				5		
Pepperell	34	21	Lovjoy	Jesse	1			1		3	1		1				7		
Pepperell	32	2	Lovjoy	Wc						1			1	1			3		
Watertown	233	25	Lowd	Edward	1			1		1		1					4		
Natick	246	45	Lowton	Saml	1			1		1		1					4		
Natick	246	44	Lucus	Abrm				1						1			2		
Natick	246	43	Lucus	Henry				1					1				2		
Waltham	114	24	Lyman	Theodore	2	1	2	2	1			6	2				16		
Ashby	36	4	Lymond	James	2	1	1			1		1	1				8		
Malden	95	23	Lynde	Benja'	1	1		1		2	2		1				8		
Malden	95	22	Lynde	Jabez	1			1					1				3		
Malden	95	24	Lynde	Jos'				1			1	1		1			4		
Malden	95	28	Lynde	Jos' Jr			1										1		
Malden	95	25	Lynde	Jso'	1		1			1		1					4		
Malden	95	21	Lynde	Mary									1				1		
Malden	95	26	Lynde	Nathn		1		1					1		2		5		
Malden	95	27	Lynde	Nathn Jr	3		1	1		1	1	1	1				9		
Malden	95	20	Lynde	Rachl								1	1				2		
Hopkinton	242	32	Lyon	Orpheus		1		1				1					4		
Stoneham	139	19	Lyonds	Jebez	2			1					1				4		
Stoneham	139	20	Lyonds	Stephen	1	1	1						1				4		
Tewksbury	52	22	Mace	Benja	2	1	1		1	2	1	1	1				10		
Tewksbury	52	16	Mace	Furtam	1			1		1			1	1			5		
Marlborough	190	4	Mack	John P.	1			1		1		1					4		
Cambridge	226	15	Mackey	James	2		1						1				4		
Reading	133	14	Mackintone	Archelas			1	1		3		1	1				7		
Reading	133	16	Mackintone	Benjamin	2	2		1		1	2			1			9		
Reading	133	19	Mackintone	Ebenezer	1			1	1	3	1		1	1			9		
Reading	133	20	Mackintone	Ephraim		1		1						1			3		
Reading	133	15	Mackintone	Hezekiah	1	1	2					2	1				9		
Reading	133	21	Mackintone	John	3	1		1					1	1			7		
Reading	133	17	Mackintone	Solomon	1			1	1					1			4		
Waltham	115	4	Macomber	Zabidee	3		1	1		1			1				7		
Charlestown	87	33	Makepeace	Geo'				1					1	1			3		
Newton	122	12	Mallard	James	1			1		1			1				4		
Charlestown	87	29	Mallet	Ann									1	1			2		
Charlestown	87	26	Mallet	Isaac	2		1		1	4	1	1					10		
Dracut	48	27	Mallone	William				1					1	1			3		
Natick	247	3	Man	John	2	1	1	1		2	1		1				9		
Dracut	47	1	Manfure	J* W	2			1	1	1	3	2		1			11		
Dracut	46	40	Manfure	Samll		1	1		1		2	1	1				7		

TOWN	PG#	LN#	LAST NAME	FIRST NAME	FREE WHITE MALES					FREE WHITE FEMALES					TOTAL ALL OTHER	TOTAL SLAVES	TOTALS	DISTRICT/TOWNSHIP	NOTES
					under 10	10 to 16	16 to 26	26 to 45	45 and over	under 10	10 to 16	16 to 26	26 to 45	45 and over					
Tewksbury	52	19	Maning	Elizabeth	1	1		1	1	3			1	1			9		
Cambridge	226	29	Mannen	Samll		1		1						1			3		
Cambridge	226	16	Mannen	Wm		1		1						1			3		
Tewksbury	52	15	Manning	Hannah		1						1	1	1			4		
Billerica	176	32	Manning	Isaac				1				1		1			3		
Billerica	176	33	Manning	Jacob			1	1						1			3		
Chelmsford	170	35	Manning	Jacob	2		2	1					1				6		
Billerica	176	34	Manning	Jesse	1			1					1	1			4		
Billerica	176	42	Manning	Jesse Jr			1			1			1				3		
Ashby	37	15	Manning	John		2		1		2		1	1				7		
Charlestown	87	46	Manning	John	2		1						1				4		
Chelmsford	170	33	Manning	Jona'	1		2		1	1	2	3		1			11		
Pepperell	34	14	Manning	Peter	2			1		2	1		1				7		
Charlestown	87	24	Manning	Pheebe		2							1	1			4		
Charlestown	87	40	Manning	Rachl		1				1		1		1			4		
Townsend	27	25	Manning	Saml		1		1		1			1				4		
Tewksbury	52	18	Manning	Samll			3	1		2	2		1				9		
Medford	101	24	Manning	Sarah									1				1		
Chelmsford	170	34	Manning	Timo'			3	1		2			1				7		
Billerica	176	35	Manning	Wm		1	2	1		2	1	3		1			11		
Charlestown	87	41	Manning	Wm		1				2	1						4		
Townsend	27	26	Manning	Wm	2	1		1		1			1				6		
Charlestown	87	23	Manning	Wm H.	1			1		1			1	1			5		
Charlestown	88	1	Mansfield	Arnold			1			1		1					3		
Chelmsford	170	40	Mansfield	John		1	2	1						1			5		
Charlestown	87	39	Mansir	Eben	2	1	2	1		2	1		1	1			11		
Charlestown	87	38	Mansir	Saml	1		1	1		1		1					5		
Cambridge	226	17	Manson	Frederick		1				1		1					3		
Framingham	72	19	Manson	Frederick	1	1		1		1	1	1		1			7		Stamped pg# was x'd out
Marlborough	192	13	Manson	Loring	1		1	1		2			1				6		
East Sudbury	68	11	Maples	Ebenezer		1		1		1		1		1			5		
Dracut	44	22	Marble	David			1	1		1		1		1			5		
Stow	197	22	Marble	John	1	1	1		1	1		1	1	2			9		
Dracut	45	5	Marble	Jonath			1			1		1					3		
Ashby	37	17	March	Josh W.	3		1			1		1					6		
Ashby	37	16	March	Saml				1						1			2		
Concord	8	33	Marhsal	Robert	1		1				1	1					4		
Burlington	155	4	Marion	Isaac			1	1		1	1			3			7		
Lexington	158	15	Marrett	Amos				1		1				1			3		
Lexington	158	16	Marrett	Amos Jr		1		1		3	2		1				8		
Burlington	155	6	Marrett	John				1				1	2				4		
Hollistown	238	30	Marsh	Ezekl	1	3		1		2	1	1		1			10		
Acton	18	2	Marsh	James	2	1		1		1	1	1					7		
Hopkinton	242	39	Marsh	Lydia		3		1				1		1			6		
Chelmsford	170	32	Marshal	Abel	2	1		1		3	1		1				9		
Tewksbury	52	14	Marshal	Daniel	2	1		1		1	1	2		1			9		
Tewksbury	52	20	Marshal	Jacob	1	1	1	1		3	1	1	1				10		
Chelmsford	170	28	Marshal	James	2	1		1		2	2		1				9		
Tewksbury	52	13	Marshal	Joel	1		2		1	2	2			1			9		
Chelmsford	170	29	Marshal	Peter			2						2	1			5		
Chelmsford	170	30	Marshal	Saml				1						1			2		
Chelmsford	170	31	Marshal	Saml Jr	3		2	1		3	1	1					11		
Newton	122	15	Marshall	Catharine		1		1					1	1			4		
Framingham	78	18	Marshall	Eben				1						1			2		
Framingham	76	17	Marshall	Gilbert	1		1	1		5	1		1				10		
Billerica	176	36	Marshall	Isaac				1					1				2		
Billerica	176	37	Marshall	Isaac Jr	1		1	1		2			1				6		
Sherburn	250	36	Marshall	James				1						2			3		
Dracut	47	14	Marshall	Joshua	2	2	1	1		2	1		2				11		
Billerica	176	38	Marshall	Saml			1	1			1						3		
Weston	109	13	Marshall	Thomas		1	1	1	2	1	2	2	2	2			14		
Malden	95	31	Martin	Mary				1				1		4			6		
Cambridge	226	20	Mason	Daniel		2		1		1			1				5		
Lexington	158	33	Mason	Daniel				1					1				2		
Cambridge	226	30	Mason	Jacob	1			1		1	1		1				5		
Lincoln	13	27	Mason	Jonas				1			1	2	1	2			7		
Lexington	158	32	Mason	Joseph				1						2			3		
Cambridge	226	14	Mason	Josiah Jr			1	1				2		1			5		
Reading	133	18	Mason	Nathan		1		1				1	1				4		
Cambridge	226	19	Mason	Thadd				1		4	1		3	1			10		
Cambridge	226	24	Mason	Thos		1		1				1	1				4		
Stoneham	139	21	Mathers	Timothy				1						1			2		
Stoneham	139	22	Mathers	Timothy Jr	2			2		2		1					7		
Sudbury	61	2	Mathews	James				1		1		1					3		
Newton	122	11	Mathews	John			2	1				1		1			5		
Lincoln	15	13	Matthews	Abner	1			1			1		1				4		
Tewksbury	52	25	Matthews	John				1					1				2		
Stow	196	43	Maxwell	George	2		1						1				4		
Bedford	162	33	Maxwell	William		1			2	2	1	1	1	1			9		
Stow	196	42	Maxwell	William					1					1			2		

TOWN	PG#	LN#	LAST NAME	FIRST NAME	FREE WHITE MALES under 10	10 to 16	16 to 26	26 to 45	45 and over	FREE WHITE FEMALES under 10	10 to 16	16 to 26	26 to 45	45 and over	TOTAL ALL OTHER	TOTAL SLAVES	TOTALS	DISTRICT/ TOWNSHIP	NOTES
Charlestown	87	32	Maxwell	Wm			2			1		1					4		
Framingham	76	16	Mayhew	John	1		2		1	1	1		1				7		
Hopkinton	243	5	Mayhew	John			1					1					2		
Concord	6	36	Maynard	Aaron	1			1				1					3		
Sudbury	65	6	Maynard	Asa				1			1		1				3		
Marlborough	192	21	Maynard	Benjamin			1		1	1		1	1	1			6		
East Sudbury	67	3	Maynard	Daniel		1		1				1	1				4		
East Sudbury	67	4	Maynard	Deborah			1	2		2			1				6		
Marlborough	188	29	Maynard	Elihu	1	1			1	3		1	1				8		
Marlborough	192	24	Maynard	Ephraim	1		2		1		1	1		1			7		
Sudbury	62	20	Maynard	Gideon	2	1	1		1			1	1				7		
Marlborough	187	20	Maynard	Hezekiah	1	2	4	1	1			2		1			12		
Stow	196	26	Maynard	Jabez	1	1		1				1	1				5		
Marlborough	194	35	Maynard	John	3		1	1				2	1				8		
Sudbury	61	33	Maynard	John	2			2	1		1		1				7		
Framingham	72	23	Maynard	Jonathan	1	1		1	1	1	1	1					7		Stamped pg# was x'd out
Sudbury	65	2	Maynard	Joshua		2	1	1					1	1			6		
Marlborough	192	40	Maynard	Levina			1				1			2			4		
Marlborough	188	30	Maynard	Mary										2			2		
East Sudbury	67	5	Maynard	Micah	2		1	1				1	1				6		
Sudbury	63	15	Maynard	Moses		2	2		1			1	1	1			8		
Sudbury	62	34	Maynard	Moses Jr			1			3	1		1				6		
Sudbury	63	26	Maynard	Samuel		1				2		1		1			5		
Marlborough	192	20	Maynard	Simon	1		1		1			1		1			5		
Framingham	74	9	Maynard	William	1	1		1				1					4		
Sudbury	62	19	Maynard	Zachariah				1			1		1				3		
Medford	99	47	McClester	Phillip				1									1		
Medford	99	46	McCloud	Jno'			1			2			1				4		
Charlestown	82	16	McCluer	Peter											4		4		
Charlestown	83	9	McDonnaugh	Tho'	2	1	1		1	3	1	2	3		2		16		
Charlestown	84	45	McGoon	That'			1										1		
Burlington	155	5	McIntier	Joseph	5		1						1				7		
Charlestown	86	19	McIntire	John			1			1		1					3		
Shirley	215	11	McKenzie	Bho*				1					1				2		
Shirley	215	13	McLeod	Sarah Wid.							1	2		2			5		
Stow	196	11	McLeod	William L	1		1					1					3		
Groton	211	22	McLorn	Edward	1			1		2	2		1				7		
Charlestown	88	17	McNeal	Archb		2	2		2			5	1				12		
Waltham	115	1	Mead	Jacob	1			1					1				3		
Medford	101	26	Mead	Jno'	2	1			1	1			1				6		
Waltham	115	3	Mead	Moses	1	1	1		1	3		1	1	1			10		
Medford	101	25	Mead	Nath	1			1					1				3		
Boxborough	200	26	Mead	Oliver	2	2			1	2	1	2	1			2	13		
Waltham	114	28	Mead	Stephen	2		1	1		1			1				6		
Tewksbury	52	8	Mears	Aaron	2			1					1				4		
Tewksbury	52	9	Mears	Isaac	1		1			1		1					4		
Chelmsford	170	27	Mears	Robert			1			2			1				4		
Tewksbury	52	21	Mears	Russel	1		1						1				3		
Dracut	46	26	Mears	Samll	1		1	1		2	2	1	1				9		
Tewksbury	52	17	Mears	Samll	1			1						1			3		
Billerica	176	39	Mears	Tho'	1			1	1		1	1		1			6		
Westford	182	25	Mears	Wm	2					2	1	1	1				8		
Hopkinton	243	6	Medeay	Mathew		2	1	1		1		2		1			8		
Lexington	158	20	Meed	Josiah				1		3			1	1			6		
Lexington	158	28	Meed	Levi	1	2	1	1					1	2			8		
Bedford	162	32	Meed	Stephen			1	1					1	2			5		
Wilmington	143	13	Meers	Zebediah	1			1		2			1				5		
Framingham	76	15	Mellen	Abner	1	2		1		2	1		1				8		
Hollistown	238	21	Mellen	Jacob				1						1			2		
Hollistown	238	20	Mellen	John			2						1				3		
Hollistown	238	22	Mellen	Obediah	1		1						1				3		
Hopkinton	242	35	Mellens	Henry				1						1			2		
Hopkinton	242	38	Mellens	Henry		1					1						2		
Hollistown	238	27	Mellens	James	1	1	1		1	1	2	1	1				9		
Hollistown	238	29	Mellens	John	1		1	1		3		1	1				8		
Hollistown	238	28	Mellens	Robert		1			1					1			3		
Hopkinton	242	37	Mellens	Thos				1			1			1			3		
Hollistown	238	26	Mellens	Wm	1			1		1		1	1				5		
Weston	109	11	Melo	Cato											2		2		
Concord	7	22	Melven	Amos	2	1	1		1	1	1		1				8		
Acton	19	38	Melven	Eathon	2			1		2			1				6		
Concord	7	10	Melven	Samuel	1	1			1	3	2		1				9		
Concord	10	5	Melven	Sarah									1				1		
Chelmsford	170	38	Melvin	Benja'	2		1		1	3			1				8		
Concord	7	11	Melvin	Isaac			1			2			1				4		
Concord	7	14	Melvin	Jacob	1			1		1	1	1	2		1		8		
Tyngsborough	43	7	Melvin	Reuben	3		1	1		2		1	1				9		
Pepperell	34	15	Menihan	Robert	1			1		3			1				6		
Concord	8	2	Mercer	William			2	1				1		1			5		
Malden	95	30	Merchant	Mary										1			1		

188

TOWN	PG#	LN#	LAST NAME	FIRST NAME	FREE WHITE MALES under 10	10 to 16	16 to 26	26 to 45	45 and over	FREE WHITE FEMALES under 10	10 to 16	16 to 26	26 to 45	45 and over	TOTAL ALL OTHER	TOTAL SLAVES	TOTALS	DISTRICT/ TOWNSHIP	NOTES
Charlestown	87	22	Mercy	Sophia								1					1		
Lexington	158	35	Meriam	Benjamin				1			2		1				4		
East Sudbury	67	6	Meriam	Elisha	1		1	1		3			1	1			8		
Concord	8	4	Meriam	Ephraim	2		1	1		1			1	1			7		
Lincoln	15	18	Meriam	James				1						1			2		
Bedford	162	31	Meriam	John		1	2					1		1	1		6		
Concord	8	10	Meriam	John	3	1	1	1		1			2	1			9		
Concord	8	5	Meriam	John Jr			2							1			3		
Concord	11	16	Meriam	Joseph				1					1				2		
Concord	11	15	Meriam	Josiah		1		1					1	1			4		
Bedford	162	36	Meriam	Nathaniel				1		1				1			3		
Lexington	158	17	Meriam	Rufus	1	1	1	1		3	1	1	1				10		
Bedford	162	34	Meriam	Samuel	1	1		1		3			1				7		
Concord	4	16	Meriam	Sarah		1							1				2		
Framingham	64	1	Meriam	Timothy	3		1	1		1	2	1	1				10		Stamped pg# was x'd out
Bedford	162	30	Meriam	William		1		1			2	1		1			6		
Charlestown	87	20	Merick	Esther						4		1	1				6		
Concord	11	14	Merriam	Josiah Jr	2	1		1		2		2	1				9		
Charlestown	87	27	Merriam	Lott		1	2	1		3		1	1				9		
Littleton	204	6	Merriam	Willard		1		1						1			3		
Newton	122	16	Merrick	Abigail								1	1				2		
Concord	5	27	Merrick	Tilly	1	2		1				1	1				6		
Tyngsborough	43	6	Merril	John	1			1					1				3		
Malden	95	29	Merrill	Moses			1										1		
Tewksbury	52	24	Merrit	David				1						1			2		
Tewksbury	52	23	Merrit	David Jr	1			1		1			1				4		
Hollistown	238	23	Messenger	Cathn		1	1	2				1	1	1			7		
Hollistown	238	24	Messenger	Joseph	2		1					1					4		
Framingham	76	14	Metcalf	Levi		1		1				1		1			4		
Westford	182	26	Miat	Henry				1						1			2		
Hopkinton	242	41	Mifflin	Walter	1	1	2		2	1	1	2		1			11		
Concord	9	31	Miles	Charles	1		1	1					2	1			6		
Concord	9	30	Miles	Ezekiel			2							1			4		
Concord	9	28	Miles	James	1			1		1		1					4		
Concord	10	16	Miles	Joseph	2			1				1	1				5		
Concord	10	15	Miles	Oliver		1		1				1		1			4		
Hopkinton	242	36	Millenge	Thos			2				1	1					4		
Woburn	150	23	Miller	Job				1			2		1		2		6		
Billerica	176	40	Miller	John				1						1			2		
Billerica	176	41	Miller	John Jr			1						1				2		
Charlestown	87	36	Miller	Jos'	1		2	1		2	2		1	1			10		
Charlestown	87	37	Miller	Sarah										1			1		
Charlestown	87	21	Miller	Tho'		2	2		1		1	2		1			9		
Waltham	115	2	Miller	Thomas				1		3			1				5		
Newton	122	20	Mills	Luke			1		1	1	2		1				6		
Newton	122	21	Mills	Luke Jr	1			1				1					3		
Cambridge	226	28	Mills	Samll	1	1		1		1	1	2					7		
Charlestown	87	28	Mincher	Edw'			1			3		1					5		
Lincoln	12	4	Minot	Abel	3			1					1				5		
Westford	182	28	Minot	Jesse	5	2		1			1			1			10		
Chelmsford	170	39	Minot	John				1						1			2		
Westford	182	27	Minot	John				1						1			2		
Concord	9	27	Minot	John	1		1	1		1				1			5		
Concord	8	12	Minott	George	1	1		1		1	1		2	1			8		
Concord	8	11	Minott	Jonas	1		1	1		2			1	1			7		
Concord	8	1	Minott	Jonas Jr			1	1		2		1	1				6		
Concord	5	13	Minott	Stephen			2	1					1				4		
Concord	2	4	Minott	Timothy		1		1				1	1	1			5		
Charlestown	87	25	Mirick	Benja'	2			1			1	2		1			7		
Watertown	233	29	Mitcham	John	3	1		1		1		1		1			8		
Charlestown	87	30	Mitchel	Ann	1							1		1			3		
Newton	122	19	Mitchell	Edward				1		3	1		1				6		
Framingham	72	18	Mixer	John		2	1		1		1	1		2			8		Stamped pg# was x'd out
Watertown	233	27	Mixter	Josiah		1	1	1			1	2		1			7		
Bedford	162	35	Moar	John & Bradley B	1	1		1	2				1	1	1		8		
Sudbury	58	9	Mone	Joel	1	1					1	1					4		
Pepperell	34	13	Montague	Seth			1										1		
Lexington	158	22	Moor	Robert		1		1						2			4		
Shirley	215	12	Moore	Abel	3		1	1		2			1				8		
Marlborough	192	36	Moore	Bezaleel				1					1	1			3		
East Sudbury	67	9	Moore	Caleb	1			1		1		1	1				5		
Marlborough	188	22	Moore	Carley	2			1			1		1				5		
Natick	247	6	Moore	David	2	4	1	1		1		2	1				12		
Marlborough	189	35	Moore	Edmond	1			1		2	1	1		1			7		
Sudbury	62	6	Moore	Ephraim	1	1	1						1	1			7		
Cambridge	226	21	Moore	Francis			1		1	1	1			1			5		
Sudbury	58	4	Moore	Isaac	2			1			1		1	1			6		
East Sudbury	67	2	Moore	Israel	3			1		2	1		1				8		
Charlestown	87	44	Moore	John				1		2		1					4		
Sudbury	60	17	Moore	John		1	1		1		1	1		1			6		

189

TOWN	PG#	LN#	LAST NAME	FIRST NAME	FREE WHITE MALES under 10	10 to 16	16 to 26	26 to 45	45 and over	FREE WHITE FEMALES under 10	10 to 16	16 to 26	26 to 45	45 and over	TOTAL ALL OTHER	TOTAL SLAVES	TOTALS	DISTRICT/ TOWNSHIP	NOTES
Boxborough	200	12	Moore	Jonathan	1	1		1		2			1				6		
Sudbury	59	35	Moore	Jonathan	1	2		1	1			1		1			7		
Chelmsford	170	36	Moore	Jos'					1				1	1			3		
Groton	211	16	Moore	Joseph Esq		2	3	1	3	1	1	2		1			14		
Cambridge	226	23	Moore	Josiah		2	3		1		2		1	2			11		
Groton	211	21	Moore	Lydia Wid.									1				1		
Chelmsford	170	37	Moore	Mial	3			1		1			1				6		
Sudbury	60	21	Moore	Olive			1					1	1				3		
Marlborough	191	9	Moore	Phinehas				1					1				2		
Newton	122	13	Moore	Reuben	1	2			1	3		1	1				9		
Sudbury	60	24	Moore	Reuben			1	2				1	1				5		
Sudbury	61	10	Moore	Timothy	2			1		1	1		1	1			7		
Sudbury	61	24	Moore	William	2		1		1	3			1				8		
Charlestown	87	42	Moore	Wm			1	1		1			1				4		
Charlestown	87	43	Moore		1			2		4		1	1	1			10		
Cambridge	226	18	Moredoc	Jacob W	1		1						1				3		
Watertown	233	28	Moredoe	Artimas	1			1	1	1	1	1					6		
Dracut	45	39	Morgan	Jona	3	1		1			1		1				7		
Wilmington	143	12	Morriel	Doratha								2	1				3		
Wilmington	143	11	Morriel	Nathaniel	2	2	2	1		2	1		1				11		
Acton	19	24	Morse	Abel		1		2					1				4		
Groton	211	18	Morse	Abel		1		1					1				3		
Natick	246	46	Morse	Adam	1	2	1	1		3	1		1				10		
Cambridge	226	27	Morse	Arnold		1				2		1					4		
Framingham	72	20	Morse	Asa	1	1	1		1	1	1			1			7		Stamped pg# was x'd out
East Sudbury	66	12	Morse	Asarelah			1	1		1	1		1				5		
Weston	109	14	Morse	Beniah	3			1		2			1				7		
Boxborough	200	35	Morse	Benjamin	1			1		1	1		1				5		
Groton	211	17	Morse	Benjm Doct.		1		1					1				3		
Framingham	78	14	Morse	Daniel	2			1		2			1				6		
Natick	247	7	Morse	Daniel				1					1				2		
Hopkinton	243	2	Morse	Elisha	3		1	1		1			1				7		
Natick	247	2	Morse	Elisha	1		1		1		1	1		1			6		
Marlborough	190	7	Morse	Francis		1			1		1	1	1				5		
Natick	247	8	Morse	Gershom			1					1					2		
Natick	247	4	Morse	Henry	3	2	1	1		2	1		1				11		
Sherburn	250	34	Morse	Hezekh	3		1			1	1		1				7		
Sherburn	250	38	Morse	Hezekh	2			1		1			1	1			6		
Hollistown	238	25	Morse	Isaac	1	1	1		1	2	1		1				8		
Framingham	72	21	Morse	James				2		1	1	1	2				7		Stamped pg# was x'd out
Newton	122	18	Morse	James											4		4		
Sherburn	250	40	Morse	Jason	1				1			1		1			4		
Charlestown	87	45	Morse	Jedh	2			1				1	2				6		
Hopkinton	242	40	Morse	Joel	1			1		1			1				4		
Sherburn	250	35	Morse	Jona				1					1				2		
Hopkinton	243	1	Morse	Joseph	1	1		1		3	1		1				8		
Sherburn	250	37	Morse	Levi				1			1		1				3		
Waltham	114	29	Morse	Levi			1	3		2			1				7		
Waltham	114	27	Morse	Luther	1			1		2			1				5		
Sherburn	250	39	Morse	Moses				1					2	1			4		
Hopkinton	242	43	Morse	Parrias		2	2	1					1				6		
Groton	211	19	Morse	Saml	3	1		1		1			1				7		
Natick	247	1	Morse	Saml	2	2	3		1	2	1		1	2			14		
Sherburn	250	41	Morse	Saml				1		3			1				5		
Marlborough	194	6	Morse	Stephen	3			3		2		2	1	1			12		
Cambridge	226	26	Morse	Susanna	1		1		2	2	1	2	1	1			11		
Cambridge	226	22	Morse	William				1									1		
Marlborough	194	32	Morse	William		2		1			1			1			5		
Marlborough	188	21	Morse	Windsor	3			2		1			1	1			8		
Natick	247	5	Morse	Wm	1			2		2		2	1				8		
Hopkinton	243	4	Morting	Jame			1						1				2		
Hopkinton	243	3	Morting	Nathan		1		1				1	1				4		
Tewksbury	52	26	Morton	Amos	2	1		1		1	1		1				7		
Stow	198	28	Moses	Anna	1					1			1				3		
Marlborough	194	30	Moses	Nanna								1	1				2		
Ashby	37	42	Mosman	Mathias	1	1		1	1	2	1	2		1			10		
Weston	109	12	Mosman	Micah			1			2			1				4		
Sudbury	62	31	Mosman	Moses	1		2		2	1		2		1			9		
Sudbury	62	25	Mosman	Silas		2		1		4			1	1			9		
Hopkinton	242	42	Motten	John	1			1		2	1		1				6		
East Sudbury	67	13	Moulton	Aaron	1				2					1			4		
East Sudbury	67	10	Moulton	Caleb			1		1		1	1		1			5		
Framingham	72	22	Moulton	Caleb	1			1		2		1	1				6		Stamped pg# was x'd out
East Sudbury	69	18	Moulton	Daniel	2			1		2			1				6		
East Sudbury	67	11	Moulton	William				1					1				2		
East Sudbury	67	12	Moulton	Windsor	2		1	1					1				5		
Cambridge	226	25	Mullen	John	1	1		1		2		1	1				7		
Charlestown	87	35	Mullet	Eprm	4	2	2	1		1	1		1				12		
Burlington	155	7	Mullet	Robert	1		1			1			1				4		
Townsend	27	27	Mulliken	Amos					1				1				2		

TOWN	PG#	LN#	HEADS OF HOUSEHOLD		FREE WHITE MALES					FREE WHITE FEMALES					TOTAL ALL OTHER	TOTAL SLAVES	TOTALS	DISTRICT/ TOWNSHIP	NOTES
			LAST NAME	FIRST NAME	under 10	10 to 16	16 to 26	26 to 45	45 and over	under 10	10 to 16	16 to 26	26 to 45	45 and over					
Townsend	27	24	Mulliken	Isaac	1			1				1	1				4		
Concord	6	10	Mulliken	Joseph			1	1		3			1				6		
Lexington	158	21	Mullikin	John	1	1	2	1		1	2		1	1			10		
Lexington	158	31	Munro	Abigail	3								1	2			6		
Lexington	158	30	Munro	Ebenezer		1		1				2		1			5		
Burlington	155	3	Munro	Ishmael	1		1	1	1	1			2				7		
Lexington	158	24	Munro	John				1				2	1				4		
Woburn	150	24	Munro	Jonas	2			1		1			2				6		
Lexington	158	25	Munro	Joseph	2			1		1	1		1				6		
Lexington	158	23	Munro	Nathan	2		1		1		2		1	1			8		
Lexington	158	27	Munro	Phil*n	2	3			2	3			1				11		
Lexington	158	14	Munro	Thaddeus	2		1	1						1			5		
Lexington	158	34	Munro	William		1	2	1				3	1				8		
Lexington	158	26	Munro	William Jr		2		1		3	1		1				8		
Lincoln	14	19	Munroe	Benjamin	1	1		1	1	1			1				6		
Stow	198	7	Munroe	Benjamin		1		1	1		1		1				5		
Marlborough	193	43	Munroe	David	1	1	1		3				2	1			9		
Marlborough	188	4	Munroe	David Jr	1		3			1	1	1					7		
Carlisle	22	8	Munroe	Jonas	1	1	2	1	4	2	1		1	1			14		
Marlborough	194	1	Munroe	Lois	2			1				1					4		
Newton	122	10	Munroe	Nathan	1			1				1					3		
Newton	122	14	Munroe	Oliver					1			1	1				3		
Charlestown	87	31	Munroe	Sal	3			1				1					5		
Groton	211	20	Munroe	Stephen	3	1	2		1	1			1	2			11		
East Sudbury	69	22	Murdock	Aaron					1				1				2		
Newton	122	7	Murdock	Elisha	1			1				1					2		
Newton	122	8	Murdock	Esther									1				1		
Newton	122	9	Murdock	Jonathan			1			2			1				4		
Newton	122	17	Murdock	Robert	3	1		1					2				7		
Newton	122	6	Murdock	Saml	1		1	1		1	2	1	1				8		
Charlestown	87	34	Murray	Mary		1					1			1			3		
Lexington	158	19	Muzzy	Amos					1				1	2			4		
Lexington	158	18	Muzzy	Amos Jr	1		1			2			1	1			6		
Lexington	158	36	Muzzy	Ebenezer	1	1		1			1	1	1	2			8		
Lexington	158	29	Muzzy	John			2	1				1		1			5		
Reading	133	23	N*s	Daniel	1	1		1						1			4		
Groton	211	28	Nash	Ephm		1	1	1					1		1		5		
Charlestown	88	15	Nason	Micah			1			1			1				3		
Malden	95	37	Neagles	Ann									1				1		
Malden	95	38	Neagles	Micah	3	1		1		1	1		1	1			9		
Newton	122	24	Neal	William			1					1	1				3		
Billerica	177	1	Needham	Asa	2		1			1			1				5		
Tewksbury	52	27	Needham	John	3		1	1		3	3		1				12		
Reading	134	4	Nelson	John	2			1		1	1		1				6		
Lincoln	13	34	Nelson	Josiah		2	2	1		1		2					8		
Cambridge	229	35	Nelson	Priscilla									1				1		
Lincoln	13	35	Nelson	Thomas						1					1		2		
Burlington	155	8	Nevers	Samuel	2	2			1	3	1		1	1			11		
Charlestown	88	8	Newell	Andr'				1					1				2		
Malden	95	41	Newell	Edw'			1										1		
Charlestown	88	7	Newell	Eliphl	1			1					1				4		
Charlestown	88	4	Newell	Eliz'							1		1				2		
Malden	95	40	Newell	Eliz'	1	1	1			1			1				5		
Charlestown	88	6	Newell	Hannah								1	1				2		
Stow	198	36	Newell	Jonathan	2			1			2	1		1			7		
Littleton	202	9	Newell	Jonathan A.	1	1		1			1	1					5		
Malden	95	39	Newell	Mary									1				1		
Charlestown	88	5	Newell	Susan	1					2			1				4		
Watertown	233	34	Newhall	Artimas	2		1					1					4		
Natick	247	9	Newhall	Ebenr		1		2		3	1		1				8		
Reading	133	28	Newhall	James	2			1		1			1				5		
Charlestown	88	3	Newhall	NapR	1					1	1	1					4		
Reading	134	3	Newhall	Olive						1	1	1					4		
Pepperell	32	7	Newhall	Oliver	1		1		1	1			1				6		
Reading	133	25	Newhall	Reuben	2			1			1	1					5		
Medford	101	27	Newhall	Saml			1			1		1					3		
Hollistown	238	34	Newhall	Theodore	2			1		1			1				5		
Sherburn	250	42	Newhall	Thos	2	1		1		3			1	1			9		
Charlestown	88	2	Newhall	Wm		1		1					1				4		
Marlborough	194	33	Newton	Adonijah				1			1		1				3		
Framingham	66	2	Newton	Ephraim		1		1		3		1	1				7		Stamped pg# was x'd out
Marlborough	191	11	Newton	Jerusha				1					3				4		
Framingham	64	5	Newton	Jonas	1	1		1		1	1		1				6		Stamped pg# was x'd out
Marlborough	188	6	Newton	Joseph				1					1				2		
Marlborough	193	8	Newton	Micah		1	1	1					1				4		
Hollistown	238	33	Newton	Simeon				1						1			2		
Marlborough	194	40	Newton	William			2	1					2				5		
Lexington	158	37	Nichols	Adna	2			1		2	1	1	1				8		
Framingham	74	10	Nichols	Alpheus				1			2	2	1	1			7		Stamped pg# was x'd out
Reading	134	5	Nichols	Edmund	1	2		1		2			1				7		
Reading	134	2	Nichols	Hay			1					1					2		

TOWN	PG#	LN#	LAST NAME	FIRST NAME	FREE WHITE MALES					FREE WHITE FEMALES					TOTAL ALL OTHER	TOTAL SLAVES	TOTALS	DISTRICT/ TOWNSHIP	NOTES
					under 10	10 to 16	16 to 26	26 to 45	45 and over	under 10	10 to 16	16 to 26	26 to 45	45 and over					
Reading	133	27	Nichols	James	1			2	1		1		1				6		
Reading	133	24	Nichols	James Jr	3			1					1				5		
Reading	133	30	Nichols	Jeremiah			2	1		2	1	1	1				8		
Reading	133	22	Nichols	Jesse	2	1		1		1			1				6		
Reading	133	31	Nichols	John			1	1					1	1			4		
Reading	133	32	Nichols	John Jr		1		1		2	1		1	1			7		
Wilmington	143	14	Nichols	Jonathan			2	1			1		1				5		
Westford	182	33	Nichols	Mich'			1		1				1				3		
Reading	133	29	Nichols	Reuben		1	1		1		1		1				5		
Hollistown	238	32	Nichols	Samll	1		1				1						3		
Reading	133	26	Nichols	Simon	1	1	1		1		1	3		1			9		
Reading	134	1	Nichols	Simon Jr	1		1					1	1				4		
Westford	182	32	Nichols	Steph'	1			1					1				3		
Woburn	150	25	Nichols	William		1	1			1		1					4		
Westford	182	31	Nichols	Wm		1	1			1	1	1					5		
Carlisle	23	20	Nicklas	Isaac											4		4		
Carlisle	21	31	Nicklas	James			1	1		1	1		1				5		
Carlisle	21	33	Nicklas	Job	2		1			1		1					5		
Carlisle	21	32	Nicklas	John				1	1				2				4		
Carlisle	21	29	Nicklas	John Jr		1	1	1	1	1	1	1	1				8		
Carlisle	23	2	Nicklas	Joseph	2			1				1	1				5		
Malden	95	33	Nickols	David			1			1		1					3		
Malden	95	32	Nickols	Eben	2		1			3			1				7		
Malden	95	34	Nickols	Jno'	3			1		2		1		1			8		
Charlestown	88	11	Nickols	Jona'											3		3		
Malden	95	35	Nickols	Nathn			1			3		1	2		1		8		
Malden	95	36	Nickols	Wm	3		1	1					1	1			7		
Charlestown	88	12	Nickolson	Saml	1	3		1		2	1	3	1		2		14		
Charlestown	88	13	Niles	Silas	2			1				1		1			5		
Charlestown	88	14	Niles	Silas Jr		1	4	1		1			1				8		
Waltham	115	6	Nison	Joseph	3		4	1		2	1	2					13		
Sudbury	59	27	Nixon	John	2		1	1			1		1				6		
Framingham	72	24	Nixon	Thomas	2			1		2		1	1				7		Stamped pg# was x'd out
Stoneham	139	23	Noble	John	1			1		4	1		1				8		
Hollistown	238	31	Norcross	Asa	1			1					1				3		
Hopkinton	243	9	Norcross	Benjm				1					1				2		
Hopkinton	243	7	Norcross	Daniel		1		1		1			1				4		
Watertown	233	31	Norcross	Elijah		1	1			2		1					5		
Hopkinton	243	10	Norcross	Joel	2		1	1		1			1				6		
Watertown	233	32	Norcross	Joseph	2	1	1	1					1				7		
Newton	122	23	Norcross	Nathaniel	1	1		1		3	2	1	1				10		
Concord	2	2	Noreau	John	1	1			1	2	3	1	1				10		
Cambridge	226	33	Noreross	John			1	1		1			1				4		
Hopkinton	243	8	North	Daniel	1			1				1	1				4		
Cambridge	226	32	Norton	Elizth							1		1				2		
Watertown	233	30	Norton	Jeremiah		1							1				2		
Charlestown	88	16	Norton	Solo'		1		1		3			1	1			7		
Dracut	46	19	Norwell	Moses	1			1		1	1	1					5		
Boxborough	200	1	Nourp	John	1			1		1			1				4		
Concord	9	19	Noyes	Adam	1	1		1					1				4		
Acton	19	31	Noyes	Amos	1			2					1				4		
East Sudbury	67	18	Noyes	Anna								2	1				3		
Sudbury	62	24	Noyes	Asahel	2			1					1	1			5		
East Sudbury	67	14	Noyes	John		1	1	1	1		2	2	1		1		10		
Acton	18	5	Noyes	Josiah	1		1	1		2	1		1				7		
Sudbury	62	23	Noyes	Oliver			2		1		1			1			5		
Sudbury	61	30	Noyes	Peter	1			1						2			4		
East Sudbury	67	15	Noyes	Tabitha			1							1			2		
Acton	18	9	Noyes	Thomas		1	1	1	1	1			1				7		
Framingham	64	3	Nurse	Asa	1			1		3	3						8		Stamped pg# was x'd out
Marlborough	191	20	Nurse	Francis	1			1		1		1					4		
Framingham	64	2	Nurse	John		2		1		2	1	2	1	1			10		Stamped pg# was x'd out
Framingham	64	4	Nurse	Lawson		1		1		1	1	1	1				6		Stamped pg# was x'd out
Watertown	233	33	Nuting	Charles	1	2			1	2				1			7		
Groton	211	23	Nutting	Abijah	1	1		1		1			1				5		
Carlisle	21	36	Nutting	Amos	2			1					1				4		
Pepperell	32	8	Nutting	Benja		1	1	1			1	2		1			7		
Groton	211	30	Nutting	Daniel				1						2			3		
Westford	182	30	Nutting	Danl	2			1				2	1				6		
Tyngsborough	43	8	Nutting	David	1		1			1		1					4		
Pepperell	32	9	Nutting	Ebenr	1	1			1	1	1			1			6		
Cambridge	226	31	Nutting	Elizabeth				5	1				2			7	15		
Groton	211	27	Nutting	Ephm	1	1	1	1		4			1	1			10		
Groton	211	29	Nutting	Ezekiel	1	1		1		2			1				6		
Groton	211	31	Nutting	Isaac				1		1				1			3		
Charlestown	88	10	Nutting	John				1		1		1					3		
Pepperell	32	5	Nutting	John				1				1	1	1			4		
Pepperell	32	6	Nutting	John Jr	1		1	2		3	1	1					9		
Groton	211	26	Nutting	Jona		1		1		3	1	1	1				8		
Charlestown	88	9	Nutting	Jona'				1					1				2		
Pepperell	32	10	Nutting	Levi			1	1				1	1				5		

192

TOWN	PG#	LN#	LAST NAME	FIRST NAME	M under 10	M 10 to 16	M 16 to 26	M 26 to 45	M 45 and over	F under 10	F 10 to 16	F 16 to 26	F 26 to 45	F 45 and over	TOTAL ALL OTHER	TOTAL SLAVES	TOTALS	DISTRICT/TOWNSHIP	NOTES
Groton	211	24	Nutting	Phinehas	2			1		2			1				6		
Newton	122	22	Nutting	Samuel	1	1		1	1	2		2		2			10		
Waltham	115	7	Nutting	Samuel				1	1	1		1		1			4		
Pepperell	32	4	Nutting	Simeon	1		2		1				1	1	1		7		
Westford	182	29	Nutting	Tho'	4	2		1		1	2		1				11		
Groton	211	25	Nutting	Wm	1	1	1		1	1	1	2		1			9		
Charlestown	88	18	Oakes	Edw'			1				1		1				3		
Malden	95	42	Oakes	Edw'			1						1				2		
Malden	95	45	Oakes	Esther						1	1		1				3		
Malden	95	44	Oakes	Jona'		1	2		1	2	2		1				9		
Malden	95	43	Oakes	Nehem		1											1		
Charlestown	88	19	Oakes	Rebecca							1		1				2		
Stow	196	41	Oaks	John	2		1			1		1					5		
Charlestown	88	22	Oates	James	2		1			1			1				5		
Charlestown	88	21	Odin	Saml				1									1		
Malden	96	1	Oliver	Edw'			1	1									2		
Acton	20	1	Oliver	John											5		5		
Charlestown	88	20	Oliver	John		1		1					1				3		
East Sudbury	69	9	Oliver	John	3		1			2		1					7		
Malden	95	46	Oliver	Robt	3	2		1		1	2		1				10		
Reading	134	7	Oliver	William	2		1	1		1	1	1					7		
Billerica	177	3	Orne	Hannah						3	1	1					5		
Sudbury	61	34	Osborn	Daniel	1	2		1		1	1		2				8		
Sudbury	61	25	Osborn	Obediah	1		1					1					3		
Stow	197	19	Osbourn	David	1		1	2		1		1					6		
Stow	198	4	Osbourn	James	2	2		1		1							6		
Stow	197	18	Osbourn	Samuel				1						1			2		
Westford	182	34	Osgood	Benja'		2	3		1	2	2	1	1				12		
Medford	101	28	Osgood	David	1			1		2	1		1				6		
Chelmsford	171	1	Osgood	Eph'			1	1									2		
Dracut	44	24	Osgood	Henry C	1		1			1		1	1				5		
Reading	134	6	Osgood	Joshua			1	1		3		1	1	1			8		
Billerica	177	2	Osgood	Phins	1		1			2			1				5		
Dracut	44	23	Osgood	Solomon			1	1		1	2						5		
Ashby	37	21	P*	Jacob			2			3		1	1				7		
Wilmington	143	15	P*	John				1						1			2		
Ashby	37	45	Pa*	Elian	3		1	1		2			1				8		
Marlborough	188	18	Packard	Asa	2	1		1		3		1	1	1			10		
Chelmsford	171	28	Packard	H*z'	2	1	3	1				2					9		
Groton	211	39	Page	Benjm		2	1		1	1	1		1	1			8		
Bedford	163	2	Page	Christopher		1		1	1	1	1	1	1				7		
Bedford	163	5	Page	David		1	1		1	1	1		3				8		
Concord	6	28	Page	David	1			1		4	2		2				10		
Cambridge	227	10	Page	Jacob	2	1		1		1			1				6		
Bedford	163	7	Page	John			2	1		3			1				7		
Charlestown	88	27	Page	John			1			2			1				4		
Ashby	35	26	Page	Jona	1		1					1					3		
Charlestown	88	26	Page	Jona'	2	2	5	8	2	1	1	2	2				25		
Bedford	162	40	Page	Nathaniel		1	1	1		1	1		1				6		
Shirley	215	15	Page	Phinehas	1	1	2	1				1		1			7		
Groton	211	37	Page	Simon		1	1	1				1		1			5		
Bedford	163	6	Page	Thomas		1		1				1		1			4		
Bedford	163	3	Page	William				1						1			2		
Stoneham	139	26	Pain	Daniel				1					2				3		
Malden	96	7	Pain	Jno'			1	1					1				3		
Concord	5	28	Pain	Phenihas	2		1		1		1	4		1	2		12		
Malden	96	8	Pain	Step'				1					1				2		
Malden	96	9	Pain	Step' Jr	1		2		1		2	1		1			8		
Malden	96	10	Paine	Eben	1			1		1			1	1			5		
Waltham	115	8	Paine	William		1							1	3			5		
Townsend	28	46	Palmer	David Rev	1		1			1	1						4		
Cambridge	227	12	Palmer	John	1	3		1	1	2			1				9		
Charlestown	89	6	Palmer	Joshua			1			3			1				5		
Cambridge	227	15	Palmer	Stephen				1					1				2		
Newton	123	4	Palmer	Thomas		2			2			2		1			7		
Framingham	72	28	Parhust	Josiah		1	1		1					1			4		Stamped pg# was x'd out
Newton	123	6	Park	Cornelius	1			1		1				1			4		
Newton	123	1	Park	Joshua	2	2	1		1	2			1	1			10		
Newton	123	5	Park	Nathan	2		1			1		1					4		
Marlborough	190	27	Park	Thomas	1		1			2			1				5		
Framingham	64	9	Park	John	3		2	1		2		2	1	1			12		Stamped pg# was x'd out
Newton	122	26	Park	Amasa	1	1		1		1	1		3				8		
Groton	211	36	Park	John	2	1		1		1		1	1				8		
Reading	134	33	Parker	Aaron	2	1		1				1	1				6		
Tyngsborough	43	16	Parker	Aaron	2			1		1	1	1					6		
Westford	182	40	Parker	Aaron	2	1		1		1			1	2			8		
Groton	212	17	Parker	Abigail Wid.									1				1		
Malden	96	11	Parker	Abigl									1				1		
Pepperell	32	12	Parker	Abijah				1		1	1		1				4		
Pepperell	32	24	Parker	Abijah		1	1			1		1	1				5		
Pepperell	32	17	Parker	Abijah Jr	1			1		1			1				4		

TOWN	PG#	LN#	HEADS OF HOUSEHOLD LAST NAME	FIRST NAME	FREE WHITE MALES under 10	10 to 16	16 to 26	26 to 45	45 and over	FREE WHITE FEMALES under 10	10 to 16	16 to 26	26 to 45	45 and over	TOTAL ALL OTHER	TOTAL SLAVES	TOTALS	DISTRICT/ TOWNSHIP	NOTES
Pepperell	32	25	Parker	Abijah Jr	3	1	1	1		1	3		1				11		
Malden	96	12	Parker	Amos			1										1		
Reading	134	29	Parker	Amos	2		1	1		2		1	1	1			9		
Pepperell	32	15	Parker	Asa			1			3		1					5		
Reading	134	12	Parker	Asa			2		1		1	1		1			6		
Reading	134	13	Parker	Asa Jr	2			1		1			1				5		
Chelmsford	171	8	Parker	Benja'			1	1				1		1			4		
Westford	182	37	Parker	Benja'	2	1		1		2	1		1				8		
Reading	135	8	Parker	Benjamin	1		1	1		3	1	2	1				10		
Woburn	150	28	Parker	Benjamin		1			1	4	2		2				10		
Groton	212	15	Parker	Benjm	2	3		1		2			1				9		
Groton	212	23	Parker	Betty										2			2		
Pepperell	32	18	Parker	Caleb	1			1		1		1	1	1			6		
Dracut	46	12	Parker	Daniel	1		1			1	1	1	1				6		
Reading	134	10	Parker	Daniel				1						2			3		
Reading	134	9	Parker	Daniel Jr	1	2	1		1		1			1			7		
Charlestown	88	32	Parker	Danl	1		1	1				1	1				5		
Cambridge	227	2	Parker	David	1			1		2			1				5		
Carlisle	21	20	Parker	David				1			1		1	1			4		
Chelmsford	171	13	Parker	David			2	1	1			1		1			6		
Reading	134	18	Parker	David	1	1	2		2			2		2			10		
Westford	182	38	Parker	David	3	1	1		1	1	1			1			9		
Chelmsford	171	2	Parker	Ebenz		1	1	1		2			1				6		
Groton	212	20	Parker	Ebenzr	2	2	1		1	2	1	1		1			11		
Pepperell	32	11	Parker	Edmund				1			1		1				3		
Woburn	150	29	Parker	Edmund	2	1		1		2	1		1				8		
Groton	211	44	Parker	Eleazr	1		1	1				1	1				6		
Reading	134	19	Parker	Eliab	1			1					1				3		
Tyngsborough	43	17	Parker	Elijah	3	2		1		2	1		1				10		
Dracut	48	33	Parker	Ephraim				1				1	1				3		
Reading	135	4	Parker	Ephraim			1	1				1	1				4		
Reading	135	5	Parker	Ephraim Jr				1						1			2		
Groton	211	43	Parker	Ezekiel	1			1		1			1				4		
Medford	101	35	Parker	Farwell	1		4			1		1					7		
Chelmsford	171	6	Parker	Henry L		1						1					2		
Woburn	150	26	Parker	Ichabod	1		1	1		1	1		1	1			7		
Groton	212	2	Parker	Imla		1	1	1		1			1	1			6		
Reading	134	11	Parker	Isaac	2	1	1		1		1						6		
Westford	182	35	Parker	Isaac				1			1			1			3		
Malden	96	16	Parker	Jacob	1		2		1			1		1			6		
Groton	211	46	Parker	Jacob L.		1		1	1	2		2	1				8		
Pepperell	32	14	Parker	James	2			1		2	1		1				8		
Shirley	215	17	Parker	James		1	1	2	1		1	1		1			8		
Chelmsford	171	9	Parker	Jeduth	1			1		2	1		1				6		
Malden	96	13	Parker	Jno'		1											1		
Billerica	177	10	Parker	John	2	2	1	1	1	2			2	1			12		
Dracut	48	32	Parker	John	3			1					1				7		
Framingham	64	7	Parker	John	2			1		3	1	1	1				9		Stamped pg# was x'd out
Lexington	159	3	Parker	John	1	1		1		2	2		1	1			9		
Marlborough	192	14	Parker	John				1			1		1	1			4		
Pepperell	32	19	Parker	John	1		2			1		1					5		
Shirley	215	26	Parker	John		1			1	1				1			4		
Billerica	177	11	Parker	John Jr		3	2		1		1	1	1				9		
Dracut	46	14	Parker	John Jr		1	1					1					3		
Dracut	46	15	Parker	Jona	2			1		2		1					6		
Pepperell	32	29	Parker	Jona								1					1		
Chelmsford	171	11	Parker	Jona'	1			1		1		1		1			5		
Pepperell	32	13	Parker	Jonas	3		1	1		2	1		1	1			10		
Reading	134	34	Parker	Jonas	1	1			1	1	2		1				7		
Shirley	215	16	Parker	Jonas	1	1	1			1		1					5		
Newton	123	2	Parker	Jonathan		1	1	1			1		2				6		
Charlestown	88	31	Parker	Jos'	1		1	1					1				4		
Chelmsford	171	3	Parker	Jos'	2	1		1	1	1	1		1	1			9		
Newton	122	25	Parker	Joseph	1	1	1	1	1		1	2	1	1			10		
Reading	134	22	Parker	Joseph		1			1			2					4		
Weston	109	16	Parker	Joseph	1		1	1		3			1				7		
Wilmington	143	17	Parker	Joseph			2						2	1			5		
Groton	212	11	Parker	Joshua	2			1		2	1		1				7		
Westford	182	39	Parker	Joshua		1			1					1			3		
Woburn	150	27	Parker	Josiah	1		2		1	2		2	1				9		
Dracut	47	37	Parker	Kindal Jr	2			1		1		1		1			5		
Dunstable	217	25	Parker	Levi			1		1	1	2	1		1			7		
Pepperell	34	18	Parker	Levi	3	1			1	1				1			7		
Lexington	159	5	Parker	Mary										1			1		
Malden	96	17	Parker	May									1	2			3		
Reading	135	11	Parker	Moly	2							1		1			4		
Chelmsford	171	4	Parker	Moses	2			1		1			1				5		
Groton	211	33	Parker	Nathan				1		1			1				3		
Reading	134	31	Parker	Nathan	2	1	4		2		3		1	1			14		
Carlisle	23	5	Parker	Nathaniel		1	1		1		1	2		1			7		

194

TOWN	PG#	LN#	HEADS OF HOUSEHOLD		FREE WHITE MALES					FREE WHITE FEMALES					TOTAL ALL OTHER	TOTAL SLAVES	TOTALS	DISTRICT/ TOWNSHIP	NOTES
			LAST NAME	FIRST NAME	under 10	10 to 16	16 to 26	26 to 45	45 and over	under 10	10 to 16	16 to 26	26 to 45	45 and over					
Woburn	150	30	Parker	Nathaniel		4	1			3	1	2					11		
Pepperell	32	28	Parker	Nathl	1	1	2		1	3	1			1			10		
Lexington	159	8	Parker	Obediah		4	3	1				1					9		
Groton	212	13	Parker	Oliver	2			1		1		1					5		
Dracut	46	13	Parker	Peter	4	1		1		1	1		1				9		
Framingham	64	6	Parker	Peter	2		1	1	1	2	1		2				10		Stamped pg# was x'd out
Concord	10	11	Parker	Phinehas				1		1		2		1			5		
Groton	212	4	Parker	Phinehas	1		1		1				1				4		
Reading	134	28	Parker	Phinehas		1			1			1	1				4		
Lexington	159	4	Parker	Robert	1			1		1		1					4		
Westford	182	36	Parker	Saml S.		1				2		1					4		
Newton	123	3	Parker	Samuel		1	1		1			1		1			5		
Reading	135	1	Parker	Samuel			1	1		3	1						6		
Wilmington	143	19	Parker	Samuel				1					1				2		
Carlisle	21	15	Parker	Sarah									1				1		
Groton	212	24	Parker	Silas		1	1	1		1		1	1				6		
Burlington	155	9	Parker	Simeon			1				2		1				4		
Reading	134	14	Parker	Simeon	1			1					1				3		
Chelmsford	171	7	Parker	Simon	1	1		1		2			2	1			8		
Billerica	177	12	Parker	Steph'		1		1		3			1				6		
Reading	134	27	Parker	Thomas		1			1		1	1		1			5		
Wilmington	143	16	Parker	Thomas		1			1	1	1	1	1				6		
Dracut	48	34	Parker	Warren			1						1		1		3		
Chelmsford	171	12	Parker	Willard	1	1	2		1			1	1	1			8		
Carlisle	21	6	Parker	William	2	1	1	1		2	1	1	1				10		
Reading	134	8	Parker	William	3			1	1				1	1			7		
Reading	134	32	Parker	William Jr		1	1	1		2			2				7		
Groton	212	6	Parker	Winslow	2	2	2		1	3	1			1			12		
Chelmsford	171	5	Parker	Wm				1					1				2		
Groton	212	12	Parker	Wm	3	3		1		3	1		1				12		
Malden	96	14	Parker	Wm		1		1									2		
Townsend	27	33	Parker	Wm	3			1				1					5		
Chelmsford	171	10	Parker	Zebul'	4			1					1				6		
Dunstable	217	23	Parkhurst	Ebenz	3	1	1	1			1		1				8		
Framingham	64	10	Parkhurst	Ephraim	2	1		1		3		1	1				9		Stamped pg# was x'd out
Chelmsford	171	30	Parkhurst	Epm'		1	1		1		1			2			6		
Dunstable	217	20	Parkhurst	Joel Equ				1			1	1	1				4		
Lexington	159	6	Parkhurst	John		1	1		1			1		1			5		
Dunstable	217	21	Parkhurst	Joseph				1					1				2		
Dunstable	217	22	Parkhurst	Joseph Jr		1		1		1	1	2	1				7		
Chelmsford	171	32	Parkhurst	Josiah	3	1		1		1			1				7		
Dunstable	217	24	Parkhurst	Leonard	3		1	1		3			1				9		
Lincoln	14	12	Parkhurst	Nathaniel				1					1				2		
Chelmsford	171	31	Parkhurst	Phillip		4	1	1						2			8		
Chelmsford	171	33	Parkhurst	Saml	2	1		1		1			1				6		
Waltham	115	9	Parkhurst	Sarah	2			1					1				4		
Carlisle	20	14	Parkin	Asa		1		1					1				3		
Carlisle	20	3	Parkins	Nathan	1	1		1			1	1		1			6		
Chelmsford	171	29	Parkis	Danl'		1	1	1	1		1		1	1			7		
Concord	5	33	Parkman	William	1			1				1		1			4		
Lincoln	12	14	Parks	Charles	1		1	1		2		1					6		
Lincoln	13	2	Parks	Daniel	2			2		3	1	1					9		
Lincoln	13	6	Parks	Isaac		1	1		1		1			1			5		
Hopkinton	243	18	Parks	Joseph				1					1				2		
Lincoln	13	10	Parks	Josiah	2	1	1	1		2			1				8		
Cambridge	226	36	Parks	Leonard	2			1		4	1		1				9		
Hollistown	238	41	Parks	Samll				1					1				2		
Hollistown	238	42	Parks	Samll Jr		1	1			2		1					5		
Lincoln	13	7	Parks	Samuel		2	2		1	1	2			1			9		
Hollistown	238	40	Parks	Solomon	2			1		3	1		1				8		
Lincoln	12	16	Parks	Willard				1			1	2		1			5		
Acton	18	14	Parlin	Samuel	1		2		1	2	1		1				8		
Sudbury	60	1	Parmenter	Abel	1	1		1		1			1				5		
Framingham	72	25	Parmenter	Amos				1					1				2		Stamped pg# was x'd out
Sudbury	62	3	Parmenter	Deliverance		1		1			1			1			4		
Sudbury	61	27	Parmenter	Ebenezer	1	1		1		1	1	1	1	1			8		
Marlborough	193	27	Parmenter	Eliab	1			1		1			1				4		
Framingham	70	14	Parmenter	Ezra			1			5			1				7		Stamped pg# was x'd out
Sudbury	65	10	Parmenter	Hepzibah									1				1		
Sudbury	60	4	Parmenter	Israel	2	2			1	1	1	2		1			10		
Sudbury	61	26	Parmenter	James	1	1	1		1	2	1	1		3			11		
East Sudbury	69	10	Parmenter	Jason				1					1	1			3		
Sudbury	59	38	Parmenter	Jedediah	1		1	1	1	1		1	1				8		
East Sudbury	67	19	Parmenter	Jona	3		1		1			1	1				7		
Framingham	72	27	Parmenter	Joshua	1		2		1	1		1	1				7		Stamped pg# was x'd out
Sudbury	60	3	Parmenter	Levi			1			2			1				4		
Sudbury	60	2	Parmenter	Micah				1					1				2		
Framingham	74	4	Parmenter	Peter	2			1		2		1					6		
Framingham	74	5	Parmenter	Phinehas				1					1				2		
East Sudbury	69	23	Parmenter	Susannah							1	1		2			4		

TOWN	PG#	LN#	LAST NAME	FIRST NAME	FREE WHITE MALES					FREE WHITE FEMALES					TOTAL ALL OTHER	TOTAL SLAVES	TOTALS	DISTRICT/ TOWNSHIP	NOTES
					under 10	10 to 16	16 to 26	26 to 45	45 and over	under 10	10 to 16	16 to 26	26 to 45	45 and over					
Sudbury	60	5	Parmenter	Uriah			1		2			3		1			7		
Sudbury	65	9	Parmenter	William	2	1		1		2			1				7		
East Sudbury	69	24	Parris	Abigail										1			1		
Charlestown	89	3	Parsons	Ruth									1				1		
Carlisle	22	10	Partin	David				1						1			2		
Carlisle	22	11	Partin	David Jr	1			1		1			1				4		
Carlisle	22	14	Partin	Josiah	3			1	1	1		1		1			8		
Burlington	155	12	Pasho	John A	2	1		1		2	1		1	1			9		
Littleton	204	25	Patch	Abraham				1						1			2		
Westford	182	41	Patch	David			1					1					2		
Watertown	233	35	Patch	Ellis	2	1		1		2			1				7		
Littleton	205	5	Patch	Hannah									1	1			2		
Littleton	205	4	Patch	Isaac	1	1		1						1			4		
Westford	182	42	Patch	Isaac				1						1			2		
Westford	182	43	Patch	Isaac Jr	1	2		1		3			1	1			9		
Groton	212	19	Patch	Jacob L.		1	1		1			2		1			6		
Littleton	204	24	Patch	John		1	1		1		1	1		1			6		
Stow	197	3	Patch	John	1	2		1		2		3	1				11		
Littleton	204	26	Patch	Moses		1			1	2	1			1			6		
Ashby	37	18	Patch	Stephen	1	2	1		1	1	1	1		1			9		
Ashby	34	14	Patche	Abrm	2	1	1		1	1	1	3		1			11		
Billerica	177	15	Patten	Asa		2			1			2		1			6		
Westford	182	45	Patten	Isaac	4	2	1	1				1	1	1			13		
Billerica	177	13	Patten	John			2		1			2		1			6		
Billerica	177	14	Patten	John Jr	2	1		1		1	1		1				7		
Medford	101	43	Patten	Mary									1	1			2		
Watertown	233	40	Patten	Thos		1	1	2	1	1				1			7		
Billerica	177	16	Patten	Wm		1	1		1			1		1			5		
Framingham	72	29	Patterson	David	1		1	1	1		1	1		2			8		Stamped pg# was x'd out
Shirley	215	14	Patterson	Hezekiah		1		1					1	1			4		
Cambridge	226	35	Patterson	Joseph			1						1				2		
Charlestown	89	5	Paul	Clerk			1					1					2		
Malden	96	3	Paul	John				1	1					1			3		
Shirley	215	25	Pays	Jonas		1	3		1	4	2	2		1			14		
Shirley	215	24	Pays	Oliver	3	1		1	1	1			1	1			9		
East Sudbury	68	10	Payson	Joseph				1			1	2		1			5		
Charlestown	88	24	Payson	Phillips	2			1		1		1	1				6		
Charlestown	88	23	Payson	Saml	3			1		2	1		2				9		
Charlestown	88	25	Payson	Tho'	1			1		2	1	2	1				8		
Dracut	48	1	Peabody	*	1			1		1			1	1			5		
Dracut	48	2	Peabody	*	3	1		1		1	1		1				8		
Wilmington	143	22	Peabody	Joseph				1				1					2		
Shirley	215	27	Peabody	Thomas	3	1			1	2			1				8		
Lexington	159	1	Peak	John	1	1	1		1	1	1	1		1			8		
Tyngsborough	43	19	Pear	William	2			1	2	1	1			1			7		
Stoneham	139	25	Pearce	Ephraim	2	1	1		1	1	2			1			9		
Wilmington	143	18	Pearson	Aaron	2		1	1		1		2					7		
Wilmington	143	20	Pearson	Isaac															Name crossed out
Wilmington	143	21	Pearson	Moses	4	3	1		1	1			1				11		
Cambridge	227	13	Pearsons	Eliphalet	1	1	1		1		2	2	1				9		
Cambridge	227	16	Pearsons	Gorom		1	1	1		1		4	1				9		
Cambridge	227	17	Pearsons	Thos	2			1		3	1	1					8		
Marlborough	189	8	Pease	Levi		1		1		4	1		1	1			9		
Lincoln	14	7	Peirce	Abijah		1		1				1	1	1			5		
Medford	101	38	Peirce	Abner	2		2	1		1	1	1					8		
Chelmsford	171	16	Peirce	Hannah									1	1			2		
Charlestown	88	43	Peirce	James				1									1		
Chelmsford	171	19	Peirce	James		1	1	1		2	1		1				7		
Marlborough	192	28	Peirce	John	1		1	1	3			1					7		
Townsend	27	32	Peirce	Jona		1	1				1	1					4		
Lincoln	14	22	Peirce	Jonas	1	1		1	1	1	1		1	1			8		
Malden	96	15	Peirce	Jos'		1											1		
Medford	101	39	Peirce	Jos'		1					1						2		
Charlestown	88	44	Peirce	Mary								1					1		
Chelmsford	171	14	Peirce	Oliver		1		1		1	2			1			6		
Chelmsford	171	20	Peirce	Rebecca									1	1			2		
Chelmsford	171	18	Peirce	Robert	2	1	1	1		1				1			7		
Charlestown	88	42	Peirce	Saml		1											1		
Chelmsford	171	17	Peirce	Silas			1		1		2	1	2				7		
Townsend	27	38	Peirce	Solo	3	1			1	1	1			1			8		
Chelmsford	171	15	Peirce	Steph'	3	2	1		1	1	1			1			10		
East Sudbury	68	27	Peirce	Thomas		1		1					1				3		
Chelmsford	171	37	Pelsuc	Benja'	1	1	2		1	1	1		1				9		
Billerica	177	17	Pemberton	Ebenz'	1	2			1	1			1	1			7		
Wilmington	143	23	Pence	Isaac	1	1	2		1	3		1		1			10		
Lexington	159	9	Penney	David	1	2			1	1	1	1	1				8		
Bedford	162	38	Penniman	Mesheck				1				1		1			3		
Tyngsborough	43	11	Perham	Elijah		1		1		2			1				5		
Pepperell	32	20	Perham	Ezekiel				1				1	1				3		
Pepperell	32	21	Perham	John	1			1		2		1					5		
Tyngsborough	43	9	Perham	John		1	1		2	3		1	1				9		

TOWN	PG#	LN#	HEADS OF HOUSEHOLD LAST NAME	FIRST NAME	FREE WHITE MALES under 10	10 to 16	16 to 26	26 to 45	45 and over	FREE WHITE FEMALES under 10	10 to 16	16 to 26	26 to 45	45 and over	TOTAL ALL OTHER	TOTAL SLAVES	TOTALS	DISTRICT/ TOWNSHIP	NOTES
Chelmsford	171	34	Perham	Jona'		2		1					1	1			5		
Tyngsborough	43	12	Perham	Jonathan		2	3		1	2	2	1	1				12		
Tyngsborough	43	14	Perham	Joseph	1			1				2	1				5		
Tyngsborough	43	10	Perham	Peter		1		1					1				3		
Tyngsborough	43	13	Perham	Willm	1	1		1		2	1		1				7		
Malden	96	5	Perkins	Jacob	4	1	2		1	2	2		1	1			14		
Hopkinton	243	29	Perkins	Reubin	2			1					1				4		
Stow	198	25	Perlin	Isaac	1		1	1				2					5		
Natick	247	11	Perrey	Louis				1					1				2		
Marlborough	193	21	Perrigo	John		1	1						1				3		
Natick	247	13	Perry	Abial		1		1					1				3		
Natick	247	12	Perry	Abial Jr		1	1	1		2			1				6		
Hollistown	238	36	Perry	Abner		1		1				1		1			4		
Hollistown	238	37	Perry	Abner Jr	3	1		1			1		1				7		
Charlestown	88	40	Perry	Cushman	2			1				1					4		
Sherburn	251	6	Perry	Daniel	2			1		1			1				5		
Natick	247	15	Perry	Elijah	1	1	1	1		1			1				6		
Cambridge	226	34	Perry	James	1	1						1		1			5		
Hollistown	238	38	Perry	James				1			1	1		1			4		
Sudbury	62	4	Perry	John	1		1	1	1	1		1	1				7		
Carlisle	23	4	Perry	Jonathan	2		1		2			1					6		
Charlestown	88	41	Perry	Jos'	2	1			2	2	1						9		
Hopkinton	243	20	Perry	Moses			1	1	4	1		1					8		
Sherburn	251	2	Perry	Moses				1			1	1	1				4		
Sherburn	251	4	Perry	Moses 3rd		2	1	1		2			1				7		
Sherburn	251	3	Perry	Moses Jr		1	1		1		3						6		
Hopkinton	243	11	Perry	Nathan	1			1					1				4		
Westford	182	46	Perry	Obadiah	2			1	1	1			1				6		
Natick	247	17	Perry	Saml		1	1	1				2		1			6		
Natick	247	14	Perry	Saml Jr.	4			1		1			1				7		
Sherburn	251	5	Perry	Tiler		1	1	1		3		1	1				8		
Sherburn	251	1	Perry	West	1			1		2			1				5		
Lexington	159	7	Perry	Widow									1				1		
Tewksbury	52	28	Persons	Wm	4			1		1			1				7		
Reading	134	25	Peters	Benjamin	1		1	1		1			1				5		
Reading	135	12	Peters	Ezra		1			1			1					3		
Burlington	155	11	Peters	Phillip			1		2	3		1					7		
Reading	135	15	Peters	Samuel	3		1				2						6		
Chelmsford	171	22	Pettengail	Nathl	1		1	2	2			1					7		
Hopkinton	243	19	Pettis	James	2		1	1	1			1	2				8		
Townsend	27	37	Petts	John	1		1		1		1						4		
Townsend	27	30	Petts	Leml		1		1					2				4		
Townsend	27	36	Petts	Leml Jr	3		1	1	1	1		1					8		
Shirley	215	20	Phelps	Jacob			1		1	1							3		
Shirley	215	19	Phelps	John			1		1			1					3		
Marlborough	188	16	Phelps	Roger	3		1	1	1	1		1					8		
Marlborough	191	3	Phelps	Stephen	1			1	2			1					5		
Shirley	215	18	Phelps	Timothy				1		1			1				3		
Weston	109	18	Philemon	Pegg											1		1		
Boxborough	199	17	Phillips	Ebenezer				1					1				2		
Malden	96	4	Phillips	Fra'	1	1							2				5		
Groton	212	21	Phillips	Jonas	1		1			1		1					5		
Concord	4	18	Phillips	Lemuel				1	1	1		1					4		
Cambridge	227	19	Phillips	Nathan	3			1		1			1				6		
Marlborough	188	13	Phillips	Nathaniel				1					1				2		
Pepperell	34	27	Phillis	*											5		5		
Lexington	159	2	Phinney	Benjamin	1		1		1		1	1	1				6		
Hollistown	238	35	Phipps	Aaron	1	2		1		1			1				6		
Hopkinton	243	17	Phipps	David		1							1				2		
Sherburn	251	7	Phipps	Jedeh	1			1		1		1		1			5		
Sherburn	251	8	Phipps	John	2			1			1		1				5		
Charlestown	88	28	Phipps	Jos'		2	2	1		1	2		1				9		
Charlestown	88	29	Phipps	Saml	2			1		1			1				5		
Hopkinton	243	14	Phipps	Saml	1	1		1				1	1	1			6		
Charlestown	88	30	Phipps	Solo'		2		1		3		1	1				8		
Chelmsford	171	36	Picking	John		2	1	1				2	1				7		
Hopkinton	243	23	Pierce	Aaron	2			1		1			1				5		
Hopkinton	243	24	Pierce	Aaron Jr	2			1				1	1				5		
Weston	109	22	Pierce	Abel	3	1		1		1	2		1				9		
Woburn	150	33	Pierce	Abel	2	1		1		1			1				6		
Woburn	150	31	Pierce	Abigail									2	1			3		
Lexington	159	11	Pierce	Abijah		1	2						2				5		
Groton	211	41	Pierce	Abner			1		3			1					5		
Waltham	115	14	Pierce	Abraham		1	1	2	1				1				6		
Weston	109	19	Pierce	Amos	2	2		1		1	1		1				8		
Weston	109	10	Pierce	Benj															Enumeration blank
Weston	109	15	Pierce	Benjamin	2			1		2	1	1	1				8		
Hopkinton	243	22	Pierce	Ebenz	1			1		1			1				4		
Pepperell	32	26	Pierce	Edward	1	1	1						1				4		
Groton	211	34	Pierce	Elijah	2								1				4		

TOWN	PG#	LN#	LAST NAME	FIRST NAME	FREE WHITE MALES under 10	10 to 16	16 to 26	26 to 45	45 and over	FREE WHITE FEMALES under 10	10 to 16	16 to 26	26 to 45	45 and over	TOTAL ALL OTHER	TOTAL SLAVES	TOTALS	DISTRICT/ TOWNSHIP	NOTES
Pepperell	32	23	Pierce	Ephm	1		1		1	2		2		1			8		
Waltham	115	13	Pierce	Ephraim		1	1			2	1	1	1				7		
Hopkinton	243	25	Pierce	Francis				1					1				2		
Hopkinton	243	35	Pierce	Icabud	1		1			1			1				4		
Lexington	159	13	Pierce	Isaac		1		1		2	1		1				6		
Waltham	115	15	Pierce	Isaac	2		1	1				1		1			6		
Weston	109	17	Pierce	Jacob	1			1		1			1				4		
Woburn	150	32	Pierce	Jacob	1	1	1	2			2		1		3		11		
Westford	182	44	Pierce	Jona		2		1			3		2				8		
Cambridge	227	1	Pierce	Jonas	2		1	1		4			1				9		
Hopkinton	243	15	Pierce	Jonas				1					1				2		
Watertown	233	41	Pierce	Joseph	2		4	1				1	1				9		
Weston	109	23	Pierce	Joshua		1	1	1		1				1			6		
Hopkinton	243	30	Pierce	Nathan	3			1		2	1		1				8		
Woburn	150	34	Pierce	Nathan	3	1		1		2			1				8		
Lexington	159	12	Pierce	Reuben	1			1				1	1	1			5		
Groton	211	35	Pierce	Saml	1	1				1			1				5		
Hopkinton	243	26	Pierce	Saml	1					3	2		1				8		
Waltham	115	10	Pierce	Samuel			1	2	2	1	1	1		1			9		
Woburn	151	3	Pierce	Samuel	1	1	1	1	2		1						7		
Cambridge	226	37	Pierce	Solomon		1	3	1		1		2		1			9		
Weston	109	20	Pierce	Thaddeus	3			1		2			1				7		
Waltham	115	11	Pierce	William	3	1		1		1		1					7		
Hopkinton	243	28	Pierce	Wm		1		1				1	1	2			6		
Hopkinton	243	16	Piercing	Jonas	3			1		2			1				7		
Newton	122	28	Pigeon	Elizabeth	2	1	1			3	1	1	1				10		
Newton	122	29	Pigeon	Jane				1				1		1	1		4		
Newton	123	8	Pigeon	John	2			1		3	1		1				8		
Hopkinton	243	12	Pike	Aaron	4		1			4		1					10		
Newton	123	7	Pike	Hannah	1									1			2		
Tyngsborough	43	15	Pike	Isaac			1		1			1		1			4		
Bedford	162	37	Pike	John	2			1			1		1				5		
Hopkinton	243	33	Pike	Jona			2			1	2	2	1	2			10		
Hopkinton	243	31	Pike	Jona Jr			1						1				2		
Hopkinton	243	32	Pike	Nathan			1		1			2	1	2			7		
Hopkinton	243	34	Pike	Timothy					1					1			2		
Charlestown	89	7	Pilsbury	Saml	2			1			1	1					5		
Littleton	203	4	Pingery	Stephen	3	1		1	1	2		1	1	1			11		
Waltham	115	12	Piper	Filly M.	1			1		3	1		1	1			8		
Ashby	37	20	Piper	Jona	1	1			1	1			2				6		
Concord	4	17	Piper	Joshua	1			1						1			3		
Concord	9	12	Piper	Lucy										1			1		
Dracut	47	33	Piper	Samll	2		1		1	2	3	1	1				11		
Acton	16	29	Piper	Silas	1	1	1	1		5		1	1	1			12		
Tyngsborough	43	18	Pitts	John				1			2		2		3		8		
Chelmsford	171	21	Pitts	Saml	1	1	3	1	1		1	1	1				10		
Sudbury	61	19	Plympton	Ebenz	4	1				2	2	1	2				13		
Woburn	150	35	Plympton	Sylvanus	2			1		1	1		1				6		
Stoneham	139	24	Poland	John	1			1		1			1				4		
Billerica	177	7	Pollard	Edw'		1		1						1			3		
Sudbury	60	33	Pollard	John			1						1	1			3		
Woburn	151	1	Pollard	John	1			1			1		1	1			5		
Billerica	177	8	Pollard	Jona'				1			1	1	1				4		
Billerica	177	4	Pollard	Jona' P.	3	2		1		1		1	1				9		
Bedford	163	1	Pollard	Matthew		1		1						2			4		
Bedford	163	4	Pollard	Oliver		2		1		1	1		1				6		
Billerica	177	5	Pollard	Sols'		1	1	1						2			5		
Billerica	177	6	Pollard	Wm			1						1				2		
Charlestown	89	4	Pollard		5		1	1			1		1				9		
Charlestown	88	37	Polly	Geo'											3		3		
Medford	101	36	Polly	Josiah	1	1		1				1					5		
Charlestown	88	38	Polly	Robt				1					1				2		
Malden	96	2	Polly	Saml	1		1	1		2	1		1				7		
Medford	101	44	Polly	Sampson											4		4		
Cambridge	227	18	Pomson	Samll	1	3		5	1	1	2	3	2				18		
Sherburn	251	11	Pond	Aplos		1		1					1				3		
Hollistown	238	39	Pond	Jona				1		2		1	1				5		
Hopkinton	243	36	Pond	Painjm	1	1	1	1		2	1		1				8		
Sherburn	251	13	Pond	Theodore			1					1					2		
Hopkinton	243	27	Pond	Zadoc				1		2			1				4		
Reading	134	26	Pool	Elizabeth									1				1		
East Sudbury	67	21	Pool	Hannah			1	1					1				3		
Reading	135	6	Pool	Jonathan	1		2		1		1	1		2			8		
Reading	134	23	Pool	Thomas		1	2		1		1	1					6		
Reading	135	7	Pool	Timothy			1			1	1	1					4		
Woburn	151	2	Poole	Thomas	1			1		1			1				4		
Malden	96	6	Popkins	Jno'	1	1			1	2	2	2		1			10		
Waltham	115	16	Poriet	Sally	1		1						1				3		
Newton	123	9	Porter	Amasa	1			1		3			1		1		7		
Cambridge	227	11	Porter	Israel	1	2	1		1	1		2		1			9		

TOWN	PG#	LN#	LAST NAME	FIRST NAME	FREE WHITE MALES					FREE WHITE FEMALES					TOTAL ALL OTHER	TOTAL SLAVES	TOTALS	DISTRICT/ TOWNSHIP	NOTES
					under 10	10 to 16	16 to 26	26 to 45	45 and over	under 10	10 to 16	16 to 26	26 to 45	45 and over					
Littleton	203	5	Porter	John	1	1			1			1		1			5		
Medford	101	34	Porter	Jona'	2		1		2	2		2	1				10		
Cambridge	227	14	Porter	Joseph		1						1	1				3		
Medford	101	37	Porter	Rufus			1			2		1					4		
Bedford	162	39	Porter	William		2		1		3	1	1	1				9		
Lexington	159	10	Porter	William		1			1	1	1	2		1			7		
Concord	5	14	Potter	Ephraim		1			1				1				3		
Marlborough	193	34	Potter	Ephraim		1	1						1				3		
Concord	5	22	Potter	Ephraim Jr	2			1		1		1	1				6		
Concord	5	21	Potter	Jonas	2	1		1		1	1			1	1		8		
Concord	5	20	Potter	Samuel	4			1		1			1				7		
Marlborough	193	36	Potter	Stephen	1			1		2	1		1				6		
Watertown	233	38	Potts	Wm	1		1					1					3		
Charlestown	89	8	Powars	Batting	2		1	1	8	6		2	5	6	1		32		
Pepperell	32	27	Powers	Hannah									1	1			2		
Littleton	201	7	Powers	Robert				1				1		1			3		
Pepperell	32	30	Powers	Wm	1		1	1					1				4		
Natick	247	16	Pratt	Jacob	1		1			1		1					4		
Framingham	64	8	Pratt	Aaron	2		1			3		1					7		Stamped pg# was x'd out
Reading	135	3	Pratt	Amos	1		1			2		1					5		
Medford	101	31	Pratt	Benja'		1	1			2		1					5		
Reading	134	16	Pratt	Benjamin	1	1	1	1		3		1					8		
Townsend	27	31	Pratt	Benl		1		1		4	1		1				8		
Framingham	72	26	Pratt	Benoni	1	1		2	2	2	1	1	1	1			12		Stamped pg# was x'd out
Reading	134	17	Pratt	Daniel			1	1				1	1				4		
Reading	135	2	Pratt	David	2		1			2		1	1				7		
Sherburn	251	10	Pratt	Ebenz	1	1	1			1		1					5		
Shirley	215	21	Pratt	Ebenzr				1		1				1			3		
Framingham	78	8	Pratt	Ephraim	2		1			4		1					8		
Reading	134	20	Pratt	Ephraim	4	2		1			1	1					9		
Shirley	215	22	Pratt	Hannah	1					1			1	1			4		
Sherburn	251	14	Pratt	Henry	3	2		1				1					7		
Charlestown	88	34	Pratt	Isaac			1	1				1					3		
Medford	101	30	Pratt	Isaac	2		1			2		1					6		
Reading	134	15	Pratt	Isaac		1	1	1		1	2		1				7		
Westford	183	4	Pratt	Isaac		1	1			1		1					4		
Malden	96	21	Pratt	Jacob	1	2	3	1		2		1	1				11		
Sherburn	251	9	Pratt	Jacob				1				1		1			3		
Malden	96	24	Pratt	Jacob Jr		1											1		
Dunstable	217	30	Pratt	Jerathmul C.			1			1		1					3		
Framingham	64	12	Pratt	John	3	1		1			2	1					9		Stamped pg# was x'd out
Malden	96	18	Pratt	John	1	1		1		1	1	2					7		
Malden	96	19	Pratt	John	1	2	1	1		3	1		1				10		
Framingham	78	15	Pratt	John Jr	3			1		3			1				8		
Groton	212	22	Pratt	Jona				1					1				2		
Framingham	78	10	Pratt	Jonathan			1			2	1	1					6		
Reading	135	9	Pratt	Jonathan	1		1						1				3		
Medford	101	29	Pratt	Jos	1			1						1			3		
Marlborough	193	1	Pratt	Mary						1		1					2		
Hopkinton	243	13	Pratt	Moses			1			2	1						4		
Malden	96	20	Pratt	Nath'	3		1	1		1			1				7		
Framingham	78	16	Pratt	Nathl	1	1	1			2	1	1					7		
Weston	109	21	Pratt	Paul		1		1		3	2	1	1				9		
Pepperell	32	16	Pratt	Robert	1	1		1		1		1	1				6		
Natick	247	10	Pratt	Silas	1		1			3		1					6		
East Sudbury	67	20	Pratt	Simeon	2	1		1		1	1	1	1				8		
Malden	96	22	Pratt	Tho'				1						1			2		
Malden	96	23	Pratt	Tho' Jr		1											1		
Charlestown	88	33	Pratt	Tho' W.	1	1		1					1				4		
Newton	122	27	Pratt	Thomas	2		1	1				2	1				8		
Medford	101	32	Pratt	Timo'			1			1		1					3		
Reading	134	24	Pratt	William			2					1					3		
Charlestown	88	39	Pratt	Wm	2		1			2		2	1				8		
Watertown	233	36	Prentice	Benjm			1	1						2			4		
Groton	211	38	Prentice	Daniel				1									1		
Cambridge	227	9	Prentice	Ebenz	1	1		1		1			1				5		
Charlestown	89	1	Prentice	Geo'				1				1	1				3		
Cambridge	227	7	Prentice	George	1	1	1	1	1		2	1					9		
Watertown	233	37	Prentice	Hannah	1			1				1	1				4		
Cambridge	227	4	Prentice	Henry		3		1					1				5		
Cambridge	227	6	Prentice	Henry			1	1		2	2						6		
Cambridge	227	3	Prentice	John	2			1		2		1					6		
Charlestown	89	2	Prentice	Mary									1	1			2		
Charlestown	88	45	Prentice	Nath'		1	1		1	1	1	1	1				7		
Newton	123	10	Prentice	Robert		2		1		2	1		2				8		
Hopkinton	243	21	Prentice	Saml	1		1	1					1	1			5		
Cambridge	227	8	Prentice	Soloman				1					1				2		
Sherburn	251	12	Prentice	Stephen	2			1				1					4		
Watertown	233	39	Prentice	Thos				1					1				2		
Cambridge	227	5	Prentice	Wm		1		1		2			1				5		
Marlborough	187	16	Prentiss	Nathaniel S.	3		1			1	1	1					7		

TOWN	PG#	LN#	LAST NAME	FIRST NAME	FREE WHITE MALES					FREE WHITE FEMALES					TOTAL ALL OTHER	TOTAL SLAVES	TOTALS	DISTRICT/ TOWNSHIP	NOTES
					under 10	10 to 16	16 to 26	26 to 45	45 and over	under 10	10 to 16	16 to 26	26 to 45	45 and over					
Reading	134	30	Prentop	Caleb Rev	3		2		1	3	1	1	1	1	1		14		
Concord	4	10	Prescott	Abel		1		1			1	1		1			5		
Groton	212	8	Prescott	Abel	2		1	1		1		1	1				7		
Concord	8	8	Prescott	Abel Jr	1			1		2			1				5		
Pepperell	32	22	Prescott	Abigail								1	1	1			3		
Westford	183	13	Prescott	Abra'	1	1		1	1	1		2					7		
Westford	183	7	Prescott	Amos				1		3	1	1					6		
Concord	4	21	Prescott	Benajmin Jr	2			1		2			1				6		
Acton	16	2	Prescott	Benjamin			1	2				1		2			6		
Concord	4	20	Prescott	Benjamin		1		1						1			3		
Concord	9	29	Prescott	Charles				1									1		
Groton	212	9	Prescott	David	1			1		1	1	1		1			6		
Westford	183	10	Prescott	Ebenz		1	2	1		2	1	1		1			9		
Westford	183	11	Prescott	Ebenz Jr			1						1				2		
Ashby	37	19	Prescott	Elijah			1			1		2					4		
Groton	212	18	Prescott	Isaac	1			1		2			1				5		
Westford	183	5	Prescott	Isaiah	1	1		1		4			1				8		
Westford	183	14	Prescott	James		1	2	1		3		1	1				9		
Concord	8	6	Prescott	John				1				1	1				3		
Westford	183	8	Prescott	John	1	1	4	1			1	1		1			10		
Groton	212	7	Prescott	Jonas				1				3		1			5		
Westford	183	9	Prescott	Jonas			3	1					2				6		
Westford	183	12	Prescott	Joseph			2			1	1			1			6		
Groton	212	3	Prescott	Oliver Esq			2	1			1	2		3			9		
Groton	211	32	Prescott	Oliver Jr Esq	2	1	3	1		3		2	1				13		
Concord	6	27	Prescott	Rebecka		1				4			1				6		
Groton	212	10	Prescott	Samson	2		1			3			1				8		
Concord	8	7	Prescott	Samuel	1			1				1					3		
Groton	212	1	Prescott	Susanna Wid.			2					2	1				5		
Westford	183	6	Prescott	Timo'				1			1	2		1			5		
Concord	4	3	Prescott	Willoughby		1		1		2	2	1	1				8		
Bedford	163	8	Preston	Amaraiah	2			1		1	1	1					7		
Concord	9	24	Price	James	1	1	1	1	1	1	1				2		10		
Concord	10	19	Price	Joel			1		1			1	1	1			5		
Natick	247	18	Price	Jonas		1		1		1		1					4		
Marlborough	191	34	Priest	Abraham			1	1		1			1				4		
Marlborough	191	32	Priest	Benjamin	3	1		1		1		1					7		
Littleton	201	9	Priest	Jacob	3	2	1	1		1		2					10		
Marlborough	189	34	Priest	Shadrick	2		1					1					4		
Groton	211	45	Priest	Timothy		1	1	1				1	1				5		
Medford	101	40	Prince	James	1			1		1	1	1	1		1		7		
Concord	5	16	Prison				2	6	8						1		17		
Billerica	177	9	Pritchard	Burly		1											1		
Medford	101	33	Pritchard	Lucy	1								1				2		
Acton	19	27	Procter	Abel	2			1		2	1		1				7		
Chelmsford	171	23	Procter	Amos	1			1					1				3		
Westford	182	47	Procter	Cha'			1		1		2			1			5		
Chelmsford	171	25	Procter	Danl'			1		1					1			3		
Chelmsford	171	26	Procter	Eldad	2	1		1		1			1				6		
Chelmsford	171	27	Procter	Elijah			1		1			3		1			6		
Carlisle	23	1	Procter	Ezekiel	1			1		2			1				5		
Concord	7	8	Procter	John				1				1	1				3		
Chelmsford	171	24	Procter	Levi				1				1	1				3		
Westford	183	3	Procter	Mary			1			1	1		1				4		
Westford	183	2	Procter	Pheeb								1	1				2		
Westford	183	1	Procter	Phin				1									1		
Burlington	155	10	Procter	Ruth			1			2		1	3				7		
Dunstable	217	27	Procter	Gershom	2	2		1		1		1	1				8		
Groton	212	5	Procter	James Jr		1	1	1		2			1				7		
Littleton	203	21	Procter	John	2			1		2			1				6		
Dunstable	217	26	Procter	Jonas	1	1	1		1		1			1			6		
Dunstable	217	28	Procter	Nathan	1			1			2	1					5		
Littleton	202	17	Procter	Nathaniel				1					1				2		
Littleton	202	18	Procter	Nathaniel Jr.	2	1		1		1	1	1	1				8		
Townsend	27	29	Procter	Oliver		2		1				1		1			5		
Dunstable	217	29	Procter	Peter	1		2	1		1			1				6		
Littleton	203	42	Procter	Simeon				1						1			2		
Littleton	203	41	Procter	Simeon Jr	1			1		3	1		1				7		
Littleton	203	43	Procter	William		1		1					1				3		
Shirley	215	23	Procter	Wm				1		1	1		1				4		
Groton	212	16	Protor	Ebenzr	1			1		1			1				4		
Stow	197	12	Puffer	Mary		1	2	1					1				5		
Groton	212	14	Pushey	John				1		1			1				3		
Groton	211	42	Pushey	John Jr	3			1					1				5		
Groton	211	40	Pushey	Jonas	1		1			1		1					4		
Stow	198	26	Putman	Asa	4			1		1	1	1					8		
Stow	198	30	Putman	Nathan		2	1			1	1	1		2			9		
Charlestown	88	36	Putnam	Aaron	1	1	2	1		1	1		2				9		
Townsend	27	34	Putnam	Andrew				1		1	1		1				4		
Chelmsford	171	35	Putnam	Danl'	1	1		1		2	1		1	1			8		

200

TOWN	PG#	LN#	LAST NAME	FIRST NAME	FREE WHITE MALES under 10	10 to 16	16 to 26	26 to 45	45 and over	FREE WHITE FEMALES under 10	10 to 16	16 to 26	26 to 45	45 and over	TOTAL ALL OTHER	TOTAL SLAVES	TOTALS	DISTRICT/ TOWNSHIP	NOTES
Medford	101	41	Putnam	Eleazer	1				1					1			3		
Medford	101	42	Putnam	Henry			1										1		
Reading	134	21	Putnam	Henry	1	1	3	1	1	2		2	1				12		
Dracut	44	31	Putnam	John			5	1		1			1				8		
Charlestown	88	35	Putnam	Susan									1	1			2		
Townsend	29	7	Putney	Joseph				1						1			2		
Groton	212	25	Quailes	Charles		1		1		1		1		1			5		
Carlisle	20	4	Raimond	Daniel	2			1		1	1		1				6		
Malden	96	29	Ramsdal	John				1					1				2		
Malden	96	30	Ramsdal	John Jr	2			1					1				4		
Groton	212	32	Ramsdel	Rebekah Wid.								1		1			2		
Acton	17	26	Ramsdell	Abigail						1		1	1	1			4		
Charlestown	89	21	Rand	Abra'	1			1			1		1				4		
Charlestown	89	22	Rand	Anna	1									1			2		
Weston	109	28	Rand	Benjamin	2	2			1	2	1		1				9		
Charlestown	89	19	Rand	Caleb		1		1						1			3		
Weston	109	27	Rand	Daniel	2	1		1		1			1				6		
Stow	195	8	Rand	David	1		1		1	2	2	1	1				9		
Malden	96	28	Rand	Edmd				1					1				2		
Malden	96	27	Rand	Edmd Jr			1										1		
Stow	198	10	Rand	Ephraim			1						1				2		
Charlestown	89	24	Rand	Esther									2	2			4		
Charlestown	90	8	Rand	Eunice	1					1			1				3		
Charlestown	89	23	Rand	Hepz'										1			1		
Hopkinton	243	43	Rand	Jona	2			1		2			1				6		
Medford	102	1	Rand	Jos	3	1		1		2	1		1				9		
Stow	198	9	Rand	Lucy									1				1		
Charlestown	89	18	Rand	Mary									1				1		
Medford	102	2	Rand	Mary								1	1				2		
Charlestown	89	16	Rand	Nath'	1			1		1			1				4		
Stow	198	22	Rand	Oliver	1			1		1			1				4		
Charlestown	90	7	Rand	Prince											5		5		
Charlestown	89	17	Rand	Richd			1					1	1				3		
Charlestown	89	12	Rand	Tho'			1	1					1	1			4		
Charlestown	89	20	Rand	Tho'		1		1					1				3		
Charlestown	89	25	Rand	Tho'	3	2		1		2			1	1			10		
Charlestown	89	26	Rand	Tho' Jr		1						1					2		
Weston	109	26	Rand	Thomas			3	1				2	1				7		
Stow	197	41	Randell	Abraham	1	2	2	1		1	1		1				9		
Stow	197	17	Randell	Josiah		1	1	1		2	2		1				8		
Stow	198	8	Randell	Silas	1	1	4	1		1	1	1	1				11		
Malden	96	31	Rantam	Mary									1				1		
Stow	196	24	Ray	Abner		1		1				1					3		
Stow	196	23	Ray	Abraham	2			1					1				4		
Charlestown	89	33	Raymond	Bartho'		1		1					1				3		
Charlestown	89	34	Raymond	Bartho' Jr	1		1						1				3		
Ashby	37	27	Raymond	Daniel	2	1		1		1	2		1				8		
Charlestown	89	32	Raymond	Danl	1		1	1		2	1		1				7		
Westford	183	21	Raymond	Danl		1			1		2			1			5		
Westford	183	22	Raymond	John	3			1		2	1		1	1			10		
Boxborough	199	12	Raymond	Joseph	1				1	1	1		1	1			6		
Littleton	202	35	Raymond	Joseph	3			1					1				5		
Boxborough	199	7	Raymond	Molly	1					1		1					3		
Medford	102	5	Raynard	James	3			1		2			1				7		
Charlestown	89	11	Rayner	Ann								1		1			2		
Charlestown	89	38	Rayner	Ann										1			1		
Reading	135	19	Rayner	John	2		1	1	1	1			1	1			8		
Tewksbury	52	33	Rea	Percie R	1	1		1		1	3	2					9		
Sudbury	58	2	Reed	Abel	2	1		1		2	1		1				8		
Westford	183	38	Reed	Abel	1			1		2			1				5		
Westford	183	34	Reed	Abijah		1	2	1		3	1		1				9		
Westford	183	30	Reed	Amos	4			1		1			1	1			9		
Medford	101	45	Reed	Benjm	1		2	1		2	1	1		1			9		
Reading	135	26	Reed	Berzellai		1	1						1				3		
Dunstable	217	32	Reed	Caleb	2			1		1			1				5		
Littleton	202	1	Reed	Daniel		1		1	1		1		1				5		
Woburn	151	4	Reed	Daniel			1	1					1	1			4		
Woburn	151	5	Reed	Daniel Jr	1			1		2			1				5		
Charlestown	89	37	Reed	Danl				1				1		1			3		
Charlestown	89	36	Reed	Danl Jr	1		1			2	1	1					6		
Bedford	163	9	Reed	David	1	1			1	1		1	1	1			7		
Woburn	151	6	Reed	Ebenezer			1	1				1		1			4		
Westford	183	31	Reed	Eleaz'	2	1		1		1			1				6		
Dunstable	217	31	Reed	Eleazr				1	1	1		2					5		
Lexington	159	27	Reed	Elizabeth		1	1			1		1		2			5		
Hopkinton	243	42	Reed	Ephm	1	1		1		2	1		1	1			8		
Burlington	155	15	Reed	George		1		1						1			3		
Lexington	159	19	Reed	Hammond			1	1					1	1			4		
Lexington	159	20	Reed	Hammond Jr		1		1		2			1				5		
Reading	135	25	Reed	Hannah							1	1		1			3		
Westford	183	28	Reed	Hannah									1	1			2		
Sudbury	58	3	Reed	Isaac	1		1	1		2		1	1				7		

TOWN	PG#	LN#	LAST NAME	FIRST NAME	M under 10	M 10 to 16	M 16 to 26	M 26 to 45	M 45 and over	F under 10	F 10 to 16	F 16 to 26	F 26 to 45	F 45 and over	TOTAL ALL OTHER	TOTAL SLAVES	TOTALS	DISTRICT/TOWNSHIP	NOTES
Woburn	151	33	Reed	Isacc	3	3	1	1					1	1			10		
Woburn	151	32	Reed	Jacob				1						2			3		
Burlington	155	17	Reed	James	1	2	1		1	1	1		2	1	1		10		
Cambridge	228	4	Reed	James				1						1			2		
Dracut	48	10	Reed	James	2		1		1					1			5		
Malden	96	25	Reed	James				1		1	1	1					4		
Burlington	155	18	Reed	James Jr	2	1		1		3		3	1				11		
Acton	19	33	Reed	John	2	1		1		2			1				7		
Bedford	163	15	Reed	John			1	1		1		1	1				5		
Groton	212	37	Reed	John	1			1		2		1					5		
Bedford	163	16	Reed	John Jr	2			1		1	1		1				6		
Burlington	155	16	Reed	Jonas		2		1		3			1				7		
Burlington	155	14	Reed	Jonathn	3			1		2			1				7		
Charlestown	89	35	Reed	Jos'		1	3				1	2					7		
Cambridge	227	33	Reed	Joseph				1		1	2			1			5		
Sudbury	60	26	Reed	Joseph Jr		1				2		1	1	1			6		
Lexington	159	22	Reed	Joshua		1	1	1				1	2	1			7		
Westford	183	24	Reed	Joshua				1						1			2		
Woburn	151	7	Reed	Joshua	1		1	1			1		1	1			6		
Woburn	151	8	Reed	Joshua Jr	3			1					1				5		
Cambridge	227	37	Reed	Josiah				1					2				3		
Newton	123	26	Reed	Josiah			1						1				2		
Westford	183	32	Reed	Leon'		2		1				2		1			6		
Lexington	159	17	Reed	Nathan	1		2	1	1		2	2		1			10		
Bedford	163	10	Reed	Oliver				1						1			2		
Bedford	163	11	Reed	Oliver Jr		1	1				1		1				4		
Littleton	203	31	Reed	Peter	2			1		4	1		1				9		
Littleton	201	15	Reed	Potter		1		1		3			1	1			7		
Burlington	155	13	Reed	Prudence										1			1		
Bedford	163	12	Reed	Reuben	3		1	1		2			1				8		
Groton	212	33	Reed	Saml			1						1				2		
Westford	183	26	Reed	Saml'	1			1		2			1				5		
Westford	183	27	Reed	Saml' Jr	2		2	1		3	2		1				11		
Burlington	155	19	Reed	Samuel				1						1			2		
Littleton	203	35	Reed	Samuel		1	2	1						1			5		
Westford	183	37	Reed	Silas	3		2	1		1	2	1		1			11		
Lexington	159	28	Reed	Sweethen				1		2	1		2				6		
Lexington	159	25	Reed	Thaddeus	3	1	1		1	2			1				9		
Westford	183	33	Reed	Tho'	2		1		1	3		2					9		
Littleton	203	33	Reed	Thomas		1		1		1	2		1				6		
Littleton	202	2	Reed	Thomas Jr	2			2		2			1				7		
Westford	183	35	Reed	Willard	1		2		1	1	1	1		1			8		
Westford	183	36	Reed	Willard Jr		1							1				2		
Acton	16	31	Reed	William		1		1				1		1			4		
Lexington	159	24	Reed	William				1		2			1	1			5		
Westford	183	29	Reed	Wm	1	1			1	2	1		1	1			8		
Westford	183	25	Reed	Zach'	1	1	1	1		1			1	1			7		
East Sudbury	67	31	Reeves	Nathaniel		1		1		1			1				4		
Watertown	234	2	Remington	John	1		1		1	1		3					7		
Charlestown	89	47	Reynolds	Hannah									1				1		
Malden	96	32	Reynolds	Jno'				1									1		
Charlestown	89	44	Reynolds	Jona'				1									1		
Ashby	37	41	Rice	Asa		1							1				2		
Marlborough	188	14	Rice	Benjamin		1	1	1	1	1			1	1			7		
Sudbury	57	1	Rice	Benjamin	2			1		1	1	1		1			7		
Stow	198	35	Rice	Buckminster	2			1			1		1				5		
East Sudbury	69	11	Rice	Daniel	1		1	1		1			1				5		
Littleton	202	7	Rice	Daniel	2	1			2	3	1		1	1			11		
Framingham	77	1	Rice	David	2			1	1			1		1			6		
Natick	247	19	Rice	David		1		1		2	1	1	1				7		
East Sudbury	67	32	Rice	Edmund	2	1			1	2	2		1				9		
Marlborough	189	19	Rice	Eli			1					1					2		
East Sudbury	68	2	Rice	Elisabeth						1				1			2		
East Sudbury	67	33	Rice	Elisha	2			1		2	2		1				8		
Marlborough	192	3	Rice	Elisha	2			1		2	1		1				7		
Marlborough	188	23	Rice	Ephraim B.	1			1		2	1	1					6		
East Sudbury	68	1	Rice	Ezekiel		1		1				1	1	1			6		
Framingham	64	13	Rice	Ezekiel				2		1				1			4		Stamped pg# was x'd out
Framingham	77	8	Rice	Ezra	3			1		1			1				6		
Marlborough	189	4	Rice	Gershom	1		2	1		1	1		1				7		
Hopkinton	243	41	Rice	Hezekiah			1	1				1	1	1			5		
East Sudbury	67	29	Rice	Isaac		1	1	1			1			1			5		
Sudbury	63	28	Rice	Ithemer	1	1	2		1	2	1		1				9		
Marlborough	188	35	Rice	Jabez	1	1			2			1		1			6		
Marlborough	194	5	Rice	Jabez Jr				1									1		
Natick	247	21	Rice	James		1		1				1	1	1			5		
Hopkinton	243	37	Rice	Jason				1						1			2		
Marlborough	189	20	Rice	Joel				1						1			2		
Ashby	37	24	Rice	John		1		1		2		1					5		
Natick	247	24	Rice	John	3			2		1		2					8		

TOWN	PG#	LN#	LAST NAME	FIRST NAME	FREE WHITE MALES					FREE WHITE FEMALES					TOTAL ALL OTHER	TOTAL SLAVES	TOTALS	DISTRICT/ TOWNSHIP	NOTES
					under 10	10 to 16	16 to 26	26 to 45	45 and over	under 10	10 to 16	16 to 26	26 to 45	45 and over					
Natick	247	20	Rice	Jona				1		4	2		1				8		
Marlborough	189	24	Rice	Jonah	2		1		1		2	1		1			8		
Sudbury	62	13	Rice	Jonathan			2		1					1			4		
Framingham	77	4	Rice	Josiah				1									1		
Stow	197	11	Rice	Mallethias				1						1			2		
Hopkinton	243	38	Rice	Moses	2	1		1		4		1	1				10		
Sudbury	59	10	Rice	Nahum			1			2		1					4		
Marlborough	189	27	Rice	Nathan	1		1						1				3		
East Sudbury	65	5	Rice	Nathaniel	3			1		1			1				6		
Marlborough	188	9	Rice	Noah	1	2	2		1	2	2	1		3			14		
Framingham	77	3	Rice	Peter	1			1	1	1	2	1	1	1			9		
Marlborough	189	18	Rice	Peter		1	1		1				1	1			5		
Framingham	77	7	Rice	Phinehas		2	2	1		4			1	1	1		12		
Sudbury	61	3	Rice	Reuben	3	3	1	2	1	1		1	1				13		
Ashby	37	23	Rice	Saml	2	2			1			1	1				7		
Ashby	37	25	Rice	Saml Jr			1			2	1		1				5		
Framingham	64	17	Rice	Samuel	3		1	1		2	1		1				9		Stamped pg# was x'd out
Marlborough	189	13	Rice	Seth	1		1					1					5		
Stow	198	19	Rice	Solomon			1	1		2			1				5		
Charlestown	90	9	Rice	Tho'	2	1		1		1		1	1				7		
Framingham	77	2	Rice	Thomas	4			1		2	1		1				9		
Marlborough	189	17	Rice	Thomas	2	2	1		1			3	1	1			11		
Marlborough	187	10	Rice	William		1		1				1	1				4		
Sudbury	61	5	Rice	William			2		1	2				2			7		
Concord	4	13	Richard	Louis			1			5			1				7		
Newton	123	13	Richards	Aaron	1	1	1		1	1		1	1				7		
Newton	123	17	Richards	Daniel		1	3	1			2		1	1			9		
Newton	123	16	Richards	James		1	2		1	1	2		1				8		
Hopkinton	243	44	Richards	Joseph	1	1	1	1		3	2		1				10		
Charlestown	89	39	Richards	Peaton			1										1		
Charlestown	90	10	Richards	Saml			1						1				2		
Newton	123	18	Richards	Solomon	1	1	1		2			1	1	1			8		
Newton	123	15	Richards	Thaddeus	1		1	1		2		1	1	1			8		
Framingham	64	14	Richards	Thomas	4		1	1		2			1				9		Stamped pg# was x'd out
Ashby	37	28	Richardson	Abel	2	1			1	2	1		1	1			9		
Woburn	151	9	Richardson	Abel		1	2		1					1			5		
Woburn	151	10	Richardson	Abel 3rd	3			1					1				5		
Woburn	151	39	Richardson	Abel Jr	2	1	2		1	1	1		1				9		
Westford	183	17	Richardson	Abijah		1	1	1				2	1				6		
Dracut	48	23	Richardson	Acquilla	1			1		1			1				4		
Groton	212	34	Richardson	Alpheus	2	1	1						1				5		
Billerica	177	27	Richardson	Asa	2			1		1	1	1	1	2			9		
Charlestown	89	41	Richardson	Asa			1				1	2	1				5		
Reading	135	20	Richardson	Asa	1	1		1		2			1				6		
Charlestown	89	42	Richardson	Asa Jr			1					1					2		
Woburn	151	13	Richardson	Barnabas				1									1		
Woburn	151	14	Richardson	Barnabas Jr	1	1		1		1	1		1				6		
Woburn	151	16	Richardson	Bartholomew				1					1	1			3		
Woburn	151	18	Richardson	Bartholomew 3rd	1		1	1		1			1				5		
Woburn	151	17	Richardson	Bartholomew Jr	1	1	1		1	1		2		1			8		
Stoneham	139	34	Richardson	Benjamin		1		1				1		1			4		
Newton	123	20	Richardson	Benjm	4		1	1					1	1			8		
Malden	96	33	Richardson	Bradbury		1											1		
Stoneham	139	27	Richardson	Caleb	1		3	1	1			1		1			8		
Woburn	151	34	Richardson	Calvin			1						1				2		
Stoneham	139	33	Richardson	Charly		1		1		1			1	1			5		
Newton	123	24	Richardson	David	1		2	1		1			1	1			7		
Billerica	177	25	Richardson	Eben'				1						1			2		
Billerica	177	26	Richardson	Eben' Jr	1	2	1		1	3	2	1	1				12		
Newton	123	25	Richardson	Ebenz	1	1	1	1		2			1				7		
Reading	135	23	Richardson	Edward	1		2						1				4		
Woburn	151	20	Richardson	Edward		1	1		1		1			1			5		
Chelmsford	171	41	Richardson	Eleazer															Enumeration blank
Woburn	151	22	Richardson	Eleazer	1				1			1		1			4		
Cambridge	227	35	Richardson	Elias	1	1		1		4		1	2	1			11		
Chelmsford	171	39	Richardson	Elijah			1	1				1	1				4		
Stoneham	139	28	Richardson	Elijah		1	1		1			1		1			5		
Dracut	48	26	Richardson	Ephm		1		1				1		3			6		
Woburn	151	24	Richardson	Ethan	3			1		1			1	1			7		
Watertown	234	4	Richardson	Fisher				1		2		1					4		
Sudbury	61	1	Richardson	Gideon	2	1		1		3	1		1				9		
Cambridge	227	34	Richardson	Giles	3			1	1	1	1		2				9		
Reading	135	17	Richardson	Harburt	3	1		1		2			1	1			9		
Townsend	27	43	Richardson	Herh				1				3		1			5		
Townsend	27	44	Richardson	Herh Jr			1						1				2		
Woburn	151	19	Richardson	J*	1			1		1			1				4		
Billerica	177	31	Richardson	Jacob		1	3		1		2	1	1	1			10		
Woburn	152	2	Richardson	Jacob	1	2	2	1		1	1		1	1			10		
Woburn	151	11	Richardson	James	4	1	1		1	1	1		1				10		
Woburn	151	29	Richardson	Jedu*					1		1	2		1			5		

TOWN	PG#	LN#	LAST NAME	FIRST NAME	FREE WHITE MALES					FREE WHITE FEMALES					TOTAL ALL OTHER	TOTAL SLAVES	TOTALS	DISTRICT/ TOWNSHIP	NOTES
					under 10	10 to 16	16 to 26	26 to 45	45 and over	under 10	10 to 16	16 to 26	26 to 45	45 and over					
Medford	102	3	Richardson	Jedun		1		1		2		1	1				6		
Groton	212	29	Richardson	Jephh Capt.	1		4	1			1	1	1				9		
Newton	123	14	Richardson	Jeremiah		1	1		1			2		1			6		
Shirley	215	31	Richardson	Jeremiah				1		1			1				3		
Woburn	151	42	Richardson	Jerusha		1	1			1			1				4		
Woburn	151	27	Richardson	Jese				1		1				1			3		
Woburn	151	37	Richardson	Jese	1	2	1	1		3	1		1				10		
Woburn	151	28	Richardson	Jese Jr				1		1		1					3		
Reading	135	18	Richardson	Jethro			1		1	1	2	2	1				8		
Woburn	152	3	Richardson	Jethro			2			1			1				4		
Billerica	177	24	Richardson	John	2	1		1		1	1		1				7		
Concord	5	15	Richardson	John		1		2		2		3					8		
Charlestown	89	40	Richardson	Jona'	2	1		1		2			1				7		
Chelmsford	171	38	Richardson	Jona'				1						1			2		
Westford	183	19	Richardson	Jona'		1		1		4	1		1	1			9		
Dracut	46	4	Richardson	Jonathan	3	2		1		2	1	1	1				11		
Woburn	151	12	Richardson	Joseph			2	1					1				4		
Woburn	151	15	Richardson	Joseph Jr	1			1		1			1				4		
Hollistown	239	6	Richardson	Joshua Jr			1	1		1	2	1	1				7		
Billerica	177	28	Richardson	Josiah			1		1	1	1			1			5		
Billerica	177	32	Richardson	Josiah			1						1				2		
Chelmsford	171	42	Richardson	Josiah				1	1					1			3		
Sudbury	59	9	Richardson	Josiah	2		1	1	1	1			1	1			8		
Townsend	27	40	Richardson	Josiah	1	2			1	1	2			1			8		
Woburn	151	43	Richardson	Josiah		1	1	1	1					1			5		
Chelmsford	171	43	Richardson	Josiah Jr		1		1		3			1				6		
Woburn	152	1	Richardson	Josiah Jr					1								1		
Wilmington	143	25	Richardson	Jude	1	1		1					1				4		
Wilmington	143	26	Richardson	Lowammer	4			1		1			1				7		
Westford	183	18	Richardson	Lydia									1	1			2		
Stoneham	139	32	Richardson	Mallechy	1			1		2			1				5		
Woburn	151	40	Richardson	Mary			1				1			1			3		
Acton	18	4	Richardson	Moses	2	2	1		2		1			1			9		
Dracut	46	3	Richardson	Moses				1						1			2		
Woburn	151	38	Richardson	Nathan			1		1			1		1			4		
Dracut	46	2	Richardson	Obadiah	1			1		3	3	1					9		
Dracut	49	1	Richardson	Obadiah Jr	1		1					1					3		
Billerica	177	20	Richardson	Oliver		1	1		1		1	2		5			11		
Chelmsford	171	40	Richardson	Oliver	3	1	1	1		1	1		1				9		
Stoneham	139	29	Richardson	Oliver				1						2			3		
Stoneham	139	30	Richardson	Oliver Jr	1		1			1		1					4		
Woburn	152	7	Richardson	Peter			1	1	1			1	1				5		
Cambridge	227	32	Richardson	Raham	2		1						1				4		
Woburn	151	41	Richardson	Rebekah	1			1		1			1	1			5		
Dracut	46	5	Richardson	Reuben	3			1		2			1	1			8		
Woburn	152	5	Richardson	Reuben				1					1	1			3		
Woburn	152	6	Richardson	Richard	1		1			1			1				4		
Cambridge	227	36	Richardson	Richd	3	1	5		1	1	1	1	1				14		
Dracut	46	18	Richardson	Robert	2			1		1			1				5		
Billerica	177	22	Richardson	Saml				1						1			2		
Dracut	45	1	Richardson	Saml	1			1		1			1				4		
Westford	183	16	Richardson	Saml		1	1	2				1	1				6		
Billerica	177	23	Richardson	Saml Jr		1	1	1		1	1		1				6		
Newton	123	19	Richardson	Samuel	1			1				1		1			4		
Woburn	151	25	Richardson	Samuel		1		1		1	1		1				5		
Woburn	152	4	Richardson	Samuel T		1							1				2		
Billerica	177	29	Richardson	Silas	1	1		1					1				4		
Westford	183	15	Richardson	Silas	1	1		1		1		1	1				6		
Townsend	27	39	Richardson	Simeon	1	2	1		1	3				2			10		
Billerica	177	30	Richardson	Steph'			1					2	2				5		
Woburn	151	26	Richardson	Stephen	1			1		3		1	1				7		
Dracut	48	24	Richardson	Stephen		1		1			1			1			4		
Dracut	47	2	Richardson	Stephen Jr	2	2		1		3	1		1				10		
Stoneham	139	31	Richardson	Thadeous	1	2	2	1	1		1	1	1	1			11		
Billerica	177	21	Richardson	Tho'	1	1	1		1	2	1	4		1			12		
Charlestown	89	43	Richardson	Tho'				1		2			1				4		
Westford	183	20	Richardson	Tho'		1	2	1				1	1				6		
Woburn	151	30	Richardson	Thomas		1		1		1		1					4		
Dracut	46	28	Richardson	William	2	2		1		3			1				9		
Malden	96	26	Richardson	Wm		1											1		
Groton	212	35	Richardson	Wm M.			3	1		1		1	1				7		
Townsend	27	45	Richardson	Zach	1			1					1				3		
Dunstable	217	35	Richardson	Zachariah		1							1				2		
Woburn	151	35	Richardson	Zachariah				1						2			3		
Woburn	151	36	Richardson	Zachariah Jr		1		1		1			1	1			5		
Woburn	151	21	Richardson	Zadock			1	1		1			1				4		
Woburn	151	23	Richardson	Zadock Jr	1			1		1			1				4		
Hollistown	239	1	Rider	Asa			1	1		1	1	1					5		
Framingham	77	5	Rider	Jonas		1		1				1		2			5		
Hollistown	238	43	Rider	Joseph				1						1			2		

204

TOWN	PG#	LN#	HEADS OF HOUSEHOLD		FREE WHITE MALES					FREE WHITE FEMALES					TOTAL ALL OTHER	TOTAL SLAVES	TOTALS	DISTRICT/ TOWNSHIP	NOTES
			LAST NAME	FIRST NAME	under 10	10 to 16	16 to 26	26 to 45	45 and over	under 10	10 to 16	16 to 26	26 to 45	45 and over					
Concord	6	3	Ripley	Ezra	1	1	1		1	1		2		1			8		
Shirley	215	28	Ritter	Moses					1	1				1			3		
East Sudbury	68	4	Rivers	Jacob	3	2	1	1		1	1		2	1			12		
Charlestown	89	29	Robbins	Aaron	1		1					1					3		
Cambridge	228	3	Robbins	Anna									1				1		
Carlisle	21	8	Robbins	Benjamin				1				2	1	1			5		
Littleton	204	15	Robbins	Benjamin				1					1	1			3		
Boxborough	200	2	Robbins	Daniel			1		1	2		1		1			6		
Charlestown	89	27	Robbins	Eben			1	1		1				1			4		
Dunstable	217	34	Robbins	Elijah	4			1					1				6		
Newton	123	12	Robbins	Eliphalet				1						1			2		
Boxborough	200	14	Robbins	Elisha	2				1	1		1	2	1			8		
Cambridge	227	40	Robbins	Elisha	1			1		3				1			6		
Carlisle	21	7	Robbins	Ephraim	1			1		2			1	1			6		
Acton	17	10	Robbins	George		1	1		1	1	1	1		4			10		
Stow	199	5	Robbins	Israel	1			1		2			1				5		
Westford	183	40	Robbins	Jacob			1		1			1	1				4		
Watertown	234	1	Robbins	James	2	1	3		1	1	3	1	1				13		
Acton	18	38	Robbins	John	1	1		1		3		1	1				8		
Carlisle	20	20	Robbins	John		1	1		1	1		3		1			8		
Charlestown	89	28	Robbins	John			2					2					4		
Groton	212	31	Robbins	John				1				1		1			3		
Shirley	215	29	Robbins	John		1	1	1		1		1					5		
Carlisle	21	2	Robbins	John 4th		1						1					2		
Acton	18	6	Robbins	John Jr			1						3				4		
Carlisle	20	15	Robbins	John Jr			2	1		1			1				5		
Groton	212	38	Robbins	John Jr	1		2			1		1					5		
Charlestown	89	31	Robbins	Jona'			1										1		
Charlestown	89	30	Robbins	Jos'	2			1						1			4		
Littleton	204	11	Robbins	Joseph				1					1		1		3		
Stow	197	10	Robbins	Martha									1	1			2		
Cambridge	227	20	Robbins	Nathan	1	1	1					1					4		
Littleton	204	12	Robbins	Peter				1									1		
Cambridge	227	39	Robbins	Philemon	1	1		1		2		1	1				7		
Acton	16	17	Robbins	Phillip		1		1				1	1	1			5		
Acton	19	25	Robbins	Rebekah	1						1			1			3		
Acton	19	1	Robbins	Ruth			2					1		1			4		
Newton	123	11	Robbins	Silas				1						1	1		3		
Lexington	159	26	Robbins	Stephen		2	1	2		1		2	1				9		
Charlestown	89	9	Robbins	Tho'			1	1	1	1		3	1	1			9		
Lexington	159	14	Robbins	Thomas		1		1	1			1	1	1			6		
Acton	17	11	Robbins	Tilg			1			1			1				3		
Groton	212	36	Robbins	Willard	2			1		1		1	1	1			7		
Westford	183	39	Robbins	Benja'	3	1		1		1	1	1	1	1			10		
Concord	11	26	Robbinson	Cesar											3		3		
Lexington	159	16	Robbinson	Jacob	4		1	1		1			1				8		
Bedford	163	13	Robbinson	Jesse	1			1		1		1					4		
Westford	183	23	Robbinson	John			2		1			1		1			5		
Lexington	159	29	Robbinson	Jonathan				1					1				2		
Lexington	159	21	Robbinson	Joseph		1		1				1	2				6		
Concord	10	23	Robbinson	Keen	2		1	1		2			1				7		
Acton	19	40	Robert	Chaffin	2		1		1	1	2	1	1				9		
Weston	109	30	Roberts	Joseph	2	1		1	1				1				6		
Sudbury	63	3	Robins	Eunice							1	1		1			3		
Concord	6	21	Robinson	Jeremiah	1		1	1				1		1			6		
Sudbury	60	32	Robinson	Jona			1		1				1	1			4		
Sudbury	57	4	Robinson	Paul	1		1			1			1				4		
Dunstable	217	33	Roby	Joseph W		1		1				1		1			4		
East Sudbury	67	27	Roby	William	2			1		1		1	1	2			8		
Hopkinton	243	40	Rocket	Josiah			1	1				1	1	1			6		
Hopkinton	243	39	Rocket	Nathan	1			1		2			1				5		
Hollistown	239	2	Rockwood	Asa				1		1			1	1			4		
Natick	247	22	Rockwood	Elisha		1	1					1					3		
Groton	212	27	Rockwood	Joseph		1	1					2		1			6		
Groton	212	28	Rockwood	Joseph Jr	3		1	1		1	1		1				8		
Hollistown	239	3	Rockwood	Naham				1				1					2		
Groton	212	26	Rockwood	Saml Dea.	3	1	2		1		1		2				10		
Hollistown	239	4	Rockwood	Timothy			2		1				1	1			5		
Hollistown	239	5	Rockwood	Timothy Jr	1	2	1		1			1	1	1			8		
Concord	4	28	Rogers	Abigail							1			1			2		
Stow	195	17	Rogers	Abraham F.	2	1		1		2	1			1			8		
Newton	123	27	Rogers	Caleb	1	1	1						1				4		
Littleton	201	27	Rogers	Daniel		1			1	2	1						5		
Tewksbury	52	31	Rogers	David	1	1	1	1				1	1		1		7		
Charlestown	90	2	Rogers	Israel					1			1	2	1			5		
Billerica	177	38	Rogers	John	3			1					1				5		
Newton	123	22	Rogers	John	1	1		1					1				4		
Newton	123	23	Rogers	John Jr	3		2		1	2			1				9		
Billerica	177	37	Rogers	Josiah	3	3	1	1		2		1	1				12		
Billerica	177	35	Rogers	Micaijah	1	1	1	1				1	1				6		

205

TOWN	PG#	LN#	LAST NAME	FIRST NAME	M under 10	M 10 to 16	M 16 to 26	M 26 to 45	M 45 and over	F under 10	F 10 to 16	F 16 to 26	F 26 to 45	F 45 and over	TOTAL ALL OTHER	TOTAL SLAVES	TOTALS	DISTRICT/TOWNSHIP	NOTES
Tewksbury	52	30	Rogers	Philip P	1			1		2	1		1				6		
Billerica	177	36	Rogers	Tho'	2		1	1		1			1	1	1		8		
Tewksbury	52	29	Rogers	Timo			2		1	1		2	1	1			8		
Billerica	177	39	Rogers	Wm	3		4	1	1	2		1	1				13		
Charlestown	90	1	Rogers	Wm			1	1		1		1	1		1		6		
Tewksbury	52	32	Rogers	Zadoch			2					1	1	1			5		
Billerica	177	33	Rogers	Zeb					1				1				2		
Billerica	177	34	Rogers	Zeb Jr	3	1			1	1			1				7		
Reading	135	16	Rold	Daniel	1		1				2						4		
Reading	135	21	Rolf	Stephen		1	2		1				1				5		
Charlestown	89	15	Romny	James					1				1				2		
Reading	135	14	Roop	Jesse			1					1					2		
Reading	135	13	Roop	John	1		2					1					4		
Reading	135	10	Roop	Oliver	3	1	2	1		2	1		1				11		
Concord	3	10	Ross	James	1			1		2			1				5		
Bedford	163	14	Ross	John					1	1				1			3		
Ashby	37	26	Ross	Jona	2			1		1		1					5		
Newton	123	21	Ross	Silas			3			1		1	1				6		
Charlestown	89	45	Roulston	Andr'	3	1		1			2						7		
Charlestown	89	46	Roulston	James	2		1	1		1		1					6		
Cambridge	228	1	Row	Isaac	4	2		1		1	1		1				10		
Cambridge	228	2	Row	James	2		2		1		3		2	1			11		
Stoneham	139	35	Row	William A	1	1	1	1		2	1		1				8		
Medford	102	4	Rowson	Wm			2		7	23	12	3	1				48		
Wilmington	143	24	Ru*nd	Re* Freegrace	1		1	1		1		1					5		
Sudbury	63	24	Ruffer	Asahel		1	1			2		1					5		
Sudbury	62	14	Ruffer	Daniel			2		1	1		1		1			6		
Sudbury	63	23	Ruffer	Isaac		1			1			1		1			4		
Sudbury	63	21	Ruffer	James	2		1		1	1		1		1			7		
Sudbury	63	16	Ruffer	James Jr		1		2	1			2		1			7		
Sudbury	63	19	Ruffer	Phinehas		1			1			1		1			5		
Sudbury	62	36	Ruffer	Samuel	4	1	1	1	1		3		1	1			13		
Sudbury	63	5	Ruffer	Samuel Jr	3			1		2	1		1	2			9		
Sudbury	62	32	Ruffer	Silas	3	2		1		2	1		1				10		
Framingham	64	15	Rugg	Jonathan		1	2		1	1	1	1					7		Stamped pg# was x'd out
Billerica	177	19	Ruggles	Joseph					1				1				2		
Townsend	27	42	Rumerell	Joseph	2	1		1		1			1	1			7		
Townsend	27	41	Rumerell	Wi*	1					1		2	1				5		
Charlestown	89	14	Runey	Hannah						1		1	1				3		
Charlestown	89	13	Runey	John	2	1	1	2		1		3	1				11		
Billerica	177	18	Rupell	Benja		1		1		1			1				4		
Reading	135	24	Russel	Stephen		1				1	1						3		
Reading	135	22	Russel	Timothy				1					1		2		4		
Weston	109	25	Russell	Abner	2	1		1					1	1			6		
Burlington	155	20	Russell	Amos		1		1		3		1					6		
Carlisle	20	11	Russell	Amos					1				1				2		
Woburn	151	31	Russell	Bill		4	1	1			1	1					8		
Cambridge	227	24	Russell	Daniel				1				1					2		
Cambridge	227	38	Russell	David	2			1		1			1				5		
Cambridge	227	21	Russell	Edward	1	1		1		3			1	1			8		
Cambridge	227	23	Russell	Elizth			1						1				2		
Stow	198	39	Russell	Ephraim	1	1			1	2		2	2		1		10		
Watertown	234	3	Russell	Hubbard	1	1		1	1				1				5		
Cambridge	227	27	Russell	Ichabod			1	2				2					5		
Carlisle	21	38	Russell	James	1		1		1	1			1				8		
Charlestown	90	5	Russell	James		2	3	2			1	2	1				11		
Carlisle	22	1	Russell	James Jr	1		1	1				1					4		
Natick	247	23	Russell	Joel				1				1	1				3		
Billerica	177	40	Russell	John	1			1		1			1	1			5		
Littleton	202	37	Russell	John			1		1		1			3			6		
Sherburn	251	15	Russell	Jona			1	1		1	2		1				6		
Lexington	159	23	Russell	Joseph				1				1	1				3		
Weston	109	24	Russell	Joseph	2	1	1	1	1		1	2		1	1		11		
Lexington	159	18	Russell	Joshua		1	6	3				1		1	1		12		
Cambridge	227	22	Russell	Josiah	1			1		2		1					5		
Charlestown	89	10	Russell	Mary						1		2					3		
Burlington	155	21	Russell	Molly						1			1				2		
Cambridge	228	5	Russell	Mongo											3		3		
Cambridge	227	26	Russell	Nathan	2	1		1				2	1				7		
Lexington	159	15	Russell	Nathan	3	1		2	1			1	1				9		
Marlborough	193	38	Russell	Nathaniel P.	1	1			1	1	1			2			7		
Cambridge	227	31	Russell	Noah	1	1		1		2	1	1	1				8		
Marlborough	189	9	Russell	Oliver	2	1	2		1	2		1	1				9		
Cambridge	227	25	Russell	Patten					1					1			2		
Groton	212	30	Russell	Peteliah	1		1	1		1	1	1					7		
Charlestown	90	4	Russell	Philm	3		2	1				1	1				8		
Cambridge	227	28	Russell	Samll				1					2				3		
Weston	109	29	Russell	Samuel	2			1					1				4		
Shirley	215	30	Russell	Solomon		1		1		2	1		2				7		
East Sudbury	68	3	Russell	Thadeus		1			1		1			1			4		
Littleton	202	39	Russell	Thomas					1		1		1	1			4		

TOWN	PG#	LN#	LAST NAME	FIRST NAME	FREE WHITE MALES					FREE WHITE FEMALES					TOTAL ALL OTHER	TOTAL SLAVES	TOTALS	DISTRICT/ TOWNSHIP	NOTES
					under 10	10 to 16	16 to 26	26 to 45	45 and over	under 10	10 to 16	16 to 26	26 to 45	45 and over					
Cambridge	227	30	Russell	Thos			2		1			2		1			6		
Charlestown	90	6	Russell	Walter	2	1	3	1		2	1		1				11		
Cambridge	227	29	Rust	Wallis		1	1	1		2		1					6		
Charlestown	90	3	Ryan	Rehica									1	1			2		
Charlestown	90	42	Sampson	Amos	2	1			1	3	2		1				10		
Weston	110	1	Samson	John		1	1		1		1		1	1			6		
Reading	136	20	Sanburn	Peter Rev				1		1		2					4		
Townsend	28	31	Sanders	Jacob	2	2			1		1	3		2			11		
Townsend	28	8	Sanders	James	1		2	1	1		1			1			7		
Townsend	28	27	Sanders	Jonas			1					1		2			4		
Townsend	28	43	Sanders	Perly							1		1				2		
Townsend	28	21	Sanders	Solo	3		1		1		1	1		1			8		
Townsend	28	38	Sanders	Wm	1		1			1		1					4		
Watertown	234	22	Sanders	Robert			1			1				1			3		
Weston	110	2	Sanderson	Abijah	1	1		1		2	1	1	1				8		
Waltham	115	25	Sanderson	Abner		1	1		1		1	1		2			7		
Weston	110	22	Sanderson	Abraham				1	1				3	1			6		
Weston	110	26	Sanderson	Abraham Jr		1		1		3	1		1				7		
Shirley	215	34	Sanderson	David	2			1		2			1				6		
Weston	110	29	Sanderson	Jacob	2			1		3			1				7		
East Sudbury	68	12	Sanderson	James	1	1	1		1			2		1			7		
Waltham	115	17	Sanderson	John			1	2	1			3	1	1			9		
Weston	110	15	Sanderson	Jonas			1	1					1	1			4		
Weston	110	16	Sanderson	Jonas Jr			1	1		1			1				4		
Waltham	115	23	Sanderson	Jonathan	3	2		1		2	1		1				10		
Waltham	115	31	Sanderson	Josiah	1		1	1	1			2	1				7		
Watertown	234	19	Sanderson	Josiah	1	1			1	1	1	1		1			7		
Waltham	115	30	Sanderson	Mary									2				2		
Waltham	115	29	Sanderson	Nathan	4	1	1		1	2	1	1					11		
Littleton	203	3	Sanderson	Samuel	1			1		1	1		1				5		
Watertown	234	25	Sanger	Abigail										1			1		
Watertown	234	15	Sanger	Abraham			1			1			1				3		
Sherburn	251	22	Sanger	Asa		3			1	2	1		1				8		
Sherburn	251	24	Sanger	Calven				1					1				2		
Framingham	77	12	Sanger	Daniel				1				1	1	1	1		5		
Watertown	234	21	Sanger	Daniel	2		3	1		1	1	1					9		
Framingham	64	11	Sanger	Daniel Jr	1			1		2		1					5		Stamped pg# was x'd out
Littleton	202	30	Sanger	David	2		1						1				4		
Sherburn	251	23	Sanger	David			1			1		1					3		
Watertown	234	24	Sanger	David		1		2			1		1				5		
Sherburn	251	17	Sanger	John			2	1		1	1	1					6		
Watertown	234	27	Sanger	John	1			1		2	1	1					6		
Framingham	77	10	Sanger	Joseph		2		1		1	1		1		1		7		
Newton	124	14	Sanger	Nathan			1			2	1						4		
Watertown	234	26	Sanger	Richard				1		2		1					4		
Sherburn	251	25	Sanger	Samll			1		1			3	1				6		
Townsend	28	3	Santell	Simeon			4	1		2	2			2			10		
Malden	96	39	Sargeant	Amos	3	1	1	1		1	1		1	1			10		
Malden	96	47	Sargeant	Benja'		1				1							2		
Malden	96	36	Sargeant	David				1					2	1			4		
Malden	96	38	Sargeant	David 3rd		1				1		1					3		
Malden	96	37	Sargeant	David Jr				1		2	2	1		1			7		
Malden	96	35	Sargeant	Debor'										3			3		
Malden	96	34	Sargeant	Ezra	1		1	1				1		2			6		
Charlestown	91	4	Sargeant	Jesse				1		3		1					5		
Malden	96	43	Sargeant	Jos'				1									1		
Malden	96	40	Sargeant	Mary									1				1		
Malden	96	44	Sargeant	Nath'		1											1		
Malden	96	42	Sargeant	Ruth									1				1		
Charlestown	90	23	Sargeant	Saml G.			1			2		1	1				4		
Charlestown	90	22	Sargeant	Saml L.	1		1			2			1				5		
Woburn	152	18	Sargeant	Samuel	3	1		1			1		1				7		
Malden	96	41	Sargeant	Winslow		1	1	1	1		1	2		1			8		
Townsend	28	1	Sarles	*			2		2		1		1	1			7		
Townsend	29	37	Sarles	Azubah	1					1			1				3		
Townsend	28	5	Sarles	James	1			1		3			1				6		
Townsend	28	2	Sarles	Saml	3	1		1		1	2		1				9		
Townsend	29	41	Sarles	Uriah			1						1				2		
Townsend	28	20	Sartell	Ephm			1			2			1				4		
Pepperell	33	31	Sartill	Nathl		1		1				1	1				4		
Tewksbury	53	8	Saunders	Amos	3			1		1			1	1			7		
Tewksbury	53	7	Saunders	Benja	1	2		1		3	2		1				10		
Billerica	178	12	Saunders	Hannah							1			2			3		
Billerica	178	11	Saunders	John	1				1			1		1			4		
Charlestown	91	5	Saunders	John		1											1		
Tewksbury	53	11	Saunders	Samll			1			1		1					3		
Tewksbury	53	9	Saunders	Timo	2			1		3		1	1				8		
Westford	183	46	Saunderson	Wm	1	1			1					1			4		
Medford	102	10	Savel	Tho'					1					1			2		
Medford	102	11	Savel	Tho' Jr			1						1				2		

TOWN	PG#	LN#	LAST NAME	FIRST NAME	FREE WHITE MALES					FREE WHITE FEMALES					TOTAL ALL OTHER	TOTAL SLAVES	TOTALS	DISTRICT/ TOWNSHIP	NOTES
					under 10	10 to 16	16 to 26	26 to 45	45 and over	under 10	10 to 16	16 to 26	26 to 45	45 and over					
East Sudbury	68	33	Sawin	Benjm	1		1	1					1				4		
Sudbury	59	15	Sawin	Benjm	2	2			1	1		2		1			9		
Marlborough	187	12	Sawin	John	1		1	1			1			1			5		
Marlborough	187	11	Sawin	Mannings				1						1			2		
Watertown	234	12	Sawing	Daniel	1			1					1				3		
Natick	247	30	Sawing	Ezekiel	2			1		2	1		1				7		
Natick	247	39	Sawing	Fracs	2	1		1		1				1			6		
Natick	247	36	Sawing	John			1	1			2		1				5		
Cambridge	228	16	Sawing	Joseph			1			1			1				3		
Natick	247	29	Sawing	Moses	1	1		1		3			2				8		
Natick	247	28	Sawing	Thos	2		1		1	2	2		1				9		
Groton	212	74	Sawtell	Abel	1			1		4			1				7		
Groton	212	69	Sawtell	Elnathan	4				1	1	1	2	1				10		
Groton	212	61	Sawtell	Joseph				1				1		1			3		
Groton	212	62	Sawtell	Joseph 3rd	1		2	2		3			1	1			10		
Groton	212	48	Sawtell	Joseph Jr	3	1	1	1	1			1	1	1			10		
Littleton	202	27	Sawtell	Mercy	1								1	1			3		
Groton	212	67	Sawtell	Nathl			1						1				2		
Groton	212	41	Sawtell	Richard		1		1		1	1	1	1				6		
Groton	212	42	Sawtell	Richard Jr		1		1		2			1				5		
Dracut	48	19	Sawyer	Caleb	4			1		1			1				7		
Stow	196	34	Sawyer	Caleb	1			1		2	1		1				6		
Tyngsborough	43	25	Sawyer	David	1	1		1		3	1	1	1				9		
Dracut	46	22	Sawyer	Eben	2			1		3	2		1				9		
Dracut	46	17	Sawyer	Henry	1			1		3		1					6		
Boxborough	200	30	Sawyer	Lemuel	1				1				1				3		
Dracut	46	20	Sawyer	Nathan		1	1			1		1					4		
Boxborough	200	39	Sawyer	Nathaniel		2			1		1	1	1				6		
Marlborough	191	14	Sawyer	Phinehas	1			1		4			1				7		
Reading	135	28	Sawyer	Thomas		2	1	1		2	1		1				8		
Reading	135	27	Sawyer	William		1	1					1					3		
Dracut	46	21	Sayer	Reuben	1			1					1	1			4		
Tewksbury	53	16	Scarlet	Molly		1	1			1			1				4		
Pepperell	33	11	Scott	Aaron		1	1	1				2	1				6		
Pepperell	33	47	Scott	Eunice						1			1				2		
Sudbury	61	11	Scott	Jacob	2			1					1				4		
Charlestown	90	31	Scott	John			1				1	1					3		
Charlestown	90	32	Scott	Robt				1				1					2		
Woburn	152	9	Scotts	John				1				1		1			3		
Tyngsborough	43	23	Scrivner	Matthew	2	2	1		1	1	3		1	1			12		
Townsend	28	35	Seales	Natha	1				1	1	2	1					7		
Townsend	28	19	Seales	Nathn		1	1	1		1			1				5		
Boxborough	199	8	Searjants	Samuel	2			1			1	1					6		
Stow	197	9	Searjents	Nathaniel		1	1	1			1	1	1				6		
Cambridge	228	25	Seaver	Ebenz		2		1			1		1				5		
Newton	124	2	Seavern	Elisha		1	1	1					1				4		
Newton	124	4	Seavern	Richard		1						1					2		
Newton	124	9	Seaverns	Abijah	1	7	2			2		1	1				14		
Weston	110	17	Seaverns	Joseph	1		1	1		3	1		1	1			9		
Weston	110	13	Seaverns	Josiah		1	1	1				2		1	1		8		
Groton	212	39	Seever	Herman	1		2	1				2	1				7		
Watertown	234	16	Seger	Ebenz	1				1	2	3	2	1				10		
Acton	18	19	Sergeant	Solomon	1			1	1	1	1		1				5		
Hopkinton	244	17	Serridge	Isaac	2			1	1	1		1	1	1			8		
Townsend	28	16	Sever	Thos			1		1			2		2			6		
Townsend	28	17	Sever	Thos Jr		1		1				1					3		
Marlborough	195	1	Sewell	Ephraim	2	1	1	1		2			1				8		
Tewksbury	53	12	Shad	Jacob		1	1	1		1	1		2				7		
Tewksbury	53	14	Shad	Joel	1	2		1		1	2		1				8		
Tewksbury	53	2	Shad	Jona Jr	2	1	1	1		2	1		1				9		
Tewksbury	53	1	Shad	Joseph	2	1		2	1	1		2		1			10		
Pepperell	32	47	Shattuck	Abijah				1		1			1				3		
Pepperell	32	48	Shattuck	Abijah	1		1	1		2			1				6		
Pepperell	34	16	Shattuck	Amaziah	1			1				1					3		
Pepperell	33	28	Shattuck	Asa	1	1	1	1		2		1	1	1			9		
Groton	212	72	Shattuck	Daniel		1	1	1		1	1	1					6		
Pepperell	33	24	Shattuck	David			1	1						1			3		
Pepperell	33	26	Shattuck	Ebenr	3	1		1			2	1	1				9		
Ashby	37	35	Shattuck	Elias Jr	1	1	2		1	1	2	1					10		
Pepperell	33	25	Shattuck	Elijah		1	2	1			1	1	1				7		
Pepperell	33	9	Shattuck	Emerson	2	1		1		2			1	1			8		
Groton	212	63	Shattuck	Ezekiel	2	1		1		2	1	1	1				9		
Pepperell	33	29	Shattuck	Israel	1	2		1		3		1	1				9		
Pepperell	32	31	Shattuck	James				1				1		1			3		
Pepperell	33	4	Shattuck	James Jr		1		1		1	1		1				5		
Groton	212	76	Shattuck	Jeremiah	3		1			1			1				6		
Pepperell	33	21	Shattuck	Jerh					1	1	1	2		1			6		
Pepperell	32	43	Shattuck	Jesse	3			1		1			1				6		
Groton	212	57	Shattuck	Job Capt.			1		1			1		2			5		
Groton	212	59	Shattuck	Job Jr	1	2	1	1		1		1	1	1			9		

TOWN	PG#	LN#	LAST NAME	FIRST NAME	FREE WHITE MALES under 10	10 to 16	16 to 26	26 to 45	45 and over	FREE WHITE FEMALES under 10	10 to 16	16 to 26	26 to 45	45 and over	TOTAL ALL OTHER	TOTAL SLAVES	TOTALS	DISTRICT/TOWNSHIP	NOTES
Groton	212	73	Shattuck	John			1			1		1					3		
Pepperell	32	40	Shattuck	John				1					1				2		
Pepperell	32	38	Shattuck	Jona				1					1				2		
Pepperell	33	2	Shattuck	Jona 3rd	1		1			2			1	1			6		
Pepperell	32	39	Shattuck	Jona Jr			2	1					1	1			5		
Pepperell	32	34	Shattuck	Joseph		1	1	1		1	1			1			6		
Pepperell	33	30	Shattuck	Junia				1		2			1				4		
Pepperell	32	35	Shattuck	Moses	3	1		1		2	2	2		1			12		
Groton	212	70	Shattuck	Nathl	1			1		1	2			1			6		
Pepperell	33	10	Shattuck	Nathl	2		1			2	1		1				7		
Groton	212	58	Shattuck	Noah	1		1	1		1		1		2			7		
Townsend	28	34	Shattuck	Noah	1			2		1			1				5		
Pepperell	33	23	Shattuck	Oliver			1							1			2		
Pepperell	32	37	Shattuck	Philip		2		1				1					4		
Pepperell	32	33	Shattuck	Reuben		1	3	1				1		1			7		
Pepperell	33	12	Shattuck	Reuben Jr	1		1	1				1					4		
Pepperell	32	36	Shattuck	Saml				1				1		1			3		
Townsend	28	11	Shattuck	Solo	3	1		1		2	1		2				10		
Pepperell	32	32	Shattuck	Thos				1				1		1			3		
Townsend	28	33	Shattuck	Zach			1	1					1	1			4		
Charlestown	90	39	Shattuck			1											1		
Concord	6	37	Shaw	Joseph		1		1		1			1				4		
Concord	5	1	Shaw	Joseph Jr		1						1					2		
Concord	8	37	Shaw	William				1					1				2		
Pepperell	33	5	Shed	Daniel				1		1			1				3		
Pepperell	32	41	Shed	David		1		1					1				3		
Pepperell	32	42	Shed	David Jr	1		1					1					3		
Charlestown	90	46	Shed	Eben				1			1	1	1				4		
Chelmsford	172	39	Shed	Ebenz	2	1	1	1					1				6		
Chelmsford	172	40	Shed	Eliza'									1				1		
Pepperell	33	27	Shed	Esther	1		2			1			1				5		
Cambridge	228	17	Shed	Frances			2				1						3		
Cambridge	228	14	Shed	John	3	1		1		1			1				7		
Billerica	178	14	Shed	Jos'	1			1		2	1	1					6		
Groton	212	64	Shed	Joseph		1		1					1				3		
Cambridge	228	21	Shed	Nathan		1	4	2	1			2					10		
Groton	212	49	Shed	Oliver			1	1					1				3		
Charlestown	90	47	Shed	Saml				1			1		1				3		
Charlestown	91	2	Shed	Saml		2		1					1				4		
Burlington	155	31	Shed	Samuel	1	1		1		2			1				6		
Billerica	178	15	Shed	Tho'				1					1				2		
Pepperell	32	46	Shed	Willard		1	1					1					3		
Billerica	178	13	Shed	Zach	3		1	1		3			1				9		
Waltham	116	10	Shed	Zacheus	2	1	1		1	3	1		1				10		
Medford	102	17	Shed	Zachh	2			1		2		1	1				7		
Hopkinton	244	7	Sheffield	Daniel	2			2			1		1				6		
Medford	102	19	Shelbeck				1				1	2	1				5		
Pepperell	32	49	Shepard	Francis	1	1	1	1		1	1		1				7		
Pepperell	33	1	Shepard	Jona			2	1						1			4		
Groton	212	60	Sheple	James	2	2	1		1			1		1			8		
Groton	212	65	Sheple	John	1	2		1						1			5		
Groton	212	54	Sheple	Jona	1				1	1	2		1				6		
Groton	212	50	Sheple	Wilder	1	2		1					1	1			6		
Groton	212	55	Sheple	Wm				1					1				2		
Groton	212	56	Sheple	Wm Jr	1	1		1		1		1					5		
Pepperell	33	6	Shepley	John	1			1		2		1			1		6		
Pepperell	33	8	Shepley	Sarah								1		1			2		
Westford	183	45	Sheppard	Chri'				1				1		1			3		
Charlestown	91	11	Sheppard	Leml															
Charlestown	91	1	Sheppard	Saml	2			1		1	1						5		
Dracut	44	13	Sherborn	James	2		1						1				4		
Chelmsford	172	30	Sherburn	Saml			1						1				2		
Tyngsborough	43	39	Sherburne	Samll	1			1		2	1						5		
East Sudbury	68	8	Sherman	Edward				1					1				2		
East Sudbury	68	9	Sherman	Ephraim	2	2		1			1		1				7		
Marlborough	187	13	Sherman	Isaac	1			1		2	1			1			6		
East Sudbury	68	7	Sherman	Jona		1		1		1	1		1	1			6		
Lincoln	12	18	Sherman	Jonas	1	1		1		1	1			1			6		
Marlborough	194	20	Sherman	Micah	1		2	2		1		2	1				9		
Marlborough	194	2	Sherman	Moses	3			1		1			1				6		
East Sudbury	68	6	Sherman	Reuben	2			1		2			2				7		
East Sudbury	68	5	Sherman	Timothy	1		1	1			1	1		1	1		8		
Townsend	28	6	Sherwin	H* P.	2		1	1		3			1				8		
Townsend	28	36	Sherwin	John	1	1	1	1		2			1				7		
Townsend	29	5	Sherwin	Salome	1					1		1	1				4		
Townsend	29	35	Sherwin	Zemry			1	1		3		2	1				8		
Ashby	36	5	Shid	Betty		1		1			2			1			5		
Littleton	203	7	Shierer	William			1							1			2		
Reading	135	29	Shilden	Nathaniel		1			2	1	1	1	1	1			8		
Reading	135	30	Shilden	Russel	2		1	1				1					7		

TOWN	PG#	LN#	LAST NAME	FIRST NAME	FREE WHITE MALES					FREE WHITE FEMALES					TOTAL ALL OTHER	TOTAL SLAVES	TOTALS	DISTRICT/ TOWNSHIP	NOTES
					under 10	10 to 16	16 to 26	26 to 45	45 and over	under 10	10 to 16	16 to 26	26 to 45	45 and over					
Townsend	28	7	Shinvin	Levi			2						1				3		
Acton	16	5	Shirland	James	3			1					1				5		
Sudbury	65	3	Shirtliff	Joseph	1		1			1	1		1				5		
Hopkinton	244	20	Show	Saml	1			1				1	1	1			5		
Townsend	28	4	Shriver	Daniel						1					1		2		
Malden	97	16	Shute	Eben				1									1		
Malden	97	10	Shute	Geo'	1		1			1			1				4		
Malden	97	9	Shute	Han'										4			4		
Malden	97	17	Shute	Isaac		1											1		
Malden	97	14	Shute	Jacob		1		1					1				3		
Malden	97	7	Shute	Pheebe									1				1		
Malden	97	15	Shute	Richd		1	1		1			1	1	1			6		
Malden	97	8	Shute	Saml			1			1			1				3		
Malden	97	11	Shute	Solo'			1			1			1				3		
Malden	97	13	Shute	Tho'		1											1		
Malden	97	12	Shute	Wm		1											1		
Westford	184	5	Simmes	Tho'		1		1		2			1				5		
Concord	8	25	Simmon	Micah	1	3	2	1	1		1		1				10		
Groton	212	75	Simmons	Moses	1			1		3	2		1				8		
Bedford	163	18	Simonds	Aaron			2			1		1					4		
Woburn	152	13	Simonds	Benjamin	2	1	4		1			1	1				10		
Burlington	155	28	Simonds	Caleb	3	2	1	1		2	1		1				11		
Burlington	155	30	Simonds	Calvin	2	2	2			1			2	1			11		
Lexington	159	33	Simonds	David	1			1	1	2			1	1			7		
Burlington	155	24	Simonds	Gideon	2			1		2	1		1				7		
Watertown	234	28	Simonds	James		1		1		1	1	1	1	1			7		
Billerica	177	41	Simonds	John	2		1		1	1			1				6		
Groton	212	43	Simonds	John		1	1					1	1				5		
Lexington	159	34	Simonds	John		1		1				1	1	1			5		
Burlington	155	29	Simonds	Jonathan		1		1		3	2		1				8		
Lexington	159	37	Simonds	Joseph	1	1	1	1		1			1				6		
Lexington	159	35	Simonds	Joshua		1		1			1	1	1	1			6		
Lexington	159	36	Simonds	Joshua Jr	2			1		1	1		1				6		
Chelmsford	172	31	Simonds	Josiah			1						1				2		
Bedford	163	22	Simonds	Lemuel		1		1					1				3		
Woburn	152	14	Simonds	Nathan		1		1	1	1		1	1	2			8		
Lexington	159	38	Simonds	William		1				1	1						3		
Townsend	28	24	Simons	James		1		1					1	1			4		
Townsend	29	2	Simons	James Jr				1					1				2		
Groton	212	66	Simson	Benjm	1					3			1				5		
Hopkinton	244	18	Singletery	Ebenz		1	1	1		1			1				5		
Burlington	155	27	Skilton	Dayz	2		2	1		1	1		1				8		
Bedford	163	20	Skilton	Dryz	4	1	1						1				7		
Billerica	177	43	Skilton	John		1	1	1		2			1				6		
Burlington	155	25	Skilton	Matthew	2	1		1		1			1				6		
Burlington	155	32	Skilton	Matthw Jr		1					1						2		
Charlestown	91	9	Skilton	Saml			1					1	1				3		
Burlington	155	26	Skilton	Thomas		2		1			1		1				5		
Acton	18	21	Skinner	Abraham	3			1		1	1		1				7		
Charlestown	91	7	Skinner	John	2			1		2			1				6		
Woburn	152	20	Skinner	Mary	1								1				2		
Charlestown	91	8	Skinner	Richd	1		1			2							4		
Reading	136	1	Slack	John	2			1					1	1			5		
Cambridge	228	24	Slever	John				2					1				3		
Townsend	28	23	Sloan	James	3	1	1		2	1			1				9		
Westford	183	43	Sloan	John				1					1				2		
Lincoln	15	1	Smith	*amiah	2	2	1		1			2	1				9		
Hopkinton	244	14	Smith	Aaron	2			1			1		1				5		
Tyngsborough	43	26	Smith	Aaron	1		3	1		2	1	1					9		
Lexington	160	11	Smith	Abel	2			2					1				5		
Sudbury	63	1	Smith	Abel	1	1	1	1	1	3	2	1	1				12		
Hopkinton	244	16	Smith	Abiel			1	2				1	1	1			6		
Lexington	160	10	Smith	Abraham	1	1		1					2				5		
East Sudbury	68	32	Smith	Alexander	1			1		4	1		1				8		
Waltham	115	18	Smith	Amos	2	2	1	1		2	1		1				10		
Charlestown	90	16	Smith	Ann											1		1		
Sudbury	63	37	Smith	Asahel		1		1			1			1			4		
Stow	197	25	Smith	Benjamin		2		1				1		1			5		
Woburn	152	8	Smith	Benjamin		2		1					1	1			5		
Hopkinton	244	13	Smith	Benjm		1		1	1	1			1				5		
Cambridge	228	19	Smith	Cathn								3		1			4		
Sudbury	63	22	Smith	Daniel N.		1	2			2			1				6		
East Sudbury	68	14	Smith	David	1			1		2			1	1			6		
Pepperell	34	22	Smith	David				1		2			1	1			5		
Reading	136	4	Smith	David			4	1	1	1			1	1			9		
Waltham	116	11	Smith	David	1	1	3		1			2	1	2			11		
Dracut	48	21	Smith	Dudley		1		1		1	1		1				6		
Charlestown	90	17	Smith	Eben				1						1			2		
Acton	17	2	Smith	Eben		1		1					1				3		
Charlestown	91	10	Smith	Ebz' Jr			1			1							2		

TOWN	PG#	LN#	LAST NAME	FIRST NAME	FREE WHITE MALES					FREE WHITE FEMALES					TOTAL ALL OTHER	TOTAL SLAVES	TOTALS	DISTRICT/ TOWNSHIP	NOTES
					under 10	10 to 16	16 to 26	26 to 45	45 and over	under 10	10 to 16	16 to 26	26 to 45	45 and over					
Woburn	152	11	Smith	Elias	1			1		2			1				5		
Waltham	115	19	Smith	Elijah	4	2	1	1		1		1	1				11		
Waltham	116	4	Smith	Elijah Jr		1		1				1					3		
Concord	10	22	Smith	Elisha			1										1		
Charlestown	90	18	Smith	Eliza'									1				1		
Newton	124	1	Smith	Enoch	2	1		1		2			1				7		
East Sudbury	68	16	Smith	Ephraim		2	2		1		1	1		1			8		
Natick	247	26	Smith	Henry	1				1	1		1					4		
Sudbury	65	1	Smith	Henry			1	2	2	1	1	1					8		
Hollistown	239	13	Smith	Isaa	1		1		1	1	2		1				7		
Bedford	163	23	Smith	Isaac		1	1			1		2					5		
Charlestown	90	15	Smith	Isaac	1		1			1		2					5		
Hollistown	239	11	Smith	Israel	1		1		1			1	1				5		
Sudbury	61	12	Smith	Israel		1		1		1			1	2			6		
Lexington	160	12	Smith	James	1	2		2		1	1	1	1		1		10		
Reading	136	27	Smith	James				1			1		1				3		
Weston	110	25	Smith	James				1		2			1				4		
Sudbury	61	13	Smith	Jedediah	1	1	1	1		1			1				6		
Weston	110	3	Smith	Joel	2	1	1		1			2	2				9		
Marlborough	191	29	Smith	John		1	1	1					1				4		
Reading	136	26	Smith	John	2		1	1		1			1				6		
Weston	110	4	Smith	John	1			1					1				3		
Lexington	160	8	Smith	Jonas		1		1		1		1					4		
Marlborough	191	31	Smith	Jonas	1		1		1	1	1		1				6		
Waltham	115	20	Smith	Jonas				1					1				2		
Burlington	155	23	Smith	Jonathan	1			1		1		1		1			5		
Reading	136	28	Smith	Jonathan	1			1		1	1	1	1				6		
Sudbury	63	33	Smith	Jonathan			3	1				1		2			7		
Lincoln	14	28	Smith	Jonathan		1		1		2			1				5		
Lexington	159	39	Smith	Jonathan Jr	2		1		1	2		1	1				8		
Medford	102	12	Smith	Jos'		1	1		1				1				4		
East Sudbury	68	13	Smith	Joseph				1				1	1				3		
Hopkinton	244	12	Smith	Joseph	1			1		1		1	1	1			6		
Lexington	160	9	Smith	Joseph	2	2	2	1	2	1		2		1			13		
Reading	136	30	Smith	Joseph	2	1		1		1		1					6		
Lexington	160	7	Smith	Josiah	1	1	1		1	1	1		1				7		
Watertown	234	14	Smith	Jubel	2		1			2			1				6		
Malden	97	6	Smith	Lydia								1					1		
Reading	136	12	Smith	Mary									1				1		
Shirley	215	33	Smith	Mary Wid.								1		1			2		
Hopkinton	244	15	Smith	Moses				1		1		1					3		
Stow	198	16	Smith	Nahum	2			1		1		1	1				6		
Lexington	160	5	Smith	Nathan	2		1	2	1			1	1				8		
Weston	109	31	Smith	Nathan	1			1					1				3		
Waltham	115	26	Smith	Nathan	2	1	1	1		3	1	1	1				11		
Shirley	215	35	Smith	Nathan Capt.				1			1		1				3		
Reading	136	5	Smith	Noah		1						1					2		
Hollistown	239	9	Smith	Richard				1			2		1				4		
Hopkinton	244	3	Smith	Richard			3	1		1	2		1				8		
Shirley	215	36	Smith	Salvinas Capt.				1				1	1				3		
Shirley	215	37	Smith	Salvinas Jr	1		1			1		1					4		
Weston	110	23	Smith	Samuel	3		1	1		2			1				8		
Charlestown	91	3	Smith	Sarah									1				1		
East Sudbury	68	25	Smith	Simeon				1		1				2			4		
Acton	19	30	Smith	Solomon	2			1		2	1	1					7		
Westford	183	44	Smith	Tho'	1	1	1		1	2	1		1				8		
Acton	17	5	Smith	Thomas	2			1		2		1					6		
Waltham	116	9	Smith	Thomas	2	1	1		1	3		2		1			11		
Natick	247	25	Smith	Timothy				1						2			3		
Natick	247	27	Smith	Timothy Jr.			1						1				2		
Lexington	160	4	Smith	William				1					1				2		
Marlborough	191	30	Smith	William	2		1	1		2	3		1	1			11		
Sudbury	63	32	Smith	William	1		1	1		1	1		1				6		
Lexington	160	6	Smith	William Jr		1		1		1	1		1				5		
Marlborough	188	25	Smith	Zeduthun	1			1		1		1					4		
Dracut	46	29	Snell	David	3		1		1	1	1	1					8		
Hollistown	239	8	Snell	John				1					1				2		
Hopkinton	244	2	Snell	John				1					1				2		
Hopkinton	244	1	Snell	Saml	2		1			4		1					8		
Westford	183	42	Snow	James	1		1			1		1					4		
Billerica	178	10	Snow	John	2			1				1	1				5		
Chelmsford	172	38	Snow	Jona'		1		1		3		1					6		
Westford	183	41	Snow	Levi'	2	1	1	1		1	1	1		1			9		
Charlestown	90	41	Snow	Mary									1				1		
Woburn	152	19	Snow	Ruth								1		1			2		
Watertown	234	18	Soden	Saml	1	1		1			1		1				5		
Billerica	178	9	Soley	John				1				1			1		3		
Charlestown	90	40	Soley	Saml	1		1			1	1	1					5		
Stow	199	3	Soper	Jacob	1		1	1		2	1	1					7		
Reading	136	21	Souker	Enoch			1					1					2		

TOWN	PG#	LN#	LAST NAME	FIRST NAME	FREE WHITE MALES					FREE WHITE FEMALES					TOTAL ALL OTHER	TOTAL SLAVES	TOTALS	DISTRICT/ TOWNSHIP	NOTES
					under 10	10 to 16	16 to 26	26 to 45	45 and over	under 10	10 to 16	16 to 26	26 to 45	45 and over					
Watertown	234	32	Souldier	John T.	3				1	1	1		1				7		
Marlborough	188	7	Souther	Lucy		1	1						1	1			4		
Littleton	202	32	Spalding	David				1					1				2		
Littleton	202	31	Spalding	Isaac				1						1			2		
Tyngsborough	43	21	Spalding	Joel		1		1		1	1		1				5		
Tyngsborough	43	22	Spalding	Jonah	1			1		3			1				6		
Natick	247	34	Sparrowhawk	Beriah			1	1					1	1			4		
Cambridge	228	23	Sparrowhawk	David			1	1		1		1	1		1		6		
Cambridge	228	26	Sparrowhawk	Hannah	2	2	2	1				1	2	1			11		
Sherburn	251	21	Sparrowhawk	Jacob	1		1	1					1				4		
Cambridge	228	22	Sparrowhawk	Mary										2	1		3		
Cambridge	228	27	Sparrowhawk	Saml			1						2				3		
Townsend	28	10	Sparrowhawk	Saml	1	2		1		2	1		2				9		
Sherburn	251	26	Sparrowhawk	Timth		2		1		1	1			1			6		
Watertown	234	17	Sparrowhead	Blake	2	1		1		2	1	1		1			9		
Concord	6	13	Spauldin	Ithamar			1				1	1					3		
Carlisle	21	12	Spauldin	Jonas	1		1			2	1	1	1				7		
Carlisle	22	30	Spauldin	William			1	1		1		1	1				5		
Carlisle	21	17	Spauldin	Zebulon		1	2	1		1		2	3	1			11		
Dunstable	217	42	Spaulding	Abel		1		1				2		1			5		
Pepperell	33	13	Spaulding	Abel	3	1	1	1	2	1		1	1				11		
Chelmsford	172	8	Spaulding	Abijah			1							1			2		
Chelmsford	172	24	Spaulding	Andrew			1	1		4	2		1				9		
Billerica	178	20	Spaulding	Asa			2	1	2				2	1			8		
Chelmsford	172	1	Spaulding	Az'	1	1	1	1				1	1				6		
Townsend	27	28	Spaulding	Benja	1	1		1		2	1	1	1				8		
Chelmsford	172	25	Spaulding	Benja'		1		1		1		3	1				7		
Townsend	28	9	Spaulding	Benja Jr	2			1		1		1	1				6		
Billerica	178	19	Spaulding	Benoni	1	1		1		5			1				9		
Ashby	36	6	Spaulding	Eleazer	3			1			1	1					6		
Townsend	28	28	Spaulding	Eleazer				1						1			2		
Chelmsford	172	27	Spaulding	Eli			1										1		
Chelmsford	172	6	Spaulding	Ephm		1		1					1				3		
Chelmsford	172	29	Spaulding	Esther								1		2			3		
Chelmsford	172	23	Spaulding	Henry	2	1		1		1	1	2		2			10		
Chelmsford	172	18	Spaulding	Henry Jr			1						1				2		
Chelmsford	172	21	Spaulding	Hevz'			1						1	1			3		
Chelmsford	172	26	Spaulding	Ira	1			1		2			2				6		
Chelmsford	172	11	Spaulding	Jesse	2			1		3		1	1				8		
Townsend	28	30	Spaulding	Jesse				1		2			1				4		
Chelmsford	172	9	Spaulding	Job			1	1	1					1			4		
Chelmsford	172	10	Spaulding	Job Jr	1	1		1		1		1	1				6		
Chelmsford	172	4	Spaulding	Joel			2	1				1	1	1			6		
Townsend	28	25	Spaulding	Joel			1			1			1				3		
Chelmsford	172	16	Spaulding	John				1						1			2		
Tewksbury	53	6	Spaulding	John			1	1					1	1	1		5		
Chelmsford	172	17	Spaulding	John Jr	3	1		1		1		1	1	1			9		
Townsend	28	13	Spaulding	Jona	1	1		1				1		1			5		
Chelmsford	172	7	Spaulding	Jona'			2	1				1	1	1			6		
Chelmsford	172	20	Spaulding	Joseph	2		2	1		1				1			7		
Dunstable	217	43	Spaulding	Joseph	1	2		1		1			1				6		
Pepperell	33	3	Spaulding	Josiah	1			1		2			1				5		
Pepperell	33	22	Spaulding	Leml			1	1		1		1		1			5		
Chelmsford	172	3	Spaulding	Micah	4	1	1	1		1		1	1	1			11		
Chelmsford	172	5	Spaulding	Noah			1	1		1	1	1	1				6		
Chelmsford	172	28	Spaulding	Peter				1	1					1			3		
Chelmsford	172	13	Spaulding	Peter Jr				1									1		
Westford	184	4	Spaulding	Phillip				1						1			2		
Chelmsford	172	22	Spaulding	Robert	4	1		1		1	2		1				10		
Chelmsford	172	19	Spaulding	Saml	2			1					1				4		
Townsend	29	42	Spaulding	Sarah										2			2		
Chelmsford	172	2	Spaulding	Simeon	1	1		1		3	1		1				8		
Westford	184	1	Spaulding	Sola'	2	2		1		1	1			1			8		
Chelmsford	172	12	Spaulding	Steph'				1									1		
Billerica	178	21	Spaulding	Tho'	1		1	1		2				1			6		
Pepperell	33	7	Spaulding	Thos	1		1	1		1				1			5		
Townsend	28	29	Spaulding	Thos	1			1		1			1				4		
Groton	212	71	Spaulding	Timothy		1		1			1	2					5		
Chelmsford	172	14	Spaulding	Zebul'		1		1			1	2		1			6		
Chelmsford	172	15	Spaulding	Zebul' Jr	2			1		1			1				5		
Watertown	234	30	Spear	Francis	1			1		1			1	1			5		
Cambridge	228	18	Spooner	Andrew		1		1	1	1	3	1					8		
Malden	97	2	Sprague	Cotton		1		1		3			1				6		
Littleton	203	11	Sprague	Hezekiah	1			1						1			3		
Bedford	163	21	Sprague	John	1	1	1	1	1	3	2	1	1	1			13		
Malden	96	45	Sprague	John	2	1	1		1	1		1	1				8		
Malden	97	5	Sprague	John Jr			1										1		
Malden	97	3	Sprague	Jona	1	2		1		3	1		1				9		
Charlestown	90	14	Sprague	Jos'			1	1					1	2			5		
Billerica	178	17	Sprague	Levi		1		1		3	1		1				7		

TOWN	PG#	LN#	LAST NAME	FIRST NAME	under 10	10 to 16	16 to 26	26 to 45	45 and over	under 10	10 to 16	16 to 26	26 to 45	45 and over	TOTAL ALL OTHER	TOTAL SLAVES	TOTALS	DISTRICT/ TOWNSHIP	NOTES
			HEADS OF HOUSEHOLD		FREE WHITE MALES					FREE WHITE FEMALES									
Billerica	178	18	Sprague	Mary	1					1	1		1				4		
Malden	96	46	Sprague	Phins				1					1				2		
Malden	97	1	Sprague	Phins Jr	1		1	1		2	1	1		2			9		
Charlestown	90	13	Sprague	Saml	2			1		1		1	1				6		
Stoneham	139	37	Sprague	Samuel				1				1		1			3		
Malden	97	4	Sprague	Step'	4			1		1	1		1				8		
Weston	110	27	Spring	Amasa				1			1			1			3		
Watertown	234	5	Spring	Marshall	2		1	1					3	2			9		
Hopkinton	244	8	Spring	Thadeus	2			1					2				5		
Ashby	37	31	Sta*	Abel	1	2		1		1			1				6		
Weston	110	11	Stack	John	2	1	1		1	2	2	1	1				11		
Wilmington	143	28	Stanly	Abraham	4			1					1				6		
Wilmington	143	27	Stanly	Elijah		1		1					1				3		
Wilmington	143	29	Stanly	Jonathan					1			1		1			3		
Charlestown	90	38	Stanton	John					1				1	1			3		
Weston	110	8	Starr	Abigail		1							1	2			4		
Newton	124	15	Starr	Ebenezer	1					2			1				5		
Weston	110	7	Starr	Josiah		1	1	1					1				4		
Tewksbury	53	10	Staton	Benja				1		1	1		1				4		
Weston	110	28	Stearns	*	1	1		1		3			1				7		
Lexington	159	30	Stearns	Asahel	4	3	1		1	1	1	1	1				13		Joel Smith included on line
Lexington	160	2	Stearns	Benjamin			2	1		2			1				6		
Lincoln	15	2	Stearns	Charles	2	2			2	2	2	1	1	1			13		
Weston	110	10	Stearns	Charles	3		1	2		1			1	1			9		
Waltham	115	21	Stearns	Daniel	1			1					1	1			4		
Waltham	115	24	Stearns	David	2	3	4	2					1	1			13		
Watertown	234	6	Stearns	David				1		2	1	2	1				7		
Bedford	163	19	Stearns	Elijah		1		2					1	1			5		
Billerica	178	1	Stearns	Elijah				1		1			1				3		
Watertown	234	29	Stearns	George	4		1	1		1		1		1			9		
Billerica	178	4	Stearns	Isaac				1					1	1			3		
Lexington	160	3	Stearns	Isaac	3		1	1		1		1		1			8		
Billerica	178	3	Stearns	Isachar	2		1	1		2			1				7		
Waltham	115	28	Stearns	Ismael	1			1		1			1	1			5		
Weston	110	6	Stearns	Jepthah		1	1						1	1			4		
Billerica	178	6	Stearns	John			1										1		
Chelmsford	172	37	Stearns	John	2			1		1			1				5		
Framingham	74	10	Stearns	John				1									1		
Waltham	116	7	Stearns	John	3		1	1		2	1	1					9		
Billerica	178	8	Stearns	Jona	3			1		1			1				6		
Hopkinton	244	6	Stearns	Jona	2	3		1		2	2		1				11		
Waltham	116	2	Stearns	Jonathan	3	2	1		1	1	1	2	1				12		
Billerica	178	7	Stearns	Joseph	2	1		1		2			1				7		
Waltham	115	22	Stearns	Joseph			1						1				2		
Waltham	116	3	Stearns	Joshua	1				1	3	2	2		1			10		
Waltham	115	27	Stearns	Juda			1	1				3	2	1			8		
Newton	124	13	Stearns	Luther	8	10	2	1		1		1	3	1			27		
Boxborough	200	37	Stearns	Miriam						1				1			2		
Weston	110	24	Stearns	Nathan	2				1	2				1			6		
Carlisle	21	19	Stearns	Nathaniel	2				1	2			1				6		
Concord	5	3	Stearns	Peter	1			⊥		3			1				6		
Billerica	178	2	Stearns	Saml					1				1	2			4		
Bedford	163	17	Stearns	Samuel			1			1			4		1	1	8		
Waltham	116	5	Stearns	Samuel		1	1	1					3		1		7		
Waltham	116	8	Stearns	Samuel Jr	1			1					1				3		
Waltham	116	1	Stearns	Silas			2	1					1	1			5		
Weston	110	14	Stearns	Silas	1			1					1	1			4		
Cambridge	228	28	Stearns	Stephen	1	1		1						1			4		
Waltham	116	6	Stearns	Thomas	1		1						1				3		
Ashby	37	30	Stearns	Thos				1						1			2		
Billerica	178	5	Stearns	Timo'	2	1							1				5		
Framingham	72	32	Stearns	Timothy				2						1			3		Stamped pg# was x'd out
Framingham	73	1	Stearns	Timothy 3	2			1		2			1				6		
Framingham	72	31	Stearns	Timothy Jr				1			1			1			3		Stamped pg# was x'd out
Concord	6	34	Stebins	John				1		1		1					3		
Cambridge	228	20	Stedman	Ebenz	1	1	1	1	1	1		3		1			10		
Hollistown	239	14	Stedman	John			2	1			2			1			6		
Woburn	152	10	Steel	James		1	2	1		1		1	1	1			8		
Weston	110	12	Steoman	Hannah	1			1				1		1			4		
Stoneham	139	36	Stephens	John H	1	1		1		3			1				7		
Hopkinton	244	19	Stepherd	Timothy		1		1	1	3	2		2				10		
Cambridge	228	15	Sterley	Saml M.				1					1				2		
Charlestown	90	43	Stetson	David	1	1	9	2		1		1	2				17		
Charlestown	90	44	Stetson	Jos'	2		1	2				1	1				7		
Chelmsford	172	32	Stevens	Abel			1										1		
Dracut	48	8	Stevens	Benja	1	2			1	3	1		1				9		
Boxborough	200	20	Stevens	Benjamin	2	1	1		1	1	1		1				8		
Sudbury	60	29	Stevens	Benjm		1	1			1		1					4		
Westford	184	2	Stevens	Bill W.	2			1		1				1			5		
Marlborough	190	36	Stevens	Daniel		1		1		2		3		1			8		

TOWN	PG#	LN#	LAST NAME	FIRST NAME	FREE WHITE MALES under 10	10 to 16	16 to 26	26 to 45	45 and over	FREE WHITE FEMALES under 10	10 to 16	16 to 26	26 to 45	45 and over	TOTAL ALL OTHER	TOTAL SLAVES	TOTALS	DISTRICT/ TOWNSHIP	NOTES
Marlborough	189	38	Stevens	Daniel Jr	1		1	1		1		1	1				6		
Charlestown	90	20	Stevens	Eliza'								2	1	1			4		
Marlborough	187	6	Stevens	Francis			2		2	1	1			1			7		
Burlington	155	22	Stevens	Jedidiah			3			1		1					5		
Dunstable	217	45	Stevens	Jesse	2		1	1		1			1				6		
Charlestown	90	19	Stevens	John	4	2	1	1				1		1			10		
Townsend	28	39	Stevens	John		2		1		1		1					5		
Groton	212	68	Stevens	Jona	1			1		3	1		1				7		
Townsend	28	26	Stevens	Jona		1			1			2		1			5		
Chelmsford	172	36	Stevens	Jona'	1				1	1	1		1				5		
Pepperell	32	45	Stevens	Joseph	1		2					1					4		
Dunstable	217	47	Stevens	Josiah		3	1			3		1	1				9		
Chelmsford	172	34	Stevens	Lampron	1			1		3			1				6		
Dunstable	217	46	Stevens	Parker		1		1				1	1				4		
Charlestown	90	21	Stevens	Pelet'	2		1			2		1					6		
Chelmsford	172	35	Stevens	Saml		1	1	1		1			1				5		
Dunstable	217	44	Stevens	Saml Capt.			2		1		1		1				5		
Chelmsford	172	33	Stevens	Simeon		1			1	3			1				6		
Pepperell	32	44	Stevens	Simon	3		1	1					1	1			7		
Townsend	28	14	Stevens	Solo		1			1					1			3		
Townsend	28	15	Stevens	Solo Jr	2	1		1					1				5		
Tyngsborough	43	24	Stewart	Robert		1		1		1				1			4		
Tewksbury	53	3	Stickney	Abran		1	1			1		1			1		5		
Tewksbury	53	15	Stickney	Amos	2			1		1		1					5		
Tewksbury	53	4	Stickney	Eleazer		2		1		1		1		1			6		
Billerica	177	42	Stickney	Jona'		1		1				1	2				5		
Townsend	28	37	Stickney	Joseph	1			1		2		1					5		
Charlestown	90	11	Stimpson	Andri'	2		1		1	2	1	1					8		
Hopkinton	244	11	Stimpson	Ebenz	1		4					1	1				8		
Hopkinton	244	4	Stimpson	Jeremh	1	1	1		1	3	1		1		1		10		
Watertown	234	20	Stimpson	John	1			1		1		1					4		
Watertown	234	31	Stimpson	John	1			1		1		1					4		
Hopkinton	244	10	Stimpson	Saml		1		1		2	2		2				8		
Newton	124	3	Stimpson	Samuel	1	1	2	2			1	1	1				9		
Shirley	215	32	Stimpson	Stephen	1	1	2		1	2	1	1		1			10		
Reading	136	6	Stimpson	Thomas					1								1		
Reading	136	7	Stimpson	Thomas Jr	3			1				1					5		
Reading	136	15	Stimpson	William	1				1				2				4		
Reading	136	16	Stimpson	William Jr	3			1	1	1			2				8		
Charlestown	90	12	Stimpson	Wm	1	1			1	2			1				6		
Hopkinton	244	9	Stimpson	Saml Jr	3		1			2			1				7		
Weston	110	9	Stimson	James		1		1		1			1				4		
Westford	184	3	Stoddard	Ann									1				1		
East Sudbury	68	18	Stone	Aaron	1		1					1					3		
Watertown	234	9	Stone	Abijah		1			1	5	2			3			12		
Framingham	73	5	Stone	Abner	1		2		1		1		1	1			7		
Groton	212	47	Stone	Amos	1	2	1		1	2	1	2		1			11		
Framingham	73	7	Stone	Benjamin			1					1					2		
Framingham	73	9	Stone	Daniel			1				1		1				3		
Framingham	73	10	Stone	Daniel Jr	1			1		2	1		1	2			8		
Newton	124	7	Stone	David				1				1	1				4		
Watertown	234	13	Stone	David		1	2						1	1			5		
Townsend	28	12	Stone	Ebenz	1			1	1	2	2		1				8		
Reading	135	34	Stone	Eliab Jr	2		1	1		2	1		1	1			9		
Reading	135	33	Stone	Eliab Rev	1	1		1	1			1		1	1		7		
Framingham	77	9	Stone	Elijah		1	2	1		1	2	1	1				9		
Lincoln	14	3	Stone	Gregory	1			1		4	1	1					8		
Framingham	77	11	Stone	Isaac		1	2		1	1	2			1			8		
East Sudbury	68	19	Stone	Isabel	2	1	1	1		1			1	2			9		
Hollistown	239	7	Stone	James	1	1		1		1		2	1				7		
Newton	124	6	Stone	James		2	1	1		1		3	2				10		
Charlestown	90	45	Stone	John	1	2		1		2		2	2				10		
East Sudbury	68	17	Stone	John				2				2		1			5		
Hollistown	239	10	Stone	John		1			1				1	1			4		
Hopkinton	244	5	Stone	John	1	2	1	1		1	3		1				10		
Newton	124	5	Stone	John			1	1				2		1			5		
Ashby	37	32	Stone	John E.	3	1		1					1				6		
East Sudbury	68	26	Stone	John Jr	3	1	2	1		1	1	2	3				14		
Hollistown	239	12	Stone	John Jr			1						1				2		
Ashby	37	29	Stone	John L.	1		1						1				3		
Groton	212	45	Stone	Jona	1				1			1		1			4		
Watertown	234	8	Stone	Jona	2	2	4		1	2	1	1	1	1			15		
Groton	212	46	Stone	Jonas		1			1			2		2			6		
Lexington	159	32	Stone	Jonas		1			1	1				2			5		
Newton	124	10	Stone	Jonas		1			1	1				2			5		
Newton	124	11	Stone	Jonas Jr		1			1					2			5		
Groton	212	51	Stone	Joseph	1		2						1				4		
Weston	110	5	Stone	Joseph	1			1		2		1		1			6		
Ashby	37	33	Stone	Josh	2			1		2			1				6		
Concord	5	11	Stone	Joshua	2				1	1			1				5		

TOWN	PG#	LN#	LAST NAME	FIRST NAME	FREE WHITE MALES under 10	10 to 16	16 to 26	26 to 45	45 and over	FREE WHITE FEMALES under 10	10 to 16	16 to 26	26 to 45	45 and over	TOTAL ALL OTHER	TOTAL SLAVES	TOTALS	DISTRICT/ TOWNSHIP	NOTES
Framingham	73	8	Stone	Josiah	1	2	1	1		2	1		1	1			10		
Groton	212	44	Stone	Levi	2	2			1	1	1	3	1	1			12		
Concord	3	15	Stone	Martha		1		1				4		2	1		9		
Cambridge	228	10	Stone	Mary	1					3	3	1		3	1		12		
Framingham	73	6	Stone	Micah		1			1		1			1			4		
Newton	124	8	Stone	Moses	3	1		1		2		1	1				9		
Sudbury	59	34	Stone	Moses	2	1	1		1				2	2			9		
Watertown	234	10	Stone	Moses	2	2	2		1	1	2			1			11		
Groton	212	53	Stone	Natha Wid.							1			1			2		
Watertown	234	11	Stone	Nathl	2	1	1	1		2	1		1				9		
Framingham	73	4	Stone	Peggy							1		1				2		
Townsend	28	22	Stone	Peter	1	3			1	3			1				7		
East Sudbury	68	20	Stone	Purchas	1	1		1		2			1				6		
Framingham	78	5	Stone	Rebeckah		1	1						1	1			4		
Ashby	37	34	Stone	Saml					1					1			2		
Natick	247	38	Stone	Saml					1	1		1					3		
Townsend	28	32	Stone	Saml		1			1	1	2	2	1				8		
Lexington	159	31	Stone	Samuel	3	1		1					1				6		
Boxborough	200	21	Stone	Silas		1	2		1		1	2	2	1			10		
Sherburn	251	20	Stone	Silas	5	1			1	1	2	1	1				12		
Stow	196	18	Stone	Stephen					1					1			2		
Framingham	73	17	Stone	Thomas Jr	3			1	1	1			1				7		
Newton	124	12	Stone	Timothy		2	1	1		1		1					6		
Natick	247	35	Stone	Wm	1	1	1			3	1	3		1			11		
Watertown	234	7	Stone	Wm	1	1	1		1	4	2	1	1				12		
Framingham	73	3	Stones	Thomas					1					2			3		
Cambridge	228	29	Storier	Charles	1	1		1		1	1		1				6		
Marlborough	194	13	Stow	Abraham	2	1			1	2	1			1			9		
Marlborough	192	19	Stow	Hannah		1						1	1				3		
Marlborough	193	22	Stow	Heman	1		2		1	1	1	2		1			9		
Stow	196	19	Stow	Ichabod	3	1	2	1		1		1	1				10		
Marlborough	194	16	Stow	Jabez Jr			1	1		2			1				5		
Marlborough	191	40	Stow	Joab		1	2	2		1	1	1					8		
Concord	4	12	Stow	Joseph					1					1			2		
Marlborough	194	15	Stow	Josiah					1					1			2		
Concord	4	33	Stow	Nathan		1			1			2		2			6		
Marlborough	194	7	Stow	Samuel					1					1			2		
Reading	136	10	Stowel	Eli*	1	2			1					1			5		
Marlborough	195	3	Straten	Moses			1			1			1				3		
Cambridge	228	8	Straton	Nathan				1					1				2		
Natick	247	40	Stratten	Abijah		1	1		1				2				6		
Natick	247	37	Stratten	Daniel	2				1	2	1			1			7		
Natick	247	32	Stratten	Elijah	1	1			1	3	1		1				8		
Natick	247	31	Stratten	James	1			1		1		1					4		
Natick	247	33	Stratten	Saml	1		1	1	1	1	1		1				7		
Sherburn	251	16	Stratton	Abijah	1	1	1						1				4		
Weston	110	21	Stratton	Daniel	1	1	1		1	3		2		1			10		
Weston	110	18	Stratton	Elisha	3	1				1	1	1		1			9		
Concord	5	2	Stratton	Elizabeth									1	1			2		
Weston	110	19	Stratton	Isaac	3	1			1	3	1						9		
Weston	110	20	Stratton	John		1	1	1	1	1			1				6		
Sherburn	251	18	Stratton	Nathan		1		1					1				3		
Sherburn	251	19	Stratton	Nathan Jr	3			1		2	1	1					8		
Watertown	234	23	Studson	Ebenz				1					1				2		
Reading	136	17	Swain	Benjamin	2		1	1					2				6		
Reading	136	22	Swain	Hannah							1			1			2		
Reading	135	31	Swain	John	1	2	5		2	2	2	1	2	1			18		
Reading	136	29	Swain	John Jr	1		1				1		1				4		
Reading	135	32	Swain	Oliver	4			1			1		1				7		
Reading	136	19	Swain	Thomas				1		1			1				3		
Reading	136	2	Swain	Thomas Jr			1						1	1			3		
Tewksbury	53	13	Swain	Walter	1			1		1			1				4		
Dunstable	217	41	Swallow	Abraham	2	1		1		2			1				7		
Dunstable	217	36	Swallow	Amiziah		1			1		1			1			4		
Dunstable	217	40	Swallow	Asa	2		1	1		2			2				8		
Dunstable	217	37	Swallow	Benjm			1	1				1	1	1			5		
Dunstable	217	39	Swallow	Jonas	1			1		3	1		1				7		
Dunstable	217	38	Swallow	Peter	1		1				1	1		1			6		
Groton	212	52	Swallow	Rachel Wid.						3			1				4		
Tyngsborough	43	20	Swan	Benja		1		1				1		1			4		
Charlestown	90	25	Swan	Benja B.	1		1					1					3		
Woburn	152	12	Swan	Caleb	1		2		1	2	1	1					8		
Cambridge	228	12	Swan	Ebenz	1			1					1	1			4		
Cambridge	228	6	Swan	George	1	1	1		1	1		1	2				9		
Cambridge	228	13	Swan	Gershom	2		3	1		2	2		1				11		
Charlestown	90	28	Swan	John		1	3		1		1	1		1			8		
Lexington	160	1	Swan	Joshua								1	2	1			4		
Charlestown	90	24	Swan	Saml		1		1						1			3		
Medford	102	18	Swan	Saml		3	2		1		1	2	2				11		
Charlestown	90	26	Swan	Saml Jr			1					1					2		

215

TOWN	PG#	LN#	LAST NAME	FIRST NAME	FREE WHITE MALES under 10	10 to 16	16 to 26	26 to 45	45 and over	FREE WHITE FEMALES under 10	10 to 16	16 to 26	26 to 45	45 and over	TOTAL ALL OTHER	TOTAL SLAVES	TOTALS	DISTRICT/ TOWNSHIP	NOTES
Cambridge	228	7	Swan	Sarah	1								1	1			3		
Charlestown	90	27	Swan	Tho'	1		1			1		1					4		
Cambridge	228	11	Swan	Timf	4			2		1			1				8		
Cambridge	228	9	Swaney	Willm			1	1			2	1		1			6		
Reading	136	14	Sweet	Phinehas		1	1	1			2		1	1			7		
Reading	136	18	Sweetser	Cornelius	1	1	1		1		1			1			6		
Reading	136	8	Sweetser	Daniel	2		1	1		2		2	1				9		
Reading	136	24	Sweetser	Ezra	2		1					1		1			5		
Reading	136	9	Sweetser	John		1	1	1	1	1		1	2	1			9		
Reading	136	13	Sweetser	Mary										2			2		
Reading	136	25	Sweetser	Moses	2			1					2				5		
Reading	136	11	Sweetser	Paul	1		3		1	2	2		1				10		
Reading	136	23	Sweetser	Thomas	3	1			1				1	1			7		
Reading	136	31	Sweetser	Timothy			1		1	1			2				4		
Charlestown	90	36	Sweetsin	Benja					1			1		1			3		
Charlestown	90	33	Sweetsin	Caleb			2			1	1		1				5		
Charlestown	90	34	Sweetsin	Jos'	1	1		1		3	1			1			8		
Charlestown	90	37	Sweetsin	Pheebe							1	1					2		
Charlestown	90	35	Sweetsin	Richd	2		1					1		1			5		
Malden	97	18	Sweetsir	James	1			1		1		1		1			5		
Stow	198	15	Swift	Luther	1		1						1				3		
Townsend	28	18	Sylvester	Caleb	2	3	1		1	1			2		1		11		
Medford	102	16	Symmes	Danl'			2										2		
Medford	102	13	Symmes	Jno'	4	2	1	1		1	1		1				11		
Medford	102	14	Symmes	Josiah					1								1		
Woburn	152	16	Symmes	Samuel	1	2	2		1	1				1			8		
Billerica	178	16	Symmes	Steph'		1			1					1			3		
Medford	102	15	Symmes	Timo'			1	1					2				4		
Woburn	152	17	Symmes	William		1		1		1		1					4		
Woburn	152	15	Symmes	Zachariah			1	1				1		1			4		
Tewksbury	53	5	Symmon	Wm	2			2	2	2	3	2		2			15		
Groton	212	40	Symms	Caleb	2	1		1		2	1		1	1			9		
Medford	102	6	Symonds	Danl'	2			1		1			1				5		
Medford	102	8	Symonds	Eben	2		1		1	1	2		1				8		
Sudbury	60	25	Symonds	John	2			1		2			1				6		
Charlestown	91	6	Symonds	Jos'	2			1					1				4		
Medford	102	9	Symonds	Joshua		1			1	1	2			1			6		
Medford	102	7	Symonds	Jude					1	1	2	1					5		
Charlestown	90	30	Symonds	Silas	1			1					1				3		
Reading	136	3	Symonds	Thomas		1	1		1	1		1	1	1			7		
Charlestown	90	29	Symonds	Wm	1	2	1						1				5		
Watertown	234	34	Tainter	Benjm	2	2			1	2	1		1				9		
Cambridge	228	34	Tapley	Isaac	2			1					1				4		
Charlestown	91	33	Taply	John	1		1						1				3		
Cambridge	228	36	Tappan	David	1	2	1		1	2			1	1			9		
Groton	212	81	Tarbell	Benjm		1		1				1		1			4		
Pepperell	33	16	Tarbell	David				1						1			2		
Pepperell	33	17	Tarbell	David Jr	1			1		1			1				4		
Groton	212	80	Tarbell	Eben				1		2	1		1				5		
Pepperell	33	14	Tarbell	James			1		1			1		1			4		
Groton	212	82	Tarbell	John		1	1	2	1			1	1	1			8		
Groton	212	84	Tarbell	Mary Wid.		1				2			1				4		
Groton	212	85	Tarbell	Nehh				1				1		1			3		
Pepperell	33	20	Tarbell	Sewall				1					1				2		
Groton	212	78	Tarbell	Solomon	1			1		1			2				5		
Groton	212	79	Tarbell	Thomas		1		1	1	2	1		1				7		
Groton	212	83	Tarbell	Wm	1	1	1	1		3			1				8		
Pepperell	33	15	Tarbell	Wm		1	2		1	1	1			1			7		
Westford	184	8	Tarble	Abijah	2	1	1	1		1			1				7		
Westford	184	7	Tarble	Saml				1	1	1			1	1			4		
Billerica	178	23	Tarble	Wm	1		1		1	1		1		1			6		
Billerica	178	24	Tarble	Wm Jr			1										1		
Townsend	29	39	Tarbox	Daniel				1				1		1			3		
Woburn	152	36	Tay	Comfort	2					2			1				5		
Woburn	152	25	Tay	John	3	1		1		1		1					7		
Woburn	152	22	Tay	Joshua	1		1	1	1	1		1	1	1			8		
Reading	137	4	Tay	Nathaniel	1	1		1					1				4		
Woburn	152	24	Tay	Samuel		1	2	1				1		1			6		
Woburn	152	21	Tay	William	1		1	1					2	3			8		
Burlington	155	35	Tay	Isaiah	1			1					1				3		
Sudbury	57	3	Tayler	John	1		1	1		1			1				5		
Ashby	36	9	Taylor	Abel		1		1		2			1				5		
Carlisle	22	19	Taylor	Abel				1				1		1			3		
Stow	197	20	Taylor	Abel		1		1	1			1	1	1			6		
Stow	197	31	Taylor	Abigail				1						2			3		
Carlisle	22	18	Taylor	Abraham	1	1		1		1			2				6		
Ashby	37	46	Taylor	Abram					1			1	1	2			5		
Dunstable	217	48	Taylor	David			1	1					1	1			4		
Marlborough	193	3	Taylor	David	1					1		1					3		
Littleton	205	12	Taylor	Elizabeth									1				1		
Boxborough	200	16	Taylor	Ephraim		1	1		1			1		1			5		

TOWN	PG#	LN#	LAST NAME	FIRST NAME	FREE WHITE MALES					FREE WHITE FEMALES					TOTAL ALL OTHER	TOTAL SLAVES	TOTALS	DISTRICT/ TOWNSHIP	NOTES
					under 10	10 to 16	16 to 26	26 to 45	45 and over	under 10	10 to 16	16 to 26	26 to 45	45 and over					
Boxborough	200	24	Taylor	Hezekiah			1					1					2		
Dracut	48	13	Taylor	Isaac	5			1		1		1					8		
Boxborough	199	2	Taylor	Israel	1	1		1		1	1	1	1				8		
Reading	137	5	Taylor	James	1		1				1	3		1			7		
Burlington	155	33	Taylor	John	1		1						1				3		
Dracut	48	14	Taylor	John	1				1	1		1	1	1			6		
Marlborough	190	18	Taylor	John	2			1					2				5		
Dunstable	217	49	Taylor	Jonas		1						1	1				4		
Reading	137	6	Taylor	Joseph			1				1		1				3		
Boxborough	200	23	Taylor	Mary										1			1		
Cambridge	229	3	Taylor	Mical	1		1	1					1				4		
Boxborough	200	22	Taylor	Oliver	1		2		1	1				1			6		
Stow	196	9	Taylor	Paul	1		1			3			1				6		
Billerica	178	29	Taylor	Richd			1						1				2		
Townsend	28	40	Taylor	Robert	2	2		1		2			1				8		
Boxborough	199	1	Taylor	Silas	1	1	1	1			1	2		1			8		
Stow	196	8	Taylor	William			1	1		4	1		1				7		
Charlestown	91	41	Taylor	Wm	2		1					1	1				5		
Marlborough	191	28	Tayntor	John	3			1			2		1				7		
Marlborough	192	6	Tayntor	Jonathan				1				1		1			3		
Marlborough	192	7	Tayntor	Joseph			1					1					2		
Medford	102	21	Teal	Benja		1		1		2	2		1				7		
Charlestown	91	30	Teal	Blany	3			1				1	1				6		
Medford	102	22	Teal	Gershom	3	1	1	1		3	1	2	1				13		
Charlestown	91	31	Teal	Jona'	3	1	1		1	1	1	2	1				11		
Medford	102	20	Teal	Saml		1		1				1		1			4		
Hopkinton	244	26	Temple	Abner	1	3		1		2	1		1				9		
Concord	7	32	Temple	Benjamin				1			1		1				3		
Reading	137	3	Temple	Daniel	1	1	1	1		2			2	1			9		
Marlborough	187	19	Temple	David		1		2	1		1		1				6		
Marlborough	193	32	Temple	Isaac			1				1		1				3		
Reading	137	2	Temple	Jabez	1		1			3	2	1					8		
Marlborough	194	38	Temple	John	2		2		1	2	2	1		1			11		
Reading	136	33	Temple	John	1			1				1	1				4		
Marlborough	194	25	Temple	John Jr		1		1	1				1				4		
Reading	136	34	Temple	John Jr	2		2	1		2	1	1					9		
Marlborough	194	21	Temple	Jonas			1		2	1	1	2		1			8		
Reading	136	35	Temple	Jonathan	1			1		3			1				6		
Framingham	77	14	Temple	Josiah		2	1	1	1		1	1		1			8		
Marlborough	194	22	Temple	Moses	2			1		1		1					5		
Concord	7	31	Temple	Peter	2	1	2		1		1	1					9		
Reading	137	1	Temple	Richard	1		1						1				3		
Acton	19	15	Temple	Samuel	3			1		1	2		1				8		
Marlborough	194	29	Temple	Silas		1	1			3		1	1				7		
Reading	136	32	Temple	William	1			1	1			1		2			6		
Littleton	204	33	Tenney	Cheney				1					1	1			3		
Littleton	203	34	Tenney	John	1		1	1		3			1				7		
Littleton	204	4	Tenney	Stephen	2			2		1			2				7		
Littleton	204	5	Tenney	William				1						1			2		
Hollistown	239	15	Thair	Elim			2		1		1	3		1			8		
Cambridge	228	35	Thatcher	Mary			1			1		3		1			6		
Hopkinton	244	21	Thayer	Araba		1		1			1	1					4		
Newton	124	21	Thayer	Eleazer	1			1		2				1			5		
Dracut	46	1	Thayer	Elizabeth	2			1		1		1					5		
Cambridge	228	31	Thayer	Richard	1		1	1		1			1				5		
Charlestown	91	37	Thayer	Zenas			1										1		
Dracut	48	35	Thissell	Joshua	3			1					2	1			7		
East Sudbury	68	23	Thomas	Josiah	1	1	1	1	2		1		1	2			10		
Acton	16	12	Thomas	Sarah	1						1		1				3		
East Sudbury	66	1	Thompson	Abel	2			1		2	2		1				8		
Woburn	152	30	Thompson	Abijah		1	2	1	1		2			1			8		
Woburn	152	31	Thompson	Abijah Jr	3			1		1	1		1				7		
Tyngsborough	43	29	Thompson	Asa		1				1	1		1				5		
Wilmington	143	30	Thompson	Benjamen				1			1		1				3		
Wilmington	144	3	Thompson	Benjamen Jr	3	1	1	1		1	1		1				9		
Wilmington	144	1	Thompson	Ebenezer				1		1	1	1	1				5		
Cambridge	228	30	Thompson	Ebenz	1		1	1		1	1	1	1				7		
Tyngsborough	43	28	Thompson	Ezra		1		1	1	2	1		1	1			8		
Woburn	152	28	Thompson	Hiram	1			1		1	1		1				4		
Charlestown	91	42	Thompson	Hugh	2		1	1					1				5		
Woburn	152	29	Thompson	Jaber	1			1						1			3		
Sudbury	59	18	Thompson	James	2			1	1	1			2				7		
Woburn	152	27	Thompson	Jonathan	1	1	1	1		3			1				8		
Dracut	45	18	Thompson	Leonard		1		1		1		1					4		
Woburn	152	32	Thompson	Leonard	2	1		1		1	1		1				7		
Tyngsborough	43	27	Thompson	Nathan	1				1				2	1			5		
Medford	103	4	Thompson	Saml		1	1			1	1		2	1			7		
Tewksbury	53	21	Thompson	Samll	3			1		2			1				7		
Woburn	152	26	Thompson	Samuel		1			1		1		1	1			5		
Charlestown	91	39	Thompson	Timo'	3		4		1	2	2			1			13		
Charlestown	91	40	Thompson	Timo' Jr	2		2						2				6		

217

TOWN	PG#	LN#	HEADS OF HOUSEHOLD		FREE WHITE MALES					FREE WHITE FEMALES					TOTAL ALL OTHER	TOTAL SLAVES	TOTALS	DISTRICT/ TOWNSHIP	NOTES
			LAST NAME	FIRST NAME	under 10	10 to 16	16 to 26	26 to 45	45 and over	under 10	10 to 16	16 to 26	26 to 45	45 and over					
Billerica	178	22	Thompson	Wm			2		1	1				1			5		
Watertown	234	36	Thompson	Wm	3		1		1	1		1	2				9		
Medford	103	7	Thoring	James				1				1					2		
Tewksbury	53	19	Thorndike	Hezeh	2	2		1		2	1	1	1				10		
Tewksbury	53	18	Thorndike	Paul		1	2		1		2			1			7		
East Sudbury	69	12	Thorning	John	2				1	1				1			5		
Lexington	160	16	Thorning	William	3	2		1		2	1		1				10		
Acton	19	9	Thorpe	Thomas	2	1		1			2		1				7		
Hopkinton	244	24	Tidd	Daniel	1	1	1	1		2		1					7		
Hopkinton	244	25	Tidd	John	2	2			1	1		2	1	1			10		
Lexington	160	14	Tidd	John		1	1		1	1		2					6		
Westford	184	6	Tidd	John	3	1			1			1		1			7		
Woburn	152	33	Tidd	Jonathan	1	1		1				1	1				5		
Bedford	163	24	Tidd	Samuel				1					1	1			3		
Woburn	152	34	Tidd	Samuel	1	2		1				1	1				6		
Lexington	160	15	Tidd	William				1						1			2		
Cambridge	229	1	Tiliston	Josiah		2							1				3		
Hopkinton	244	23	Tilton	Abrm	1		1	1	1	2	1	1	1	1			10		
East Sudbury	68	21	Tilton	John			2		1		1	1	1	2			8		
East Sudbury	69	1	Tilton	John Jr		1	3						1	1			6		
East Sudbury	68	22	Tilton	Samuel	1		1	1						1			4		
Acton	16	32	Tinney	Peter	1	1		1		1		1					5		
Hopkinton	244	29	Titus	Primas											3		3		
Malden	97	27	Todd	Joshua		1											1		
Marlborough	193	14	Toflin	Thomas				1		1				2			4		
Lincoln	12	6	Toleman	Elisha	1		3	1		1			1	1			8		
Medford	103	6	Toleman	Nath'	1			1					1				3		
Newton	124	16	Tolman	Thomas				1						1			2		
Framingham	77	15	Tombs	Nathan	1			1		2			1				5		
Framingham	77	17	Torry	Reuben				1			1		1				3		
Woburn	152	35	Tottingham	Elisha					3					5			8		
Sudbury	61	8	Tower	Abel	1	1	1	1		2		1	1	2			10		
Stow	198	37	Tower	Augustus	1		1	1		2		1	1	1			8		
Lincoln	14	32	Tower	Daniel				1					1				2		
Concord	11	24	Tower	Elizabeth										2			2		
Lincoln	14	36	Tower	Jonathan	3			1		1			1				6		
Newton	124	17	Tower	Jonathan	2				1	1			1				5		
Framingham	77	16	Tower	Joseph					1			1		2			4		
Carlisle	21	3	Tower	Sarah	2					2			1	1			6		
Sudbury	61	7	Tower	Silas	2	1		1		3	2		1				10		
Waltham	116	13	Townsend	David		2	4	2	1	3	3		2				17		
Malden	97	24	Townsend	Eben		1											1		
Malden	97	26	Townsend	Esther								1		1			2		
Charlestown	91	32	Townsend	Ezra			1			2		1					4		
Medford	103	5	Townsend	Jethro		2	1			1							4		
Malden	97	25	Townsend	John	1			1		3	1		1				7		
Marlborough	194	37	Townsend	Joseph			1		1		1		1	2			6		
Cambridge	229	4	Townsend	Saml		1			1	1				1			4		
Charlestown	91	12	Townsend	Saml			1	1		1			2				5		
Weston	110	34	Townsend	Tho. H.			1	1		2	1	1	1		1		8		
Hopkinton	244	28	Townsend	Timothy	1	1		1	1	2		1	2	1			10		
Weston	110	33	Train	Arthur	1	1		1		1			1				5		
Weston	110	31	Train	Enoch	1	1		2		1	1		1				7		
Weston	110	30	Train	Nahum	3		1	1	1	2	1	1	1	1			12		
Weston	110	32	Train	Samuel Jr	3	1	2		1				1	1			9		
Charlestown	91	36	Trask	Isaac				1		1				1			3		
Stow	197	33	Trask	John	2			1		1			1				5		
Charlestown	91	35	Trask	Nath'	2	1	2	1		1		1	1				9		
Natick	247	41	Travis	Daniel	3			1	1				1	2			8		
Natick	247	42	Travis	David		1								2			4		
Weston	111	1	Travis	Elijah	1			1		2	1	1	1				7		
East Sudbury	69	21	Travis	Joel				1		3			1	1			6		
Littleton	202	48	Treadwell	Tane		1						2		1			4		
Malden	97	28	Trevalley	John	3			1					1				5		
Marlborough	192	18	Trobridge	Joseph	1	1		1		2			1				6		
Pepperell	33	19	Trobridge	Thos	1			1		3	1		1				7		
Groton	212	87	Trowbridge	Abigail Wid.	1	2	1	1					1	1			7		
Newton	124	23	Trowbridge	Edmund	2				1				1	1			5		
Framingham	73	11	Trowbridge	John		1		1		1			1				4		
Framingham	73	12	Trowbridge	John Jr	1		1	1					1				4		
Framingham	73	13	Trowbridge	Joshua			1	1		1			1				4		
Newton	124	24	Trowbridge	Saml	2	1			1	2		1	1				8		
Groton	212	88	Trowbridge	Thomas				1		1				1			3		
Billerica	178	28	Trull	David	1			1	1	1	1		1	1			7		
Sudbury	60	19	Trull	David	1			1		2				4			8		
Billerica	178	27	Trull	Elijah	1		1	1					1	1			6		
Charlestown	91	38	Trull	Joel		1											1		
Billerica	178	26	Trull	Saml				1						1			2		
Burlington	155	34	Trull	Soloman			1			3			1				5		
Charlestown	91	43	Trumbal	Fra'								1	1				2		

218

TOWN	PG#	LN#	LAST NAME	FIRST NAME	FREE WHITE MALES under 10	10 to 16	16 to 26	26 to 45	45 and over	FREE WHITE FEMALES under 10	10 to 16	16 to 26	26 to 45	45 and over	TOTAL ALL OTHER	TOTAL SLAVES	TOTALS	DISTRICT/ TOWNSHIP	NOTES
Charlestown	91	13	Trumbal	Richd			1	1	2					1	1		6		
Burlington	155	37	Tu*	Edward		1	1		1	3		1					7		
Burlington	155	36	Tu*	Timothy					1				1				2		
Framingham	77	13	Tucker	Abel			1			1			1				3		
Pepperell	33	18	Tucker	Benja	2		1						1	1			5		
Tewksbury	53	20	Tucker	David	3		1	1		1			1	2			9		
Watertown	234	37	Tucker	John	3	2		1		2	2		1				11		
Sherburn	251	27	Tucker	Wm		2			1			1	1	1			6		
Tewksbury	53	17	Tuell	Jesse	2		1	1		1			1	1			7		
Charlestown	91	19	Tufts	Ammi	1			1		2			1				5		
Charlestown	91	27	Tufts	Amos	2		2	1		2	1		1				9		
Charlestown	91	21	Tufts	Ann									1	1			2		
Groton	212	77	Tufts	Asa	2			1		2	1		1				7		
Medford	102	30	Tufts	Benja'				1					1				2		
Medford	102	31	Tufts	Benja' Jr	2		1	1		1			1				6		
Medford	102	26	Tufts	Cha'				1									1		
Charlestown	91	25	Tufts	Danl		1	3	1				1	1				7		
Malden	97	20	Tufts	David	4	2			1		2		1				10		
Medford	102	41	Tufts	Eben'		1			1				1	1			4		
Groton	212	86	Tufts	Ebrakim	1			1		3	1		1				7		
Medford	102	43	Tufts	Eliza						1				1			2		
Billerica	178	25	Tufts	Geo	1	1		1		3			1				7		
Medford	102	29	Tufts	Gershom	2	1		1		4			1				9		
Medford	102	32	Tufts	Hutch			1		1			2		1			5		
Medford	102	33	Tufts	Hutch Jr	1			1		1			1				4		
Charlestown	91	45	Tufts	Isaac			1	1		2		1					5		
Medford	102	27	Tufts	Isaac			1		1			2		1			5		
Medford	102	38	Tufts	Jacob	3		1	1		1			1				7		
Medford	102	28	Tufts	James		1	1		1	2	2			1			10		
Cambridge	228	33	Tufts	John		1	1			1		1		1			5		
Charlestown	91	22	Tufts	John	2	1	3		1	1		2	2	1			13		
Medford	102	24	Tufts	Jona'	4	1		1					1	1			8		
Charlestown	91	20	Tufts	Jos'	1	2	1	1		4	2		1				12		
Charlestown	91	46	Tufts	Jos'			1			1		1					3		
Medford	102	25	Tufts	Jos'	1		1			1			1				4		
Medford	102	42	Tufts	Jos'	2		1						1				4		
Charlestown	91	28	Tufts	Jos' Jr			1			1			1				3		
Malden	97	22	Tufts	Josiah	1	1		1	2				1				6		
Malden	97	19	Tufts	Mary			2							1			3		
Medford	102	40	Tufts	Mary										1			1		
Medford	102	39	Tufts	Nath			1		1	1				1			4		
Charlestown	91	26	Tufts	Nath'		2	1	1				1	1				6		
Medford	102	23	Tufts	Peter	1	1	1		1	2	1	2	1				10		
Charlestown	91	29	Tufts	Peter Jr	1	1	1			1			1				5		
Charlestown	91	47	Tufts	Saml		1			1			1	2	1			6		
Malden	97	23	Tufts	Saml	1	1	1	1		1	2		1				8		
Medford	102	35	Tufts	Saml'					1			1	1				3		
Medford	102	37	Tufts	Saml' 3rd	2				1	2	1			1			7		
Charlestown	91	48	Tufts	Saml' Jr			3			1	1	1					6		
Medford	102	36	Tufts	Saml' Jr		1	2	1		1		1	1				7		
Charlestown	91	24	Tufts	Simon	1			1		3			1				6		
Malden	97	21	Tufts	Step'	1	1			1	1	1		1	1			7		
Cambridge	228	32	Tufts	Stephen	1		1					1					3		
Medford	102	34	Tufts	Tabitha										1			1		
Lexington	160	13	Tufts	Thomas	1	1	1	1		1			1				6		
Charlestown	91	44	Tufts	Timo' Esq					1					1			2		
Charlestown	91	23	Tufts	Timo' Jr	2	2		1		1	1	1					8		
Littleton	203	24	Tulle	Samson					1	2	1	1					5		
Hopkinton	244	22	Tumbs	Joseph	2	1			1	2	2		1				9		
Medford	103	1	Turner	*	1			1					1				3		
Charlestown	91	16	Turner	Barnab		1	1	2			1		1				6		
Charlestown	91	17	Turner	Benja'			1					1					2		
Lincoln	14	34	Turner	Henry	2				1	1				1			5		
Charlestown	92	1	Turner	James	3			1				2	1				7		
Charlestown	91	14	Turner	John					1			2		1			4		
Charlestown	91	15	Turner	John Jr	2	1		2		1	1		1				8		
Concord	6	33	Turner	Joseph			2	1					1				4		
Townsend	29	8	Turner	Luther	1					1	2		1				6		
Charlestown	91	18	Turner	Nath'			1	1		1		1					4		
Townsend	27	35	Turner	Simon		1		1		1		1	1				5		
Concord	5	32	Turner	Thomas	2				1			1	1	2			7		
Littleton	204	22	Tuttle	Daniel	2	1	1		1			1	1				8		
Littleton	204	23	Tuttle	Jeremiah	2		1	1					1				5		
Littleton	201	4	Tuttle	John			1		1	2	2	2	1	1			10		
Medford	103	3	Tuttle	Mary	1								1				2		
Acton	19	37	Tuttle	Samuel			2	1			1		1				5		
Littleton	202	12	Tuttle	Samuel	1	1			1	3		1	1	1			10		
Chelmsford	172	44	Tuttle	Sarah			1					1	1	1			4		
Acton	18	17	Tuttle	Simon	1				1	1				2			5		
Acton	18	18	Tuttle	Simon Jr	4		2	3		1			1	1			12		
Watertown	234	33	Tuttle	Stephen	2			1		3			1				7		
Acton	16	28	Tuttle	Thaddeus	1					1							4		

TOWN	PG#	LN#	LAST NAME	FIRST NAME	FREE WHITE MALES					FREE WHITE FEMALES					TOTAL ALL OTHER	TOTAL SLAVES	TOTALS	DISTRICT/ TOWNSHIP	NOTES
					under 10	10 to 16	16 to 26	26 to 45	45 and over	under 10	10 to 16	16 to 26	26 to 45	45 and over					
Littleton	202	10	Tuttle	William	3	1	2		1	1		3	1				12		
Wilmington	144	2	Tw*	James		1			1				2				4		
Cambridge	228	37	Twing	Amos	1			1		2		1					5		
Newton	124	22	Twing	James	3			1		1	1	1	1	1			9		
Newton	124	19	Twing	John		1	2		1				3	2			9		
Newton	124	20	Twing	John Jr	4		2	1			1		2				10		
Cambridge	229	2	Twing	Nathl	3				1	1	1		1				7		
Newton	124	18	Twing	Nicholas	3	1		1		2			1				8		
Cambridge	228	38	Twing	Thos		1		1					1	1			4		
Watertown	234	35	Twist	Elias	1	1	1	1		2			1				7		
Waltham	116	12	Twist	Timothy	2			1					1				4		
Hopkinton	244	27	Twitchel	Jonas	1	1		1						1			4		
Sherburn	251	29	Twitchell	John	1	1		1	1	1	1		1	1			8		
Sherburn	251	28	Twitchell	Peter	2	1	1	1		1		1	1				8		
Chelmsford	172	43	Tyler	Jos'	4	2	1		1		1		1				10		
Chelmsford	172	41	Tyler	Mary									1	1			2		
Chelmsford	172	42	Tyler	Nathan	5	1	1	1		1	1	1	1				12		
East Sudbury	67	26	Tyler	Othneil	2			1			1		1				5		
Woburn	152	23	Tylor	Jonathan	3		1	1		3	1	2	3				14		
Charlestown	91	34	Tyng	Danl	1			1					1				3		
Medford	103	2	Tysick	Jos'				1		3				1			5		
Tyngsborough	43	31	Underwood	Asa	3			1				1					5		
East Sudbury	69	13	Underwood	Benjm	2			1		2			1				6		
Hopkinton	244	30	Underwood	Daniel	1			1		1			1				4		
East Sudbury	68	29	Underwood	Jona	1		1		1			1	1	1			6		
East Sudbury	68	30	Underwood	Jona Jr	1	1		1		1	1		1				6		
Framingham	73	14	Underwood	Jonas		1		1					1	1			4		
Charlestown	92	4	Underwood	Jos'	1			1					1	1			4		
Concord	5	24	Underwood	Joseph	1			1					1				5		
Lexington	160	18	Underwood	Joseph			3		1		2	2		1			9		
Hollistown	239	16	Underwood	Joshua Jr		1			2	2				1			6		
Lincoln	14	30	Underwood	Moses				1	1	1		1		1			4		
Framingham	73	15	Underwood	Nathan	2			1		2			1	1			7		
Lincoln	13	1	Underwood	Peter	1			1		2			2				6		
Lincoln	13	5	Underwood	Peter				1			1		1				3		
Malden	97	33	Upham	Amos		1	1	1		1			1				5		
Malden	97	34	Upham	Amos Jr	2		1			1							4		
Malden	97	36	Upham	Jesse		1		1					1				3		
Malden	97	30	Upham	Lois									1				1		
Malden	97	32	Upham	Lydia									1				1		
Weston	111	2	Upham	Lydia		2		1				1	1				5		
Weston	111	3	Upham	Martha		1						1	1				3		
Waltham	116	14	Upham	Nathan		1		1		1		1					4		
Malden	97	35	Upham	Saml L.	1		1			1		1					4		
Malden	97	31	Upham	Sarah	1					2			1				4		
Reading	137	14	Upham	Tammey		1							1				2		
Malden	97	29	Upham	Wm		1		1		1	1		1				5		
Reading	137	9	Upton	Amos		1	1	1		1			1				5		
Reading	137	8	Upton	Benjamin		3	1	1				2		1			8		
Reading	137	17	Upton	Benjamin Jr		1		1			1		1	1			5		
Reading	137	7	Upton	Daniel	1	1		1		2			1	2			8		
Reading	137	12	Upton	David	1	1	1	1				1		2			7		
Reading	137	13	Upton	David Jr	1			1		2		1	1		1		7		
Reading	137	15	Upton	Elijah				1					1				2		
Reading	137	10	Upton	Hezekiah		1	1	1					1				5		
Reading	137	16	Upton	Jabez				1					1				2		
Wilmington	144	5	Upton	Jethro			1	1			1		1				4		
Tyngsborough	43	30	Upton	Joseph			1					1	1				3		
Reading	137	11	Upton	Nathaniel	1	2	1		1	3		1	1				10		
Wilmington	144	6	Upton	Raul	1	2		1		2				1			7		
Wilmington	144	4	Upton	Thomas R			2	1				2	1	1			7		
Medford	103	8	Usher	Susan							1		1				2		
Dracut	44	35	Varnum	Daniel	2		1	1		3		1					8		
Dracut	45	17	Varnum	James		1	2		1	1	1	2	1				9		
Pepperell	33	33	Varnum	John		1	1	1		1	1		1				6		
Dracut	44	26	Varnum	Jona			2		1			1		1			5		
Dracut	44	27	Varnum	Jona Jr			1					1					2		
Dracut	47	16	Varnum	Jonas	1	2			1	1	1	1	1				8		
Pepperell	33	32	Varnum	Jonas				1					1				2		
Dracut	45	19	Varnum	Joseph			2			1			1				4		
Dracut	45	21	Varnum	Joseph Brett	1		1				1	1		1			5		
Dracut	44	32	Varnum	Joseph M	2	3	1		1	1		2		1	1		12		
Chelmsford	173	1	Varnum	Lucy						1		1					2		
Dracut	44	1	Varnum	Parker	1	2		2	1	2	2	3			1		14		
Dracut	46	38	Varnum	Prescot	2		1	1	2	4	1		1				12		
Pepperell	33	34	Varnum	Spaulding			1					1					2		
Dracut	44	28	Varnum	Thomas	3	1	1		1	2	2		1	1			12		
Cambridge	229	6	Vaughan	Charles	2			1				2					5		
Townsend	29	4	Verde	George	3			1					1				5		
Charlestown	92	3	Veron	Stephn	2	1		1	1	2		1		1			9		

TOWN	PG#	LN#	LAST NAME	FIRST NAME	FREE WHITE MALES under 10	10 to 16	16 to 26	26 to 45	45 and over	FREE WHITE FEMALES under 10	10 to 16	16 to 26	26 to 45	45 and over	TOTAL ALL OTHER	TOTAL SLAVES	TOTALS	DISTRICT/ TOWNSHIP	NOTES
Waltham	116	16	Viles	Irena	1		1	1			2	1	1				7		
Lexington	160	17	Viles	Joel	1	1	1		1	1	1	2		1			9		
Waltham	116	15	Viles	John	3				1	3	1			1			9		
Watertown	234	38	Villey	Daniel	2			1		2			1				6		
Littleton	203	30	Vinal	Christian		1								1			2		
Watertown	234	39	Vinal	John	2			1		2			1	1			7		
Littleton	203	40	Vinal	Luftanus	1			1					1				3		
Littleton	203	36	Vinal	Melzer	2			1	1	3			1	1			9		
Stoneham	140	4	Vinton	Ezra	2	2			1	2		3	1				11		
Reading	137	18	Vinton	John			1	1				1					3		
Reading	137	19	Vinton	John Jr	1		1			2	1		1				6		
Malden	97	37	Vinton	Mary								1		1			2		
Stoneham	140	2	Vinton	Thomas			1	1						1			3		
Stoneham	140	3	Vinton	Timothy				1			1			1			3		
Watertown	234	40	Vole	Ebenz	2			2		3			1				8		
Hopkinton	244	33	Vollentine	Joseph		1	1			1		1					4		
Hopkinton	244	34	Vollentine	Saml	2	1	1	1		3				1			9		
Hopkinton	244	32	Vollentine	Wm	3	3	1		2			1	3	1			14		
Hopkinton	244	31	Vollentine	Wm Jr	3	1	1						1				6		
Sudbury	61	6	Vorce	Reuben				1						1			2		
Charlestown	92	2	Vose	Danl			1			1		1					3		
Concord	5	9	Vose	John	1	1	1							2			6		
Cambridge	229	5	Vose	Robert	1		3	2		2	1	1	1	1	1		13		
Charlestown	92	20	Wade	Eben			1			2							3		
Woburn	152	37	Wade	Ebenezer			2	1					1				4		
Malden	98	19	Wade	Edw	1		1		1	1		1		1			6		
Malden	98	26	Wade	Fitch			1										1		
Medford	103	33	Wade	John	1		1	1		2	1		1				7		
Woburn	152	38	Wade	Nathaniel	1		1	1		2			1				6		
Malden	97	44	Wait	Aaron	1		1					1					3		
Malden	97	43	Wait	Andr'			1					1					2		
Charlestown	92	19	Wait	Benja'			1										1		
Malden	98	16	Wait	Benja'	1				1	1				2			5		
Malden	98	14	Wait	Danl	1		2	1		1			1				6		
Malden	97	47	Wait	David				1									1		
Malden	98	4	Wait	Eben			1		1			1		1			5		
Malden	98	6	Wait	Ezra			2	1		1				1			5		
Malden	98	15	Wait	Ezra Jr	1	1	1	1		1	1		1				7		
Medford	103	14	Wait	Fra'	1	1		1		1		2					6		
Malden	98	1	Wait	Isaac				1									1		
Medford	103	15	Wait	Jacob		2		1						1			4		
Malden	98	3	Wait	James	2		1						1				4		
Malden	97	40	Wait	Jno' 3rd	1			1		2			1				5		
Malden	97	39	Wait	Jno' Jr				1						1			2		
Malden	97	38	Wait	John				1									1		
Natick	248	3	Wait	John			1			2			1				4		
Malden	98	8	Wait	Mary										1			1		
Malden	98	2	Wait	Micah	1		3		1	1	1			1			8		
Malden	98	13	Wait	Nathn	1		1		1				2	1			6		
Malden	98	7	Wait	Pheebe						2		1					3		
Groton	212	90	Wait	Phinehas		1		1		1			1	1			5		
Malden	98	9	Wait	Ruth										1			1		
Malden	97	41	Wait	Saml				1					1	1			3		
Malden	97	42	Wait	Saml' Jr			1			1	1	1					4		
Malden	98	10	Wait	Sarah										1			1		
Malden	98	11	Wait	Step'			1							1			3		
Malden	98	12	Wait	Step' Jr			1						1				2		
Malden	98	5	Wait	Tho'		1		1				1		1			4		
Malden	97	45	Wait	Wm				1						1			2		
Malden	97	46	Wait	Wm Jr	1					1	2		1				6		
Stow	198	20	Wakefield	Mary										1			1		
Reading	137	23	Wakefield	Timothy		2	1	1		1			1	1			7		
Stow	195	6	Walcutt	Frederick		1		1						1			3		
Stow	195	7	Walcutt	John	1		1	1		1			1				5		
Stow	196	6	Walcutt	Jonathan	2		1	1		1			1		1		7		
Stow	195	2	Walcutt	Silas	1		1						1				3		
Stow	195	1	Walcutt	William	1			1		2			1				5		
Hopkinton	244	36	Walken	Henry	3			1			1		1	1			7		
Hollistown	239	18	Walkens	Elijah	1			1					1				3		
Woburn	153	18	Walker	Abel	1	1				3			1				7		
Lexington	160	26	Walker	Abiel			1						1				2		
Sudbury	60	13	Walker	Abner			1	1			1		1				4		
Ashby	36	28	Walker	Asa		1	1	1						1			4		
Ashby	36	36	Walker	Asa Jr	1			1		1			1				4		
Boxborough	199	19	Walker	Augustus	2			1		1			1				5		
Chelmsford	173	3	Walker	David		1		1				1		1			4		
Billerica	178	34	Walker	Dudly	1	1	1	1		3			1	1			9		
Burlington	156	10	Walker	Edward	1	1	2	1		4	1	1	1				12		
Chelmsford	173	2	Walker	Ezek'			1		1	1			1				4		
Ashby	36	27	Walker	Isaac	1					1			1				5		

TOWN	PG#	LN#	LAST NAME	FIRST NAME	M under 10	M 10 to 16	M 16 to 26	M 26 to 45	M 45 and over	F under 10	F 10 to 16	F 16 to 26	F 26 to 45	F 45 and over	TOTAL ALL OTHER	TOTAL SLAVES	TOTALS	DISTRICT/ TOWNSHIP	NOTES
Townsend	29	1	Walker	Isaac Jr	1	2	1			3			1				8		
Hopkinton	245	2	Walker	Israel		1	2		1		1		1				6		
Burlington	156	8	Walker	James				1			1		1				3		
Burlington	156	16	Walker	John	1	2		1		1			1				6		
Shirley	215	42	Walker	John	1	1	1	1	1	3			1				9		
Hopkinton	244	38	Walker	Joseph		1		1			1		1				4		
Hopkinton	245	8	Walker	Joseph	2	2		1		2			1				8		
Townsend	29	15	Walker	Joseph	1			1		2			1				5		
Burlington	156	5	Walker	Josiah				1					1	2			4		
Natick	247	45	Walker	Josiah		1				1	1	1					4		
Burlington	156	6	Walker	Josiah Jr		1	1			1			1				4		
Framingham	70	8	Walker	Matthias	2		1			2	1		1	2			9		Stamped pg# was x'd out
Sudbury	60	14	Walker	Paul	3		1			2			1				7		
Cambridge	230	15	Walker	Saml	1	1		1		1	1		1				6		
Burlington	156	9	Walker	Samuel	2	1		1		2	2		1				9		
Framingham	73	16	Walker	Samuel	2			1		1	3		1				8		
Hopkinton	244	40	Walker	Sarah								1		1			2		
Townsend	28	41	Walker	Silas				1						1			2		
Hollistown	239	25	Walker	Solomon		1		1		1	1	1					5		
Sudbury	60	12	Walker	Thomas				1					1				2		
Charlestown	92	31	Walker	Timo'	1	2	2	2		2		1	1				11		
Hopkinton	245	3	Walker	Timothy	3	1		1		5	1	1	1				13		
Wilmington	144	7	Walker	Timothy			2	1	1					1			5		
Ashby	36	26	Walker	Zach	1	2			2		1	2		1			9		
Hopkinton	244	43	Walkins	Jona			1			1		1					3		
Framingham	70	6	Walkup	William		1	2		1	1		1	2	1			9		Stamped pg# was x'd out
Charlestown	92	6	Wallace	Susan									2	1			3		
Ashby	36	25	Waller	Benja	2			1		3	1		1				8		
Medford	103	18	Waller	Jno'	4	1		1					1				7		
Townsend	29	26	Wallis	Benja				1		1			1				3		
Townsend	29	13	Wallis	Isaac	1		1	1	1	1		1		1			7		
Townsend	29	24	Wallis	Jona	1			1		1							3		
Townsend	29	27	Wallis	Jona Jr		1	1			1			1				4		
Townsend	29	25	Wallis	Joseph	1		1					1					3		
Townsend	29	32	Wallis	Mary		1		1				3		1			6		
Townsend	29	18	Wallis	Wm	3	1		1		1			1				7		
Marlborough	191	33	Walnutt	Ephraim	3			1		1			1				6		
Reading	137	35	Walton	Benjamin		1	1		2			1		2			7		
Pepperell	33	35	Walton	John	5		1	1					1				8		
Reading	138	3	Walton	Oliver	4			1	1	2	1	2	1	2			14		
Reading	138	4	Walton	Timothy		1		1				2		1			5		
Weston	111	7	Ward	Artemas	1	2	1	1	1	4			1	1			12		
Natick	247	44	Ward	Daniel	1		1						1				3		
Newton	125	14	Ward	John		1		1			1		1				4		
Hopkinton	244	41	Ward	Joseph			1	1		1		1	1				5		
Newton	124	25	Ward	Joseph	2	1	1		1	2		2	1				10		
Weston	111	14	Ward	Lucy						1	1		1				3		
Hopkinton	245	4	Ward	Peter	1			1						1			3		
Newton	124	26	Ward	Samuel	3	1	1	1		1		1	1		1		10		
Sherburn	251	37	Ware	Alpha		1				1		1					3		
Newton	125	18	Ware	Azariah	1		2	2		1		1	1				8		
Sherburn	251	38	Ware	Benjm		1	1		1		1			2			6		
Hopkinton	244	44	Ware	James				1				1	1				3		
Hopkinton	245	1	Ware	James Jr			1			2	1	1					5		
Newton	125	17	Ware	John		2	5	1		3	1	2		1			15		
Sherburn	251	39	Ware	Joseph		1	1	1			1			2			6		
Newton	125	19	Ware	Walter	1		2					1	1		1		6		
Cambridge	230	7	Warland	John		2	2	1				1	1				7		
Cambridge	229	37	Warland	Thos		1	1	1		1	2	3	1				10		
Pepperell	34	9	Warner	Joseph		1	1	1				2		1			6		
Townsend	29	16	Warner	Joseph	1			1				1					3		
Townsend	29	28	Warner	Richard	4			1		1			1				7		
Townsend	29	44	Warner	Saml		1						1					2		
Ashby	36	30	Warner	Wm				1						2			3		
Townsend	29	9	Warren	Aaron	1		1					1	1				4		
Stow	198	34	Warren	Abijah	2		1		1	2	3	1		1			11		
Charlestown	92	13	Warren	Amos		1	1	1		1		2	1				7		
Watertown	235	9	Warren	Charles	3		1				2		1				7		
Hopkinton	244	42	Warren	Daniel		1				1	1						3		
Lincoln	12	12	Warren	Daniel	1		2	1		2			1				7		
Watertown	235	3	Warren	Eliphalet				1		2			1				4		
Littleton	202	20	Warren	Elizabeth									1	1			2		
Townsend	29	11	Warren	Ephm				1		1		1					4		
Shirley	215	39	Warren	Ephraim		1		1			1		1				4		
Stow	198	24	Warren	Huldy									1				1		
Chelmsford	173	14	Warren	Isaac		1		2			2	1	1				7		
Framingham	68	8	Warren	Isaac			2					1					3		Stamped pg# was x'd out
Medford	103	31	Warren	Isaac	1	1		1					2				5		
Chelmsford	173	15	Warren	Issac Jr			1			1		1					3		
Littleton	202	3	Warren	James	1			1		2			1				5		
Weston	111	10	Warren	Jedediah	1			1		1			2				5		

TOWN	PG#	LN#	HEADS OF HOUSEHOLD		FREE WHITE MALES					FREE WHITE FEMALES					TOTAL ALL OTHER	TOTAL SLAVES	TOTALS	DISTRICT/ TOWNSHIP	NOTES
			LAST NAME	FIRST NAME	under 10	10 to 16	16 to 26	26 to 45	45 and over	under 10	10 to 16	16 to 26	26 to 45	45 and over					
Chelmsford	173	17	Warren	Jerem'	1			1		2	1		1				6		
Shirley	215	46	Warren	John			1			2			1				4		
Weston	111	9	Warren	John			1				1	1	1	2			7		
Weston	111	4	Warren	Jona	1	1			1		1	1		1			6		
Chelmsford	173	16	Warren	Jos'			1		1	2	1	1	1				7		
Chelmsford	173	18	Warren	Jos' Jr	1	1		1		4		1		1			9		
Boxborough	199	11	Warren	Joseph		1			1	1		1		1			5		
Cambridge	230	16	Warren	Joseph	2	1	3	2		2		1		1			12		
Pepperell	34	4	Warren	Joseph			2		1		1			1			5		
Cambridge	230	13	Warren	Josiah	1			1		2			1				5		
Framingham	70	1	Warren	Josiah	3	1		1				1	1				7		
Weston	111	6	Warren	Micah	1				1				1				3		
Townsend	29	12	Warren	Moses	1	1	2	2		3	1	1	1				12		
Watertown	235	8	Warren	Moses	1		1	1		2			1				6		
Hopkinton	244	39	Warren	Naham			1		1		1			1			4		
Weston	111	5	Warren	Nathan	2	1		1		3	1	1	1				10		
Waltham	116	20	Warren	Peter	4	1	2			2	1	1	1				13		
Littleton	202	44	Warren	Samson		2	1		2	1	1	2	1	1			11		
Medford	103	32	Warren	Silas	1		1	1					1				4		
Marlborough	194	9	Warren	Thaddeus		1	1		1	2	1	2		1			9		
Cambridge	230	11	Warren	Wm	1		2						1				4		
Shirley	215	47	Warren	Wm			1		1	1							3		
Natick	247	1	Washman	Saml	2	1	1		1	2	1			3			11		
Cambridge	229	34	Waterhouse	Benjn	3	2			1	2	2	2		1			13		
Ashby	36	33	Waters	*	2	1		1	1	2	2	2	1				12		
Charlestown	92	21	Waters	Abra'	1			1				1	1				4		
Cambridge	230	25	Waters	Bettern	2	2	5	3	1	3	2	4	1	5	4		32		
Malden	98	21	Waters	Danl		1	2		1			1		1	1		7		
Carlisle	20	16	Waters	John		1		1	1			1	1	1			6		
Hollistown	239	24	Watkins	Andrew			1		1			1		1			4		
Hopkinton	244	35	Watkins	Moses	1	1			1	1	1	3		1			9		
Cambridge	229	28	Watson	Daniel				1					1				2		
Cambridge	229	27	Watson	Jacob	1				1	1				1			4		
Cambridge	229	38	Watson	Jacob Jr	1			1	2	2		1	1	1			9		
Cambridge	230	4	Watson	John	1		3		1				1	1			7		
Charlestown	92	5	Watson	Moses	2	1	2	1					1	1			8		
Cambridge	229	26	Watson	Nathan	1			1	1			2	1	1			7		
Cambridge	229	30	Watson	Nathl P.	2			1					1				4		
Cambridge	229	29	Watson	Saml			1		2	1							4		
Cambridge	229	17	Watson	Wm	2	1			1	1	1	3	1				10		
Malden	98	27	Watts	Isaac	1			1				1	1				3		
Medford	103	11	Watts	Nath'	1	1			1	2			1				6		
Medford	103	12	Watts	Nath' Jr			1				1						2		
Medford	103	13	Watts	Nathan	1			1		3	2		1				8		
Townsend	28	45	Waugh	John				1					1				2		
Townsend	29	22	Waugh	John	2	2		1	1	2	1		1	1			11		
Weston	111	11	Way*	Nero											2		2		
Concord	11	13	Wayman	John	3		1	1	1	2	1		1				10		
Malden	98	18	Wealer	Ann										1			1		
Malden	98	25	Wealer	Isaac	2			1					1				4		
Medford	103	26	Wealer	Jona'	1			1		1	1						4		
Malden	98	24	Wealer	Saml	1	1		1			1		1				5		
Charlestown	92	9	Wealer	Simon				1					1				2		
Ashby	36	24	Weatherbee	Israel	2	1	1		1	1	1		1				8		
Townsend	29	34	Weatherbee	Jacob	1	1		1		3	1		1				8		
Billerica	178	36	Weatherly	John	1			1		1			1				4		
Hopkinton	244	37	Weatin	Levi	1			1		2	1		1				6		
Littleton	203	29	Webber	Job	2			1		2			1		1		7		
Bedford	163	27	Webber	John			2		1					1			4		
Bedford	163	28	Webber	John Jr		1		1		2			1				5		
Bedford	163	32	Webber	Joseph	1			1		1			1				4		
Billerica	178	38	Webber	Leonard		1											1		
Cambridge	229	36	Webber	Saml	3			1		3	1	2	2	1			13		
Carlisle	21	26	Webber	Thomas				1	1	2			1				5		
Bedford	163	30	Webber	William	2			1	1	1			1				6		
Marlborough	189	5	Webster	James				1		3			1				5		
Dracut	47	15	Webster	William	2	1		1		3			1				8		
Marlborough	193	28	Weeks	John	1			2		3	1		1				8		
Marlborough	193	33	Weeks	Jonathan	2	1	1		1	1	1	2		2			11		
Marlborough	189	21	Weeks	William	2	1		1		2	1	1					8		
Sudbury	63	4	Weighton	John				1									1		
Waltham	116	22	Wellington	Abraham	1			1		1		1					4		
Ashby	36	18	Wellington	Amos					1			3	1				5		
Ashby	36	17	Wellington	Benja		1	1		1			3	1				7		
Ashby	36	19	Wellington	Elias Jr			1	1				1					3		
Ashby	36	37	Wellington	Elias Jr			1	1		1	2	2	1				8		
Charlestown	92	11	Wellington	Josiah		1	1		1				1	1			5		
Ashby	36	31	Wellington	Oliver	4	1		1		1	1		1				9		
Ashby	35	27	Wellington	Roger					1					1			2		
Waltham	116	21	Wellington	William	1	2		1		1		2		1	1		10		
Waltham	116	17	Wellington	William Jr			1	1		1	1	1					5		
Cambridge	230	2	Wells	Ebenz	4	2	1		1	3	1		1				13		

TOWN	PG#	LN#	LAST NAME	FIRST NAME	FREE WHITE MALES					FREE WHITE FEMALES					TOTAL ALL OTHER	TOTAL SLAVES	TOTALS	DISTRICT/ TOWNSHIP	NOTES
					under 10	10 to 16	16 to 26	26 to 45	45 and over	under 10	10 to 16	16 to 26	26 to 45	45 and over					
Charlestown	92	28	Welman	John				1					1				2		
Charlestown	92	17	Welsh	Eunice									1				1		
Charlestown	92	16	Welsh	Ezra	3			1		1	1		1				7		
Newton	125	22	Welsh	Michael		1	1	1					1				4		
Waltham	116	18	Welsh	William	1	1		1				1	1				5		
Westford	184	24	Wendal	Jacob	1	1		1				1	1				5		
Cambridge	230	3	Wendall	Cathn				1				1		1			3		
Weston	111	16	Wentworth	Elijah		1		1		2		1		1			6		
Newton	125	11	Wentworth	Isaac				1				2		1	3		7		
Stow	196	29	Werthinton	Samuel	3	1		1		1	2	1		1			10		
Hopkinton	245	5	Wesson	Aaron			2					2					4		
Hopkinton	245	6	Wesson	Abiel	3			1		1				1			6		
Marlborough	192	22	Wesson	James		1	1	1				1	1				5		
Hopkinton	245	9	Wesson	John		1		1						1			3		
Townsend	29	14	Wesson	Wm	1			1		1	1	1					6		
Charlestown	92	29	West	Saml		1											1		
Sherburn	251	33	Westbury	Edward		1		1				3		1			6		
Reading	137	30	Weston	Abijah	1			1		2			1	1			6		
Lincoln	15	3	Weston	Daniel	2			1		1				1			5		
Reading	138	7	Weston	Ephraim	2	1		1		1				1			6		
Medford	103	22	Weston	Esther									1				1		
Reading	137	31	Weston	Jabez	2			1		2			1	1			7		
Reading	137	24	Weston	James	1	1			1	1	2		1				7		
Reading	137	26	Weston	James 3rd	2			1		1			1				5		
Reading	137	27	Weston	James 4th				1		1		1					3		
Reading	137	25	Weston	James Jr	2	1		1		3			1				8		
Reading	137	28	Weston	John		1	1	1			1		1				6		
Reading	137	29	Weston	John Jr	2			1					1				4		
Reading	137	32	Weston	Jonathan	1		3	1			1		1				7		
Lincoln	14	6	Weston	Nathan	4	1			2		1		1	1			10		
Billerica	178	42	Weston	Saml				1					1				2		
Reading	137	33	Weston	Samuel	4			1		1			1				7		
Medford	103	23	Weston	Wymond				1				1	2				4		
Lincoln	15	4	Weston	Zacariah			2	1					2	1			6		
Waltham	116	24	Weston	Zachariah		1	3	1		1	1	1	1				9		
Acton	19	2	Wetherbee	Edward	1	1	2		1	2	1	1		1			10		
Groton	213	9	Wetherbee	Parker				1				1	1				3		
Medford	103	19	Wetherton	Henry	1			1		2		1	1				6		
Carlisle	22	22	Wheat	Daniel	1			1		3			1				6		
Bedford	163	34	Wheeer	Abner	1			1		1	1		1				5		
Concord	9	1	Wheeler	Abel	2				1	2	2	2	1				10		
Sudbury	61	32	Wheeler	Abel	1		1						1				3		
Framingham	70	13	Wheeler	Abner	1			1					2				4		Stamped pg# was x'd out
Lincoln	15	26	Wheeler	Abner	1	1	3	1				2	1	1			10		
Groton	212	93	Wheeler	Asa				1		1	1	1		1			5		
Marlborough	189	22	Wheeler	Asa	3			1	1	1			1				7		
Sudbury	61	21	Wheeler	Asahel	1			1	1	1		1	1				7		
Pepperell	34	8	Wheeler	Benja			2	1						1			4		
Townsend	29	30	Wheeler	Benja				1				1					2		
Woburn	153	17	Wheeler	Benjamin	1		1	1					1				5		
Sudbury	63	2	Wheeler	Caleb	2	1		1		4	2	3	1				14		
Concord	11	20	Wheeler	David		1	2	1			2		1				7		
Concord	11	21	Wheeler	David Jr	3		1	1			2		1				8		
Lincoln	15	16	Wheeler	Edmund		1	2	1					1				5		
Stow	198	38	Wheeler	Ephraim		1		1		1			1				4		
Concord	8	19	Wheeler	Ephraim Jr		1		1		1		2					5		
Sudbury	61	20	Wheeler	Israel	1	2		1			1	2		1			8		
Sudbury	60	11	Wheeler	Israel Jr	1		1	1		1		1					5		
Acton	17	33	Wheeler	John		2		1		1			1				5		
Ashby	37	47	Wheeler	John	2			1		2	1		1				7		
Carlisle	20	9	Wheeler	Joseph P	1			1		1	1		1				6		
Concord	11	22	Wheeler	Jotham		2		1		1			2				6		
Carlisle	22	29	Wheeler	Judah				1									1		
Acton	17	27	Wheeler	Kiah	2			1		1	1	1	1				7		
Stow	196	40	Wheeler	Levi		1		1		1	1		1				5		
Sudbury	63	25	Wheeler	Loring	1			1					1				3		
Concord	9	25	Wheeler	Mary									1				1		
Concord	10	12	Wheeler	Mary		1		1				1	1				4		
Acton	17	30	Wheeler	Nathan		1	1	1					1				4		
Carlisle	21	37	Wheeler	Nathan	1			1		3	1		1				7		
Concord	10	7	Wheeler	Noah		1	3	1		2		1	1	1			10		
Carlisle	20	7	Wheeler	Oliver				1					1				2		
Boxborough	200	44	Wheeler	Peter	4	1		1		1	1		1				9		
Concord	5	6	Wheeler	Peter	1	2	1		1	1	1	1	1				9		
Littleton	204	31	Wheeler	Peter				2						1			3		
Acton	19	13	Wheeler	Phinehas			1						1				2		
Concord	10	17	Wheeler	Phinehas		1	2	1			2	1		1			8		
Acton	16	27	Wheeler	Rebekah										3			3		
Carlisle	20	8	Wheeler	Reuben	4			1		2			1				8		
Acton	17	31	Wheeler	Roger								1	1	1			4		
Carlisle	20	5	Wheeler	Sampson					1					1			2		

TOWN	PG#	LN#	HEADS OF HOUSEHOLD		FREE WHITE MALES					FREE WHITE FEMALES					TOTAL ALL OTHER	TOTAL SLAVES	TOTALS	DISTRICT/ TOWNSHIP	NOTES
			LAST NAME	FIRST NAME	under 10	10 to 16	16 to 26	26 to 45	45 and over	under 10	10 to 16	16 to 26	26 to 45	45 and over					
Acton	17	29	Wheeler	Samuel					1					2			3		
Concord	10	8	Wheeler	Samuel	2	1	2		1				1	1			8		
Carlisle	20	6	Wheeler	Simon	1			1		1		1					4		
Townsend	29	23	Wheeler	Solo	2			1		3			1				7		
Concord	8	32	Wheeler	Thomas		1		1				1		2			5		
Lincoln	15	17	Wheeler	Thomas	1	1		1		1			1				5		
Littleton	204	19	Wheeler	Thomas	2			1			2		1	1			7		
Acton	16	13	Wheeler	Timothy B.	3			1					1				5		
Sudbury	65	4	Wheeler	William	3	1	1	1		1			1				8		
Concord	5	29	Wheelock	Jonathan			1	1		2			1				5		
Medford	103	20	Wheelwright	Jos'	1			3		1			1				6		
Concord	8	18	Wheler	Ephraim				1					1	1			3		
Cambridge	230	19	Whipple	Joseph	1				2			2	1				6		
Stow	197	5	Whit	Dorothy									1				1		
Boxborough	200	25	Whitcomb	Abel	1	1			1	1	2	1		2			9		
Stow	196	17	Whitcomb	Abraham	1	1	1	1		1		1					6		
Littleton	205	10	Whitcomb	Daniel		1			1				1				3		
Boxborough	199	24	Whitcomb	Ephraim		1	1		1		1	1		2			7		
Boxborough	199	27	Whitcomb	Ephraim Jr	1			1			1	1					4		
Stow	196	28	Whitcomb	Hezekiah	2	1		1		3			1	1			9		
Littleton	201	23	Whitcomb	John	3	2		1			1	1	1				9		
Littleton	203	8	Whitcomb	Jonathan		2	2	1	1	1	4	1	1				13		
Boxborough	200	32	Whitcomb	Jotham				1		1		1	1	1			5		
Boxborough	200	13	Whitcomb	Moses	2			1		3			1				7		
Littleton	201	22	Whitcomb	Oliver				1		1			2	1			5		
Stow	195	5	Whitcomb	Oliver			1			1		1					3		
Boxborough	199	13	Whitcomb	Samuel	2	1	1					1	1	1			7		
Stow	195	3	Whitcomb	Silas			1			3			1	1			6		
Stow	195	4	Whitcomb	Simeon	1		1							1			4		
Marlborough	193	6	Whitcomb	Timothy	1			1	1	1			2	1			7		
Boxborough	200	31	Whitcomb	William				1				1		1			3		
Stow	196	16	Whitcomb	William		1			1	1				1			4		
Marlborough	193	4	Whitcomb	Zelotes	2			1						1			4		
Westford	184	29	White	Aaron		1						1					2		
Westford	184	30	White	Abel		1							1				2		
Watertown	235	6	White	Andrew			1						1				2		
Watertown	235	7	White	Andrew Jr	2			1		2			1				6		
Cambridge	230	20	White	Charles		1	1	1				2		2			7		
Acton	19	20	White	Daniel	2	1	1	1			1		1				7		
Cambridge	230	23	White	Daniel A		1											1		
Pepperell	34	6	White	David			1	1		4			1	1			8		
Cambridge	230	21	White	Easter									2				2		
Newton	124	27	White	Eleazer	2	1		1	1	3		1	1				10		
Littleton	203	16	White	Elenor							1	1	1				3		
Cambridge	230	17	White	Elijah	1		2			1	1	1					6		
Hollistown	239	21	White	James	1		1	1			2						5		
Billerica	178	35	White	John				1			1		2				4		
Concord	2	1	White	John		1			1	1	1	1	1				6		
Littleton	203	14	White	John	1			1		2			1				5		
Watertown	235	15	White	Jonas		2	3	2	1			4		1			13		
Cambridge	230	22	White	Joseph		3						1					4		
Littleton	203	27	White	Joseph	2			1		3			1				7		
Pepperell	34	7	White	Josh		1	1					2		1			5		
Newton	125	9	White	Loas	1			1		2	1		1				6		
Tyngsborough	43	40	White	Mark		1						1					2		
Billerica	178	30	White	Mary									1		1		2		
Watertown	235	21	White	Moses	3		2		1	1	1	1	1	1			11		
Watertown	235	18	White	Saml	3	1		1		1			1				7		
Watertown	235	20	White	Saml		1		1		1							3		
Acton	19	6	White	Samuel	1	1		2				1	1	1			7		
Littleton	203	15	White	Samuel	1	1		1		5			1				9		
Tewksbury	53	28	Whitemore	Isaac	2	1				1	1		1				6		
Pepperell	33	49	Whiting	Benja		1	3		1			1		1			7		
Lincoln	13	3	Whiting	Hosea	1		1			1	1		1				5		
Chelmsford	173	7	Whiting	Phin'		1	1				2	1			3		8		
Ashby	37	40	Whiting	Saml		1					1						2		
Billerica	178	37	Whiting	Saml	1	4	1	1		2	1	1		1			12		
Watertown	235	22	Whiting	Samuel		1				2	1		1				5		
Concord	6	8	Whiting	Thomas	1	1		1		2	1		1				7		
Westford	184	28	Whiting	Wm	2	1		1					1				5		
Stow	198	1	Whitman	Charles				1						2			3		
Stow	198	2	Whitman	Charles Jr		1	1			1	1	1					5		
Stow	198	18	Whitman	Joseph		1	1			1	1	1					5		
Groton	212	105	Whitman	Nehh	1			1		1	3		1				7		
Stow	198	3	Whitman	Thomas	1	1	2		1	1	2		1				9		
Newton	125	12	Whitmore	Jona W.		1	1	1		2			1				6		
Sherburn	251	31	Whitney	Aaron	1		1		1		1		1				5		
Weston	111	15	Whitney	Abijah	2	2		1		2		1	1	1			10		
Stow	196	13	Whitney	Abraham				1					1				2		
Stow	196	14	Whitney	Abraham Jr	2	1			2	1		1	1				9		

225

TOWN	PG#	LN#	LAST NAME	FIRST NAME	FREE WHITE MALES under 10	10 to 16	16 to 26	26 to 45	45 and over	FREE WHITE FEMALES under 10	10 to 16	16 to 26	26 to 45	45 and over	TOTAL ALL OTHER	TOTAL SLAVES	TOTALS	DISTRICT/ TOWNSHIP	NOTES
Watertown	235	10	Whitney	Abrm		1			1	2				1			5		
Newton	125	21	Whitney	Amasa	1			1		4	1		1				8		
Charlestown	92	32	Whitney	Amazh	2			1		2		1	1				7		
Chelmsford	173	12	Whitney	Amos	1			1					1				3		
Townsend	29	19	Whitney	Asa	3			1		3			1				8		
Sherburn	251	30	Whitney	Daniel	1				1		1			1			4		
Stow	197	4	Whitney	Daniel	4	2	3		1		1	2	1				14		
Watertown	234	42	Whitney	Daniel	1		2		1		2	2		2			10		
Hollistown	239	22	Whitney	David	2	2	1		1	1	1		2	1			11		
Natick	248	2	Whitney	El*	1			1		2			1				5		
Wilmington	144	10	Whitney	Elda			20	13		1		1	1				36		
Stow	196	36	Whitney	Elias				1						1			2		
East Sudbury	68	28	Whitney	Elisabeth								1		1			2		
Watertown	235	11	Whitney	Ezekl	1		1		1					1			4		
Watertown	235	14	Whitney	Ezekl	3		1			2			1				7		
Watertown	235	12	Whitney	Francis				1									1		
Stow	196	35	Whitney	Hezekiah		1		1	1	2	1		2	1			9		
Ashby	36	23	Whitney	Isaac		2		1		4			1				8		
Stow	197	8	Whitney	Jacob	2	3	1	1		1		1	1	1			11		
Tyngsborough	43	38	Whitney	James	3		1			2		1					7		
Natick	247	43	Whitney	Jason		2		1		1	1		1				6		
Sherburn	251	35	Whitney	John		1		1			1		1				4		
Watertown	234	43	Whitney	Jona	1		1		1		1		1				5		
Watertown	235	1	Whitney	Jona Jr	3			1		1		1					6		
Sherburn	251	34	Whitney	Joseph	2	1		1		2	1		1				8		
Boxborough	199	10	Whitney	Joshua	3	1		1					1				6		
Ashby	36	21	Whitney	Josiah	1	2	1		1			1		1			7		
Waltham	116	23	Whitney	Josiah		1		1	1			1	1				5		
Ashby	36	8	Whitney	Josiah Jr	2	1		1		2	1		1				8		
Ashby	36	29	Whitney	Judah	1			1		2			1				5		
Stow	197	2	Whitney	Lemuel				1					1				2		
Townsend	29	20	Whitney	Levi				1					1				2		
Newton	125	3	Whitney	Moses				1					1				2		
Watertown	235	13	Whitney	Moses			1			1			1				3		
Watertown	235	19	Whitney	Nathl R.	3	3	2	1		1		2	2				14		
Watertown	234	41	Whitney	Saml		1		1						2			4		
Hollistown	239	19	Whitney	Samll			1	1			1		1				4		
Wilmington	144	9	Whitney	Samson	2			1		1			1	1			6		
Ashby	36	22	Whitney	Selas		1	2	1		3	1		1				9		
Sherburn	251	36	Whitney	Susanna		1	1			2			1				5		
Newton	125	1	Whitney	Thaddeus		1			1	2		1		1			6		
Marlborough	191	8	Whitney	Thomas	1	1		1		1		1					5		
Shirley	215	38	Whitney	Thomas Esq	1		1	1				1	1				5		
Newton	125	2	Whitney	Timo	1		1		1		1		1				5		
Reading	137	21	Whitridge	William				1			1		1				3		
Reading	137	22	Whitridge	William Jr	2			1		1			1	1			6		
Ashby	37	37	Whitson	Jonah	1			1		2			1				5		
Weston	111	12	Whittemore	Aaron	1	1		1			1		1				5		
Cambridge	229	25	Whittemore	Amos	2		1	1		3	2	1	1				11		
Weston	111	13	Whittemore	Israel				1						1			2		
Cambridge	229	15	Whittemore	Jona		1	3	2		3			1				10		
Malden	98	22	Whittemore	Jos'		1		1					1				3		
Cambridge	230	24	Whittemore	Josiah	2	1		3		3	2	1	1	1			14		
Charlestown	92	25	Whittemore	Nathan		1	1	1		2	2		1				8		
Charlestown	92	34	Whittemore	Phillip	2	1		1		3	1		1				9		
Cambridge	229	10	Whittemore	Saml		1		4		2		2					9		
Cambridge	229	13	Whittemore	Saml	3		1				1	1					6		
Cambridge	229	14	Whittemore	Thos	1	2		1	1	2	1		1				9		
Cambridge	229	12	Whittemore	Wm	1				1		1	1	1				5		
Cambridge	229	24	Whittemore	Wm	3			2		2	2	1	2				12		
Charlestown	92	15	Whittemore	Wm			1			1		1					3		
Hopkinton	245	10	Whuler	Saml	1			1		2			1				5		
Stoneham	140	1	Wi*	Mathew				1		2			1				4		
Hollistown	239	23	Wier	George	2		1		1				1				5		
Sudbury	60	34	Wier	Isaac		2		1					1				4		
Watertown	235	25	Wild	Nathl		1	2	1	1		1	2	2	1			11		
Ashby	36	20	Wilden	Rufus	1		1		1		2	1		1			7		
Marlborough	191	4	Wilder	Eunice									1	1			2		
Townsend	29	3	Wilder	Isaac		2	1		1	1	1	1		1			8		
Shirley	215	48	Wilds	Ivery		1	2	1	3			5	7	6			25		
Reading	138	9	Wiley	Edmund	2			1		3		1	1				8		
Reading	138	2	Wiley	Eli	1		1			1		1					4		
Reading	137	34	Wiley	James		1	2		1	2			1				7		
Medford	103	29	Wiley	John	1			1		2	1		4		4		13		
Reading	138	5	Wiley	Nathaniel				1						1			2		
Reading	138	6	Wiley	Nathaniel Jr	3	1	2	1		1	1	2	1	1			13		
Stoneham	140	5	Wiley	Phinehas	1	1	1	1		3	2	1	1				11		
Reading	138	11	Wiley	Samuel	2		2	1					1				6		
Charlestown	92	22	Wiley	Wm	1	1	1	1		3	1		1				9		
Carlisle	22	21	Wilkin	Timothy Jr	1	1		2		2			1				7		
Marlborough	192	30	Wilkins	David	2	1		1		3	2		1				10		
Marlborough	192	33	Wilkins	Edward	1			1		1		2	2	1			8		

226

TOWN	PG#	LN#	LAST NAME	FIRST NAME	FREE WHITE MALES under 10	10 to 16	16 to 26	26 to 45	45 and over	FREE WHITE FEMALES under 10	10 to 16	16 to 26	26 to 45	45 and over	TOTAL ALL OTHER	TOTAL SLAVES	TOTALS	DISTRICT/ TOWNSHIP	NOTES
Carlisle	22	27	Wilkins	Isaac				1				1		1			3		
Carlisle	22	26	Wilkins	James	1			1		3	1		1				7		
Watertown	235	2	Wilkins	John	1			1		3			1				6		
Marlborough	192	34	Wilkins	Jonas	2		1			2	1	1	1				8		
Westford	184	26	Wilkins	Robert	2			1		1			1				5		
Carlisle	22	31	Wilkins	Timothy	3		2		1	1		1	1	1			10		
Billerica	178	39	Wilkins	Wm	2		4	1		2	1	1	1				12		
Sudbury	62	2	Will	Asahel	2			1			1	1					5		
Marlborough	191	22	Will	Ebenezer	1			1		2		1					6		
Shirley	215	40	Willard	Israel	1			1	1	1	1	2	1	1			9		
Sudbury	57	2	Willard	John			1	1					1	1			4		
Boxborough	200	5	Willard	Joseph		1			1		2	5		1			10		
Cambridge	230	6	Willard	Joseph	1	1	2		1	2	2	4	1	1			15		
Cambridge	230	5	Willard	Mary	1			1				1	1	1			5		
Shirley	215	41	Willard	Nathan			5	4	8			7	21	4			49		
Ashby	37	39	Willard	Tarbill		1						1					2		
Chelmsford	173	6	Willey	Andr		1			1		1			1			4		
Cambridge	229	9	William	Gershom		1	2		1		1		2	1			8		
Concord	8	17	William	John	1			1		2			1				5		
Concord	6	26	William	Oliver			1				1						2		
Groton	212	91	Williams	Aaron				1			1						2		
Cambridge	229	32	Williams	Amasa	2		1			1		1					5		
Pepperell	34	20	Williams	Benja	1			1					1				3		
Chelmsford	173	8	Williams	Benja'	2		1				1						4		
Marlborough	190	2	Williams	Betty						1			1	1			3		
Groton	212	96	Williams	Daniel	3	2			1	1		1	1				9		
Medford	103	9	Williams	Eben		1	1						1				4		
Lexington	160	28	Williams	Elizabeth		1				1				2			4		
Marlborough	190	1	Williams	George		1	1	1	3	1			1	1			9		
Medford	103	10	Williams	Gershom	1		1			1			1				4		
Chelmsford	173	11	Williams	Isaac	2			1		1	1						5		
Pepperell	33	37	Williams	Isaac				1						1			2		
Pepperell	33	38	Williams	Isaac Jr	1	1		1			1		1				5		
Groton	212	97	Williams	Jacob L.	2	2	1			1		1	1				8		
Malden	98	23	Williams	Jane						2		1					3		
Groton	212	95	Williams	Jason		1		1			1	1	1				5		
Groton	212	99	Williams	John Capt.	1			1		1	2	1	1	1			8		
Chelmsford	173	9	Williams	Jona'	1	1	3		1		1	2		1			10		
Pepperell	33	39	Williams	Jonah	1		1	1		5	1	1	1				11		
Marlborough	194	8	Williams	Joseph			2		2		1	2		1			8		
Littleton	202	8	Williams	Miriam											1		1		
Stow	198	27	Williams	Robert		2	4		1					1			8		
Chelmsford	173	10	Williams	Seth			1			1		1					3		
Dracut	47	22	Williams	Simeon	1		1		1					2			5		
Groton	212	98	Williams	Simeon Capt.	1			1		2		1	1	1			7		
Marlborough	193	25	Williams	Stephen			1					1					2		
Pepperell	33	36	Williams	Tho	2	1		1		2			1				7		
Marlborough	187	9	Williams	Thomas	2		1						1				4		
Cambridge	229	23	Williams	Thos		1		1									2		
Reading	138	1	Williams	William	1	1	1		1	1	1		1				7		
Reading	138	12	Williams	William Jr	1		1					1					3		
Shirley	215	45	Williams	Wm	2	1	1	1		2	1		1				9		
Lexington	160	25	Willington	Benjamin		2	2		1	1			1	2			9		
Watertown	235	5	Willington	Edmund	2			1		2			1				6		
Lincoln	14	14	Willington	Elijah	2	1			1	2	2		1				9		
Cambridge	229	7	Willington	Jedun		1	1		3	2	1			2			10		
Watertown	235	24	Willington	Joel	2				1	2			2	1			8		
Concord	9	6	Willington	Lucy	1					1	2		1				5		
Watertown	235	26	Willington	Saml		1	2		2	2	3	1		1			12		
Watertown	235	4	Willington	Thos	1				2					5			8		
Sudbury	62	12	Willis	Abel	2	1		1	1	2			1				8		
Medford	103	30	Willis	David				1						1			2		
Malden	98	20	Willis	Eliakm				1						1			2		
Sudbury	62	16	Willis	Elisabeth		1	1						1	1			4		
Sudbury	62	17	Willis	Hopestill	1			1			2			1			5		
Sudbury	62	18	Willis	Jedediah	1	1		1		1	1		1				6		
Sudbury	62	21	Willis	Jesse	2	1		1	1	1	1	1		1			9		
Sudbury	62	22	Willis	Jesse Jr	2			1		2			1				7		
Sudbury	62	1	Willis	Sarah			1				1			1			3		
Marlborough	192	29	Willkins	Levi	2	1		1		2	2		1				9		
Stoneham	140	10	Willy	James		1			1			1	1				4		
Reading	137	20	Willy	John	1	2	5			1		2					11		
Stoneham	140	6	Willy	Nathan	3	1	2	1	1	2	2		3				15		
Littleton	202	38	Wilson	Charles	1			1		3			1				6		
Dracut	45	4	Wilson	David	1	1	1	1		1	1	1					7		
Littleton	202	14	Wilson	Henry	1			1		2			1				5		
Westford	184	25	Wilson	Isaac	2			1		3			1				7		
Bedford	163	31	Wilson	James		1	2		1			1		1			6		
Burlington	156	18	Wilson	James		1				1			1				3		
Framingham	70	10	Wilson	James			1			1	1	1	1				5		Stamped pg# was x'd out
Townsend	29	17	Wilson	James	1		1		1		1		1				5		

227

TOWN	PG#	LN#	LAST NAME	FIRST NAME	FREE WHITE MALES under 10	10 to 16	16 to 26	26 to 45	45 and over	FREE WHITE FEMALES under 10	10 to 16	16 to 26	26 to 45	45 and over	TOTAL ALL OTHER	TOTAL SLAVES	TOTALS	DISTRICT/ TOWNSHIP	NOTES
Billerica	178	32	Wilson	John				1				1		1			3		
Tyngsborough	43	37	Wilson	John	2	1	2	1		2	1		1				10		
Hopkinton	245	13	Wilson	John O.	2	1	1	1	1	2	1	1	1				11		
Billerica	178	33	Wilson	Jos'	2			1		2			1				6		
Dracut	47	24	Wilson	Joseph		1	2		1		1		1				6		
Cambridge	229	8	Wilson	Josiah	1	2		1	1				1				6		
Medford	103	17	Wilson	Miles			1			2		1					4		
Newton	125	4	Wilson	Moses				2				1					3		
Burlington	156	11	Wilson	Rebekah								1	1				2		
Chelmsford	173	13	Wilson	Saml				1									1		
Malden	98	17	Wilson	Saml	1	1	1	1		1			1				6		
Carlisle	21	18	Wilson	Samuel	2			1	1					1			5		
Billerica	178	31	Wilson	Seth	3	1		1		1			1	1			8		
Chelmsford	173	4	Wilson	Simeon	1			1		2			1				5		
Townsend	28	42	Wilson	Thos	1			1				1					3		
Townsend	29	31	Win	Hezh	2			1		3			1				7		
Newton	125	10	Winch	Ebenezer	3	1		1	1	1		1	2				9		
Framingham	70	7	Winch	Jesse		1		1		2			1				5		Stamped pg# was x'd out
Framingham	70	3	Winch	Joseph	3			1	1	2	1		1	1			10		Stamped pg# was x'd out
Framingham	70	11	Winch	Josiah	3			1			1		1				6		Stamped pg# was x'd out
Framingham	70	4	Winch	Nathan			1		1			1		1			4		Stamped pg# was x'd out
Framingham	74	1	Winch	Rebeckah									1				1		
Framingham	72	30	Winch	Reuben	1			1		2		1					5		Stamped pg# was x'd out
Framingham	70	2	Winch	Silas				1				3	1				5		Stamped pg# was x'd out
Newton	125	13	Winchester	Amos		1	1			1	1	1					6		
Marlborough	192	15	Winchester	Caleb		2		1					1				4		
Newton	125	23	Winchester	Ichabod	1			1		1			1				4		
Watertown	235	16	Winchester	Wm	1	1		2		3			1				8		
Burlington	156	19	Winn	Abel			1			2			1				4		
Burlington	156	12	Winn	David	1	1		2			1	2		1			8		
Burlington	156	15	Winn	Jeremiah			1	1		1							2		
Reading	138	8	Winn	Jeremiah	1		1			1		1					4		
Burlington	156	7	Winn	Joseph				1			1	2		1			5		
Carlisle	23	11	Winn	Peter		1				1		1					3		
Burlington	156	13	Winn	Timothy		3	1	1		1		1	1	3			11		
Ashby	36	35	Winship	Abel	1	2		1		1	1	1					7		
Lincoln	13	33	Winship	Benjamin		2		1					1				4		
Cambridge	230	12	Winship	Edmund	2			1		1	1		1	1			7		
Charlestown	92	10	Winship	Henry	1	2		1		1			1				6		
Lexington	160	22	Winship	Isaac	1		1		1	1	1	1					6		
Hollistown	239	20	Winship	Jacob	1			1		1			1				4		
Woburn	153	12	Winship	Joel	3			1					1				5		
Cambridge	229	19	Winship	John	1	1		1					1				4		
Cambridge	230	18	Winship	Jona		3	5	1			1	3		1	1		15		
Charlestown	92	18	Winship	Jona'			1										1		
Lexington	160	23	Winship	Jonathan	1			1	1	1	1	1	1	2			9		
Medford	103	16	Winship	Moses			1						1				2		
Cambridge	230	10	Winship	Saml	2			1		2			1				6		
Lexington	160	21	Winship	Simon	2		1		1	1		1	1				7		
Lexington	160	27	Winship	Stephen	1		1	1		5			2				10		
Watertown	235	17	Winship	Thos		1		1		2			2				6		
Cambridge	229	21	Winship	Wm			3	1			1		1				6		
Cambridge	229	22	Winship	Wm Jr			1			1	1		1				4		
Cambridge	229	18	Winthrop	James				1									1		
Cambridge	229	20	Winthrop	Wm		1		1		1			1				4		
Framingham	70	12	Winzell	John	1	1		1	2	2			1	5			13		Stamped pg# was x'd out
Marlborough	193	35	Wiswall	Oliver				1					1				2		
Newton	125	7	Wiswell	Elizabeth	1					4		1					6		
Newton	125	5	Wiswell	Jeremiah			1	2					1				4		
Newton	125	6	Wiswell	Jeremiah Jr	4	2		1				1	1				9		
Hollistown	239	17	Wiswell	Jona	1			1				1	1				4		
Waltham	115	5	Wiswell	Moore &		2	9					5	1				17		
Stow	195	14	Witherbee	Ephraim		2	1	1		1		2	1				8		
Stow	195	19	Witherbee	Jonas		2							1				3		
Stow	199	6	Witherbee	Judah	2		1	1		2	2	1	1				10		
Boxborough	200	7	Witherbee	Levi		1		1		1	1		1				5		
Boxborough	200	9	Witherbee	Phinehas				1					1				2		
Boxborough	200	10	Witherbee	Phinehas Jr		1		2	1				2	1			7		
Boxborough	200	15	Witherbee	Reuben	1			1		1			1				4		
Boxborough	200	27	Witherbee	Samuel				1					1				2		
Boxborough	200	29	Witherbee	Samuel Jr		1		1		2			1				5		
Boxborough	200	3	Witherbee	Silas				1					1				2		
Boxborough	200	28	Witherbee	Simeon	1		1	1		3			1				7		
Marlborough	193	5	Witt	Josiah			1	2					2				5		
Marlborough	193	24	Witt	Samuel	3	1	1	1		1			2				9		
Shirley	215	44	Wodd	Aaron		1	1	1				1	1				5		
Waltham	116	19	Wolcott	Edward K	1		1	1			1	1		1	1		7		
Pepperell	33	48	Wood	Aaron		1	2				1	1	1				6		
Concord	10	1	Wood	Abigail									1				1		
Dracut	46	6	Wood	Abijah		1		1					1				3		
Concord	8	35	Wood	Amos				2					1				3		
Dracut	48	31	Wood	Amos	1	1		1		2			1				6		

TOWN	PG#	LN#	LAST NAME	FIRST NAME	FWM under 10	FWM 10 to 16	FWM 16 to 26	FWM 26 to 45	FWM 45 and over	FWF under 10	FWF 10 to 16	FWF 16 to 26	FWF 26 to 45	FWF 45 and over	TOTAL ALL OTHER	TOTAL SLAVES	TOTALS	DISTRICT/TOWNSHIP	NOTES
Concord	8	36	Wood	Amos Jr	2	1		1			1	1					6		
Townsend	29	29	Wood	Benja				1		1			1	1			4		
Concord	7	15	Wood	Daniel	4	1		1		1			1				8		
Dracut	48	30	Wood	Daniel	3			1		1			1	1			7		
Groton	212	107	Wood	Daniel				1					1				2		
Stow	199	4	Wood	Daniel				1		1			1				3		
Ashby	36	7	Wood	David	1	1	1					1					4		
Charlestown	92	23	Wood	David				1				1	1	1			4		
Burlington	156	17	Wood	Edward	2			1				1	1	1			6		
Tewksbury	53	27	Wood	Edward				1		1	1			1			4		
Concord	8	28	Wood	Ephraim		1		1		1			1	1			5		
Dracut	46	7	Wood	Hiram	1		1						1				3		
Littleton	203	12	Wood	Jane		1				1				1			3		
Burlington	156	1	Wood	John		1		1		1				1			4		
Charlestown	92	8	Wood	John			1										1		
Groton	213	4	Wood	John	1			1		3			1				6		
Littleton	205	13	Wood	John	1		2	1		1		2		1			8		
Groton	212	106	Wood	John A.				1									1		
Burlington	156	2	Wood	John Jr	1	1	1	1		2	1	1	1				9		
Charlestown	92	7	Wood	Jona'			1						1				2		
Stow	197	28	Wood	Jonathan			2	1		2	2			1			8		
Dracut	49	11	Wood	Joseph	2			1		2				2			7		
Stow	197	30	Wood	Joseph			2	1		1			2	1			7		
Tewksbury	53	29	Wood	Joseph				1					1				2		
Littleton	203	23	Wood	Josiah	1			1					1				3		
Littleton	201	8	Wood	Martin				1									1		
Concord	10	30	Wood	Moses			1										1		
Concord	5	19	Wood	Nathan	2		1	1				1		1			6		
Boxborough	199	6	Wood	Oliver	1	1	2		1	2	2		2	1			12		
Marlborough	187	2	Wood	Peter				1		1				1			3		
Newton	125	8	Wood	Ryal				1				1		1			3		
Westford	184	27	Wood	Saml	2			1		3	1	1					8		
Littleton	203	22	Wood	Samuel		1	1	1			1			1			5		
Woburn	152	39	Wood	Seth		1	1	1	3			1	1	2			10		
Dracut	48	29	Wood	Solomon	2			1		3	2			1			9		
Concord	3	3	Wood	Stephen	1		1	1				1	1				7		
Woburn	152	40	Wood	Sylvann	1	1		1		1			1				5		
Concord	7	7	Wood	Thadeus		1		1		1	1	2		1			7		
Tewksbury	53	26	Wood	Thos	1	1	2		1	2	2	1					10		
Dracut	49	7	Wood	William			1						1				2		
Charlestown	92	33	Wood	Wm		1				1	1		1				4		
Hopkinton	245	7	Wood	Wm	3			1		2	2	1					9		
Groton	212	92	Wood	Mary Wid.	1	1				1		1		1			5		
Tewksbury	53	25	Wood	Eben				1					1				2		
Acton	19	10	Wood	Moses	2		1	1		3		2	1				10		
Pepperell	33	40	Woodard	Benja				1					1				2		
Shirley	215	43	Woodbury	Benjm				1					1				2		
Newton	125	20	Woodcock	Nathan	3		1			1			1				6		
Groton	212	101	Woods	Abel				1					1				2		
Groton	213	2	Woods	Caleb	2		1			4			1				8		
Cambridge	230	14	Woods	Coolidge	2		1	1	1	2		1		1			9		
Groton	212	103	Woods	Eber	1		1			2			1				5		
Pepperell	34	1	Woods	Henry				1						2			3		
Pepperell	34	2	Woods	Isaac				1				2		1			4		
Pepperell	34	10	Woods	Isaac Jr			1					1					2		
Pepperell	34	3	Woods	James	1			1		1			1				4		
Groton	212	104	Woods	John		1		1				2		1			5		
Groton	213	7	Woods	Jona	1	1		1		1			1				5		
Watertown	235	23	Woods	Jonas	1		2			1	1	1					6		
Groton	213	3	Woods	Jotham	1	1		1		3			1				7		
Pepperell	34	12	Woods	Leml		1		1						1			3		
Pepperell	34	5	Woods	Levi	3		1		1	1	2	2		1			11		
Marlborough	187	21	Woods	Moses	1		1	1	1			2		1			7		
Groton	212	102	Woods	Nahum	1	1	1	1		3	2		1	1			11		
Lincoln	13	4	Woods	Nehemiah	1		1			2	1		1	1			7		
Groton	213	5	Woods	Oliver				1			2			1			4		
Littleton	202	28	Woods	Phillips			1			1	1						3		
Groton	212	89	Woods	Samson Maj.	1		2	1		2	1	1	1				9		
Marlborough	187	7	Woods	Sarah		1								1			2		
Pepperell	33	46	Woods	Stephen	1			1					1				4		
Pepperell	34	11	Woods	Thos	1			1		3			1				6		
Groton	212	100	Woods	Timothy				1		1	2		1	1			6		
Acton	18	36	Woodson	Ebenezer			1			1		1					3		
Bedford	163	33	Woodward	David				1					2		2		5		
Newton	125	15	Woodward	Ebenezer		1						2	1				4		
Newton	125	16	Woodward	John				1					1	1			3		
Tyngsborough	43	33	Woodward	John	2	1		1		1			1				6		
Reading	138	10	Woodward	John G			1			2			1				4		
Tyngsborough	43	32	Woodward	Jona			1	1						1			3		
Tewksbury	53	22	Woodward	Joseph	2	2		1		1		2	1		2		11		

					FREE WHITE MALES					FREE WHITE FEMALES									
TOWN	PG#	LN#	LAST NAME	FIRST NAME	under 10	10 to 16	16 to 26	26 to 45	45 and over	under 10	10 to 16	16 to 26	26 to 45	45 and over	TOTAL ALL OTHER	TOTAL SLAVES	TOTALS	DISTRICT/TOWNSHIP	NOTES
Marlborough	188	2	Woodward	Moses			1				1						2		
Framingham	74	11	Woolson	Pervis								1	1				2		
Tewksbury	53	24	Wooster	Eldad	4	1		1				1	1	1			9		
Tyngsborough	43	35	Wooster	Francis	2	1	1		1		1	2	1				9		
Tyngsborough	43	36	Wooster	Jonath	1				1	3		1					6		
Tewksbury	53	23	Wooster	Samll	2	1	1	1	2	2	3		1	1			14		
Tyngsborough	43	34	Wooster	Samll		1			1		1		1				4		
Chelmsford	173	5	Worcester	Osgood	1			1			1	1					4		
Hopkinton	245	12	Works	James	1			1				1					3		
Hopkinton	245	11	Works	Jane			3		1		1	1		2			8		
Littleton	204	20	Worster	Benjamin		1	1		1			1	1	2			7		
Littleton	204	21	Worster	Bridges	1			1					1				3		
Ashby	37	38	Worth	Joseph					1				1				2		
Ashby	36	16	Worth	Levi	3	1		1		1	1		1				8		
Cambridge	229	31	Worth	Saml	1		1			1		1					4		
Ashby	36	34	Woster	Joseph Jr	1			1			1	1					4		
Ashby	36	11	Wright	Abel	2			1		1		1	1				6		
Westford	184	19	Wright	Abel	2		1	1		1			1	1			7		
Pepperell	33	50	Wright	Abel	2		2		1	2	1			1			9		
Westford	184	14	Wright	Abijah		1	1			1		1		2			6		
Ashby	36	13	Wright	Abram B.	2			1					1				4		
Westford	184	11	Wright	Amos		2			1			2		2			7		
Westford	184	17	Wright	Asa	2	1		1		2	1		1				8		
Charlestown	92	27	Wright	Benja'			1						1	1			3		
Billerica	178	41	Wright	Danl		1	1		1		1		1	1			6		
Pepperell	33	44	Wright	David			2		1	1			1	1			6		
Pepperell	33	42	Wright	Edmund				1		1	1	1	1				5		
Westford	184	21	Wright	Eleazer	3			1		1			1				6		
Ashby	36	12	Wright	Elijah				1		3			1				5		
Littleton	203	6	Wright	Ephraim	3			1		1	2		1				8		
Littleton	202	26	Wright	Ezekiel	3			1		3			2	1			10		
Cambridge	230	1	Wright	Hannah									2	2			4		
Ashby	36	10	Wright	Henry Jr					1	1			1				3		
Ashby	37	44	Wright	Henry Jr		1			1	1			1				4		
Bedford	163	25	Wright	James			2		1	1	1		1				6		
Westford	184	18	Wright	James		1			1	1		1		1			5		
Woburn	153	11	Wright	James							1						1		
Bedford	163	26	Wright	James Jr	1		2				1	1					5		
Billerica	178	40	Wright	John	1	1	1	1		1	1	1	1				8		
Medford	103	21	Wright	John			2		1	2	1			1			7		
Stoneham	140	8	Wright	John	1		2			2		1					6		
Westford	184	12	Wright	John			1					1	1				4		
Groton	213	8	Wright	John C.	1	1		1		1			1	2			6		
Westford	184	20	Wright	John T.	1	1	1			1		1					5		
Concord	9	23	Wright	Jonas	3		1	1			1	1					7		
Charlestown	92	12	Wright	Jos'			1										1		
Westford	184	16	Wright	Jos'		2		1				2		1			6		
Concord	9	22	Wright	Joseph				1					1				2		
Pepperell	33	43	Wright	Josiah	2	2			1	2	2			1			10		
Woburn	152	41	Wright	Josiah		1	2	1	1			1		1			7		
Littleton	203	28	Wright	Jotham			1					1					2		
Westford	184	23	Wright	Levi'	2			1		1			1				5		
Pepperell	34	23	Wright	Natha	1	1	1		1		1			1			6		
Westford	184	15	Wright	Nathan	5	1		1					1				8		
Pepperell	33	45	Wright	Noah	2	3		1					1				7		
Groton	213	1	Wright	Oliver	1			1		1	1	1	1				6		
Littleton	202	49	Wright	Peter	3			1		2	1		1				8		
Woburn	153	10	Wright	Philemon	2	1	1	1		2	1		1	1			10		
Westford	184	13	Wright	Reuben	3	1		1		2				1			8		
Pepperell	33	41	Wright	Saml			2			2	2		1	1			8		
Westford	184	22	Wright	Saml			1		1	1	1	2					7		
Acton	16	1	Wright	Samuel	1	1		1	2		1		1				7		
Ashby	36	14	Wright	Stephen	1	1		1		3			1				7		
Stoneham	140	7	Wright	Timothy		1	1	1					1	1			5		
Stoneham	140	9	Wright	Timothy Jr	1			1		1		1					4		
Townsend	29	21	Wright	Washn	1		1			1		1					4		
Pepperell	34	19	Wright	Wc B				2					1	1			4		
Chelmsford	173	19	Wright	Zach'	1	1		1				1	1				5		
Westford	184	9	Wright	Zach'		2	1		1		1			1			6		
Westford	184	10	Wright	Zach' Jr				1		1			1				3		
Woburn	153	19	Wyer	Abigail										1			1		
Medford	103	27	Wyer	Danl'	2			2					1				5		
Charlestown	92	24	Wyer	David		1	1		1	1		3		1			8		
Medford	103	28	Wyer	David	1			1		1			1				4		
Charlestown	92	26	Wyer	Lydia							1	2		1			4		
Billerica	178	43	Wyer	Martha		3	2					1		2			8		
Townsend	29	10	Wyer	Richard		1			1			1		2			5		
Cambridge	230	9	Wyeth	Ebenz	1	4			1		1			1			8		
Cambridge	230	8	Wyeth	Jacob	1	2		2			1	2					8		
Lexington	160	19	Wyeth	John				1					1				2		

230

TOWN	PG#	LN#	LAST NAME	FIRST NAME	FREE WHITE MALES					FREE WHITE FEMALES					TOTAL ALL OTHER	TOTAL SLAVES	TOTALS	DISTRICT/ TOWNSHIP	NOTES
					under 10	10 to 16	16 to 26	26 to 45	45 and over	under 10	10 to 16	16 to 26	26 to 45	45 and over					
Cambridge	229	33	Wyeth	Jonas		1	1	1	1			1		1			6		
Cambridge	229	16	Wyeth	Noah	2	1	1						1	1			7		
Sherburn	251	32	Wyeth	Tapley				1		1	1			1			4		
Burlington	156	3	Wyman	Abel		2	3		1	1		2		1			10		
Ashby	36	15	Wyman	Abijah	2		2	1	1		1	2	1	2			12		
Burlington	156	14	Wyman	Ahira					1					1			2		
Woburn	153	1	Wyman	Benjamin	2		1	1		2	1		1				8		
Wilmington	144	8	Wyman	Catharine						1		1					2		
Woburn	153	2	Wyman	Daniel	2		1		1	2	2	1	1		1		11		
Woburn	153	15	Wyman	David	3	3	2		1	1		1	1	3			15		
Woburn	153	3	Wyman	Eunice			1				1	1		1			4		
Burlington	156	4	Wyman	Ezra					1		1	1	2	1			6		
Weston	111	8	Wyman	Hezekiah			3		1			1		1			6		
Lexington	160	24	Wyman	James	2	1			1			3		1			8		
Medford	103	25	Wyman	James		1		1	1				1	1			5		
Woburn	153	16	Wyman	James	1		1					1					3		
Lexington	160	20	Wyman	James Jr	1			1				1	1				4		
Woburn	153	4	Wyman	Jesse				1		3			1				5		
Woburn	153	7	Wyman	Jonathan	4	1		1		1			1				8		
Medford	103	24	Wyman	Joseph	2	1	1	1			1		1	1			8		
Woburn	153	5	Wyman	Joshua		1	1	1	1					1			5		
Woburn	153	6	Wyman	Joshua Jr	1	1	2			1		1					6		
Woburn	153	13	Wyman	Nathan					1					1			2		
Woburn	153	14	Wyman	Nathan Jr	1	1	1		1	1	1	1	1				8		
Bedford	163	29	Wyman	Nathaniel		1			1		2	1		1			6		
Woburn	153	20	Wyman	Nathaniel	1	1	2			1		2					7		
Charlestown	92	30	Wyman	Nehm		3	1	1		4			1				10		
Boxborough	199	9	Wyman	Oliver					1			1		1			3		
Concord	2	5	Wyman	Oliver		1	1	1		1		5					9		
Woburn	153	8	Wyman	Paul		1			1				1	1			4		
Cambridge	229	11	Wyman	Saml		1		1		1		1					4		
Woburn	152	42	Wyman	Samuel E	3			2		2			2				9		
Charlestown	92	14	Wyman	Seth	1		1	1	1	2		2	1	1			10		
Ashby	36	32	Wyman	Stephen				1			1		1				3		
East Sudbury	68	24	Wyman	William	2	1	1		1	1		2	1				9		
Woburn	153	9	Wyman	Zebadiah			2					2					4		
Townsend	29	33	Wyman	Zebn					1					1			2		
Groton	213	6	Wythe	Jonathan	1		1					1					3		
Groton	212	94	Wythe	Joseph					1			1		1			3		
Reading	138	13	Young	Benjamin	1	1		1		1	2		1				7		
Groton	213	10	Young	Elisha	1				1	3	1	1	1				8		
Hopkinton	245	14	Young	John	3					2	2		1	1			9		
Malden	98	28	Young	Tho'					1								1		
Littleton	202	34	Young	William		1			1		2	1	1				6		
Woburn	153	21	Young	William		1			1			2		1			5		
Concord	11	29		Zilpah											1		1		

NOTES